T5-AGP-509

*A Critical Bibliography of
French Literature*

A Critical Bibliography of French Literature

D. C. CABEEN

General Editor

VOLUME IV

THE EIGHTEENTH CENTURY

Edited by

GEORGE R. HAVENS

Ohio State University

DONALD F. BOND

The University of Chicago

SYRACUSE UNIVERSITY PRESS

1951

Printed in Belgium

To the memory of

GUSTAVE LANSON

GENERAL INTRODUCTION

" Qui scit ubi scientia sit, ille est proximus habenti."
Ferdinand Brunetière, *Manuel de l'histoire de
la littérature française (Avertissement)*

THERE EXISTS today no adequate guide for the selection of the best articles or books
of scholarly criticism devoted to French literature.   Most of the existing bibliographies,
whether they cover a single author, a literary movement, or a larger period, aim to
achieve completeness.   They thus impose upon the user a difficult choice among
the numerous items they list, and, in the absence of qualitative indications, he must
often make such a selection intuitively.

The present bibliography is doubly critical.   First, it is selective, for it gathers
together only that information which is essential to the specialist, the advanced student,
or the cultivated amateur of French literature.   Every item listed is, in the opinion
of the compilers, valuable to anyone undertaking further studies.   Secondly, the bibliography is critical in form, since each collaborator has briefly appraised the books
or articles with which he deals.   The object has consistently been to point out what
still remains valid and important in a work of whatever date.

A bibliography whose guiding principle is that of critical selectivity must be objective.
In so far as possible, each author or subject has been treated by a scholar who is known
in the United States for his interest in that author or subject.   But no collaborator
has worked in a vacuum : his judgments have been influenced by consultation with
the individual Volume Editors and with the General Editor.   And yet, everyone who
has taken part in this enterprise knows that it must inevitably be marred by errors
and omissions, which the Editors earnestly beg all users of the bibliography to call
to their attention.   Such a complex work as this can always bear improvement.

It is hoped that this bibliography will prove to be a constructive force, suggesting
by implication which subjects have been comparatively neglected or inadequately
treated and which aspects of a writer, a group, or a period require reinterpretation
today.   In the future, scholarly writing can hardly fail to benefit from a critical
bibliography which obviates the need for many of the preliminary explorations hitherto

necessary.   Under normal circumstances, indeed, the bibliography should so stimulate new works as to be itself soon outdated—and no result could more deeply gratify the compilers.

Finally, it is especially significant that the present work is at once American in inspiration and co-operative in nature.   Undertaken in the United States when Europe was being shaken by the first clashes of a devastating war, continued in spite of the difficulties and delays of uneasy later years, this *Critical Bibliography* bears witness to the conviction of its American and French contributors that French literature is the common heritage of the civilized world.

THE EDITORS

GENERAL EDITOR'S NOTE

THE BIBLIOGRAPHICAL forms adopted for this volume, as well as for the series as a whole, have been selected with a view to giving the greatest amount of information compatible with clearness and brevity. To this end, the forms of the H. W. Wilson Company, with some slight modifications, were chosen for periodicals, and those of the Library of Congress for books.

The strongest argument for the use of the Library of Congress forms is that its catalogue is the one source available to all collaborators working on this project. Thus the main entry for the late Professor Van Roosbroeck is Van Roosbroeck, G. L., although Columbia University, where he last taught, carries his name as Roosbroeck, G. L. van, which we print as a cross-reference. On the other hand, the Library of Congress has : Bengescu, George; but we use : Bengesco, Georges, because most Voltaire specialists prefer and use this French spelling.

In many cases, the General Editor (who compiled the Index) would have liked to give in more detail the information used in the Library of Congress catalogue in identifying authors and other proper names appearing in an entry. Often this information is priceless and is not available elsewhere, since it has been obtained by literary, historical, and genealogical research which has never been equaled in a large-scale project for scope, thoroughness, and precision. But the need to economize on space forbids complete reproduction of this valuable material.

A somewhat more detailed explanation of the Index than the brief note which heads it seems called for. Any index so simple and obvious as to need no explanation would also be the easiest to compile, but in a volume like this would be too cumbersome to use to the best advantage. Lack of space has also rendered it impossible to attempt an analysis comparable in scope and value to the magnificent two-volume Index in Moland's famous edition of Voltaire (No. 1628).

The Index of the present volume attempts a compromise which, like all compromises, is never entirely satisfactory. The great proportion of the indexed subjects appear less than three times, and it is not difficult for the reader to look up three or fewer serial numbers in order to find the one needed. No doubt the presence of an identifying word before the serial numbers of items which appear more than three times will save a substantial amount of trouble, if the user will take the few moments necessary to understand the mechanics of the Index. Thus, under the subject heading of " Voltaire " we find : Montesquieu : 1557, *1609-11*. The fact that the numbers *1609-11* are in italics shows that Voltaire is the author of the items they identify; 1557, not being italicized, indicates that it is probably a comparison between Voltaire and Montesquieu, as it is. However, innumerable items do not lend themselves so neatly to brief identification, even by specialists on the given subject, but the loss of time devoted to consulting the item itself seemed hardly sufficient to justify the substantial amount of extra printing required for more complete identification. Based on the idea that if a name is worth mentioning in an analysis, it should be listed under that item, the Index attempts to be as complete as possible. In a very few cases this leads to an excessively large number of references under a given item, but this was unavoidable and of minor significance.

In general, subject headings in the Index are given in English, except in cases where a translation would be inadequate or too lengthy (e.g., *philosophe*).

In the main body of this volume there has been no effort to eliminate duplicate titles. In fact, some items appear several times. Usually the first appearance of the study carries the full entry, and subsequent ones only the title, with a cross-reference to the first mention. Usually also the annotations of items after the first occurrence offer material of further interest. Even when nothing new is presented, the mere presence of an item in a given section adds something to the subject by acting as a significant reminder. In the Index, however, it was not found practicable to indicate a distinction between the main item and cross-references to it.

Last names of eighteenth-century writers are abbreviated to an initial only in sections devoted to them. When a book was published in Paris, no place of publication is given.

I wish here to express my sincere thanks to the Carnegie Corporation, whose generous grant has rendered inestimable service to this volume and to the whole project. This volume is greatly indebted also to the Graduate School of the Ohio State University for kindly providing funds, and to Mrs. Luigi Cognasso for effective aid in the difficult task of proof reading. Finally, I am most grateful to the Reference Departments of the Columbia University Library, and of the New York Public Library, and particularly to MM. A. P. DeWeese, Walter Pilkington, and James Tobin of the latter institution for their valuable assistance on many knotty problems. Scholarship in the United States owes an immense debt to Reference Librarians for their patience, courtesy, tenacity of purpose, and unusual technical knowledge.

David C. Cabeen

FOREWORD

ONE OF THE OUTSTANDING achievements of modern scholarship has been the recognition of the eighteenth century in French literature as worthy of attention in its own right. It is still not so long ago that the century of Voltaire, of Rousseau, of Diderot, of Montesquieu, was regarded merely as a kind of interlude between the great classic period and the rich, varied flowering of the nineteenth century. In the colleges and the universities of the United States, it was too often nearly or completely ignored. The exploratory lectures of Villemain and the brilliant series of portraits by Sainte-Beuve first pointed the way to a more serious study, to be followed in turn by the penetrating work of Bersot and Brunetière and the stimulating essays of Faguet. The real credit for the change, however, is due to the sound scholarship of one man, who recognized the artistic integrity and the intellectual significance of the eighteenth century and who, by precept and example, advanced immeasurably our understanding of its literature and thought. That man was Gustave Lanson.

Although Lanson was a master of the whole broad pageant of French literature from the Renaissance to his own day, the eighteenth century was his field of predilection. The *Histoire de la littérature française*, first published in 1894 and frequently revised and reprinted, is more than a classic manual : it provides an almost unique example of a profound and exact knowledge of facts combined with rare interpretative power, clarity, and concision. It demonstrates, too, a quality only too rare even among scholars, the ability to appreciate open-mindedly and objectively men of the most diverse talents and points of view. Some of the footnotes in which Lanson frankly modified, in successive editions, too hostile evaluations of Montesquieu, Voltaire, and others, while leaving his original opinion intact before the eyes of the reader, afford a remarkable lesson in selfless integrity. They show, also, a widening maturity which, even in a man of his precocious attainments, never ceased to grow. One of our greatest American scholars (in a field other than the eighteenth century) when asked where he learned his almost impeccable methods of scholarship, replied : " From Lanson's *Histoire*." There is indeed no better source.

Lanson's *Nivelle de La Chaussée et la comédie larmoyante*, his doctoral thesis of 1887, was an early and important contribution to eighteenth-century studies. His series of articles on the " Origines et premières manifestations de l'esprit philosophique en France," published in the *Revue des cours et conférences* from 1907 to 1910, and his " Questions diverses sur l'histoire de l'esprit philosophique en France avant 1750," in the *Revue d'histoire littéraire de la France* of 1912, underlined the importance, for a true understanding of eighteenth-century writers, of their pragmatic and experimental approach to intellectual problems, even though their incomplete knowledge of the facts did not always permit them to reach sound conclusions. These articles possess great value as a refutation of Taine's hostile view that the *philosophes* were misled by an abstract and *a priori* attitude toward the complex problems of humanity.

If the series of articles on "l'esprit philosophique " demonstrated a mastery of factual research and interpretation of ideas, Lanson proved in *L'Art de la prose* (1908) that he was equally capable—in his study of the prose rhythms of Voltaire, of Rousseau, and Bernardin de Saint-Pierre—of artistic analysis. His *Voltaire* (1906), in the *Grands Écrivains Français* series is a model of brevity, insight, clearness, and rapidity of movement not unworthy of the great author of *Candide* himself. The scholar who would learn to carry his erudition lightly and well can find no better mentor than Lanson in these 221 small but tightly packed pages.

Lanson's best known contribution is perhaps the indispensable *Manuel bibliographique de la littérature française moderne*, published in 1909-1914, with an extensive *Supplément* in 1921. No one can study French literature effectively without constant recourse to this basic work of reference. We can only marvel that a man like Lanson, whose chief interest was literature and whose own writings were all marked by distinguished literary quality, should have been willing to sacrifice time and effort to the uninspiring but necessary task of getting together, with the aid of students, the list of books and articles essential to the serious study of modern French literature. Occasional errors of detail do not detract from the extraordinary value of Lanson's accomplishment, and this *Manuel* of over 1800 pages remains a monument of devotion from which we can still profit greatly. The present volume is, in some sense, a continuation and development of Lanson's work, but with a high degree of selectivity and the addition of critical evaluations.

Lanson could be devastating at times, it is said, and bitterly sarcastic in his excoriation of careless or insincere workmanship. It was the fierce anger, no doubt, of a man of unflinching integrity, exacting for himself as for others. Yet, whoever has sat on a Saturday morning in his hospitable office in the *rue d'Ulm*, listening to the quiet, slow, poised speech of the bearded director of the École Normale Supérieure, can only carry away the vivid memory of a friendly and kindly man who, behind his plain eyeglasses, wore his high distinctions with the simplicity of the truly great.

Bon travail, he wrote succinctly many years ago as he began his review of an American doctoral thesis, and tempered with a gentleman's courtesy such criticisms of detail as followed. His procedure might well be a lesson to reviewers since his time who do not always remember that honesty and urbanity are not of necessity mutually exclusive.

To a young American graduate student starting his dissertation he once said encouragingly, after amazingly putting him at his ease : " Oh ! you will soon know much more about this subject than I do," and then proceeded with his calm and penetrating counsel. To another American, seeking a thesis subject, he, after a few days' reflection, suggested five—all so interesting, the man later said, that he was only sorry he could not select them all. But Lanson's carefully thought-out suggestion, in the course of the years, resulted in several fruitful volumes by his young disciple. Similar incidents could doubtless be multiplied.

To listen to Lanson give an *explication de texte* was a revelation of what the printed word may mean to those able to understand with something of his keen intelligence, broad background, and sympathy. Both *sensitivity* and *learning*, he was fond of pointing out, are essential to the comprehension of a work of literature—a statement which many scholars and critics of today might well take to heart. For an understanding of Lanson's method there are three brief essays which are worth very close study : the *Avant-propos* to his *Hommes et Livres* of 1895, the lecture delivered at the University of Brussels in 1909 entitled " L'esprit scientifique et la méthode de l'histoire littéraire "(reprinted in his *Méthodes de l'histoire littéraire*, 1925), and the article, " La Méthode de l'histoire littéraire," published in the *Revue du Mois* of October 10, 1910 (pp. 385-413).

Lanson's distinguished pupils, Pierre-Maurice Masson, Georges Ascoli, M. Daniel Mornet, M. André Morize, and others, have made able contributions to eighteenth-century studies which are evaluated in this volume. Many an American scholar, directly or indirectly influenced by Lanson, also carries on in some measure his high tradition. Most of them are represented among our contributors, and of them it would be neither fitting nor necessary to speak here. Their most important books and articles are discussed in the following pages. They show clearly that the methods and ideals of French scholarship have long since crossed the ocean and spread their sound influence abroad. In the midst of intolerance and tyranny, modern man has, as never before, urgent need of objectivity, knowledge, and a deep feeling for those humane values which are the distinctive marks of the best French scholarship.

The eighteenth century in France was a decisive period in the realm of ideas. Montesquieu, Voltaire, Rousseau, and Diderot—to mention only the leaders—have left an indelible imprint on the mind of modern man. The basic questions were then raised, on such matters as the meaning of progress, the division of governmental powers, individual freedom in relation to the authority of the State, economic and social equality, the relations between reason and emotion, the esthetics of art and of literature. On these and a host of other problems, wit, irony, and brevity were employed in the service of intelligence. The result is a series of unrivalled masterpieces, clothed in trenchant prose. They still speak to us, through the censorship of the *ancien régime*, with clear and authoritative voice.

The man of letters of the eighteenth century did not live in an ivory tower; he took a bold and vigorous part in the life of his time. In sharing some of his ideas, we too can better understand our own turbulent day. Literature is human thought, action, and feeling in its most vivid and vital expression; and scholarship is the means by which we can better understand human life. The editors of this volume join with the many devoted collaborators in the hope that their work, arid as it must appear in form, may in substance serve to aid and inspire many studies, which, in contributing to a better comprehension of the life and thought of the eighteenth century, will contribute also notably to our own.

GEORGES R. HAVENS
The Ohio State University

DONALD F. BOND
The University of Chicago

LIST OF ABBREVIATIONS USED IN VOLUME IV

APSLB	American philosophical society, Library bulletin
APSP	American philosophical society, Proceedings
APSR	American political science review
APST	American philosophical society, Transactions
Ar	Arche
Archeion	Archeion; Archivo di storia della scienza
Archiv	Archiv für das Studium der neueren Sprachen und Literaturen (Herrig)
AS	American speech
ASM	Institut de France. Académie des sciences. Mémoires
ASP	Annales des sciences politiques
ASSM	Annales de la Société historique et archéologique de l'arrondissement de Saint-Malo
AST	Reale accademia delle scienze di Torino, Memorie, Scienze morali, storiche e filologiche
Ath	Athenaeum
Atl	Atlantic monthly
AUG	Annales de l'Université de Grenoble
AUL	Latvijas universitatis Raksti, Acta universitatis Latviensis, Filologijas un filozofijas fakultates
AUP	Annales de l'Université de Paris
BA	Books abroad
BACF	Académie des sciences, belles-lettres et arts de Clermont-Ferrand; Bulletin historique et scientifique de l'Auvergne
BBB	Bulletin du bibliophile et du bibliothécaire
Bbib	Bulletin of bibliography
BCP	Bibliothèque du Congrès international de philosophie; histoire de la philosophie
Bcr	Bulletin critique
BDA	Bulletin des arts
Beibl	Beiblatt zur Anglia
BHM	Bulletin de la Société française d'histoire de la médecine
BHT	Bulletin de la Société des historiens du théâtre
BibG	Bibliothèque universelle de Genève
BioM	Biographie universelle, by J. F. and L. G. Michaud, ed. *See* 42
Bit	Bulletin italien
BJ	Basler Jahrbuch
Bl	Blackwood's magazine
BLS	Faculté des lettres de Strasbourg, Bulletin
BM	British museum
BMF	Bullettino di bibliografia e di storia delle scienze matematiche e fisiche
BN	Bibliothèque nationale
BNYPL	Bulletin of the New York Public Library
BRLC	Bibliothèque de la Revue de littérature comparée
BSC	Bulletin de la Société des lettres, sciences et arts de la Corrèze
BSF	Bulletin de la Société archéologique du Finistère
BSFP	Bulletin de la Société française de philosophie
BSHL	Bulletin de la Société historique et archéologique de Langres
BSHM	Bulletin de la Société française d'histoire de la médecine
BSHP	Bulletin de la Société de l'histoire du protestantisme français
BSLP	Bulletin de la Société de linguistique de Paris
BSP	Papers of the Bibliographical society of America

BU	Bibliothèque universelle et Revue suisse
Cal	Caliban
CathHR	Catholic historical review
CBEL	The Cambridge bibliography of English literature
CCP	Collection des classiques populaires
CDHF	Collection de documents inédits sur l'histoire de France
CDS	Cahiers du Sud
CF	Canada-français
Cfor	Canadian forum
CHR	Canadian historical review
Cint	Cooperazione intellettuale
CL	Comparative literature
CLF	Chronique des lettres françaises
CLNL	Comparative literature news-letter
CLR	University of Chicago law review
CLS	Comparative literature studies
Cméd	Chronique médicale
CML	Calendar of modern letters
CNL	Comparative news letter
Conn	Connoisseur
Cornhill	Cornhill magazine
Corr	Correspondant
Cox	E. G. Cox, A reference guide to the literature of travel, *see* 2515
CPMP	University of California publications in modern philology
Cpr	Cahiers de la presse; revue trimestrielle de l'Institut de science de la presse de l'Université de Paris
Cr	Critique
Crev	Contemporary review
Crit	La critica
CSE	Columbia university studies in English and comparative literature
Cult	Cultura
CW	Catholic World
Diss	Dissertation
Dlit	Deutsche Literaturzeitung
DR	Deutsche Rundschau
DUJ	Durham university journal
DUV	Dichtung und Volkstum
DV	Deutsche Vierteljahrschrift für Literaturwissenschaft und Geistesgeschichte
EA	Études anglaises
EdM	L'éducateur moderne
EdR	Edinburgh review
EF	Educational forum
EHR	English historical review
Eit	Études italiennes
EJ	Economic journal
EJHR	Essays in intellectual history dedicated to James Harvey Robinson by his former seminar students. New York, Harper, 1929
Elo	Eloquenza
Emon	Elliott monographs in Romance languages and literatures

EprR	État présent des études sur Jean-Jacques Rousseau. *See* 1859
ER	English review
ES	Englische Studien
ESS	Encyclopaedia of the social sciences
EssAF	Essays in honor of Albert Feuillerat. New Haven, Yale Univ. press, 1943. (Yale romanic studies, 22)
Est	English studies
Euph	Euphorion
EvL	Everyman's library
ExL	Ex libris
FAR	Franco-American review
FCHQ	Filson club history quarterly
Feu	Le feu
FI	Friends' intelligencer
FJE	Feuilleton du Journal de l'Empire
FL	Folk-lore
FM	Fraser's magazine
Fmod	Le français moderne
Fo	Fontaine
FortR	Fortnightly review
FQ	French quarterly
FR	French review
FrAR	French American review
FS	French studies
Gav	Gavroche
GBA	Gazette des beaux-arts
GDL	Gazette des lettres
GE	Giornale degli economisti
GEF	Grands écrivains français series
Geg	Die Gegenwart
GEL	Les grands événements littéraires series
GJa	Goethe-Jahrbuch
GQ	German quarterly
GR	Grande revue
Gren	La grande encyclopédie (1886-1902)
Grev	Germanic review
GRM	Germanisch-romanische Monatschrift
GSF	German studies presented to Professor H. G. Fiedler. Oxford, Clarendon press, 1938
GSLI	Giornale storico della letteratura italiana
HAHR	Hispanic American historical review
HB	Historische Bibliothek
Hip	Hippocrate, revue d'humanisme médical
Hisp	Hispania
HLR	Harvard law review
HLS	Hand- und Lehrbuch der Staatswissenschaft
HR	Hispanic review
HRen	Humanisme et Renaissance
HS	Historische Studien

HSCL	Harvard studies in comparative literature
HTB	New York Herald Tribune books
HZ	Historische Zeitschrift
ICC	Intermédiaire des chercheurs et curieux
IGB	Institut national genevois, Bulletin
IJE	International journal of ethics
IMG	Internationale Musik-Gesellschaft
ISLL	University of Illinois studies in language and literature
Ital	Italica
JAFL	Journal of American folk-lore
JCL	Journal of comparative literature
Jdéb	Journal des débats
JE	Journal des économistes
JEGP	Journal of English and Germanic philology
JFM	Jahrbuch über die Fortschritte der Mathematik
JGen	Journal de Genève
JGG	Jahrbuch der Goethe-Gesellschaft
JHI	Journal of the history of ideas
JHS	The Johns Hopkins studies in Romance literatures and languages
JIBA	Journal of the Royal institute of British architects
JIH	Journal de l'Institut historique
JIHS	Journal of the Illinois State historical society
JMH	Journal of modern history
JMP	Jahrbuch der Musikbibliothek Peters
JPE	Journal of political economy
Jph	Journal of philosophy
JS	Journal des savants
JSH	Journal of Southern history
JSSP	Société de statistique de Paris, Journal
LA	Living age
Lab	Labyrinthe
LB	Leuvensche bijdragen
LC	Library of Congress
LE	Das litterarische Echo
LeA	Les lettres et les arts
Leo	Leonardo
LGRP	Literaturblatt für germanische und romanische Philologie
LHM	American Society Legion of honor magazine
LHQ	Louisiana historical quarterly
Libr	The library; a quarterly review of bibliography. (Transactions of the Bibliographical society, London.)
Litt	Litteris
LM	London Mercury
Lmen	Larousse mensuel
Lmod	Les langues modernes
LQ	Library quarterly
LR	Les lettres romanes
MAA	Académie des sciences, des lettres et des arts d'Amiens. Mémoires
MAC	Académie (impériale) des sciences, arts et belles-lettres de Caen. Mémoires

MAL   Mémoires de l'Académie des sciences, belles-lettres et arts de Lyon
MARB   Mémoires de l'Académie royale des sciences, des lettres et des beaux-arts. (Brussels.)
             Classe des lettres et des sciences morales et politiques
Marz   Marzocco
MAS   Institut de France.   Mémoires de l'Académie (royale) des sciences
MAT   Mémoires de l'Académie des sciences, inscriptions et belles-lettres de Toulouse
MAV   Académie de Versailles; Mémoires de la Société des sciences morales, des lettres
             et des arts de Seine-et-Oise
MB   More books.   Bulletin of the Boston public library
MBRP   Marburger Beiträge zur romanischen Philologie
MC   Monthly criterion, later Criterion
MCG   Geisteskultur; Monatshefte der Comenius-Gesellschaft für Geisteskultur und Volks-
             bildung
MDU   Monatshefte für deutschen Unterricht
MélAL   Mélanges offerts à Abel Lefranc.   Droz, 1936
MélBB   Mélanges d'histoire littéraire et de philologie offerts à Bernard Bouvier...   Geneva,
             Société anonyme des éditions Sonor, 1920
MélFB   Mélanges d'histoire littéraire générale et comparée offerts à Fernand Baldensperger.
             Champion, 1930.   2 v.
MélGL   Mélanges offerts par ses amis et ses élèves à M. Gustave Lanson.   Hachette, 1922
MélHH   Mélanges de philologie, d'histoire et de littérature offerts à Henri Hauvette.   Les
             presses françaises, 1934
MélHL   Mélanges Henri Lichtenberger, Stock [c1934]
MerF   Mercure de France
Mfran   Muse française
MHM   Maryland historical magazine
MHR   Missouri historical review
MHSC   Missouri historical society collections
MidA   Mid-America
Min   Minotaure
Minerve   La Minerve française
ML   Modern languages
MLA   Modern language association of America
Mlet   Music and letters
MLF   Modern language forum
MLJ   Modern language journal
MLN   Modern language notes
MLQ   Modern language quarterly
MLR   Modern language review
MLS   Mémoires lus à la Sorbonne; histoire, philologie et sciences morales
MM   Monde moderne
MNG   Abhandlungen zur mittleren und neueren Geschichte
MP   Modern philology
MQ   Musical quarterly
Mser   Milano Sera
MSM   Proceedings of the Association of history teachers of the Middle States and
             Maryland
MSSO   Mémoires de la Société des sciences morales, des lettres et des arts de Seine-et-Oise.
             See MAV

MTL	Mémoires et travaux publiés par les professeurs des facultés catholiques de Lille
MVHR	Mississippi Valley historical review
NA	Nuova antologia
NAR	North American review
Ncent	Nineteenth century and after
NE	New Englander
Necc	Nouvelles ecclésiastiques, ou Mémoires pour servir à l'histoire de la Constitution Unigenitus
Neo	Neophilologus
NEQ	New England quarterly
NHS	New Haven colony historical society. Papers
NL	Nouvelles littéraires
NNY	Nation, New York
n.p.,	No place of publication given
NQ	Notes and queries
NR	New Republic
NRE	Nouvelle revue encyclopédique
Nrev	Nouvelle revue
NRF	Nouvelle revue française. (nrf)
NRI	Nouvelle revue d'Italie
NRM	Nouvelle revue du Midi
NRT	Nouvelle revue de théologie
ns	new series
NSL	Univ. of Nebraska studies in language, literature and criticism
NSN	New statesman and nation
NSp	Neueren Sprachen
NY	New Yorker
NYW	New York World
Obs	L'observateur
OC	Open court
Olib	Oise libérée
PAHS	Publications de l'Académie internationale d'histoire des sciences
Par	Paru
PBA	Proceedings of the British Academy
PBSA	Papers of the Bibliographical society of America
PFS	Strasbourg, Université, Faculté des lettres, Publications
Phil	Philosophy
Phist	Pennsylvania history
PhR	Philosophical review
PLPS	Proceedings of the Leeds philosophical society, literary and historical section
PMHB	Pennsylvania magazine of history and biography
PMLA	Publications of the Modern language association of America
PNor	Paris Normandie
Poly	Polybiblion
PQ	Philological quarterly
PrA	Preussische Akademie der Wissenschaften. Histoire de l'Académie royale des sciences et belles-lettres. Classe de philosophie expérimentale
PrJ	Preussische Jahrbücher
PSM	Popular science monthly

PSO	Société académique d'archéologie, sciences et arts du Département de l'Oise, Publications
PSP	American philosophical society, Proceedings
PSQ	Political science quarterly
Psy	Psyché (Paris)
QQ	Queens quarterly
QR	Quarterly review
QRB	Quarterly review of biology
RAA	Revue anglo-américaine
Ranth	Revue anthropologique
RAu	Revue d'Auvergne
RBE	Revue bourguignonne de l'enseignement supérieur
RBelgique	Revue de Belgique
Rbib	Revue des bibliothèques
RBP	Revue belge de philologie et d'histoire
RCC	Revue des cours et conférences
RCI	Revue critique des idées et des livres
RCL	Revue des cours littéraires
RCLN	Revue critique des livres nouveaux
Rcont	Revue contemporaine
Rcr	Revue critique d'histoire et de littérature
RDF	Revue historique du droit français et étranger
RDH	Revue des documents historiques
RDM	Revue des deux mondes
RDP	Revue du droit public et de la science politique en France et à l'étranger
RDS	Revue du dix-huitième siècle
REC	Revue des études coopératives
Rech	Recherches philosophiques
REH	Revue des études historiques
RELV	Revue de l'enseignement des langues vivantes
Ren	Renaissance
Renc	Revue encyclopédique
REP	Revue d'économie politique
RépF	République française
RER	Revue des études rabelaisiennes
RES	Review of English studies
Rev	Revue (ancienne Revue des revues)
Revue	La revue : hommes et mondes
Rfil	Rivista filosofica
RFor	Romanische Forschungen
Rfr	Révolution française, revue d'histoire moderne et contemporaine
RFrance	Revue de France
RG	Revue germanique
Rgén	Revue générale (Brussels)
RH	Revue de Hollande
RHB	Revue historique de Bordeaux
RHDE	Revue d'histoire des doctrines économiques et sociales
Rheb	Revue hebdomadaire
RHEM	Revue d'histoire, rédigée à l'État-major de l'armée

RHES	Revue d'histoire économique et sociale
Rhisp	Revue hispanique
Rhist	Revue historique
RHL	Revue d'histoire littéraire de la France
RHLE	Revista crítica de historia y literatura españolas
RHM	Revue d'histoire moderne et contemporaine
RHP	Revue d'histoire politique et constitutionnelle
RHph	Revue d'histoire de la philosophie (till 1931); continued in 1933 as : Revue d'histoire de la philosophie et d'histoire générale de la civilisation (ns)
RHRF	Revue historique de la révolution française
RHV	Revue historique vaudoise
RIE	Revue internationale de l'enseignement
RIF	Rivista italiana di filosofia
Rin	Rinascita
RIS	Revue internationale de sociologie
RivI	Rivista d'Italia
RivP	Rivista pedagogica
RKHS	Register of the Kentucky state historical society
RLA	Revue de législation ancienne et moderne, française et étrangère
Rlat	Revue latine
RLav	Revue de l'Université Laval
RLC	Revue de littérature comparée
RLH	La revue : littérature, histoire, arts et sciences des deux mondes
RLille	Revue de Lille
Rliv	Revue des livres anciens
RLJ	Revue critique de législation et de jurisprudence
RLR	Revue des langues romanes
RMM	Revue de métaphysique et de morale
Rmod	Revue moderne
Rmois	Revue du mois
Rmond	Revue mondiale
Rmus	S. I. M., revue musicale. (Société internationale de musique, section française)
RN	Revue du Nord
RNS	Revue néo-scolastique. (Louvain)
RO	Revue occidentale
Rom	Romania
RP	Revue de philosophie
RPar	Revue de Paris
RPB	Revue philomathique de Bordeaux et du Sud-Ouest
RPC	Revue de pathologie comparée et d'hygiène générale
Rpéd	Revue pédagogique
RPF	Revue de philologie française et provençale; after 1897 Revue de philologie française et de littérature
RPFE	Revue philosophique de la France et de l'étranger
Rph	Revue philosophique
RPL	Revue politique et littéraire. (Revue bleue)
RPP	Revue politique et parlementaire
RPyr	Revue des Pyrénées
RQH	Revue des questions historiques

RQS	Revue des questions scientifiques (Louvain)
RR	Romanic review
Rrel	Review of religion
Rrét	Revue rétrospective
Rsav	Revue savoisienne
Rsc	Revue scientifique
RSH	Revue de synthèse historique
RSLF	Revue de science et de législation financières
Rsoc	Revue sociale
Rsyn	Revue de synthèse
RU	Revue universitaire
Runiv	Revue universelle
SAA	Société d'agriculture, sciences et arts d'Agen. Recueil des travaux
SAB	South Atlantic bulletin
SAQ	South Atlantic quarterly
SatR	Saturday review (of politics, literature, science and art) (London)
Sbio	Studies of a biographer
SCM	South Carolina historical and genealogical magazine
ScRR	Scritti varii di erudizione e di critica in onore di Rodolfo Renier. Turin, Bocca, 1912
SFDY	Studies by members of the French Department of Yale University, edited by Albert Feuillerat. Decennial volume. New Haven, Yale univ. press, 1941. Yale romanic studies, 18
SFELT	Société française des éditions littéraires et techniques
SFLQ	Southern folklore quarterly
SHF	Société de l'histoire de France
ShJ	Shakespeare-Jahrbuch
SHTB	Société des historiens du théâtre, Bulletin
SIM	Internationale Musik-Gesellschaft. Sammelbande.
SJ	Solicitors' journal and weekly reporter
SM	Scientific monthly
SNA	Société académique de Nantes et du Département de la Loire-inférieure, Annales
SP	Studies in philology
Spect	Spectator
SR	Sociological review
Srev	Sewanee review
SRL	Saturday review of literature
SSML	Smith college studies in modern languages
SSQ	Société académique des sciences, arts, belles-lettres, agriculture & industrie de Saint-Quentin; Travaux
StGS	Studies and essays in the history of science and learning offered ... to George Sarton. New York, Schuman [1946]
SVL	Studien zur vergleichenden Literaturgeschichte
SVR	Saggi raccolti a cura della Società filologica romana e dedicati a Vittorio Rossi. Florence, Sansoni, 1937
Symp	Symposium
Sz	Századok (Budapest)
TB	Temple bar
TBR	New York Times book review
TF	Les textes français

TFM	Société des textes français modernes
Th	Thought
TLF	Textes littéraires français
TLS	London Times literary supplement
TMLA	Transactions of the Modern language association of America
Tmod	Temps modernes
TNC	Neuvième Congrès international de philosophie. Travaux
TPMLA	Transactions and proceedings of the Modern language association of America
Tro	Table ronde
TSE	University of Texas studies in English
TT	Time and tide
TWA	Wisconsin Academy of arts and letters. Transactions
UTQ	University of Toronto quarterly
VKA	Kommunisticheskaia akademiia, Vestnik. Moscow. (Messenger of the Communist Academy)
VQR	Virginia quarterly review
WMQ	William and Mary college quarterly historical magazine
YHP	Yale historical publications : manuscripts and edited texts
YLG	Yale university library gazette
YR	Yale review
YRS	Yale romanic studies
YWML	The year's work in modern language studies
ZDA	Zeitschrift für deutsches Altertum und deutsche Literatur
ZDK	Zeitschrift für Deutschkunde
ZDP	Zeitschrift für deutsche Philologie
ZFEU	Zeitschrift für französischen und englischen Unterricht
ZFSL	Zeitschrift für französische Sprache und Literatur
ZIM	Internationale Musik-Gesellschaft. Zeitschrift
ZNSL	Zeitschrift für neufranzösische Sprache und Literatur
ZOG	Zeitschrift für österreichischen Gymnasien
ZRP	Zeitschrift für romanische Philologie
ZSG	Zeitschrift für schweizerische Geschichte
ZVL	Zeitschrift für vergleichende Literaturgeschichte

LIST OF CONTRIBUTORS TO VOLUME IV *

ALBERT BACHMAN
  Gettysburg College

CHANDLER BAKER BEALL
  University of Oregon

ARMAND G. BÉGUÉ
  Brooklyn College

MORRIS G. BISHOP
  Cornell University

DONALD F. BOND
  University of Chicago

GABRIEL BONNO
  University of California, Berkeley

CLARENCE DIETZ BRENNER
  University of California, Berkeley

DAVID CLARK CABEEN
  Formerly of Vanderbilt University

ALESSANDRO S. CRISAFULLI
  Catholic University of America

LESTER G. CROCKER
  Goucher College

FRANCIS J. CROWLEY
  University of California, Los Angeles

JEAN DAVID
  University of Washington

HERBERT DIECKMANN
  Harvard University

JEAN DUFRENOY
  University of California
  College of Pharmacy, San Francisco

OTIS E. FELLOWS
  Columbia University

WOLF FRANCK
  New York City

MARGARET GILMAN
  Bryn Mawr College

FRANCIS WEST GRAVIT
  Indiana University

HENRY ALEXANDER GRUBBS
  Oberlin College

GEORGE R. HAVENS
  Ohio State University

WILLIAM C. HOLBROOK
  Northwestern University

ANNE C. JONES
  Wellesley College

* Names are given here in most cases, as in the MLA "List of Members," as of February, 1949.

HUNTER KELLENBERGER
  Brown University

HARRY KURZ
  Queens College

J. ROBERT LOY
  University of California, Berkeley

JOHN FRANCIS MCDERMOTT
  Washington University

DOROTHY M. MCGHEE
  Hamline University

KENNETH N. MCKEE
  *Washington Square College,
  New York University*

ROBERT B. MICHELL
  University of Wisconsin

ANDREW R. MOREHOUSE
  Yale University

† THOMAS E. OLIVER
  University of Illinois

CLIFFORD H. PRATOR, Jr.
  University of California, Los Angeles

HENRY H. H. REMAK
  Indiana University

ARNOLD H. ROWBOTHAM
  University of California, Berkeley

DONALD S. SCHIER
  Carleton College

ALEXANDER HERMAN SCHUTZ
  Ohio State University

EDWARD D. SEEBER
  Indiana University

JOSEPH R. SMILEY
  University of Illinois

PAUL MERRILL SPURLIN
  University of Michigan

CHARLES N. STAUBACH
  University of Michigan

ROBERT EDWARD TAYLOR
  *Washington Square College,
  New York University*

NORMAN LEWIS TORREY
  Columbia University

FERNAND VIAL
  Fordham University

IRA OWEN WADE
  Princeton University

JAMES R. WADSWORTH
  Formerly of University of Nebraska

† Deceased.

TABLE OF CONTENTS
VOLUME IV

† Deceased.

CHAPTER I. BACKGROUND MATERIALS

(Nos. 1-400)

ALBERT BACHMAN, MORRIS BISHOP, DONALD F. BOND, DAVID C. CABEEN, WOLF FRANCK, MARGARET GILMAN, GEORGE R. HAVENS, DOROTHY M. McGHEE, and ALEXANDER H. SCHUTZ

Bibliographies
(Nos. 1-58)

DAVID C. CABEEN and DONALD F. BOND

Apollinaire, Guillaume, Fernand Fleuret, Louis Perceau. L'enfer de la Bibliothèque nationale; bibliographie méthodique et critique de tous les ouvrages composant cette célèbre collection avec une préface, un index des titres et une table des auteurs. Nouvelle édition. Bibliothèque des curieux, 1919. 415 p.   1

Descriptive bibliography of the 930 volumes in reserved section (" cage ") of the BN. While principally devoted to bibliographical detail, annotations contain much material of value to student of literary history.

Barbier, Antoine Alexandre. Dictionnaire des ouvrages anonymes. 3. éd. Tome I [-IV]. Suite de la 2. éd. des *Supercheries littéraires dévoilées*, par J. M. Quérard, publiées par MM. Gustave Brunet et Pierre Jannet. Tome IV [-VII] Daffis, 1872-79. 4 v.   2

See, Quérard, (51).

Belin, J. P. Le commerce des livres prohibés à Paris de 1750 à 1789. Belin, 1913. 129 p. *See* 357, 359.   3

Essential book in its field; divided into six parts, by chapters, as follows : I. *La censure;* II. *L'impression à l'étranger et en province;* III. *Paris. L'entrée des livres. Les imprimeries clandestines;* IV. *La vente des livres prohibés;* V. *Après la publication. Les condamnations. La police;* VI. *L'administration de la librairie.* No index, but several interesting illustrations; useful footnotes.

Reviews : D. Mornet in RHL 20:957-60, 1913; L. Villat in RSH 27:196-97, 1913.

— Le mouvement philosophique de 1748 à 1789; étude sur la diffusion des idées des philosophes à Paris, d'après les documents concernant l'histoire de la librairie. Belin, 1913. 381 p. (Diss., Paris). *See* 360, 1024, 1293.   4

The 8-page bibliography does not pretend to cover subject, but merely to list sources consulted by author. Lack of alphabetical list of proper names greatly lessens value of book as work of reference.

Reviews : D. Mornet in RHL 20:957-60, 1913; L. Villat in RSH 27:195-96, 1913.

Besterman, Theodore. A world bibliography of bibliographies. Oxford, University press, 1939-40. 2 v.   5

Standard bibliography, covering all subjects in all languages. Second and greatly augmented edition, 1947-49. 3 v. (v. 1). No critical annotations. Lists nearly 64,000 volumes in over 45 languages.

The bibliographic index : a cumulative bibliography of bibliographies. New York, Wilson, 1938.   6

Fullest current bibliography of bibliographies. " Issued quarterly, March, 1938 . . ., with annual cumulations, and larger cumulations at intervals, the first covering 1937/42." (From the LC card.)

Bibliographie der Rezensionen, nach Titeln (Alphabet der Verfasser) geordnetes Verzeichnis von Besprechungen deutscher und ausländischer Bücher und Karten, etc. Leipzig, [etc.], Dietrich, 1901-44.   7

Invaluable reference source for book reviews in years covered. Reviews in non-German language periodicals published in separate volumes. Curious compilation in that reviews of books by important authors, in well-known journals, are frequently not mentioned, while minor studies, or reviews in obscure sources, are often to be found listed only here.

1

Bond, Donald F. American scholarship in the field of eighteenth-century Anglo-French studies. RR 29:141-50, 1938.   8

Critical survey with bibliographical references.

— Anglo-French and Franco-American studies : a current bibliography. RR 29:343-72, 1938.   9

Continued annually with John F. McDermott, Joseph E. Tucker, J. M. Carrière, and E. D. Seeber, 1939-1948; in FrAR, 1949—.

Bonno, Gabriel. Liste chronologique des périodiques de langue française du dix-huitième siècle. MLQ 5:3-25, 1944.   10

See 35.

Book review digest; annual cumulation. New York, Wilson, 1905—.   11

Useful reference source. Gives extracts, usually well chosen, from book reviews published in better-known American and British literary periodicals, and from a very few scholarly ones.

Brenner, Clarence D. A bibliographical list of plays in the French language, 1700-1789. Berkeley, California, 1947. 229 p., double column.   12

Essential work, listing more than eleven thousand dramatic compositions. Scope, and necessary limitations of the compilation explained in brief but careful and scholarly preface. Lithoprint : fine but clear type.

Brunet, Jacques Charles. Manuel du libraire et de l'amateur de livres. 5th ed. Didot, 1860-65. 6 v. Supplément by P. Deschamps and G. Brunet, Didot, 1878-80. 2 v.   13

Valuable for detailed descriptions of first and other early editions, *éditions de luxe*, etc. Especially useful for books in French and Latin of the 16th, 17th, and 18th centuries. Arranged by author, with subject index in v. 6. An inadequate supplement was published in 1878-80.

Cahen, Léon. A propos des origines intellectuelles de la Révolution française : la librairie parisienne et la diffusion du livre français à la fin du XVIIIᵉ siècle. Rsyn, 17:159-79, 1939. *See* 2891.   14

An attempt to add to findings of Mornet, (45). Warns reader against attributing too great a role to literature as one of the causes of the Revolution.

Calot, Frantz, and **Georges Thomas.** Guide pratique de bibliographie, suivi d'un memento analytique des principales bibliothèques publiques de Paris. Delagrave, 1936. 320 p.   15

Excellent book : well organized and thorough. Many items followed by descriptive annotations; a few by critical ones. Has an : *Index des auteurs et des anonymes,* and another : *Index alphabétique abrégé des matières.*

Caron, Pierre, and **Marc Jaryc.** Répertoire des périodiques de langue française, philosophiques, historiques, philologiques et juridiques. Fédération des sociétés françaises des sciences philosophiques, historiques, philologiques et juridiques.   1935, 351 p. First supplement, 1937-39, 2 v.   16

Cohen, Henri. Guide de l'amateur de livres à vignettes du dix-huitième siècle. 4th ed., Rouquette, 1880. 591 p.   17

As title implies, volume intended for bibliographer, book dealer and collector; has little or no bearing on matters of literary content.

— Guide de l'amateur de livres à gravures du XVIIIᵉ siècle. 6th ed., revised, etc. by Seymour de Ricci. Rouquette, 1912. 2 v.   18

Covers much the same ground as preceding work, but in far greater detail, with extensive reports on sales of rare and special editions, etc.

Contades, Gérard de, *comte.* Bibliographie sportive : le driving en France (1547-1896). Rouquette, 1898, 208 p.   19

Gives interesting data on vehicles, by centuries, each century sub-divided by year of publication and author of each work, with excellent descriptive and often critical annotations. Section on 18th century has 68 pages, with several illustrations.

Cross, Tom Peete. Bibliographical guide to English studies. 9th ed., with an index. Chicago, Univ. of Chicago press, 1947. 74 p.   20

Has no section devoted specifically to French literature, but a most useful handbook for bibliography and related subjects.

Dictionnaire de biographie française. Ed. by J. Balteau *et al.* Letousey & Ané, 1933-39.   21

Brief signed biographical sketches.

Fascicule XIX (1941) has not finished letter *A*. Will be of special value in tracing complicated family relationships : thus, gives sketches of 17 members of D'Argenson family, and of length calculated to indicate importance of each.

Dubosq, Y. Z. Le livre français et son commerce en Hollande de 1750 à 1780. Amsterdam, H. J. Paris, 1925. 166 p. (Diss., Amsterdam). *See* 363.   22

Conveniently divided into three parts : first, on dealers, such as Luzac, Rey, and others, on censorship, etc.; second, on circulation of French books (listed by authors) in Holland; third, on commercial relations of French books printed in Holland with other European countries. Useful work which, however, lacks an index.
Review : D. Mornet in RHL 34:606-07, 1927.

Du Peloux, Charles, *vicomte*. Répertoire général des ouvrages modernes relatifs au dix-huitième siècle français (1715-1789). Grund, 1926. 306 p. Supplément, table méthodique. Grund, 1927. 62 p.   23

Though incomplete, inaccurate, and badly arranged, this work must be consulted by students planning any thorough survey of an 18th century author, since it gives many useful references.
Review : D. Mornet in RHL 36:140-41, 1929; G. B. Watts in MLN 42:423, 1927; Anon in RLC 6:695, 1926.

Ersch, Jean Samuel. La France littéraire, contenant les auteurs français de 1771 à 1796. Hambourg, Hoffmann, 1797-98. 3 v. 1st supplement, 1802; 2nd supplement, 1806.   24

Still of use, especially for minor and generally forgotten authors.

Faÿ, Bernard. Bibliographie critique des ouvrages français relatifs aux Etats-Unis (1770-1800). Champion, 1924. 108 p. (Diss., Paris). (BRLC, 7). *See* 3130.   25

Useful work, classified chronologically; any other approach by user, however, made difficult by lack of index.

Fortescue, G. K. Subject index of the modern works added to the library of the British Museum... 1881-1900. London, 1902-03. 3 v. Continued at five-year intervals.   26

Valuable universal subject-index ("... le meilleur répertoire méthodique quin-

quennal de bibliographie universelle qui existe..." Langlois, No. 39, p. 30, n. 3.) Latest volume (1945) covers years 1936-40.

[Franklin, Alfred]. Guide des savants, des littérateurs et des artistes dans les bibliothèques de Paris, par un vieux bibliothécaire. Welter, 1908. 219 p.   27

Useful work : gives location, history, type of contents and fields of specialization of each of more important libraries of Paris, and of many lesser ones.
Review : Anon in Archiv 123:454-55, 1909.

Fuchs, Max. Une bibliothèque provinciale au xviiie siècle. RHL 32:580-87, 1925.   28

Library is that of Huguenot family of Costelongue; is by no means limited to works on Protestant theology, though well supplied in that field.

Fürstenberg, Hans. Das französische Buch im achtzehnten Jahrhundert und in der Empirezeit. Weimar, Gesellschaft der Bibliophilen, 1929. 431 p.   29

Of interest principally to bookcollector, bibliographer, and dealer in rare and illustrated books. Amply and carefully indexed from several points of view.

[Gay, Jules]. Bibliographie des ouvrages relatifs à l'amour, aux femmes, au mariage, et des livres facétieux, pantagruéliques, scatalogiques, satyriques, etc. Par le Cte d'I*** 4th ed., by L. Lemonnyer. Lemonnyer, 1893-1900. 4 v.   30

Lemonnyer edition improves in every respect upon its predecessors, and can render useful service to serious research workers in a number of fields.
Review : G. Vicaire in BBB 1893:596-98.

Georgi, Gottlieb. Allgemeines europäisches Bücher-lexicon. Leipzig, Georgi, 1742-53. 8 v.   30A

Part V : French books to 1749. ("... vraiment unique pour l'ensemble de la littérature européenne, depuis le commencement du xvie siècle jusqu'en 1739; la 5e partie, consacrée aux livres français, est très bonne..." Langlois, (No. 39, p. 16, n. 1.) Three-volume supplement brings work up to 1757. Work best known for 17th century German bibliography.

Giraud, Jeanne. Manuel de bibliographie littéraire pour les xvie, xviie, et xviiie siècles français, 1931-1935. Vrin, 1939. 304 p. 30B

Supplement to Lanson's bibliography, which gives no references beyond 1921. Well made and, in general, reliable work, by trained librarian.
Review : J. Bonnerot in BBB 1939, p. 281-82.

Gottschalk, Louis. Studies since 1920 of French thought in the Period of the Enlightenment. JMH 4:242-60, 1932.   31

Valuable study, too little known. Lays especial emphasis upon contributions of Sée, Mornet, Kingsley Martin, Schinz, and Carcassonne, with briefer mention of many others.

Grässe, Johann G. T. Trésor de livres rares et précieux. Dresden, Kuntze, 1859-69. Berlin, 1922. 7 v.   32

Especially useful in locating translations of editions described. Designed to supplement Brunet, (13), but contains more German entries.

La grande encyclopédie, inventaire raisonné des sciences, des lettres et des arts. Lamirault, [1886-1902]. 31 v.   33

Excellent biographical and critical articles, by able collaborators, followed by brief but well selected bibliographies.

Harrisse, Henry. Les De Thou et leur célèbre bibliothèque, 1573 - 1680 - 1789, (d'après des documents nouveaux) BBB 1903:465-77, 537-48, 577-89, 648-62; 1904: 72-90, 165-71, 259-67, 327-39, 392-400, 487-97, 541-50. Reprinted as : Le président de Thou et ses descendants, leur célèbre bibliothèque, leurs armoiries et les traductions françaises de J.-A. Thuani Historiarum sui temporis. Leclerc, 1905. 274 p.   34

Hatin, Louis Eugène. Bibliographie historique et critique de la presse périodique française. Didot, 1866. 660 p. See 2764. 35

See Bonno, 10.

Hébrail, Jacques, and **Joseph de La Porte.** La France littéraire. Duchesne, 1769-84. 4 v.   36

A mine of interesting and often useful information on all sorts of literary activities : names and membership of learned societies, etc., bibliographies of authors' works, locations of éloges upon them, etc. Information arranged without much system, and often incomplete and inaccurate.

Hœfer, J. C. F. Nouvelle biographie générale. Didot, 1853-70. 46 v.   37

More condensed than Michaud (42), more factual, less literary, and less interesting reading. Contains more names than Michaud, and in its author bibliographies gives titles in original languages, whereas Michaud translates them into French.

Jones, S. Paul. A list of French prose fiction from 1700 to 1750. New York, Wilson, 1939. 150 p. (Diss., Columbia.) See 700.   38

Indispensable in its field.   25-page Introduction gives many valuable facts on literature of period covered.
Reviews : E. R. Briggs in MLR 34: 639-40, 1939; E. Joliat in PQ 19:220, 1940; D. Mornet in RHL 46:128-29, 1939; A. Schinz in RR 31:175-76, 1940.

Langlois, Ch. V. Manuel de bibliographie historique. 2nd ed., Hachette, 1901. 239 p.   39

Intended primarily for students of history, but extremely valuable for students of literature as well. See particularly Part I *(Instruments bibliographiques)*, which covers bibliography of bibliography as well as universal bibliography.

Lanson, Gustave. Manuel bibliographique de la littérature française moderne, xvie, xviie, xviiie et xixe siècles. New ed., Hachette, 1921. Le dix-huitième siècle, p. 531-923. Supplément, p. 1620-1660. 40

Indispensable work, remarkable for clear, logical arrangement; especially good for 18th century. Though not without incomplete and inaccurate references, inevitable in undertaking of such scope, work as whole unequaled for value in its field, and starting point for all serious research in French literature.
Reviews : G. Cohen in RLC 2:499-504, 1922; A. Monglond in RSH 26:123-30, 1913.

La Vallière, Louis César de La Baume Le Blanc, *duc* de. Catalogue des livres de la bibliothèque de feu M. le duc de La Vallière. Bure, 1783-88. 9 v. See 696. 41

Mine of valuable information on manuscripts, first and *de luxe* editions, rare books, etc. Was prepared for sale of library, which lasted from Jan. 12th,

1784, to May 5th. Much of catalogue included in Brunet's *Manuel*, (13). Has elaborately classified table of contents.

Michaud, J. F. and **L. G. Michaud.** Biographie universelle, ancienne et moderne. Vivès, 1842-65. 45 v. 42

Sketches, written by able scholars, in general, reliable, and of real historical and critical value. Often less objective, and contain more human-interest material than similar biographical work today.

Monaghan, Frank. French travellers in the United States, 1765-1932. New York, New York Public Library, 1933. 114 p. 43

Indispensable in its field. Many items have descriptive annotations, and a few have critical ones. Copies of all books listed are located.
Review : *See* 3133.

Monglond, André. La France révolutionnaire et impériale. Grenoble, Arthaud, 1930-38. v. 1-5. (In progress). 44

Indispensable for its period. V. I, 1789-90; v. II, 1791-93; v. III, 1794-96; v. IV, 1797-99; v. V, 1800-02. Detailed work, veritable mine of information, listing pamphlets, books, and articles dealing with period.

Mornet, Daniel. Les origines intellectuelles de la Révolution française, 1715-1787. Colin, 1933. 552 p. 45

A veritable encyclopedia upon its subject; for evaluation as a whole, see : Wade (57). Bibliography of nearly 1600 titles. Book's great usefulness would have been increased by index of proper names. *See* 1062.
Reviews : H. Metzger in Rph 117: 301-03, 1934; A. Meynier in Rfr 87:5-17, 1934.

Nitze, W. A. and **E. Preston Dargan.** Bibliography [of the 18th century]. *In their :* History of French literature from the earliest times to the present. 3rd ed., New York, Holt, [c1938]. p. 816-23. *See* 76. 46

So rigidly selective as to constitute almost a minimum list.
Reviews : C. Gauss in MLN 39:35-45, 1924; K. Glaser in ZFSL 51:473-74, 1928; A. Schinz in MP 21:215-20, 1923-24.

Palfrey, Thomas R., J. G. Fucilla, and **W. C. Holbrook.** The XVIIIth century. *In their :* Bibliographical guide to the

Romance languages and literatures. 3rd. ed., Evanston, Ill., Chandler, 1946. p. 41-42. 47

Two pages devoted to French 18th century list (with cross-references) many bibliographical items essential in any thorough study of period. This list of titles, since it contains only a few annotations, and these of briefest descriptive nature, far wider in scope than that treated in present chapter.
Review : R. Levy in FR 14:233-36, 1940-41.

Peddie, Robert A. Subject index of books published up to and including 1880, A-Z. London, Grafton, 1933. 2nd ser., 1935; 3rd ser., 1939; New Series, 1948. 48

Analytical subject index of books in English and other languages; " ... no headings have been used which can be found in ordinary Author Catalogues..." (ed. of 1933, p. xiv.)
Review : TLS, Aug. 7, 1948, p. 448.

Petit de Julleville, Louis, *ed.* Histoire de la langue et de la littérature françaises des origines à 1900. Colin, 1896-99. 8 v. *See* 77. 49

Bibliographies which follow sketch of each writer in 18th century volume (v. 6, 1898) well selected for content value, but not annotated, and need supplementing in their bibliographical detail before they may safely be cited as references.

Petzholdt, Julius. Bibliotheca bibliographica : kritisches Verzeichniss der das Gesammtgebiet der Bibliographie betreffenden Literatur des In- und Auslandes, in systematischer Ordnung bearbeitet... mit alphabetischem Namen- und Sachsregister. Leipzig, Engelmann, 1866. 939 p. 50

Each item listed followed by brief but precise critical and analytical annotation. " La première, la meilleure, la seule qu'on doive consulter pour tout ce qui est antérieur à 1866..." (Langlois, no. 39, p. 67.) " ... a work of scholarship, displaying... erudition, critical faculty..." (Besterman, no. 5, 1st ed., I, viii.)

Quérard, Joseph-Marie. La France littéraire, ou dictionnaire bibliographique. Didot, 1827-64. 12 v. 51

Indispensable work. Vols. 11 and 12 are supplements, containing corrections and additions, authors, pseudonyms, and anonyms. Covers 18th century and 19th to 1826. Gives biographical notes, titles of works, place and date of publication. Interesting bibliographical and historical notes given on many works.

— Les supercheries littéraires dévoilées. Galerie des écrivains français de toute l'Europe qui se sont déguisés sous des anagrammes, des astéronymes, des cryptonymes, des initialismes, des noms littéraires, des pseudonymes facétieux ou bizarres, etc. 2. éd., considérablement augm., publ. par MM. Gustave Brunet et Pierre Jannet. Suivie 1. du Dictionnaire des ouvrages anonymes par Ant.-Alex. Barbier. 3. éd., rev. et augm. par M. Olivier Barbier. 7 v. Daffis, 1869-79.   52

"Barbier, connected with this edition of Quérard by the phraseology of the title page, is issued separately and has special title : *Dictionnaire des ouvrages anonymes.*" (No. 2) (Quoted from the analytic of the LC card.) Essential work in its field.

Ritchie, R. L. Graeme, *ed.* France : a companion to French studies. 4th ed., London, Methuen [c1946]. 514 p.   53

Preface carefully delimits scope of the work : " ... to supply... the information about France which is necessary as a background to French reading and travel...", beginning with 17th century, in fields of French thought, history, literature, institutions, architecture, and painting. (p. v.) Text gives useful bird's-eye view for non-specialist. Bibliographies which follow most chapters are excellent starting points for research in subjects treated.
Review : Anon in TLS, March 6, 1937, p. 158.

Stein, Henri. Manuel de bibliographie générale (Bibliotheca Bibliographica nova). Picard, 1897. 895 p.   54

Aims at completeness, with omission of outdated works. Has elaborate and methodical system of classification of material by subjects, supported by alphabetical subject-author index.

Stewart, John Hall. France, 1715-1815; a guide to materials in Cleveland. Cleveland, Western Reserve univ. press, 1942. 522 p.   55

Valuable selective bibliography of both primary and secondary materials. Emphasis on historical works, but includes much on 18th century literature.

Tchemerzine, Avenir. Bibliographie d'éditions originales et rares d'auteurs français des xve, xvie, xviie et xviiie siècles. Plée, 1927-34. 10 v.   56

Valuable work; gives detailed bibliographical description of first and rare editions, with complete transcription of titles, showing line endings, title page decorations, and other means of identifying editions. Many facsimiles of title pages.

Wade, Ira O. The clandestine organization and diffusion of philosophic ideas in France from 1700 to 1750. Princeton, Univ. press, 1938. 329 p. *See* 2915.   57

Appendix lists, by libraries, documents consulted; brief bibliography of works used in preparation of book.
Reviews : T. E. Jessop in Phil 14:106-07, 1939; J. Lough in MLR 34:105-06, 1939; A. R. Morehouse in MP 37:214-17, 1939-40; N. L. Torrey in RHL 45; 529-31, 1938.

Watt, Robert. Bibliotheca britannica : or, A general index of British and foreign literature. In two parts : Authors, and Subjects. Edinburgh, Constable, 1824. 4 v.   58

Invaluable subject-index, particularly for 17th and 18th century materials.

Histories of Literature
(Nos. 59-83)

GEORGE R. HAVENS

Abry, E., C. Audic, et P. Crouzet. Histoire illustrée de la littérature française. Didier, 1912. New revised ed., 1929. Distributed in USA by Heath, Boston and New York. 746 p.   59

Excellent manual with systematic arrangement of materials under bold-face headings. Convenient for ready reference to leading facts about each author, his dates and important works. Gives brief citations illustrative of ideas, characteristics, or style. Rather " choppy " for extended reading at one sitting. Best for reference.
Review : D. S. Blondheim in MLN 28:59-61, 1913.

Bédier, Joseph, et Paul Hazard. Histoire de la littérature française illustrée. Larousse, 1923-24. 2 v. Revised ed. 1948-49. 2 v.   60

Two beautifully illustrated volumes in

large format. Some illustrations in color. Excellent text by different authors. 18th century chapters (II, 31-150; revised ed., II, 1-64) by Georges Ascoli and Daniel Mornet, French Revolution (II, 151-57; revised ed., II, 166-75) by Paul Hazard, three outstanding authorities. More recent in text and bibliography than classic Lanson (No. 70). Admirable work in every respect.
Review : K. Glaser in ZFSL 49:183-86, 1927.

Braunschvig, Marcel. Notre littérature étudiée dans les textes. Colin. v. II, 1921. 844 p. 61

Volume II contains 18th and 19th centuries. Brief *morceaux choisis* with useful introduction and commentary on each author. Valuable for survey purposes or for *explication de textes.* Note *Corrections et additions.* p. 841-42.

Brunetière, Ferdinand. Manuel de l'histoire de la littérature française. 8th ed., Delagrave, 1921. 531 p. 62

Most useful for extensive notes, comprising full half of each page. Notes indicate chief original sources, raise interesting questions unsolved by author and often still in doubt, and suggest to attentive reader promising lines of further research or study. As dogmatic thinker, not too friendly to ideas of 18th century, Brunetière should, however, be approached with wholesome skepticism.
Review : H. P. Thieme in MLN 13 : columns 490-506, (p. 245-53), 1898.

Cherel, Albert. De Télémaque à Candide. Gigord, 1933. 526 p. (VI in series ed. by J. Calvet under title : Histoire de la littérature française.) *See* 1033. 63

Faguet, Emile. Histoire de la littérature française. Plon-Nourrit, 1901. 2 v. 64

Brief survey by intelligent and penetrating critic. " Ce qui fait que l'humanité aura toujours beaucoup de complaisance pour le xviiie siècle, c'est que le xviiie siècle ressemble beaucoup à l'humanité " (II, 311). Numerous illustrations and facsimiles of autographs.

Hanotaux, Gabriel. Histoire de la nation française. Société de l'histoire nationale and Plon. v. 13, 1923. p. 379-433 by Fortunat Strowski. 65

Brief and rapid survey, but contains suggestive observations of intelligent and penetrating critic.

Hémon, Félix. Cours de littérature. Delagrave, 1889-1919. 9 v. 66

Old, but useful manuals, several of which deal with 18th century. More detailed than most similar texts. Numerous quotations from works of authors treated. *Jugements* of later critics.

Hervier, Marcel. Les écrivains français jugés par leurs contemporains. Mellottée, 1911-39. v. 2 (Le 18e siècle), 1931. 274 p. 67

Treats great figures, Montesquieu, Voltaire, Rousseau, Buffon, and Diderot. Valuable compilation of contemporary opinions.

Hettner, Hermann. Literaturgeschichte des achtzehnten Jahrhunderts, 6th ed., Braunschweig, Vieweg. Revised by H. Morf, 1912. 3 v. *See* 3192. 68

While older work, still notable for breadth of coverage and comparative point of view. V. 1 deals with English, v. 2 with French, and v. 3 with German literature in 18th century, tracing progress of Enlightenment from one country to another in that order.
Review : Anon in MLN 11 : columns 191-92 (p. 96), 1896.

Jasinski, René. Histoire de la littérature française. Boivin, 1947. 2 v. 69

New manual (1947); follows as strictly as possible chronological order as representing development closest to actual facts. Treats more secondary figures than most similar books. Particularly good for Montesquieu and Diderot among great names of 18th century. Occasional slight errors of dates or facts, as is almost unavoidable in a first edition, but very good and most recent over-all history up to present writing (1948).
Review : L. A. Bisson in MLR 43: 118-19, 1948.

Lanson, Gustave. Histoire de la littérature française. 12th ed., Hachette, 1912 (or later reprintings). 1204 p. 70

23rd ed. (n.d.) has 1266 p. and Appendix with some revisions or additions not incorporated in text. Classic work. Greatest single-volume history of French literature at advanced level. Keen, penetrating, authoritative, open-minded, with appreciation of viewpoints of widely-differing authors. See notes to Montesquieu, Voltaire, and Rousseau which indicate frank modifications of opinion with reasons, while leaving original state-

ment in text for record, remarkable evidence of intellectual integrity. Work written with clarity and verve, but not for elementary student since it assumes some knowledge of authors and their background as well as general philosophical preparation in history of ideas.
Review : A. T[erracher] in MLN 27: 128, 1912.

— Histoire illustrée de la littérature française. Hachette, 1923. 2 v.   71

Two admirably illustrated volumes of large format, preceding slightly and rivaling the famous Bédier and Hazard (No. 60). Many illustrations in full color. Same text as standard single-volume Lanson (No. 70), and same general evaluation applies.
Reviews : K. Glaser, in ZFSL 49:183-86, 1927.

— et **Paul Tuffrau**. Manuel d'histoire de la littérature française. Hachette, 3rd ed., 1932. 813 p. USA, Heath, Boston and New York.   72

Reworking of original Lanson (no. 70), at *lycée* level. Authoritative, interesting, clear. Gives summaries of important works and makes effective use of boldface type for headings. Useful questions at end of each chapter and brief list of supplementary readings. One of best introductory manuals.

Lavisse, Ernest. Histoire de France. V. 8 (Part 2) : Le règne de Louis XV (1715-74). Hachette, 1909. V. 9 (Part 1) : Le règne de Louis XVI (1774-89). Hachette, 1911. *See* 99.   73

Good brief discussion of intellectual, literary, economic, scientific, and artistic movements in 18th century. Occasional minor errors in dates, etc. Citations not always strictly accurate in wording, but difficult to check because references are not given.

— **and Alfred Rambaud.** Histoire générale du IVe siècle à nos jours. V. VII : Le XVIIIe siècle, 1715-1788. Colin, 1896. 1051 p. *See* 100.   74

Chapter 14 (p. 681-725) on French literature is by Emile Faguet and presents valuable survey in less than 50 rapidly-moving pages. Last 2 pages contain brief bibliography, no longer, of course, up to date. Chapters 13, 15, and 16 discuss respectively : *La France économique*, *Les sciences en Europe*, and *L'art en Europe*, written by different specialists.

Mornet, Daniel. Histoire générale de la littérature française (Exposée selon une méthode nouvelle). Larousse, n.d. 2 v. 75

Vol. 1 treats in succinct fashion leading authors and tendencies; Vol. 2 concentrates on a few great works. Thus, for 18th century, Vol. 2 presents Voltaire's *Lettres philosophiques* and *Candide*, Diderot's *Lettres à Mlle Volland* and *Le neveu de Rameau*, and Rousseau's *Nouvelle Héloïse* and *Emile*. Work of master in 18th century French literature. Particularly valuable for beginning student who needs to orient himself and not get lost in multiplicity of authors, works, and tendencies offered by more extensive studies.

Nitze, William A., and E. Preston Dargan. A history of French literature. New York, Holt, 1922; 3rd ed., revised, 1938. 818 p. *See* 46.   76

18th century chapters are by Dargan, an authority on period. His work begins with Part III, *Modern times, The quarrel of the ancients and moderns* (p. 337) (cf. Preface, p. IV). Most recent over-all study of French literature in English. May be used with confidence. A valuable bibliography by chapters at end of volume, with titles of outstanding importance starred.
Reviews : M. P. Brush, FR 2:85-87, 1928; C. Gauss, MLN 39:35-45, 1924; H. C. L[ancaster], *ibid.*, 43:211-12, 1928.

Petit de Julleville, Louis. Histoire de la langue et de la littérature françaises des origines à 1900. Colin, 1895-99; 3rd and 4th printing, 1908-12. 8 v. V. VI, 1909. 901 p. *See* 49.   77

Whole of volume VI is devoted to 18th century. 16 chapters are by different specialists. One of older works, but still very good and complete. Brief bibliographical indications at end of each chapter.

Roustan, Mario. La littérature française par la dissertation. Mellottée, n.d. V. II, Le dix-huitième siècle. 370 p.   78

Stimulating suggestions on topics for written discussion. Numerous hints on reading. Much to provoke thought on part of professor or student.

Shipley, Joseph T. ed., Dictionary of world literature; criticism, forms, technique. New York, Philosophical Library, 1943. 633 p.   79

Useful reference work containing much material in compact form. Many different contributors. See articles : *French criticism, eighteenth century*, (p. 265-68), by G. R. Havens; *Diderot*, by Herbert Dieckmann, and various definitions : *Alexandrine, drame, tragédie*, etc. Review : H. Kurz in FR 17:229, 1943-44.

Saintsbury, George E. B. A short history of French literature. 3rd ed. Oxford, Clarendon, 1889. 608 p. 80

An older history, but written by keen critic of broad and deep learning and vigorous mentality. Author known also for his remarkable article on French literature in 11th ed. of the *Encyclopaedia Britannica* (1910-11), Vol. 11, p. 110-54, and for numerous articles on individual French writers scattered through same edition of same work. Article on French literature and those on Montesquieu, Voltaire, and Rousseau, with some from other periods, have been reprinted under title : *French literature and its masters*, by George Saintsbury, ed. by Huntington Cairns, *See* 1594.

Suchier, Hermann, and Adolf Birsch-Hirschfeld. Geschichte der französischen Literatur. 2nd ed., Leipzig, Bibliographisches Institut, 1913. 2 v. 81

Standard German manual, copiously illustrated. Only a few over 100 pages are devoted to 18th century. Review : W. Küchler in ZFSL 42²: 114-16, 1917.

Villemain, Abel François. Cours de littérature française; tableau de la littérature au XVIIIe siècle. New ed., Didier, 1859. 4 v. 82

Broad survey, including much attention to English background. By modern standards, tends toward superficiality. Has defects of spoken lectures unrevised for publication. Merits attention, however, as one of first exploratory studies in immense field.

Wright, C. H. C. A history of French literature. New York, Oxford university press, 1912. Revised ed., 1925. 990 p. 83

Standard work, but sometimes better for factual information than for interpretation which, in the case of 18th century, is inclined to be more sensitive to defects than to qualities of greatness. Recent studies of Diderot have largely

superseded treatment here. Excellent brief paragraphs, however, treat influence of Montesquieu's *Esprit des lois* on American Constitution. 2nd ed. states : " For this new edition the author has rewritten the final chapter, on contemporary authors, and has thoroughly revised the bibliography " (p. x). Reviews : [O.] Schultz-Gora in ZFSL 43²: 65-71, 1915; A. Terracher in MLN 28:121-24, 1913; A. Tilley and H. Oelsner in MLR 8:121-30, 277, 1913.

Historical and Political Background*
(Nos. 84-107)

DAVID C. CABEEN and GEORGE R. HAVENS

Original Source Materials

Argenson, René Louis de Voyer de Paulmy, marquis d'. Journal et mémoires. Ed. by E. J. B. Rathery. Renouard, 1859-67. 9 v. (SHF, 100, 104, 107, 111, 117, 122, 129, 131, 138). 84

Best edition of these important memoirs of a caustic and radical observer of 18th century abuses, not blinded by his high rank. Saw poverty and suffering of peasantry and thought revolution just around corner as early as middle of century. Commented on Louis XV's loss of popularity and government's nervous orgy of miscellaneous arrests to suppress seditious remarks. Some allowance must be made for author's extreme pessimism and desire for radical reform.

Bachaumont, Louis Petit de. Mémoires secrets pour servir à l'histoire de la république des lettres en France. London, Adamson, 1783-89. 36 v. 85

Edition described and criticized by Paul Lacroix, under his pseudonym *Le bibliophile Jacob*, in the *Préface* (p. I-XIX) of his edition of these *Mémoires* (Delahays, 1859, 468 p.) This latter edition carries all of Bachaumont's own entries, from 1762 till his death in 1771.

* Because of the great amount of material available upon the subject of this section, it is more rigidly selective than any other on a general topic; its compilers regret the number of fine studies which must necessarily be omitted. Lanson, *Bibliographie* (no. 40), p. 43-44, 48, 538-54, 903-23 and the *Supplément* (no. 40, p. 1541-42, 1622-24 and 1656-60) and Du Peloux, *Répertoire général*, etc. (no. 24) *Supplément*, 1927, p. 40-49, offer many further titles.

Barbier, Edmond Jean François. Chronique de la régence et du règne de Louis XV (1718-1765) ou Journal de Barbier, avocat au Parlement de Paris. Charpentier, 1857. 8 v.   86

First complete edition based on author's manuscript. Brief introduction and footnotes. Indispensable source of political and social information by this lawyer-observer of 18th century. Not much on literature. Each chapter deals with a single month. Useful chapter summaries and Index. A *Journal de police sous Louis XV* (1742-43) follows the *Journal de Barbier* (8:129-348).

Buvat, Jean. Journal de la régence (1715-1723). Plon, 1865. 2 v.   87

Useful 29-page introduction by archivist Emile Campardon. Scanty footnotes; adequate index. Covers period from Sept., 1715 to Jan., 1724. Detailed account of illness and death of Louis XIV and maneuvers by which Duc d'Orléans gained Regency. Indispensable source with dates from day to day, sometimes with exact hour of significant happenings. According to James Breck Perkins, *France under the regency*, (no. 102, p. 461, n. 2), this journal has been published " ... with so many and so injudicious omissions that any student of the time had best consult the MS."

Barthélemy, Edouard Marie, *comte de.* Les correspondants de la marquise de Balleroy. Ed. by Count Edouard de Barthélemy. Hachette, 1883. 2 v.   88

Extensive Introduction on Caumartin and Balleroy families. These letters by various hands are valuable direct source of information on early years of 18th century from 1705 to 1724. Of particular importance for Regency of Duc d'Orléans. Details on wild speculation under John Law. Disorder due to false arrests (II, 159-60). " On vole ici et on assassine beaucoup " (II, 138).

Garat, Dominique Joseph, *comte.* Mémoires historiques sur la vie de M. Suard. Belin, 1820. 2 v.   89

No footnotes or index. Jean Baptiste Suard (1733-1817) arrived in Paris in 1750 at seventeen, and became journalist. Revolution left him, like many another survivor, disillusioned with reign of disorder and bloodshed. Garat has given interesting record of ideas and opinions during second half of 18th century, with some reflections on their influence on leaders of Revolution. Valuable analytical Table of contents at beginning.

Marais, Mathieu. Journal et mémoires... sur la régence et le règne de Louis XV (1715-1737). Didot, 1863-68. 4 v.   90

Adequate, 102-page biographical and critical introduction on Marais by M. F. A. de Lescure. Scanty footnotes; excellent, detailed analytical index. Like Jean Buvat, Marais begins with death of Louis XIV and first colorful events of Regency. Memoirs end with October, 1727, followed by extracts from Marais' *Correspondance* with President Bouhier from 1724 to 1737. Some rather scanty information on literary events. Scornful attitude toward escapades of young Arouet (Voltaire). Marais, like Barbier, was a lawyer of the Parlement, inclined to be conservative; but was a hardheaded observer of events. His *Journal* is, within its limits, classic source of firsthand information.

Marmontel, Jean François. Mémoires. Didot, 1884. 447 p.   91

Introduction of eleven pages by F. Barrière. Marmontel (1723-99), one of lesser *philosophes*, wrote his *Mémoires* in 1798 for instruction of his children. Favorable to Diderot, hostile to Rousseau. Interesting testimony on great literary personalities of 18th century, on reform of declamation in theater, etc. Must of course be read critically with due allowance for author's limitations and prejudices.

[Métra, François]. Correspondance littéraire secrète. Neuwied, Société typographique, 1775-1793. 19 v. Also entitled : Correspondance secrète, politique et littéraire. London, Adamson, 1787-1790. 18 v.   92

Voluminous, gossipy, but at times gives interesting and significant details on events and opinions during tragic reign of Louis XVI. First edition so rare that even *Bibliothèque nationale* possesses only a few volumes of it. The other edition, which stops with 7th October 1785 and is not identical with first, more common. Cf. Quérard, *La France littéraire* (no. 51), and Barbier, *Dictionnaire des ouvrages anonymes* (no. 2). For more extended description, cf. also Hatin, *Bibliographie de la presse*, (no. 2764, p. 68), and his *Histoire de la presse*, (no. 2762, 3:483).

Morellet, André. Mémoires inédits sur le dix-huitième siècle et sur la révolution. L'advocat, 1821. 2 v. 2nd ed., 1822.   93

V. I has 22-page *éloge* of Morellet which was the *Discours de réception* of his successor in the *Académie française*, P. E. Lemontey. No footnotes. Abbé André Morellet (1727-1819) left valuable record of ideas, personalities and events from 1750 to coming to power of Napoleon in early years of 19th century. Rather hostile to Rousseau, though less categorically than Marmontel, and an admirer of Diderot. Disillusioned by violence of the Revolution.

Saint-Simon, Louis de Rouvroy, *duc* **de.** Mémoires de Saint-Simon, ed. by A. de Boislisle. Hachette, 1879-28. 42 v. (GEF)   94

Fine edition; ample, scholarly footnotes; convenient marginal subject headings. 2-volume index detailed, analytical, and accurate. Saint-Simon was vivid, passionate observer of decline of Louis XIV and rise of Regency. No such record exists elsewhere. Detailed descriptions of leading personalities of time. Due allowance must be made for author's volcanic temperament and towering prejudices, but, particularly for last half of age of Louis XIV, his record seems essentially true in its main lines. Indicates hard-working virtues as well as narrow vision of the great King. Review: J. C. in RQH 3rd ser. 12: 230-31, 1928.

Modern Discussions

Barni, Jules. Histoire des idées morales et politiques au dix-huitième siècle. Baillière, 1865-73. 3 v.   95

In modest foreword, author explains that these volumes are intended for instruction of young students. General ideas are brought out in discussion of individual authors. Treats important questions from sanely liberal point of view and, without any effort to be either profound or brilliant, is still of more intrinsic value today than many books which attempt to be both.

Caro, Elme. La fin du dix-huitième siècle; études et portraits. Hachette, 1880. 2 v. 96

Important and interesting work. Portraits of individuals are valuable; chapters which begin each volume have direct bearing on subject of present section

V. I opens with: *L'opinion publique au dix-huitième siècle* (19 pages) : v. II : *Paris et la société française de 1765 à 1775* (42 p.). Few books study as profitably both literature and political history and their relationship because Caro is both able historian and penetrating literary critic, with sufficiently balanced temperament, for example, to render justice both to Montesquieu and to Rousseau.

Houssaye, Arsène. Galerie du XVIIIe siècle. Dentu. v. I, La régence, 1874. 362 p. V. 2, Louis XV. 1874. 370 p. V. 3, Louis XVI, 1875. 370 p.   97

Approaches study of history through personalities. Reader may expect lively and interesting portraits of individuals rather than penetrating analysis of causes.

Janet, Paul. Histoire de la science politique dans ses rapports avec la morale. 3rd ed. Alcan, 1887, 2 v.   98

Still essential book. Only four chapters (V, VI, VII and X of v. II) directly concern 18th century France, though some of book's most valuable material treats predecessors and contemporaries, in Italy, England, and Germany, of *philosophes*, and influence of these foreign thinkers on latter. Treatment of Montesquieu (1573) especially valuable; one of best available comparisons of him with Rousseau is found on p. 465-77.

Lavisse, Ernest. Ed. Histoire de France depuis les origines jusqu'à la révolution. Hachette, 1900-11. 9 v. V. 8, part 1, Louis XIV; la fin du règne, (1685-1715), part 2, Le règne de Louis XV. v. 9, part 1, Le règne de Louis XVI (1774-1789). *See* 73.   99

In the opinion of a leading British authority : " Lavisse's great cooperative *History of France* incorporates the latest researches down to 1789, and renders the older narratives without exception obsolete." (G. P. Gooch, *History and historians in the nineteenth century.* 3rd ed. London and New York, Longmans, Green [1935] p. 225. Essential work, by able body of specialists. Excellent, detailed table of contents, made easy to use by marginal topic headings. Last volume, (v. 9, part 2), is admirable subject and proper name index.

Reviews : H. E. Bourne in AHR 15: 857-58, 1909-10 (v. 8, part 2), and *Ibid.* 16:615-16, 1910-11 (v. 9, part 1); T. F. T. in EHR 25:408-09, 1910 (v. 8, part 2) and 26 : 425, 1911 (v. 9, part 1); J. W. Thompson in AHR 14:579-81, 1908-09 (v. 8, part 1).

— and **Alfred Rambaud.** Histoire générale du IVᵉ siècle à nos jours. Colin, 1893-1901. 12 v. V. 6, Louis XIV (1643-1715). V. 7, Le XVIIIᵉ siècle (1715-1788). V. 8, La révolution française (1789-1799). *See* 74.
100

Essential work. Each principal subject treated by competent specialist, each an authority in his respective field. Valuable selective bibliographies follow chapters. Much better in dealing with French writers than with foreign writers. In v. 8 Aulard is especially good on French Revolution, on which period he is one of leading authorities of his time.
Reviews : E. Bernheim in HZ 86 (ns 50) : 470-75, 1901; E. D. in PrJ 104: 531-34, 1901; G. Monod in Rhist 63:137-38, 1897; H. M. Stephens in AHR 3: 349-52, 1897-98 (v. 7) and 715-18, (v. 8).

Lefebvre, Georges. The coming of the French revolution. Trans. by R. R. Palmer, Princeton, Princeton Univ. press, 1947. 233 p.
101

Author considered by translator as ablest and most balanced living authority on French Revolution. Respected by both conservatives and radicals. Study popular in tone. Appeared in 1939 as *Quatre-vingt-neuf,* to celebrate 150th anniversary of Revolution, and was later suppressed by Vichy. Good preface and notes by translator.
Reviews : P. H. Beik in SRL 31:30-31, Feb. 21, 1948; M. Spahr in APSR 42:388, Apr., 1948; L. Woolf in NSN 35:339, Apr. 24, 1948.

Perkins, James Breck. France under the regency. Boston and New York, Houghton, Mifflin, 1892. 603 p.
102

Well-balanced, well-written account of events, though not remarkable for either profound or brilliant analyses of underlying historical causation. More than half of book deals with reign of Louis XIV. Treatment of John Law's speculations excellent.
Reviews : G. B. A[dams] in YR 1: 317-18, 1892-93; Anon in Atl 71:682-85, May, 1893; Anon in NNY 55:307-08, Oct. 20, 1892; A. F. Pollard in EHR 8:791-93, Oct., 1893.

— France under Louis XV. Boston and New York, Houghton, Mifflin, 1897. 2 v.
103

Just, moderate appraisal of the *régime;* stronger on historical narrative than on tendencies in national life, and better at showing industrial progress than in analysis of political philosophies.
Reviews : Anon in NNY 66:188-89, March 10, 1898; H. E. Bourne in AHR 3:535-37, 1897-98.

Sée, Henri. Les idées politiques en France au XVIIIᵉ siècle. Hachette, 1920. 264 p.
104

Interesting work, especially useful for way in which it outlines principal characteristics of political thinking of 18th century, and suggests its relationship to literature of Revolution. Greater part of work devoted to treating political ideas as exposed and illustrated in writings of their leading exponents : Montesquieu, D'Argenson, Voltaire, Rousseau, Diderot, Helvétius, D'Holbach, the Physiocrats, Mably, and Condorcet.
Review : F. M. Fling in AHR 26:507-09, 1920-21.

Ségur, Pierre Marie Maurice Henri, *marquis* de. Au couchant de la monarchie. V. I. Louis XVI et Turgot (1774-1776). Calmann Lévy, [1909]. 372 p. V. II. Louis XVI et Necker (1776-1781). *Ibid.,* [1913] 461 p.
105

Sound history, written with distinction. In v. I, author expresses belief that Turgot, " ... le plus honnête homme de son temps..." (p. 365) yet hastened fall of monarchy by his lack of experience and of realism. Book is rich in pen portraits; the historian, a liberal aristocrat in the best tradition of his caste, succeeds in being just toward those less well endowed than himself. *See* no. 2495. These volumes, sound and interesting as history, touch literature only indirectly.
Reviews : Anon in RHEM 51:181-83, July, 1913; J. Dureng in RDS 1:333, 1913.

Tocqueville, [Alexis, etc.]. Histoire philosophique du règne de Louis XV. 2nd ed., Amyot, [c1847] 2 v.
106

Author attempts to cover almost whole history of this reign, with considerable detail, in somewhat less than 1000 pages. Succeeds fairly well, and presents material in clear, readable form, though interpretations of events necessarily foreshortened, and therefore oversimplified. Detailed table of contents in each volume, but no index.

Vaughan, Charles Edwyn. Studies in the history of political philosophy before and after Rousseau. Manchester, Univ. press; London and New York, Longmans, Green, 1925. 2 v. *See* 1604, 2149, 3077. 107

Brilliant, but often subjective and abstract interpretations and analyses of political philosophies as seen in light of various figures whom Vaughan considers. Contains many fine ideas, such as study of role of expediency in politics, but numerous inadequacies, among them failure to trace relationships between thinkers and their environment. Especially able on Montesquieu, and his relationship with Vico. (*See* also no. 1582).
Reviews : Anon in TLS, May 7, 1925, p. 307; C. D. B[urns] in IJE 36:107, 1925-26; H. J. Laski in NNY 121:45-46, July 1, 1925; C. Schmitt in Dlit 46² : 2086-90, Oct. 24, 1925.

Letter Writers and Authors of Memoirs

Letters Writers
Mademoiselle Aïssé,
Mademoiselle de Lespinasse,
Madame du Deffand
(Nos. 108-135)

Margaret Gilman

Charlotte Elisabeth Aïssé

Aïssé, Charlotte Elisabeth. Lettres portugaises, avec les réponses. Lettres de Mademoiselle Aïssé, suivies de celles de Montesquieu et de Madame du Deffand au chevalier d'Aydie, etc. Revues avec le plus grand soin sur les éditions originales, accompagnées de nombreuses notes, suivies d'un index et précédées de deux notices biographiques et littéraires par Eugène Asse. Charpentier, 1873. 423 p. 108

Biographical introduction and valuable notes (including Voltaire's notes published in the 1787 edition) on persons and events referred to in letters. Appendix contains letters about A., prefaces to first edition, and information on Calendrini and Aydie families.

[Aimery de Pierrebourg, Marguerite, baronne]. Mademoiselle Aïssé et son tendre chevalier. Fayard [1930]. 259 p. Author's pseud., Claude Ferval, at head of title. 109

Popular biography of A. and the Chevalier d'Aydie. Differs from Sainte-Beuve and Asse on probable relations between A. and M. de Ferriol.

Asse, Eugène. Le baron de Ferriol et mademoiselle Aïssé. Rrét ns 8:1-48, 97-144, 169-202, 1894. 110

Chiefly on Ferriol, but his will, published here for first time, establishes certain previously doubtful facts and dates in A.'s life.

Bouvier, Emile. La genèse de l'Histoire d'une Grecque moderne. RHL 48:113-30, 1948. *See* 785. 111

Shows convincingly that Prévost's novel is a *roman à clef*, based on *l'histoire scandaleuse* of A. and M. de Ferriol, which is discussed in detail.

Ferval, Claude, *pseud., See* : Aimery de Pierrebourg. 112

Gosse, Edmund. Mademoiselle Aïssé. *In his :* French profiles. New York, Dodd Mead, 1905. p. 35-67. 113

Puts A. among greatest French letter-writers, together with Mme de Sévigné and Mlle de Lespinasse.

Ritter, Eugène. Notes sur les Lettres de Mademoiselle Aïssé. MélGL p. 313-18. 114

Notes on date of A.'s birth, and on a number of Genevans mentioned in her letters.

Sainte-Beuve, C. A. Mademoiselle Aïssé. RDM ns 13:294-320, Jan. 15, 1846. *Also,* with additions and corrections, *in his :* Portraits littéraires, Garnier, nd. 3:129-83. 115

Published also as foreword to : *Lettres de Mademoiselle Aïssé à Madame Calendrini.* 5th ed., Gerdès, 1846. 311 p. Biographical and psychological study, supplemented by unpublished documents and letters.

Julie Jeanne Éléonore de Lespinasse

Lespinasse, Julie Jeanne Eléonore de. Lettres de Mademoiselle de Lespinasse, suivies de ses autres œuvres et de lettres de Madame du Deffand, de Turgot, de Bernardin de Saint-Pierre, revues sur les éditions originales, augmentées des variantes, de nombreuses notes, d'un appendice comprenant les écrits de d'Alembert, de Guibert, de Voltaire, de Frédéric II, sur Mademoiselle de Lespinasse, d'un index, et précédées d'une notice biographique et lit-téraire par Eugène Asse. Charpentier, 1876. lxxix + 409 p.   116

Text of letters to Guibert superseded by 1906 edition, and introduction by Ségur's biography, but this edition still indispensable for notes and supple-mentary material on L.

— Correspondance entre Mademoiselle de Lespinasse et le comte de Guibert, publiée pour la première fois d'après le texte original par le comte de Villeneuve-Guibert. Cal-mann-Lévy, 1906. 563 p.   117

Described by F. Vandérem in BBB ns 9:49-51, 1930, as " la seule édition complète et intégrale " (p. 50).

Asse, Eugène. Mademoiselle de Lespinasse et la marquise du Deffand, suivi de docu-ments inédits sur Mademoiselle de Lespi-nasse. Charpentier, 1877. 108 p.   118

Gives proofs that L.'s mother was Comtesse d'Albon. Documents include L.'s acte de baptême, will, inventory, etc.

Beaunier, André. La vie amoureuse de Julie de Lespinasse. Flammarion, 1925. 191 p.   119

Popular biography, tending to over-emphasize romantic side of L.

Bonnefon, Paul. Mademoiselle de Lespi-nasse : l'amoureuse et l'amie. RHL 4:321-65, 1897.   120

Chief interest is unpublished letters from L. to Jean Devaines.

Eliac, Georges. Un après-midi chez Julie de Lespinasse. Préface du marquis de Ségur. Émile-Paul, 2nd ed., 1912. See 278.   120A

Imaginative reconstruction, from letters and memoirs, of L.'s salon, done, as Ségur says in preface, with " une vérité poussée jusqu'au scrupule " (p. v).

Royde-Smith, Naomi. The double heart, a study of Julie de Lespinasse. New York, Harper, 1931. 287 p. See 280.   121

As author says, no new material, but fresh point of view, seeing in L. " a strange necessity of her own nature that makes love for her synonymous with du-plicity" (p. 11). Evidence not convincing.

Sainte-Beuve, C. A. Lettres de Made-moiselle de Lespinasse. In his : Causeries du lundi. Garnier, nd. 2:121-42.   122

Somewhat unsympathetic, but in ge-neral fair picture of L. as victim of " genre de passion et de mal sacré rare en France."

Ségur, Pierre Marie Maurice Henri, mar-quis de. Julie de Lespinasse. RDM 75th year, 5th per. 26:515-58, April 1, 1905; 860-902, Apr. 15, 1905; 27:867-906, June 15, 1905; 28:51-86, July 1, 1905; 29:74-116, Sept. 1, 1905, 824-67, Oct. 15, 1905; 30: 102-45, Nov. 1, 1905. Also : Calmann-Lévy, [1906]. 651 p.   123

— Julie de Lespinasse. Trans. by P. H. Lee Warner, New York, Holt, 1907. 403 p. See 282.

Most complete biography of L. and basis for all later ones. First to identify L.'s father as Gaspard de Vichy. Sym-pathetic study of L. as a " mélange de chaleur et de retenue." Pages (104-10) on Taaffe superseded by W. H. Smith in his introduction to Letters to and from Madame du Deffand and Julie de Lespi-nasse. (No. 126.) Appendix contains many previously unpublished documents and letters of L. to the Vichy family, and D'Alembert's correspondence with the Duc de Villa-Hermosa.

La Marquise Marie Anne
(de Vichy-Chamrond) du
Deffand de la Lande

Du Deffand de la Lande, Marie Anne (de Vichy-Chamrond) marquise. Correspon-dance complète de Madame du Deffand avec la duchesse de Choiseul, l'abbé Barthé-lemy et M. Craufurt, publiée avec une introduction par M. le marquis de Sainte-Aulaire. Nouvelle édition revue et con-sidérablement augmentée. Michel Lévy, 1866. 3 v. A 3rd edition (Lévy, 1877) revised and enlarged.   124

Introduction contains some useful in-formation, but shows little understanding of D. and is distinctly moralizing in tone.

— Correspondance complète de la marquise du Deffand avec ses amis le président Hé-nault, Montesquieu, D'Alembert, Voltaire, Horace Walpole, classée dans l'ordre chro-nologique et sans suppressions, augmentée des lettres inédites au chevalier de l'Isle, précédée d'une histoire de sa vie, de son salon, de ses amis, suivie de ses œuvres diverses et éclairée de nombreuses notes par M. de Lescure. Plon, 1865. 2 v. 125

Lescure's introduction still most useful and detailed biography of D., especially valuable for wealth of quotations from contemporary memoirs. But tends to underrate importance of D.'s correspondence with the Choiseul family and with the Barthélemy, first published by Sainte-Aulaire in 1859.

— Letters to and from Madame du Deffand and Julie de Lespinasse, edited by Warren Hunting Smith. New Haven, Yale univ. press, 1938. 97 p.   126

Contains 31 letters, of which 18 (from W. S. Lewis collection) are entirely unpublished. Most illuminating for early relations of D. and L., and for L.'s affair with John Taaffe.

[Aimery de Pierrebourg, Marguerite, baronne.] Madame du Deffand, l'esprit et l'amour au xviiie siècle. Fayard, [1937]. 415 p. Author's pseud., Claude Ferval, at head of title. See 216.   127

Popular, somewhat sentimental, but well-documented biography. Account of break with Mlle de Lespinasse puts latter completely in wrong, and is far from fair.

Walpole, Horace. Horace Walpole's Correspondence with Madame du Deffand and Wiart, edited by W. S. Lewis and Warren Hunting Smith. New Haven, Yale univ. press, 1939. 6 v. (The Yale edition of Horace Walpole's Correspondence, v. 3-8). See 215, 3029.   128

Admirable edition, containing in addition to letters published in Toynbee edition of 1912, about 15 pages of unpublished letters, Walpole's Paris journals, D.'s Journal (1779-80), her will and inventory, and " portraits " of and by her. Full notes, including information on practically everyone mentioned in letters. Introduction contains : discussion of previous editions (inferior to Toynbee's treatment); life of D., establishing for first time date of birth and of legal separation, and details of financial status; brief but excellent study of D. and Walpole; account of manuscripts of letters and of D.'s bequest to Walpole and of new material in present edition; bibliography of works by and on D.
Reviews : See 3029.

Bradford, Gamaliel. Madame du Deffand. In his : Portraits of women. Boston, Houghton Mifflin, 1916. p. 135-54.   129

Unsympathetic study, finding in D.'s affection for Walpole " the most marked symptom of health in a character otherwise erratic, distorted and unsound." (p. 154).

De Koven, Anna. Horace Walpole and Madame du Deffand : an eighteenth century friendship. New York, Appleton, 1929. 199 p.   130

Attempts to justify Walpole, emphasizing the happiness he and D. enjoyed when they were together, and maintaining that " he loved her better than he knew " (p. vi). Frequent errors in translations of letters.

Ilchester, [G. S. H. F.] 6th earl of. Madame du Deffand to Walpole. TLS June 19, 1948, p. 348.   131

Text of important letter from D., annotated by Walpole, dated Dec. 26, 1770, and giving detailed account of the Duc de Choiseul's fall from power. This letter, listed as missing in the Yale edition of Walpole's correspondence (IV, 497), was discovered during a recent rearrangement of manuscripts evacuated from Holland House.

Naughton, A. E. A. Some literary opinions of Madame du Deffand. Stanford studies in language and literature. Stanford University, Cal., [1941]. p. 257-74.   132

Good summary of D.'s reading, but analysis of her taste less sure and discriminating than Sainte-Beuve's.

Sainte-Beuve, C. A. Lettres de la marquise du Deffand. In his : Causeries du lundi. Garnier, nd. 1:412-31. See 225.   133

Penetrating psychological study, bringing out both classical and pre-romantic sides of D. A fuller knowledge of D.'s correspondence with Walpole has made conclusions on Walpole " rigueurs plus apparentes que réelles " highly questionable. Study dated March, 1850.

— Correspondance inédite de Madame du Deffand. In his : Causeries du lundi. Garnier, nd. 14:218-37.   134

Especially interesting for its very sympathetic study of the Duchesse de Choiseul, who " a bien les honneurs de cette correspondance." Study dated May, 1859.

Ségur, Pierre Marie Maurice Henri, marquis de. Madame du Deffand et sa famille. RDM 5th per. 36:353-401, Nov. 15, 1906. Also in his : Esquisses et récits, Calmann-Lévy, [1908]. p. 1-136. See 228.   135

Important material gathered from provincial archives, including number of letters from D. to members of her family, which add greatly to knowledge of her life before 1750.

Authors of Memoirs

d'Argenson, Bachaumont, Duclos
(Nos. 136-174)

Dorothy M. McGhee

René Louis de Voyer de Paulmy, marquis d'Argenson

Argenson, René Louis de Voyer de Paulmy, marquis d'. Considérations sur le gouvernement ancien et présent de la France. Amsterdam [*i.e.* Paris], Rey, 1765. 312 p.   136

Argenson, René Louis de Voyer de Paulmy, marquis d'. Les loisirs d'un ministre, ou, essais dans le goût de ceux de Montaigne, composés en 1736. Plomteux, 1787. 2 v. in I.   137

— Journal et mémoires. *See :* 84.   138

La France au milieu du XVIIIe siècle (1747-1757) d'après le Journal du marquis d'Argenson. Extraits publiés avec une notice bibliographique par Armand Brette et précédés d'une introduction par Edme Champion. Colin, 1898. 411 p.   139

Introduction stresses modification of ministerial ideas after 1750.

Alem, André. Le marquis d'Argenson et l'économie politique au début du dix-huitième siècle. Rousseau, 1900. 188 p.   140

Though repetitive, the volume offers a panoramic scene of author and century, forerunners of the physiocrats, with d'A. as relatively conservative. Paucity of notes and references makes analytical reading difficult.

Aubertin, Charles. Le marquis d'Argenson. *In his :* L'esprit public au XVIIIe siècle. Didier, 1873. p. 192-233. *See :* 1021.   141

Valuable study. Interprets era through *Mémoires* of great and versatile mind which evaluated shadings in liberalism. Believes that a d'A. less completely absorbed in political life might have become great figure in literature.

Batiffol, Louis. Les vrais bibliophiles; Le marquis de Paulmy d'Argenson. *In :* Cantinelli, Richard, and Emile Dacier, Les

trésors des bibliothèques de France. Van Oest, 1933. 4:124-34.   142

In this volume, d'A. is revealed as true collector. Portrait engraving. Samples of library which he permitted scholars to see, after 1767.

Broglie, Albert, *duc* de. Maurice de Saxe et le marquis d'Argenson. Calmann-Lévy, 1891. 2 v.   143

Meticulously documented, making ample use of *Mémoires*, these two volumes present direct, readable exposition of events leading up to the Minister's dismissal.

Champion, Edme. Le marquis d'Argenson. Rfr 36:97-115, 1899.   144

A cumulative plea, through d'A. drama, to examine all history with sanity and balance. View that minister was essentially moderate; that criticism has often been over-recriminatory.

Durand, Karl. Die Memoiren des Marquis d'Argenson. Berlin and Leipzig, Rothschild, 1908. 100 p. (MNG, v 6).   145

Careful documentation and concision of form; has usual material on composition of *Memoirs;* discusses d'A.'s difficulty in reconciling internal policy with foreign.

Flassan, Gaëtan des Raxis, *comte* de. [D'Argenson]. *In :* Histoire générale et raisonnée de la diplomatie française. Treuttel et Würtz, 1811, 5:331 et sq.   146

Background study, copiously documented, basic for diplomatic motivations of d'A.'s works. Clarifies circumstances of Marquis' dismissal, and his subsequent declaration of mental independence.

Lichtenberger, André. [D'Argenson]. *In his :* Le socialisme au XVIIIe siècle. Alcan, 1895. 471 p. p. 93-103, *passim.*   147

Interesting as giving motivations which by implication enter character of d'A. *See* 1052.

Ogle, Arthur. The marquis d'Argenson, a study in criticism. Stanhope Essay, Oxford, 1893. London, Fisher Unwin, 1893. 262 p.   148

Expansive, leisurely promenade among attitudes, promises, characteristics, and literary style of d'A. Extremely readable; appreciative of austere and powerful dignity of Louis' minister.

Rankin, Reginald. The marquis d'Argenson and Richard II. London, Longmans, Green, 1901. 300 p. 149

Adeptly expressed presentation of d'A. as paradox, in revolt against very public opinion he professed to cherish; shown as uncompromising minister, becoming apostle of decentralization, and as *philosophe* still devoted to principle of monarchy. Copiously annotated.

Sainte-Beuve, Charles-Augustin. Le marquis d'Argenson d'après les manuscrits. *In his :* Causeries du lundi, Nov. 3, 10, and 17, 1855. Garnier, 1857. 12:93-156. 150

Praise for what seemed 18th century paradox,—adroitness and integrity within state ministry. Interest in remarks more often inheres in Sainte-Beuve's own predilections than in d'A.'s activities.

— Journal et mémoires du marquis d'Argenson, publiés d'après les manuscrits de la Bibliothèque du Louvre, by [J. B.] Rathery. *In his :* Causeries du lundi, June 20, 1859. Garnier, s.d. 14:238-59. 151

Continued interest in d'A.'s apparent complexity of spirit.

Sée, Henri. D'Argenson. *In his :* Les idées politiques en France au xviiie siècle. *See :* 104. p. 51-65. 152

A study which shows with clarity and force that d'A.'s ideas were by no means abstractions, when examined in connection with panorama of century.

— Les idées politiques et sociales du marquis d'Argenson. RIS 32:136-47, 1924. 153

Useful summary of ways in which d'A. announced his democratic principles, not so much as theorist, but as one imbued with them and living them.

Zévort, Edgar. Le marquis d'Argenson et le ministère des affaires étrangères, du 18 nov. 1744 au 10 janv. 1747. Baillière, 1880. 415 p. 154

Precision and clarity, in focusing upon numerous missions, clouded thinking and agreements of doubtful value during d'A.'s ministry. Useful sources, appendices and catalogue of Correspondence, making impartial judgment a possibility.

Louis Petit de Bachaumont

Bachaumont, Louis Petit de. Mémoires secrets pour servir à l'histoire de la république des lettres en France. Ed. by F. Pidansat de Mairobert and Moufle d'Angerville. London, Adamsohn, 1777-89. 36 v. *See :* 85. 155

Aubertin, Charles. Mémoires de Bachaumont. *In his:* L'esprit public au xviiie siècle. Didier, 1873. p. 374-99. *See :* 1021. 156

Evaluates B. as a type complementary to that of d'Argenson—completely dilettante, but important because he excluded nothing from his *Mémoires* and criticized Voltaire constructively.

[Boyer d'Eguilles, A. J. B. ed.]. Un protégé de Bachaumont; correspondance inédite du marquis d'Eguilles. Rrét 3:95-168, 217-40, 1886; 4:121-44, 217-40, 1886; 5:73-96, 1887. 157

Documented from Arsenal notes, and salon of Mme Doublet, this correspondence evokes an entire scene : fascinating, corrupt, pampered; a circle in which B. moved at ease, dispensing interesting advice.

Goncourt, Edmond and Jules de. Bachaumont. *In their :* Portraits intimes du xviiie siècle. Dentu, 1857. p. 7-47. 158

A conversational, journalized account, which, in treating B. as " l'anecdotier parfait " of his century (p. 8) fails to concede that Mercier has any claim to that title. Is, however, profitably detailed, well-rounded portrait.

Nougaret, P. J. B. Anecdotes secrètes du xviiie siècle, rédigées avec soin d'après la correspondance secrète, politique et littéraire, pour faire suite aux Mémoires de Bachaumont. Colin, 1808. 2 v. 159

In the same genre as B., but infinitely dull in telling. Satires on Academy form only particular appeal.

Hatin, Eugène. Bachaumont. *In his :* Bibliographie historique et critique de la presse française, (No. 2764), p. 66-68. *Also in his :* Histoire politique et littéraire de la presse en France, (No. 2762), v. 3. p. 464, 471-83, and especially 478-83. 160

Charles Pinot Duclos

Duclos, Charles Pinot. Œuvres complètes. Colnet, 1806. 10 v. 161

— Histoire de Louis XI. *In his :* Œuvres complètes, Guérin, 1745-46. 2:3-609. 162

— Mémoires secrets sur les règnes de Louis XIV et de Louis XV. *In :* Petitot,

Claude B., ed. Collection des mémoires relatifs à l'histoire de France. Foucault, 1819-29. 2nd ser., v. 76-77.   163

The *Notice sur Duclos*, 76:3-38, contains rather ordinary biographical material— which is presented more attractively by Sainte-Beuve. (no. 174). Texts of D. and Abbé Le Grand are collated.

— Mémoires sur la vie de Duclos, écrits par lui-même. *In :* Mémoires biographiques et littéraires. Ed. by M. F. A. de Lescure. Firmin-Didot, 1881. 37:1-37.   164

Rather mediocre as study, but useful for its survey of material.

Barni, Jules. Duclos; l'homme : sa vie. *In his :* Les moralistes français du dix-huitième siècle. Germer Baillière, 1873. p. 71-115.   165

Extremely readable account of D.'s circle; text carries air of authority.

Bondois, P. M. Crébillon et Duclos à la Bibliothèque du Roi. RHL 38:599-602, 1931.   166

Treatment of custom of sinecures for important authors—custom which accounts for some of the official signatures by D.

Brunel, Lucien. Duclos et d'Alembert entrent à l'Académie. *In his :* Les philosophes et l'Académie française au dix-huitième siècle. Hachette, 1884. p. 28-43; also : p. 44-58. *See :* 1029.   167

Meticulous and clear presentation of the Academy's role in philosophic movement, its respect for hard work, and its unfortunate disregard for innovation. Throughout, D. is viewed as taking constructive attitude toward future of Academy.

Gilbert, Pierre. Une résurrection littéraire : Charles Pinot-Duclos. RCI 16:670-88, 1912.   168

Appreciative of some elements that made for D.'s popularity among his own, —independence, lack of affectation. Correlatively, exposes smug pretensions of many of *philosophes.*

Dimoff, Paul. Les relations de J.-J. Rousseau et de Duclos. MerF 178:5-19, Feb.-Mar., 1925.   169

Concisely expressive account of a lifelong friendship that often evaluated the Rousseau works in manuscript. (*Le devin du village; La Nouvelle Héloïse; Emile.*)

Henriot, Émile. Un honnête homme au XVIIIe siècle, — Duclos. Nrev 3rd per. 17:553-64, Sept.-Oct., 1910; 3rd per. 18: 124-33, Nov.-Dec., 1910.   170

Biographically superseded by more detailed studies, but this is of superior penetration. Masterful evocation of salon spirit.

— Duclos. RPar 32^2:596-609, Apr., 1925.   171

Lacking other merits, D. deserves appreciation as *portraiteur.*

Le Bourgo, Léo. Un homme de lettres au XVIIIe siècle; Duclos, sa vie et ses ouvrages. Bordeaux, Gounouilhou, 1902. 233 p. (Diss., Rennes). *See :* 991.   172

Basic work from many standpoints; extensive bibliography; editions; direct, yet conversationally pleasant evaluation of D.'s fame in respect to his life, rather than works. Accompanying arguments of significance :—Preciosity surviving into 18th century; D. as early exponent of Utilitarianism.

McCloy, Shelby T. Duclos, historian and philosopher. SAQ 38:60-74, 1939.   173

Article for layman, stressing D.'s sociological views.

Sainte-Beuve, C. A. Duclos. *In his :* Causeries du lundi. Garnier, nd, 9:204-61. *Also in his :* Galerie de portraits littéraires; écrivains politiques et philosophes. Garnier, 1893. p. 19-63.   174

A study impressive for its balanced judgments. D. pictured at once as prime *causeur,* bitter, humble, of Utopian turn of mind (short of revolution); of doubtful integrity in acknowledging literary debts.

The Salons
(Nos. 175-301B)

Morris Bishop

Studies on French 18th century society and salons in general are listed first in this section, alphabetically by name of authors. Next come items under individual *salonnières* in alphabetical order, and under the name of each, in alphabetical order by name of the author of the study. To save space only enough Christian names are given to permit identification (i.e., the first two). Dates of birth and death of the leaders of salons are printed because a knowledge of their ages at a given date in an author's life may be material, or at least of interest. When possible these names and dates are taken from the LC catalogue; otherwise, from Hœfer. (F. Hœfer, *Nouvelle biographie générale*. Didot, 1853-70. 46 v. *See :* 37.) In several cases, the dates given for the salons are approximate.

General Studies
(Nos. 175-197)

Abrantès, Laure Junot, *duchesse* **d'.** Histoire des salons de Paris. 3rd ed. Ladvocat, 1836-38. 6 v. 175

Mostly of later period. But has long accounts of salons of Mme Necker and Mme Genlis. Vivid recollections, artfully reorganized, with aid of creative imagination, one suspects.

Bertaut, Jules. Egéries du XVIIIe siècle. Plon, 1928. 257 p. Mme Suard, Mme Delille, Mme Helvétius, Mme Diderot, Mlle Quinault. Pleasant, popular reading, based on authorities. 176

Review : D. Mornet in RHL 36:300-01, 1939.

Bradford, Gamaliel. Portraits of women. Boston and New York, Houghton, Mifflin, 1916. 202 p. 177

" Psychographs " of Mme du Deffand (p. 133-54) and Mme de Choiseul, (p. 155-76), among others. Bradford tried, with much success, to find those habits of action which make characters. Attempts also to be an American Sainte-Beuve. Valuable studies, well pondered, well written. Chapter on Mme du Deffand appeared with title : *Portrait of a lady :—Madame du Deffand* in NAR 201:567-79, 1915.

Broc, [Hervé] de, *vicomte.* Les salons au XVIIe et XVIIIe siècles. *In his :* La France sous l'ancien régime. Part II : Les usages et les mœurs. Plon-Nourrit, 1889. p. 435-527. 178

Chapter on the salons is rather heavy; is a summary of the inevitable series. Includes some lesser known figures : comtesse de Rochefort, marquise de Montesson, Mme Helvétius.

Glotz, Marguerite, and Madeleine Maire. Salons du 18e siècle. Hachette, 1945. 288 p. 179

Delightful little book; admirable introduction to whole subject. 64-page chapter on *maîtresses de maison, hôtes des salons, sujets de conversation, art de la conversation.* Then chief salons pass in review.

Based on memoirs and letters, with unhackneyed anecdotes and details. Well informed, well ordered, piquant.

Clergue, Helen. The salon; a study of French society and personalities in the 18th century. New York and London, Putnam, 1907. 359 p. 180

Chapters on evolution of salon, Mme du Deffand, Mme D'Epinay, Julie de Lespinasse, Mme Geoffrin, retold from modern French writers. Long and dull.

— Phases of France on the eve of the Revolution. London, Cape, 1922. 224 p. 181

Chapters on duchesse du Maine and Mme Necker. Good secondary book, taken from obvious available authorities.

Du Bled, Victor. La société française avant et après 1789. Lévy, 1892. 337 p. 182

Treats Lauzun and Mme de Coigny, duchesse de Gramont, duchesse de Polignac, *les salons de la Terreur*, etc. Anecdotes strung together by accomplished gossip writer. Excellent *petite histoire*, as authentic as author's sources, which he treats respectfully, not critically.

— La société française du XVIe siècle au XXe siècle. 5th série : XVIIIe siècle. Perrin, 1905. 312 p. 183

Studies of Mme des Ursins, the marquise de Lambert, Mme de Tencin, and *La cour sous Louis XV et Louis XVI*. Lectures, written with lecturer's effort to keep auditors *en haleine*. Though author will go out of his way for good story, he is conscientious in his treatment of sources. Very readable.

Ducros, Louis. La société française au 18e siècle. Hatier, 1922.
— French society in 18th century. Trans. by W. de Geijer. London, Bell, 1926. 354 p. 184

Has chapter on salons, treating them rather from social than literary point of view.

Feuillet de Conches, F. S. Les salons de conversation au 18e siècle. Chavaray, 1882. 227 p. 185

Gay, rococo, mischievous book by one who loved 18th century. Useful for accounts of minor *salonnières* and for quaint and *recherché* anecdotes.

Fischer, Carlos. Les salons. Seheur, [1929]. 120 p. (La vie au 18e siècle, series). 186

Picture-book of unfamiliar paintings and engravings of century. Text is pleasant re-evocation of social life, with special interest in background, furniture, costumes, *décor*. Florid, but colorful and useful as corrective to books treating of mind of salons, without hint of their physical setting.

Goncourt, Edmond and Jules de. La femme au dix-huitième siècle. Didot, 1862. 461 p. 187

Long chapter on *La société — les salons*, plus many glimpses of social life in other chapters. Deals with salons of nobility : Palais-Royal, Temple, Mesdames de Boufflers, Luxembourg, Beauvau, Choiseul, etc., also describes *salons de finance*. Typical of Goncourts' enormous documentation, with their taste for picturesque, sometimes falsifying picture.

Grands salons littéraires, XVIIe et XVIIIe siècles, Les. Conférences du Musée Carnavalet, 1927. Payot, 1928. 176 p. 188

Mme de Tencin, by Paul Reboux. Racy, very amusing lecture—but unimportant. " Excusez-moi, je vous parle moins du salon de Madame de Tencin que de sa chambre à coucher." Mme Geoffrin, by Nozière : sprightly, witty, well informed. *See :* no. 247. Good on her relations with painters. Mme du Deffand, by André Bellessort : brilliant, penetrating study—what Gamaliel Bradford used to call a psychograph. Book contains excellent unusual illustrations. *See :* no. 217.

[Hall, Evelyn Beatrice]. The women of the salons. By S. G. Tallentyre [*pseud.*]. New York and London, Putnam, 1926. 235 p. 189

Includes Mesdames du Deffand, Geoffrin, d'Epinay, Necker, and Mlle de Lespinasse. Good little sketches, but external, treating subjects as quaint, amusing foreigners. *Madame du Deffand* appeared in LA 225 (ser. 7, v. 7) : 510-18, 1900.

Mason, Amelia Gere. The women of the French salons. New York, Century, 1891. 286 p. 190

Not bad review of salons through two centuries. In spite of American-feminine-Protestant-1890 moralizing, shows real sympathy for salon life. Many illustrations.

Maugras, Gaston. Le duc de Lauzun et la cour intime de Louis XV. Plon, 1893. 469 p.
— Le duc de Lauzun et la cour de Marie-Antoinette. Plon, 1893. 551 p. 191

Mostly court society. But some literary figures inevitably enter (Walpole, Hume, Franklin). Excellent chapters on background of *mœurs*. Well told, very readable.

— La cour de Lunéville au XVIIIe siècle. Plon, 1904. 473 p.
— Dernières années du roi Stanislas. Plon, 1906. 461 p. 192

Curious account of the *cour de Lorraine*. Voltaire, of course; and provincial salons of Mme de Graffigny and others. Ample, vivacious account of Saint-Lambert, Devau, Desmarets, etc. Fine background material. Conscientious, largely based on unprinted sources; well written, like all of Maugras.

Nicolardot, Louis. Les cours et les salons au 18e siècle. Dentu, 1879. 319 p. 193

Author, pro-clerical, reviews anecdotal literature of century for examples of licence of nobles and especially of *philosophes* and intelligentsia. Accepts every scurrilous tale without question. Despite title, has nothing much on salons.

Picard, Roger. Les salons littéraires et la société française, 1610-1789. New York, Brentano, 1943. 363 p. 194

Pleasant review, agreeably written, with sufficient comment. Adequate introduction to whole field. Based on best authorities, from whom much material and phrasing is borrowed without acknowledgment. Author roundly accused of plagiarism by André Morize in review (below).
Review : A. Morize in Ren 2-3:498-504, 1944-45.

Putnam, Emily J. The lady of the salon. Crev 98:284-99, 1910. 195

Good discussion of various theories of politeness.

Sainte-Beuve, Charles Augustin. La femme au XVIIIe siècle. *In his :* Nouveaux lundis. Calmann Lévy, 1870-83. 4:1-30. 196

Brief laudatory description of the Goncourts' book. Then a study of duchesse de Boufflers, later maréchale de Luxembourg, exceeding bounds of Goncourts.

Conclusion : " Société française, ancienne société tant regrettée,... j'aurais voulu, moi aussi, te traverser et te connaître, mais non pas me renfermer en toi et y mourir!"

Tinker, C. B. The salons and English letters. New York, Macmillan, 1915. 290 p. 197

Review of French salons, routine. Chapter on English authors in Parisian salons assembles available facts, makes some interesting generalizations.
Review : G. L. Hamilton in RR 6: 458-61, 1915. (Unfavorable.)

Salonnières
(Nos. 198-301B)

Boufflers-Rouveret, Marie Charlotte, etc. *comtesse* **de.** 1725-1800. 198

Salon : 1752-80.

Sainte-Beuve, Charles Augustin. La comtesse de Boufflers. *In his :* Nouveaux lundis. 4:163-236. 199

Discusses especially her relations with prince de Conti, Hume and Rousseau. Engaging description of her visit to England; she was the first great French lady to make such a visit out of mere curiosity.

Schazmann, P. E. La comtesse de Boufflers. Roches, 1933. 320 p. 200

Friend of Rousseau, Hume, Gustave III of Sweden. Not precisely *salonnière*, though she ruled the prince de Conti's assemblies in the Temple and at l'Isle-Adam, and later had her intellectual villa in Auteuil, across from Mme Helvétius. Not to be confused with her cousin, marquise de Boufflers, nor with duchesse de Boufflers, who became maréchale de Luxembourg. Good, conscientious, readable book.

Choiseul Stainville, Louise Honorine, etc. *duchesse* **de.** 1734-1801. 201

Salon : 1758-81.

Maugras, Gaston. Le duc et la duchesse de Choiseul. Plon-Nourrit, 1904. 473 p.
— Les dernières années du duc et de la duchesse de Choiseul. Plon-Nourrit, 1903. 527 p. 202

Mme de Choiseul was the faithful friend and correspondent of Mme du Deffand, friend of Voltaire and Walpole, patroness of Barthélemy. Good social and family history, but not much about salons, in special sense.

Mazade, Charles de. La duchesse de Choiseul et Mme du Deffand. RDM 2nd per. 24:677-97, Dec. 1, 1859. 203

Taken mostly from the newly published *Correspondance inédite* of Mme du Deffand.

Condorcet, Marie Louise, etc. *marquise* **de.** 1764-1822. 204

Salon : 1787-1792.

Guillois, Antoine. La marquise de Condorcet : sa famille, son salon, ses amis, 1764-1822. Ollendorff, 1897. 255 p. *See :* 1415. 205

Chapter on her salon of Hôtel des Monnaies, opening in 1786. Frequented by Chamfort, Beaumarchais, Roucher, Garat, Chénier, Cabanis, Morellet, La Fayette, Volney, Suard. Another chapter on her salon at beginning of Revolution. But mostly on visitors; not much on conduct of salon itself.
Reviews : R. Doumic in RDM 4e pér. 139:921-32, Feb. 15, 1897; G. V[icaire] in BBB 64:583-86, 1897.

Léger, Charles. Captives de l'amour. Gaillandre, 1933. 263 p. 206

Based on unpublished letters of Mme de Condorcet and Mme de Coigny, which were written later than our period. Good summary of precedent life of Mme de Condorcet.

Créqui, Renée Caroline, etc. *marquise* **de.** 1714-1803. 207

Salon : 1748-89.

Tisseau, Paul. La marquise de Créqui. Emile Paul, 1926. 234 p. 208

Friend of Rousseau, and intimate of Sénac de Meilhan. Her salon frequented by chevalier d'Aydie, d'Alembert, Fontenelle, Marmontel, duc de Penthièvre, Pompignan, Florian, Delille, etc. A compilation, written without much grace. Some *inédits*.
Reviews : G. Ascoli in Rcr 95:163, 1928; D. Mornet in RHL 39:129-30, 1932.

Du Deffand, Marie Anne, etc. *marquise.* 1696-1780. 209

Salon : 1730-80.

— Letters of the Marquise du Deffand to the Hon. Horace Walpole... from the year 1766 to the year 1780. To which are added letters of Madame du Deffand to Voltaire, from

the year 1759 to the year 1775. London, Longmans, 1810. 4 v. Ed. by Mary Berry.
210

Invaluable in its time, but not by our standards : first editor, Mary Berry, placidly burned matter to Walpole's and Mme Du Deffand's discredit.

— Correspondance complète avec ses amis : le président Hénault. Montesquieu, d'Alembert, Voltaire, Horace Walpole. *See* 125.
211

— Correspondance complète de Mme du Deffand avec la duchesse de Choiseul, l'abbé Barthélemy et M. Craufurt.
212

— Lettres de la marquise du Deffand à Horace Walpole (1766-1780). Introduction and notes by Mrs. Paget Toynbee. London, Methuen, 1912. 3 v.
213

Thoroughly admirable edition, with excellent notes, and introduction, model of judicious condensation, dealing with history of letters, with Mme du Deffand, and with Walpole. Adds nearly 500 unpublished letters.

— Lettres à Voltaire; Introduction et notes de Joseph Trabucco. Bossard, 1922. 273 p.
214

Readable re-edition, without scholarly pretensions. Introduction is good character sketch of Mme du Deffand.

Walpole, Horace. Correspondence with Mme du Deffand and Wiart. *In :* Horace Walpole's correspondence with Madame du Deffand. (No. 128) p. 407, 439, 461, 497, 502, 561.
215

Superb edition, perfectly edited, nobly produced. Because nearly all of Walpole's letters were destroyed, work consists mostly of Mme du D. Includes Walpole's Paris *Journals*, 1865-75, Mme du D.'s *Journal*, 1779-80. Introduction deals brilliantly with Mme du D.'s life, her relations with Walpole, etc. Facsimiles and unusual portrait illustrations. Full and careful notes. Final volume contains appendices of varying interest. Whole book a marvel of exactness, thoroughness, acumen.

[Aimery de Pierrebourg, Marguerite]. Madame du Deffand; l'esprit et l'amour au XVIIIᵉ siècle. (*Pseud.*, Claude Ferval). *See* 127.
216

Probably best book on Mme du D. Fine treatment of background; excellent story-telling and analysis of character;

limpid style. (Ferval is a novelist.) Apparently accurate; but no acknowledgments, references to sources, or bibliography.

Bellessort, André. Le salon de Madame du Deffand. *In :* Les grands salons littéraires (XVIIᵉ et XVIIIᵉ siècles). Conférences du Musée Carnavalet. (1927) Payot, 1928. p. 145-76.
217

Shrewd and sympathetic. *See* 188.

Caro, Elme-Marie. Deux types de femmes de l'autre siècle : Mme du Deffand, Mme Roland. RDM 2nd per. 92:256-73, Mar. 15, 1871.
218

The two women differed with their times. Interesting comparison.

[Herpin, Clara Adèle Luce]. Le président Hénault et madame du Deffand. Calmann Lévy, 1893. 548 p. By Lucien Perey [*pseud.*].
219

Ample volume, leisurely and rich. Much quotation of unpublished letters. Pleasant nostalgic evocation of "... cette pléiade de mondains cultivés et amoureux des lettres." Not displaced by Lion's book, (no. 222).

Hervé, Georges. Les correspondantes de Maupertuis. Dix lettres inédites de Mme du Deffand. RPar 18th year, 5:751-78, 1911.
220

Graceful and well-informed introduction.

Irvine, Lyn Ll. Walpole and Mme du Deffand. *In his :* Ten letter-writers. London, Hogarth press, 1932. p. 49-65. 221

Good : not essential.

Lion, Henri. Un magistrat homme de lettres au XVIIIᵉ siècle : le président Hénault. Plon, 1903. 446 p.
222

Good book on Mme du Deffand's lover. Descriptions of salons of duchesse du Maine, Mme du Deffand, maréchale de Luxembourg, Mme de Rochefort, princesse de Conti, Mme de Mirepoix, princesse de Beauvau. Material mostly secondary.

Mazé, Jules. Histoire de deux vieilles maisons : l'Hôtel de Brienne et le Couvent de Saint-Joseph. Champion, 1927. 109 p. 223

Author describes old houses, quarters (1927) of Ministry of War. Exact record of decoration, furniture, etc. Two chapters on Mme du Deffand and her *cercle* in the *Couvent de Saint-Joseph.* Fine background material for novelist or reconstructor of period.

Rageot, Gaston. Mme du Deffand. Michel, [1937]. 251 p. 224

No new facts on the biography of Mme du Deffand, but sympathetic, readable psychological study.

Sainte-Beuve, Charles Augustin. Correspondance inédite de Madame du Deffand. *See* 134. 225

Review of publication (1859) of her letters, edited by marquis de Sainte-Aulaire. Long extracts. More about duchesse de Choiseul than about Mme du D.

— Lettres de la marquise du Deffand. *See* 133. 226

Rather descriptive than analytical, with long quotations and suggestions for further reading. But character of Mme du D. emerges, sharply defined. Fine sympathetic treatment of Walpole and his relations with Mme du Deffand.

Scherer, Edmond. Le roman de Mme du Deffand. *In his:* Études sur la littérature contemporaine. Calmann-Lévy, 1885-95. v. 3:191-218. 227

Good study.

Ségur, Pierre Marie Maurice Henri, *marquis de. Madame du Deffand et sa famille. *See* 135. 228

Invaluable for background, youth, and early years of D. Based on manuscript sources, organized with good sense, presented with charm.

Smith, Warren Hunting, ed. Letters to and from Madame du Deffand and Julie de Lespinasse. *See* 126. 229

Thoroughly admirable edition of interesting letters.

Strachey, [Giles] Lytton. Madame du Deffand. *In his:* Books and characters. New York, Harcourt, Brace, 1922. [81]-111. 230

Delightful, naturally, but contains nothing new.

Egmont, Sophie Jeanne, etc., *comtesse* d, 1740-1773. 231

Salon : 1760-71.

Armaillé, Marie de Ségur, *comtesse* d'. La comtesse d'Egmont. Perrin, 1890. 305 p. 232

Daughter of maréchal de Richelieu and subject of some romances; protectress of Rousseau and friend of Marmontel, Horace Walpole, Spanish diplomats. Especially friend and correspondent of Gustave III of Sweden. Book based in good part on her correspondence with Gustave, preserved in Swedish archives.

Buffenoir, Maximilien. Sur les pas de la comtesse d'Egmont, ou les beaux jours de Braine au XVIIIe siècle. Soissons, Société archéologique, 1930, 275 p. 232A

Contributions on the Countess's platonic affection for the King of Sweden. Her hatred of despotism. Picture of a philosophical salon in the provinces. Review : D. Mornet in RHL 40:127-28, 1933.

Epinay, Louise Florence, etc., *marquise* d'. 1726-1783. 233

Salon : 1750-73.

[Herpin, Clara Adèle Luce.] Une femme du monde au XVIIIe siècle. La jeunesse de madame d'Epinay... by Lucien Perey [*pseud.*] and Gaston Maugras. 7th ed., Calmann-Lévy, 1898. 544 p. 234

— Une femme du monde au XVIIIe siècle. Dernières années de madame d'Epinay, son salon et ses amis. 3rd ed., Calmann-Lévy, 1883. 607 p. *See* 2383.

1150 pages on Mme d'Epinay, many of them taken from *inédit* material in public and private libraries. Solid and well done; great storehouse of material, though much of it trifling. Valuable chapter on her salon, and many historical references. The authors are thorough partisans for Mme d'Epinay against the world, especially against Rousseau. But *see* under Rousseau. Review : B. E. in BBB 49:432-34, 1882.

Scherer, Edmond. Mme d'Epinay. *In his:* Études sur la littérature contemporaine. Calmann-Lévy, 1885-95. v. 3:47-131. 235

Good study.

Anon. Mme d'Epinay and her circle. EdR 195:157-88, 1902. 236

Well based and understanding.

Genlis, Stéphane Félicité, etc. *comtesse* de. 1746-1830. 237

Salon : 1772-89.

Bourgain, M. P. La Jeunesse d'une femme célèbre : Mme de Genlis. RDM 5ᵉ pér. 52:844-75, 1909.   238

Good detailed account of her life to time of her marriage.

Dobson, Austin. Madame de Genlis. *In his :* Four Frenchwomen. London, Chatto & Windus, 1893. p. [105]-189.   239

Fine example of *vulgarisation*, done with affection, knowledge, intelligence. But his 1890 *mignardise*, though suitable to his subject, may now seem over-quaint.

Rostand, Rosemonde Gérard, Mme Edmond. La vie amoureuse de madame de Genlis. Flammarion, 1926. 185 p.   240

Salon life, mostly at Palais-Royal, appears only incidentally. Book is sympathetic, engaging, unimportant.

Geoffrin, Marie Thérèse. 1699-1777. 241
Salon : 1730-76.

Geoffrin, Mme Marie Thérèse (Rodet), and Stanislaw II, August, king of Poland. Correspondance inédite (1764-1777). Ed. by Charles de Mouÿ. Plon, 1875. 529 p.   242

Invaluable collection. Interest more political and historical than literary. The King unburdened himself of his and Poland's troubles in letters to his " *maman.*" Excellent 96-page politico-literary introduction.
Review : C. de Mazade in RDM 3rd per. 12:266-84, Nov. 15, 1875.

Aldis, Janet. Madame Geoffrin, her salon and her times, 1750-1777. London, Methuen; New York, Putnam, 1905. 372 p.
243

Pleasant enough compilation, from Ségur, Tornezy, etc. Much local color, determined vivacity and broadminded disapproval.

Brown, Harcourt. Madame Geoffrin and Martin Folkes : six new letters. MLQ 1:215-41, 1940.   244

Mme Geoffrin gives news of scientific experiments and of gossip of the salons, 1742-1743. Not intrinsically of much importance.

Goncourt, Edmond and Jules de. Madame Geoffrin. *In their :* Portraits intimes du dix-huitième siècle. Charpentier, 1880. p. [129-46.] Édition définitive, Flammarion, 1925. v. I, p. 149-66.   245

Chapter includes letters, *inédites* at time of book's publication, in the original astonishing orthography of Madame Geoffrin.

[Herpin, Clara Adèle Luce]. Comment on crée un salon : madame Geoffrin. *In her :* Figures du temps passé. By Lucien Perey [pseud.]. Calmann-Lévy, 1900. p. 283-358.
246

Good chapter, but not essential if one has Ségur's book (no. 250).

Nozière. Le salon de Madame Geoffrin. *In :* Les grands salons littéraires (XVIIᵉ et XVIIIᵉ siècles). Conférences du Musée Carnavalet. (1927) Payot, 1928. p. 107-44. English translation by Mabel Robinson, London, 1930, p. 137-77.   247

Agreeable but secondary.

Pilon, Edmond. Le salon de Mme Geoffrin, et le sentimentalisme philosophique. *In his :* Portraits français I. Bibliothèque internationale d'édition, 1904. p. 79-93.   248

Sympathetic, lively, with all obligatory anecdotes.

Sainte-Beuve, Charles Augustin. Madame Geoffrin. *In his :* Causeries du lundi. Garnier. 2:309-29.   249

Chiefly a shrewd, " stracheyan " analysis of Mme Geoffrin's character and charm. She is taken as illustration of philosophic mood of mid-century. Usual *trouvailles* of thought and statement : thus, Mme Geoffrin is called " le Fontenelle des femmes."

Ségur, Pierre Marie Maurice Henri, *marquis* de. Le royaume de la rue Saint-Honoré : Mme Geoffrin et sa fille. Lévy, 1897. 503 p.   250

Essential book on Mme Geoffrin. Based largely on manuscript sources, especially rich archives of Estampes family, inheritors of the papers of Mme Geoffrin and her daughter. Hundred page appendix includes letters from Grimm to St. Petersburg, correspondence with Empress Catherine, etc. Ségur shrewdly chronicles little incidents of salon life with exact concern, as if dealing with tremendous matters. But he lets us understand that he knows, at heart, their unimportance. He plays the game with the *salonnières* and with us. Incidentally, he destroys legend of stupidity of M. Geoffrin.
Reviews : R. Doumic in RDM 4th per. 141:917-28, June 15, 1897; C. Woeste in Rgén 68:74-100, 1898.

Tornezy, A[lbert]. Un bureau d'esprit au XVIIIe siècle; le salon de madame Geoffrin. Lecène, Oudin, 1895. 274 p.   251

> Unpretentious, uninspired, even a little naïve. But it will do, for essential facts and characters and obligatory anecdotes. Review : R. Mahrenholtz in ZFSL 18²:36-37, 1896.

Tourneux, Maurice. Mme Geoffrin et les éditions expurgées des Lettres familières de Montesquieu. RHL 1:52-64, 1894.   252

> *Lettres inédites* on various matters, including expurgation of a note written to Montesquieu, derogatory to Mme Geoffrin.

Graffigny, Françoise d'Issembourg, etc. de. 1695-1758.   253

> Salon : 1748-58.

Noël, Georges. Une " primitive " oubliée de l'école des " Cœurs sensibles " : Mme de Graffigny. Plon, 1913. 399 p. (Diss., Paris).   254

> Serious, careful, well-written book about Mme de Graffigny, " *cœur sensible*," friend of Voltaire. Excellent chapter on her Paris salon. But in fact not much record subsists of its activities. Review : D. Mornet in RHL 22:610-11, 1915.

Helvétius, Anne Catherine, etc. 1719-1800.   255

> Salon : 1751-89.

Guillois, Antoine. Le salon de Madame Helvétius. Calmann-Lévy, 1894. 340 p.   256

> Salon of the *philosophes* and the *idéologues*, where freer tone of discussion reigned than at Mme Necker's and Mme Geoffrin's. Good sound book, well based on *inédits* and on all available printed materials. But a little lacking in *vues d'ensemble*. Fine chapter on Revolution and its effects on salon's *habitués*, Condorcet, Cabanis, etc. Review : G. V[icaire] in BBB 61:331-33, 1894.

Stenger, Gilbert. La société de Mme Helvétius à Auteuil. Nrev ns 26:48-60, 1904.   257

> Pleasant.

Houdetot, Élisabeth Françoise, etc. *comtesse* d'. 1730-1813.   258

> Salon : 1755 ?-89 ?

Buffenoir, Hippolyte. Les grandes dames du XVIIIe siècle. La comtesse d'Houdetot, une amie de J.-J. Rousseau. Lévy, 1901. 356 p. *See* 1964.   259

> Not much about Mme d'Houdetot as a *salonnière*, though some information about her friends and visitors at Sannois. Rather ecstatic in manner.

— La comtesse d'Houdetot; sa famille; ses amies. Leclerc, 1905. 314 p. *See* 1965.   260

> Buffenoir's first book on Mme d'Houdetot led to the discovery of many family papers, here presented. Seven letters of Voltaire, eighteen of Rousseau, etc. Several *inédit* portraits, well reproduced. Not much on salons. Review : E. Ritter in ZFSL 29²:258-61, 1906.

Chinard, Gilbert. Les amitiés américaines de Madame d'Houdetot. Champion, 1924. 62 p. (BRLC, 8.).   261

> Includes a number of letters and documents previously published but dispersed; also unpublished Frankliniana and Jeffersoniana from American Philosophical Society and Library of Congress. Excellent example of such work, with sufficient, but not excessive, commentary. Review : *See* 3151.

Stenger, Gilbert. A Sannois chez Mme d'Houdetot. Nrev ns 23:495-506, 1903. 262 Agreeable.

Du Bled, Victor. Un client de l'ancien régime : I. De l'Isle, Mme de Choiseul et ses amis. RDM 3rd per. 100:877-912, Aug. 15, 1890.
— II. Mme de l'Isle : le salon de la duchesse de Polignac. RDM 3rd per. 101:351-86, Sept. 15, 1890.   263

> Lively articles, apparently not reprinted.

Lambert, Anne Thérèse, etc. *marquise de.* 1647-1733.   264

> Salon : 1698-1733. *See also below*, Chapter X, nos. 2737-2760.

Boulan, Émile. Mme la marquise de Lambert. *In his :* Figures du dix-huitième siècle; les sages : Fontenelle et Mme de Lambert. Leyden, Sijthoff, 1920. p. 111-86.   265

> The study of Mme de Lambert is chiefly analysis of her character and writings. Little on salons. Lectures; vivacious.

Reynold, Gonzague de. Madame de Lambert et son salon. *See* 2736.   266

The 1929 booklet has several interesting illustrations of building, adjoining *Bibliothèque nationale*, which housed her salon.

Sainte-Beuve, Charles Augustin. Madame de Lambert. *In his :* Causeries du lundi. Garnier. 4:217-39.   267

Sympathetic, perceptive study of her character and writings. Not much on her salon. Excellent analysis of her ideas, especially on rights of women to intellectual consideration.

Zimmermann, J. P. La morale laïque au commencement du XVIIIᵉ siècle; Mme de Lambert. RHL 24:42-64, 440-66, 1917.   268

Useful generalizations on social ethics, drawn from details in works of Mme de Lambert.

Lespinasse, Julie Jeanne etc., de. 1732-1776.   269

Salon : 1764-74.

Lespinasse, Julie de. Lettres de Mlle de Lespinasse, suivies de ses autres œuvres et de lettres de Mme du Deffand, de Turgot, de Bernardin de Saint-Pierre. Notes et notice biographique par Eugène Asse. *See* 116.   270

Has a long (79 p.) *notice*, valuable in its time, but now superseded.

— Lettres inédites de Mademoiselle de Lespinasse à Condorcet, à Guibert, au comte de Crillon. Publiées avec des lettres de ses amis, des documents nouveaux et une étude par M. Charles Henry. Dentu, 1887. 408 p.   271

Good edition.

— Letters of Mlle de Lespinasse, with notes on her life and character by d'Alembert, Marmontel, de Guibert, etc. Translated by Katherine Prescott Wormeley. Boston, Hardy, Pratt, 1901. 342 p.   272

A selection for American taste of 1900.

— Love letters of Mlle de Lespinasse to and from the Comte de Guibert. Trans. with introduction by E. H. F. Mills. London, Routledge, [1929]. 553 p.   273

Intelligent brief introduction.

Beaunier, André. La vie amoureuse de Julie de Lespinasse. *See* 119.   274

Beaunier does not really like Julie; she fills him with irritation and pity. He treats her with modern common sense; thus treated she looks absurd. Those who still adore her do so, they say, because she loved more greatly than we do. No, says Beaunier, she did not love more greatly; just differently. Refreshing book for the tough-minded, the anti-Romantics.

Bonnefon, Paul. Mlle de Lespinasse, l'amoureuse et l'amie : lettres inédites. *See* 120.   275

Good commentary.

Bordeaux, Henry. Julie de Lespinasse. *In his :* Portraits de femmes et d'enfants. Plon-Nourrit, [1909]. p. 235-68.   276

A retelling of Ségur, (no. 123) with a few unimportant reflections.

Bradford, Gamaliel. Eve and Adam. Mademoiselle de Lespinasse. *In his :* Daughters of Eve. New York, Book League of America, 1930. p. 67-86.   277

Makes a real effort to tell her story and docket her character. Intelligent and well written; but one becomes irritated with Bradford's assured cataloguing of souls.

Éliac, George. Un après-midi chez Julie de Lespinasse. (In 1912 ed., Georges.) *See* 120A.   278

Series of dialogued scenes, not *jouables*, but an ingenious pastiche, made up mostly of authentic quotations from letters and memoirs. Introduced with high praise by Ségur, who says that " George Éliac " is probably pseudonym.

Jebb, Camilla. A star of the salons; Julie de Lespinasse. New York, Putnam; London, Methuen, 1908. 343 p.   279

Very good example of a secondary book in English. Author, heavily in debt to Ségur, etc., makes a book by adding background of manners and customs (excellent), sympathetic speculations on character, and graceful style. Author has feminine awareness of clothes, health, physical conditioning of emotional drama. Selections appeared in Ncent 54:257-68, 1903, with title : *Some facts about Mademoiselle de Lespinasse*.

Royde-Smith, Naomi. The double heart, a study of Julie de Lespinasse. *See* 121. 280

Psychological study, based on Ségur (no. 282). The well-known novelist recreates Julie and her friends, with novelist's sympathy, understanding and freedom. Beautifully written; work of art rather than scholarship.

Review : in TLS, Sept. 3, 1931, p. 659.

Sainte-Beuve, Charles Augustin. Lettres de Mademoiselle de Lespinasse. *See* 122.
281

Brief summary of life of Mlle de Lespinasse, bare mention of her career as *salonnière*, and extended analysis of her character as revealed in letters to Guibert. Sainte-Beuve takes her as type of great lover, victim of *mal sacré*, which, he says, is very rare in France. She is a *Nouvelle Héloïse en action*. Brilliant characterizations and generalizations.

Ségur, Pierre Marie Maurice Henri, *marquis* de. Julie de Lespinasse. *See* 123. 282

Best book on Julie. Based on a wealth of *inédits*, especially original *lettres* of Julie in the archives of the Guibert family, manuscript journals of her relatives, documents from the Mora family, etc. Author knows social life of the century as do few others of our times. Admirable portraits of minor figures. Ségur's affection for heroine animates his pages with feeling.

Luxembourg, Madeleine Angélique, etc. *duchesse* de. 1707-1787.
283

Salon : 1750-87.

Buffenoir, Hippolyte. La maréchale de Luxembourg (1707-1787); souvenirs, documents, témoignages. Emile-Paul, 1924. 255 p. *See* 1966.
284

Mostly about Rousseau. Useful chapters on *maréchale's* salon and friends. Good quotations from contemporaries. Reviewer describes book as " ... aimable et pittoresque." (p. 123).

Review : D. M.[ornet] in RHL 33:123-24, 1926.

Maine, Anne Louise, etc. *duchesse* du. 1676-1753.
285

Salon : 1704-47.

Birrell, Francis. La duchesse du Maine. London, Gerald Howe, 1929. 96 p. 286

Her life and character, in summary. Birrell would make her a link between Louis XIV and Revolution, by her breaking down of caste lines at Sceaux. Bold hypothesis. But author's chief interest is pointing out her absurdities, and fantasticalities of her salon. Amusing, mannered style.

Desnoiresterres, Gustave. Les cours galantes. Dentu, 1860-64. 4 v. v. 4, 346 p.
287

Fourth volume deals largely with the duchesse du Maine and the *Cour de Sceaux*. Good gossip, by an *anecdotier* thoroughly at home in 18th century. Pleasant garrulity, giving page references.

Jullien, Adolphe. Les grandes nuits de Sceaux; le théâtre de la Duchesse du Maine. Baur, 1876. 75 p. 288

Jullien strives to be vivacious, but the dusty ancient gayeties he evokes sound dreary and taste insipid. Some *inédits*, on war of songs between Academy and Malézieux. Good deal on production of Voltaire's *Comte de Boursoufle* and other plays. Curious items on marionette plays.

Maurel, André. La duchesse du Maine. Hachette, 1928. 254 p. 289

More readable, but less scholarly than Philpin de Piépape (no. 289A). Adds a few new documents. Fine summary of *duchesse's* character. Altogether, excellent example of secondary work which adds art and sympathy to facts exhumed by others.

Philpin de Piépape, Léonce M. G. La duchesse du Maine. Plon-Nourrit, 1910. 387 p. New ed., Plon, 1936. 316 p. — A princess of strategy : the life of Anne Louise Bénédicte de Bourbon-Condé, duchesse du Maine. Trans. by J. Lewis May. London, Lane, 1911. 415 p. 289A

More politico-historic than literary. But there are good chapters on the two *Cours de Sceaux*. Serious and scholarly, a little heavy for its subject. Trustworthy and conscientious, it makes salons seem dull.

Sainte-Beuve, Charles Augustin. La duchesse du Maine. *In his :* Causeries du lundi. Garnier. 3:206-28. 290

One of Sainte-Beuve's little gems : gay, discerning, leading to this memorable conclusion : " L'homme a beau retourner et renverser les situations, il ne change pas ses défauts ni ses travers; on les voit bientôt reparaître tous; seulement ils se produisent, selon les temps, sous une forme plus ou moins noble, polie et agréable; et cette forme-là, qui combinait l'excès de l'égoïsme avec la délicatesse d'esprit et la politesse, est plutôt celle du passé."

[**Vincens, Cécile**]. La duchesse du Maine. by Arvède Barine, [pseud.]. LeA 4: 268-88; 353-81, 1889. *Also in her :* Princesses et grandes dames. Hachette, 1893. p. 215-91. Author's *pseud.*, Arvède Barine, at head of title.
— The Duchess of Maine. *In her :* Princesses and court ladies, by Arvède Barine, [pseud.]. New York and London, Putnam, 1906. p. 210-87.   291

Model of re-evocation. Style is simple, *coulant.* All the zest which authors, who must be complete and exhaustive, lose, is here retained.

Necker, Suzanne Curchod. 1739-1794. 292 Salon : 1765-88.

Gambier-Parry, Mark. Madame Necker, her family and friends. Edinburgh and London, Blackwood, 1913. 366 p.   293

Compilation from good authorities, sober and conscientious, all well enough. But somehow lifeless and dull.

Haussonville, Gabriel P. O. *comte* d'. Le salon de Madame Necker. Lévy, 1882. 2 v.
— The salon of Madame Necker. Trans. by H. M. Trollope. London, Chapman and Hall, 1882. 2 v.   294

Indispensable. Author used very rich archives of Coppet. Revealed much on Gibbon, Marmontel, Morellet, Grimm, Diderot, D'Alembert, Mlle de Lespinasse, Galiani, Bernardin de Saint-Pierre, Mme Geoffrin, maréchale de Luxembourg, Mme du Deffand, comtesse d'Houdetot, Buffon, etc. Charmingly written. Author dares even to confess boredom when he is bored. " Je sentais en quelque sorte peser sur moi le poids de ces monceaux d'oubli qui se sont accumulés sur tant de souvenirs." (v. I, p. 6).

Sainte-Beuve, Charles Augustin. Madame Necker. *In his :* Causeries du lundi. Garnier, 4:240-62.   295

Good summary of life, with harsh treatment of language of her *Mélanges.* Though article is complement of and pendant to Sainte-Beuve's *causerie* on Mme de Lambert, it does not contain much by way of comparison to her.

Rochefort, Marie Thérèse, etc. *comtesse* **de.** 1716-82.   296 Salon : 1742-74.

Loménie, Louis de. La comtesse de Rochefort et ses amis. [Lévy, 1870]. 371 p.   297

Bel esprit, amie of the duc de Nivernais, friend of Mme du Deffand, Walpole, Mirabeau *père,* Duclos, cardinal de Bernis, etc. Singers from opera frequented salon in *Hôtel du Luxembourg.* Much about *comédies de société* at *Hôtel de Brancas ;* several reproduced in book. Book is based on unpublished letters in Mirabeau documents. Author very prim about 18th century gallantries.

Suard, (M... Panckoucke, Mme). 1750-1830.   298

Salon : 1771-91.

Doumic, René. Lettres d'un philosophe et d'une femme sensible; Condorcet et Mme Suard, d'après une correspondance inédite. RDM 6e pér. 5:302-25, Sept. 15, 1911; 835-60, Oct. 15, 1911; 7:57-81, Jan. 1, 1912. *See* 1407.   299

From the collection of Mlle Valentin Stapfer.

Tencin, Claudine Alexandrine Guérin de. 1682-1749.   300

Salon : 1716-49.

Coynart, Charles de. Les Guérin de Tencin. (1520-1758). Hachette, 1910. 424 p.   301

Necessary supplement to Masson (no. 301A). Mostly about Mme de Tencin and her brother, the disreputable Cardinal. Not exactly a rehabilitation, though it destroys a good many legends. Rich, packed with facts, details, documentary evidence, references to provincial archives. Model of its kind; but rather exacting reading.

Masson, Pierre Maurice. Une vie de femme au xviiie siècle : Mme de Tencin (1682-1749). 3rd ed., Hachette, 1910. 339 p.   301A

Model for the writer in this *genre.* Based on comprehensive research, largely in manuscript sources; appendix of *inédits ;* invaluable critical bibliography. But text itself shakes off critical baggage; astounding Tencins are shrewdly analyzed, importance of the salon appraised; whole told with rare raciness and gusto. Reviews : G. Ascoli in RSH 20:376-78, 1910; D. Mornet in RHL 16:624-27, 1909.

Reboux, Paul. Madame de Tencin. RFrance 7th yr., v. 4:86-105, July 1, 1927. With title : Le salon de Madame de Tencin, *is*

also in : Les grands salons littéraires (xviie et xviiie siècles). Conférences du Musée Carnavalet, (1927). Payot, 1928. p. 79-106.

301B

Slight, light, and amusing.

Music
(Nos. 302-356)

WOLF FRANCK

At no time nor in any country has music been discussed as much as in 18th century France. Yet this extensive activity has never been thoroughly investigated, not even in connection with the literature of the century with which these musical discussions were, of course, closely linked. For to explain music by means of words involves literary problems *per se*, and in the literary-minded 18th century France almost every writer had something to say about music. Besides the literary significance, the philosophical and aesthetic implications are obvious in the age of the Encyclopedists.

Any student of this period is therefore confronted with the task of becoming acquainted with this material. To collect and analyze all of it exceeds, however, by far, the internal and external boundaries of the present undertaking. Our bibliographical attempt therefore constitutes only a first step into this vast territory. We have tried, however, to cover as wide a field as possible with respect to kinds of material and periods of the century. For this reason original material has been included to a large extent; other items were selected mainly from the viewpoint of their introductory, general, or bibliographical value. Many important original items, however, had to be omitted because of the writer's obvious connection exclusively with music, as in the case of Rameau, or because extensive, though necessary, investigation would be required, as for instance in the cases of a periodical like the *Mercure de France* or the various *Correspondances*. In other cases, special studies already exist which direct the reader to the original material, as Ecorcheville's *De Lulli à Rameau*, Kretzschmar's essay on Grimm or van der Straeten's *Voltaire musicien*. In other instances, no valuable contribution was at hand, as in the case of Beaumarchais. The lack of availability of material proved also to be a serious limitation. No item has been included which could not be directly examined. Freedom of selection could therefore not be exercised for the material as a whole, but nevertheless the main basic trends have been illustrated.

In any case, the compiler trusts that the selection will sufficiently open up the field to the serious student. The length of the annotations does not necessarily indicate the importance of the items discussed but it corroborates to a certain degree the need for further investigation. The study, general or special, of the relationship of music and literature in 18th century France is still in its infancy but is, therefore, the more rewarding.

Wolf Franck.

Beyle, Marie Henri. Vies de Haydn, de Mozart et de Métastase; texte établi et annoté par Daniel Muller; préface de Romain Rolland. Champion, 1914. 492 p. (Œuvres complètes de Stendhal, publiées sous la direction d'Edouard Champion). 302

Stendhal's first publication (1814) reveals the deep lyrical and musical sensitivity of the author, elsewhere so carefully hidden by him. Rolland, in his preface, shows how for Stendhal music was " la langue d'une aristocratie du cœur et de la volupté," culminating, for him, in 18th century *bel canto* and represented at its best by Cimarosa, Mozart, Paisiello, Pergolesi and later Rossini. Haydn, Mozart and Metastasio were chosen in this book as representatives of instrumental and dramatic music and musical poetry. We know that the study on Haydn was a blunt plagiarism of *Le Haydine* by Carpani, and in the appendix this edition gives all the documents relating to the public polemic ensuing from this plagiarism. The study on Mozart is based essentially on a biographical sketch by Winckler (not on the one indicated by Stendhal himself) while the part on Metastasio is entirely Stendhal's own work. Throughout the whole book Stendhal gives his opinions on music and musicians in general and on the state of music in Italy at his time in particular. It is not surprising that we are also given many revealing critical sidelights on French musical life. The *avant-propos bibliographique et critique* by Daniel Muller informs us about the different editions of the book (including the English translation of 1817) and about the careful procedures in the establishment of this edition.

Bingham, Alfred Jepson. Marie-Joseph Chénier, early political life and ideas (1789-1794). New York : privately printed, 1939. 210 p. (Diss., Columbia). 303

A poet like his elder brother André, M.-J. Chénier, who reported to the Convention about the project which eventually became the *Conservatoire de musique*, offers excellent opportunity to study the place and role of a prominent writer within the turmoil of the French Revolution. As Chénier wrote the text of many a celebrated hymn, including the words to the *Chant du départ*, the place of music in the revolutionary set-up plays an important part in such a study. All these relations are shown by Bingham in a lively, well-documented manner. The detailed table of contents and extensive bibliography, however, do not make up for the want of an index.

Brenet, Michel. La librairie musicale en France de 1653 à 1790, d'après les Registres de privilèges. *In :* IMG Sammelbände 8: 401-66, 1906-07. 304

Covering period from 1654 to 1789 these documents, reprinted from manuscripts in *Bibliothèque nationale,* relate history of music publishing in France and thereby offer valuable cultural background. Noteworthy is the fact that the documents of 18th century comprise seven times more pages than those of last half of preceding century. List contains printing privileges granted for music as well as for books on music, and the student thus can follow currents and trends which dominated the French musical scene, particularly in Paris, during 18th century. We not only meet names of native and foreign composers who, at one time or another, were in vogue, but also many unfamiliar composers who complete the picture, and literary names like Rousseau and d'Alembert. Introduction and ample footnotes.

Bricaire de La Dixmerie, Nicolas. Les deux âges du goût et du génie français sous Louis XIV et sous Louis XV; parallèle des efforts du génie et du goût dans les sciences, dans les arts et dans les lettres, sous les deux règnes. Amsterdam, Vlam, 1770. 387 p. 305

Comprehensive picture of culture of two ages, first part giving general survey, second dealing with single disciplines. Author's contention is that age of Louis XIV sowed the seed while age of Louis XV reaped the harvest. The sections specifically treating music are : *La musique* (p. 181-92) which concentrates on opera; *La musique instrumentale* (p. 362-67) and *Le chant* (p. 373-76) both for most part devoted to virtuosos; *Scène lyri-comique* (p. 376-78) and *La danse* (p. 378-82) which deal with comic opera and ballet respectively. Documentary value of these studies is enhanced

by fact that they are incorporated into panorama of the whole cultural scene.

Carlez, Jules. Framery, littérateur-musicien (1745-1810). Caen,·Delesques, 1893. 58 p. 306

Framery, active as poet, journalist, librettist, composer, translator, and author of a volume of a musical encyclopedia, offers good example of vital role intellectual life played in social development of France in 18th century. The different intellectual interests of Framery centered in music and Carlez ably presents the many aspects of Framery's life and activities.

Castel [Louis Bertrand]. Esprit, saillies et singularités. Amsterdam & Paris; Vincent, 1763. 393 p. 307

Posthumous collection of those writings of general interest by this Jesuit father, (1688-1757), mathematician by profession. Although he dealt with philosophical, moral, literary, and musical questions, today he is interesting mainly because of his project of a *Clavecin oculaire* which he developed first in *Mercure de France* in 1725 and ten years later in *Mémoires de Trévoux.* A passage in Newton's *Optics* led Castel to idea of similarity in quantitative relationship between the colors of the spectrum and the tones of the scale. He thus suggested construction of color instrument which would offer the eye what a music instrument offers the ear. Castel spent much effort on the practical realization of this project which, however, never materialized, and went even so far as to suggest a combination instrument for all the senses which would have, in addition to other features, a set of perfumes which could be " composed " and " played " *ad libitum.* This volume gives Castel's main ideas, particularly on *Clavecin pour les yeux* (p. 278-348) which was much discussed throughout 18th century and was for instance translated into German by Telemann (1739).

[Chabanon, Michel Paul Guy de]. Observations sur la musique, et principalement sur la métaphysique de l'art. Pissot, 1779. 215 p. 308

— De la musique considérée en elle-même et dans ses rapports avec la parole, les langues, la pensée, et le théâtre. Pissot, 1785. 459 p.

Chabanon (1730-92), violinist, composer and writer who became member of

Académie française in 1780, conceived in these two works what is probably most advanced musical aesthetics written anywhere in 18th century. Second work is revision of first with addition of a second part which applies principles developed in first part to the particular problems of the relationship between music and language. Chabanon's great accomplishment was to leave behind ideas of rationalism and imitation of effects and replace them with a theory of autonomy and intangibility of music. Bases music on genius instead of reason, and proclaims, in opposition to Rousseau, priority of instrumental over vocal music and underlines pre-eminence of melody which affects state of the soul with an inherent kind of indefiniteness. In relation to poetry, music is rhythmically independent, and poet and composer have to further each other mutually in their common work.

Chabanon, toward end of his second work (p. 393-96), reproduced and commented on four *Chansons des sauvages de l'Amérique septentrionale.*

[Contant, d'Orville, André Guillaume]. Histoire de l'opéra bouffon, contenant les jugemens de toutes les pièces qui ont paru depuis sa naissance jusqu'à ce jour. Pour servir à l'histoire des théâtres de Paris. Amsterdam, Grangé, 1768. 2 v.   309

Chronological survey of operas and plays with the music produced in Paris outside the *Opéra* during period from 1753-67. This chronique gives a good notion of artistic and intellectual climate of Parisian stage in middle of 18th century through description and analysis of works, presentation of plots, occasional quotation of couplets, enumeration of actors' or singers' names, and critical evaluations.

Cucuel, Georges. La critique musicale dans les revues du XVIIIe siècle. Amus 2:127-203, 1913.   310

Term "*revue*" as used in this study means those theatrical productions which consisted of a number of scenes without content connection. Cucuel proposes "d'étudier simplement la manière dont les pièces satiriques du XVIIIe siècle ont parlé de la musique et des musiciens de leur temps." (p. 187). In other words, actual events are mirrored in these plays, especially aspects of Parisian life of the time. Period dealt with extends from 1690 to 60's of next century. Chronological table of the *revues* constitutes not only index of material investigated but also serves as a succinct survey of the 70 odd plays, their authors, theaters, and sources.

— La Pouplinière et la musique de chambre au XVIIIe siècle. Fischbacher, 1913. 457 p. (Diss., Paris).   311

La Pouplinière (1693-1762), for more than forty years *fermier général,* was one of the most brilliant patrons of art under *ancien régime.* This connection with the old social order gave him means to bring together in his salon, one of the most splendid of the time, the most progressive spirits in literature and music like Voltaire, Rousseau, Rameau, Stamitz, and Gossec. Cucuel's study, which has become standard work, shows this interrelation of social and artistic life during the reign of Louis XV in the most striking way, the more so as it was conceived and written with utmost scholarly sobriety and exactness.

— Sources et documents pour servir à l'histoire de l'opéra-comique en France. Amus 3:247-82, 1914. *See* 491.   312

Critical bibliography of 18th century sources, documents, and writings relating to *Opéra comique,* one of the most important social and artistic creations of period. First part deals with unpublished material, second with printed sources such as historical works, reminiscences and correspondences, aesthetic considerations, and social observations. Despite its bibliographical character and its limited topic, study throws light on manifold forces which brought French comic opera to the fore.

Diderot, Denis. Beaux-arts. Deuxième partie (Musique). *In his:* Œuvres complètes. Assézat ed. Garnier, 1875-77. 12: 135-534.   313

Divided into two groups, the first part (p. 143-70) consists of following three pamphlets : *Arrêt rendu à l'amphithéâtre de l'opéra; Au prophète de Bœhmischbroda, au grand prophète Monet ; Les trois chapitres ou La Vision de la nuit du mardigras au mercredi des cendres.* All three belong to the year 1753 in which began famous *querelle des bouffons* concerning superiority of French or Italian music. Diderot's position rather neutral; full meaning of his arguments can be understood only in light of whole contemporary pamphlet literature on this question.

Second group contains the *Leçons de*

clavecin et principes d'harmonie par M. Be-metzrieder (p. 171-524). Bemetzrieder was the teacher of Diderot's daughter. The *Leçons*, first and most successful of Bemetzrieder's theoretical works, present this instruction in form of dialogues. Their stylistic brilliancy is due to editor-ship of Diderot who himself figures in the dialogues as the *philosophe*. Book contains not only elements of musical theory of its time (published in 1771) but also has remarkable sidelights on proper teaching methods and on composers of third quarter of 18th century. Again, neutrality between the different camps is maintained on these pages, being based on the *philosophe's* considerations on music as an art to master souls. [*maître les âmes*].

Following the *Leçons* (p. 525-34) is an article about them which Diderot pub-lished in 1771 in Grimm's *Correspondance littéraire*.

— Rameau's Neffe; ein Dialog von Diderot. Aus dem Manuscript übersetzt. *In :* Goethes Werke. Weimar Ausgabe. Böhlau, 1887-1919. v. 45. p. 1-217.   314

Diderot's masterpiece, *Le neveu de Rameau*, was published for first time in this translation of Goethe, in 1805, twenty-one years after the author's death. In a dialogue between author and Rameau's nephew, probably written in the early 1760's, social aspects of the life of an artist and of art at this time are discussed from every angle, music being the Ariadne thread in labyrinth of moral interpreta-tions. Diderot clearly indicates his criticism of Rameau as representative of an obsolete kind of musicianship and his predilection for Duni as representative of adequate melodic expression of human affections and feelings. Goethe in his *Anmerkungen über Personen und Gegenstände, deren in dem Dialog Rameau's Neffe erwähnt wird* (p. 159-217) presents comments of the greatest interest on French music and literature of 18th century and on musical and cultural questions in general, paying high respect to Diderot and his masterpiece.

Écorcheville, Jules. De Lulli à Rameau 1690-1730; l'esthétique musicale. Fortin, 1906. 172 p.   315

Discussion of French theory of aesthet-ics from Bossuet to the writers of the *Mercure de France*. Although musical side of question is emphasized, aesthetics of rising French rationalism in general

comes to fore as basis of the growing new ideas. Bibliography of contemporary French sources presents valuable survey of aesthetic philosophy during period.

Faller, Max. Johann Friedrich Reichardt und die Anfänge der musikalischen Jour-nalistik. Kassel, Bärenreiter, 1929. 101 p.   316

Although Reichardt (1752-1814) played an important role as a composer, con-ductor, and aesthetician, his main signi-ficance lies in his insatiable drive to report whatever he heard and saw. Unrestricted by any convictions, he was quick and superficial in his reporting but he embraced almost everything of musical and general cultural interest. As he spent some time in Paris on at least four occasions, and was admitted into all important circles, we are indebted to him for many details about manifold intellec-tual life of French capital, found parti-cularly in his *Vertraute Briefe über Frankreich, auf einer Reise im Jahr 1792 geschrieben* (1792/93), 2 v.) and his *Vertraute Briefe aus Paris geschrieben in den Jahren 1802 und 1803* (no. 348). Faller presents the many involved jour-nalistic ventures of Reichardt in a well-organized and documented manner and heightens usefulness of his essay by chronological survey of Reichardt's wri-tings.

Font, Auguste. Essai sur Favart et les ori-gines de la comédie mêlée de chant. Tou-louse; Privat, 1894. 355 p. (Diss., Paris). *See* 493.   317

Good and detailed survey of develop-ment of musical comedy and vaudeville in France since beginning of 17th century and evaluation of Favart's place in this development which finally led to rise of French comic opera. Integration of comedy, music, and public taste is clearly brought out and ample documentation is judiciously used. Chronology of Favart's plays with indication of places of per-formance and first editions is very useful, but unfortunately general bibliography and index are wanting.

Gaudefroy-Demombynes, Jean. Les juge-ments allemands sur la musique française au XVIIIᵉ siècle. Maisonneuve, 1941. 457 p.   318

French music of 18th century seen through eyes of contemporary German critics. The five sections of the book deal with opera, comic opera, vocal music, instrumental music, and theory, that is, aesthetics. Many sidelights are thrown on French musical life and thought, and particular angle of this study stresses many features in instructive new way. Reader should be cautious with respect to small items, especially dates, although scholarly approach prevails throughout. An extended bibliography of 18th century German and French books on musical and general aesthetics, and of German periodicals of the time is of special value.

Goldschmidt, Hugo. Die Musikästhetik des 18. Jahrhunderts und ihre Beziehungen zu seinem Kunstschaffen. Zürich und Leipzig, Rascher, 1915. 462 p. 319

Only book up to present day on music aesthetics of 18th century. Divided in two parts, first general, second devoted to aesthetics of opera. Work gives detailed, chronological, and ideological survey of main musical aesthetic theories and arguments which were brought forth in Europe throughout whole century. Although Goldschmidt pays due tribute to German, Italian, Spanish, and English contributions, his study centers around France from Boileau to the Encyclopedists and then to Chabanon and Lacépède. Despite fact that Goldschmidt's evaluations are superseded today by more objective approach, his book is still invaluable through comprehensive presentation of most complex and important topic.

Gradenwitz, Peter. Questions musicologiques : Johan Stamitz et le Petit prophète de Bœhmischbroda. RMUS 19:62-70, 1938. 320

Excellent and amply documented analysis of those pamphlets of *Guerre des bouffons* which deal with Bohemian musicians. Gradenwitz believes that *Petit prophète de Bœhmischbroda* is a poetic synthesis of Gluck and Johann Stamitz, founder of Mannheim School, who went to Paris in 1754 and made deep impression on Parisian public, particularly as director of concerts given in house of Leriche de la Pouplinière in Passy.

Grétry, André Ernest Modeste. Mémoires, ou essais sur la musique. L'imprimerie de la République, Pluviôse, an V (1797). 3 v. 321

— Réflexions d'un solitaire. Manuscrit inédit... avec une introduction et des notes par Lucien Solvay et Ernest Closson. Brussels & Paris : Librairie nationale d'art et

d'histoire, van Oest, 1919-22. 4 v. (Œuvres complètes de Grétry publiées par le Gouvernement belge).

In field of French opera, Grétry's achievement represents the counterpart to the achievement of his contemporaries, the Encyclopedists : he brought naturalness and the virtues of bourgeois life to fore on operatic stage. Highly esteemed by Louis XVI as well as by leaders of Revolution and Napoleon I, Grétry represented nevertheless pre-revolutionary world. Dwindling of his creative power as composer, hastened by his personal misfortunes, led him to concentrate his activity on writing during last two decades of his life, although first volume of his *Mémoires* had already been published in 1789. These and the *Réflexions* (of which several chapters are lost) are personal account of his thoughts, experiences and reflections. Although only the volume published in 1789 is autobiographical in stricter sense of word and although the writing is often wordy, especially in the *Réflexions*, all these volumes reflect atmosphere of a whole epoch, dealing with everything from love to influence of political institutions on music, and they are written by a man who enjoyed company of Voltaire, Rousseau, Diderot, Marmontel, Grimm and many other distinguished people. The *Mémoires* and *Réflexions* are therefore filled with literary considerations, often based on first-hand experience. It is symbolical that Grétry wrote his *Réflexions* at Rousseau's *Ermitage* in Montmorency, which he acquired in 1798 and where he died fifteen years later. Unfortunately the *Réflexions* are published without index; the *Mémoires*, however, have one that is most complete.

Guiet, René. L'évolution d'un genre : le livret d'opéra en France de Gluck à la Révolution (1774-1793). Northampton, Mass. 199 p. (Smith College studies in modern languages, v. XVIII, nos. 1-4. October, 1936-July, 1937.) *See* 478, 3287. 322

Owing to decisive role opera played in intellectual life of 18th century France, Guiet is able to show how the opera libretto, after Gluck's French operas, truly mirrored the divergent cultural tendencies which finally converged in French Revolution. Aesthetic, social and political forces equally concurred in this development, which is presented here with clarity and circumspection. The minute bibliography, a list of operas not performed in the period dealt with, and the index enhance value of this study.

Hirschberg, Eugen. Die Encyklopädisten und die französische Oper im 18. Jahrhundert. Leipzig : Breitkopf & Härtel, 1903. 145 p. (Publikationen der Internationalen Musikgesellschaft. Beihefte. Heft X). (Diss., Leipzig).   323

First systematic attempt to show the contributions of the Encyclopedists to the victory of the Bouffons and Gluckists in France. Despite much more recent study of Oliver (no. 337), it is still valuable through presentation in separate sections of work on music, done outside the *Encyclopédie* itself, by several prominent Encyclopedists, especially Grimm, Diderot and d'Alembert. Voltaire is dealt with in beginning of last chapter. Detailed index considerably enhances usefulness of book.

Iacuzzi, Alfred. The European vogue of Favart; the diffusion of the opéra-comique. New York, Institute of French studies, 1932. 410 p. (Diss., Columbia). *See* 565.   324

Role Favart played in creation of the French comic opera cannot be underestimated, and spread and influence of his work throughout Europe during latter half of 18th century is equally important. Thus : the most famous example is the parody of Rousseau's *Devin du village; Les amours de Bastien et Bastienne* (by Favart, Mme Favart and Harny de Guerville) whose German adaptation by Weiskern the twelve-year-old Mozart set to music. Favart's works were adapted, used and often newly set to music not only in Austria, but in England, Germany, Italy, Spain, and Northern Europe as well. Iacuzzi gives well-documented survey of this influence. Especially valuable is chronology of Favart's plays and their translations and imitations, a section which considerably improves and enlarges chronology of Font (no. 317). Selective bibliography and detailed index complete usefulness of book.

Jansen, Albert. Jean-Jacques Rousseau als Musiker. Berlin, Reimer, 1884. 482 p. 325

Still most detailed study of Rousseau the musician. Especially valuable is appendix (p. 455-79), with unpublished material. Noteworthy is fragment of letter of Rousseau to Grimm on French and Italian opera, written in 1750, in which author of *Lettre sur la musique française* (1753) clearly underlines superiority of French music. Another interesting docu-

ment is extract of a survey Rousseau made about his activity as music copyist during last years of his life. *See* 2106.

Kretzschmar, Hermann. Die Correspondance littéraire als musikgeschichtliche Quelle. JMP 10:77-92, 1903.   326

Due respect is paid to significance of Grimm's *Correspondance littéraire* as source for development of arts and sciences under *ancien régime* in Kretzschmar's survey of Grimm's activity as music critic. Grimm's main interest lies in opera; he was one of the most embittered partisans of Italian opera. But Kretzschmar emphasizes that his reports chronicle not only Parisian opera from Rameau to Cherubini but also give lively account of response, taste, and attitude of public. Kretzschmar shows richness of the *Correspondance* as musical source if seen with critical eyes.

Lacépède [Bernard Germain Etienne Laville], *comte* **de.** La poëtique de la musique. Imprimerie de Monsieur, 1785. 2 v.   327

Lacépède, eminent naturalist, studied music with Gossec and was active as composer. Importance of his *Poëtique de la musique* lies above all in fact that it represents first systematization of musical aesthetics brought about by the reform operas of Gluck. His work is almost entirely devoted to discussion of lyric tragedy. Like Gluck, Lacépède wants music to remain in service of the dramatic poem but he develops from this principle several postulates which as a result confronted music with rather modern tasks for this period. Above all Lacépède demands unity which combines different musical elements into one integrated whole in accordance with action and poetry. In this respect his request for motivic connections is noteworthy. Another important demand is the appropriate and consequential characterization of personages. Overture, arias, orchestral interludes, recitatives, choral passages have all to be musically interrelated. Although Lacépède still advocates rational theory of imitation, he is by no means dogmatic and always puts emphasis on adequate musical expression of actual dramatic situations. He thus presents complete aesthetics of the highest, and in its way unsurpassed type of French serious opera in 18th century.

La Laurencie, Lionel de. La grande saison italienne de 1752. Les bouffons. SIM 8, no. 6, p. 18-33, no. 7-8, p. 13-22. 1912. 328

Very detailed and well-documented study of historical and aesthetic background and circumstances of appearance of the Italian opera troupe in Paris which in 1752, particularly through the performance of Pergolesi's *Serva padrona*, brought about the *Guerre des bouffons*.

Landormy, Paul and Joseph Loisel. L'Institut de France et le Prix de Rome. *In :* Encyclopédie de la musique et Dictionnaire du Conservatoire. Part 2. Delagrave, 1931. p. 3479-3575.

Maurat, Edmond. L'enseignement de la musique en France et les Conservatoires de province. *ibid.*, p. 3576-3616.

Peytel, A. Les théâtres musicaux subventionnés. *ibid.*, p. 3748-3833.   329

These three studies in the great standard French encyclopedia of music are of different value but nevertheless indispensable to student of interrelationship between music and literature. The first essay contains succinct history of *Académie des Beaux-Arts* with particular emphasis on its music section, giving an analysis of its organization and complete lists of different categories of members with biographical sketches of full members. Essay on music instruction in France represents well-documented history of its intellectual and social setting, especially with respect to foundation of *Conservatoire*. Third essay complements second with special emphasis on operatic institutions. Complete chronology of the works given at the Paris Opera constitutes valuable supplement to text proper. All three contributions bring to fore the musical development within general cultural scene. Lacks bibliography.

Leblond, Gaspard Michel. Mémoires pour servir à l'histoire de la révolution opérée dans la musique par M. le chevalier Gluck. Naples and Paris : Bailly, 1781. 491 p.   330

Leblond (1738-1809) like many of his compatriots gives evidence of vital role music played in intellectual life of 18th century France. Archeologist and librarian of Mazarin Library in Paris, he was merely amateur in music. He sensed, however, the great significance of work of Gluck and thus compiled this volume which up to present day represents the only comprehensive collection of the pamphlets, articles and notes, published in France between 1772 and 1780, concerning quarrel between the Gluckists and Piccinnists. The part literature played in this musical feud becomes easily evident when we meet among the authors such writers as Rousseau, La Harpe, Marmontel, and many others.

Leclerc, J. B. Essai sur la propagation de la musique en France, sa conservation, et ses rapports avec le gouvernement. Imprimerie nationale, 1796. 66 p.

Framery, N. E. Avis aux poètes lyriques, ou De la nécessité du rythme et de la césure dans les hymnes ou odes destinés à la musique. Imprimerie de la République [1796]. 36 p.   331

Two pamphlets typical of approach of revolutionary period to artistic problems, the first written by a member of the Convention and later President of the *Conseil des 500* for the Committee of Public Instruction, the second published by same Committee to be distributed to Conservatories and Associations of writers and artists.

Both pamphlets presuppose subordination of art to public interest which is incarnated in the people and represented by the authorities. For Leclerc music has to serve moral ends of society, in particular welfare of the people. Music should not be separated from poetry as it is too vague and therefore an easy outlet for dangerous passions. Marches and dances for instance should be played by instruments alone only after their music has been originally set to a text. All musical activity down to smallest detail is to be regulated by law; the Legislative has to decide about acceptance or rejection of any new composition. As music is either solely destructive or solely beneficial, latter end can be guaranteed only by its full subjection to complete public control.

In similar spirit Framery wants music to serve patriotism, virtue and reason. Only *genre* satisfactory to this end is secular hymns which are to be kept at level of musically uneducated people in interest of public function of music in festivals, during work and for recreation. Hence, works of poets as well as composers must be simple and easy.

Marmontel, Jean François. Essai sur les révolutions de la musique en France. *In :* Œuvres complètes de Marmontel, new ed., Verdière, 1818-20. v. 10. p. 393-426.   332

Marmontel's very active interest in music cannot be better characterized than by fact that it was he who adapted

Quinault's *Roland* for first French opera of Piccinni whom the anti-Gluckists had called to Paris. This *Essai* is his credo in favor of Italian music, written at same time (1777) as Piccinni's *Roland* in Paris. Although Marmontel tries to express his ideas in restrained way, he cannot hide his hostility toward Gluck.

Marpurg, Friedrich Wilhelm, ed. Historisch-kritische Beyträge zur Aufnahme der Musik. Berlin, 1754-78. 5 v.   333

This periodical, published at such irregular intervals that the last issue followed preceding one by sixteen years, constitutes the first attempt to present historical and critical approach in writing on music. Representing the important Berlin School which worked under a monarch passionately devoted to French culture as well as to music, the *Beyträge* critically reflect aesthetic-literary discussions on music taking place in neighboring France. On the one hand, the periodical published without comment translations of several French investigations on music of antiquity but, on the other hand, it submitted the theories of Batteux, reigning at this time all over Europe, to critical examination from first volume until last. That Marpurg kept his readers informed about the *Guerre des bouffons*, goes without saying. In general the *Beyträge* permit us to observe how predominating French doctrines of art were put to scrutiny in a country which was on its way to its own classical art.

Masson, Paul Marie. L'opéra de Rameau. Laurens, 1930. 595 p. (Diss., Paris).   334

Standard work on Rameau who, as theoretician and composer alike, was the most prominent figure in French musical life in 18th century. Although Masson investigates only the dramatic work of Rameau, he is concerned with historical criticism rather than with descriptive history and is thus compelled to pursue general aesthetic conceptions of the time and their development. The student of French intellectual history in first half of 18th century is therefore richly rewarded by detailed musical analysis, combined with presentation of the essential trends " dans l'état d'esprit et dans les habitudes artistiques du temps." That the work satisfies highest scholarly requirements is shown also by elaborate index of proper names, feature not too frequent in French studies.

Noverre, Jean-Georges. Lettres sur la danse et sur les ballets. 2nd ed. London & Paris : Dessain, 1783. 368 p.   335

Humanization of the ballet is Noverre's great contribution to the magnificent progress of the arts made in France during 18th century. Dancer and ballet master in Paris, Berlin, London, Lyons, Stuttgart, Vienna and finally again in Paris, he brought to fore over all Europe his principle of satisfying equally mind and heart in the ballet. These letters, published in 1760 while he was in Lyons, and afterwards re-edited several times, quickly became standard work because they developed under all its different aspects problem of composing for and performing of ballets. Taking imitation of nature as guiding principle, Noverre asks for integration of dance, setting, action, costumes, gestures, and especially music. His book gives not only convincing account of his principles but also good insight into mechanical stiffness which predominated in French ballet in middle of century. At same time, by discussions of literary, musical, and scenic principles, he often introduces the thought-world of such of his progressive contemporaries in music and literature as Rameau and Diderot.

[Nougaret, Pierre Jean Baptiste]. De l'art du théâtre où il est parlé des différents genres de spectacles, et de la musique adaptée au théâtre. Cailleau, 1769. 2 v.   336

First great work about French lyric scene which clearly advances postulates of rising middle class. Nougaret demands combination of nature and truth, of pleasant and useful, and presentation of plain people and their problems on stage. Although title of his work promises consideration of all different kinds of theatrical production, their discussion only serves to underline the significance of *Opéra-Bouffon* which he evaluates as the real art form of his own and future times. Poetry and literature, past and present, are scrutinized with respect to their use on stage. Last book of work, covering larger part of second volume, is devoted to an investigation of role of music, which according to author, has only to serve the pleasure of the spectator. Detailed table of contents in each volume.

Oliver, Alfred Richard. The Encyclopedists as critics of music. New York, Columbia univ. press., 1947. 227 p. (Diss., Columbia). *See* 1317.   337

Places emphasis on literary rather than musical aspects. Author understands his task to be a compilation as comprehensive as possible of available material without any particular viewpoint of his own. Quotations are unfortunately presented in translation only. Helpful are : *Index of articles on music in the Encyclopedia* and bibliographical list of *Authorities on music in the Encyclopedia*. Extensive bibliography and index.

Pierre, Constant. Les hymnes et chansons de la Révolution; aperçu général et catalogue avec notices historiques, analytiques et bibliographiques. Imprimerie nationale, 1904. (Ville de Paris. Publications relatives à la Révolution française). 1040 p. 338

Comprehensive work of first-rate importance, entirely based on original documents and sources, covering period from 1789 to 1802. First part gives factual history of origin and rôle of the songs and hymns of the Revolution, biographies of poets and composers, description and evaluation of documents and sources, as well as of public and private collections. Second part lists in four sections, with all desirable bibliographical accuracy, the hymns, the popular songs, the songs taken from dramatic works and the instrumental music. Indexes of titles, first lines, authors, melodies, and a general one which refers to preceding indexes, make this work nearly perfect.

— Musique des fêtes et cérémonies de la Révolution française; œuvres de Gossec, Cherubini, Lesueur, Méhul, Catel, etc. recueillies et transcrites. Imprimerie nationale, 1899. 582 p. (Ville de Paris. Publications relatives à la Révolution française). 339

Presents 148 pieces of music, 38 written for instruments, covering period mainly from 1790 to 1800. Pierre offers here only collection giving us a comprehensive view of music of the Revolution. Although accompaniments as well as purely orchestral music are reduced to piano arrangements, completeness of presentation, especially texts in their entirety, is of inestimable value to student of intellectual history of the Revolution. Pierre gives exhaustive survey of sources and documents, of authors and composers as well as of his own working methods, and collection is indexed under every aspect, which makes it useful in many ways. Reader who wishes to trace all variants of a piece, can easily supplement

his study by consulting Pierre's *Catalogue* (no. 338).

Pochon, Alfred. J.-J. Rousseau musicien et la critique; essai de mise au point. [Montreux, Corbaz]. Les éditions du mois suisse, 1940. 53 p. 340

This little study, though far from exhaustive, is valuable largely because of second of its three chapters in which Pochon reviews a number of critics of Rousseau the musician from time of great Frenchman up to our century. In his conclusions, Pochon underlines role music played for Rousseau and his work.

Prod'homme, Jacques Gabriel. Diderot et la musique. ZIM 15:156-62, 177-82, 1913-14. 341

A survey in chronological sequence of Diderot's writings on music. Author doubts Diderot's authorship of the three pamphlets in v. 12 of the *Œuvres complètes* (no. 313). He attributes to Diderot progressive ideas on music which find their confirmation and fulfillment in the works of Grétry and Gluck. *See* 2285.

— Les frères Parfaict, historiens de l'opéra. Rmus 11:110-18, Feb. 1, 1930. 342

Detailed study of background, lives, and literary activities of the two brothers whose *Histoire générale du théâtre français depuis son origine (1734-49, 15 v.)*, *Mémoires pour servir à l'histoire des spectacles de la Foire par un acteur forain (1743, 2 v.)* and *Dictionnaire des théâtres de Paris (1756-67, 7 v.)* contain wealth of information not only for student of French theater in general but particularly for one interested in rise and development of lyric stage. Close interaction of literature and music is characteristic, and although Prod'homme's paper emphasizes lives of the two brothers rather than their work, his rich documentation forms good introduction to this relationship.

— Pierre de Jélyotte (1713-1797). SIM 3: 686-717, 1901-02. 343

Jélyotte, brilliant tenor of the Paris Opera from 1733-1754, most understanding interpreter of Rameau and the first Colin in Rousseau's *Devin du village*, offered Prod'homme a welcome opportunity to depict the involvement of court and opera life under Louis XV. In describing the life and circumstances of Jélyotte, Prod'homme acquaints us not only with many well-known musicians of the time but also with Rousseau, Mme de Pompadour, Mme d'Epinay, Marmontel, Marquis d'Argenson and many others. Rich documentation, including list of all roles performed by Jélyotte at the Opera, enhances general cultural value of study.

— La position sociale des musiciens avant la Révolution. Musique 3:8-18 and 75-80, 1929.   344

Well-documented study of way in which musicians made living in 17th and 18th century France. Composers as well as performers, and publishing as well as instruction are discussed. Social changes which took place during the two centuries are presented with respect to their significance within intellectual life of nation as well as their movement towards economic establishment of musician in rising bourgeois society.

Prunières, Henri. Lecerf de La Viéville et l'esthétique musicale classique au XVIIe siècle. SIM 4:619-54, 1908.   345

Comprehensive analysis of aesthetics of Lecerf de La Viéville who with his *Comparaison* (no. 346) opened, on the French side, great quarrel about French and Italian music in 18th century France. Prunières shows whole cultural background of Lecerf de La Viéville's position and thus gives reader good insight into significance of musical achievements of age of Louis XIV.

Raguenet, François. A comparison between the French and Italian music. MQ 32:411-36, 1946.   346

Storer, Mary Elizabeth. Abbé François Raguenet, deist, historian, music and art critic. RR 36:283-96, 1945.

Raguenet (c. 1660-c. 1722) foreshadows many intellectual trends which only came to full blossom in course of 18th century. In field of music his *Paralele* [sic] *des Italiens et des François en ce qui regarde la musique et les opéra* [sic], published in 1702, is first principal attack on French music in favor of Italian music. Our translation is the annotated English version of 1709, modernized by Oliver Strunk, and offers good introduction to argumentation which eventually led to the *Guerre des bouffons* and the *querelle* between the Gluckists and Piccinnists. Raguenet's work provoked Le Cerf de La Viéville's *Comparaison de la musique italienne et de la musique française*, published in three volumes, 1704-

1706, which constitutes extensive historical and critical defense of French music. Third volume contains answer to Raguenet's *Défense* of his *Parallele* against Le Cerf de La Viéville; in other words, the literary quarrel about music was already coming into full swing in beginning of century.

Miss Storer's somewhat diffuse paper discusses Raguenet's literary, historical and critical works and thus offers good picture of manifold interests and achievements of the Abbé whose musical views are closely connected with his general cultural outlook. She evaluates Raguenet as a precursor of Diderot in the history of art criticism.

Récy, René de. La critique musicale au siècle dernier; Rameau et les Encyclopédistes. RDM 3ème pér. 76:138-64, 1886.   347

On the basis of six books published between 1873 and 1884, Récy discusses career of Rameau and antagonism of Encyclopedists. He condemns the unjust evaluation of Rameau by his contemporaries in France and finds justification of Rameau's theoretical and operatic work in fact that the ideas of this Frenchman were recognized and bore fruit outside France, particularly in Germany.

Reichardt, Johann Friedrich. Vertraute Briefe aus Paris geschrieben in den Jahren 1802 und 1803. Hamburg, Hoffmann, 1805. 3 v. (v. 1-2. 2nd corrected ed.) 348

Reichardt, conductor to Frederick the Great as well as to King Jérôme of Westphalia, prolific composer, and concert manager, is today mainly remembered for having been first music journalist in modern sense of word in that he wished to publish news for its newsworthiness and not because of its meaning. The many, mostly short-lived, periodicals he founded and directed, and his travel descriptions give evidence of this and are still valuable as contemporary sources. His *Vertraute Briefe* were result of his last journey to Paris and furnish us with lively and colorful, though superficial, picture of the French capital under the First Consul. Although Reichardt puts emphasis on theater, and in this respect, of course, on operas, his description of political, social, scientific, and general artistic life after storms of the Revolution gives us a good insight into intellectual atmosphere of Paris at end of 18th century.

Rolland, Romain. Musiciens d'autrefois.
2nd ed. Hachette [1908]. 306 p. *See* 1320.
Voyage musical au pays du passé. *ibid.*
[1920]. 246 p.   349

Rolland, father of modern French
musicology, had the almost unique gift
of combining with the art of writing
great scholarship in his special field and
broad outlook on civilization in general.
Essays of these two volumes show to
reader, in most instructive and readable
way, interrelation of music with the other
arts and social life. The *Musiciens d'autrefois* deals partly with 18th century by
means of separate studies on Gluck,
Grétry and Mozart, while the *Voyage
musical au pays du passé* is almost entirely
devoted to that period. Portraits of
Kuhnau, Bach's predecessor at Leipzig,
of Handel, Telemann, and Metastasio are
combined with study on origins of
" classic style " in music of 18th century
and musical journey through 18th century
Europe, i.e., through Italy and Germany.
Against background of intellectual and
social forces shaping course of 18th century, and specifically in France, reader
gains clear insight into important place
music held within this framework.

— La Marseillaise en Allemagne. In : Goethe
et Beethoven. Éditions du Sablier [c. 1930]
p. 243-51.   349A

Due to the fact that the spread eastward
of the *Marseillaise* forms part of the
dissemination of ideas of French Revolution outside France, these few pages
from the second volume of Rolland's
great work on Beethoven (6 v., 1928-45)
acquire special importance. Rolland
shows how *Marseillaise*, as a whole or as
text and melody separate, was introduced
or adapted in Germany during first
decade after its composition. He points
to use of the melody by Richard Wagner
and to a threefold adaptation by Schumann,
but emphasis rests on its spread during
last years of 18th century. In this
respect Rolland's note is a unique contribution to the intellectual history of the
Revolution.

Rousseau, J.-J. Écrits sur la musique. *In
his :* Œuvres complètes. Furne, 1835.
3:447-874.

— Le devin du village. *ibid.* p. 248-55.

— Pygmalion, scène lyrique. *ibid.* p. 220-23.
                                                  350

Music runs like a thread through the

life of Rousseau, whether he earned a
living as a simple copyist, or composed
the prototype of the French " singspiel "
in his *Le devin du village* (1752), or created
melodrama (monodrama) in his *Pygmalion*
(1770). It is therefore not surprising to
find not only many remarks on music in
his works but to see several of his writings
devoted entirely to music. They can be
conveniently divided into three groups,
and although this is not the place to
describe them extensively, their general
trend at least can be indicated. The first
group comprises Rousseau's attempt at
new notation of music, based on numbers,
his *Projet concernant de nouveaux signes
pour la musique*, which he read to the
Académie des sciences in 1742 and which
he presented to the public in more
elaborate form in his *Dissertation sur la
musique moderne* the following year. The
next group is made up of the many
pamphleteering letters, most of which
served to establish Rousseau's position
in the " guerre des bouffons." Their
gist, in favor of Italian music, especially
Italian opera, might best be deduced from
last sentence of the most famous letter,
the *Lettre sur la musique française* (1753) :
" D'où je conclus que les François n'ont
point de musique et n'en peuvent avoir,
ou que, si jamais ils en ont une, ce sera
tant pis pour eux." About twenty years
later Rousseau paid due respect to the
famous opera reform of Gluck in his
remarks on latter's operas *Alceste* and
Orphée. The third group consists of two
major works. First is the *Essai sur l'origine des langues, où il est parlé de la mélodie
et de l'imitation musicale* (written about
1760 and originally entitled *Essai sur le
principe de la mélodie*). Rousseau develops
his favorite theory that music is essentially
rooted in melody and song and that this
art has been gradually lost by man.
Second work is the *Dictionnaire de musique*
(1767) which is a revision and enlargement
of his articles on music for the *Encyclopédie*. Rousseau's place in the history of
French music has been said to be the
link between Rameau and Gluck. This
holds true when we think less of actual
music than of theoretical and aesthetical
conceptions. Even then we have to add
that Rousseau's views on music represent
a curious mixture of quite antiquated and
radical ideas. All this comes out clearly
in his *Dictionnaire*, which is a dictionary
of musical topics and not biographical.
But its great value lies precisely in fact
that it provides reader with an insight
into this mixture of ideas prevalent in

middle of 18th century in France and into the musical mind of Rousseau himself. And it is not the smallest merit of this work that it is the best written music dictionary up to present day.

Straeten, Edmond van der. Voltaire musicien. Baur, 1878. 299 p.   351

In fourteen essays Straeten investigates " ... l'immixtion de Voltaire dans presque toutes les branches de l'art musical " (p. 1) with due consideration of fact that Voltaire was musical amateur as well as genius curious about every kind of human experience. Picture of Voltaire given here shows his musical interests, including use of musical metaphors in his language and his endeavours in acoustics; also his encounter with young Grétry and the failure of young Mozart to meet the Sage of Ferney. All this is presented in conversational tone, but is well documented. Index includes only names of musicians.

Tiersot, Julien. Beethoven, musicien de la Révolution française. RPar 17:733-60, Jan.-Feb., 1910.   352

Ideas and ideologies of the French Revolution, especially ideas of liberty and fraternity, as expressed in work of Beethoven. Particularly the songs, the 3rd, 5th, 6th, and 9th symphonies, *Fidelio*, the music of *Egmont*, the *Battle Symphony* and the *Missa solemnis* are treated. The political and intellectual forces which influenced Beethoven are emphasized.

—. Les fêtes et les chants de la Révolution française. Hachette, 1908. 323 p.   353

Shows how music gave expression to feelings of the people during the French Revolution by presenting public appeal of music and its materialization in revolutionary songs and *fêtes*. Vividly described are the close interrelationship and collaboration between different branches of intellectual activity from 1789 until end of century and the manifold fluctuations of these efforts in connection with the revolutionary events. Has an elaborate appendix with sources, documentary and bibliographic material, and index.

—. Gluck and the Encyclopedists. MQ 16: 336-57, 1930.   354

Survey of intellectual battle in France concerning superiority of French or Italian opera from *Guerre des bouffons* (1752) to production of Gluck's reform operas in Paris more than twenty years later. Gluck's development is presented with particular emphasis on causes which brought him to France, and the reasoning of the Encyclopedists is given as well as that of the minor figures of controversy around Gluck's operas like Abbé Arnaud, Suard, Marmontel, La Harpe. In conclusion, Tiersot considers Gluck as the continuator of French operatic tradition who completed the work of Lulli and Rameau.

— J.-J. Rousseau, 2nd rev. ed. Alcan, 1920. 280 p. (Les maîtres de la musique). *See* 337.   355

Comprehensive study of Rousseau : music teacher, copyist, writer on music, and composer. Important place music held in life and work of Rousseau as well as his great contribution to French musical life and thinking of 18th century presented in an equally readable and thoroughly documented way. Bibliography especially valuable through complete listing of Rousseau's compositions (including those lost), of his musical writings, and survey of libraries possessing music autographs of Rousseau.

Varnum, Fanny. Un philosophe cosmopolite du XVIIIe siècle; le chevalier de Chastellux. Rodstein, 1936. 269 p. (Diss., Paris).   356

Detailed, well-documented study of life and works of Chastellux, who became director of French Academy and participated in American War of Independence. Deeply interested in music, he took part through several writings in animated public debate in France on opera, and translated Algarotti's *Saggio sopra l'opera in musica.* Ably analyzes (p. 35-48) musical views of Chastellux who decidedly favored Italian way of subordinating the drama to the music in opera but did not deny, like Rousseau, a future to French music. Thanks to the many-sidedness and progressive ideas of Chastellux the integration of music in development of 18th century France clearly emerges from this study. Rich bibliography.

Review : *See* 2920.

Censorship
(Nos. 357-372)

ALBERT BACHMAN

Bachman, Albert. Censorship in France from 1715-1750; Voltaire's opposition. New

York, Institute of French studies, 1934. 206 p. (Diss., Columbia). 357

This dissertation fills the lacuna between Macpherson's *Censorship under Louis XIV (1661-1715)* and Belin's *Le commerce des livres prohibés à Paris de 1750 à 1789* (nos. 3 and 359). Extensive use has been made of manuscript source material of BN. Historical setting is sufficiently evaluated, but chief merit of study centers around *permission tacite*, which practice has been traced back to 1725. Research on literary activities of the Abbé d'Olivet might further elucidate genesis of that semi-official deceptive device. Reviews : H. L. Brugmans in RR 27: 42-44, 1936; D. Mornet in RHL 43: 130-31, 1936; A. Schinz in RHL 42:450-53, 1935.

Bayle, Paule, and Jacques Herblay. Journalisme au xviiie siècle. Nrev ns 37:213-35, Nov. 15, 1905, 395-413, Dec. 1, 1905. 358

First article bears subtitle *La présidente Doublet* and the second *Les bulletins et la police*. Mme Doublet de Breüillepont is described as the outstanding representative of *nouvelles à la main* journalism. Among her *habitués* are mentioned MM. de Caylus, Mirabeau, Foncemagne, Rigault, Largillière, Helvétius, Marivaux, etc.

Belin, Jean Paul. Le commerce des livres prohibés à Paris de 1750 à 1789. *See 3.* 359

Author analyzes with considerable skill mechanism of censorship and its manifold subterfuges : clandestine printing in Paris, provincial France, abroad, etc. Chapter dealing with Malesherbes's administration is too summarily treated, but still remains only *ouvrage d'ensemble* for second half of 18th century.

— Le movement philosophique de 1748 à 1789; étude sur la diffusion des idées philosophiques à Paris, d'après les documents concernant l'histoire de la librairie. *See 4.* 360

A daring enterprise within framework of a dissertation. After methodical and sagacious examination of widely scattered manuscript material, author was able to give his study the appropriate sub-title *Etude sur la diffusion des idées philosophiques à Paris.* Belin draws heavily upon Bachaumont, Métra, and other manuscript collections of BN. Belin owes also debt of gratitude to Pellisson

(no. 369). There are a few errors and at times too hasty conclusions.

Brunetière, Ferdinand. La direction de la Librairie sous M. de Malesherbes. RDM 3rd per. 49:567-612, Feb. 1, 1882. *See 2874.* 361

The first critical and scholarly treatment of 18th century censorship. Brunetière made wide use of the Anisson-Duperron Collection. Host of details fit into general picture. At certain periods he evaluates the conflict between rival authorities. Author falls somewhat short in full evaluation of Malesherbes's role as *Directeur de la Librairie* ; that important chapter still remains to be written.

Coyecque, Ernest. Inventaire de la collection Anisson sur l'histoire de l'imprimerie et la librairie, principalement à Paris, du xviie au xviiie siècle. Leroux, 1900. 2 v. 362

Represents valuable guide for 18th century research worker. There are detailed indications for each entry, but in view of great mass of marginal material, which is not classified, it pays diligent scholar to examine the dossiers for what they are worth. At end of vol. 2 is supplement and complete list of the *Fonds français, nouvelles acquisitions.* This part of collection contains many dossiers on the *Librairie sous M. de Malesherbes.*

Dubosq, Yves Zacharie. Le livre français et son commerce en Hollande de 1750 à 1780. *See 22.* 363

Work was originally designed as a contribution to a comprehensive study of the Dutch booktrade. Part I deals more with Dutch literature; Part II, *Le livre français en Hollande de 1750 à 1780 ;* and Part III, *Le commerce du livre français en Hollande de 1750 à 1780,* belong rather to field of comparative literature. New light is thrown on the *supplément* publication of the *Encyclopédie* as directed by *Une association hollandaise.* A very readable book.

François, Alexis. La correspondance de J.-J. Rousseau dans la querelle littéraire du xviiie siècle. RHL 33:161-79, 355-69, 1926. 364

Based on *documents inédits* of library of Neuchâtel, and throws light on personal relationship which existed between Rousseau and Malesherbes.

Gordon, D. H. and N. L. Torrey. The censoring of Diderot's Encyclopédie and the re-established text. New York, Columbia univ. press, 1947. 124 p. *See* 1308. 365

Two introductory chapters tell how this rare volume of corrected proofs of the *Encyclopédie* got into Germany from Russia and finally into the United States, and recount Le Breton's " great publishing venture." Next two chapters analyze the motives of self-appointed censor and deal with nature of the censored material, which is of interest only to specialist. Russian incident may well be only first step to further discoveries, once Count Stroganoff manuscript and book collections become available. Reviews : D. F. Bond in MP 45:142-43, 1947-48; A. Guérard in PR 362-64, 1947; G. R. Havens in Rrel 13:199-203, 1949; L. W. Tancock in FS 2:272-75, 1948.

Malesherbes, Chrétien Guillaume de Lamoignon de. Mémoires sur la librairie et sur la liberté de la presse. Agasse, 1809. 435 p. 366

Malesherbes devotes five *mémoires* to study of 18th century booktrade. *Mémoires sur la librairie* were completed in 1759, whereas *Mémoire sur la liberté de la presse* appeared as piece of propaganda shortly before convocation of *Etats généraux* in 1789. Comprehensive in scope, yet many generalizations tend to distort historical perspective. Last *Mémoire* concludes with prophecy that " ... la liberté de la presse est le fondement de la liberté des nations." Columbia University has copy of Malesherbes' book in its Rare book division.

Mellottée, Paul. Histoire économique de l'imprimerie. Tome I, L'imprimerie sous l'ancien régime, 1439-1789. Hachette, 1905. 531 p. 367

Rather extensive study of printing in France during the *ancien régime;* illustrates two principal features of 18th century French booktrade (1) concentrating larger capital in fewer hands and (2) tendency towards centralization. Author shows how royal power had established unwittingly, through customary procedure of giving special privileges, *les premières assises de la propriété littéraire.* Excellent bibliography.

Molinier, Auguste. Inventaire sommaire de la collection Joly de Fleury. Picard, 1881. 114 p. 368

Collection of lesser importance but in many ways supplements the *Collection Anisson.* The *Joly de Fleury* collection, preserved in MS Division of BN, contains, for greater part, the archives of the *procureurs-généraux.*

Pellisson, Maurice. Les hommes de lettres au XVIIIe siècle. Colin, 1911. 311 p. *See* 1064. 369

After much analytical spade work, author has welded huge mass of material into splendid *livre de synthèse.* Main strength of book lies in chapters *Les hommes de lettres et la loi* and *Les hommes de lettres et le pouvoir;* chapter on *Les hommes de lettres et les libraires* is superseded by subsequent study of Belin, (no. 4 and no. 360).

Review : D. Mornet in RHL 19:693-95, 1912.

Taschereau, Jules Antoine, Ed. Revue rétrospective, ou Bibliothèque historique, contenant des mémoires et documents authentiques inédits et originaux, pour servir à l'histoire proprement dite, à la biographie, à l'histoire de la littérature et des arts. Fournier, 1833-38. 20 v. 370

An exceedingly helpful collection. Consists of *morceaux inédits* such as *Détentions de Voltaire, chronique du règne de Louis XV, Chronique secrète de Paris sous le règne de Louis XVI,* etc. Excellent index.

Venturi, Franco. Le origini dell'Enciclopedia, Florence. Edizioni U. 1946. 164 p. 371

Scholarly work; based largely on manuscript material of Anisson collection of BN. Chap. III forms heart of study; D'Alembert's position is clearly shown. Venturi claims that Diderot's suppleness and courage saved enterprise; Malesherbes's role falls short of our expectations.

Review : N. L. Torrey in RR 39:167-69, 1948.

Werdet, Edmond. Histoire du livre en France depuis les temps les plus reculés jusqu'en 1789. Dentu, 1861-64. 4 v. in 5. 372

First systematic *ouvrage d'ensemble* on French booktrade during *ancien régime.* V. 3 of Part II deals more specifically with 18th century. Many interesting side lights, but author prefers *aspect littéraire* to scholarly approach.

History of the Language
(Nos. 373-400)

ALEXANDER H. SCHUTZ

Eighteenth-Century Source Materials

Encyclopédie. (*See* nos. 1288-1322). 373

Despite the use of many linguistic items by historians of the French language, there is as yet no connected story of its material or policies from the philologic viewpoint. *For a brief exploration see, however,* 1322. A list of important articles follows : *Alphabet, Articles, Cas, Concordance, Conjugaison, Consonne, Construction, Datif, Détermination, Dialecte, Dictionnaire, Figure, Formation, Français, Futur, Gallicisme, Genre, Grammaire, Idiotisme, Langue (& Langue françoise), Lettres, Méthode, Mot, Néographique, Néologique, Nombre, Orthographe, Partitif, Patois, Phrase, Pléonasme, Proposition, Prosodie, Régime, Romane (langue), Style, Syllabe (-ique), Transitif, Troubadour.* Through *Figure* the articles are signed by the grammarian Du Marsais (his spelling), with exception of *Dictionnaire,* which, because of its general character, bears signature of D'Alembert. Bulk of the others are work of Beauzée, whose initial is regularly followed by letters E.R.M. *(Ecole royale militaire),* strange base of operations. Noteworthy exception is article *François* by Voltaire. It is odd that the closely related *Langue françoise* has as its author the Chevalier de Jaucourt, who is likewise responsible for *Langue romane* and *Syllabique.* Some articles are unsigned : *Patois,* insignificant paragraph reflecting prevailing idea that dialects are " corruptions "; *Transitif,* called *Terme de grammaire hébraïque; Proposition,* whose non-linguistic paragraphs alone indicate their respective authors.

The scission between grammar and what we now call stylistics, the utter lack of correlation between the rare items on the older literatures of the French domain (e.g., *Troubadour, Trombadour*) and linguistics are subjects for further study.

Encyclopédie méthodique. 374

By the adjective *méthodique* is to be understood that articles of the older *Encyclopédie* are presented by topics. For our purposes, cf. those volumes entitled *Grammaire et littérature,* published by Panckoucke in Paris and by Plomteux in Liége. Forming volumes 80-82 of series, they are nevertheless numbered I-II-III, dated, respectively, 1782-1784-1786. Included are not only what title indicates but large number of purely lexicographic notes. Authors are difficult to find, there being no index. Some items are joint productions. Abbé Girard, among others, is responsible for certain ones. Comparison has still to be made between the other *Encyclopédie* and the *Méthodique* to see whether there were any revisions.*

[Desfontaines, Pierre François Guyot]. Dictionnaire néologique à l'usage des beaux esprits du siècle avec l'éloge historique de Pantalon-Phœbus par un avocat de province. Amsterdam, Le Cène, 1728. 468 p. 375

Interesting as piece of satire, but valuable also for author's judgment on words or expressions misused by contemporaries or appearing for first time in given sense. More study on data provided here would be profitable.

Lacombe, François. Dictionnaire du vieux langage françois. Panckoucke, 1766. Vol. 1, 498. Vol. 2, 588 p. 376

Two editions of same date, in one volume and in two, second volume being really a *Supplément.* Interesting as one of early Old French dictionaries. There is an allusion to author's troubadour selection, from materials communicated by La Curne de Sainte-Palaye. Latter's influence never adequately treated anywhere; his pioneering calls for a monograph.

Court de Gébelin [Antoine]. Histoire naturelle de la parole ou Précis de l'origine du langage et de la grammaire universelle. Chez l'auteur, Boudet, Valleyre (the printer), Duchesne, Saugrain, Ruault, 1776. 400 p. 377

Book deserving more frequent consultation in original. Its data are too often known to us from secondary sources. Fantastic and significant are side by side; on one hand, queerest of notions on relation of sounds and facial expression, on other, a foreshadowing of comparative linguistics. Much of interest for the then prevailing anthropological conceptions, also for language and aesthetics. Preoccupation with " origines " is characteristic—and fatal.

* Information on this work, I owe to Dr. A. C. Keller, University of Washington, who consulted the *Encyclopédie méthodique* at the New England Deposit Library.

Domergue, Urbain. Journal de la langue française, soit exacte, soit ornée. Lyon, l'auteur du Journal, 1784-87; Knapen (l'auteur), 1790-91.   378

Distinction between " *langue exacte* " and " *langue ornée* " seems based on that between grammar, phonetics, lexicography, on one hand, and stylistics on other. The *Journal* is full of interesting details, ranging from Domergue's plea for *vous* vs. *tu* to his " examen " of J.-J. Rousseau (1791 vol., p. 163). Despite utilization by Brunot (6 : pp. 912, 1045, *et al.*), Domergue deserves a monograph, since last word has not been said about development of his doctrine. Work difficult to secure in this country. Only the volume published in Paris is available at Library of Congress.

Féraud, l'abbé Jean-François. Dictionnaire grammatical de la langue française. Nouvelle édition, Delalain, 1788. vol. 1 (A-H), 463 p., 2 (I-Z), 538 p.   379

" *Grammatical* " used to include Phonetics and Prosody. Pioneer phonetic dictionary, perhaps more heavily weighted on this aspect than on syntax. Brunot uses the augmented form, the *Dictionnaire critique* of 1788, considering, however, only those parts that fall within scope of his work. Thus he gives a good evaluation of Féraud's syntactic contributions (6:2, 897), but only casual references to phonetic transcriptions, worth developing, with more systematic treatment of Féraud's different editions. Of interest are comments on changes of pronunciation since days of Ménage, also such remarks as these : (s.v. *Imparfait*) : " Mr. de Voltaire écrit *ais, ais, ait*, au lieu de *ois, ois, oit*, mais cette manière d'écrire ne prend pas."

Rivarol, [Antoine]. Discours sur l'universalité de la langue française. Delagrave, 1929. 143 p. Édition critique, avec une introduction et des notes par Marcel Hervier. *See* 2720.   380

" Cette édition du célèbre *Discours* de Rivarol se présente d'abord comme la première édition critique de son texte." (p. 5) Two sets of notes; one, at bottom of page, devoted to editor's critical remarks; the other, at end of text, is Rivarol's own commentary. Index alone explains which set is author's and which editor's. Variants show evolution of Rivarol's own style. Especially valuable is Ch. III of Introduction : *Comparaison*

des langues et la question de l'universalité avant Rivarol.

Modern Studies

Baldensperger, Fernand. Comment le dix-huitième siècle expliquait l'universalité de la langue française. *In his :* Études d'histoire littéraire. Hachette, 1907. p. 1-54.   381

Old but not outmoded. Considering brevity of treatment, still practical source for comprehension of century's linguistic standards, especially those of France. But for rest of Europe, Brunot is better. Review : D. Mornet in RHL 15:541-45, 1908.

Brunot, Ferdinand. Histoire de la langue française. V. 6, Le dix-huitième siècle. Part II, by Alexis François : La langue postclassique. Colin, 1932. 541 p.   382

Thorough, but hard to use because of confusing indices. One for proper names would have saved much labor; the *Index lexicologique* could have included more material in previous sections of Vol. 6. Reader is not informed till the last fascicle that such an index is available. Reviews : E. Bourciez in Rcr ns 100: 135-37, 1933; G. Esnault in MerF 246: 704-10, 1933; M. Frey in Archiv 166:273-75, 1934-35; E. G[amillscheg] in ZFSL 57:254-56, 1933; K. Glaser in LGRP 54: 22-24, 1933, 55:234-36, 1934; A. Meillet in BSLP 33:78-81, 1932; W. von W[artburg] in ZRP 55:682-85, 1935.

— Histoire de la langue française. V. 6, Première partie, Fascicule premier. Colin, 1930. 519 p.   383

Subtitle is self-explanatory : *Le mouvement des idées et les vocabulaires techniques.* Latter range from Philosophy to Finance. Mine of information without equal in this domain for thoroughness of treatment and results of highest value. Reviews : F. Gaiffe in RPF 42:232-38, 1930; K. Glaser in LGRP 52:124-25, 1931; A. Meillet in BSLP 31:125-29, 1931; G. Rohlfs in Archiv 161:119-20, 1932; W. von Wartburg in ZRP 51:603-07, 1931.

— Histoire de la langue française. Vol. 7 : La propagation du français en France jusqu'à la fin de l'ancien régime. Colin, 1926. 360 p.   384

An *essai de philologie sociologique* on nature of difficulties encountered by French language in its efforts to become national. Far surpasses anything of its kind previously published. Indispensable. Reviews : E. Bourciez in Rcr ns. 93-311-14, 1926; L. Clédat in RPF 38:70, 1926; C. Guerlin de Guer in RN 12:227-233, 1926; A. Meillet in BSLP 27:96-99, 1927; D. Mornet in RHL 34:446-49, 1927; H. Yvon in RU 35²:237-39, 1926.

— Histoire de la langue française. Vol. 8 : Le français hors de France au XVIIIe siècle. Part I : Le français dans les divers pays d'Europe. Colin, 1934. 768 p.   385

Acknowledgments are made to Max Fuchs and other students of Brunot for chapters done by them. Indispensable not alone for linguistic data but also for light shed upon general intellectual relations of France at this period. The *Avertissement*, taken by itself, is lesson in methodology. Reviews : E. Bourciez in Rcr ns 102: 146-49, 1935; M. Frey in Archiv 169: 111-13, 1936 and 170:250-52, 1936; K. Glaser in LGRP 61:100-03, 1940; A. Meillet in BSLP 36:65-67, 1935.

François, Alexis. Les origines lyriques de la phrase moderne au dix-huitième siècle. Presses universitaires, 1929. 61 p.   386

Sub-title is self-explanatory : *Etude sur la prose cadencée dans la littérature française au 18e siècle.* The work is not superseded by Brunot, Vol. 6, part 2 (no. 382). Its literary emphasis is greater than in Brunot. Chapter headings are worth noting : I. *La question du nombre poétique et du nombre oratoire.* II. *La question du vers blanc.* III. *La question de la prosodie.* IV. *La question du double rhythme.* Good treatment of Rousseau's attack on musicality of French language.

Kuehner, Paul. Theories on the origin and formation of language in the eighteenth century in France. Philadelphia, Univ. of Pennsylvania, 1944. 54 p. (Diss., Pennsylvania, 1941).   387

I. Traditional theory (i.e., biblical), II. Conventional theory (i.e., innate ideas, Reason), III. Sensationalist theory (Condillac). Treatment of relations between Condillac and Rousseau could be clearer. Bibliography throughout excellent. Works listed in notes, often of first importance, not always listed at end of book. Recent date makes the monograph especially valuable.

Gazier, Augustin Louis. Lettres à Grégoire sur les patois de France (1790-94). Durand et Pedone-Lauriel, 1880. 353 p.   388

Despite incorporation of many of its results into Brunot (Vol. 9), this book still has value for anyone interested in primary sources. Letters deal with the revolutionary government's investigation into the state of the dialects.

Hunt, H. J. Logic and linguistics; Diderot as *grammairien philosophe.* In MLR 33: 215-33, 1938.   389

Later than François and Brunot. Excellent statement of weaknesses in *grammaire raisonnée*, by a man with background in both philosophy and modern linguistics. Shows Vendryes' attraction to Diderot's theory of gestures, also how near latter came to discovering the social aspects of language which are the foundations of the Meillet school. Traces effects of 18th century thought on modern philology.

Le Bidois, Georges. Observations sur la langue du XVIIIe siècle. *In :* J. Calvet, Histoire de la littérature française. V. 6. Ed. by Albert Cherel : De Télémaque à Candide. p. 443-82. Gigord, 1933. *See* 1033.   390

Comprehensive survey of known facts by capable linguist with eye to relations between language and literature. Supersedes in part articles of Brunot in Petit de Julleville (V. 6) (nos. 49, 77). There is little that Le Bidois misses. First-rate performance. Could have benefited by more careful proofreading (e.g., misspellings of *Le pour et contre,* p. 450-456).

Masson, Pierre-Maurice. Contribution à l'étude de la prose métrique dans La nouvelle Héloïse. AJJR 5:259, 1909.   391

Brunot remarks (6:2112, n. 4) : " On peut trouver singulier que P.-M. Masson cherche à prouver que certains fragments de *La nouvelle Héloïse* ont été préalablement versifiés, hypothèse qui n'est ni vraisemblable, ni appuyée sur des faits certains." In his brief treatment, he nevertheless uses Masson's notation for the cadenced prose of Rousseau. Masson probably right that " La prose métrique de *La nouvelle Heloïse* mériterait toute une étude." In conjunction with the more specialized presentation of Masson one may read with profit Lanson's chapter XIV : *Deux phrases artistiques du XVIIIe siècle,* in his *Art de la prose.* Librairie des annales, 1909, (p. 195).

Morel, Jean. L'essai sur l'origine des langages. *In his :* Recherches sur les sources du Discours sur l'inégalité. AJJR 5:150-60, 1909.   392

Discusses relation of Rousseau and Condillac on origin of language. While Brunot (no. 382, 6:909) uses data on Condillac's views, his interest is in French rather than general language. Morel's stress is also more on literary and philosophic aspects.

Roumiguière, Henriette. Le français dans les relations diplomatiques. [Berkeley, Univ. of California press], 1926.   340 p. [Diss., California). Published also as: Univ. of California publications in modern philology, v. 12, no. 4.   393

In most respects superseded by Brunot. Author's list of documents (p. 282) remains of interest, also her argument that it was diplomacy, as practiced by first great modern state, which advanced French language (p. 313), rather than converse.
Reviews : A. D[auzat] in RPF 41:228-29, 1929; P. Fouché in RLR 65 (7th ser. 5):125-26, 1927-28.

Sckommodau, Hans. Der französische psychologische Wortschatz der zweiten Hälfte des 18 Jahrhunderts. *In:* Leipziger romanistische Studien, 1, Heft 2. Leipzig, Selbstverlag des romanischen Seminars, 1933. 176 p.   394

Semantic discussion of words like *sensible, machine, organes,* with emphasis on connotations rather than formal definitions. Has headings like *Die leiblichen Äusserungen seelischen Erlebens, Die Begriffe für seelisches Erleben.* Serious lack of historical perspective. Cumbersome indices, one being list of authors in order of citation. Word index refers to page numbers. Bibliography lists citations by author. Second part of bibliography provides meager list of reference works. Useful book.
Reviews : P. Fouché in RLR 67:204-05, 1933-36; E. G[amillscheg] in ZFSL 58:126 (short notice), 1934.

Sahlin, Gunvor. César Chesneau du Marsais et son rôle dans l'évolution de la grammaire générale.   Presses universitaires, [1928]. 490 p.   395

The *Avant-propos* is of 1928, date being important since author refers to timeliness of his work, now that the " théories grammaticales sont remises en question." A. François observes that his chapter had been written when he came to know

Sahlin (Brunot, no. 382, 6(2) : 900, n. 1). Author indulges in a bit too much special pleading on behalf of Du Marsais. Full bibliography, p. 77-8, and *Appendice* containing selection from the *Logique et principes,* which uses an *Idylle* of Mme Deshoulières as material for grammatical comment.
Review : H. Yvon in RPF 40:217-19, 1928.

Sautebin, Hippolyte. Un linguiste français du xviiie siècle; le président de Brosses. Berne, Staempfli, 1899.   110 p.   (Diss., Berne).   396

Used by Brunot (no. 383, 6:910), but for his special purpose, hence selectively. This book still necessary for connected idea of contribution of De Brosses to etymological research, of which he came near to making a scholarly pursuit " ni inutile ni incertain." Goes astray on onomatopœia and the like. Relationship to *Encyclopédie* needs cautious revaluation in several details of linguistic history.

Sicard, Roch Ambroise. Éléments de grammaire générale appliqués à la langue française.   2nd ed.   Déterville, An X, 1801. 2 v.   397

Vol. 1, typical grammar based on " des lois dont la raison consacra les principes." Features question and answer method (" Que fait la détermination de l'étendue ? " " Elle applique le nom appellatif à l'individu qu'on veut désigner," p. 122), also a system for graphic demonstration of modifying adjectives : PrAoPuIgEeR (i.e., Papier rouge), perhaps influenced by his work with deaf-mutes. Vol. 2 has phonetics and versification, plus a list of definitions. This is second edition; the first of 2000 copies, was sold out in 18 months, showing popularity. Unfortunate that Fouquet never finished his projected study on *grammaire générale,* where this work might have received attention due it.

Souriau, Maurice. La langue de Voltaire dans sa correspondance.   RHL 28:105-31, 279-88, 423-49, 1921.   *See* no. 1841.   398

Brunot (no. 382, 6(2):1134) makes some use of these articles, apropos of *Néologie,* but does not cite them in introductory bibliography of volume. Article contains worth-while lists of words that did not fit in with strictest puristic standards. e.g., " low," archaic, technical, dialectal. Third article devoted to syntax. Souriau's viewpoint is that of literary critic, not of linguist by profession. Some items are made more interesting thereby (*honnête homme*, p. 279) while others are less trustworthy and require caution (*entrepris*, p. 282). The latter, in the sense of *gêné*, is acceptable Old French.

Vernier, Léon. Étude sur Voltaire grammairien et la grammaire au XVIIIe siècle. Hachette, 1888. 261 p. (Diss., Paris). *See* no. 1808. 399

Superseded by Brunot (383, 6:870 ff.) for most part. Still worth consulting for sidelights on Voltaire's interest in the " grand siècle." Vernier describes a state of affairs much like our " mechanist-mentalist " controversy, at the time captioned " méchanique " and " métaphysique " (p. 22 ff.) with which, of course, Brunot does not concern himself. Despite title, there is surprisingly little on Voltaire as a grammarian. Cf. nos. 1739, 1808.

Review : G. Paris in Rom 19:365, 1890.

Wade, Ira Owen. Studies on Voltaire. Princeton univ. press, 1947. 244 p. *See* nos. 1812, 3126. 400

Of interest for this section is Chap. III, p. 124-28, brief exposition of Mme du Châtelet's grammatical work and the three surviving chapters of her treatise, p. 209-43. Supplementary to history of *grammaire raisonnée*, which doctrine she modified through her acquaintance with Locke, with current French usage, and with other languages. Comes near to suggesting functional grammar : Ch. 7, *Un père est toujours père*, the last word considered adjectival (not noted by Wade).

CHAPTER II. POETRY
(Nos. 401-445)

HENRY A. GRUBBS

General Studies
(Nos. 401-412)

Cameron, Margaret M. L'influence des Saisons de Thomson sur la poésie descriptive en France (1759-1810). Champion, 1927. 201 p. (Diss., Paris).   401

Useful analyses of works of French descriptive poets of 18th century, especially Saint-Lambert, Delille, Léonard, and Roucher. Critical judgments conventional, but of some value.
Review : *See* 3026.

Chaponnière, Paul. L'esprit mondain et la poésie lyrique au xviiie siècle. RDS 2:40-55, 1914.   402

Well-documented demonstration of not too surprising fact that *esprit mondain* was not conducive to production of lyric poetry.

Faguet, Emile. Histoire de la poésie française de la renaissance au romantisme. Boivin, nd. [1923-36]. 11 v. v. 6-11.   403

Reprinted from course of lectures published in RCC, those concerning 18th century appearing in RCC 7, part 1, 1898-99, to 16, part 1, 1907-08. Unsatisfactory work. Contains much biographical, historical, and other information on men who wrote poetry. A few sound critical judgments, many unsound ones. Has not been reviewed completely, but a few reviews of separate volumes, e.g., H. Bibas, in YWML 6:63-64, 1934-35, says, referring to v. 9 : " properly speaking this is not a history of poetry at all."

Fusil, Casimir A. La poésie scientifique de 1750 à nos jours : son élaboration, sa constitution. Éditions scientifica, 1917. 320 p.   404

Mornet claims it should be entitled *Réflexions sur l'inspiration scientifique dans la poésie française de 1750 à nos jours.* Says it is not sufficiently complete or scientific.

Review : D. Mornet in RHL 27:132-36, 1920.

Ganay, Ernest de, comte. Poésie et jardins au xviiie siècle. RPar 38e année, 3:414-32, 1931.   405

Analysis of Delille's *Jardins,* some useful bibliographical information about it, analysis of a number of very obscure poems on gardens.

Grubbs, Henry A. Voltaire and rime. SP 39:524-44, 1942.   406

Contemporary accusations that Voltaire used poor rimes are more or less justified; this is not surprising, since he, like many others in his time, considered rime at best a necessary evil.

Lote, Georges. La poétique classique du dix-huitième siècle. RCC 31[1] : 60-74, 156-71, 262-75, 464-80, 1929-30.   407

Study, based on both principles and practice of poets, of versification, rhythm, harmony, imitative harmony, etc. Useful, but value somewhat marred by author's uncritically contemptuous attitude toward 18th century technique and poets.

Mornet, Daniel. L'alexandrin français dans la deuxième moitié du xviiie siècle. Toulouse, Privat, 1907. 95 p.   408

Shows important role of certain poets (notably Delille and Roucher) in " dislocating " Alexandrine.
Review : G. Lanson in RHL 15:170, 1908.

— La question des règles au xviiie siècle. RHL 21:241-68, 592-617, 1914.   409

Amplification of material found in *Le Romantisme en France au XVIIIe siècle,* Part III. Valuable analysis of critical treatises. General divisions : I. *La critique philosophique,* II. *Les débuts de la critique historique,* III. *La critique de sentiment,* IV. *Le dogmatisme latent.*

Potez, Henri. L'élégie en France avant le Romantisme. (De Parny à Lamartine). 1778-1820. 1897. 488 p. (Diss., Paris). 410

Best general study of poetry in latter part of century. Its critical attitude (that Romantic poetry is summit of French poetry) dates it, but in spite of that fact is very useful.

Ranscelot, Jean. Les manifestations du déclin poétique au début du xviiie siècle. RHL 33:497-520, 1926. 411

Useful analysis of little-known works—thus supplementing well-known " manifestations " found in Fontenelle, Fénelon, and Lamotte.

Thérive, André. La poésie au xviiie siècle. Mfran 4:359-65, 1925. 412

Brief and full of common sense. 18th century poets should be judged for what they are, not for what they are not.

André Chénier
(Nos. 413-435)

Chénier, André. Œuvres complètes. Foulon, 1819. 396 p. 413
First edition, edited by Henri de Latouche.

— Œuvres complètes, publiées par Paul Dimoff. Delagrave, 1908-19 (v. I, 1908, v. II, 1910, v. III, 1919), Reprinted 1926-27. 414

Generally accepted as definitive edition; contains all of author's poetical works, including all fragments found in mss. Editor's classification of poems and fragments accepted (with some reservations) by critics; he is accused of relatively few errors in transcription or interpretation.
Review: D. Mornet in RHL 15:545-48, 1908, and RHL 28:135-36, 1921.

— Œuvres inédites, publiées d'après les manuscrits originaux, par Abel Lefranc. Champion, 1914, 292 p. 415

Contains all prose works found in mss.

— Œuvres, publiées avec une introduction et des notices par Henri Clouard. Cité des livres, 1927, 3 v. 416

Comes nearest of any edition to containing complete works, poetry, and prose (does not contain Malherbe commentary). Follows Dimoff's classification of poems most of time, but not always, and does not by any means contain all

fragments. Omits scholarly and critical apparatus (notes, variants, etc.) Less useful to student than Dimoff's edition.

— Œuvres en prose, nouvelle édition revue sur les textes originaux, précédée d'une étude sur la vie et les écrits politiques d'André Chénier et sur la conspiration de Saint-Lazare, accompagnée de notes historiques et d'un index, par L. Becq de Fouquières. Charpentier, 1872. 408 p. 417

Not based upon the manuscripts, and hence does not contain prose works published later by Lefranc. Valuable for biography after 1790, not given in Dimoff.

— Œuvres complètes. Texte établi et commenté par Gérard Walter. NRF 1940. 933 p. (Bibl. de la Pléiade, v. 57). 418

Only complete edition of C.'s works. Gives poetry in an arrangement different from that of Dimoff (less convenient but better for general reader), prose works, Malherbe commentary and correspondence, including three hitherto unpublished letters.

Poésies de François de Malherbe, avec un commentaire inédit par André Chénier, précédé d'une notice sur la vie de Malherbe et d'une lettre sur le commentaire. Publiées par Latour. Charpentier, 1842. 324 p. 419

This commentary has not been published in any of the collective editions of C.'s works except in no. 418.

Poésies de F. Malherbe, accompagnées du commentaire d'André Chénier, publiées par L. Becq de Fouquières. Charpentier, 1874. 331 p. 420

Only reprint of C.'s Malherbe commentary.

Becq de Fouquières, Louis. Documents nouveaux sur André Chénier, et examen critique de la nouvelle édition de ses Œuvres. Charpentier, 1875. 372 p. 421

Valuable for biography after 1790, not given in Dimoff's study of C.

Dimoff, Paul. La vie et l'œuvre d'André Chénier jusqu'à la Révolution française (1762-1790). Droz, 1936, 2 v. 422 and 423

Has detailed analytical table of contents, complete indexes, extensive bibliography—not only of Dimoff's authorities, but of C. in general up to 1790. Essential work on C.; supersedes all preceding studies of life and works *for period covered*.

Period limitation unfortunate and not entirely wise; general study of C.'s poetry loses some of its point since the great poems written in 1793-94 are not treated. Dimoff's work a critical synthesis of all earlier studies, completed by author's own not inconsiderable research. Defects principally in presentation : unnecessarily difficult to read, much too long, much too diffuse. Dimoff's judgments as to C.'s greatness as poet weakened because of his own misconception as to what constitutes greatness in poetry.

Faguet, Emile. André Chénier. Hachette, 1902. 188 p. (GEF).   424
Has neither index nor bibliography.
Review : P. Morillot in RHL 10:147-52, 1903. Morillot says Faguet's thesis that there were three successive stages in C.'s poetry (i.e., 1, bucolics, 2, elegies, 3, " modern " poems) is contradicted by the facts.

Glachant, Paul. André Chénier critique et critiqué. Lemerre, 1902. 432 p.   425
A study of C.'s critical and literary theories, followed by a bibliography.
Morillot says bibliography not complete, because it lacks iconography and does not give complete history of text and of publication of poems; that study exaggerates importance of C. as literary theorist.
Review : P. Morillot in RHL 10:147-50, 1903.

Kramer, C. André Chénier et la poésie parnassienne; Leconte de Lisle, Champion, 1925. 300 p.   426
Over-abundance of material to show that C. influenced Leconte de Lisle; no attempt to show why; no conclusions reached. Has neither index nor bibliography.
Reviews : E. Estève in RHL 35:128-30, 1928; D. G. Larg in MLR 23:242-43, 1928.

Maurras, Charles. André Chénier. In his : Poésie et vérité. Lyon, Lardanchet, 1944, 18-85. (Reprinted from RPar 46ᵉ année, 2:241-67, 494-515, 1939).   427
First general study written since Dimoff. Thought-provoking attempt at revaluation, marred, in latter part especially, by predominance of Maurras' anti-romantic, traditionalist monomania. Has thesis that had C. lived longer he would have created a poetic tradition that would have prevented errors and excesses of Romanticism.

Morillot, Paul. André Chénier. Lecène, Oudin, 1894. 239 p. (Collection Les classiques populaires).   428
Best of semi-popular, general studies of C. Has neither index nor bibliography.

Sainte-Beuve, Charles-Augustin. André Chénier, homme politique. In his : Causeries du lundi. Garnier, n.d. 4:144-69. 429
Study dated 1851.

— Mathurin Régnier et André Chénier. In his : Portraits littéraires. Garnier, 1862. 3 v. 1:159-75.   430 and 431
Study dated 1829.

— Documents inédits sur André Chénier. In his : Portraits littéraires. Garnier, 1862, 1:176-208.   432
Study dated 1839.

— Un factum contre André Chénier. In his : Portraits contemporains. Lévy, 1870-71, 5:300-24.   433
Study dated 1844.

— Poésies d'André Chénier. In his : Nouveaux lundis, M. Lévy, 1870, 3:330-39. 434
Study dated 1862. This and four preceding studies, along with unpublished fragments, and allusions to C. found elsewhere in Sainte-Beuve's works, have been published in volume, Les grands écrivains français, études des Lundis et des Portraits classées selon un ordre nouveau et annotées par Maurice Alem : XVIIIᵉ siècle. Auteurs dramatiques et poètes. Beaumarchais, Florian, André Chénier. Garnier, 1930, p. 80-199; 219-81. These writings have been to large extent superseded by studies by Becq de Fouquières and Dimoff. Useful for one interested in vogue of C., they are also of interest for light they throw on Sainte-Beuve as critic and polemist.

Walter, Gérard. André Chénier, son milieu et son temps. Laffont, 1947. 360 p. 435
Most complete biography to date. Stresses C.'s participation in politics during Revolution.
Review : [R.] Etiemble in Tmod 2: 686-704, 1947.

Jacques Delille
(Nos. 436-442)

Cherel, Albert. Un souvenir de l'Homme des champs dans Les méditations. RHL 17:617-18, 1910.   435A

This reminiscence is found in Lamartine's *L'automne*.

Delaruelle, L. Lamartine lecteur de Delille. RHL 18:417-18, 1911.   436

Passage on autumn in *Les jardins* compared to passages in *L'isolement* and *L'automne*.

Downs, John A. The poetic theories of Jacques Delille. SP 37:524-34, 1940. 437

Based partly upon Souza, but also claims that D. was precursor as regards his ideas on relations of literature and society.

Maigron, Louis. Un manuscrit inédit de Remard sur Delille. RHL 14:330-58, 1907; 15:518-40, 722-54, 1908; 17:620-33, 839-58, 1910; 19:900-10, 1912; 20:924-51, 1913; 21: 720-45, 1914; 22:578-601, 1915.   438

Publishes portions of a *Supplément nécessaire aux Œuvres complètes de Jacques Delille*, unpublished manuscript by Charles Remard, librarian at Fontainebleau in early 19th century. Detailed study of " emprunts " of Delille, that is, his sources. Maigron has published portions dealing with *Discours sur les Géorgiques*, *Géorgiques* and *Énéide*, also Remard's preface.

Sainte-Beuve, Charles Augustin. Delille. *In his :* Portraits littéraires. Garnier, 1862, 2:64-105.   439

This article, written in 1837, in spite of its claims to impartiality, is a polemic, attacking D. violently. The article is discussed in detail in Souza's *Le cas Delille et Sainte-Beuve* (no. 442).

Schinz, Albert. Victor Hugo et Delille. MLN 59:37-39, 1944.   440

Strong probability that D.'s verses on sufferings of French royal family *(Malheur et pitié)* inspired some of early work of Hugo.

Souza, Robert de. Un préparateur de la poésie romantique : Delille.   MerF 285: 298-327, July 15, 1938.   441

The most genuinely constructive recent study of D. Somewhat overenthusiastic, but in this case overenthusiasm is to be preferred to uncritical, ignorant disdain.

— Le cas Delille et Sainte-Beuve.   MerF 287:99-118, Oct. 1, 1938.   442

Examination of Sainte-Beuve's article on D., refutation of much of it, and denunciation of general tendency by which each literary movement tends to knife its immediate predecessors. Souza claims French lyric poetry is a continuous chain, all links of which are essential.

Jean-Baptiste Rousseau
(Nos. 443-445)

Grubbs, Henry Alexander. The vogue of Jean-Baptiste Rousseau. PMLA 55:139-66, 1940.   443

Examination of growth and decline of vogue of J.-B. R. and an attempt to explain phenomena noted.

— Jean-Baptiste Rousseau; his life and works. Princeton univ. press, 1941. 310 p.   444

Detailed biography of J.-B. R. based partly upon new documents, followed by brief chapters discussing works. Final chapter attempts general appraisal of J.-B. R.'s rank as poet. Has index and bibliography of authorities.
Reviews : H. C. Lancaster in MLQ 2:342-43, 1941; L. W. Tancock in MLR 40:63-64, 1945; N. L. Torrey in RR 32: 426-29, 1941; A. J. Whallon in MP 39: 436-37, 1941-42.

Sainte-Beuve, Charles Augustin. Jean-Baptiste Rousseau. *In his :* Portraits littéraires. Garnier, 1862, 1:128-44.   445

First published in RPar in 1829, this article, which struck serious blow at J.-B. R.'s vogue, is adroit polemic, rather than impartial judgment.

CHAPTER III. DRAMA

(Except Voltaire and Diderot)
(Nos. 446-692)

CLARENCE D. BRENNER, HARRY KURZ, KENNETH N. McKEE, and IRA O. WADE

Drama and Dramatists
(Nos. 446-620)

CLARENCE D. BRENNER

General Studies

Note : All works listed below, unless otherwise indicated, are in the Library of the University of California at Berkeley. An (*) indicates that no copy has been located in an American library.

Almanach des spectacles de Paris [After 1754 entitled Les spectacles de Paris]. 1752-1815. 46 v.   446

Kind of yearbook of officially subsidized theaters. Gives repertory of each theater during preceding year, with outline of plot of most plays. Lists names of actors and members of orchestras. Items of miscellaneous information. Valuable feature is up-to-date list of living authors with titles of their plays, published and unpublished. Important.

Léris, Antoine de. Dictionnaire portatif, historique et littéraire des théâtres. Jombert, 1754. 557 p. 2nd ed. 1763.   447

Only second, revised and augmented edition should be used. Type of Maupoint, *Bibliothèque des théâtres*, Prault, 1733, (now obsolete), but more complete and accurate. Competent work for its time and not to be neglected. Contains many bits of information not found elsewhere.

Frères Parfaict (François and Claude) and Godin d'Abguerbe. Dictionnaire des théâtres de Paris. Lambert, 1756. 7 v. 2nd ed. 1767-70. 7 v.   448

V. 7 is supplement containing additions and corrections and should be used along with other volumes. Alphabetical list of French plays from 1552 to date, including operas. Synopses of many unpublished plays, excluding those given by *Comédie-*

Française, which are to be found in *Histoire du Théâtre-Français* by same authors. Devotes most attention to *Théâtre-Italien*. Major part of material supplied by T. S. Gueullette. Usually gives essential bibliographical details. Most comprehensive of 18th century dictionaries of plays.

[Attr. to L. F. C. Marin, J. Capperonnier, P. J. Boudot, B. Mersier]. Bibliothèque du théâtre français depuis son origine, contenant un extrait de tous les ouvrages composés pour ce théâtre, depuis les mystères jusqu'aux pièces de Pierre Corneille, [et] une liste chronologique de celles composées depuis cette dernière époque jusqu'à présent. Dresden, Groell, 1768. 3 v.   449

Really catalogue of plays in library of Duc de la Vallière. Usually catalogued under his name. 18th century plays in v. 3. Not very extensive list. Carefully compiled and often with quite full bibliographical data. Synopses of some plays. Many plays by known authors are given as anonymous. Of most value for earlier periods of theater.

[Lacroix, Paul]. Catalogue de la bibliothèque dramatique de Monsieur de Soleinne, by the Bibliophile Jacob [*pseud.*] Administration de l'Alliance des arts, 1843-45. 5 v.   450

Auction sale catalogue of magnificent library. 18th century plays and works relating to that period scattered through various sections of v. 2 to 5. Most extensive listing of French plays available. For most part hastily compiled. Full of errors and misprints. V. 5 contains index of authors.

Brunet, Charles. Table des pièces de théâtre décrites dans le catalogue de la bibliothèque de Monsieur de Soleinne. Morgand, 1914. 491 p.   451

Indispensable, not only for using Soleinne catalogue, but also as rapid check list of plays. Carefully compiled, but badly proof-read.

Duval, Henri. Dictionnaire des ouvrages dramatiques. Manuscript in Bibliothèque Nationale, fonds français 15048-61. 14 v. Microfilm copy in Library of Congress. 452

Compiled during 2nd quarter of 19th century. Plays catalogued by genres. Imposing list, though very far from complete for 18th century. Especially important because compiler consulted records of police censor and discovered number of unknown plays, most of which were destined for *théâtres des boulevards*. Greatly extends knowledge of repertories of these theaters. Some plays are listed under several genres, with variations in detail.

Douay, A. Catalogue Douay. Manuscript in Bibliothèque de l'Arsenal. 453

Compilation similar to Duval's, but less extensive. Arranged chronologically, 11 volumes being devoted to 18th century. Contains some items not found elsewhere. Most entries lacking in some of most elementary bibliographical details. Very difficult to use because written in almost illegible hand.

Brenner, Clarence D. A bibliographical list of plays in the French language, 1700-1789. *See* 12. 454

Lists over 11,600 plays. Anonymous plays listed alphabetically. Author list similarly arranged. Gives essential bibliographical information. Preface explains necessary limitations on this information. Index of titles.
Review : H. C. Lancaster in MLN 63: 358-59, 1948.

Aghion, Max. Le théâtre à Paris au XVIIIe siècle. Librairie de France [1926]. 442 p. *See* 669. 455

Popular and entirely unoriginal. Only book which endeavours to give comprehensive picture of 18th century theater in all its aspects. Many interesting illustrations.

Lecomte, L. Henri. Histoire des théâtres de Paris, 1402-1904. Notice préliminaire. Daragon, 1905. 60 p. *See* 681. 456

Convenient table for dates of founding of various theaters.

Bossuet, Pierre. Histoire des théâtres nationaux. Éditions et publications contemporaines, [1910], [1928]. 505 p. 457

Factual history chiefly concerned with organization and administration. Very well documented. Comprehensive bibliography.

Hallays-Dabot, Victor. Histoire de la censure théâtrale en France. Dentu, 1862. 340 p. *See* 678. 458

Represents original research on subject whose importance is often overlooked. Supplemented by more recent investigations, but still of value.

Fuchs, Max. La vie théâtrale en province au XVIIIe siècle. Droz, 1933. 218 p. (Société des historiens du théâtre. Bibliothèque, No. 3). 459

Well-documented work dealing with construction of theaters. their technical equipment, and legislation governing them.

Fontaine, Léon. Le théâtre et la philosophie au XVIIIe siècle. Versailles, Cerf, 1878. 262 p. 460

Most material has received fuller and more scholarly treatment in later works, but it is still of some value for its brief indications of numerous plays in which philosophical ideas found expression. Difficult to use for lack of index.

Wade, Ira O. The *philosophe* in the French drama of the eighteenth century. Princeton, Princeton univ. press, 1926. 143 p. (Diss., Princeton). 461

Shows importance of role played by theater in " philosophic " struggle. Traces with precision steps in development of *philosophe* movement and in evolution of meaning of term. Full and valuable bibliography.
Review : M. E. I. Robertson in MLR 24:110-11, 1929. Believes that Wade's position not clear as to the exact object of the monograph, as a result of eliminating all but one class of *philosophe*.

Moore, Alexander P. Le *genre poissard* and the French stage in the eighteenth century. New York, Institute of French studies, [c 1935]. 422 p. 462

Fairly complete inventory of *poissard* plays, with considerable reference to other *poissard* literature. Leaves something to be desired on critical side and in knowledge of general background.
Review : M. Fuchs in RHL 43:441-42, 1936.

Brenner, Clarence D. Dramatizations of French short stories in the eighteenth century, with special reference to the *contes* of La Fontaine, Marmontel and Voltaire. Berkeley, Univ. of California press, 1947. 33 p.   462A

Attempts to demonstrate that *conte* was most important single printed source of material for playwrights of this century. Review : O. Fellows in RR 38:358-59, 1947.

Theaters, Dramatic Theory, etc.
(Nos. 463-533)

Théâtre-Français

See : Campardon, 526; Lecomte, 456; Bossuet, 457.   463

Joannidès, A. La Comédie-Française de 1680 à 1900. Dictionnaire général des pièces et des auteurs. Plon, 1901. 136, [274] p. 464

Accurate and complete list of plays by title and author, and with yearly total of performances for each play.

Frères Parfaict (François and Claude). Histoire du Théâtre-Français depuis son origine jusqu'à présent. Le Mercier, 1745-49. 15 v.   465

Only v. 14 and 15 concern 18th century. Chronological history. First attempt at scholarly research in French theater. Produced much that had not before been published. Gives synopses of many plays, often with extracts from text. Pioneer work.

Genest, Emile, and E. Duberry. La maison de Molière, connue et inconnue. Fischbacher, 1922. 330 p.   466

Popular account. Interestingly written and based on considerable research. Best modern general history of this theater.

Jullien, Adolphe. Les spectateurs sur le théâtre; établissement et suppression des bancs sur les scènes de la Comédie-Française et de l'Opéra. Detaille, 1875. 32 p.   467

Most detailed account of this practice. Does not sufficiently explain its effect on development of French theater.

Berret, Paul. Comment la scène du théâtre du XVIIIe siècle a été débarrassée de la présence des gentilshommes. RHL 8:456-59, 1901.   468

Adds some new facts to Jullien's account.

Théâtre-Italien

See : Campardon, 527; Courville, 528; Gueullette, 573; Font, 493, Grannis, 545; Moore, 462; Cucuel, 491; Bossuet, 457; Parfaict, 448; Lecomte, 456; Arnoldson, 615, etc.

Nouveau Théâtre italien de Luigi Riccoboni, dit Lélio. Coustelier, 1716.   469

Nouveau Théâtre italien ou Recueil général de toutes les pièces représentées par les comédiens de S. A. R. Mgr. le duc d'Orléans. Coustelier, 1718. 2 v. Flahaut, 1723, 3 v.; 1725, 4 v. Subsequent editions published, Briasson, 1729, 8 v.; 1733, 8 v.; 1753, 10 v.   470

Briasson editions contain the *Parodies*. Last most complete. Earlier editions are *recueils factices*, so that almost no two copies are alike.

Les parodies du Nouveau théâtre italien. Briasson, 1730, 1731. 3 v. New ed., 1738. 4 v.   471

Registres de l'Opéra-Comique. Manuscript records of Théâtre-italien, later including those of Opéra-Comique after two troupes were combined in 1762. *In :* Bibliothèque de l'Opéra. Microfilm copy in Library of Congress.   472

Runs from 1717 down into 19th century. A number of volumes are missing. Contains financial statement for each performance, minutes of meetings of troupe, records of business dealings, etc.

[Desboulmiers, Jean-Auguste Julien, known as]. Histoire anecdotique et raisonnée du Théâtre-italien depuis son rétablissement jusqu'en 1769. Lacombe, 1769. 7 v.   473

Kind of continuation of Frères Parfaicts' history of same theater. Most valuable for synopses of plays. Historical and bibliographical comments rather summary and of varying value. Should be checked. Vol. VII contains catalogue of plays, authors, actors not mentioned in previous pages, repertory of all plays, etc.

Origny, Antoine Jean Baptiste Abraham d'. Annales du Théâtre-italien, depuis son origine jusqu'à ce jour. Duchesne, 1788. 3 v.   474

Careful compilation. Based in part on registers of this theater. Most trustworthy of older works on this subject.

Gueullette, Thomas Simon. Notes et souvenirs sur le Théâtre-italien au XVIIIe siècle,

publiés par J. E. Gueullette. Droz, 1938.
217 p. 475

Anecdotes and recollections of this troupe assembled about 1750 by one who was intimately acquainted with its members. Much of material used in Frères Parfaicts' *Dictionnaire*.

Opéra

See : Jullien, 467; Polinger, 610; Hazard, 1043. 476

Campardon, Emile. L'Académie royale de musique au XVIIIe siècle. Berger-Levrault, 1884. 2 v. 477

Material, arranged in dictionary form, consists in large part of unpublished legal documents bearing on theater itself and on members of troupe. Of slight value for repertory.

Guiet, René. L'évolution d'un genre : le livret d'opéra en France de Gluck à la révolution. *See* 322, 3287. 478

Valuable study, interestingly presented and well documented. Demonstrates importance attached to librettos and their close relations to certain literary forms. Reviews : H. C. Lancaster in MLN 53:228, 1938. Valuable contribution. Asks whether Guiet should not have more thoroughly considered music of operas, since it must have influenced librettos. D. Mornet in RHL 44:136-37, 1937. Gives *livret* important place in history of literature. New and interesting conclusions. A few unimportant inaccuracies and omissions. W. D. Patton in RR 29:396-98. 1938.

Prod'homme, J. G. L'Opéra (1669-1925). Delagrave, 1925. 165 p. 479

Handbook of factual information. including complete repertory. Much needed work. Unfortunately not done with greatest care.

Tavenol, L. and Durey de Noinville. Histoire du Théâtre de l'Académie royale de musique en France depuis son établissement jusqu'à présent. 2nd ed., Barbou, 1753. 2 v. 480

Pioneer work on subject. Almost encyclopedic in its detail of various aspects of this theater and those who were associated with it. Some errors and misprints, but still remains valuable source.

Theaters of fairs and boulevards;
Opéra comique

See : Barbaret, 624; Bossuet, 457; Gaiffe, 542; Grannis, 545; Guiet, 478; Iacuzzi, 565; Lanson, 546; Lavedan, 529; Lecomte, 497, 681; Marandet, 566; Moore, 462; Mooser, 523; Salvatore, 567. 481

Le Théâtre de la foire ou l'opéra-comique. Amsterdam, 1721-34, 10 v. 2nd ed., Gandouin, 1737, 9 v. 482

Plays mostly by Lesage, Fuzelier, D'Orneval. V. 10 devoted to plays by Carolet, omitted from 2nd ed. V. 1 contains important preface by Lesage.

Théâtre des boulevards ou Recueil des parades. Mahon, Langlois, 1756. 3 v. Reprinted by G. d'Heylli. Rouveyre, 1881. 2 v. 482A

Contains 28 *parades*. Since most *parades* have remained unpublished, this collection is one of few easily available sources for examples of this popular genre. *Parades* long attributed to Salé are now thought to be work of T. S. Gueullette.

Carmody, Francis J. Le Répertoire de l'opéra-comique en vaudevilles de 1708 à 1764. Berkeley, Univ. of California press, 1933. 66 p. 483

Useful but incomplete list. Lacking many small factual details. A number of other details are in error or of questionable accuracy.

*[Attr. to J. J. Mussot, dit Arnould]. Almanach forain. 1773-74. 2 v.

*Nogaret, François Félix. Les Spectacles des foires et des boulevards, 1776.

*— Les Spectacles de la foire. 1777-78. 2 v.

*— Les Petits spectacles de Paris. 1786-87. 2 v. 484

These four publications, usually referred to collectively as the *Almanach forain*, are modelled on the *Almanach des spectacles*. They attempt to give for smaller, popular theaters information similar to that provided for large theaters in latter publication. Especially valuable for listing productions of smaller theaters whose repertory has never been established. No complete set is known to exist anywhere.

Albert, Maurice. Les théâtres de la foire (1660-1789). Hachette, 1900. 312 p. 485

More or less popular treatise. Contains much interesting material, but lacks scholarly precision and detail. Of little value for repertory.

Batcave, Louis. Les Petits Comédiens du roi au Bois de Boulogne (1778-1779). Schemit, 1909. 44 p.   486

Offers fairly well-documented history of this theater, but repertory as given by no means complete.

Campardon, Emile. Les spectacles de la foire. Berger-Levrault, 1877. 2 v.   487

Kind of dictionary of actors and theaters, based to considerable extent on unpublished documents. Little information on repertory. Valuable compilation, though it contains many errors in dates, titles, etc. Preface dated 1871.

Chaponnière, Paul. Les comédies de mœurs du théâtre de la foire. RHL 20:828-44, 1913.   488

Limited to first quarter of 18th century. Emphasizes realism of this theater and its lack of scruples as vehicle for social satire. Lively sketch which must be taken largely on faith for want of examples. A few generalizations may be questioned, but on whole good article.

Cucuel, Georges. Les créateurs de l'opéra-comique français. Alcan, 1914. 243 p. 489

Devoted mostly to musical aspects of this type of play. Many inaccuracies in dates and other details. Short bibliography.

— Le Moyen-âge dans les opéras-comiques du XVIIIe siècle. RDS 2:56-71, 1914. 490

Rather summary account of a few typical plays.

— Sources et documents pour servir à l'histoire de l'opéra-comique en France. *See* 312.   491

Kind of critical bibliography of a number of manuscripts and printed sources. Of most value for manuscript material. Estimates of printed works often quite uncritical. Has thoroughly unscholarly faith in accuracy and general reliability of 18th century printed works. This is most comprehensive listing of source material in this field.

[Desboulmiers, Jean-Auguste Julien, known as]. Histoire du théâtre de l'opéra-comique. Lacombe, 1769. 2 v.   492

Up to 1756 based on Frères Parfaicts' works. Ends with year 1761. Analyzes 106 plays and makes anecdotal comments on them. Practically everything in this work is copied literally from other sources. Full of errors and of minimum value.

Font, Auguste. Essai sur Favart et les origines de la comédie mêlée de chant. Toulouse, Privat, 1894. 355 p. Republished Paris, 1894, with title Favart, l'opéra-comique et la comédie-vaudeville au XVIIe et XVIIIe siècles. Fischbacher, 1894. 355 p. (Diss., Toulouse). *See* 317.   493

Various aspects of subject have been more thoroughly treated since publication of this book, but it still remains best general account. Carefully done. Author missed some bibliographical items.

Genest, Emile. L'Opéra-comique connu et inconnu. Fischbacher, 1925. 351 p. 494

Excellent general account of history of this theater. Not intended for scholarly public. Based on accurate compilation of published material.

Heulhard, Arthur. La Foire Saint Laurent, son histoire et ses spectacles. Lemerre, 1878. 317 p. [Yale].   495

Good account of various aspects of subject, somewhat condensed, but done with considerable care.

Hugot, Eugène. Histoire littéraire, critique et anecdotique du Théâtre du Palais Royal, 1784-1884. 3rd ed. Ollendorff, 1886. 308 p.   496

Only three short chapters devoted to 18th century. Based on minimum of research. Of little or no value for repertory.

Lecomte, L. Henri. Les variétés amusantes. Daragon, 1908. 262 p. *See* 681. 497

Fairly accurate history of this theater as far as it goes. Repertory as given is far from complete. Synopses of a good many plays.

Lindsay, Frank W. Dramatic parody by marionettes in eighteenth century Paris. New York, King's crown press, 1946. 185 p. (Diss., Columbia).   497A

Intelligently and, on whole, carefully presented study of rather minor aspect of the theater. Useful also for bibliography and factual material on marionette plays and the *théâtres de la foire*.

Reviews : C. D. Brenner in RR 38:

80-82, 1947; H. C. Lancaster in MLN 61:486-88, 1946.

Frères Parfaict (François and Claude). Mémoires pour servir à l'histoire des spectacles de la foire, par un acteur forain. Briasson, 1743. 2 v.   **498**

Covers period 1697-1742. Brief history of these theaters by years. Vol. 2 contains lists of plays, authors, and troupes. Based on considerable amount of research and first-hand information. Lists not complete. Many inaccuracies. Little criticism of plays. Most of factual material reproduced in *Dictionnaire des théâtres* of same authors.

Péricaud, Louis. Le Théâtre des petits comédiens de S. A. S. Monseigneur le comte de Beaujolais. Jorel, 1909. 129 p. *See* 686.   **499**

Product of superficial research. No mention of considerable part of repertory of this theater.

— Le Théâtre de " Monsieur." Jorel, 1908. 152 p.   **500**

Adequate account of history of this theater. A few misstatements of fact.

Private Theaters

See : Moore, 462; Desnoiresterres, 538; Lintilhac, 541; Barthélemy, 557A; Collé, 555; Gueullette, 573.   **501**

Du Bled, Victor. La comédie de société au XVIIIᵉ siècle. Lévy, 1893, 326 p. *Also in :* La société française du XVIᵉ au XXᵉ siècle. VIIIᵉ série. Perrin, 1911. p. 1-212.   **502**

Probably best of number of general accounts of this theater, all of which are similar in ground covered. Devotes great deal of space de Madame de Genlis.

Gofflot, L. V. Le théâtre au collège, du moyen-âge à nos jours. Champion, 1907. 336 p.   **503**

Material in several chapters covering 18th century is informative but of necessity quite condensed. Good bibliography. Comprehensive study of this subject for this period remains to be written.

Jullien, Adolphe. La comédie à la cour. Les Théâtres de la société royale pendant le siècle dernier. Firmin-Didot, [1885]. 321 p.   **504**

Collection of three long articles previously published separately. Each

presented with considerable amount of accurate detail.

Lebègue, Raymond. Les ballets des Jésuites. RCC 37²:127-39, 209-22, 321-30, 1936.   **505**

Supplements Gofflot. Concerned mostly with subject matter of ballets. Material on influence of exoticism especially interesting.

Dramatic theory

Borgerhoff, E. B. O. The evolution of liberal theory and practice in the French theater, 1680-1757. Princeton, Princeton univ. press, 1936. 117 p. (Diss., Princeton).   **506**

Satisfactory demonstration of early development of " anti-classical " attitude, with much material taken from little-used sources.

Review : H. C. Lancaster in MLN 53: 227-28, 1938. Believes that Borgerhoff is interested in exception, not rule. Also, that almost all daring innovations had been made in more daring manner before 1680.

Frederick, Edna C. The plot and its construction in eighteenth century criticism of French comedy; a study of theory with relation to the practice of Beaumarchais. Bryn Mawr, 1934. 128 p. (Diss., Bryn Mawr). *See* 648.   **507**

Careful presentation of subject. Might have been more extensively documented, though that would not have modified author's line of reasoning. Supplements Mornet and others.

Review : D. Mornet in RHL 43:453-54, 1936. " ... travail précis et judicieux, dont les résultats sont neufs et assez importants." More complete bibliography would be useful.

Jourdain, Eleanor F. Dramatic theory and practice in France, 1690-1808. London, Longmans, 1921. 240 p.   **508**

Unscholarly. Presents various lines of development in hazy and confused manner. Full of errors and inaccuracies, many resulting from insufficient investigation and documentation. Not recommended.

Review : G. Rudler in FQ 5:81-83, 1923.

Melcher, Edith. Stage realism in France between Diderot and Antoine. Bryn Mawr, 1928. 189 p. (Diss., Bryn Mawr).   **509**

Section on 18th century is for most part superficial, incomplete, and often uncritical.
Review : Anon. in RLC 10:535-36, 1930.

Mornet, Daniel. La question des règles au XVIIIᵉ siècle. *See* 409.   510

Rather brief discussion of rules affecting tragedy (p. 250), unities (p. 265-67), and *drame* (p. 614-16).

The Art of Representation
[staging, costume, declamation, etc.] 511

Adequate estimate of various aspects of this subject may be formed only from consideration of the numerous works published on them, especially in 18th century. The limitations imposed upon this volume make such extensive listing impossible. For titles of such works, and in some cases criticisms, consult : Aghion, 455; Berret, 468; Borgerhoff, 506; Courville, 528; Gaiffe, 542; Gofflot, 503; Guiet, 478; Jourdain, 508; Jullien, 467; Lanson, 536; La Villehervé, 550; Melcher, 509; Soleinne, 450-51.

Morality in the theater; the status of actors

Barras, Moses. The stage controversy in France from Corneille to Rousseau. New York, Institute of French studies, 1933. 358 p. (Diss., Columbia). *See* 2030. 512

Very extensive documentation presented painstakingly, though sometimes without critical discrimination. Excellent bibliography. Traces controversy from 17th century classical period with special attention to development of shift from theological to humanitarian argumentation in early decades of 18th century. *See also :* 2111.
Review : P. Jourda in Rcr 100:150-51, 1933.

Bourquin, Louis. La controverse sur la comédie au XVIIIᵉ siècle et la Lettre à d'Alembert sur les spectacles. RHL 26: 43-86, 555-76, 1919; 27:548-70, 1920; 28: 549-74, 1921.   513

Excellent and carefully documented series of articles, unfortunately never finished because of author's death in First World War.

Foreign influences

See : Dejob, 534; Courville, 528; Gaiffe, 542; Guiet, 478; Lion, 1779; Martino, 2561; Reynaud, 3254-55, and Chapter XI. 513A

Baldensperger, Fernand. [Esquisse d'une

histoire de Shakespeare en France. *In his :* Études d'histoire littéraire. 2nd series. Hachette, 1910. p. 155-216. *See* 3007. 514

Adds some facts and anecdotal material to Jusserand's book (no. 518). Contains a few inexcusably bad errors.

Dargan, E. Preston. Shakespeare and Ducis. MP 10:137-78, 1912-13. *See* 3008. 515

Not only best account of Ducis' plays, but also good brief consideration of number of other adaptations of Shakespeare.

Haines, C. M. Shakespeare in France; criticism : Voltaire to Victor Hugo. London, Oxford univ. press, 1925. 170 p. *See* 3014.   516

Very good chronological analysis of this criticism.

Huszár, Vilmos. L'influence de l'Espagne sur le théâtre français des XVIIᵉ et XVIIIᵉ siècles, par Guillaume Huszár. Champion, 1912. 190 p. *See* 3313.   517

Far from being complete study of subject. Discusses only Lesage, Marivaux, and Beaumarchais.
Review : F. Baldensperger in Rcr 75: 55-56, 1913.

Jusserand, J. J. Shakespeare en France sous l'ancien régime. Colin, 1898. 389 p. English translation by author, Shakespeare in France under the *ancien régime*. London, Unwin, 1899. 496 p. *See* 804, 3015. 518

Very readable book based on generally sound scholarly investigation. Places Shakespearean influence in proper relation to other aspects of anglomania. Exaggerates Prévost's enthusiasm for Shakespeare (*see* 804, 812).

The French theater in European countries

Bruce, H. L. Voltaire on the English stage. Berkeley, Univ. of California press, 1918. 152 p. (CPMP, v. 8, no. 1); *see :* Inklaar, 549.   518A

Faber, Frédéric. Histoire du théâtre français en Belgique. Brussels, Olivier, 1878-80. 5 v.   519

Valuable compilation marred by careless workmanship. Often in error or incomplete in detail. Should be checked against Liebrecht's work (no. 522).

Fransen, J. Les comédiens français en Hollande au XVIIᵉ et au XVIIIᵉ siècle. Champion, 1925. 472 p. (Diss., Paris).   520

Important and scholarly work, assembling much new material. Seems to have missed a few plays.

Review : H. C. Lancaster in MLN 42: 416-17, 1927.

Kunz-Aubert, Ulysse. Spectacles d'autrefois (à Genève au XVIIIe siècle). Geneva, Atar, n.d. 108 p.   521

Gives about all there is to be said on this limited subject. Reproduces a number of documents and a short play that may be of interest to historians of the theater.

Liebrecht, Henri. Histoire du théâtre français à Bruxelles au XVIIe et au XVIIIe siècle. Champion, 1923. 377 p.   522

Important work. Very carefully done. Based largely on unpublished material. Review : G. Cohen in RLC 5:183-89, 1925.

Mooser, Robert Aloys. Contribution à l'histoire de la musique russe. L'opéra-comique français en Russie au XVIIIe siècle. Conches-Geneva, The Author, 1932. 56 p.   523

Olivier, Jean-Jacques. Les comédiens français dans les cours d'Allemagne au XVIIIe siècle. Soc. fran. d'imprimerie et de librairie, 1901-05. 4 v.   524

Much interesting information, though not as complete as it might be. There are a few bad factual errors.

Witzenetz, Julia. Le théâtre français de Vienne (1752-1772). Szeged, 1932. 138 p.   525

Most complete, but not a definitive, presentation of subject. Some errors and omissions.

Actors

See : Burnet, 581; Campardon, 477, 487; Gueulette, 475; Olivier, 524; *Registres de l'Opéra-comique,* 472.   525A

Campardon, Emile. Les comédiens du roi de la troupe française. Champion, 1879. 336 p.   526

Collection of unpublished legal documents (1613-1789) relating to a number of these actors.

— Les comédiens du roi de la troupe italienne. Berger-Levrault, 1880. 2 v.   527

Collection of material similar to preceding item.

Courville, Xavier de. Un apôtre de l'art du théâtre au XVIIIe siècle, Luigi Riccoboni dit Lélio. Droz. Vol. I, L'expérience italienne (1676-1715), 1943; Vol. II, L'expérience française (1716-1731), 1945. A separate volume entitled Introduction et Bibliographie, 1943. 65 p.   528

Only second volume concerns us here. Really a detailed history of *Théâtre italien* for first 15 years after its reestablishment in 1716. Outstanding contribution to history of the theater. By carefully investigating the Italian repertory, author has turned up much new material. One important result is considerably revised estimate of Marivaux's plays.

Lavedan, Henri. Volange, comédien de la foire, 1756-1808. Tallendier, 1933. 192 p. Originally published in Les œuvres libres, Fayard [c1932]. v. 129, p. 5-54.   529

Interesting and entertaining account, but, according to Max Fuchs in his *Lexique des troupes de comédiens au XVIIIe siècle,* no. 530A, p. 207, it is merely pretentious expansion of article by Dumersan in *Le monde dramatique* for Aug. 5, 1837.

Lyonnet, Henry. Dictionnaire des comédiens français. (Ceux d'hier) Biographie, Bibliographie, Iconographie. Jorel, n.d., 2 v.   530

Biographical sketches of members of the *Comédie française* that vary greatly in length and in value. Handy reference work of special worth for the more obscure names listed.

Originally published in *fascicules* by the *Bibliothèque de la Revue universelle internationale illustrée,* Geneva, 1902-1908. Apparently bound up by Jorel and sold over his imprint.

Fuchs, Max. Lexique des troupes de comédiens au XVIIIe siècle. Droz, 1944. 231 p.   530A

Lists some 2,600 actors and actresses known to have been members of troupes outside of Paris. Information is summary, but there are numerous references to sources. Supplemented by *Table des noms par villes* and *Table des troupes.* Valuable reference work based on extensive researches in local archives, local histories, etc. Covers period 1714-1791. For this period it largely replaces Lyonnet's *Dictionnaire des comédiens français* (no. 530).

Manne, Edmond Denis de and **C. Méné-trier.** Galerie historique des comédiens de la troupe de Nicolet. Lyons, Scheuring, 1869. 414 p. 531

Sketches of careers of better-known actors of this troupe, of whom some were also playwrights, e.g., Audinot, Dorvigny, Mayeur de Saint-Paul, Taconnet. Work of some value even though not always accurate in detail.

Olivier, Jean-Jacques. Henri Louis Le Kain de la Comédie française (1729-1778). Société française d'imprimerie et de librairie, 1907. 351 p. 532

Like all works by this author, scholarship is a trifle amateurish. Nevertheless good book, with number of interesting illustrations.

Review : F. E. Schneegans in LGRP 35:61, 1914.

Barrière, F. Mémoires de Mlle Clairon, de Lekain, de Préville, de Dazincourt, de Molé, de Garrick, de Goldoni, avec avant-propos et notices par F. Barrière. Firmin-Didot, 1857. 468 p. (Bibliothèque de mémoires relatifs à l'histoire de France pendant le XVIIIᵉ siècle, tome VI). 533

Handy collection in one volume of *mémoires* and other documents by and about persons named. All material previously published. The *avant-propos* of no value, but notes are useful as far as they go.

Tragedy, Comedy, *Drame*, Proverb
Plays, and Parody
(Nos. 534-547)

Dejob, Charles. Études sur la tragédie. Colin, [1896]. 414 p. 534

Italian tragedy in France in 18th century is discussed, p. 151-91. Very summary treatment devoted largely to popularity and influence of Metastasio.

Chaponnière, Paul. L'influence de l'esprit mondain sur la tragédie au XVIIIᵉ siècle. RHL 19:547-69, 1912. 535

Attempts to show that sterility, lack of imagination and idealism, *nature*, in 18th century tragedy reflect attitude of mind of *mondains* for whom it was written. Resulting product is smug, insincere, filled with blasé conventionalism and devoid of finer emotions. Much truth in article, but author neglects other contributing factors.

Lancaster, Henry Carrington. French tragedy in the time of Louis XV and Voltaire, 1715-1774. Baltimore, Johns Hopkins press, 1950. 2 v. 662 p. 535A

Follows general plan of author's previous histories. Discussion limited to tragedies acted by Comédie Française. Extensive use made of *registres* of this troupe. First chapter, using new facts from this source, gives in concise form the most authentic picture of all aspects of this theater. Detailed analysis and criticism of tragedies, with addition of new factual information. Important is careful attention given to sources of plot material. Nowhere else has Voltaire the tragic dramatist received such thorough and intelligent attention.

Summary and estimate on p. 607 ff is best survey of Voltaire's contributions in this field. Final *Conclusion* presents best outline of history of 18th century French tragedy to be found anywhere. A few misprints in dates easily recognizable. Though essentially reference work, it will at same time probably remain definitive study of development of tragedy in this period.

Lancaster, Henry Carrington. Sunset ; a history of Parisian drama in the last years of Louis XIV, 1701-1715. Baltimore, Johns Hopkins press, 1945. 365 p. 535B

Detailed studies of Regnard, Dancourt, and other transitional dramatists who lead into the 18th century. Factual, authoritative, indispensable.

Lanson, Gustave. Esquisse d'une histoire de la tragédie française. New York, Columbia univ. press, 1920. 155 p. 2nd ed., Champion, 1927. 194 p. 536

Second edition contains a few very minor revisions of 18th century section. Syllabus offering excellent outline of development of tragedy in all its aspects.

Review : H. C. Lancaster in MLN 36: 98-103, 1921.

Comedy
(Nos. 537-541)

See : Courville, 528; Gaiffe, 542; Lanson, 546, 575; Lemaître, 558; Martino, 2561; Origny, d', 474. 536A

Dejob, Charles. Les femmes dans la comédie française et italienne du XVIIIᵉ siècle. Fontemoing, 1899. 414 p. 537

Series of lectures analyzing many types. Covers wide range of material with considerable penetration.

Desnoiresterres, Gustave. La comédie satirique au XVIII⁰ siècle; histoire de la société française par l'allusion, la personnalité et la satire au théâtre. Perrin, 1885. 458 p. *See* 672. 538

Subtitle indicates character of book. Valuable for large number of factual details. Various aspects of society of period illustrated by allusion to many plays. Little criticism of plays themselves.

Lanson, Gustave. La comédie au XVIII⁰ siècle. *In his :* Hommes et livres. Lecène, Oudin, 1895. p. 215-60. 539

Point of departure is criticism of Lenient's *La comédie en France au XVIII⁰ siècle.* (*See* no. 540.) After disagreeing with Lenient's method of attack, Lanson outlines what he considers true development of comedy. Only comedies of Marivaux, Beaumarchais, and possibly Sedaine have any intrinsic value. 18th century comedy is totally lacking in *le sens de la vie*, nor is it even " *philosophique.*" Much penetrating criticism. Exception may be taken to some details and to general conclusions.

Lenient, C. La comédie en France au XVIII⁰ siècle. Hachette, 1888. 2 v. 540

Traces development of comedy and *opéra-comique* in a series of *essais* on authors, arranged in somewhat confusing order. Criticism often superficial. Lacks clear perspective. Review : G. Lanson in *La comédie au XVIII⁰ siècle, see* no. 539, p. 215 ff.

Lintilhac, Eugène. Histoire générale du théâtre en France : v. 4 La comédie, dix-huitième siècle. Flammarion, [1909]. 488 p. 541

Chapters on various types of comedy, illustrated with many scenes from plays. Considerable amount of interesting factual material. More descriptive than critical. Useful bibliography and footnotes. Sections on *parade* and on Beaumarchais of some importance.

Drame
(No. 542)

See : Béclard, 598; Diderot, 2209; Fontaine, 460; Guiet, 478; Hazard, 1043; Jourdain, 508; Lanson, 574. 541A

Gaiffe, Félix. Le drame en France au XVIII⁰ siècle. Colin, 1910. 600 p. *See* 676. 542

Wealth of material about subject matter, sources, staging, etc. of large number of

plays. In this mass of material, author, at times, loses his general perspective. Number of *drames* are missing from bibliography. Reviews : F. Baldensperger in Rcr 70: 64-67, 1910; G. Lanson in RHL 17:644-45, 1910; W. Martini in ZFSL 37:35-39, 1911.

Proverb Plays
(Nos. 543-544)

See : Moore, 462; Collé, 553; Lavedan, 529. 542A

Recueil général des proverbes dramatiques en vers et en prose, tant imprimés que manuscrits. London & Paris, 1785. 16 v. [Library of Congress]. 543

Representative collection of 118 plays, most of them anonymous, though authors of many are known. Some of these plays were performed at public theaters.

Brenner, Clarence D. Le développement du proverbe dramatique en France et sa vogue au XVIII⁰ siècle. Avec un proverbe inédit de Carmontelle. Berkeley, Univ. of California press, 1937. 56 p. 544

Reviews : C. A. Bevans and A. Taylor in MP 36:73-74, 1938-39. " Brenner has succeeded in doing what he set out to do and has left to some later comer a small task of continuing his study." H. C. Lancaster in MLN 53:229, 1938. Suggests a little additional illustrative material. D. Mornet in RHL 44:563-64, 1937. Praises study. Offers suggestion, of dubious value, that Brenner supplement this work with an analysis of the subject matter of plays.

Parody
(Nos. 545-547)

See : Levy, 553; Moore, 462; Gaiffe, 542; Lenient, 540. 544A

Grannis, Valleria B. Dramatic parody in eighteenth century France. New York, Institute of French studies, [c1931]. 428 p. 545

Somewhat loosely written. Explanatory material contains inaccurate general statements and unsubstantiated statements of detail. Chapter on *drame* is particularly bad in this respect. Bibliography of parodies requires some corrections.

Lanson, Gustave. La parodie dramatique au XVIII⁰ siècle. *In his :* Hommes et livres, Lecène, Oudin, 1895, 261-93. 546

Essay presenting outline of origin and development of this type. Has formed basis for later studies of subject.

Lecomte, L. Henri. Table chronologique des parodies représentées ou seulement imprimées en France du 10 février 1694 au 31 décembre 1912. Manuscript in Rondel collection, Bibliothèque de l'Arsenal.   547

Useful list, but, like all of Lecomte's work, incomplete and not always accurate.

Dramatists (Dancourt, Destouches, Marivaux, Regnard, Sedaine, etc.) (Nos. 548-620)

Note. For Beaumarchais, Diderot, Lesage, Rousseau, and Voltaire see the special sections on those authors.

Autreau, Jacques, see 470.

Schwarz, H. S. Jacques Autreau, a forgotten dramatist. PMLA 46:498-532, 1931.   548

A sufficiently comprehensive account for most reference purposes. Suggests certain influences which merit consideration.

Arnaud, François Thomas de Baculard d'. *See :* Cucuel, 490; Haines, 516, 3014.

Inklaar, Derk. François Thomas de Baculard d'Arnaud, ses imitateurs en Hollande et dans d'autres pays. 's-Gravenhage, Smits, 1925. 426 p. *See* 980.   549

Best discussion of Baculard's plays. Omits mention of some of his minor dramatic efforts. Inklaar is so obsessed with Baculard's faults that he overlooks certain merits.
Review : D. Mornet in RHL 34:607-09, 1927.

La Villehervé, Bertran de. François Thomas de Baculard d'Arnaud; son théâtre et ses théories dramatiques. Champion, 1920. 168 p.   550

Incomplete, posthumous publication. Immature in scholarship. Indicates certain neglected aspects of Baculard's theater and offers some interesting suggestions that merit further consideration.
Review : D. Mornet in RHL 32:316-18, 1925.

Boissy, Louis de.

Zeek, Charles F., Jr., Louis de Boissy, auteur comique (1694-1758). Grenoble, Allier, 1914. 265 p. (Diss., Grenoble).   551

Mediocre work. Based on inadequate

research. Zeek missed five plays entirely. Failed to locate manuscripts of ten others, of which eight are in BN and two in the Archives du Théâtre-français.

Carmontelle, Louis Carrogis. *See :* Brenner, 544; *Recueil général des proverbes dramatiques,* 543.

Gaiffe, Félix. Carmontelle, peintre des mœurs. RDS 2:1-16, 1914.   552

Good article, stressing large number of types portrayed by Carmontelle.

Thierry, A. Augustin. Trois amuseurs d'autrefois : Paradis de Moncrif, Carmontelle, Charles Collé. Plon-Nourrit, 1924. 231 p.   552A

Intended for general public. Based on fairly accurate documentation as far as it goes.

Carolet, D. *See :* Grannis, 545; Moore, 462; *Le théâtre de la foire,* 482; Chaponnière, 488.

Levy, Bernard. The unpublished plays of Carolet. New York, Institute of French studies [c1931]. 269 p. (Diss., Columbia).   553

Meritorious effort that produces some new information on an obscure author. Further bibliographical investigation would have resulted in more definite information on certain plays. Some inconsistency in dates given in text.
Review : D. Mornet in RHL 38:633-35, 1931.

Chénier, Marie Joseph. *See :* Haines, 516, 3014.

Liéby, Adolphe. Étude sur le théâtre de Marie-Joseph Chénier. Société française d'imprimerie et de librairie, 1901. 514 p. *See* 3038.   554

Very detailed and scholarly study. Lacks comprehensive bibliography.
Review : J. Bury in RHL 10:698-708, 1903.

Collé, Charles. *See :* Fontaine, 460; *Recueil général des proverbes dramatiques,* 543; Gaiffe, 542; Thierry, 552.   555

Crébillon, Prosper Jolyot de.

Dutrait, Maurice. Étude sur la vie et le théâtre de Crébillon. Bordeaux, Cadoret, 1895. 568 p. (Diss., Bordeaux).   556

Careful and detailed study to which later research has added little.

Dancourt, Florent Carton. *See :* Lenient, 540; Lintilhac, 541; Lanson, 575.

Barthélemy, Charles. La bourgeoisie et le paysan sur le théâtre du xviie siècle : la comédie de Dancourt (1685-1714), étude historique et anecdotique. Charpentier, 1882. 380 p. 557

Pretentious title is misleading; study simply consists of scenes from Dancourt's comedies to serve as documents illustrating various aspects of society of his day.

Lemaître, Jules. La comédie après Molière et le théâtre de Dancourt. Hachette, 1882. 247 p. 2nd ed., Leipzig, Welter, 1903. (Diss., Paris). 558

Rather brief discussion of types of characters in Dancourt's comedies with some brief comments on philosophy, dialogue, etc.

Destouches, Philippe Néricault. *See :* Gaiffe, 542; Lanson, 539, 575; Lenient, 540; Lintilhac, 541; Schwarz, 548.

Burner, A. Philippe Néricault Destouches 1680-1754); essai de biographie. RHL 38:40-73, 177-211, 1931. 559

Purports to be careful and judicious weighing of all evidence. Best attempt so far at a biography, but still incomplete in some respects. Has useful but incomplete bibliography.

Hankiss, Janos. Philippe Néricault Destouches; l'homme et l'œuvre. Debreczen, Csáthy, 1918; Hegedüs & Sandor, 1920. 443 p. 560

Leaves much to be desired from bibliographical standpoint. Very full discussion of plays, their sources, influence, etc. Much valuable material, though inaccurate on some minor points. Reviews : H. C. Lancaster in MLN 38:231-34, 1923; H. Tronchon in RHL 29:498-500, 1922; J. Wihan in Euph 26: 297-98, 1925; W. Wurzbach in LGRP 44:234-36, 1923.

Dufresny, Charles, sieur de La Rivière. *See :* Jamati, 608; Moore, 462; Lintilhac, 541.

Vic, Jean. Les idées de Charles Rivière Dufresny. RDS 3:121-41, 1916; 4:235-53, 1917. 561

Amateurish study. Some biographical information of value. Indicates numerous ideas borrowed by 18th century dramatists from Dufresny, especially by Beaumar-

chais. Makes out far too good a case. Attributions should be taken with greatest reserve.

Fagan de Lugny, Barthélemy Christophe. *See :* D'Origny, 474; Lenient, 540; Lintilhac, 541.

Clerc, Albert. Barthélemy-Christophe Fagan, auteur comique (1707-1755). Boccard, 1933. 226 p. 562

Well-documented monograph that presents careful and sufficiently thorough treatment of subject, except for Fagan de Lugny's connection with *parade*, where Clerc too readily accepts traditional ascriptions.

Favart, Charles Simon. *See :* Lenient, 540; Grannis, 545; Heulhard, 495; Martino, 2561.

— Mémoires et correspondance littéraire, dramatique et anecdotique. Colin, 1808. 3 v. 563

Section devoted to Favart's correspondence with Durazzo, 1759-70, is of moderate importance; more so for the latter than for Favart. Rest of miscellaneous correspondence and short literary compositions of little consequence.

Font, A. Essai sur Favart et les origines de la comédie mêlée de chant. *See :* 317, 493. 564

Iacuzzi, Alfred. The European vogue of Favart; the diffusion of the opéra-comique. *See* 324. 565

Adequate presentation of subject. Excellent bibliography of Favart's plays contains a few inconsequential omissions. Date of first editions omitted for many plays. Review : F. Desonay in RBP 13:249-50, 1934.

Marandet, Amédée. Manuscrits inédits de la famille Favart, de Fuzelier, de Pannard et de divers auteurs du xviiie siècle, Jorel, 1922. 139 p. 566

Detailed description of major part of Favart manuscripts in *Bibliothèque de la Ville de Paris.* Offers important additions to our knowledge of works of authors mentioned in title. Valuable, though incomplete, chronological lists of plays of Pannard and Fuzelier.

Salvatore, Paul J. Favart's unpublished plays; the rise of the popular comic opera. New York, Institute of French studies, 1935. 407 p. (Diss., Columbia). 567

Full discussion of Favart's unpublished plays, with a few omissions. Seems unaware of Marandet's work and the *Théâtre choisi*. Some slight inaccuracies and much bad proof reading. Subtitle not justified.

Review : M. Fuchs in RHL 43:442-43, 1936. Very severe. "... le travail... dépasse les limites de la négligence pardonnable... ce livre est à refaire. Conseillons à M. Salvatore de le reconstruire sur un meilleur plan..."

Grafigny, Françoise d'Issembourg d'Happoncourt de. *See :* Gaiffe, 542.   568

Noël, Georges. Une " primitive " oubliée de l'école des " cœurs sensibles " : Madame de Grafigny (1695-1758). *See* 254.   569

Reduces to proper proportions Mme de Grafigny's very limited talent as dramatist. Judicious criticism.

Gresset, Jean-Baptiste Louis. *See :* Fontaine, 460; Lenient, 540; La comédie; Lintilhac, 541; Lanson, 575.   570

Wogue, Jules. J.-B. L. Gresset; sa vie, ses œuvres. Lecène, Oudin, 1894. 349 p.   571

Careful analyses of Gresset's plays. Does not overrate their importance. Inclined to make critical statements based on questionable premises or on lack of detailed knowledge of development of 18th century comedy. No bibliography.

Gueulette, Thomas Simon. *See : Théâtre des boulevards*, 542; Gueullette, 475; Courville, 528.   572

Gueulette, J. E. Un magistrat du xviiie siècle, ami des lettres, du théâtre et des plaisirs. Th. S. Gueulette. Droz, 1938. 200 p.   573

Careful, though somewhat amateurish study. Offers interesting new theory on development of *parade*. Missed several manuscripts of Gueulette's plays in *Bibliothèque de la Ville de Paris*.

Review : [M. Fuchs] in BHT 6:74-76, July-Sept., 1938.

La Chaussée, Pierre Claude Nivelle de. *See :* Fontaine, 460; Gaiffe, 542; Lanson, 539; Lenient, 540; Lintilhac, 541.   574

Lanson, Gustave. Nivelle de la Chaussée et la comédie larmoyante. Hachette, 1887, 295 p.; 2nd ed., 1903. 322 p. (Diss., Paris).   575

Model of scholarship and lucid exposition. Criticism sometimes made that

Lanson has attributed too much importance to La Chaussée is based largely on difference of definition and point of view. A bibliography would have added to usefulness of book. Second edition preferable because of better arrangement of material, and some revision.

La Motte, Antoine Houdar de. *See :* Hazard, 1043; Mornet, 409, 510; Guiet, 478.   576

Dupont, Paul. Un poète-philosophe au commencement du dix-huitième siècle; Houdar de La Motte (1672-1731). Hachette, 1898. 318 p. (Diss., Paris).   577

Thorough analysis of La Motte's dramaturgy and theories. Dramatic compositions other than tragedies receive little attention. No detailed study of individual plays. No bibliography of La Motte's works.

Review : [H.] Potez, in RHL 8:693-95, 1901.

La Place, Pierre Antoine de. *See :* Dargan, 515; Baldensperger, 514; Jusserand, 518; Haines, 516.   578

Cobb, Lillian. Pierre Antoine de La Place; sa vie et son œuvre (1707-1793). Boccard, 1928. 226 p. (Diss., Paris). *See* 2926.   579

Careful, well-documented study, giving as much detail as subject merits.

Review : P. van Tieghem in RHL 36: 142-43, 1929.

Le Grand, Marc-Antoine. *See :* Courville, 528.   580

Burnet, Mary Scott. Marc-Antoine Legrand, acteur et auteur comique (1673-1728). Droz, 1938. 199 p. (Diss., Paris,)   581

Pains taking but uninspired study projected against background of which author has insufficient knowledge.

Review : M. Fuchs in RHL 45:386-87, 1938; H. C. L[ancaster] in MLN 53: 612-13, 1938.

Le Tourneur, Pierre Prime Félicien. *See :* Dargan, 515; Baldensperger, 514; Jusserand, 518; Haines, 516.   582

Cushing, Mary Gertrude. Pierre Le Tourneur, New York, Columbia univ. press, 1908. 317 p. (Diss., Columbia).   583

Unscholarly and uncritical. Author lacks familiarity with background of 18th century theater. Tries to prove Le Tourneur a genius. Same data could just as well be used to demonstrate that he was nothing but a moderately good professional translator.

Marivaux, Pierre Carlet de Chamblain de.

Baldwin, Edward C. Marivaux's place in the development of character portrayal. PMLA 27:168-87, 1912.   584 and 585

Misleading title; is chiefly a comparison of M. with Addison's *Sir Roger de Coverly papers* and a discussion of the *Spectateur français*.

Deschamps, Gaston. Marivaux. Hachette, 1897. 191 p. (GEF)   586

Good short summary of M.'s life and works, but contains nothing new. Follows general pattern of this series.

Durry, Marie-Jeanne. Quelques nouveautés sur Marivaux. RCC 40:97-113, 206-18, 419-28, 1938-39. Reprinted, Boivin, 1939. 46 p.   587

Based largely on research in archives. Offers a few new biographical details of no great consequence.

Fleury, J. F. B. Marivaux et le marivaudage. Plon, 1881. 416 p.   588

General, and on the whole unscholarly, treatment of subject. Soon superseded by Larroumet's work (no. 592). Appendices, which reprint *La provinciale* and Riccoboni's *Suite de Marianne*, of some value.

Grimm, Charles. Encore une fois la question Marivaux-Richardson. RLC 4:590-600, 1924.   589

Claims Richardson's letter to Aaron Hill was a hoax; that Richardson had read *Marianne* and was inspired by it to write *Pamela*. For opposite point of view see F. C. Green, *Minuet*, (no. 1042), p. 399-430.

Jaloux, Edmond. Marivaux. NRF [46]: 533-40, Apr. 1, 1936.   590

Believes that M.'s dominant trait was *la pudeur*, which produced excess both of *sensibilité* and *amour-propre*.

Jamieson, Ruth K. Marivaux, a study in eighteenth-century sensibility. New York, King's crown press, 1941. 202 p. (Diss., Columbia).   591

Careful and thorough investigation concerned largely with M.'s novels.

Fresh approach which adds much to understanding of subject. Good bibliography.

Review : I. O. Wade in MLQ 4:104-07, 1943.

Larroumet, Gustave. Marivaux, sa vie et ses œuvres. Hachette, 1882. 640 p. 2nd ed., Hachette, 1894. 520 p.   592

First edition provided with copious notes and extensive bibliographical appendix which are of considerable value. Despite all scholarly apparatus, work suffers from over-enthusiasm and an uncritical approach which have served to distort estimates of M. ever since. Second edition has been condensed about one-third by suppression of most signs of erudition and by other simplifications. For a more accurate estimate of M. see more recent works of Courville, Tilley, and others.

Poulet-Malassis, Auguste. Théâtre de Marivaux; bibliographie des éditions originales et des éditions collectives données par l'auteur. Rouquette, 1876. 24 p.   593

Omits mention of three published plays. Entirely unreliable for dates of first performances.

Tilley, Arthur. Marivaux. *In his :* Three French dramatists : Racine, Marivaux, Musset. Cambridge, (England), University press, 1933. p. 78-136.   594

Essay which indicates what scholarly reappraisal of M.'s theater might accomplish.

Review : M. A. Ruff in RHL 42:128-30, 1935.

— Marivaudage. MLR 25:60-77, 1930. 595

Fresh examination of subject, which demonstrates that M.'s contemporaries attributed two types of *marivaudage* to him, neither of which is much in evidence in his plays or novels. Reveals how much loose thinking there has been on subject.

Marmontel, J. F.

Lenel, S. Un homme de lettres au XVIIIe siècle. Marmontel, d'après des documents nouveaux et inédits, Hachette, 1902. 512 p. (Diss., Paris)   595A

A scholarly and comprehensive survey of Marmontel's life and works. Most of Marmontel's plays have received more detailed treatment elsewhere.

Price, Lawrence M. The vogue of Marmontel on the German stage. Berkeley and Los Angeles, Univ. of California press, 1944. p. 27-123. (*On cover :* University of California publications in modern philology. v. 27, no. 2),   596

Mercier, Louis Sébastien. *See :* Fontaine, 460; Lanson, 539, 575; Gaiffe, 542.   597

Béclard, Léon. Sébastien Mercier, sa vie, son œuvre, son temps, d'après des documents inédits. Champion, 1903. 810 p. *See* 2934.   598

Scholarly work of first order. Presents not only very careful and complete study of M.'s life and work, but also gives excellent picture of literary and social background of period and his relation to it. Carried only to year 1789. Projected second volume never published. Manuscript material for it, including two completed chapters, in *Bibliothèque de l'Arsenal.*

Palissot de Montenoy, Charles. *See :* Fontaine, 460; Wade, 461.   599

Delafarge, Daniel. La vie et l'œuvre de Palissot (1730-1814). Hachette, 1912. 554 p. (Diss., Paris).   600

Very detailed and scholarly study. Review : D. Mornet in RHL 20:451-53, 1913.

Vier, J. A. L'activité d'une académie provinciale au xviiie siècle; l'Académie de Stanislas de 1750 à 1766. RHL 33:337-54, 1926.   601

See p. 350-52 for Palissot's *Le cercle.*

Pannard, Charles François. *See :* Grannis, 545; Heulard, 495; Marandet, 566; Théâtre de la foire, 482.   602

Junge, Ernst. Charles François Pannard. Leipzig, Seele, 1911. 200 p. (Diss., Leipzig).   603

Incomplete and wholly unsatisfactory study.

Piron, Alexis. *See :* Heulard, 495; Lanson, 539; Lenient, 540; Lintilhac, 541.   604

Chaponnière, Paul. Alexis Piron; sa vie et ses œuvres. Geneva, Imprimerie du Journal de Genève, 1910. Reissued, with new title page, Geneva, Jullien, and Paris, Fontemoing, 1910. 463 p. (Diss., Geneva).   605

Piron's plays for fairs receive scant attention. More serious plays are given

sufficient consideration. Bibliographical information on plays might be more complete.

Regnard, Jean François. *See :* Martino, 2561; Lenient, 540; Moore, 462; Lintilhac, 541.   606

Hallays, André. Regnard. Berger-Levrault, 1929. 166 p.   607

Popular, unoriginal. Good general account. Better as biography than as criticism.

Jamati, Georges. La querelle du Joueur; Regnard et Dufresny. Messein, 1936. 158 p.   608

Inept title. Slight, unoriginal, but carefully written account of Regnard, Dufresny, and the theater of their time. Only one chapter devoted to quarrel. Offers no solution of its problem.

Toldo, Pierre. Études sur le théâtre de Regnard. RHL 10:25-62, 1903; 11:56-87, 1904; 12:424-52, 1905.   609

Best discussion of Regnard's plays, though not the last word on the subject. Not much attention given to Regnard's life.

Roy, Pierre Charles.

Polinger, Elliot H. Pierre Charles Roy, playwright and satirist (1683-1764). New York, Institute of French studies, 1930. 367 p. (Diss., Columbia).   610

Incomplete picture of Roy's dramatic activity, concentrating on important works. Some compositions not mentioned. Considerable bibliographical information on Roy's works lacking.

Rozoi, Farmin de.

Estrée, Paul d'. Farmin de Rozoi. RHL 25:211-42, 408-22, 562-79, 1918.   611

Interesting and well documented.

Sedaine, Michel Jean.

Curzon, Henri de. Actualités bibliographiques; M. J. Sedaine, 1719-1797. La bibliographie moderne 2:63-68, 1898.
612 and 613

Sedaine, Michel Jean. Le philosophe sans le savoir. Variorum and critical edition. Ed. by T. E. Oliver, Urbana-Champaign, Ill. University press [c1913]. 200 p.   614

The University studies. University of Illinois, IV, p. 242-416, 1913.

Arnoldson, Mrs. Louise (Parkinson). Sedaine et les musiciens de son temps. Éditions Véga, 1934. 251 p. (Diss., Paris). 615

Based on extensive documentation, including some new manuscript material, but amateurishly written. Shows inability to estimate comparative worth of sources. Best work is on Sedaine as librettist. A few slight inaccuracies in bibliography of Sedaine's works.

Günther, Ladislas. L'œuvre dramatique de Sedaine. Larose, 1908. 342 p. (Diss., Paris). 616

Thin. Author shows inexperience in field of theater and lack of knowledge of 18th century background. Many misprints. Some errors in bibliography. Not without merit if used judiciously. Review : D. Mornet in RHL 16:826-29, 1909.

Rey, Auguste. Notes sur mon village; la vieillesse de Sedaine. Champion, 1906. 114 p. 617

Well-documented little work. Still best biography of Sedaine. Throws new light on several plays.

Wade, Ira O. The title of Sedaine's Le philosophe sans le savoir. PMLA 43:1026-38, 1928. 618

Plausibly refutes widely held belief that original title was Le duel. Offers interesting interpretation of play. Throws light on working of censorship and on place of this play in " philosophic " struggle.

Vadé, Jean Joseph. See : Moore, 462. 619

Müller, Max. Jean Joseph Vadé (1719-1757) und das Vaudeville. Greifswald, Abel, 1911. 174 p. (Diss., Greifswald). 620

Incomplete and superficial study. Review : W. von Wurzbach in ZFSL 40:198-200, 1912-13.

Alain René Lesage
(Nos. 620A-626)
(For Lesage's Novels see Chap. IV)

Harry Kurz

Brunetière, Ferdinand. Autour de Turcaret. In his : Conférences de l'Odéon; les époques du théâtre français (1636-1850). 7th ed. Hachette, p. 181-204. 620A

Masterly analysis of influence of Molière and La Bruyère; sets Turcaret in its literary place. Notes on the epoch of 1709—l'argent est roi. In general, says that L. was an observer, not a thinker. Why Turcaret had no imitators, and why L. did not repeat his success; reasons lie in social and theatrical conditions of time. The comédie de mœurs ended, the novel will take over task of social satire.

Gutkind, Curt S. Lesages Komödie, Turcaret. ZFSL 55:308-24, 1931-32. 621

Turcaret given 7 times in 1709, great success. Yet withdrawn till 1730. Analysis of reasons for this. Cue in disappearance of Le financier from printed title. Power of the traitant, historical analysis from 1675 into XVIIIth century. Difference between Molière's Jourdain and successors. New role of money. Contemporary documents revealing financial stringency in France in 1708. Hence Turcaret (Turc + arrêt) dangerously timely. Excellent article adding to stature of L. as daring satirist substituting for mild Crispin realistic upstarts.

Sarcey, F. Turcaret. In his : Quarante ans de théâtre. Bibliothèque des annales, 1900. v. 2, p. 341-50. 622

Turcaret today less a play than a pamphlet in dialogue. This due to change in our point of view. Role of the traitant in 18th century. Such portraits interesting, informative, but dated. Yet dialogue remains delightful.

Van Kempen, C. R. Brest. A propos du nom de Turcaret. Neo 16:6-9, 1930. 623

(a) The Turc was well known as brigand even by Cyrano and Molière. But (b) Breton has vocable teurk (tique), a leach sucking blood from cattle. By 1709, this word was coming into use for a usurer; in 1718 it is approved by the Dictionary of the Academy.

(b) is source of L.'s character name.

Barbaret, V. Lesage et le théâtre de la foire. Nancy, Sordoillet, 1887. 266 p. (Diss., Paris). Inscribed to Petit de Julleville. 624

Pictures théâtre forain before L. Analyses of L.'s plays, sources, subjects, satirical motives, types of roles. Table chronologique of L.'s pièces foraines, followed by appendix of documents on persecutions suffered by Foire at hands of grands théâtres. Description of how plays were staged and conditions of commedia dell'arte in L.'s time. Essential book warmed by author's love of subject matter.

Review : E. Lintilhac in Rcr ns 27: 91-95, 1889.

Kurz, Harry. Canada in French plays of the eighteenth century. QQ 1924, p. 371-87. 625

Analysis of L.'s play *Les mariages du Canada* and its relation to his *Beauchesne*.

— European characters in French drama of the eighteenth century. New York, Columbia univ. press, 1916. 329 p. *See* 3314. 626

Analysis of L.'s farces for the *Théâtre de la foire*. Index contains some 20 references to his various foreign characters. Reviews : L. Roustan in Rcr 89:138-40, 1922; C. F. Zeek in MLN 32:113-16, 1917.

Beaumarchais
(Nos. 627-667)

IRA O. WADE

Cordier, Henri. Bibliographie des œuvres de Beaumarchais. Quantin, 1883. 143 p. 627

This work which contains some 522 bibliographical items is indispensable for anyone working on B. Cordier utilized resources of the BN as well as the BM. Work none the less far from complete. There are notable features. Has endeavored to give, for instance, parodies, translations, and adaptations of B.'s plays in English, German, Swedish, and Dutch, with a Russian item here and there. One section entitled Biographies is an attempt to make a list of biographies which had appeared in encyclopedias as well as in book form down to 1883.

Beaumarchais. Œuvres complètes de Pierre Augustin Caron de Beaumarchais. Collin, 1809. 7 v. 628

This edition, published by B.'s friend, Gudin de la Brenellerie, is first full edition of B.'s works, although two other editions of so-called *Œuvres complètes* had appeared in 1775 (3 v.) and in 1780 (4 v.). For contents of this edition, *see* no. 467 in Cordier (no. 627).

— Théâtre. Lettres relatives à son théâtre. Texte établi et annoté par Maurice Allem. (Nouvelle revue française, 1934). 718 p. 629

Contents are as follows : *Avertissement* of M. Allem, *Essai sur le genre dramatique sérieux, Eugénie, Les deux amis, Lettre modérée, Le barbier de Séville, Le mariage de Figaro, Tarare, La mère coupable, 41 lettres, Notes et variantes, Note bibliographique.*

Texts of *Eugénie, Les deux amis* and *Le mariage de Figaro* are from first edition of each play; texts of *Tarare* and *La mère coupable* are from second edition of each; text of the *Barbier de Séville* is from third edition. Letters selected from published correspondence of B. Only those related to his plays chosen. Notes and variants, p. 603-706, valuable, particularly in so far as they concern manuscripts of the plays. Variants were copied from the G. d'Heylli edition mentioned below (no. 639). The *note bibliographique* is merely a selection of various editions of plays and of complete works, in which Cordier (no. 627) is largely used. This edition makes handy text for all plays and complementary material.

— Le barbier de Séville, ou La précaution inutile, comédie en quatre actes. Représentée et tombée sur le Théâtre de la Comédie françoise aux Tuileries, le 23 de Février, 1775. 1775. 88 p. 630
See Cordier, 627, No. 46.

— L'autre Tartuffe, ou La mère coupable. Drame en cinq actes, en prose; Par P. A. Caron-Beaumarchais. Remis au Théâtre de la Rue Feydeau, avec des changements, et joué le 16 Floréal, an V (5 mai 1797) par les anciens acteurs du Théâtre français. " On gagne assés dans les familles, Quand on en expulse un méchant." Dernière phrase de la pièce. Rondonneau, 1797. 128 p. 631
See Cordier, 627, No. 272.

— Les deux amis, ou Le négociant de Lyon. Représenté pour la première fois sur le Théâtre de la Comédie française à Paris, le 13 janvier 1770. " Qu'opposerez-vous aux faux jugements, à l'injure, aux clameurs ? — Rien." Les deux amis, Acte IV, Scène vii. Le Prix est de 36 sols. Duchesne, 1770. 163 p. 632
See Cordier, 627, No. 28.

— Eugénie, " Une seule démarche hasardée m'a mise à la merci de tout le monde." Eugén., Acte III, Scène iv. Merlin, 1767. 72 p. 633
See Cordier, 627, No. 1.

— La folle journée, ou Le mariage de Figaro. Représentée pour la première fois par les Comédiens français ordinaires du Roi, le Mardi 27 Avril 1784. " En faveur du

badinage, Faites grace à la raison." Vaud.
de la pièce. Ruault, 1785. 237 p.   634
See Cordier, 627, No. 128.

— Lettres à Madame de Godeville, 1777-
1779. Lemerre, 1928. 233 p.   635
    Edited with an *Avertissement* by Maxime
Formont. There is a fac-simile of one
of the letters. 107 Letters which B.
wrote to one of his mistresses. They have
no great historical or literary value.

— Lettres de jeunesse (1745-1775); publiées
par Louis Thomas. Boccard, 1923. 292 p.
                             636
    Collection of 167 letters written to or
from B. during years 1745-1775. In a
préface Thomas explains that he proposes
to publish complete *Correspondance* of B.
Plan not executed. Letters published not
altogether unknown. In this edition,
based upon archives of Beaumarchais
family, however, text has been corrected.
Notes not extensive.

— Lettres inédites de Beaumarchais, de
Mme de Beaumarchais, et de leur fille
Eugénie, publiées d'après les originaux de
la Clements Library par Gilbert Chinard.
Margraff, 1929. 139 p.   637
    Contains letters of B. and his family
which throw light upon various incidents
of B.'s biography. Letters of B. concern
purchase of forest of Chinon, one of his
early unfortunate enterprises. Letters to
Théveneau de Grancy reveal B.'s relationship with the American Congress. Those
of Mme B. give indications of the years
when B. was in exile. Chinard, in a clear
and succinct introduction, calls attention
of scholars to rich collection of B.'s works
now at Clements Library of the University of Michigan. Introduction supplemented by explanatory material placed
at beginning of each group of letters.

— Lettres de vieillesse de Beaumarchais.
Ed. by L. Thomas. RBelgique 2nd. ser. 43-
45:301-16, 1905; 2nd ser. 46-48:51-65, 1906.
                             638
    Unpublished letters taken from MS 933
of Public library of Lille. Letters (there
are three groups of them) were addressed
to B.'s commercial correspondents in
America during years 1797-98.

— Théâtre complet de Beaumarchais, réim-
pression des éditions princeps, avec les
variantes des manuscrits originaux publiées
pour la première fois par G. d'Heylli [*pseud.*]
et F. de Marescot. Académie des bibliophiles, 1869-71. 4 v.   639

Not in Cordier (no. 627). This edition,
elegantly printed, remarkable not only for
text which has been established upon
first editions of plays, and collated upon
manuscripts of B. when possible, but also
for extremely interesting introductions to
each play by either G. d'Heylli or F. de
Marescot. Each play followed by detailed
list of variants. While not thoroughly
critical, this edition is none the less very
important.

Marsan, Jules. Beaumarchais et les affaires
d'Amérique (Lettres inédites). Champion,
1919. 62 p.   640
    Collection of 30 unpublished letters
concerning B.'s commercial and political
enterprises in America during the Revolution. Letters well edited and furnish an
interesting supplement to Gudin's and
Loménie's account of these enterprises.

Arneth, Alfred von. Beaumarchais und
Sonnenfels. Vienna, Braumüller, 1868.
107 p.   641
    Interesting account of B.'s escapades
in Austria in 1774, based on material in
Vienna national library. Material had
been largely used by Loménie (no. 662).
Documents utilized by Von Arneth
(letters and reports) are published in their
entirety, p. 65-107.

Beaugeard-Durand, M. T. Portrait de
Madame *** RPL 4th ser. 20:161-63,
Aug. 8, 1903.   642
    Contains an unpublished *Portrait de
Madame* from collection of Alfred Morrison. Original is the Baronne de Burmane,
who, according to author, was the none
too faithful mistress of B. and of several
other notables of the time.

Bettelheim, Anton. Beaumarchais, eine Biographie. Frankfurt a/M., Rütten and
Loening, 1886. 659 p.   643
    Forthright and rather complete bio-
graphy of the author. Bettelheim had
access to B.'s papers at the BN., *Archives
nationales, Affaires étrangères,* and *Comédie française.* He has not, however,
used them exhaustively. Also used the
papers of Loménie. Literary aspects of
B. receive much less treatment than they
do in Lintilhac. Appendix contains seven
unpublished letters of B.

Brunetière, Ferdinand. Le mariage de
Figaro. *In his:* Les époques du théâtre
français. Hachette, 1896. p. 315-37.   644

Attempt to put the *Mariage* in its
proper place in development of French
theater and to mark what is imitation and
what is originality in play. Good analysis
of play's import, done along rather general
lines. Good example of dogmatic academic criticism.

[Cousin d'Avallon, Charles Yves Cousin,
called]. Vie privée, politique et littéraire
de Beaumarchais. Michel, 1802.   645

Work has distinction of being earliest
biography of B. Is rare, and said by
Tourneux to be unknown both to Quérard
and the BN. Was reprinted with additions and suppressions under the title :
*Beaumarchaisiana, ou Recueil d'anecdotes...
et autres pièces peu connues de Caron de
B., avec des notes et éclaircissements précédés de la vie de l'auteur.* 1812. See
Gudin de la Brenellerie : *Histoire de
Beaumarchais* (no. 651), p. iii.

Dalsème, René. La vie de Beaumarchais.
12th ed. Gallimard, 1928. 376 p.   646

Translated by Hannaford Bennett, New
York, 1929. Romanced history of the life
of B., not unpleasantly told but not
particularly interesting to scholars. Author
had access to B. correspondence now at
the BM.

Francastel, Pierre. La première version du
monologue de Figaro. Jdéb [Ed. hebdo-
madaire] 34:932-35, June 10, 1927.   647

Francastel publishes the version of
monologue read before Louis XVI by
Mme Campan. Version had already
been discussed in part by Lintilhac,
without, however, giving text. Analysis
of Francastel more solid.

Frederick, Edna C. The plot and its
construction in the eighteenth century
criticism of French comedy; a study of
theory with relation to the practice of
Beaumarchais. *See* 507.   648

Very interesting and carefully documented account of emphasis placed upon
plot-construction in comedy of 18th
century (both in theory and practice) and
role of B. in this movement. Portion
(p. 102-111) dealing with relationship
between B.'s theory and practice in plot-
construction and Diderot's theories on
drame especially significant.
Review : E. Melcher in MLN 50:
404-05, 1935.

Frischauer, P. Beaumarchais, adventurer in
the century of women. Translated by

M. Goldsmith. New York, Viking press,
1935. 312 p.   649

Lengthy, chatty, romanced history for
anyone who wishes to gain knowledge and
pastime, both without effort. Reasonably
instructive bibliography, p. 307-08.

Gaiffe, F. Le mariage de Figaro. Amiens,
Malfère, 1928. 173 p. [Les grands événements littéraires].   650

Succinct but well-documented account
of composition, performance, criticism,
and influence of the *Mariage*, by scholar
who best understood drama of 18th
century. In opening chapter there is a
brief but very creditable biography of B.
Review : D. Mornet in RHL 36:141-
42, 1929.

Gudin de la Brenellerie, P. P. Histoire
de Beaumarchais [Ed. Tourneux]. Plon,
1888. 508 p.   651

Gudin was secretary of B. and as such
was well placed to know intimate activities
of B.'s life. His enthusiasm and loyalty
to B. do not always make for clarity of
judgment. Even facts at times need to
be controlled. *Notice préliminaire* of
Maurice Tourneux well done.

Hallays, André. Beaumarchais. Hachette,
1897. 188 p. (GEF).   652

Clear, well-written biography of B. and
criticism of his works. Adequate for early
acquaintance with B. Now somewhat
superseded by work of Gaiffe (650).

Huot, Paul. Beaumarchais en Allemagne;
révélations tirées des Archives d'Autriche.
Lacroix, 1869. 218 p.   653

Much of material of this work had
already been utilized by Loménie (no. 662)
and Arneth (no. 641).

Johnson, M. Leah. Beaumarchais and his
opponents; new documents on his lawsuits.
[Richmond, Va.], 1936. 278 p. (Diss.,
Columbia).   654

Miss Johnson has analyzed pamphlets
and factums in Goëzman, Kornman, and
other affairs, and extracted liberally from
them. At end of her work is an excellent
bibliography, especially of pamphlets
which took their origins in these affairs.
Review : M. Fuchs in RHL 45:265-66,
1938.

Jones, Florence N. Beaumarchais and
Plautus : the sources of the Barbier de
Séville. Chicago, Scott, Foresman, 1908.
29 p. (Diss., Chicago).   655

Studies relationships between *Miles gloriosus* and *Barbier*. Difficulty of establishing direct relationships between two works shown by Miss Jones's interesting, but by no means complete, treatment of "guardian and ward" comedy in 17th and 18th centuries. Interesting note added in Appendix upon *Mariage de Figaro* and *Casina*.

Kite, Elizabeth S. Beaumarchais and the war of American independence... with a foreword by James M. Beck. Boston, Badger, [1918]. 2 v. 656

Appreciative and not very critical biography by an American admirer. Only chapters XVI-XXII deal with B.'s activity in Revolutionary War. Book, however, not without importance; has utilized some of documents which Marsan published in 1919. In addition, she had access to *Congressional Papers*. Fairly interesting bibliography.

Lafon, Roger. Les années d'activité maritime de Beaumarchais. MerF 204:75-93, May 15, 1928. 657

Account of B.'s activity in War of American Independence founded on documents now at *Comédie française* and *Archives nationales*. Analysis of some of the memoirs of B. shows his astuteness.

— Beaumarchais, le brillant armateur. Société d'éditions géographiques, maritimes et coloniales, 1928. 316 p. 658

Good presentation of one episode in life of B., the fitting out of boats in the Revolutionary War. A few of the documents are published in an appendix.

Latzarus, Louis. Beaumarchais. Plon, [1930]. 390 p. 659

No. 31 of series *Le roman des grandes existences*. Interesting but not very new.

Lemaitre, Georges. Beaumarchais. New York, Knopf, 1949. 362 p. 659A

Most recent biography in English, based upon standard authorities. Bibliography and Index. More emphasis upon chequered life than on literature.
Reviews : C. Brinton in NYT, May 8, 1949; L. Gottschalk in SRL 32:15-16, May 21, 1949.

Lintilhac, Eugène François. Beaumarchais et ses œuvres, précis de sa vie et histoire de son esprit, d'après des documents inédits, avec un portrait et un fac-similé. Hachette, 1887. 447 p. 660

Good working biography of "*vie et œuvres*" type, full and explicit. Second part : *Examen critique des œuvres de Beaumarchais* especially helpful, since few critics have given adequate attention to B. as writer. *Appendice* at end of volume should be consulted by those working on any aspect of B. Cf : D. Mornet in RHL 36:463, 1929 : "La thèse de Lintilhac est copieuse et surtout extrêmement confuse."

— La comédie satirique et Beaumarchais. *In his* : Histoire générale du théâtre en France. Flammarion, n.d., 4:391-471. 661

Best treatment of B.'s *Barbier* and *Mariage* which places B. and his works in development of 18th century French comedy. Citations are long and not always apt. Discussion is sometimes confused. Relationship between *Barbier* and *Jean Bête* not entirely clear. Comparison between first draft and second of Figaro's monologue complicated by innuendos of historical nature. All in all, however, solid piece of literary criticism. Lintilhac's statement concerning what remains to be done in publication of *Beaumarchais inédit* (p. 440-1) should be pondered carefully.

Loménie, Louis L. de. Beaumarchais et son temps. 2nd ed. Michel Lévy, 2 v. Translated (in part) by Henry S. Edwards, New York, Harper, 1857. 4th ed., revised and corrected, 1880. 2 v. 662

Loménie's biography, though diffuse, still remains fullest and best work on B. As was characteristic of time in which it was written, dwells at considerable length upon picturesque incidents and social background. Critical judgments of B.'s literary productions rather inadequate. Much of Loménie's work had already appeared in the RDM, Oct. 1, 1852 to Feb. 15, 1854. See Cordier (no. 627), p. 126, No. 502. There is a lengthy notice of work in EdR 104:453-490, Harpers (by J. Bonner) 14:76, and in FM 49:330. Cf : D. Mornet in RHL 36:463, 1929 : "Les deux gros volumes de Loménie... sont déjà un peu anciens."

Mary-Lafon, Jean Bernard. Beaumarchais est-il le seul auteur de ses ouvrages ? JIH 1:73-77, 212-15, 1834. 663

Substance of this article discussed in Tourneux's edition of Gudin de la Brenellerie's *Histoire de Beaumarchais*, p. xiii of the *Notice préliminaire*. Mary-Lafon attributed B.'s plays to a collaboration of B. and Gudin. Articles on this controversy reprinted by Mary-Lafon in his *Cinquante ans de vie littéraire*, 1882.

Mérimée, Paul. Une critique espagnole du Mariage de Figaro. RLC 16:195-223, 1936.
664

Letter, written in 1785, possibly by García de la Huerta, to an unknown lady, criticizing at length and vehemently B.'s *Mariage*.

Rivers, John. Figaro : the life of Beaumarchais. London, Hutchinson [1922]. 314 p.
665

Author declares he wrote his work because he found both Loménie and Gudin had given legendary character to their account of B. Then proceeds to give his own account frequently drawn from Gudin or the Bachaumont *Mémoires secrets*. Not badly done in novelistic style of Dalsème, Frischauer, Latzarus.

Valles, Charles de. Beaumarchais, magistrat. Oliven [c1927]. 329 p.
666

Work relates details of B.'s activity in the *Tribunal de la Capitainerie*. Material drawn from the *Archives nationales*.
Review : D. Mornet in RHL 36:462-63, 1929.

Vic, Jean. Les idées de Charles Rivière Dufresny. *See* 561.
667

Shows B.'s debt to Dufresny's *Le jaloux honteux* in *Le mariage*. Figaro is said to have first been traced in character of Gusmand of *Le double veuvage*. Subject of *Le mariage* can be found in *La noce interrompue*. Serious study.

Drama of the Revolution
(Nos. 668-692)

KENNETH N. MCKEE

Tourneux, Maurice. Bibliographie de l'histoire de Paris pendant la Révolution française. Imprimerie nouvelle, 1890-1913. 5 v.
668

This bibliography is best work of its kind to date for Revolutionary period.

Aghion, Max. Le théâtre à Paris au XVIIIᵉ siècle. *See* 455.
669

Fragmentary reference to conditions existing in theater during Revolution, with special treatment of new theaters established at end of 18th century. Book has no index or bibliography, but choice of extensive illustrations excellent.

Albert, Maurice. Les théâtres des boulevards. Société française d'imprimerie et de librairie, 1902. 381 p.
670

Reliable text for study of theater of Revolution (chapters I-VII). Author gives special attention to struggle of the *théâtres des boulevards* to break monopoly of the *Théâtre Français* and allow complete freedom to small theaters (ch. II); also shows how theaters became tools of revolutionary propagandists (ch. IV).

Brazier, Nicolas. Histoire des petits théâtres de Paris depuis leur origine. Allardin, 1838. 2 v.
671

One of less important secondary books for study in Revolutionary field. Treatment is by theater rather than by chronology; therefore, one has to search through each chapter for items relating to revolutionary period. Brazier rarely cites sources; rather, his book seems to be based on memory and hearsay.

Desnoiresterres, Gustave. La comédie satirique au XVIIIᵉ siècle. *See* 538.
672

Last four chapters deal with Revolutionary period. One of better secondary sources, although restricted in scope. No index, but good footnotes and table of contents.

Estève, Edmond. Le théâtre monacal sous la Révolution. *In his :* Études de littérature préromantique. Champion, 1923. p. 83-137.
673

Important study in literary influences. Estève shows influence of French convent plays, particularly Monvel's *Les victimes cloîtrées*, on English horror novels of Lewis and Radcliffe.

Etienne, C. G. and A. Martainville. Histoire du Théâtre-français. Barba, 1802. 4 v.
674

Chief value of this work is that authors were eye-witnesses of what they relate. They have advantage of first-hand knowledge, but also prejudices that go with it, and their style savors sometimes of gossip and calumny.

Fleury, J.-A.-B. Mémoires de Fleury. Dupont, 1836-38. 6 v. in 3.
675

Fleury's vivacious and witty account of his own experiences during Revolution and those of the troupe at the *Théâtre-français*. He is not always fair to his associates.

Gaiffe, Félix. Le drame en France au
XVIIIe siècle. *See* 542. 676

Touches only occasionally on theater
of Revolutionary period, but throws
interesting sidelights on origin of melodrama as found in " convent " plays.

Goncourt, Edmond and Jules de. Histoire
de la société française pendant la Révolution. Didier, 1864. 450 p. 677

Deals with customs, morals, and manners of Revolutionary period, and notorious personalities. Authors have no
thesis to prove—they merely examine
society of 1789-1799. Excellent study for
background material.

Hallays-Dabot, Victor. La censure pendant
la Révolution. *In his :* Histoire de la censure
théâtrale en France. p. 143-206. *See* 458.
678

This chapter adequate without being
thorough. Some footnotes, but no
bibliography.

Hérissay, Jacques. Le monde des théâtres
pendant la Révolution. Perrin, 1922. 444 p.
679

One of best studies to date in Revolutionary period. Hérissay stresses the
monde, but he brings all aspects of the
theater into his book. Work well planned,
scholarship dependable, and text well
documented.

Jauffret, Paul Eugène. Le théâtre révolutionnaire, 1788-1799. Furne, Jouvet, 1869.
431 p. 680

Necessary, though ill-made, book : no
index, notes, table of contents, or bibliography. One of few writers to survey
complete revolutionary theater in chronological order, Jauffret follows theater
from 1788 to 1799, and covers field
thoroughly, although references frequently inaccurate. Used in conjunction
with original sources, book provides much
valuable information on theater of period.

Lecomte, L[ouis] Henry. Histoire des
Théâtres de Paris : Le théâtre national. Le
Théâtre de l'égalité. Daragon, 1907. 160 p.
In same series, and with same publisher :
Les Variétés amusantes, (1908, 262 p.), and
Le Théâtre de la Cité, (1910, 300 p.). *See*
456, 497. 681

These three books offer accurate information about plays of Revolutionary
period : dates of *premières*, actors in cast,
synopses of plots, pithy criticism. Within

their narrow framework, these books are
excellent. Material arranged in chronological order, with appendix composed of
alphabetical list of plays presented in each
theater.

Lumière, Henry. Le Théâtre-français pendant la Révolution. Dentu, [1894]. 438 p.
682

Deals almost entirely with the *Théâtre-
français*, its division in 1791, and eventual
reunion in 1799. Chief value of Lumière's
study lies in wealth of detail concerning
actors and authors, their jealousies and
quarrels, and their tribulations during
Revolution. Copious footnotes.

Lunel, Ernest. Le théâtre et la Révolution.
Daragon, 1909. 160 p. 683

Composed of an assortment of revolutionary anecdotes and public events
bearing on the theater. Material arranged
by year, but has no unifying theme ; useful only *after* scholar is well oriented in
field.

McKee, Kenneth N. The role of the priest
on the Parisian stage during the French
Revolution. Baltimore, Johns Hopkins
press, 1939. 126 p. (Diss., New York
Univ.). [The Johns Hopkins studies in
Romance literatures and languages. v. 36].
684

Illustrates a method of correlating
dramatic literature with public opinion as
reflected in newspaper criticism and
new productions ; shows that plays of
anti-clerical violence did not receive popular support.

Reviews : C. D. Brenner in FR 15:
75-76, 1941-42 ; J. H. Stewart in AHR
46:634-35, 1940-41 ; N. L. Torrey in
RR 32:313-15, 1941.

Muret, Théodore. L'histoire par le théâtre,
1789-1851. v. I, La Révolution, le Consulat,
l'Empire. Amyot, 1865. 355 p. 685

First 188 pages of v. I cover Revolutionary period. Author attempts to show
how theater reflected history of times.
Occasionally successful, but limited in
number of plays analyzed.

Péricaud, Louis. Théâtre des petits comé-
diens de S.A.S. Monseigneur le comte de
Beaujolais. (Histoire de l'histoire des grands
et des petits théâtres de Paris pendant la
Révolution, le Consulat et l'Empire. 2 v.).
See 499. 686

Traces day-by-day history of the
Théâtre des Beaujolais and the *Théâtre de*

Monsieur. Interesting chiefly for details of dates, costs, etc., for *premières* and revivals. Little critical analysis of plays.

Pitou, Alexis. Les origines du mélodrame français à la fin du XVIIIᵉ siècle. RHL 18: 256-96, 1911.   687

In this admirable article, Pitou shows how melodrama started in *pantomime héroïque* of pre-Revolutionary decades; claims that anti-clerical and anti-monarchical violence of Revolution hastened and popularized development of genre.

[Quentin, Henri]. Le théâtre sous la Terreur (théâtre de la peur) 1793-1794. By Paul d'Estrée[*pseud.*]... Émile-Paul, 1913. 523 p.
                      688

Authoritative study of theater in Paris and in provinces during months of the Terror. Estrée discusses actors, authors, directors of theaters and part played by public during Revolution. Chapters on newspapers of Revolution especially important for analysis of popular reaction to plays. Complete index and table of contents.

Söderhjelm, Alma. Le régime de la presse pendant la Révolution française. Helsingfors, Hufvudstads-bladet, 1900-01. 2 v. (Diss., Helsingfors).   689

Indispensable adjunct to any research in Revolutionary theater, whose theatrical productions and propaganda are inextricably related to newspaper criticism

and public opinion. Thoroughly reliable study, well documented and skilfully written for such an unwieldy subject.

Trahard, Pierre. La sensibilité révolutionnaire (1789-1794). Boivin, [c1936]. 283 p. *See* 2147.   690

Trahard's scholarship throws much light on social and psychological milieu of Revolution, showing how intense feeling is often transformed into violence. Provides interesting corollary for theatrical excesses of period. Excellent bibliography.

Tuetey, Alexandre. Répertoire général des sources manuscrites de l'histoire de Paris pendant la Révolution française. Imprimerie nouvelle, 1890-1914. 11 v.   691

Documents dealing with theater are found in v. II, p. 151-78.

Welschinger, Henri. Le théâtre de la Révolution, 1789-1799. Charavay, 1880. 524 p.
                      692

Based largely on Pixérécourt collection of Revolutionary plays, this is best book published to date on Revolutionary theater. Welschinger groups plays by subject matter rather than in chronological order, but provides fine index. Author prejudiced in favor of Church and monarchy, but his scholarship is accurate and judgment reliable.

Reviews : F. Brunetière in RDM 3rd per. 43:474-85, Jan. 15, 1881.

CHAPTER IV. PROSE FICTION

(Except Montesquieu, Voltaire, Rousseau, and Diderot)

(Nos. 693-1018)

Arnold G. Bégué, George R. Havens, Harry Kurz, J. Robert Loy, Arnold H. Rowbotham, and Robert E. Taylor

General Studies
(Nos. 693-711)

Arnold H. Rowbotham

Montesquieu, Charles Louis, etc. Lettres persanes. Ed. by Elie Carcassonne. Roches, 1929. 2 v. (TF)   693

Introduction, v. I, p. xxxv-xxxvi, n. 2, contains list of fictional letters with Oriental background.

Rochedieu, C. A. Bibliography of French translations of English works, 1700-1800, with an introduction by Donald F. Bond. Chicago, Univ. of Chicago press, 1948. 387 p. *See* 2908.   694

This Bibliography places in hands of students of Anglo-French relations a most useful tool for quick location of references. Reviews : M. M. H. Barr in PBSA 43:98-100, 1949; J. C. Hodges in SAB 14:1, 6, 1949.

Voltaire, F.-M. A. etc. Zadig ou la destinée, histoire orientale. Critical edition, ed. by Georges Ascoli. Hachette, 1929. v. I, p. l-lxv. *See* 1653.   695

These pages of Introduction contain a list of fiction with an Oriental motif published between 1670 and 1748.

Catalogue des livres de la Bibliothèque de feu M. le duc de La Vallière, 1783-87. 2 parts (Part 1, 3 v.; Part 2, 6 v.) in 9 v. (Part II, v. 3—v. 6. of the series—p. 83-314, contains 2797 titles). *See* 41.   696

Garnier, Charles G. T. Voyages imaginaires, songes, visions et romans cabalistiques. Amsterdam and Paris, 1787-95. 39 v.   697

Valuable collection containing many of most important Extraordinary Voyages. Last three volumes form supplement containing *Histoire des naufrages...* par M. D. *See* Gove (nos. 699, 2538.)

Gay, Jules. Bibliographie des ouvrages relatifs à l'amour, aux femmes, au mariage... *See* 30.   698

Gove, Philip B. The imaginary voyage in prose fiction; a history of its criticism and a guide for its study, with an annotated check list of 215 imaginary voyages from 1700 to 1800. New York, Columbia univ. press, 1941. 445 p. (CSE, 152). *See* 2538.   699

A most useful work in its field.

Jones, S. Paul. A list of French prose fiction from 1700-50. *See* 38.   700

Careful and scholarly chronological list covering first half of century only, with notes regarding editions, etc. Index of titles and authors. Valuable introduction. Best and most complete work for period, indispensable for student in this field.

Rousseau, Jean-Jacques. La nouvelle Héloïse. Critical edition, ed. by Daniel Mornet. Hachette, 1925. 4 v. *See* 1898.   701

V. I, p. 335-85, contains list of French novels of period 1741-80, classified according to subject matter. Full but not exhaustive. Best bibliography for period covered.

Pigoreau, Alexandre Nicolas. Petite bibliographie biographico-romancière, ou dictionnaire des romanciers. Pigoreau, 1821. 354 p.   702

Early and rare bibliography. Contains useful information regarding lesser authors but is, on whole, highly untrustworthy.

Streeter, Harold Wade. The eighteenth century English novel in French translation : a bibliographical study. New York, Publication of Institute of French studies, [1936]. 256 p. (Diss., Columbia).   703

Part I deals with : (1) reception o English novel in France; (2) main channels of its diffusion and (3) extent and diversity of French translations. Part II contains list of French translations of English novels, together with list of spurious " translations." Introduction and general bibliography. Review : *See* 2910A.

Bougeant, Guillaume-Hyacinthe. Voyage merveilleux du prince Fan-Férédin dans la Romancie contenant plusieurs observations historiques, géographiques, physiques, critiques et morales. Le Mercier, 1735. 275 p.
704

Satire of novel in novelistic form, inspired by Lenglet-Dufresnoy's work (no. 708.)

Dufrenoy, Marie-Louise. L'Orient romanesque en France, 1704-1789. Montreal, Beauchemin, 1946-47. 2 v.   704A

Oriental vogue and influence in relation to 18th century French novel. V. II devoted to extensive bibliography. Amplifies, but does not supersede Martino (nos. 1055A, 2561) for period covered. Emphasizes psychological *finesse* of Crébillon *fils*, while playing down more than Martino his eroticism. Interesting treatment of Melon's *Mahmoud le Gaznévide*. Endeavors to show statistically rise and fall of oriental vogue.
Reviews : R. C. Anderson in RR 38: 78-80, 1947, and 39:255-59, 1948; P. Barrière in RLC 21:141-42, 1947; P. Langellier in FR 20:74-75, 1946-47, and 22:412, 1948-49 : G. H. McNeil in AHR 52: 175-76, 1946-47, and 53:875-76, 1947-48.

Formey, Jean-Henri-Samuel. Conseils pour former une bibliothèque peu nombreuse mais choisie, nouvelle édition corrigée et augmentée. Berlin, 1756. 352 p.
705

First edition Berlin, 1746. Subsequent editions contain number of changes. Chiefly, critical list of novels. Valuable as showing contemporary opinion.

Jacquin, Abbé Armand Pierre. Entretiens sur les romans, ouvrage moral et critique dans lequel on traite de l'origine des romans et de leurs différentes espèces tant par rapport à l'esprit que par rapport au cœur par l'abbé J... Duchesne, 1755. 396 p. 706

Jacquin gives three causes for popularity of novel : false exoticism, false standards of taste, excessive feminine liberty in France. Though not as discerning as Lenglet-Dufresnoy's work, it is valuable as summary of arguments hostile to novel.

La Chesnaye-Desbois, François-Alexandre Aubert de.   Lettres amusantes et critiques sur les romans en général, anglais et français, tant anciens que modernes adressées à Miledy W... Gissey, 1743. 707

Criticism chiefly in Letter I. Other letters are accounts of various novels. Author emphasizes didactic role of novel. (" les romans sont encore des précepteurs muets ").

[Lenglet-Dufresnoy, Nicolas-Alexandre.] De l'usage des romans, où l'on fait voir leur utilité et leurs différents caractères : Avec une bibliothèque des romans accompagnée de remarques critiques sur leur choix et leurs éditions par M. de C. Gordon de Percel (pseud. for L-D). Amsterdam, 1724. 2 v. 333, 360 p.   708

Vol. I contains best and most able defense of novel in first half of century. Author asserts superiority of genre over works of history. " Un roman est un poème héroïque en prose." Vol. 2 contains critical list of novels, with index.

— L'histoire justifiée contre les romans par M. l'abbé Lenglet-Dufresnoy. Amsterdam, Bernard, 1735. 391 p.   709

Fifty pages of *pièces citées*. Chiefly refutation of his own views favoring the novel, published anonymously (see above).

Marmontel, Abbé Jean-François. Essai sur les romans considérés du côté moral. *In his :* Œuvres complètes. Verdière, 1818-20. 10:287-361.   710

Best critical review written in second half of century. Author examines particularly moral effects of *sensibilité* on novel. More important for its historical than for its critical value.

Ratner, Moses. Theory and criticism of the novel in France from l'Astrée to 1750. [New York, De Palma] 1938. 119 p. (Diss., New York univ.).   711

Well-documented study of subject matter and structural aspects of novel. Useful though not definitive work. Bibliography and index. Author finds steady development towards modern conception of novel, although lack of status of genre, during period, results in dearth of systematic theory.

Aspects of the 18th-Century Novel
(Nos. 712-732)

Arnold H. Rowbotham

Bila, Constantin. La croyance à la magie au xviiie siècle en France dans les contes, romans & traités. Gamber, 1925. 158 p. 712

General treatment of subject. Chap. VI alone deals with novel. Author finds belief in magic widespread but consistently opposed by *philosophes*. Good bibliography.

Clapp, John M. An eighteenth-century attempt at a critical view of the novel : the Bibliothèque universelle des romans. PMLA 25:60-96, 1910. 713

Nature and contents of chief collection of prose fiction of period, chiefly significant as showing wide range of interest of novel-reading public of pre-Revolutionary France.

Chaplyn, Marjorie A. Le roman mauresque en France de Zayde au Dernier Abencérage. Nemours, Lesot, 1928. 173 p. (Diss., Paris). 714

Part II, p. 101-33, deals with 18th century. Author discusses writers who have made use of Moorish motif and concludes that genre was more popular than the number of authors using it would seem to imply.

Claretie, Léo. Le roman en France à la fin du XVIIᵉ siècle. *In his :* Le Sage, romancier. Colin, 1890. p. 103-47. 715

Contains excellent summary of condition of novel at beginning of century, emphasizing growing reaction to classical romances.

Etienne, Servais. Le genre romanesque en France depuis l'apparition de La nouvelle Héloïse jusqu'aux approches de la Révolution. Colin, 1922. 440 p. *See* 903. 716

Deals chiefly with Rousseau and *La nouvelle Héloïse*. Diffuse and obscure work, with vague conclusion, but full of stimulating ideas. Good on minor authors of Rousseauist school.

Green, Frederick Charles. French novelists, manners and ideas from the Renaissance to the Revolution. New York, Appleton, 1922. 239 p. 717

Readable and discerning treatment of subject. Deals chiefly with 18th century.

— Realism in the French novel in the first half of the XVIIIth century. MLN 38:321-29, 1923. 718

Author cites examples and quotes passages from several novels showing steady growth of realism during period. See also : *Further evidence of realism in the French novel of the eighteenth century* (no. 719).

— Further evidence of realism in the French novel of the eighteenth century. MLN 40:257-70, 1925. 719

Analysis of several lesser-known novels to prove increasing use of realism.

— The eighteenth century French critic and the contemporary novel. MLR 23:174-87, 1928. 720

Gives opinions of Desfontaines, Grimm, Marmontel, etc.

— La peinture des mœurs de la bonne société dans le roman français de 1715 à 1761. Presses universitaires de France, 1924. 259 p. 721

Value of the 18th century *roman de mœurs* as social document. Selective bibliography.

— Minuet. *See* 734. 722

Le Breton, André. Le roman français au XVIIIᵉ siècle. Boivin, [1925 ?]. 396 p. 723

Still best general treatment of novel of period. Suffers from lack of index and bibliography. Author considers novel most important literary genre of time.

McGhee, Dorothy M. The conte philosophique bridging a century. PMLA 58:438-49, 1943. 724

Brief review of *conte* in post-Voltaire period.

Merlant, Joachim. Le roman personnel de Rousseau à Fromentin. Hachette, 1905. 424 p. 725

Chaps. I-III deal with 18th century. Careful analysis of works of chief writers. Treats autobiographical novel as " vital and concentrated form of the *roman de mœurs*." Important work, especially for second-rate writers. Detailed table of contents but no index.

Morillot, Paul. Le roman au XVIIIᵉ siècle. *In his :* Le roman en France depuis 1610 jusqu'à nos jours. [1892]. p. 155-343. 726

P. 155-343 deal with the 18th century novel. Selections from chief writers with introductory notices on life and works of author. Same material, with additions from Courtilz de Sandras, Beckford and Choderlos de Laclos, published with the title : *Le roman français durant l'époque classique (1610-1800)*, London and Paris, Dent, [1922]. 347 p. In this edition p. 161-347 deal with 18th century.

Palache, John G. Four novelists of the old régime; Crébillon, Laclos, Diderot, Restif de la Bretonne. New York, Viking press, 1926. 271 p. *See* 909, 928.   727

Readable and popular treatment of these four novelists. Introduction and bibliography of little value.

Morillot, Paul. Le roman. *In :* Petit de Julleville. L, Histoire de la langue et de la littérature françaises des origines à 1900. Colin, 1896-99. 6:447-502.   728

Excellent and useful brief review of subject.

Saintsbury, George. History of the French novel (to the close of the 19th century). London, Macmillan, 1917-19. 2 v.   729

Vol. I deals with 18th century. General review of authors and works. Opinionated but fairly factual. Good for some of lesser known writers.

Singer, Godfrey Frank. The epistolary novel, its origin, development, decline and residuary influence. Philadelphia, [Univ. of Pennsylvania press], 1933. 266 p. (Diss., Pennsylvania).   730

Chapter VIII : *Epistolary fiction (particularly the novel) in France and Italy,* p. 181-94; this chapter apparently appendix to main theme. Superficial and inexact. Bibliography highly untrustworthy. Can well be ignored by student in French field.

Storer, Mary Elizabeth. Un épisode littéraire de la fin du xviie siècle; la mode des contes de fées (1685-1700). Champion, 1928. 289 p.   731

Bibliographies. Though dealing chiefly with 17th century, contains some authors who wrote also in 18th.

Van Tieghem, Philippe. La sensibilité et la passion dans le roman européen au xviiie siècle. RLC 6:424-35, 1926.   732

Rapid review of field to show that psycho-sentimental novel of 18th century cleared way for modern novel, particularly as regards elements of passion and *sensibilité.* Valuable synthesis of subject but no new material.

Foreign Influences
(Nos. 733-740)
(See also chapter XI)
Arnold H. Rowbotham

Barton, Francis B. Étude sur l'influence de Laurence Sterne en France au dix-

huitième siècle. Hachette, 1911. 161 p. (Diss., Paris).   733

Bibliography. Lacks intelligent summary. Discusses translations, imitations, and influence of Sterne on Diderot, Xavier de Maistre.
Review : *See* 3023.

Green, Frederick C. The novel. *In his :* Minuet : a critical survey of English and French literary ideas in the eighteenth century. *See* 1042, p. 302-470.   734

In general, work attacks theory of international literary influences during period, and in particular influence of Richardson on French novel. Stimulating but dogmatic.

Joliat, Eugène. Smollett et la France. Champion, 1935. 279 p.   735

Author concludes that of the four great English novelists of period Smollett was the only one who was not appreciated in France.

Killen, Alice M. Le roman terrifiant ou roman noir de Walpole à Anne Radcliffe et son influence sur la littérature française jusqu'en 1840. Champion, 1923. 255 p. *See* 2897.   736

Deals chiefly with 19th century but describes briefly vogue at end of 18th. Valuable bibliography and index.
Reviews : *See* 2897.

Mann, William Edward. Robinson Crusoë en France; étude sur l'influence de cette œuvre dans la littérature française. Davy, 1916. 290 p. (Diss., Paris).   737

Chap. IV : *Robinson Crusoë et le roman au XVIIIe siècle. Robinson Crusoë* contributed to vogue of shipwreck motif after 1730. Analytical table of contents, bibliography, and index.

Price, Lawrence M. The vogue of Marmontel on the German stage. Berkeley, Univ. of California press, 1944.   738

P. 27-123. (On cover : University of California publications in modern philology, v. 27, no. 2).

Sells, Arthur Lytton. Les sources françaises de Goldsmith. Champion, 1924. 233 p. 739

Goldsmith's genius owes much to French classicism. In novel he shows debt to Marivaux.

Texte, Joseph. Jean-Jacques Rousseau et les origines du cosmopolitisme littéraire;

étude sur les relations littéraires de la France et de l'Angleterre au XVIIIe siècle. Hachette, 1895. 466 p. (Diss., Paris). *See* 831, 2145, 2912. 740

Study of Anglo-French literary contacts. " Cosmopolitanism was born of the fruitful union between the English genius and J.-J. Rousseau." While some of Texte's views have been seriously questioned (see, for example, Green : *Minuet*, no. 734) this book still remains necessary work for student of 18th century novel. Analytical table but no index.
Reviews : *See* 2145.

Lesage
(Nos. 741-776)

HARRY KURZ
(For Lesage's plays, see Chapter III)

Le Sage, Alain René. Les aventures du flibustier Beauchêne. Ed. by Harry Kurz. New York, Century, 1926. 227 p. 741

The Introduction (p. xiii-xxviii) contains close tracing of elements of L.'s story, both Canadian and piratical, juxtaposing them with printed records available to him, and concluding that he actually transcribed them from a piratical manuscript. *See* no. 742.
Review : M. I. Protzman in MLJ 11: 125-27, 1926-27.

Chinard, G. Les aventures du Chevalier Beauchêne de Lesage. RDS 1:279-93, 1913 742
Penetrating analysis of this debated work and its two sections. Chinard shows that first part dealing with pirate recounts adventures typical of historical people like de Lussan, Hennpin, La Hontan. Second part describing an Indian Utopia fabricated by L. is forerunner of anti-clerical ideas of *philosophes*. Chinard sees clearly the distinction between these two sections and suggests that first may be an authentic record. *See* Kurz, no. 741.

Knapp, Lewis M. Smollett and Lesage's The devil upon crutches. MLN 47:91-93, 1932. 743
Copies of receipts of payments to Smollett for corrections on English translation of *Diable boiteux*, 1759, presumably made on a translation of 1750. Smollett is known as translator of *Gil Blas*—but this note establishes his connection with a rendering of L.'s other work.

Vic, Jean. La composition et les sources du Diable boiteux de Lesage. RHL 27:481-517, 1920. 744

Willers, Hermann. Le diable boiteux (Lesage) — El diablo cojuelo (Guevara). Erlangen, Junge. 100 p. (Diss., Rostock). *Also in :* RFor 49:215-316, 1935. *See* 768. 745
Thorough tracing of sources for *Diable boiteux* not only from Guevara, but Santos, Rojas Zorilla, Pérez de Montalbán, Lugo y Dávila and others. This process applied to edition of 1707 and of 1726, to which L. added five chapters. Similar tracing in La Bruyère. Diagrams for each chapter in the *Diable boiteux* show amount of borrowing. A final chapter gives useful summary of European vogue of *novela picaresca* with important selective bibliography of this genre.

Le Sage, etc., Gil Blas. Lefèvre, 1820. 3 v. 746
Editor, F. de Neufchâteau, dismisses in his introduction accusations of plagiarism; finds only two places certainly inspired by Marcos de Obregón, of which an analysis chapter by chapter is present, together with translation of Padre Isla's preface of 1787.

— Gil Blas. Garnier [1863 ?]. 2 v. Preface by Sainte-Beuve, dated 1850. *See :* Sainte-Beuve. 747
Edition contains also useful series of citations from various critics on *Gil Blas* such as : l'abbé des Fontaines, Voltaire, Marmontel, La Harpe, Saint-Marc Girardin, Sir Walter Scott, Villemain, Nisard, and, finally, a long extract from French Academy prize-winning essay by M. Patin (1922) on *Gil Blas* as ordinary mortal, rather than as *héros de roman*. This essay shared prize with that of Malitourne. A reprint of this edition (1935), with preface by Auguste Dupouy brings discussion of *Gil Blas* up to date with emphasis on authentic autobiographical elements identifiable through recent research on L. Well-documented study with good selective bibliography on *Gil Blas*.
Review (of reprint) : D. Mornet in RHL 43:128-30, 1936.

— Histoire de Gil Blas de Santillane. Ed. by A. Dupouy. Les belles lettres, 1935. 2 v. (TF). 748
Follows 1747 edition, last published in L.'s lifetime.

— The adventures of Gil Blas of Santillana. Translated into English by Henri van Laun. London, Gibbings, 1897. 4 v.   749

Introduction by van Laun useful; lists arguments since Voltaire on question of L.'s originality. Analysis of causes of Voltaire's spite, and of points made by disputants from both sides, from Isla, Neufchâteau, Llorente, and also by articles in the NAR (25:278-307, Oct. 1827) and in Bl (55:698-724, June, 1844).

— Gil Blas. A comedy. London, Francklyn, 1751. 92 p.   750

Acted at Theater Royal, Drury Lane, by Edward Moore. A five-act play with Gil Blas acting role appropriate to Scaramouche or Arlequin.

— Gil Blas; or, The boy of Santillane. A musical comedy in 3 acts, by George MacFarren. London, John Cumberland, n.d., printed from the acting copy.   750A

Version of Gil Blas in the robber cave. Cordier (no. 767) mentions (p. 577-80) four French dramatizations.

Brunetière, F. La question de Gil Blas. *In his :* Histoire et littérature. Lévy, 1891. II, p. 235-69.   751

Most penetrating and complete treatment to date, starting with Voltaire's slur on L., on through Isla, Neufchâteau, Llorente, Scott, Audiffret, Tieck, de Castro, Ticknor, Sainte-Beuve, Franceson, Baret. Urges real *édition critique* of Gil Blas and makes suggestions. Conclusion : in harmony with Sainte-Beuve's declaration that " un auteur est un homme qui prend dans les livres tout ce qui lui passe par la tête." *Gil Blas* is the French " *encyclopédie du roman picaresque.*"

Calemard, J. Une erreur littéraire à propos de Gil Blas. BBB, 1926, 351-64 and 405-18.   752

Study of editions of *Gil Blas*. Two editions of 1715 show 12 slight changes, improvements. Edition of 1730-32 (3 v.) and 1737 (4th v.) show further slight changes. Quotes Tressan who found L. at Boulogne entering changes. Final corrected version appeared 1750. Total, 90 word changes, 40 suppressions, 520 additions, many bad. Author considers 1732 edition best text.

Cordasco, Francesco. Llorente and the originality of Gil Blas. PQ 26:206-18, 1947.   753

Beginning with Voltaire's slur on the authorship (1751), article cites Padre Isla's claim (1787), Neufchâteau's defence (1818), analyzes thoroughly arguments advanced by Llorente in his *Observations sur Gil Blas* (1822), dismissing most yet admitting possibility of L.'s plagiarism, agreeing with Claretie's (1890) conclusion that true originality of *Gil Blas* still open question.

Franceson, Charles Frédéric. Essai sur la question de l'originalité de Gil Blas. Leipzig, Fleischer, 1857. 111 p.   754

Author, professor at University of Berlin, refutes Isla and especially J. A. Llorente's *Observations critiques sur Gil Blas*, 1822, in which he maintains that L. had a Spanish ms. which he adapted. In 14 chapters, lists his points which Franceson refutes in detail in first half of essay. Then proves originality of L. by various tests, absence of prolixity. Reduces possibilities of imitation to 13 elements not all certain. Translates from Marcos de Obregón, 39 pp. in appendix, containing only material L. used from Spanish.

Fullerton, W. M. Gil Blas. QR 215:335-51, 1911.   755

Good critical study of *Gil Blas* as presentation of average mankind. Picaresque form used by L. because of his acquaintance with it. L. compared to Tolstoy in attempt to picture society of his day, hence *Gil Blas* an encyclopedia of human types. Useful references to *Gil Blas*' influence on Stendhal.

Haack, Gustav. Untersuchungen zur Quellenkunde von Lesage's Gil Blas de Santillane. Kiel, Nord-Ostsee-Zeitung, 1896. 98 p. (Diss., Kiel).   756

Orderly presentation of arguments for L.'s originality. Ch. I deals with relationship between *Gil Blas* and Spanish picaresque novels, Marcos de Obregón in detail. Ch. II discusses episodes and characters found in Spanish dramas used by L. in farces, and possible borrowings in *Gil Blas*. Total, some fifty per cent of novel is conceivably based on sources, but rest is L.'s and that fifty per cent has passed through prism of his genius.

Heinz, Hans. Gil Blas und das zeitgenössische Leben in Frankreich. Erlangen, Junge, 1914. 179 p. (Diss., Munich).   757

Confrontation of social studies of 18th century in France (Taine, the Goncourts) and details in *Gil Blas* to prove that background is not Spanish but French. Tribute to L.'s accurate picturization of contemporary life. Has five chapters on government officials, plain people, literary circles, acting world, doctors. Really helpful analysis of true originality of L., realist even in such details as *toilette*.

Mouton, Léo. Un prétendu supplément du Gil Blas de Lesage : L'histoire de Don Rodriguez Vexillario. RHL 44:77-83, 1937. 758

Shows *Histoire de Don Rodriguez* a literary fake.

Ricard, Anselme. Monographie sur le Gil Blas de Lesage; étude littéraire, lexicologique et grammaticale. Prag, 1884. 38 p. 759
Useful presentation of elements in L.'s style. Lists several hundred " *expressions humoristiques* " (*foi de fripon*), a shorter group of archaisms, and some 400 picturesque locutions. Interesting indication of persistence of 18th century idiom in modern French. Grammar not discussed despite title.

Robolsky, Hermann. Sur l'originalité de Gil Blas. Stettin, 1857. 25 p. (Friedrich Wilhelmschule Programm). 760

Superficial discussion, interesting only as evidence of burning interest in Germany in Voltaire's slur on *Gil Blas* as pure adaptation, a question even then settled by Sainte-Beuve and Ticknor.

Sainte-Beuve. Gil Blas par Lesage. *In his :* Causeries du lundi. Garnier [185- ?]. Vol .2. p. 353-75. 761
Article valuable today more because of casual comment than for analyses of L.'s main works. Example : contrast between Gil Blas and René, Panurge, Figaro. Emphasis on human quality of *Gil Blas*. Superiority of vol. III over others. Translation into French of Spence's interesting comments on a visit to L. in Paris.

Saint-Victor, Paul J. R. B. Gil Blas. *In his :* Hommes et dieux; études. Lévy, 1883. p. 157-66. 762
Maintains that *Gil Blas* is sordid book at fifth reading. Analysis of Gil Blas' character to demonstrate egotistical, self-centered nature, unrelieved by any virtue except good humor. Subjective article of considerable interest.

Bizet, René. Lesage est-il romancier ? Runiv 39:170-89, 1929. 763

Biographical elements used by L. in *Gil Blas*, both Breton and Parisian. This section of article useful and suggestive. Rest answers titular question in negative on ground that L. is dramatist and best pages are comic scenes. Not the creator of the novel but essentially moralist aiming to picture vice as detestable.

Brunetière, F. Lesage. *In his :* Études critiques sur l'histoire de la littérature française. Hachette, 1887, 3:63-120. 764

Traces influence of *Mémoires* and La Bruyère on novel. Attacks Isla, Llorente fabrications. True greatness of *Gil Blas*. Relation between sequel (1724, 1735) and first part, (1715). Gil Blas lacks complexity of romantic hero and is not the *chef-d'œuvre* of French novel. 18th century not ready for birth of real novel. Makes usual error on *Beauchêne*. Clear assertive article of a master.

Claretie, Léo. Lesage. Lecène, 1894. 238 p. (Collection des classiques populaires). 765

One of series of great authors of all nations. Has 14 chapters dealing with life and individual works, with long quotations. Largely abbreviated popular rewriting of following work (no. 766) without new material or additional scholarly value. Cf. Lanson, no. 770.

— Le roman en France au début du XVIIIᵉ siècle; Lesage, romancier, d'après de nouveaux documents. Colin, 1890. 447 p. 766
Three parts, biography of L,. study of his sources, nature of his originality. Part II reviews critical work proving L.'s originality. Part III applies those considerations to style. Appendix lists 2 autographs, and editions, bibliography now entirely replaced by Cordier (no. 767), except for section VI, critical review of contemporary references to L. with complete citations such as Prévost's *Pour et contre*. Valuable also for exhaustive treatment of *Gil Blas* question. Chap. II, p. 199, with citations. Error in connection with *Beauchêne*. An essential book for L.'s novels, fair, judicial, thorough. Cf. Lanson, no. 770.
Review : E. Lintilhac in Rcr ns 33: 452-59, 1892.

Cordier, Henri. Essai bibliographique sur les œuvres d'Alain René Lesage. Librairie Leclerc, 1910. 348 p. 767

960 entries. Dependable listing of editions with descriptive comment on

collections and separate works. Includes translations. *Gil Blas* items, nos. 228-594. Essential tool for L. research. Comments extensive, detailed contents of collections, especially useful for L.'s theater, nos. 700-890. Only 205 copies printed.

Hendrix, William S. Quevedo, Guevara, Lesage, and the Tatler. MP 19:177-86, 1921-22. *See* 745.   768

Relation between *Sueños*, *Diablo cojuelo*, *Diable boiteux* and evolution of *Tatler*, *Spectator*, *Rambler* — parallelisms in thought and conclusion that *Tatler* owes more to L. than to others.

Kurz, H. Proving that when a man dies he must have lived. PQ 8:309-11, 1929.   769

Report of finding of church record attesting murder and burial of Beau-chêne, thus proving that L told truth when he asserted that pirate's widow commissioned him to rewrite an actual ms. of memoirs.

Lanson, G. Étude sur Gil Blas. *In his :* Hommes et livres. Lecène, Oudin, 1895. p. 185-214.   770

Criticism of Claretie's studies (nos. 765-66) followed by claim that L.'s originality consists in his style, despite admitted borrowing. Pot-boiling and its effect on L.'s style. He is truly great when he is himself and natural. His true master, La Bruyère. Deplores L.'s tendency to " grossir le volume." Yet *Gil Blas* persists while models have disappeared. Secret lies in L.'s style and *don de la vie*.

Lawrence, Alexandre. Influence de Lesage sur Smollett. RLC 12:533-45, 1932.   771

Inquiry into extent of indebtedness of Smollett to L. Many parallels in situation and character cited between *Gil Blas* and *Roderick Random*, even satire on doctors, though Smollett was a doctor. But Smollett transforms into English background and types suggestions received from L.; process simplified by fact that common people are alike. Satire on justice, police, bandits, prisons, cafés, easily usable. This fact gave color to Voltaire's charge of plagiarism. Hence Smollett's originality not impaired, no more than L.'s.

Lintilhac, Eugène. Lesage. Hachette, 1893. 205 p. (GEF).   772

Most penetrating analysis available of L. Part I treats man and his work, Part II the writer and his spirit. Nothing found

since 1893 invalidates this authoritative study. No error on *Beauchêne*. Claretie (nos. 715, 766) treats more exhaustively question of *Gil Blas*. Critical bibliography, p. 206.

Review : F. Hémon in Rcr ns 36:61-64, 1893.

Malitourne, Armand. Éloge de Lesage. Didot, 1822. 30 p.   773

Compares L. with Molière as moralist in theater, reveals *Turcaret* as natural successor to *Tartuffe*. Then treats *Gil Blas*, which has no 17th century French model, and enlarges upon L.'s originality. Author considers L.'s novels as manifestation in prose of his dramatic gift. Article valuable for suggestive references.

Michelmore, G., & Co. Bibliographical notes upon a unique set of Lesage's Editions originales. London, Michelmore, [192- ?].   774

Sale catalogue of first and second editions. Excellent descriptions of princeps with photographs of title pages. Includes earliest English translations, an Italian version of *Gil Blas* by Giulio Monti, Venice, 1751, 7 v. In all 54 vol. are described. Inserted : (at NYPL) a Le Sage collection : repr. from the *Times literary supplement*, London, June 16, 1921. 3 p.

Review : G. L. Van Roosbroeck in RR 19:65-66, 1928.

Potez, Henri. Deux logis d'Alain-René Lesage. MM 18:15-20, 1903.   775

Description of visit to house of his birth at Sarzeau and of his death at Boulogne. Incidental biographical references give article objective value.

Wershoven, F. J. Smollett et Lesage. Brieg, 1883. 15 p. (Brieg Ober-realschule programm).   776

Analysis of debt of Smollett to L. in *Roderick Random* and *Peregrine Pickle*. Useful, sound, well-reasoned presentation of superiority of L. *See* Lawrence, no. 771.

Abbé Prévost*
(Nos. 777-834)

George R. Havens

* For a careful analysis of a number of Prévost titles, several of which are given in this list, I am greatly indebted to Professor Alessandro Crisafulli, whose Bibliographies of

Bayle, of Fontenelle, and of Mably appear elsewhere in this volume.

Works
(Nos. 777-783)

Prévost, Abbé Antoine-François. Le pour et contre. Didot, 1733-40. 20 v. *See* 2782-86. 777

See George R. Havens, *The Abbé Prévost and Shakespeare*, (no. 804) and, *The Abbé Prévost and English literature*, (no. 805). A forthcoming study of P.'s periodical by Mysie E. I. Robertson is announced by Claire Eliane Engel, *Voyages et découvertes de l'abbé Prévost*, 1939, (no. 810), p. 245, but presumably has not been completed owing to Miss Robertson's untimely death.

— Œuvres choisies. Leblanc, 1810-1816. 39 v. 778

Standard edition of P.'s works, reprinted from edition of 1783-1785, also in 39 v.

— Manon Lescaut, Préface de M. de Lescure, eaux-fortes de Lalauze. Quantin, 1879. 779

" De toutes les éditions, celle-ci est la plus riche en indications historiques; elle met bien en relief les rapports qui unissent l'œuvre aux mœurs contemporaines." Paul Hazard, *Études critiques sur Manon Lescaut*, p. 102. (No. 807.)

— Manon Lescaut, with Introduction and Notes by Louis Landré. New York, Scribner, 1930. 209 p. 780

Excellent Introduction based on modern scholarship.
Review : M. I. Barker in FR 4:497-98, 1930-31.

— Histoire du chevalier des Grieux et de Manon Lescaut. Introduction by F. C. Green. Cambridge (England), University press (1942), 1945. 148 p. 781

Excellent brief Introduction of 18 pages. Gives P. benefit of the doubt on Miss Robertson's charges of forgery (782, 783). Wisely does not consider *Manon Lescaut* a " Jansenist novel " (see P. Hazard, no. 806). Good appreciative analysis of this great novel of love.

— Manon Lescaut. Ed. by M. E. I. Robertson. Oxford, Blackwell, 1943. 2 v. 782

Excellent edition by a well-known authority on P. Introduction and Notes based on best scholarship. Novel springs

from P.'s own experience rather than from literary sources. Guilhou (no. 798) has furnished evidence that the name Marc-Antoine Prévost was used by P. in Holland, thus confirming Miss Robertson's discoveries of charge of forgery against him in England. Editor gives text of 1753, revised by P., with variants of first ed. of 1731, which was more concrete and frank in use of the *mot propre*, often in defiance of strict *bienséances*. Brief selective bibliography at end of Introduction.

— Mémoires et avantures d'un homme de qualité. Tome V, Séjour en Angleterre, édition critique par Mysie E. I. Robertson. Champion, 1927. 233 p. (Bibliothèque de la RLC). 783

Important *Préface* (p. 5-35) with previously undiscovered documents which tend to show that P. was arrested for forgery in England and released through intervention of Sir John Eyles, of whose son P. had previously been tutor. This interpretation considered unproved by F. C. Green (no. 781).
Reviews : G. R. H[avens] in PQ 7:193-94, 1928; P. Hazard in *Études critiques* (807), p. 86-87; G. S[herburn] in MP 25:246-48, 1927-28; Anon in RLC 7:600-01, 1927; Anon in TLS, Oct. 20, 1927, p. 732.

Biography and Criticism
(Nos. 784-834)

Beaunier, André. La véritable Manon Lescaut. RDM 88th yr. 6th per. 47:697-708, Oct. 1, 1918. 784

Refutation of attempt by Baron Marc de Villiers (*Histoire de la fondation de la Nouvelle Orléans*, 1917) to identify Des Grieux with Avril de la Varenne and Manon with a Mlle (or Mme) Froget, who had voluntarily emigrated to Louisiana in 1715. " La véritable Manon, c'est dans le cœur de l'abbé Prévost qu'elle a vécu et puis est morte " (p. 706). Cf. Engel, no. 791.

Bouvier, Emile. La genèse de l'Histoire d'une Grecque moderne. *See* 111. 785

If 50 pages shorter, believes Bouvier, reputation of this novel would equal that of *Manon Lescaut* which it strongly resembles. Relation of plot and characters to romantic story of love of Chevalier d'Aydie and Mlle Aïssé. Doubtful role of aged M. de Ferriol who brought her from Constantinople to France at age of four. Bearing of P.'s own somewhat shady experiences in England and Holland. Valuable interpretative article, not wholly new, but excellent synthesis which would have been improved by use of references. Frequently repeats error of employing double article in speaking of *Le pour et le contre* instead of *Le pour et contre*, correct title of P.'s periodical.

Brunetière, Ferdinand. L'abbé Prévost. *In his :* Études critiques, 3ᵉ série. Hachette, 1904. p. 189-258.   786

Valuable general study. Forecasts later interpretations more favorable to P. as writer than to his early conduct in Paris, England, and Holland. Originally published, Feb., 1885.
Review : P. Hazard in *Études critiques*, (807), p. 104.

— [L'abbé Prévost]. *In his :* Manuel de l'histoire de la littérature française. 8th ed. Delagrave, 1921. p. 289-92, notes.   787

Succinct bibliographical indications up to time of first publication in 1897. Useful hints as to interpretation of P.'s life and work.

Chew, Samuel P., Jr. Prévost's Mémoires pour servir à l'histoire de la vertu. MLN 54:592-97, 1939. *See* no. 3058A.   788

P.'s novel a translation, not adaptation, as has previously been supposed, of Frances Sheridan's *Memoirs of Miss Sidney Bidulph* (1761). Examples of slight changes or errors, but translation more faithful than those the Abbé made of Richardson's *Clarissa* and *Grandison*.

Chinard, Gilbert. L'abbé Prévost. *In his :* L'Amérique et le rêve exotique dans la littérature française au xviiᵉ et au xviiiᵉ siècle. Hachette, 1913. 448 p. p. 280-306. *See* 3164.   789

Excellent discussion of P.'s *Cléveland* and the treatment of Louisiana in *Manon Lescaut*. Does not believe that P. shared Rousseau's " admiration aveugle " for " la bonté naturelle " and " le bon sauvage " (p. 299). Yet Rousseau must have so interpreted P., for Jean-Jacques says in *Le verger des Charmettes* (1739) (Hachette ed., 6:6) :
" Ou bien dans *Cléveland* j'observe la
                    [nature
Qui se montre à mes yeux touchante et
                    toujours pure."]

See no. 2048.

Reviews : D. Mornet in RHL 21:800-802, 1914; A. T[illey] in MLR 9:284-85, 1914.

Ducarre, J. Une " supercherie littéraire " de l'abbé Prévost : les Voyages de Robert Lade. RLC 16:465-76, 1936.   790

Voyages of Robert Lade (1744) not the story of a real voyage. Robert Lade never existed. Whole story made up, not well organized or developed, awkward interpolation of geographic description. Many of these descriptions used again, a few years later, in v. 8 of P.'s *Histoire des voyages* (1750). (Note comment of Henry Harrisse, *L'abbé Prévost* (no. 801), p. 371 : " C'est donc avec ce tome VIII que commence l'œuvre entièrement individuelle de l'abbé Prévost.") The *Voyages* of Robert Lade reveal P.'s temperament and indicate kind of pseudo-geographical knowledge familiar to French public of time.

Engel, Claire-Eliane. Des Grieux et Manon ont-ils existé ? Les sources de Manon Lescaut. Rheb 45²; 64-80, Oct. 3, 1936. 791

Charles-Alexandre de Grieux as possible real-life suggestion for P.'s hero. His heroine may be in part an idealization of P.'s mistress, the notorious Lenki Eckhardt, whom he knew in Holland in 1730 and after. Mrs. Penelope Aubin's *Illustrious French lovers* (1727) contains a Des Rouais in love with a Manon (note the name). Another creation of Mrs. Aubin's is a Des Prés (striking similarity of names introduced by Des : Des Grieux, Des Rouais, Des Prés) in love with a Mlle de l'Épine. Interesting, but unproved hypotheses. Date of significant passage from *Pour et contre :* " La malheureuse fin d'un engagement trop tendre," etc., must refer to period before P. took orders (Nov. 9, 1721), not to period of 1730 after his flight. For final conclusion, cf. Beaunier (no. 784).

— Autour du voyage de l'abbé Prévost en Angleterre. RLC 18:506-10, 1938.   792

First of these two notes shows that initial number of *Le pour et contre* could not have appeared before end of April or beginning of May, 1733. Cf. Henry Harrisse (no. 801), p. 209-10, where the *approbation* for first publication in volume form is dated " le 24 mars 1733," but only after deletion of " ce qui regarde les affaires ecclésiastiques." The *privilège* is dated the " 17 juin."

(*See* 810).   792A

Foster, James R. The Abbé Prévost and the English novel. PMLA 42:443-64, 1927.
                                        793

Great influence of P.'s novels in England, especially of *Cléveland*. His important contribution to the novels of horror, " les romans noirs." Influence upon Ann Radcliffe.

Review : P. Hazard in *Études critiques*, (807) p. 99. " Un bon article," says Hazard.

Frick, [Reinhold]. Manon Lescaut als typus. GRM 7:445-64, 1915-19.   794

Traces type of glorified courtesan from ancient Orient through modern literature to Marion Delorme, the *Dame aux camélias*, Ibsen, Tolstoy, etc. Interesting with its many ramifications from world literature. Contested, however, as to remote origins of the type, by Max J. Wolff in the following review. Wolff believes it did not, as literary motif, come from India or Egypt, but was rather product of luxurious living in Ancient Greece and Rome.
Review : Max J. Wolff, GRM 8:376, 1920.

Friedrich, Hugo. Abbé Prévost in Deutschland : ein Beitrag zur Geschichte der Empfindsamkeit. Heidelberg, Winter, 1929. 161 p.   795

Translations of P. in Germany fall into two periods : those of 1730-1735, and those of 1790's. In general, they are as faithful as language of time permitted. P. prepared way for success of English family novel and helped develop mood from which *Wilhelm Meister* sprang.

Goncourt, Edmond and Jules de. [Manon Lescaut]. *In their :* La femme au XVIIIe siècle. Charpentier, (1862), 1912. p. 303-12.   796

Portrait of Manon a mingling of reality of time and idealization due to P.'s genius. " On ne voit guère que dans le roman un grand malheur ou un grand sentiment régénérer ces femmes " (p. 307).

Green, Frederick C. Minuet : a critical survey of French and English literary ideas in the eighteenth century. *See* 734 (On Prévost, see p. 84-87, 140-42, 306-33, 472-75, and other references in Index).   797

Excellent appreciation of *Manon Lescaut*. Shows that Manon and Defoe's Moll Flanders have nothing in common. P. not Jansenist (cf. Paul Hazard, no. 806), but was superstitious in his forebodings

of evil. Discovery of rare translations of *Manon Lescaut* into English in 1743 (2nd ed., 1770), 1767, and 1786. P. and Lillo. P. and Shakespeare (cf. Havens, no. 804).

Guilhou, Etienne. L'abbé Prévost en Hollande (avec des documents nouveaux). Groningue, Wolters, or Paris, Nizet et Bastard, 1933. 47 p.   798

Newly discovered documents in Dutch show that P. left extensive debts behind him on his departure from Holland for England with his mistress about January 14 or 15, 1733. This discovery supports certain earlier charges against P.'s character and tends to confirm work of Miss M. E. I. Robertson on P.'s conduct in England. (Cf. 782-783 and Green, 781).

Hankiss, Jean. Secrets d'atelier de l'abbé Prévost. AMP July-Aug., 1933. p. 113-35.   799

Important demonstration of P.'s *méthode de travail*. His constant preoccupation with establishing veracity of his narratives : *témoins oculaires*, citation of memoirs, and pretense of use of newly-discovered documents. Journalistic weaknesses.

Harrisse, Henry. La vérité sur la mort de l'abbé Prévost. RPar, May 15, 1896 (3e série), p. 379-94.   800

Important article giving documentary demonstration that P.'s death was due to the " rupture d'un anévrisme," rather than to a surgeon's autopsy performed while the Abbé was still living, as was recounted in a legend originating 19 years after his death and accepted even by Sainte-Beuve in an early study of 1831 (no. 825), then, with more maturity, doubted by same author in 1853 (no. 827).

— L'abbé Prévost : histoire de sa vie et de ses œuvres. Calmann Lévy, 1896. 465 p.
                                        801

Basic study for all later work on P. Indispensable for its collection of essential documents and for bibliographical details on P.'s works. Too ready, however, to reject interpretations unfavorable to P.'s character.
Reviews : Anon in NNY Sept. 3, 1896, p. 174-75 ; P. Hazard in *Études critiques* (no. 807), p. 101.

— La vie monastique de l'abbé Prévost. Leclerc, 1903. *Also in* BBB, 1903, p. 57-75 ; 147-59 ; 204-14 ; 264-74.   802

Important study, over-favorable to P., but based on numerous documents, some of which previously unpublished.

Havens, George R. The date of composition of Manon Lescaut. MLN 33:150-54, 1918.
803

Interesting hypotheses in favor of composition of *Manon Lescaut* about 1722-23 instead of shortly before its publication in 1731. Necessarily inconclusive. While record of personal experience which went into this unique novel is still valid, I should incline today toward idea of slow maturing of P.'s painful memories of a bitter past mingled with a still turbulent present.

— The Abbé Prévost and Shakespeare. MP 17:177-98, 1919-20. *See* 518, 2784, 3063.
804

P.'s admiration for Shakespeare less unqualified than believed by Jusserand and other previous critics. P.'s synopses and evaluations in the *Pour et contre* are direct translations of the English critics, Rowe and Gildon. (See Jusserand, no. 518). Cf. P. Hazard, *Études critiques* (no. 807), p. 85, n. 1.

— The Abbé Prévost and English literature. Princeton, Princeton univ. press, and Paris, Champion, 1921. 135 p. (Emon no. 9) (Diss., Johns Hopkins). *See* 3064.   805

Based chiefly on *Mémoires d'un homme de qualité* and on the *Pour et contre*. P. was more moderate in his attitude toward English literature, less radical, more classic in taste, than has been thought. Reviews: F. Baldensperger in Rcr ns 88: 431-32, 1921; P. Hazard in *Études critiques* (807), p. 85-86; V. Klemperer in Archiv 146:272-74, 1923; D. G. L. in MLR 17:438, 1922; D. Mornet in RHL 29:369-70, 1922; P. Van Tieghem in RSH 34:143, 1922.

Hazard, Paul. Manon Lescaut, roman janséniste. RDM 94th yr. 7th per. 20:616-39, Apr. 1, 1924. *Reprinted in* the Études critiques sur Manon Lescaut of the same author, p. 47-69. *See* 807.   806

Interpretation of *Manon Lescaut* as strongly Jansenist in character was also suggested by F. Pauli in 1912 (no. 820A). This interpretation, plausibly supported by numerous citations, has nevertheless been questioned. " Je trouve un peu forcé le titre de Jansénisme de *Manon Lescaut* " (D. Mornet, RHL, 37:450). " Des Grieux is a better exponent of

eighteenth-century epicureanism than of Jansenism " (I. O. Wade, RR, 21:255).

— Études critiques sur Manon Lescaut. Univ. of Chicago press, 1929. 113 p.   807

This little book is essential for any study of P., his personality and style. See especially, from the bibliographical point of view : *Prévost et l'Angleterre, état des travaux*, p. 85-99; and *Bibliographie critique pour servir à l'étude de Manon Lescaut*, p. 101-09.
Reviews : G. Ascoli in Rcr ns 100: 328-29, 1933; G. Chinard in MLN 45: 184-85, 1930; J. Ducarre in RLC 10: 564-68, 1930; K. Glaser in LGRP 51:119-20, 1930; H. Kurz in FR 3:374-77, 1929-30; D. Mornet in RHL 37:449-50, 1930; M. E. I. R[obertson] in MLR 26:125, 1931; I. O. Wade in RR 21:252-56, 1930.

— L'amitié franco-anglaise ne date pas du XXᵉ siècle. Déjà l'abbé Prévost... NL March 18, 1939, p. 1.   808

P. knew England and the English well. In spite of this, however, his books owe little to English psychology. They have a tone and individuality of their own. (Cf. Havens, *L'abbé Prévost and English literature*, no. 805.)

— Un romantique de 1730 : l'abbé Prévost, RLC 16:617-34, 1936.   809

Instability of character, *ennui*, melancholy, *sensibilité maladive*, characterize P.'s heroes, who precede, not only Rousseau, but Richardson.

Engel, Claire-Eliane. Figures et aventures du XVIIIᵉ siècle : Voyages et découvertes de l'abbé Prévost. Editions " je sers," [c1939]. 272 p. *See* 3062.   810

Carefully documented study of deformations of England in P.'s novels. P. " ... n'est pas parmi les écrivains les plus anglicisés du XVIIIᵉ siècle... Outre-Manche, il a trouvé d'innombrables inspirations et pas trace d'influence." (p. 232).
Reviews : C. Barjac in Lmen 11:602-03, March, 1940; P. Dottin in EA 3:379-80, 1939; G. R. Havens in RR 31:176-78, 1940; E. Magne in MerF 296:383-86, Feb. 1, 1940; H. Roddier in RLC 20: 122-25, 1940; A. L. Sells in MLR 34: 612-14, 1939.

Heinrich, Pierre. Prévost historien de la Louisiane. Guilmoto [1907]. 79 p. (Thèse complémentaire).   811

Based on government archives, as well as on printed sources. Depicts forced transportation " des filles de mauvaise vie à la Louisiane sous le système de Law " (p. vii) and concludes in favor of general accuracy of this aspect of P.'s novel, *Manon Lescaut*. Review : Anon. in RHL 15:382, 1908.

Jusserand, Jules J. [L'abbé Prévost]. *In his :* Shakespeare en France sous l'ancien régime. p. 155-60; 173-74. *See* 518. 812

Passages portraying P. as a " vrai anglomane," as " hérétique dans l'âme," as speaking " sans respect sur les anciens et sur les règles," should be modified in the light of studies by George R. Havens (no. 804) and Claire-Eliane Engel (no. 810). Review : J. Texte in RHL 6:144-45, 1899.

Kurz, Harry. Manon Lescaut; a study in unchanging critics. *In :* Todd memorial volumes. New York, Columbia univ. press, 1930. 1:221-26. 813

Interesting summary of criticisms of morality of P.'s novel, with plea for more human understanding of Manon and Des Grieux.

Lasserre, Eugène. Manon Lescaut de l'abbé Prévost. Société française d'éditions littéraires et techniques (Malfère), 1930. 161 p. (Series : Les grands événements littéraires). 814

Excellent general study, though author seems not to know the indispensable American-published *Études critiques* (no. 807) of Paul Hazard. Lasserre believes Mysie E. I. Robertson too severe toward P. and her charge of forgery in England not proved. *See* nos. 781, 782, 783. Reviews : D. Mornet in RHL 40:443-45, 1933; J. Thomas in Rcr ns 100:209-10, 1933.

Le Breton, André. L'abbé Prévost. *In his :* Le roman au XVIIIe siècle. Société française d'imprimerie et de librairie. 1898. p. 90-179. 815

Especially noteworthy for analysis of P.'s fictional characters.

Maricourt, André. Ce bon abbé Prévost l'auteur de Manon. Hachette, 1932. 221 p. 816

Interesting popular biography with some new background material. Author relies too much on Harrisse (no. 801) and Schrœder (no. 828) and seems not to know the recent work of Hazard (no. 807) and Miss M. E. I. Robertson (nos. 782, 783).

Mézières, Alfred Jean-François. L'abbé Prévost. *In his :* Morts et vivants, 1897, p. 52-64. 817

P. " seul n'a jamais traité la passion comme un exercice oratoire ou comme un thème de littérature " (p. 63). This comment is intended to apply only to *Manon Lescaut* and is to be used in contrast to Rousseau's *Nouvelle Héloïse*, George Sand, and the Romantics generally.

Monglond, André. Histoire intérieure du préromantisme français, de l'abbé Prévost à Joubert. Grenoble, 1929. 2 v. (Also published as : Le préromantisme français, Grenoble, Arthaud, 1930). For Prévost, *see* I, p. 236-47). 818

Good characterization of " l'homme fatal " and of the " héros préromantique " in the works of P. " L'ouvrage de M. Monglond est à la fois très remarquable et, à certains égards, très discutable " (Daniel Mornet, p. 603 of the review listed below). Review : D. Mornet in RHL 36:603-10, 1929.

Mornet, Daniel. Introduction à la Nouvelle Héloïse (Vol. I of his critical edition of Rousseau's novel). Hachette, 1925. 396 p. 819

" *Le roman sombre* " of P. (p. 58-59). The limited influence of P. on Rousseau's *Nouvelle Héloïse* (p. 97-98). Reviews : P. C. in AJJR 17:252-54, 1926; D. Mornet in RHL 34:604-05, 1927. (Brief Notice).

Mouton, L. L'Hôtel de Transylvanie, d'après des documents inédits. Daragon, 1907. 81 p. 820

Identification of the *Hôtel de Transylvanie*, seat of Des Grieux's gambling exploits. Evidence of P.'s exact realism in *Manon Lescaut*. Review : P. Hazard in *Études critiques* (no. 807), p. 105.

Pauli, F. Die philosophischen Grundanschauungen in den Romanen des Abbé Prévost, im besonderen in der Manon Lescaut. Marburg, Ebel, 1912. 126 p. (Marburger Beiträge zur Romanischen Philologie, Heft VII). 820A

Important study which forecasts Hazard (no. 806) in interpreting *Manon Lescaut* as strongly reflecting Jansenist influence. (But see the reservations of Mornet and of Wade to Hazard's conclusions, above,

no. 806). Pauli also analyzes the *Mémoires d'un homme de qualité*, *Cléveland*, and the *Doyen de Killerine*.
Review : P. Hazard in *Études critiques* (no. 807), p. 106.

Parfitt, G. E.   Manon Lescaut au point de vue moral.   FQ 11:189-201, 1929.   821

Excellent discussion.   Morality of P.'s novel is found in its truthful portrayal of human weakness, not in *après-coup* justification of P.'s *Avis au lecteur*.

Prod'homme, Jacques Gabriel.   L'abbé Prévost : Manon Lescaut.   *In his :* Vingt chefs-d'œuvre jugés par leurs contemporains.   Stock, 1930.   p. 89-95.   822

Useful for its brief digest of 18th century opinions of *Manon Lescaut* and of some of P.'s other novels.   Omits Rousseau's admiration of *Cléveland* as expressed in the *Confessions* (Hachette, 8:157).

Rutherford, M. R.   Sur le pour et contre de l'abbé Prévost.   FS 2:223-39, 1948.   823

Good general summary of literary opinions of P. in his 20 volume periodical, *Le pour et contre* (1733-40).   *See* no. 777).

Rovillain, Eugène E.   L'abbé Prévost et l'Homme sauvage de Sébastien Mercier.   PMLA 45:822-47, 1930.   824

Influence of P. on Mercier more significant than that of Rousseau.   From P. come the elements of Romantic " horror," caverns, poisonings, duels, murders, etc..   (Cf. Foster, no. 793).

Sainte-Beuve, Charles-Augustin.   L'abbé Prévost.   *In his :* Portraits littéraires.   Garnier, n.d., 1:265-89.   825

Indulgent toward P.'s conduct ; somewhat exaggerates his appreciation of England and of Shakespeare, misquotes Rousseau's evaluation of P.'s personality by omitting the adjective " sombre " before " coloris " (p. 288).   (*See* Brunetière, no. 786, *Études critiques.* 3:204-05).   Accepts the now generally discredited legend of P.'s coming to life in midst of supposed post-mortem autopsy (Cf. no. 800).   Nevertheless, this appreciative essay on P. may still be read with profit.   Study dated Sept., 1831.

— L'abbé Prévost et les Bénédictins.   *In his :* Portraits littéraires.   Garnier, n.d., 3:453-65.   826

Excellent documented article with judicious commentary, basis for later studies of subject.   (Cf. Harrisse, *La vie monastique de l'abbé Prévost*, no. 802).   Author again omits significant word " sombre " before " coloris." (p. 465).   *See* no. 825.   Study dated July 3, 1847.

— Le buste de l'abbé Prévost.   *In his :* Causeries du lundi.   Garnier, n.d., 9:122-39. 827

Brief remarks on P.'s revisions of style in later edition of *Manon Lescaut*.   (Cf. Chap. V. of Hazard's *Études critiques*, no. 807.)   Publication of a letter of 1741 to M. de Maurepas and of P.'s *acte de décès*.   Prudent expression of doubt this time regarding circumstances of P.'s death.   *See* no. 825.   (Cf. Harrisse, *La vérité sur la mort de l'abbé Prévost*, no. 800).   Excellent appreciation of P.'s personality.   Study dated Nov. 7, 1853.

Schrœder, V.   L'abbé Prévost : sa vie, ses romans.   Hachette, 1898.   365 p.   828

Good general study of P. the novelist, but details of P.'s life in England and of his relation to English literature need re-examination in light of later studies.   (See especially Engel, no. 810, and Havens, nos. 804-805).   Reviews : P. Hazard in *Études critiques* (no. 807), p. 104 ; H. Potez in RHL 8:337-38, 1901.

— L'abbé Prévost journaliste.   RDS 2:128-40, 1914.   *See* 2787.   829

Interesting popular article on P.'s *Pour et contre*, his interest in Montaigne, Racine, Molière, Mme de Sévigné, d'Urfé, La Bruyère, Fénelon, Voltaire, Shakespeare, etc.   To be supplemented and, particularly in regard to Shakespeare, corrected by Havens (no. 804).   Author did not know that P.'s opinions on Shakespeare for the most part merely translate at length those of the English critics, Rowe and Gildon.

Stauber, Eugen.   Manon Lescaut, est-ce une œuvre romantique ?   ZFSL 49:94-102, 1927.   830

Manon " est une grisette."   Her love for Des Grieux is matter-of-fact, sensual, not ideal.   Des Grieux, with a Jansenist background (see Pauli, no. 820A and Hazard, no. 806), is pursued by idea of sin, a fatality, but not the mysterious fatality of Romantics.   P. is realistic, human, not essentially romantic.   Author omits mention of P.'s *sensibilité*, however.   (Cf., on the other hand, Woodbridge, no. 834, though his study hardly deals with *Manon Lescaut*.) Extreme position, but useful corrective.

Texte, Joseph. [L'abbé Prévost]. *In his:* Jean-Jacques Rousseau et les origines du cosmopolitisme littéraire. Hachette, 1895. p. 53-67, 184-86, 193-97. (An English translation, revised, appeared in 1898). 831

Classic *travail d'ensemble*, but should be somewhat revised for P. in the light of recent studies by Engel (no. 810), Havens (nos. 804-805), Robertson (nos. 782-783), and Wilcox (no. 833), all of which discuss phases of P.'s relation to England and to English literature. Reviews: L. P. Betz in ZFSL 18²:153-82, 1896; E. Faguet in RPL 4th Ser. 4:167-70, Aug. 10, 1895; S. Rocheblave in RIE 30:412-15, 1895; M. Souriau in RHL 3:128-31, 1896; *Réponse à M. Souriau* (by Texte), *ibid*, 1896, p. 286-91; L. Stephen in Sbio 4:247-79, 1902, or 4:230-59, 1907; E. M. de Vogüé in RDM 4th per, 130:676-91, Aug. 1, 1895.

Trahard, Pierre. L'abbé Prévost. *In his:* Les maîtres de la sensibilité française au XVIII⁰ siècle. Boivin [1931-33], 4 v. 1:89-235, 271-77. *See* 1077, 1806, 2283. 832

Written with much verve and understanding. Good general survey of *sensibilité* in P.'s life and work. Inaccurate in factual details of P.'s life. Details of interpretation occasionally to be accepted with caution. Valuable bibliography at end of volume and in notes. Reviews: G. Ascoli in Rcr ns 100:329-32, 1933; G. R. Havens in MLN 47:534-36, 1932; 49:268-69, 1934; M. E. I. Robertson in MLR 27:347-50, 1932; 29:97-99, 1934; 30:272, 1935.

Wilcox, Frank Howard. Prévost's translations of Richardson's novels. Berkeley, Univ. of California press, 1927. CPMP 12:341-411, no. 5. *See* 3067. 833

Doubtful whether P. translated Richardson's *Pamela*, published in French in 1742 and attributed to Aubert de La Chesnaye-Desbois. *Clarissa* and *Grandison*, unlike *Pamela*, are translated with extensive omissions and alterations in interest of more brevity, less brutal realism, and less lengthy moralizing. These alterations by P. undoubtedly aided Richardson's vogue on the Continent. Review: M. E. I. Robertson in MLR 23:114-15, 1928.

Woodbridge, Benjamin M. Romantic tendencies in the novels of the Abbé Prévost. PMLA 26:324-32, 1911. 834

Article based chiefly on P.'s *Cléveland* (1731-1739). P.'s heroes have " un cœur sensible," they find pleasure in recounting their sufferings, they feel themselves persecuted by a " malign deity," are afflicted with a mania for suicide, and believe in " the divine right of passion." P. does not, however, depict external nature in the Romantic manner. Review: P. Hazard in *Études critiques* no. 807, p. 105-06.

Marivaux, *see* Chapter III

Bernardin de Saint-Pierre
(Nos. 835-886)

ARNOLD H. ROWBOTHAM

Saint-Pierre, J.-H.-Bernardin de. Œuvres complètes. Ed. by Louis Aimé-Martin, 1818-20. 12 v. Supplément, Louvain, 1823. 835

In default of critical edition, this is best available for author's complete works. Careless and inaccurate, however.

— Correspondance. Published by Aimé-Martin, 1826. 3 v. Avec un volume de Mémoires sur Bernardin de Saint-Pierre. 836

In view of editor's habitual carelessness, this edition needs to be checked with original manuscript, where available.

— Paul et Virginie. Texte établi et présenté par Maurice Souriau. Roches, 1930. 239 p. (Les textes français). 837

Best edition of work, with introduction and variants. For other important editions see Thieme or Trahard's bibliographies (no. 883). A more complete list is found in Georges Vicaire's *Manuel de l'amateur de livres du XIX⁰ siècle*, Rouquette, 1894-1920, v. 7:35-79.

— Harmonies de la nature; le texte authentique, edited by Maurice Souriau. MAC, 1904. p. 21-71. 838

Definitive edition, from original MSS in *Bibliothèque du Havre*, with errors and omissions of Louis Aimé-Martin corrected.

— La vie et les ouvrages de Jean-Jacques Rousseau. Ed. by Maurice Souriau. Cornély, 1907. 190 p. 839

Definitive edition of this historically important work prepared from manuscripts of *Bibliothèque du Havre* with S-P's *Préface*. Introduction by editor, and footnotes.

Achard, Lucie. Rosalie de Constant, sa famille et ses amis. Geneva, Eggimann, 1902. 2:85-114; 156-58.   840

These pages concern S-P.'s relations with Rosalie de Constant. Correspondence furnishing interesting evidence of S-P.'s influence on women.

Barnum, George S. Saint-Pierre et Balzac. MLN 31:342-46, 1916.   841

Believes that Balzac " ... quite consciously imitated..." S-P.'s *Paul et Virginie* in his *Vicaire des Ardennes*. (p. 342).

Brunetière, Ferdinand. Les amies de Bernardin de Saint-Pierre. RDM 62nd yr., 3rd per. 113:690-704, Oct. 1, 1892. Also, in substance, *in his :* Nouveaux essais sur la littérature contemporaine. Calmann Lévy, 1895, p. 1-29, with title; Bernardin de Saint-Pierre.   842

Brunetière sees in story of S-P.'s relations with women the element which connects his life with his work. Article is based chiefly on Maury's volume (no. 866).

Cambray, S. Les origines d'un chef-d'œuvre : Paul et Virginie. Corr. 110:696-714, 1878.   843

Reconstruction of genesis of work, from evidence in life and works of author, to support thesis that this novel, apparently simple, is result of slow development of author's life and thought.

Dejob, Charles. Des restaurateurs sceptiques de religion; à propos de Bernardin de Saint-Pierre. RIE 21:409-30, 1891.   844

Careful study of author's hesitation between Catholicism and Deism. " Au fond... Bernardin de Saint-Pierre est un épicurien comme Jean-Jacques..." (p.428).

Charlier, Gustave. De Buffon à Bernardin de Saint-Pierre. *In his :* Le sentiment de la Nature chez les romantiques français. ABM 2nd ser. 9:128-57, Dec., 1912. 845

P. 144-57 of particular interest as showing relation of bucolic and pseudo-scientific elements in author's work. Treats S.-P. as creator of veritable exoticism.

Doumic, René. Le véritable Bernardin de Saint-Pierre. RDM 75th yr. 5th per. 28: 445-56, July 15, 1905. *Also in his :* Études sur la littérature française. Perrin, 1909, 6:119-41.   846

Article based chiefly on critical studies of Souriau (nos. 880, 881, 882).

Duchène, Albert. Les rêveries de Bernardin de Saint-Pierre. Alcan, 1935. 242 p.   847

Careful analysis of ideas of S.-P. regarding morals, religion, education, social life, etc. Good index.

Ernest-Charles, J[ean]. Bernardin de Saint-Pierre. RPL 42:23-27, Jan. 7, 1905. 848

Review of studies of Souriau (no. 880), and Brunetière (no. 842).

Estève, Edmond. Alfred de Vigny et Bernardin de Saint-Pierre; l'origine d'un symbole, à propos de La bouteille à la mer. RHL 20:817-27, 1913.   849

Influence of passage in Bernardin's fourth *Étude* on Vigny's *Déluge*, and of " bouteille de verre " passage in fifth *Étude* on *La bouteille à la mer*.

Feugère, Anatole. Rousseau et son temps. La littérature du sentiment au XVIIIᵉ siècle. X : Le disciple préféré du vicaire savoyard, Bernardin de Saint-Pierre. RCC 37 : 658-72, 1936.   850

Comparison of nature of S-P.'s and Rousseau's work. S-P. a precursor of picturesque exoticism.

Finch, M. B. and E. A. Peers. Bernardin de Saint-Pierre. *In their :* The origins of French romanticism. New York, Dutton [1920 ?]. p. 74-88.   851

Deals with elements of S-P.'s art and thought.

Gilbert, Pierre. Ce qu'on lit dans Paul et Virginie. RCI 14 : 558-98, Sept. 10, 1911. *Also in his :* La forêt des cippes. Champion, 1918. 1:73-102.   852

Catholic attack on suggestive sensuousness of work.

Haas, J. Ueber die Anfänge der Naturschilderung im französischen Roman : J. J. Rousseau, B. de St. Pierre, Chateaubriand. ZFSL 26:1-69, 1903.   853

Pp. 18-36 deal with S.-P. Careful analysis, with many quotations, of S.-P.'s art as painter of Nature.

Lafond, P[aul]. A propos du dénouement de Paul et Virginie. MerF 56:231-37, July 15, 1905. 854

Advances evidence to prove that historical prototype of Virginia was not drowned.

Lamartine, Alphonse de. L'homme de lettres; Bernardin de Saint-Pierre. *In his :* Cours familier de littérature, 1856-69. v 24, Entretiens CXL and CXLI, p. 513-667. 855

Inaccurate on account of Lamartine's reliance on Louis Aimé-Martin, (865). Valuable only as expressing the attitude of Romantic writers toward S.-P., called here " le traducteur de l'âme humaine..." (p. 666).

Lanson, Gustave. " ... la phrase pittoresque..." of Bernardin de Saint-Pierre. *In his :* L'art de la prose. Librairie des annales, 1909. p. 204-07. 856

Brief but sound analysis.

— Un manuscrit de Paul et Virginie : étude sur l'invention de Bernardin de Saint-Pierre. Rmois 5:399-431, Apr. 10, 1908. *Also in his :* Études d'histoire littéraire. Champion, 1929, p. 224-58. 857

Important article; account of S.-P.'s methods of literary composition, based on a manuscript in library of Victor Cousin. " On est stupéfait du prodigieux travail que cette nouvelle.... a coûté à son auteur." (p. 228).

Largemain, Lieutenant-Colonel, A. Bernardin de Saint-Pierre, ses deux femmes et ses enfants; documents inédits. RHL 9: 271-83, 448-68, 1902; 10:646-70, 1903; 11:654-69, 1904.

— Bernardin de Saint Pierre. RHL 12: 666-91, 1905; 16:135-57, 1909; 17:374-94, 1910. 858

These articles, based on documents in possession of the Saint-Pierre family, formed first attempt to correct some of the errors of Louis Aimé-Martin (no. 865).

Larroumet, Gustave. Origine et développement de la littérature romantique en France au XVIIIe et au XIXe siècle : Bernardin de Saint-Pierre. RCC 1¹:68-71, 101-104, 1892-93. 859

Follows general trend of criticism of author's work, emphasizing antinomy between his personality and his literary productions.

Leblond, Marius. Le rêve du bonheur dans Rousseau et Bernardin, éducateurs du XIXe siècle. *In his :* L'idéal du XIXe siècle, by Marius-Ary Leblond. Alcan, 1909. p. [35]-120. 860

Discusses S.-P.'s debt to Rousseau.

Le Breton, André Victor. L'exotisme dans le roman; Bernardin de Saint-Pierre. *In his :* Le roman français au XVIIIe siècle. Boivin, [1925 ?], p. 355-96. 861

Believes that S.-P. gives new meaning to word exoticism and prepares way for Chateaubriand and Pierre Loti.

Lemontey, Pierre Edouard. Étude littéraire sur la partie historique de Paul et Virginie avec pièces officielles relatives au naufrage du vaisseau le Saint-Géran. André, 1823. 66 p. (reprinted in Œuvres de P. E. Lemontey, 1829, 5:351-76). 862

Account of source of shipwreck incident taken from documents found on l'Ile Bourbon. 1823 edition contains copy of document.

Lokke, Carl L. France and the colonial question; a study of contemporary French opinion, 1763-1801. New York, 1932. 255 p. (Diss., Columbia). 863

Useful as showing geographical and historical setting of S.-P.'s *Voyage à l'Ile de France*, etc.

Lusch, Wilhelm. Chateaubriand in seinem Verhältnis zu Bernardin de Saint-Pierre. Heidelberg, Huber, 1912. 170 p. (Diss., Heidelberg). 864

Thorough treatment of subject, though containing nothing new. Cf. Ware (no. 886).

Martin, Louis Aimé. Essai sur la vie et les ouvrages de Jacques-Henri-Bernardin de Saint-Pierre. *In :* Œuvres complètes de Jacques-Henri-Bernardin de Saint-Pierre. Méquignon-Marvis, 1818. v. 1:1-271. 865

First published life of S.-P. For shortcomings of the work, see Souriau, (no. 880).

Maury, Fernand. Étude sur la vie et les œuvres de Bernardin de Saint-Pierre. Hachette, 1892. 675 p. 866

Good standard work on the author though lacking some of the documentary exactitude of Souriau. Valuable for study of background of Nature school. Lacks index and bibliography. For criticism

of work see Souriau, (no. 880). Introduction, XLIX-LVI.

Monglond, André.   Le vicaire de Jean-
Jacques. *In his :* Le préromantisme français.
See 818, v. 2, p. 428-43.   867

On whole, unsympathetic in tone,
emphasizing insincerity and egoism of
S.-P.'s character.

Mornet, Daniel.   Le sentiment de la nature
en France de Jean-Jacques Rousseau à Bernardin de Saint-Pierre; essai sur les rapports
de la littérature et des mœurs.   Hachette,
1907.   572 p.   (Diss., Paris).   868

Valuable for account of treatment of
nature before S.-P.   Indexes and bibliography.   See also same author's *Les sciences
de la nature en France au XVIIIe siècle.*
Colin, 1911, 291 p., for discussion of
background of nature cult.
Review : G. Lanson in RHL 15:168-70,
1908.

Pilon, Edmond.   Le roman de Madame
Poivre. RDM 103rd yr. 8th per. 18:368-83,
Nov. 15, 1933.   869

Sympathetic account of S.-P.'s affair
with Mme Poivre. The latter as prototype
of Marguerite. *See also* Souriau (no. 881).

Pradel de Lamase, Martial de.   La véritable Virginie de Bernardin de Saint-Pierre.
MerF 209:336-61, Jan. 15, 1929.   870

Examines claims of Mlle Mallet and
Mlle Caillou as originals for S.-P.'s
Virginie but attempts no solution of
problem.

Rauville, Hervé de.   Bernardin de Saint-
Pierre et Paul et Virginie. Runiv 41:747-54,
1930.   871

Account of wreck of Saint-Géran taken
from documents in *Archives maritimes.*

Rouch, J.   Le cyclone du Saint-Géran. MerF
199:714-20, Nov. 1, 1927.   872

Examination of scientific accuracy of
storm in *Paul et Virginie.* " Cette description de tempête... est loin d'être fantai-
siste, même dans ses moindres détails."
(p. 720).

Roule, Louis.   L'histoire de la nature vivante
d'après l'œuvre des grands naturalistes français : Bernardin de Saint-Pierre et l'harmonie de la nature.   Flammarion, 1930.
242 p.   873

Clearly written summary of S.-P.'s
pretensions to title of scientist. Roule

finds that in field of natural sciences
S.-P. was " vraiment un innovateur."
Chap. vi : *Le biologiste,* is noteworthy.
Probably best general work on relation
of science to imagination in S.-P., though
its value as reference work is spoiled by
lack of documentation and index.
Review : A. E. A. Naughton in RR
21:345-47, 1930.

Ruinat de Gournier, Jean.   Les fiançailles
de Bernardin de Saint-Pierre. RDM 74th yr.
5th per.   21:353-93, May 15, 1904.   874

Complete extant correspondence between S.-P. and Félicité published for
first time, with critical comments. Shows
his wife's unhappiness and presents her
husband in unfavorable light.   Souriau
(no. 880) finds the work " bien sévère
pour Bernardin " and thinks conclusions
of Ruinat de Gournier do not agree with
texts he cites.

Sainte-Beuve, C. A.   Bernardin de Saint-
Pierre. *In his :* Causeries du lundi, Garnier
n.d. 6:414-55; 514-39.   875

Review of the *Éloge* of S.-P. by Prévost-
Paradol containing discriminating appreciation of work of author, with thirteen
unpublished letters to Duval.   Review
dated Aug. 30, 1852.

— Chateaubriand et son groupe littéraire.
Calmann Lévy, 1906-13, 2 v.   876

In 8th lesson, v. I, p. 212-33, Sainte-
Beuve compares S.-P. and Chateaubriand
as descriptive writers.

— Bernardin de Saint-Pierre. *In his :* Critiques
et portraits littéraires. Renduel, 1836-39.
4:210-62. *Also in his :* Portraits littéraires.
Garnier, n.d. 2:106-40.   877

General article on S.-P.'s later life,
character, and talents.   Sainte-Beuve
believes that S.-P.'s treatment of nature
was compromise between traditional
Christian spiritualism and growing scientific cult of Nature.

Sarrailh, Jean.   Paul et Virginie en Espagne.
In his : Enquêtes romantiques; France-
Espagne. Belles-lettres, 1933. p. 3-39. 878

Account chiefly of Father Alea's translation and of Juan Francisco Pastor's
dramatic version.   " *Paul et Virginie...,*
conquiert l'Espagne et l'entraîne plus
avant dans le rêve et l'évasion." (p. 37).

Séché, Alphonse and Jules Bertaut.   Bernardin de Saint-Pierre et la Révolution

d'après des documents inédits. MerF
70:66-86, Nov. 1, 1907. 879

Based on documents in *Bibliothèque du Havre*. S.-P.'s relationships with official-dom during Revolution. Supplements material in Souriau (no. 880). Frequent quotations. The Revolution did not make S.-P. as rich as he had hoped, but it did not ruin him, as he asserts that it did.

Souriau, Maurice. Bernardin de Saint-Pierre d'après ses manuscrits. Société française d'imprimerie et de librairie. 1905. 423 p. 880

Valuable work containing scholarly introduction devoted chiefly to exposing weakness of Louis Aimé-Martin as literary executor of S.-P. Souriau accuses Martin of falsifying, changing, mutilating, sup-pressing and editing according to his fantasy. Condemns Barine (no. 885) and others for accepting Martin without consulting manuscripts. " ... Bernardin... ne ressemble ni à l'image... qu'Aimé-Martin a composée ni aux portraits plutôt sévères de la critique actuelle... L'homme vaut mieux que sa réputation, et l'artiste est encore supérieur à l'opinion qu'on s'en faisait jusqu'ici." (p. 419-20). Lacks index and bibliography. Footnotes refer to works cited in text.

— Une aventure de Bernardin de Saint-Pierre à L'Ile de France. RCC 9²:394-409, 1901. Reprinted, Société française d'imprimerie et de librairie, 1901. 18 p. 881

Story of S.-P. and Mme Poivre; S.-P. portrayed as playing pitiful though not hateful role. *See* Pilon (no. 869).

— Bernardin de Saint-Pierre, son caractère, ses qualités RCC 13¹:595-608, 707-16, 1904-05. 882

An answer to critics who found his *Bernardin de Saint-Pierre d'après ses manuscrits* too lenient with S.-P. Evidence shows that S.-P.'s good qualities out-weigh his bad ones.

Trahard, Pierre. [Bernardin de Saint-Pierre]. *In his :* Les maîtres de la sensibilité française au XVIIIᵉ siècle (1715-1789). *See* 832. 4:71-146. 883

S.-P.'s role in emancipation of senti-ment from bonds of reason and his assertion of æsthetic rights of true emotion.

Viany, Joseph. Les grands poètes de la nature en France : J.-J. Rousseau, Ber-nardin de Saint-Pierre, Chateaubriand. RCC 27¹:203-20, 1926. 884

Contains nothing new on these writers but is excellent general summary of contributions of each to descriptive art in prose. Viany believes that best of S.-P.'s talent was put into *Paul et Virginie*.

[Vincens, Cécile, " Mme Charles Vin-cens "]. Bernardin de Saint-Pierre, by Arvède Barine [*pseud.*]. Hachette, 1891. 187 p. (GEF) 885

Good popular treatment of subject following pattern of its series, based, however, on insufficient documentation. For criticism of work see Souriau (no. 880).

Ware, John N. The vocabulary of Bernardin de Saint-Pierre and its relation to the French romantic school. Baltimore, Johns Hopkins press; Paris, Les presses universitaires de France. 1927. 100 p. (Diss., Johns Hopkins). 886

Classified list of picturesque and tech-nical words with index, short bibliography and introduction of 13 pages. Author asserts his aim is " To show the contribu-tion of Saint-Pierre to the picturesque vocabulary of romanticism," particularly debt of Chateaubriand to author. As treatment of this theme, work is super-ficial and inadequate. For better treat-ment see Lusch (no. 864).

Review : P. Martino in Rcr 95:317, 1928.

Nicolas Edme Restif de La Bretonne
(Nos. 887-910)

ARMAND G. BÉGUÉ

Restif de La Bretonne, Nicolas Edme. La vie de mon père. Le Jay, ou à Neufchatel, 1779, 2 v. 887

Life story of his father, rather well-to-do farmer. Accurate and com-prehensive information on agriculture and on manners of peasants of Burgundy, together with genuine freshness in some charming and poetic passages. One of R.'s best compositions.

— Les contemporaines, Leipzig, Buschel, 1780-1783. 42 v. 888

Over 300 short stories composed and organized according to various *milieux* and professions; plots lack originality, but ways and manners of *bourgeoisie* and especially of lower classes well described. Engravings, rich in material details (shops, private houses, street life... etc.) constitute valuable source of information about time.

— La découverte australe, Leipzig, Paris, 1781, 4 v.   889

One of many Imaginary Voyages of century. R. sets up an ideal colony in some remote islands of Southern Hemisphere, where, through communism and eugenics, a happy and superior people is made to take root and develop. A plausible flying machine is described reminding one of Cyrano's imaginary voyages.

— L'andrographe, ou idées d'un homme sur un projet de réglement, proposé à toutes les nations de l'Europe, pour opérer une réforme générale des mœurs, et par elle, le bonheur du genre humain, Gosse et Pinet, La Haie, 1782. 492 p.   890

Offers plan, complete to every detail, of communist organization based upon agrarian economy and enlightened totalitarian government; luxury is forbidden, moral values help create strong social hierarchy; security, equality, and love bring happiness.

— Le paysan et la paysanne pervertis, ou les dangers de la ville. La Haie, 1784. 4 v. 891

R.'s best novel. Semi-autobiography showing evolution of two uprooted peasants, corrupted by easy pleasures and luxury which finally bring about their downfall; they are redeemed through remorse and virtue. Characters and situations are vigorous and convincing; novel reveals that curious contradiction between strong moral sense and equally strong tendency towards epicureanism which can be felt in R. himself, between his own immoral life and his well-meaning works.

— Les nuits de Paris, à Londres, et se trouve chez les libraires nommés en tête du catalogue, 1788-1794. 8 v.   892

Mosaic, made up of disconnected parts of unequal quality. Contains serious remarks, diatribes, social criticisms, and numerous small *tableaux* and scenes of Paris life (little people and *bourgeoisie* before and during Revolution). Unique documentation for historian of manners; but seldom concerned with real political or economic history. Less systematic, but more lively than Mercier's *Tableau de Paris*.

— Le thesmographe, ou Idées d'un honnête homme, sur un projet de réglement, proposé à toutes les nations de l'Europe, pour opérer une réforme générale des lois. La Haie,

chez Gosse-Junior et Changuion, libraires des États, 1789. 590 p.   893

Toned-down version of *L'andrographe*. Favors socialistic government which, while respecting more or less the political *status quo*, would secure for the people greater justice and security, through better social organization.

— Monsieur Nicolas, ou le cœur humain dévoilé, imprimé à la maison, 1794-1797. 16 v.   894

Huge autobiography, distorted at times by R.'s vanity, but often true to fact. Fine, minute psychological analysis, very modern in its sincerity; praiseworthy effort to retrace evolution of his life; wealth of documentation about country and city life. Pervading erotic obsession has often been noted by critics; but its historical and human values have not been sufficiently recognized. Written after Rousseau's *Confessions*, and before Casanova's *Memoirs*.

— Les posthumes; lettres reçues après la mort du mari, par sa femme, qui le croit à Florence, imprimé à Paris, à la maison; se vend chez Duchêne, libraire, rue des Grands-Augustins, 1802. 4 v.   895

In disorderly and absurd fashion, this imaginary voyage through all our planets in their various degrees of evolution and civilization illustrates Cosmogonic System already dealt with in *La philosophie de Monsieur Nicolas* (1796, 3 v.). Interesting social utopias; faith in progress, evolutionism, and "*métaphysique mithrique*," all systematically bound up with his moral and logical system.

— Mes inscriptions, journal intime de R. (1780-1787), Plon, 1889, 338 p.   896

These pages, discovered by Paul Cottin in 1888, are taken from R.'s authentic diary in which he put down for himself and not for publication, all the various states of his mind, health, pocket-book, all the little events of his daily life, every detail of his work and efforts as writer. More sincere, but less artistic than many modern Journals.

Bachelin, Henri. L'œuvre de Restif de La Bretonne; préface, notes et bibliographie. Éditions du Trianon, 1930-32. 9 v. 897

Excerpts are precious because R.'s works are not easily available (rare first editions), and are in many places tedious. This selection, made up mostly of autobiographical passages and observations about manners, artistically presented, and excellent for cultured public, cannot, however, satisfy scholars. It shows R. at his best as writer, amusing and picturesque. Yet it partly neglects R.'s important, but less entertaining pages of social and philosophical ideas.

Bégué, Armand. État présent des études sur Rétif de La Bretonne. Les belles lettres, 1948. 232 p. 898

Based upon previous critical studies up to 1945. Aims at objective, composite portrait of R. as human being, as writer, now original, now faithfully reflecting his time, as " reporter," accurate, but limited in scope, and as forerunner of social and literary trends. Bibliography of R.'s works, reprintings, and critical studies (p. 208-28).

[Bloch, Iwan]. Rétif de La Bretonne, der Mensch, der Schriftsteller, der Reformator. by Eugen Dühren, [pseud.]. Berlin, Harrwitz, 1906. 515 p. 899

Mere recitation of R.'s life, career, and ideas directly taken from his works.

Charpentier, Dr. Louis. Restif de La Bretonne, étude psycho-pathologique. Hip 2:577-604, Sept., 1934. 900

Pessimistic study of R.'s neuroses : eroticism, perversion, mythomania, paranoia... etc. This number of periodical devoted to R.

Cottin, Paul. Préface, notes et index to Restif's Mes inscriptions. Plon, 1889. p. i-cxxv. 901

Cottin's evaluation of R. as literary figure and as writer on social conditions (whose partial diary, 1780-1787 he had discovered in 1886) still seems fair and reasonable.

Ellis, Havelock. Restif de La Bretonne. In his : From Rousseau to Proust, Boston and New York, Houghton, Mifflin, 1935. p. 146-79. 902

Ellis is interested in R.'s complexes; however, he does not emphasize his abnormalities, but contents himself, through fine and delicate analysis, with arresting and objective presentation.

Etienne, Servais. Le réalisme et la réaction contre le conte moral—Laclos, Restif. In his : Le genre romanesque en France depuis l'apparition de la Nouvelle Héloïse jus-

qu'aux approches de la révolution. See 716, 389-407. 903

Very good pages explaining R.'s position and role in connection with literary trends of 18th century.

Funck-Brentano, Frantz. Rétif de La Bretonne; portraits et documents inédits. Michel, [1928], 424 p. 904

Biography based largely on R.'s Monsieur Nicolas, with few attempts to analyze or verify facts; unsafe approach in view of R.'s vanity and uncontrolled imagination.

Gérard de Nerval, Gérard Labrunie, known as. Les confidences de Nicolas (xviiie siècle); Restif de La Bretonne. In his : Les illuminés. Le divan, 1927. p. 111-348. 905

By softening all harshness and immorality, Gérard de Nerval gives us, in his graceful style, a charming and totally false picture of R.

Heine, Maurice. La vieillesse de Rétif de La Bretonne. Hip 2:605-33, Sept., 1934. 906

Study of R.'s neuroses.

[Lacroix, Paul]. Bibliographie et iconographie de tous les ouvrages de Restif de La Bretonne, by P. L. Jacob, bibliophile (pseud.]. Fontaine, 1875. 510 p. 907

Lengthy, minute, and excellent description of all of R.'s works. Still remains best reference book of its kind. But accompanying literary criticism is generally devoid of interest, and biographical notes contain mistakes and legends that are responsible for some of 19th century's distorted judgments about R.

Naughton, Alexander. Le tableau des mœurs dans les œuvres de Restif de La Bretonne. Presses modernes, 1929. 154 p. (Diss., Paris) 908

This essay consists essentially of a comparison of data given by R. on material aspects of his time with those given by other contemporary writers, especially Sébastien Mercier.

Palache, J. G. Restif de la Bretonne. In his : Four novelists of the old régime : Crébillon, Laclos, Diderot, Restif de La Bretonne. See 727. p. 142-266. 909

First American critic to consider R. Chiefly interested in his realism and dual personality.

Tabarant, Adolphe. Le vrai visage de Rétif de La Bretonne. Éditions Montaigne, 1936. 502 p.   909A

Biography is extremely rich and complete. Taharant's violently colored emotional approach brings out a weak and uncongenial R., and solves unfavorably some of doubtful facts and problems in R.'s life. Although extensively documented, this book makes lively and pleasant reading.

Trahard, Pierre. La formation sentimentale de Rétif de La Bretonne. *In his :* Les maîtres de la sensibilité française au XVIIIe siècle. *See* 832, 4:147-256.   910

Trahard determines with finesse and precision R.'s originality in connection with Rousseau's influential role in development of sensibility in literature.

Choderlos de Laclos
(Nos. 911-931)

J. ROBERT LOY

Laclos, Choderlos de. Les liaisons dangereuses avec une introduction de Maurice Allem. [La Pléiade, 1932]. 648 p.   911

Brief discussion of life and work, especially good for problem of prototypes for characters in novel, and for fortunes of novel. For prototypes see also A. Monglond in *Almanach dauphinois*, 1937 : *Clés dauphinoises des Liaisons dangereuses.*

— Les liaisons dangereuses avec introduction d'Edouard Maynial. Société les belles lettres, 1943. 2 v. in 1.   912

Best short *vue d'ensemble* on L., his novel, and text. Contains most complete bibliography on works of L., the author and his times, and the fortunes and criticism of his novel.

— Dangerous acquaintances, translated and with introduction by Richard Aldington. London, Routledge, [1924 ?]. 435 p.   913

Brief introduction by Aldington contains all necessary facts of L.'s life and one of best literary treatments of work. Aldington rejects ambition motivation of Dard *et al.* and sees in the *Liaisons* a sincere work written with intentions of reform. Bibliography of French editions of the novel, 1782-1920.

— Dangerous acquaintances, translated by E. Dowson and with preface by André Gide. London, Nonesuch press, 1940. 387 p.
914

The very unassuming introduction interesting for Gide's analysis of Valmont.

— De l'éducation des femmes, publié... avec une introduction... par E. Champion; suivi de notes inédites de Charles Baudelaire. Vanier, 1903. 156 p.   915

Interesting chiefly for random notes of Baudelaire on L. published here for first time. Essay itself is of limited value for comparison of women in the *Liaisons*.

— Lettres inédites de Choderlos de Laclos, publiées et avec introduction de Louis de Chauvigny. Société du Mercure de France, 1904. 331 p.   916

Both introduction and letters important for their depiction of L. as family man; Chauvigny sees in correspondence prime document for disproving generally accepted view of L. as false, ambitious, and libertine.

Arland, Marcel. Laclos et les liaisons dangereuses. *In his :* Les échanges. Gallimard, [1945]. p. 160-81.   917

Valid study of characters of novel and effect on them of chief actors, Valmont and Mme de Merteuil—image of evil incarnate. For Arland, it is not a novel of vice or *libertinage* but of evil itself —evil as human duty and mission; and, refuting Giraudoux (no. 922), he holds that it was not a happy accident in L.'s life.

Caussy, Fernand. Laclos. Société du Mercure de France, 1905. 365 p.   918

For most part, a less complete parallel of book by Dard (no. 919). Appendix contains *mémoire inédit* of L. on war and peace read before *Comité du salut public* —valuable as easily available document on L., royalist politician lately turned democrat.
Review : J. Ernest-Charles in RPL 42²:504-06, Oct. 14, 1905.

Dard, Emile. Un acteur caché du drame révolutionnaire; le général Choderlos de Laclos, auteur des Liaisons dangereuses (1741-1803). Perrin, 1905. 516 p.   919

Most complete study of L., the man, with special emphasis on the politician and man of the Revolution. In general, Dard explains all of L. by his Stendhalian ambition. Scholarly work, documented with citations of the period at expense of literary criticism. Appendix contains correspondence between L. and Mme Riccoboni.

Reviews : J. Gervais in Corr 220:832,
1905; M. Collière in MerF 54:583-84,
1905; J. Ernest-Charles in RPL 42²:504-
06, Oct. 14, 1905.

Doumic, René. Le vertueux Laclos. RDM
75th yr. 5th per. 25:445-56, Jan. 15, 1905.
                                          920

Doumic, writing on publications of
Chauvigny and Dard, sees quite definitely
in *Liaisons dangereuses* only *roman libertin.*

Friedrich, Hugo. Immoralismus und Tu-
gendideal in den Liaisons dangereuses.
RFor 49:317-42, 1935.   921

Excellent analysis of chief characters of
novel. Best study in German and one
of best in any language. Friedrich sees
L. writing *Liaisons* as nihilistic proof that
all human achievement—thought, deed,
and word—is never what it seems.
Immorality of Valmont and Mme de
Merteuil is really virtuous self-study
pushed to extreme. In common with *Le
rouge et le noir, Les liaisons* is analysis of
deception " *als einer bewusst gewollten
Existenzform.*"

Giraudoux, Jean. Choderlos de Laclos. *In
his :* Littérature. Grasset, [c1941]. p. 51-75.
                                          922
The final *remaniement* (cf. *Les Liaisons
dangereuses, préface de Giraudoux.* NRF,
1932; article in NRF : 854-70, Dec. 1,
1932; article in *Rmois :* 153-56, Jan.-Feb.,
1932), of Giraudoux' judgment of L.
Difficult article, a little exaggerated, with
general idea that L. is a minor Racine
from point of view of language and theme.
For Racinian theory of love, L. has
substituted eroticism.

Henriot, Emile. Choderlos de Laclos.
Runiv 21:497-507, May 15, 1925.   923
Rehash of Dard (no. 919) and Caussy
(no. 918) to conclude that L., the man,
still unknown quantity.

Lison, Lucien. Un précurseur de Talleyrand,
Choderlos de Laclos et l'alliance anglaise,
1789-90. ASP 19:581-96, 1904.   924
Detailed study of L., politician and
diplomat, and his attempt to guarantee
an English alliance via the *duc d'Orléans.*

Malraux, André. Laclos. *In :* Tableau de
la littérature française, XVII-XVIIIᵉ siècles.
Gallimard, 1939. p. 415-28.   925
Malraux sees the novel as battle waged
between vanity and desire but completely
in realm of mind; its chief importance is

as *roman de l'intelligence.* The new in
L. is that he paints a Don Juan and at
same time gives away his secret. Malraux
here makes L. spiritual ancestor of
Balzac, Stendhal, and Dostoievsky. Novel
lies between two domains of literature
—psychology and mythology—a mythology of *volonté et sexualité.*

Mann, Heinrich. Choderlos de Laclos. *In
his :* Geist und Tat, Franzosen, 1780-1930.
Berlin, Kiepenheuer, 1931. p. 9-30.   926
Good, concise essay on work and man.
Valid study of Valmont and Mme de
Merteuil in whom Mann sees complete
antithesis of every Romantic creation. He
finds the *Liaisons* only natural outcome
of ambition of L.—the one successful
achievement of that thwarted ambition,
and a masterpiece.

Maurois, André. Les liaisons dangereuses.
In his : Sept visages de l'amour. La jeune
Parque, n.d., p. 87-111, and in translation,
with title : Cynical love : Dangerous relations. *In his :* Seven faces of love. Trans.
by H. M. Chevalier. New York, Didier,
[c1944]. p. 85-109.   927
Essay, on whole, rather banal. Recommended only for its effort to see in
L. a moralist, reducing to absurd, in his
novel, concept of love-pleasure.

Palache, John G. Choderlos de Laclos. *In
his :* Four novelists of the old régime. *See*
727, p. 52-93.   928
Treatment of L., the man, is highly
readable *abrégé* of Dard (no. 919); rather
superficial discussion of novel and its
fortunes. Good introduction to subject
for readers limited to English.

Saint-Paul, Henri Ducup de. Essai bibliographique sur les deux véritables éditions
originales des Liaisons dangereuses. Giraud-Badin, 1928. 70 p.   929
Only scholarly work on bibliographical
problem relative to L. Supersedes article
by Arthur Symons in MerF 58:633-38,
1905. For confirmation of Saint-Paul's
hypotheses, see H. Saillard in BBB : 191-
92, 1928. For some corrections, see
P. Zorzanello in BBB : 237-39, 1928.

Thierry, Augustin. Les liaisons dangereuses
de Laclos. Société française d'éditions littéraires et techniques, 1930. 159 p.   930
Fairly modern treatment of literary man
and work. From point of view of style,
book is frequently irritating; from point

of view of criticism, often superficial. Incomplete index of editions and translations (English and Spanish) of the *Liaisons*, 1782-1929.

Weygand, Maxime. Vauban et Laclos, by Général Weygand. RDM 8th per. 18: 196-200, Nov. 1, 1933.   931

Interesting modern reaction to L.'s role in famous *affaire Vauban*.

Donatien Alphonse François, *comte, called marquis* de Sade
(Nos. 932-977)

ROBERT E. TAYLOR

Lely, Gilbert. D. A. F. de Sade. Pierre Seghers, 1948. 159 p.   932

Fine selection of S.'s writings preceded by excellent introduction based solidly on studies of Maurice Heine and by a useful outline sketch of his life. Thorough bibliography of S.'s works.
Reviews : G. G. in Gav, May 26, 1948; R. L. in GDL, June 26, 1948.

Nadeau, Maurice. Marquis de Sade, Œuvres. La jeune Parque. 1947. 421 p. 933

Perhaps best selection of S.'s writings, preceded by excellent 58 p. introduction. Outline of life as established by M. Heine also given. Selections, all with accurate indications of source, are chosen to illustrate S. as philosopher, sadist, moralist, man of politics, poet and visionary. Very important pamphlet, *Français, encore un effort si vous voulez être républicains*, given in entirety. Bibliography only of editions of S. used; no index. Supersedes selections by Balkis and Apollinaire (no. 935) and is not superseded by Lely (no. 932).
Reviews : M. Faure in Gav April 7, 1948; P. Klossowski in Par June, 1948, p. 60-63; A. Patri in Tro, 5:824-33, 1948; R. Stéphane in Nef, 43:121-23, 1948.

Amiaux, Mark. La vie effrénée du marquis de Sade. Éditions de France, 1936. 234 p.   934

Generally good biography but much of dialogue is imaginative or reconstructed and is, unfortunately, often sensational. Documentation scarce and sources almost never given. Some distortion of S.'s wife and mother-in-law in their favor. Good use of S.'s correspondence for psychological reconstructions. No notes; no bibliography; no index. Superseded by Desbordes (no. 947).

Apollinaire, Guillaume. L'œuvre du marquis de Sade. Bibliothèque des curieux, 1909. 324 p.   935

Though superseded by Nadeau (no. 933), work remains important for long introduction, largely biographical with many bibliographical references and interspersed with general comment on S. who was to become a god to later surrealists. (*See* M. Nadeau, *Histoire du surréalisme*. p. 33, 59-60). Bibliography of works of S. only.

Astorg, Bertrand, d'. [Sade]. *In his :* Introduction au monde de la Terreur. Éditions du seuil, 1945. p. 25-33.   936

Excellent comparative study of Saint-Just, S., and Blake. S.'s ideas and writings contrasted, too, with his own peaceful and humanitarian role during the Terror. Many valuable references to S. throughout book. A few bibliographical notes; no index.

Aulagne, Louis-Jean. Sade ou l'apologétique à l'envers. Psy 25:1245-64, 1948. 937

Worthwhile comments on S. as atheist, lyric stylist, educational theorist, and early sexologist. Well documented with pertinent and interesting footnotes.

Bataille, Georges. Le secret de Sade. Cr 15-16:147-60, 17:304-12, 1947.   938

Excellent article presenting S. as only great writer of Revolutionary period, and excellent review of P. Klossowski (no. 960), of J. Paulhan's edition of S.'s *Les infortunes de la vertu* (no. 969), and of the new Brussels edition of S.'s *Les cent vingt journées de Sodome*. *Secret* of S., no secret at all, is " revelation " of masochistic tendencies. Very good bibliographical notes.

Belaval, Yvon. Sade le tragique. CDS 285:721-24, 1947.   939

Points out essentially tragic personality of S., his " engagement personnel dans la contradiction vivante de la nécessité et de la liberté " (p. 722). Interesting comments on Baudelaire's interpretation.

Blanchot, Maurice. Quelques remarques sur Sade. Cr 3-4:239-49, 1946.   940

Penetrating remarks occasioned by new edition of S.'s *Idée sur les romans*, wherein author seeks to explain the paradox of freedom of individual in S.'s writings with latter's own complete enslavement. He sees S.'s literary creation as projection of his solitary prison life in which creation S. is " *plus Dieu que Dieu* " and so is called " *divin* " (p. 249).

— A la rencontre de Sade. Tmod 25:577-612, Oct., 1947. 941

Brilliant article treating S. and his conception of an *homme intégral* (p. 591), comparing different conceptions of his atheism, and analyzing his literary style " que l'on peut préférer à toute l'ironie de Voltaire et qui ne se retrouve dans aucun autre écrivain français " (p. 610). Well documented but sources not given. Some bibliographical notes.

Blin, Georges. Le sadisme de Baudelaire. Corti, 1948, 72 p. 942

Excellent study of S. as well as of Baudelaire. Detailed proof of S.'s influence on Baudelaire given for first time. Their differences clearly delineated. Many footnotes, all thorough and accurate. No index.

[Bloch, Iwan]. Le marquis de Sade et son temps. By Eugen Dühren [*pseud.*]. Michalon, 1901. 501 p. 943

First important study of S. and still best *ouvrage d'ensemble*, though superseded in certain biographical details by later discoveries. Richly documented, has served as source book for almost all later studies. Author badly prejudiced against French morals of 18th century, however, so general view and conclusions suffer. Excellent table of contents; thoroughly descriptive bibliography of 137 items that attempts completeness; complete index of names.
Review : E. Locard in AAcr 17:568-69, 1902.

Bourdin, Paul. Correspondance inédite du marquis de Sade. Librairie de France, 1929. 451 p. 944

Exceedingly important, indispensable work, despite certain lack of interest on part of Bourdin in his subject and despite his failure to include all letters he had at hand even if it meant sacrificing certain of his own comments. Volume is treasure house to all modern biographers of S.
Review : M. Heine in NRF 35:269-71, August 1, 1930.

Cabanès, [Auguste]. La folie du divin marquis [de Sade]. *In his :* Le cabinet secret de l'histoire, troisième série. Michel, [1905]. 3:417-90. 945

Appearing first in 1900, this article published many documents for first time, especially those from archives of hospital at Charenton. Still of real value and has been used as source by many later biographers. Far from supporting title, article refutes it. Good bibliographical notes.

Dawes, C. R. The marquis de Sade, his life and works. London, Holden, 1927. 240 p. 946

Most complete study of S. in English but author is more indebted to Dühren (no. 943) than he should be. Dühren's own comment : " ... an Englishman who had at least the grace to paraphrase my work, but with it the prudery that led him to expurgate all the vital issues." (*See* Bloch, Iwan, *Marquis de Sade's 120 days of Sodom and the sex life of the French age of debauchery*. New York, Falstaff Press, 1934. p. 182). Excellent bibliography of 112 items and full index.
Review : S. M. Ellis in FortR 128 (old series) : 572-73, 1927.

Desbordes, Jean. Le vrai visage du marquis de Sade. Éditions de la Nouvelle revue critique, 1939. 341 p. 947

Best biography of S. Many mysteries, such as S.'s trip to Italy with Louise before, and not after the Marseille *affaire*, cleared up for first time with thorough documentation and with newly-discovered letters. Throws new and unfavorable light on wife and mother-in-law of S. and exposes rather treacherous role of his lawyer. Some mutilated texts restored. Good bibliographical notes, but index lacking.

Flake, Otto. The marquis de Sade with a postscript on Restif de La Bretonne. London, Davies, 1931. 230 p. 948

Sound and reliable biography as whole but objectivity sometimes dulled by false moral tone of interpolated side remarks, and sources of information are rarely given. Based largely on Bloch (no. 943). No bibliography; good index of names.

F[rance,] A[natole]. Notice [on Sade]. *In :* Sade, D. A. F. Dorci ou la bizarrerie du sort. Charavay, 1881. p. 7-29. 949

Rather general, with many of inaccuracies of period; yet France, speaking as critic, is fair to S., recognizes his intelligence, critical judgment, and defends him against those who were comparing

him to Gilles de Retz. Some bibliographical notes.

Ginisty, Paul. Les lettres inédites de la marquise de Sade. Grev 3:1-31, Jan. 1, 1899.
950

Essential article and source for all
modern biographers of S. though not
always fair to him. Kind of biographical
sketch with quotes from Marquise's
letters for support; dates are unfortunately
avoided. Conclusion has become classic :
" Elle mourut à Échauffour... le 7 juillet,
1810. Elle avait largement payé son tribut
à la misère humaine " (p. 31).

Gorer, Geoffrey. The Marquis de Sade.
New York, Liveright, 1934. 264 p.   951

Fairly scholarly study of life and works
of S. One of best in English with ample
quotes from S. in support of all arguments,
though certain biographical details such
as account of S.'s journey to Italy are
inaccurate. Succeeds in main purpose of
debunking monster legend and does well
to establish S. as serious reformer and
philosopher. Remains, however, more
excellent popularization than original
study, and sources of information frequently not honored nor even mentioned
in bibliography. Complete references for
all citations; adequate table of contents;
no index.

Review : A. Guérard in HTB Jan. 6,
1935, p. 11; N. MacLaren in NSN 7:
808-10, May 26, 1934; TLS May 10,
1934, p. 346.

Heine, Maurice. Avant-propos, [on Sade].
In : Sade, D. A. F. Dialogue entre un
prêtre et un moribond. Stendhal, 1926.
p. 9-32.   952

Excellent introductory essay on S. as
atheist and representative of absolutes in
philosophy of 18th century. " Qu'on ne
perde pas de vue que Sade est un absolu
et qu'il va droit devant lui jusqu'au bout
de sa pensée, jusqu'à l'extrême limite de
ses conséquences logiques " (p. 17).

— L'affaire des bonbons cantharidés du marquis de Sade. Hip 1:95-133, 1933.   953

Author brings to light here for first
time all official documents relating to
Marseille scandal of 1772, thus making
this article an essential source for any
understanding of S.'s life. Evidence
which permits modern scholars to call S.
masochist is here.

— Le marquis de Sade et Rose Keller, ou
l'affaire d'Arcueil devant le parlement de

Paris. AMCP 13:309-66, 434-37, June, July,
1933.   954

Indispensable study publishing for first
time all documents relative to Rose Keller
affair. Letters of Mme Du Deffand and
diary of Hardy tend to be borne out as
reliable.

— Promenade à travers le roman noir. Min
5:1-4, 1934.   955

. Short study reflecting interest of surrealists in S. and in Gothic novel. Two
of original steel engravings for Juliette
reproduced. Other articles of some value
on S. throughout *Minotaure* and *Le surréalisme au service de la révolution.*

— Le marquis de Sade et le roman noir.
NRF 41:190-206, Aug. 1, 1933.   956

Excellent study of Gothic novel in
England and France, where author thinks
they developed independently. S.'s foremost position in this development is
clarified, and his critical opinions and
knowledge of English letters also studied.
" Si le roman de terreur ne peut être
proscrit de l'art littéraire, il est inévitable
que S. y regagne le rang de créateur
auquel il a droit " (p. 206).

Heine, Maurice. Le marquis de Sade.
Gallimard, 1950. 382 p.   956A

Collection of extremely important
studies on S. Much previously unpublished material from the late Heine's
private papers. Some reprinted articles.
Important sketch of S.'s life. Preface by
Gilbert Lely. Thorough notes ; no
index.

Reviews : C. Bo in Mser June 11,
1950 ; J. Brenner in PNor June 6, 1950 ;
in Obs June 15, 1950 ; J. Laprade in
Arts p. 2, June 23, 1950.

Hood, Robin [*pseud.*]. Le marquis de Sade,
libre penseur et non conformiste. *In :*
E. Armand, H. Treni, and R. Hood [all
pseud.] : Les utopistes et la question sexuelle.
L'en-dehors, 1936. p. 49-74.   957

Essay not without merit even if poorly
documented and rather sensationally presented. Treats S. successively as free
thinker, his life and works, his philosophic
and political conceptions. Little bibliographical comment and of no value.

Jacobus X. Le marquis de Sade et son œuvre
devant la science médicale et la littérature
moderne. Carrington, 1901. 480 p.   958

For biographical details this work is no more than a translation of Dühren. (*See* Iwan Bloch, *Marquis de Sade's 120 days of Sodom and the sex life of the French age of debauchery.* New York, Falstaff press, 1934. p. 182). It gives, however, full descriptions of S.'s novels and stories " qu'on peut lire " (p. 274) and makes no mention of his more important clandestine works.

Review : A. Cabanès in Cméd. 1902, p. 802-03.

Javelier, André Eugène-François Paul. Le marquis de Sade et les Cent vingt journées de Sodome devant la psychologie et la médecine légale. Le François, 1937. 81 p. (Diss., Paris.) 959

Excellent and thorough study in which author concludes that S. was precursor in many fields, most independent of 18th century philosophers, and founder of science of sexual psycho-pathology. Excellent bibliography of studies on S.; no index.

Jean, Marcel and **A. Mazei.** Sade, l'homme *and* Sade, le poète et le savant. In their : Genèse de la pensée moderne. Corrêa, 1950. p. 29-42. 959A

Aside from chapters on S. he is treated throughout book not only as a precursor but even as the creator of the original idea behind 19th century romantism. They argue that it was S. who put " l'univers dynamique, découvert au cœur de l'homme, dans un rapport étroit avec le monde extérieur " (p. 51).

Reviews : P. Lebesgue in Olib July 22, 1950 ; C. Mauriac in Tro p. 109-18, July, 1950 ; A. P. in Par p. 59-60, June, 1950.

Klossowski, Pierre. Sade mon prochain. Éditions du seuil, [1947]. 207 p. 960

Very personal essay, often mystical; lacking in objectivity. Citations not tied down exactly nor are characters clarified from whose mouths quotes are taken. Tendency to ignore novel *Aline et Valcour*, and ideas of S. before Revolution. Worth of essay is in its provocativeness; winner of *Prix Sainte-Beuve* in 1947. No bibliography; no index.

Reviews : G. Bataille in Cr 15-16:147-60, 17:304-12, 1947; M. Blanchot in Tmod 25:597-98, Oct., 1947; G. Picon in Fo 62:646-54, 1947.

[Lacroix, Paul]. Marquis de Sade. *In his :* Curiosités de l'histoire de France, by P. L. Jacob, bibliophile [*pseud.*]. 2nd ser.,

Procès célèbres. Delahays, 1858, p. 225-43. 961

Inaccurate but first attempt to get at truth behind trials of S. Used by most later biographers, is often source of their inaccuracies. However, reporting of judgments of S. by his contemporaries is of real value, and statement that S. was only " un aimable mauvais sujet " (p. 237) often quoted. Bibliography not possible at time; works of S. not mentioned.

Lely, Gilbert. Marquis de Sade, L'aigle, mademoiselle... Georges Artigues, 1949. xlvii, 222 p. 961A

First in promised series of hitherto unpublished S. letters and manuscripts, this volume is rich in prefatory notes and 78 pages of commentary. Tables ; index of names.

Reviews : C. Mauriac in Tro p. 139-47, March, 1950 ; M. Nadeau in MerF Feb. 1, 1950:304-8 ; L. Pierre-Quint in Obs May 25, 1950.

Magny, Claude-Edmonde. Sade martyr de l'athéisme. Cal, Oct., 1947, p. 41-44. 962

Interesting article not on rehabilitated S. but on 18th century rehabilitated by S. As Scève and Sponde throw light on Malherbe and the *Pléiade* so does S. illuminate and complement great writers of latter half of his century, author argues, and thus helps make period more real to us.

Manganella, Diego. Ombre nel tempo, la marchesa di Sade. NA 6th ser. 302:205-16, June 1, 1922. 963

Article perhaps more violent than subject, though comments on wife of S. are of value. No more than biographical sketch, works of S. not even mentioned, nor is his philosophy. Better part of article based on Ginisty (no. 950). No bibliographical notes or references of any kind.

Marciat, Docteur [*pseud.* of Cl. Tournier]. Le marquis de Sade et le sadisme. *In :* A Lacassagne. Vacher l'éventreur et les crimes sadiques. Masson, Lyon, Storck, 1899. p. 185-237. 964

Historically of great importance. One of first serious studies on S. Has been source of many later works, despite certain inevitable inaccuracies. Good bibliography though now outdated.

Masson, André. Note sur l'imagination sadique. CDS 285:715-16, 1947.   965

Interesting and unusual comments on Sade in whom " domine l'hyperbole d'une exigeante et saine sensualité " and on his censors " l'espèce la plus vaine parmi les hommes " (p. 716).

Monsour, Bernard. Sade et le roman. Ar 22:145-47, Dec. 1946.   966

Excellent article pointing out S. as critic who exercised " un esprit critique impitoyable et, le plus souvent, d'une stricte justesse " (p. 145). Article reviews his opinion of novels before him and his predictions " presque entièrement valable[s] " (p. 146) for course of those to follow.

Parrot, Louis. Sade blanc, Sade noir. CDS 285:707-14, 1947.   967

Excellent article comparing S. with Goethe and tracing his reputation down through admiring surrealists. Author sees various and contradictory interpretations of S. as indicative of his richness. Concludes that S. is " un des écrivains dont peut s'honorer une grande littérature " (p. 714).

Pastoureau, Henri. Sade, précurseur d'une Weltanschauung de l'ambivalence. Nef 7:39-46, 1950.   967A

Well documented article on the balanced passive and active algolagnic character of S.'s writing.

Paulhan, Jean. Sade, ou le pire est l'ennemi du mal. Lab, Aug. 15, 1945, p. 11.   968

Keen remarks on value of S. in light of world war and catastrophe. Biographical and critical comments on S. also of value. Idea advanced that S. is valuable counter-irritant or antidote who has made no one crueler and has even made some, Lamartine by his own confession, more tender.

Paulhan, Jean and M. Heine. Introduction and Notice to Sade. *In :* Sade, D. A. F. Les infortunes de la vertu. Éditions du point du jour, 1946. p. I-XLIII, 1-34.   969

Constitute very important introductions to a work of S., although introduction by M. Heine to S.'s *Cent vingt journées de Sodome*, Stendhal, 1931-5, 3 vols., I:IX-XVI, 3-82, also very important but difficult to find. Paulhan skillfully develops in this introduction idea that Justine and Juliette are really identical

and that they are S. Excellent bibliographical notes.

Review : G. Bataille in Cr 15-16:147-60, 17:304-12, 1947.

Picon, Gaetan. Sade et l'indifférence. Fo 62:646-54, 1947.   970

Thought-provoking article where S. is seen not as revolted theologian of P. Klossowski (no. 960) nor as great liberator of Apollinaire and of the surrealists (no. 935) but rather as man overwhelmed by indifference and yet driven on by frustration. Paradox is not resolved.

Praz, Mario. All'insegna del divin marchese (di Sade). *In his :* La carne, la morte e il diavolo nella letteratura romantica. Milan, Rome, Soc. editrice La cultura, 1930. p. 91-184.   971

Excellent and almost unique study of literary influence of S. Patient, scholarly treatment, complete documentation. Considerable influence shown on about thirty well-known authors of 19th century. Full bibliographical notes. Entitled *Romantic agony* in translation of Angus Davidson for Oxford Un. press, 1933.

Reviews : L. A. MacKay in CF 14:32, Oct. 1933; NR 76:193, Sept. 27, 1933; NSN 6:137, July 29, 1933; SRL 10:47, Aug. 12, 1933; H. Tronchon in RLC 13:214-15, 1933; W. Troy in NNY 137: 417-18, Oct. 11, 1933; TLS Jul 20, 1933, p. 492.

Sarfati, Salvator. Essai médico-psychologique sur le marquis de Sade. Lyon, Bosc & Riou, 1930. 187 p.   972

Thorough study of S., his biography, works, philosophy, personality, by trained psychologist and doctor. Concludes S. was man of intense imagination with mythomaniacal tendency and certain emotional disturbances, but possessing high intellectual qualities enriched by wide culture and originator of " quelques idées profondes, reprises depuis par nombre de philosophes et de savants " (p. 178). Short bibliography of value; no index.

Sérieux, Paul. L'internement du marquis de Sade au Château de Miolans. Hip 5: 385-401, 465-82, 1937.   973

Very complete account of S.'s stay at Miolans from Dec. 9, 1772, to May 1, 1773, superseding all other biographies for that period. Since S. spent in all over 28 years in prison this detailed account of one of them is most essential. Author cites numerous letters and documents from *Archives de Chambéry* not published before. Proof is ample here that it was his wife who effected his escape from Miolans.

Summers, Montague. The marquis de Sade, a study in algolagnia. *In his :* Essays in petto. London, Fortune press [1928?] p. 77-99. 974

Reliable though summary essay on life and importance of S., founded largely on H. Ellis. (*See* Havelock Ellis, *Studies in the psychology of sex.* New York, Random House, 1942. 1, part two : 105-09). Essay highlights S. as genuine precursor of modern sexology and " ... philosopher of no mean order " (p. 78). First appeared in 1920 in *British Society for the study of sex psychology.* No bibliography.

Tortel, Jean. Le philosophe [Sade] en prison. CDS 285:729-46, 1947. 975

Interesting comments on S., " l'enfant du siècle des lumières " (p. 734), as *philosophe*, with his opinions on calumny, robbery, rape, murder, and other crimes, but remarks of S. all taken from one work *La philosophie dans le boudoir* and hence do not always represent his complete opinion, sometimes not even his own opinion.

Uzanne, Octave. Préface sur l'œuvre de D. A. F. de Sade. *In :* Sade, D. A. F. Idée sur les romans. Rouveyre, 1878. p. ix-xlii. 976

Historically very important though superseded today in many biographical details. Bibliography of S.'s works and studies on him woefully incomplete but nevertheless of real importance as one of first such attempts.

Vincentiis, Gioacchino. Vite in margine, il marchese de Sade. Elo 2:314-25, Sept.-Oct., 1934. 977

Brief sketch, mostly of sensational episodes, but not without value. He reports the Victorien Sardou story of S. at Charenton throwing roses into the mud and laughing and concludes, as if Sardou had not concluded exactly the same thing : " In questo episodio è tutto il marchese de Sade " (p. 325). (Cf. *Cméd* 9:807-08, 1902). No exact bibliographical notes.

Minor Novelists
(Nos. 978-1018)

ARNOLD H. ROWBOTHAM

Arnaud, François Thomas Marie de

Baculard d'. Œuvres. Laporte, 1803. 12 v. 978

Arnaud, François Thomas Marie de Baculard d'. Les épreuves du sentiment. 5 v. (each story with separate title page and pagination). 979

Vol. I, L'Esclapart 1767 : *Fanni, ou la nouvelle Pamela ; Clary ou le retour à la vertu récompensée ; Lucie et Mélanie ou les deux sœurs généreuses ; Nancy ou les malheurs de l'imprudence et de la jalousie ; Julie ou l'heureux repentir ; Batilde ou l'héroïsme de l'amour.*

Vol. II, *Le Jay,* 1772 : *Anne Bell ; Sélicourt ; Sidney et Volsan ; Adelson et Salvini ; Sargines ou l'élève de l'amour.*

Vol. III, *Laporte,* 1795 : *Zénothémis ; Bazile ; Liebman.*

Vol. IV, no title page : *Ermance ; Pauline et Suzette ; d'Almanzi ; Makin ; Germeuil.*

Vol. V, no title page : *Daminville ; Henriette et Charlot ; Valmiers ; Amélie.*

Edition has engravings by Ch. Eisen which are excellent examples of late 18th century sensibility.

Inklaar, Derk. Romans et nouvelles. *In his :* François Thomas de Baculard d'Arnaud ; ses imitateurs en Hollande et dans d'autres pays. *See* 549, p. 85-130. 980

Inklaar accuses Arnaud of puerility, stupidity, and insincerity ; believes that his influence in Europe was extensive but not profound.

Johnston, Elise. Le marquis d'Argens ; sa vie et ses œuvres. Essai biographique et critique. [Imprimerie d'art Voltaire, 1929?] 213 p. (Diss., Paris.) *See* 3194. 981

Good general picture of life and thought of d'Argens. Very brief discussion of his fiction. Bibliography : p. 205-[213]. Index.

Barrett, Paul. Mademoiselle Javotte, ouvrage moral écrit par elle-même et publié par une de ses amies. 1757 or 1758. 982

Quérard and Michaud both give publication date as 1762, which is probably incorrect. In one edition the subtitle reads : " ouvrage peu moral... " etc. Discussed by F. C. Green in MLN 38: 327-29, 1923. The validity of his conclusion that the novel is " ... in the foremost rank of French realistic literature... " (p. 329) open to question.

La Harpe, Jacqueline de. L'abbé Laurent Bordelon et la lutte contre la superstition en France entre 1680 et 1730. Berkeley and Los Angeles. Univ. of California press, 1942. p. 123-224. (On cover : University of California publications in modern philology. v. 26, no. 2).   983

> Appendices containing list of author's works. Bibliography and index. Only separate work on this author.
> Review : H. C. Lancaster in MLN 58: 209-10, 1943. D. Mornet in RHL 49:86-88, 1949.

Cazotte, Jacques. Contes de Jacques Cazotte. Avec une notice bio-bibliographique par Octave Uzanne. Quantin, 1880. 218 p.   984

> Contains the *Mille et une fadaises, La patte du chat,* and *Contes divers.*

— Œuvres badines et morales, historiques et philosophiques de Jacques Cazotte. Bastien, 1817. 4 v.   985

> Best edition. Contains all of Cazotte's novels.

Shaw, Edward P. Jacques Cazotte (1719-1792). Cambridge, Harvard univ. press, 1942. 136 p. (Half-title : Harvard studies in Romance languages... Vol. XIX).   986

> Excellent summary of Cazotte's work in novel and of his relations with his literary contemporaries. Bibliographies : 119-30.
> Review : G. R. Havens in MLN 60: 276-77, 1945; A. Schinz in PQ 23:90-101, 1944.

Rocheblave, Samuel. Essai sur le comte de Caylus, l'homme, l'artiste, l'antiquaire. Hachette, 1889. 384 p.   987

> General work on life of author with chapters on his artistic and archeological contribution. Nothing concerning his novelistic work.

Godet, Philippe. Madame de Charrière et ses amis, d'après de nombreux documents inédits (1740-1805). Geneva, Jullien, 1906. 2 v. 511, 447 p., and Lausanne, SPES, 1927. 497 p.   988

> Thorough account of author's life and *milieu* with uncritical commentary on her novels. Annotated bibliography of works of author and index.

Sainte-Beuve, C. A. Madame de Charrière. *In his* : Portraits de femmes. Garnier [1869]. p. 411-57.   989

> General review of author's work with quotations. Sainte-Beuve finds her writings in best tradition of 18th century.

Woodbridge, Benjamin M. Gatien de Courtilz, sieur du Verger; étude sur un précurseur du roman réaliste en France. Baltimore, Johns Hopkins press, 1925. 214 p. (JHS, 6).   990

> General study of author (more commonly called Courtilz de Sandras) as precursor of realistic and picaresque novel, and his influence on historical novel in France. Detailed table of contents, but no bibliography or index.

Le Bourgo, Léo. Un homme de lettres au XVIIIe siècle : Duclos, sa vie, ses ouvrages. *See* 172.   991

> Pages 139-60 discuss his work as novelist. After analyzing his principal tales author concludes that, though justly forgotten today, they are valuable documents of French 18th century manners. Bibliography.

Sainte-Beuve, C. A. Duclos. *See* 174. 992

> Duclos mediocre but worthy adornment of literature of his time. Lacking in delicacy of sentiment and charm.

Toth, Karl. Woman & rococo in France seen through the life and works of a contemporary, Charles Pinot Duclos, translated from the German by Roger Abingdon. Philadelphia, Lippincott, 1931. 398 p.   993

> Detailed and illuminating account of Duclos' social *milieu.*

Elie de Beaumont, *Mme* Anne Louise (Morin-Dumesnil). Œuvres de Mme de Beaumont, de Mme de Genlis, de Fiévée, et de Mme de Duras... Lettres du marquis de Roselle; Mademoiselle de Clermont; La dot de Suzette; Ourika; Edouard. Garnier, 1865. 505 p.   994

> For a discussion of author's work *see* : Joachim Merlant, *Le roman personnel de Rousseau à Fromentin* (no. 725). p. 16-31.

Saillard, Gustave. Florian, sa vie, son œuvre. Toulouse, Privat. 1912. 322 p. (Diss., Toulouse).   995

> P. 159-167 deal with his prose and tales. Author shows that Florian's real talent as story-teller is marred by pomposity and artificiality of style. No bibliography.

Claretie, Léo. Florian. Lecène et Oudin, 1890. 238 p.   996

> Chapter III. *Le romancier,* 79-122. Brief discussion of Florian's work and style.

Fromaget, Nicolas. Le cousin de Mahomet, avec une notice bio-bibliographique par Octave Uzanne. Quantin, 1882. 282 p. 997

First edition was apparently dated 1720.

Genlis, Stéphanie-Félicité Ducrest de Saint Aubin, comtesse de. Les veillées du château ou cours de morale à l'usage des enfants. Maradan, 1804. 3 v. First ed. Lambert, 1782. 998

For most part Mme de Genlis' novels are on borderline between moral pedagogy and fiction.

Harmand, Jean. A keeper of royal secrets, being the private and political life of Madame de Genlis, with a preface by Emile Faguet. (Engl. trans.) London, Nash, 1913. 439 p. 999

Best general treatment of author. Part II is summary of her work as moralist, dramatist, and educationist. Work largely uncritical. Bibliography of author's works.

Bonhomme, Honoré. Madame la comtesse de Genlis, sa vie, son œuvre, sa mort (1746-1830) d'après des documents inédits. Librairie des bibliophiles, 1885. 138 p. 1000

Short and somewhat sketchy treatment of subject. Valuable material concerning life and social *milieu* of Mme de Genlis can be found in *Mémoires inédits de Madame la comtesse de Genlis sur le XVIIIᵉ siècle et la Révolution française.* 2nd ed. Ladvocat, 1825. 10 v. This work, however, should be used with care as it contains many errors.

Bruwaert, Edmond. Madame de Graffigny et Jean-Jacques Rousseau. Rheb 33rd yr. 8:567-92, Aug. 1924. 1001

Account of social and literary *milieu* of Madame de Graffigny.

Coderre, Armand Daniel. L'œuvre romanesque de Thomas-Simon Gueulette (1683-1766). Montpellier, Mari-Lavit, 1934. 183 p. (Diss., Montpellier). 1002

Gives summaries of principal tales, p. 79-138. Author considers Gueulette a very important intermediary between Perrault and Voltaire.

Gueulette, J.-E. Un magistrat du XVIIIᵉ siècle, ami des lettres, du théâtre et des plaisirs. Thomas-Simon Gueulette. See 573. 1003

Part II, chapter 1 deals with author's fiction.

Hamilton, Anthony, count. Contes, publiés avec une notice de M. de Lescure. Librairies des bibliophiles, 1873. 4v. (ed. *Petits chefs-d'œuvre*). 1004

This edition contains all five of Hamilton's tales.

— Mémoires de la vie du comte de Grammont, contenant particulièrement l'histoire amoureuse de la cour d'Angleterre, sous le règne de Charles II. Cologne, Marteau, 1713. 426 p. 1005

Original edition; for a list of other editions see 1006, p. 315-20.

Clark, Ruth. Anthony Hamilton (author of Memoirs of Count Grammont), his life and works and his family. London, John Lane, 1921. 362 p. 1006

Careful and scholarly work. Part II, chap. 3, deals with the *contes* and contains valuable discussion (p. 190-202) of the *romans prétendus historiques.* Index. Good bibliography.

Etienne, Servais. Le genre romanesque en France. *See* 716. 1006A

Summary of work of Loaisel de Tréogate, p. 362-84, *passim.*

Marmontel, Abbé Jean-François. Contes moraux. Garnery [1820]. 6 v. 1007

Most of *Contes* had appeared in the *Mercure.* For list of dates and early editions see Lenel (no. 1008), p. 565.

Lenel, S. Un homme de lettres au XVIIIᵉ siècle : Marmontel, d'après des documents nouveaux et inédits. Hachette, 1902. 572 p. (Diss., Paris). 1008

Best work on author. Chaps. VI and VII discuss the *Contes moraux,* Marmontel's predecessors and imitators. Chap. VIII discusses *Bélisaire* and *Les Incas.*

Pronger, L. J. Marmontel as a source of Stendhal. MLN 56:433-35, 1941. 1009

Smith, Horatio E. The development of brief narrative in modern French literature : a statement of the problem. PMLA 32:582-97, 1917. 1010

P. 585-89 summarize contribution of Marmontel.

Béclard, Léon. Sébastien Mercier, sa vie, son œuvre, son temps, d'après des documents inédits, Avant la Révolution, 1740-89. *See* 598. 1011

First volume only, second volume never published. Definitive account of life and works of M., discussing in detail his fiction. *Table analytique* but no bibliography.
Review : R. Doumic in RDM 73rd yr., 5th per. 16:444-55, July 15, 1903.

[Quentin, H.]   Un journaliste policier, le chevalier de Mouhy, by Paul d'Estrée, [*pseud.*].   RHL 4:195-238, 1897.   1012

Deals chiefly with life of De Mouhy : " ... le plus ennuyeux des romanciers du xviiie siècle." (p. 195).

Green, F. C.   The Chevalier de Mouhy, an eighteenth-century French novelist.   MP 22:225-37, 1924-25.   1013

Best account of novelistic work of author. Critic praises his extraordinary powers of observation. " De Mouhy is really the first French novelist to understand the mind of the bourgeois..." (p. 234).

— A forgotten novel of manners of the eighteenth century, La paysanne parvenue, by le chevalier de Mouhy.   MLR 18:309-16, 1923.   1014

Critic compares work favorably with novels of Marivaux.

Barba, J.-N.   Vie et aventures de Pigault-Lebrun publiées par J-N B(arba)*** Gustave Barba, 1836.   373 p.   1015

Uncritical life of author written by a contemporary. For modern estimate of Pigault-Lebrun see : G. Saintsbury, *A history of the French novel* (no. 729), 1:456-68. Saintsbury emphasizes importance of Pigault-Lebrun as one of first " professional " novelists of French literature.

Crosby, Emily A.   Une romancière oubliée : Madame Riccoboni; sa vie, ses ouvrages; sa place dans la littérature anglaise et française du xviiie siècle.   [Rieder], 1924.   190 p. (Diss., Paris).   1016

In series : *Bibliothèque de littérature comparée.* Most thorough treatment of subject. Bibliography. (For further discussion of author's work *see* Saintsbury, no. 729. I, 432-36 and Merlant, no. 725, Chap. I).

Sainte-Beuve, C. A.   Madame de Souza. *In his :* Portraits de femmes.   Garnier, [1869].   p. 42-61.   1017

Critic finds that works of author express best elements of society of 18th century.

Masson, Pierre-Maurice.   Une vie de femme au xviiie siècle : Madame de Tencin, 1682-1749.   *See* 301A, p. 130-72.   1018

Good bibliography and index. Above pages deal with novelistic work of Madame de Tencin.

CHAPTER V. LE MOUVEMENT PHILOSOPHIQUE

(Nos. 1019-1456A)

ALESSANDRO S. CRISAFULLI, LESTER G. CROCKER, FRANCIS J. CROWLEY, WILLIAM C. HOLBROOK, ANDREW R. MOREHOUSE, THOMAS E. OLIVER*, IRA O. WADE, and JAMES R. WADSWORTH

General Studies
(Nos. 1019-1080)

IRA O. WADE

Atkinson, Geoffrey. The extraordinary voyage in French literature from 1700 to 1720. Champion, 1922. 147 p. *See* 2517. 1019

General studies on utopic novels of Claude Gilbert, La Hontan, Max Misson, and Tyssot de Patot. Work is a continuation of author's thesis : *The extraordinary voyage in French literature before 1700*, New York, Columbia university press, 1920. Studies carefully made. Two of men treated have received fuller treatment : La Hontan in G. Chinard's edition of the *Mémoires de l'Amérique septentrionale*, and Tyssot de Patot in a thesis by D. R. McKee. These two latter works supplement but do not invalidate excellent preliminary work done by Atkinson.
Review : G. Chinard in MLN 37: 491-98, 1922.

— Les relations de voyages du XVIIᵉ siècle et l'évolution des idées; contribution à l'étude de la formation de l'esprit du XVIIIᵉ siècle. Champion, [1924]. 220 p. *See also* 2516. 1020

Excellent analysis of ideas of travel literature of 17th century very similar to those generally considered typical of 18th century thought. Arrangement of these ideas very satisfactory. Full bibliography of works used.
Review : A. H. Nethercot in MP 23: 242-43, 1925-26.

Aubertin, C. L'esprit public au XVIIIᵉ siècle (1715-1789). Perrin, 1889. 498 p. *See* 141, 156. 1021

Study of some of memoirs and correspondence of 18th century in effort to

determine trend of ideas, manners, and customs. Work, though out of date, picturesque and interesting.

Bachman, Albert. Censorship in France from 1715 to 1750. *See* 357. 1022

Work designed to fill gap between H. D. MacPherson's *Censorship under Louis XIV* and J. P. Belin's *Le commerce des livres prohibés à Paris de 1750 à 1789*, (no. 3). Treatment rather general.

Becker, C. L. The heavenly city of the eighteenth-century philosophers. New Haven, Yale univ. press, 1932. 168 p. 1023

Series of four lectures given on Storr's Foundation at Yale. Becker endeavors to show that 18th century philosophers had a religion which compared favorably in many respects with that of Christians. His paradoxical efforts to prove that in many respects the philosophical creed is the Christian creed are not entirely valid. Many generalizations in book could be contradicted. Nevertheless, facts, save in but few instances, are accurate; presentation, though not always profound, is fresh; and interpretation, paradoxical though it is, always provocative. Third lecture upon New History perhaps best. *See* no. 1743.

Belin, J. P. Le mouvement philosophique en France de 1748 à 1789. *See* no. 4. 1024

Best detailed treatment of philosophic movement in last half of 18th century. Author made ample use of *Collection Anisson-Duperron* and *Collection Joly de Fleury* at the BN, extensive use of literary correspondence of time. He was occupied not only with direction of movement but with its diffusion as well.

Bernard, Antoine. Le sermon au XVIIIᵉ siècle. Fontemoing, 1901. 608 p. 1025

Traces changes wrought in form, style, and content of ecclesiastical oratory of 18th century. Seeks causes for changes.

* Deceased.

Divides epoch into five periods : 1715-29 *(Oratoire)*, 1729-50 (return of Jesuits), 1750-1763 (impact of *philosophes*), 1763-1778 (absorption of philosophical doctrines), 1778-1789 (reaction against philosophical doctrines). Third period most important. In reality only two divisions are stressed : period of *Bulle Unigenitus* and quarrels of clergy; period of *philosophes*. Stresses turn from dogma to problems of morality (section on luxury important), to apologetics. Rather massive work, sometimes diffuse and not always clear-cut in judgments. Should be supplemented by Palmer (no. 1063) which is broader in scope.

Bertrand, Louis. La fin du classicisme et le retour à l'antique. Hachette, 1897. 425 p. (Diss., Paris).   1026

Best work which traces causes of revival of classicism in second half of 18th century, its insufficiencies and its connection with rise of romanticism. Parts of work have been superseded by later studies : for instance, chapter upon Chénier by study of Dimoff (no. 423). Still a valuable book.

Bouchard, Marcel. De l'humanisme à l'Encyclopédie. Hachette, 1930. 978 p.   1027

The sub-title : *L'esprit public en Bourgogne sous l'ancien régime* gives limits of this work. Bouchard, by a thorough control of archives of Dijon, has traced intellectual development of a provincial town which was an important center of culture from 1715 to 1760. In this way, has enlarged scope of E. Deberre : *La vie littéraire à Dijon au XVIIIᵉ siècle*, Picard, 1902, 413 p., and Emanuel de Broglie : *Les portefeuilles du président Bouhier*, Hachette, 1896, 349 p. Bouchard shows province of Burgundy preserving humanism of 16th century, enriching it with erudition of late 17th, and transforming it—or at least, helping to transform it—into *esprit encyclopédique*. Excellent model of French thesis, clearly organized, logically presented, and interminably long. Complete, solid, very erudite, with thorough control of material presented, and excellent index.

Bréhier, Emile. Histoire de la philosophie. Alcan, 1929. 6 fascicules in 2 v.   1028

Fascicules I and II of v. II deal with 17th and 18th centuries. Is standard history of philosophy of these periods, and corresponds to Lavisse in history. Extremely adequate for workers in 17th

and 18th centuries. Very strong in analysis of individual philosophies. Does not aim to trace movements of ideas. Excellent bibliographies (of French works mainly) at end of chapters.

Brunel, Lucien. Les philosophes et l'Académie française au XVIIIᵉ siècle. Hachette, 1884. 371 p. *See* 167.   1029

Attempt to measure role of Academy in philosophic movement. Period covered extends from 1746 to 1783, but there is rapid survey of Academy in early years of century. Three major academicians studied are Voltaire, Duclos, and d'Alembert. Documented from *Mémoires* and *Correspondances* of time. Packed with historical details, interlarded with anecdotes. Principal events are treated at some length. Should be consulted for events pertaining to Voltaire, Diderot, Palissot, Lefranc de Pompignan, etc. But work not very explicit in establishing role of Academy in movement of ideas from 1750 to Revolution.

Brunetière, F. Études critiques sur l'histoire de la littérature française. Hachette, v. 3, 1887.   1030

Collected essays of Brunetière upon great figures or knotty problems of French literature. Written with discernment after wide reading and intelligent thought, but with conviction and much dogmatism. Essays have aged with time, but still contain much of interest, and possess a freshness which Sainte-Beuve, Taine, and other 19th century literary critics seem to have lost. V. III of especial interest to students of 18th century. In reading these essays, it should be kept in mind that Brunetière, though exceedingly well-read in literature of the 18th century, did not approve of its ideas.

Bury, J. B. The idea of progress. London, Macmillan, 1920. 377 p.   1031

Attempt to trace genesis and growth of idea of progress from Bacon to Darwin. Introduction examines views upon progress before Bacon. About one half of work devoted to 18th century, chapters upon Fontenelle and Abbé de Saint-Pierre being especially good. Whole work very recommendable, both for facility with which it is written and accuracy of facts.

Cassirer, Ernst. Die Philosophie der Aufklärung. Tübingen, Mohr, 1932. 491 p.   1032

Volume in series *Grundriss der philosophischen Wissenschaften.* Capital work by one of outstanding historians of ideas. Attempts to put essential unity in movement of ideas rather than to present their full scope. Excellent chapters upon (1) pattern of thought in Enlightenment, (2) place of nature in thought of Enlightenment, (3) psychology and epistemology, (4) Religion, (5) conquest of history, (6) Political and social thought, and (7) fundamental æsthetic problem. Difficult work to grasp but well worth trouble.

Cherel, Albert. De Télémaque à Candide. *See* 63. 1033

Volume in series of J. Calvet, *Histoire de la littérature française,* by a distinguished scholar upon Fénelon (cf. *Fénelon au XVIII*e *siècle*). Traces aspects of French literature from 1699 to 1759. Properly speaking is not literary history, but rather series of chapters upon literary subjects. Early chapters on taste are simple but penetrating. Chapter on lyricism perhaps best. Chapters on movement of ideas less successful, perhaps because ghost of Fénelon moves unduly through whole work. Chapter on Voltaire unimportant. Nonetheless, a distinguished work which integrates lesser writers into literary tendencies of century. Short bibliography at end of chapters evidences good, solid judgment, and keen penetration.

Chinard, G. L'Amérique et le rêve exotique dans la littérature française au XVII*e* et au XVIII*e* siècle. *See* 789. 1034

Very carefully documented study in evolution of primitivistic thought and its relationship with general current of philosophic ideas in 17th and 18th centuries.

Cresson, André. Les courants de la pensée philosophique française. Colin, 1927, 2 v. 1035

Traces evolution of French thought from Montaigne to present. Especially helpful in two respects : traces evolution of philosophic thought, rather than that of philosophers, hence is more than history of philosophy. Places 18th century thought in its proper position in that evolution. Treatment general, but surprising amount of detail in compact two volumes. Bibliographies for further investigation.

Delbeke, François, *baron.* L'action politique et sociale des avocats au XVIII*e* siècle. Lou-

vain, Librairie universitaire, 1927. 302 p. 1036

More a study of education and social position of lawyers than of their political importance. Their influence upon philosophic movement which was promised in second volume, occupies only last chapter. A lengthy chapter discusses the Calas, Sirven, and La Barre cases.

Delvaille, Jules. Essai sur l'histoire de l'idée du progrès jusqu'à la fin du XVIII*e* siècle. Alcan, 1910. 761 p. (Diss., Paris). 1037

Thorough treatment of idea of progress, much more complete than that of Bury (1031), but more involved and not so interesting for general readers. Early chapters treat in considerable detail various points only casually mentioned in Bury (No. 1031). On other hand, Delvaille's study stops at end of 18th century, whereas Bury attempted to trace some implications of movement in 19th. No bibliography, although very thorough index of proper names. Review : L. Davillé in RHM 15:383-84, 1911.

Dorn, W. L. The age of enlightenment. *In his :* Competition for empire: 1740-1763. New York, Harper, 1940. p. 178-250. 1038

Synthesis of political, economic, and cultural history of middle 18th century cutting across national boundaries. Drawn for most part from secondary, rather than primary sources. Has many interesting general views, although they are not always substantiated by facts. Incidentally, facts not always accurate. Treatment particularly weak in origins of movement, and there is noticeable tendency to explain everything by " Reason " without explaining what reason is. Rather full bibliography of secondary works, selected with too little discrimination. Still, has good control over German works upon subject.

Dunning, William A. A history of political theories from Luther to Montesquieu. New York, Macmillan, 1905. 459 p. 1039

Second volume of three-volume *History of political theories.* Followed by volume : *A history of political theories from Rousseau to Spencer.* New York, Macmillan, 1920. 446 p. Excellent presentation of major aspects of political thinkers of 16th, 17th, and 18th centuries. Work less complete than Sée (no. 1072), but broader in scope. Each chapter followed by list of selected references, which now needs considerable revision.

Folkierski, Wladyslaw. Entre le classicisme et le romantisme. Champion, 1925. 604 p.
1040

Subtitle of this excellent work is *Étude sur l'esthétique et les esthéticiens du XVIIIᵉ siècle.* Folkierski has traced the æsthetic trend in literature from Dubos through Lessing. Not only are currents of æsthetic ideas traced, but works which contributed to this current are analyzed and position of each author in movement established. Folkierski's range of knowledge broad. English, German, Italian, as well as French æstheticism treated. Arrangement topical. Part I devoted to *Pensée générale du siècle;* Part II, entitled *Intervention d'une forte personnalité* analyzes Diderot's ideas on art and is best treatment ever accorded Diderot's æsthetics; Part III, devoted to Lessing, much shorter than other two parts and probably less important. Perhaps only serious defect of this treatise is too narrow conception of romanticism. Folkierski inclined to stress technical devices rather than psychological aspects. Question of rules seems to him more indicative of romanticism than *l'âme sensible.* None the less, most important contribution, far superior to T. M. Mustoxidi's *Histoire de l'esthétique française, 1700-1900.* Champion, 1920. 240 p.

Gillot, H. La querelle des anciens et des modernes en France. Champion, 1914. 610 p.
1041

Study of quarrel from Renaissance to *Parallèles* of C. Perrault. Second volume devoted to second phase of Quarrel and its extension to England and Germany was promised but has not appeared. Hence, this study only partially replaces work of Rigault (no. 1068). Gillot has, however, enlarged scope of Quarrel and given it more than purely literary significance. Book more thorough but less readable than Rigault.

Green, F. C. Minuet; a critical survey of French and English literary ideas in the eighteenth century. London, Dent, [1935]. 489 p. *See* 734, 2893.
1042

Excellent study of literary conditions in France and England in 18th century done by scholar familiar with both fields and not overly enthusiastic about rights and prerogatives of comparative literary critics. Work by no means tendentious,

is pleasant, fresh, and shows penetration not often met in 18th century studies. Only direction of all these facts, ideas, judgments not clear.

Hazard, Paul. La crise de la conscience européenne (1680-1715). Boivin, 1935, 3 v. *See* 2894, 3190.
1043

One of really significant recent contributions to 18th century studies. Hazard has undertaken to demonstrate two things: (1) ideas which we usually associate with period 1750-89 can be found in ferment in period 1680-1720, so much so that real crisis in thought which we attach to French Revolution occurred some three generations earlier; (2) this crisis was not peculiarly French, was European in scope. Hazard studies with great sympathy and much charm causes of this crisis and results produced, and since he has great ability as writer as well as competent scholarship, his work, though it depends for its information upon many dry monographs, is both new and interesting. Third volume contains excellent critical bibliography and justificatory notes. Work makes excellent introduction to Mornet's *Les origines intellectuelles de la Révolution française* (no. 45) which studies subsequent period 1715-89. Hazard's book should be read at least twice. Some paradoxes and generalizations upon first reading assume too much importance. Second reading reduces them to their normal position in treatise.

Review : *See* 2894.

— La pensée européenne au XVIIIᵉ siècle; de Montesquieu à Lessing. Boivin [c1946] 3 v. *See* 2895, 3191.
1044

Companion work to *Crise de la conscience européenne* (no. 1043). Written with same charm and deep understanding. Work divided into three parts : *Le procès du christianisme, La cité des hommes* and *Désagrégation.* Third volume contains excellent bibliography, extensive and up to date. Well-organized, well-presented. Shows some fatigue and some discouragement, but otherwise graceful and accurate.

Hearnshaw, F. J. C. (ed.) The social and political ideas of some great French thinkers of the Age of reason. London, Harrap, 1930. 252 p.
1045

Work comprises series of lectures delivered by various scholars at University of London in 1928-29. Lectures followed in each case by selected bibliography. Abbé de Saint-Pierre, Montesquieu, Rousseau, Voltaire, Helvétius, D'Holbach, Morelly, and Mably receive attention. Pleasant reading, somewhat uneven, and not free from error.

Lanson, Gustave. Questions diverses sur l'histoire de l'esprit philosophique en France avant 1750. RHL 19:1-29, 293-317, 1912.
1046

Inquiry into circulation of works in manuscript form during first half of century and their influence upon evolution of philosophic thought. Material which Lanson controlled for this investigation not at all complete. Nor are deductions which he makes always accurate. Point of view is none the less extremely interesting and Lanson's discoveries very important.

— Origines et premières manifestations de l'esprit philosophique dans la littérature française de 1675 à 1748. RCC 16¹:289-98, 450-60, 601-13, 721-34, 1907-08; 16²:1-15, 145-56, 241-54, 409-22, 481-93, 625-37, 738-52, 817-29, 1908; 17¹:61-74, 113-26, 145-57, 210-23, 259-71, 357-65, 499-508, 721-36, 1908-09; 17²:65-75, 211-18, 309-20, 433-42, 549-56, 657-66, 713-20, 796-804, 843-57, 1909; 18¹:22-32, 106-15, 257-66, 534-44, 734-43, 1909-10.
1047

Published notes of Lanson's course at Sorbonne; indispensable for any one beginning work in 18th century. Some of individual lectures should be supplemented by work done later by others, but general development of ideas treated still thoroughly sound.

Lanfrey, Pierre. L'église et les philosophes au dix-huitième siècle. Pagnerre, 1857. 382 p.
1048

Interesting, picturesque, and selective treatment of this subject. Work does not give vue d'ensemble but rather small sketches of important works, or of important events. Not useless to workers in field, but chatty, general, and diffuse. Should be supplemented by more recent, documented, and serious works of Monod (no. 1057), Belin (no. 1024), etc.

Laski, H. J. The rise of liberalism. New York, Harper, 1936. 327 p.
1049

Subtitle The philosophy of a business civilization gives central idea of this important work. Laski, eminent English economic historian, makes economic problem core of development of liberal ideas. This presentation not false, but one-sided. Work deals with economic theory from Renaissance to 18th century. Chapter III deals with Enlightenment. Laski understands English movement more thoroughly than he does French movement.

Laurent, François. La philosophie du xviiie siècle et le christianisme. Librairie internationale, 1866. 599 p.
1050

Little-known but meritorious work written from anti-catholic point of view, but containing surprising insights into philosophic movement. Should be read with caution. Author presents thesis that foundation of 18th century thought can be found in opposition of doctrine of progress to doctrine of infallibility and immutability of church. Struggle between these two forces shown in Book II. Altogether interesting presentation, exaggerated, and wordy, but fundamentally original and sound.

Lévy-Bruhl, Lucien. History of modern philosophy in France. Chicago, Open court, 1899. 500 p.
1051

Neat history of development of philosophic ideas in France from Descartes to naturalists. Part dealing with 18th century extends from p. 107 to p. 321. Treatment is by authors except for chapter on Encyclopédistes and another on Idéologues. Very readable book, succinct and well-arranged, but not to be compared with Cresson (no. 1035). Analysis of works treated excellent for beginners.

Lichtenberger, André. Le socialisme au xviiie siècle. See 147, 2097.
1052

Still best vue d'ensemble of movement, although much has been done since with various persons treated in work. (See for utopic novels : Chinard, von der Mühll; for Meslier : Petitfils, and Morehouse; for Montesquieu : Barckhausen; for Rousseau : Vaughan; etc.). Work has merit of sticking to texts. General conclusions need to be controlled with some care.

Lovejoy, A. O. The parallel of deism and classicism. MP 39:281-99, 1931-32. 1053

Interesting presentation of characteristics of deism (uniformitarianism, rationalistic individualism, appeal to consensus gentium, cosmopolitanism, antipathy to enthusiasm and originality, intellectual equalitarianism, rationalistic anti-intellectualism, and rationalist primitivism) as characteristics also of neo-classic æsthetic.

Ingenious and suggestive, but one-sided and very general.

Martin, Gaston. Manuel d'histoire de la franc-maçonnerie française. Presses universitaires de France, 1929. 278 p.   1054

Brief history of masonic movement in France. First two parts deal with 18th century. Last chapter of Part II treats influence of Masons upon Revolution. This was subject of Martin's thesis in 1927 (cf. : *La franc-maçonnerie française et la préparation de la Révolution*). Present work very adequate with its short summaries, small bibliographies (not overly trustworthy in titles of works), and supporting texts which occur at end of each chapter.

Martin, Kingsley. French liberal thought in the eighteenth century. Boston, Little, Brown, 1929. 313 p.   1055

Thoroughgoing and very accurate synthesis of movement of thought in century, by Englishman who was much interested in 20th century socialism. This tendency on part of author does not highly color his work, which is very readable. *See* no. 2105.

Martino, Pierre. L'Orient dans la littérature française au xviie et au xviiie siècle. Hachette, 1906. 378 p. *See* 2561.   1055A

Basic general study of subject. Voyages, commercial, political, and religious relations between Europe and Orient. Beginnings of oriental studies. Influence on fashions. Tragedy, comedy, and the novel in relation to Orient. Satire, philosophy, and fine arts. Cf. Dufrenoy, no. 704A.
Review : G. Lanson in RHL 13:545-47, 1906.

Monglond, A. Histoire intérieure du préromantisme français de l'abbé Prévost à Joubert. *See* 818.   1056

Lengthy and, for most part, well-documented study of period 1789 to 1815. When author attempts to study years preceding 1789 he is, except for case of Rousseau, who figures greatly in work, somewhat deficient. His thesis is, to say the least, original. Book, although original and using method not employed by Mornet, far from being useless. Distinction between Monglond's conception of romanticism and that of Mornet and his group lies in term *intérieure* in title of this work.
Review : D. Mornet in RHL 36:603-10, 1929. Review noteworthy.

Monod, Albert. De Pascal à Chateaubriand ; les défenseurs français du Christianisme de 1670 à 1802. Alcan, 1916. 606 p.   1057

Thorough treatment of religious movement in France in 18th century. Work essential, since most of works upon thought of 18th century are concerned with the *philosophe* and inclined to forget opponents. Results of this study based upon some 900 religious treatises. Monod defines broadly defenders of Christianity. Even Spinoza and Lévesque de Burigny find a place in movement. Work, though not easy reading, indispensable for student of 18th century.
Review : C. Charrot in RHL 26:446-75, 1919.

Mornet, Daniel. Le sentiment de la nature en France de Jean-Jacques Rousseau à Bernardin de Saint-Pierre. *See* 868.   1058

Study of changing attitude toward nature between 1750 and beginning of Revolution, and roles of Rousseau in these changes. Besides Rousseau current which Mornet studies carefully to show just what is new in his attitude and what he held in common with general movement toward nature, Mornet studies such influences as country house, walks in country, English and Chinese gardens, eclogue, mountains, sea, etc. Whole movement he treats as a sociological as well as literary movement. Also weighs carefully counter-movement, that is to say, contemporary criticism and opinions which still express classical attitude or protest against faddism or insincerity or exaggeration. Method, new at time of this work, can be applied successfully only by man like Mornet whose enormous erudition and thorough acquaintance with works of 18th century make him the leader of 18th century studies.

— Les sciences de la nature en France au xviiie siècle. Colin, 1911. 290 p.   1059

Sketch of popularity and diffusion of scientific studies in 18th century and problems (of social or psychological order) to which they gave rise. Thus, this is in no respect history of achievements of science. Well-documented, as all studies of Mornet are, with excellent bibliography of scientific treatises in 18th century.
Review : P.-M. Masson in RHL 19:944-51, 1912.

— Le romantisme en France au xviiie siècle. Hachette, 1912. 286 p.   1060

Carefully documented study of psychological aspects of pre-romantic movement. In a way, work completes Mornet's *Les sciences de la nature* (no. 1059) and *Le sentiment de la nature* (no. 1058). Third section of work entitled *La poétique romantique* elaborated in article *La question des règles au XVIIIe siècle. See* no. 409.
Reviews : C. Gauss in MLN 29:109-115, 1914; A. Monglond in RHL 20: 205-08, 1913. (Should be read in connection with Mornet's review of Monglond's no. 1056).

— La pensée française au XVIIIe siècle. Colin, 2nd ed., 1929. 220 p.   1061
Small, compact book of *Collection Armand Colin*, well-written and accurate. Short *Notices historiques* at beginning of sections which contain elementary facts. These *Notices* followed by interpretation and supplementary material. Whole work excellent. *Cinquième partie* entitled *La diffusion de l'esprit nouveau,* especially good.
Review : G. Chinard in MLN 42:124-25, 1927.

— Les origines intellectuelles de la Révolution française, 1715-1789. *See* 45.   1062
Long and involved work, very thorough and very complete. Much of its material drawn from Mornet's own investigations. Some, taken from detailed investigations of other scholars. Latter portion should be used cautiously, since, in spite of enormous labor expended by author, errors have inevitably crept in. Organization of all the massive material superb, interpretation excellent. Mornet has once and for all effectively laid ghost as to whether *philosophes* are responsible for French Revolution. But cf. H. Peyre, no. 2126. Has gigantic bibliography, well-ordered and complete.

Palmer, R. R. Catholics and unbelievers in eighteenth century France. Princeton, Princeton univ. press, 1939. 236 p.   1063
One of few books which have intelligently studied orthodox thought of century in effort to show that it was neither as foolish nor as insignificant as *philosophes* wanted to believe. Palmer proves conclusively that there was wave of enlightenment which permeated clergy also. Interesting study carefully presented, perhaps with slight " *anti-philosophe* " bias.
Reviews : G. R. Havens in PhR 50: 85-86, 1941; A. R. Morehouse in RR 32:219-23, 1941.

Pellisson, Maurice J. Les hommes de lettres au XVIIIe siècle. *See* 369.   1064
General synthesis dealing with relationship of man of letters and magistrate, book-publisher, actor, upper society, and public opinion. Picturesque, not complete, but interesting.

Picavet, François. Les idéologues; essai sur l'histoire des idées et des théories scientifiques, philosophiques, religieuses, etc., en France depuis 1789. Alcan, 1891, 628 p.   1065
Very detailed account of the culmination of doctrines and theories of Condillac, Helvétius, and Condorcet in period of Revolution, and their projection into 19th century. Work does not trace too well the contributions of Condillac, Helvétius, and Condorcet to movement. Presents well ideological synthesis of Revolution and studies minutely Destutt de Tracy, Cabanis, Volney, Andrieux, etc. Capital book for studying extension and transformation of 18th century ideas in 19th century. Should be supplemented by Emile Cailliet, *La tradition littéraire des idéologues,* a later work, distinguished by excellent foreword by Gilbert Chinard.

Pinot, Virgile. La Chine et la formation de l'esprit philosophique en France, 1640-1740. Geuthner, 1932. 480 p.   1066
An attempt to connect popularity of China with philosophic movement. Section on chronology of Chinese, particularly portion dealing with Fréret, well done. Other two sections are (1) relationship of religion and morals and (2) relationship of morals and government.
Review : A. H. Rowbotham in MP 31: 210-13, 1933-34.

Préclin, Edmond. Les Jansénistes du XVIIIe siècle et la constitution civile du clergé; le développement du richérisme; sa propagation dans le bas clergé, 1713-1791. Gamber, 1928. 578 p.   1067
History of complicated movement in ecclesiastical history of 18th century which involves Calvinism, Ultramontanism, and Jansenism. Good corrective to common assumption that Catholic religion offered unified front to philosophic movement. Well-documented work.

Rigault, E. Histoire de la querelle des anciens et des modernes. Hachette, 1856. 490 p.   1068

Classic, though somewhat outmoded, work upon Quarrel. What is not outmoded is analysis of works which appeared during Quarrel. These are excellent.

Rocquain, Félix. L'esprit révolutionnaire avant la Révolution, 1715-1789. Plon, 1878. 543 p.   1069

Work has given rise to much discussion. Rocquain, by studying *registres* of *Conseil d'État* and Parlements along with *mémoires* of D'Argenson, Barbier, Marais, etc., showed that religious struggles over *Bulle unigenitus* and political struggles between royalty and Parlements were directly responsible for Revolution. *Philosophes* were assumed in Rocquain's work to have played secondary role. Excellent work, well-documented, not always accurate in dates. Should be supplemented by Mornet's *Origines* (no. 45). There is (p. 489-535) a *Liste des livres condamnés de 1715 à 1789* arranged chronologically.

Rosenfield, Mrs. Leonora Cohen. From beast-machine to man-machine : animal soul in French letters from Descartes to La Mettrie. New York, Oxford univ. press, 1941. 353 p. (Diss., Columbia) *See* 1215.
1070

Systematic survey of impact of Descartes' views of animal machine upon writers and thinkers from 1640 to 1750. Full and factual, with detailed analyses of works. Extensive bibliography. General directions of movement clearly presented, but consequences not sufficiently treated. Reviews: F. Baldensperger in MLF 26: 168-70, 1941; G. R. Havens in MLN 57:681-83, 1942; H. Kurz in RR 33:84-87, 1942.

Roustan, Mario. Les philosophes et la société française au xviiie siècle. Hachette, 1911. 387 p.   1071

Good synthesis of position of *philosophe* in society of his time. Work a complement of Pellisson mentioned above (no. 1064). Roustan is a partisan of theory that philosophical ideas of 18th century produced French Revolution. Hence, a study is made of opinions of *philosophes* concerning royalty, King's mistresses, nobility, magistrates, *financiers, bourgeoisie*, and *tiers état*. *Idée force* theory of Roustan not so widely accepted at present time. For much more carefully documented treatment of same subject see D. Mornet, *Les origines intellectuelles de la Révolution française* (nos. 45, 1062).

Sée, Henri. L'évolution de la pensée politique en France au xviiie siècle. Giard, 1925. 398 p.   1072

Excellent treatment. After Introduction on concept of absolutism in 18th century and opening section on reaction to this concept and influence of English political theories, there follow very explicit and clear analyses of political thought of Montesquieu, D'Argenson, Voltaire, Rousseau, Diderot, Physiocrats, Helvétius, D'Holbach, Turgot, Mably, Condorcet, and Raynal. Final chapters on diffusion, scope, and influence of their political thought. Work well-documented for student from texts of authors treated. Small, carefully chosen bibliographical notes.
Review : D. Mornet in RHL 34:450-51, 1927.

— La France économique et sociale au xviiie siècle. Colin, 1925. 193 p. [Collection Armand Colin, 64].   1073

Clear and very useful exposition of the economy of France during 18th century. Careful study is also made of social classes, their composition, aims, and manner of living. For those who believe that responsibility for Revolution rests entirely with *philosophes*, this exceedingly well-documented little book offers a very interesting antidote. Picture which Sée presented more valid for period 1770-1789 than for earlier part of century. A tendency to shape whole picture in light of French Revolution. On the whole, a most interesting and valuable little book, succinct and well-written.

Smith, Preserved. A history of modern culture. New York, Holt [c1930-c1934]. Vol. II. The Enlightenment, 1687-1776. 703 p.   1074

Presentation of aspects of 18th century from science to art and music. Very full in treatment, not free from broad generalizations. None the less, best synthesis of its kind in English. Excellent bibliography.

Stryienski, Casimir. Le dix-huitième siècle. Hachette, 1920. 375 p.   1075

Volume belongs to collection *L'histoire de France racontée à tous* published under general direction of Funck-Brentano. Good, straightforward history of France during 18th century, less thorough than scholarly Volume VIII of Lavisse's *Histoire de France*, less controversial than

18th century section of Bainville's *Histoire de France*, and less anecdotal than interesting books of Perkins, *France under the Regency and under Louis XV*.

Tilley, A. The decline of the age of Louis XIV. Cambridge, University press, 1929. 458 p. 1076

Excellent appreciation of literature and thought of period 1687-1715, written with discernment and distinction. Reviews : M. F. Jerrold in MLR 25: 224-26, 1930; H. C. Lancaster in MLN 45:183-84, 1930.

Trahard, Pierre. Les maîtres de la sensibilité française au XVIIIe siècle (1715-1789). *See* 832. 1077

Study of growth of *sensibilité* from Regency to Revolution. Trahard distinguishes three phases of this growth : 1720-40, 1740-70, and 1770-89. Vol. I studies first period, treating Marivaux, Prévost, and Voltaire's theater. Vol. II, after the preliminary work with La Chaussée, Vauvenargues, and Duclos, devoted largely to Diderot. Vol. III treats Rousseau. Vol. IV terminates with Bernardin de Saint-Pierre, Laclos and Rétif de la Bretonne. Main value of whole work lies in insistence upon continuous, though not consistent, movement of *sensibilité* throughout century. Studies of individual authors treated separately are worth more than book's general thesis.

Vial, Francisque, and Louis Denise. Idées et doctrines littéraires du XVIIIe siècle. Delagrave, 1936. 436 p. 1078

Selections from writers of 18th century arranged to bring out literary ideas. Useful work for teachers working in literary criticism.

Wade, Ira O. The clandestine organization and diffusion of philosophic ideas in France from 1700-1750. *See* 57. 1079

Finding list, by titles and libraries, with analytical and critical notes, of manuscript treatises which were in circulation in France in first half of 18th century. Designed as aid to further research; each chapter aims to form basic documentation for a monograph.

Weulersse, Georges. Les physiocrates. Doin, 1931. 332 p. 1080

Simplified condensed account of *Le mouvement physiocratique en France de*

1756 à 1770. (*See* no. 2505, by same author.) First chapter an historical account of formation of school and its fortunes. Remaining chapters devoted to doctrine of school. Final chapter discusses its relations with general movement of ideas.

Pierre Le Pesant, *sieur* de Boisguillebert
(Nos. 1081-1087)

ANDREW R. MOREHOUSE

Boislisle, A. M. de. Correspondance des contrôleurs généraux des finances avec les intendants des provinces (1683-1715). Imprimerie nationale, 1874, 1883, 1897. 3 v. 1081

Volumes II and III contain important source material in correspondence of Boisguillebert with succession of finance ministers, Pontchartrain, Chamillart, and Desmaretz, covering years from 1700 to 1713. Analytical index.

— Boisguillebert et les contrôleurs généraux. *In :* Mémoires de Saint-Simon. *See* 94, XIV, appendix XII, p. 573-99. 1082

Boislisle pioneer in Boisguillebert studies. He discovered and published latter's correspondence with Louis XIV's finance ministers and wrote a *mémoire* in competition for prize offered by *l'Académie des sciences morales et politiques* in 1866, which was never published. In this article he utilizes both correspondence and that part of his memoir which dealt with Boisguillebert's life and the genesis and history of his economic writings; and as editor of Saint-Simon's *Mémoires* he corrects and elucidates remarks of Saint-Simon concerning Boisguillebert's career. A succinct, authoritative study.

— Mémoire sur le projet de dîme royale et la mort de Vauban. AMP 104:229-47, 522-51, 1875. *See* 1100. 1083

Although articles deal primarily with Vauban, Boislisle weaves into his narrative a number of quotations from Boisguillebert's correspondence (p. 531-37), which reveal his behaviour when his *Factum de la France* was proscribed and he was condemned to exile. Implications are that, if Boisguillebert was an economic genius, he was not to be compared morally with Vauban's heroic dignity in his time of trouble.

Cadet, Félix. Pierre de Boisguilbert, précurseur des économistes, 1646-1714; sa vie, ses travaux, son influence. Guillaumin, 1871. 442 p.   1084

First complete and authoritative study of B. to appear since his death, and important source for all subsequent studies. Discusses impartially B.'s life, his judgments on reign of Louis XIV, his economic theories, and his influence in 18th and 19th centuries. Shows parallels between his *Détail de la France* and writings of physiocrats. Full bibliography of B.'s printed and ms. works and of works about him given with brief annotations (p. 423-32). Valuable because it lists studies of B. from time of his death to 1870. Subject headings at top of every other page. Detailed table of contents. No index.

Daire, E. Economistes financiers du 18e siècle : Vauban, Projet d'une dîme royale. Boisguilbert, Détail de la France, Factum de la France, et opuscules divers. Jean Law, Considérations sur le numéraire et le commerce. Melon, Essai politique sur le commerce... Guillaumin, 1851. 932 p. (1st ed. 1843).   1085

In absence of critical editions, Daire's collection of B.'s important works (p. 150-416) valuable, useful, and well printed. Contains notice on his life and works and, in addition to above titles, text of B.'s *Traité des grains* and *Dissertation sur la nature des richesses*. Notes elucidate text. No index, but detailed tables of contents after each section devoted to particular writer.

Horn, I. E. Vie de Boisguillebert; écrits de Boisguillebert. *In his :* Économie politique avant les physiocrates. Guillaumin, 1867. p. 44-89, *passim*.   1086

Académie des sciences morales et politiques, which crowned his work in 1866, gives just appraisal : " Le travail de M. Horn est d'une haute importance... c'est un véritable traité d'économie politique; il a parfaitement montré ce qu'il y a de neuf et de hardi dans les idées de Boisguilbert au sujet de la richesse et de l'argent, de la rente du sol, du commerce des grains, du régime financier, et il a indiqué la filiation des principes posés par ce vigoureux penseur, et développés par les physiocrates... Son mémoire possède une valeur scientifique incontestable." (no. 1084, p. VI), *Appendices* give a number of source documents. No index.

Roberts, Hazel V. Boisguilbert, economist of the reign of Louis XIV. New York,

Columbia univ. press, 1935. 378 p. (Diss., Columbia).   1087

Full-length study of B.'s life, works, and economic theories, with frequent citations from works themselves, translated into idiomatic English. Author interprets B. as great pioneer, inventor of economic science, originator of *laissez-faire*, and precursor of physiocrats. Emphasizes similarities between B. and Adam Smith, who, she believes, was influenced by B.'s *Dissertation sur la nature des richesses* in conception and composition of *Wealth of nations*. Complete bibliography of works by and about B., p. 364-69. Index.

Review : E. A. J. Johnson in AER 26:720-21, 1936.

Henri, *comte* de Boulainvilliers
(Nos. 1088-1093)

ANDREW R. MOREHOUSE

Lanson, Gustave. L'influence de Spinoza à la fin du 17e siècle. RCC 16²:245-54, Apr. 16, 1908.   1088

See p. 245-53 for analysis of B.'s ideas concerning Spinoza. Lanson believes that B.'s ideas " sont orientées vers la destruction de la morale chrétienne et de la psychologie qui la fonde..." (p. 248). However, B. " est moins un spinoziste qu'un homme curieux de Spinoza, et qui se sert de Spinoza pour légitimer les attitudes nouvelles vers lesquelles il est porté..." (p. 249).

Simon, Renée. Henry de Boulainviller [*sic*]; historien, politique, philosophe, astrologue, 1658-1722. Boivin, n.d. [1939]. 702 p. 1089

Enlightening, erudite, and authoritative book, only thorough and complete study of B., who is depicted for first time in all facets of a gifted and original mind. All texts author could procure are analyzed and discussed in great detail and in relationship to ideas of age. Her study hence will stand as primary source book, because majority of B.'s texts in ms. and printed form not easily available. She was concerned primarily with B. in his works, and not in details of his influence. References to secondary works hence very scarce. Wade's study on B. (no. 1093) as fountainhead of Spinozism is unmentioned and should also be consulted. Miss Simon's conclusions at variance with Wade's. B. not essentially an encyclopedist, critical deist, and convert to

Spinoza, but 16th century humanist and 17th century *honnête homme*. No index.

— A la recherche d'un homme et d'un auteur; essai de bibliographie des ouvrages du comte de Boulainviller [*sic*]. Boivin, n.d. 51 p. 1090-1091

Miss Simon arranges systematically bibliography essential for preparation and completion of her exhaustive study on B. (no. 1089). B.'s works chronologically identified and arranged; titles of B.'s mss. found in important catalogues given with information, if any, as to present fate of works referred to. Lists and discusses attributed works and translations, and in final section gives her general bibliography, in which Wade's important work on B. (no. 1093) is omitted. Nevertheless, most complete bibliography in existence.

Spinoza, Benedictus de. Ethique; traduction inédite du comte Henri de Boulainvilliers. Publiée avec une introduction et des notes par F. Colonna d'Istria. Armand Colin, 1907. 374 p. 1092

Manuscript, edited and published by Colonna d'Istria, is first French translation of *Ethics*. Introduction (p. VII-XLIII) contains study of B.'s ideas in relation to those of Spinoza. B. translated the *Ethics* because " Spinoza apportait à Boulainvilliers un système complet, une conception du monde et de la nature humaine, une morale qui pouvaient prendre la place de la foi et de la morale chrétiennes " (p. XL). Hence, he found in him a powerful ally in his attacks against supernaturalism of Christianity and all metaphysical systems. B. is then identified as a precursor of Voltaire, Diderot, Helvétius, and d'Holbach. Appendices. No index.

Wade, Ira O. The works of Boulainvilliers. *In his :* The clandestine organization and diffusion of philosophic ideas in France from 1700 to 1750. *See* 57, 1079. p. 97-123. 1093

Chapter gives useful bibliographical information, summarizes B.'s religious and philosophical ideas, and reveals him primarily as a critical deist, a convert to Spinozism, and as the founder of a *coterie philosophique* with Mirabaud, Fréret, Dumarsais and others, forty years before the *coterie holbachique*. Bibliography, p. 326-27, gives references to location of B.'s manuscripts and to relatively few works about him.

Sébastien Le Prestre de Vauban
(Nos. 1094-1108)

ANDREW R. MOREHOUSE

The third centenary of V.'s birth (1933) was occasion of numerous articles on V. in journals and newspapers. For list, cf. Jeanne Giraud, *Manuel de bibliographie littéraire pour les 16e, 17e et 18e siècles français, (1921-1935). See* 30B., p. 182-83. 1094

Vauban. Abrégé des services du maréchal de Vauban, fait par lui en 1703, publié par M. Augoyat. Anselin, 1839. 31 p. 1095

Succinct chronological summary of V.'s military services written by himself, with additional comments by Augoyat. Indispensable as source work.

— Lettres intimes (inédites) adressées au marquis de Puyzieulx (1699-1705). Bossard, 1924. 139 p. Collection des chefs-d'œuvre méconnus. 1096

Introduction (p. 11-62) and notes by Hyrvoix de Landosle give biographical and background material for comprehension of the letters. Were written during Puyzieulx's ambassadorship in Switzerland and reveal primarily V.'s concern for Louis XIV's diplomatic policies that were leading to the War of the Spanish Succession. Number of letters deal with problems of Switzerland's neutrality in such a war; others are critical of Revocation of the Edict of Nantes. V. makes passing comments on his *Dîme royale* and on its favorable reception at court.

— Oisivetés de M. Vauban. 1097

Cf. Rochas d'Aiglun, no. 1106, V. I., for full extracts and p. 81-100 for full history of the *Oisivetés*. Were published under above title by Colonel Augoyat, 1842-1845, in three volumes.

Vauban, Sébastien Le Prestre de. Projet d'une dixme royale, suivi de deux écrits financiers... publiés d'après l'édition originale et les manuscrits. Avec une introduction et des notes par E. Coornaert. Alcan, 1933. 295 p. 1098

Dîme royale given in critical text, that of first edition, of 1707, essential for understanding of V.'s most important economic work. Introduction gives valuable information concerning purpose of publication, salient ideas, and subsequent fate of *Dîme royale*, with summary of V.'s life, brief history of

Louis XIV's fiscal troubles and of 17th century economic reformers, especially Boisguillebert. Complete bibliography (pp. XLII-LVI), covering MSS. and printed editions and works concerning *Dîme royale*. Contains detailed subject index and explanatory notes. Gives text of V.'s *Projet de capitation* and *Description géographique de l'élection de Vézélay*.
Review : B. Lavergne in REC 13:341-42, 1933-34.

Blomfield, *Sir* **Reginald.** Sébastien le Prestre de Vauban, 1633-1707. London. Methuen, [1938]. 216 p.   1099

Interesting account of V.'s life and works, based on Lazard (no. 1103) and Rochas d'Aiglun (no. 1106). More concerned with V. as engineering and military genius, than as economic reformer. Contains number of sketches, drawn by author, of fortresses built by V. Bibliography, p. 207-08. Index.
Review : Anon in JIBA 45:761, June 13, 1938.

Boislisle, A. M. de. Mémoire sur le projet de dîme royale et la mort de Vauban. *See* 1083.   1100

Important study, based on documents, conclusions of which have often been used by subsequent scholars. Boislisle gives history of origins, composition, printing, distribution, proscription, and fate of V.'s *Dîme royale*, with details concerning his tragic death. Boislisle believes that Louis XIV cannot escape responsibility for disgrace and death of V. P. 538-51 contain source documents, made up primarily of judicial interrogations of those suspected as involved in affair of *Dîme royale*, and undertaken by Marc-René d'Argenson in 1707 in his capacity as *Lieutenant-général* of police.

Daire, E. Economistes financiers du 18ᵉ siècle : Vauban, Projet d'une dîme royale... *See* 1085.   1101

Contains good readable text of *Dîme royale*, with notices on V.'s life and works, p. 1-154. Superseded, however, by Coornaert's critical edition (no. 1098). No index; but detailed table of contents.

Fels, Marthe de. Terre de France, Vauban. Gallimard. [1932]. 140 p.   1102

Brief and sincere tribute to V.'s greatness, conceived in lyric phrases (" et vous, Le Prestre de Vauban, vous faisiez de la France comme un autre des fables..."). She succeeds in portraying V.'s rare quality and integrity of character, and extent of his contribution to welfare of France. No bibliography, no index.
Review : J. Norel in MerF 240:643, Dec. 15, 1932.

Lazard, P. Vauban (1633-1707). Alcan, 1934. 659 p. (Diss., Paris).   1103

Fully documented, authoritative biography of V. with summaries and discussions of his works, by a Colonel of the French Army attached to Engineering corps. V. portrayed as engineer, economist, tactician, and above all, *honnête homme* of great integrity in an age of universal corruption. Remarks on *Dîme royale*, p. 563-74. Final chapter good study of V.'s character. Contains detailed bibliography of documents pertaining to V., his works, their location, and of works by and about him, with list of titles on science of fortification. Index of proper names, but not sufficient to cover adequately range of Lazard's work.
Reviews : C. T. Atkinson in EHR 50: 716-17, 1935; P. Feyel in RPL 74:744-45, Nov. 7, 1936.

Lohmann, Friedrich. Vauban, seine Stellung in der Geschichte der Nationalökonomie und sein Reformplan. Leipzig, Duncker and Humblot, 1896. 172 p.   1104

Criticism of views on V.'s position in history of economics. He is not adversary of mercantilism, not follower of liberal economic views, but mercantilist himself. The *Dîme royale* is primarily political, not economic work. V. argues in *Dîme royale* that wars, financial system and poor harvests are cause for decrease in population. Hence, it should be purpose of State to remove these evils.

Michel, Georges et André Liesse. Vauban économiste. Plon, 1891. 112 p.   1105

Succinct statement of V.'s economic ideas, valuable primarily as introduction. Has chapters on V.'s biography, economic and financial condition of France, culminating in summary of leading ideas in *Dîme royale*. " Ouvrage couronné par l'*Académie des sciences morales et politiques*." No index, but detailed table of contents.

Rochas d'Aiglun, Albert de. Vauban, sa famille et ses écrits, ses oisivetés et sa correspondance, analyses et extraits. Berger-Levrault, 1910. 2 v.   1106

" Ouvrage remarquable qui constitue une des meilleures documentations sur

Vauban... C'est un véritable monument historique qui doit servir de base et de guide à toute étude sur Vauban " (Lazard, no. 1103, p. 642). Contains much source material relating to V.'s life and career, bibliographical data, and extracts from his *Oisivetés*, which are a series of studies covering wide range of subjects from military, political, and colonial problems to conservation of forests and animal husbandry. V. 2 contains large extracts of his official correspondence with Louvois and successors, with biographical index of persons referred to in correspondence.

Review : Anon in RHEM 45:344-45, 1912.

Sauliol, René. Le maréchal de Vauban, sa vie, son œuvre. Charles Lavauzelle, 1924. 146 p.   1107

Succinct study by military specialist, editor-in-chief of *Revue d'études militaires*, and author of numerous works on military subjects. For biographical details Halévy is principal authority cited. Part 2 treats of military problems. *Dîme royale* hardly discussed. Readable but thin in comparison to Rochas d'Aiglun (no. 1106), Lazard (no. 1103), and Blomfield (no. 1099). Contains map of France in 1698 and sketches of fortifications. No index.

Vignes, J.-B. Maurice. Histoire des doctrines sur l'impôt en France. Les origines et les destinées de la dixme royale de Vauban. Giard and Brière, 1909. 525 p.   1108

Detailed, important, and interesting history of fiscal policies in 18th century France with Vauban's *Dixme royale* as central point of reference. Vignes takes its leading ideas (tax in goods, proportional tax and abolition of exemptions) and traces their 17th century origins, evolution and fate in 18th century up to Revolution, with references to 19th century. Contains full bibliography of 18th century publications on *Dixme royale* in text and notes, especially p. 81-105.

Pierre Bayle*
(Nos. 1109-1166)

ALESSANDRO S. CRISAFULLI

* This bibliography does not include studies on Bayle found in histories of French literature, histories of philosophy, encyclopedias and, with few exceptions, in other works of a general nature in which Bayle may be treated. A list of such studies can easily be compiled from bibliographies in the books annotated here. Omitted also are works not available for annotation, those not written in English, German, or Romance languages, and items which in the opinion of the compiler are of minor importance. All books, unless otherwise noted, are found in the Union Catalogue.

Works

Œuvres diverses de M. Pierre Bayle, professeur en philosophie et en histoire, à Rotterdam : contenant tout ce que cet auteur a publié sur des matières de théologie, de philosophie, de critique, d'histoire et de littérature excepté son Dictionnaire historique et critique. Nouvelle édition augmentée. La Haye (Trévoux), Compagnie des libraires, 1737. 4 v. folio.   1109

Most complete edition of *Œuvres diverses*. Includes all previously published correspondence and group of B.'s letters to his family, not published before. Many other letters have been published since 1737. For list of them, see bibliography in Courtines' book (no. 1123).

— Dictionnaire historique et critique de Pierre Bayle. Nouvelle édition augmentée de notes extraites de Chauffepié, Joly, La Monnoie, Leduchat, L. J. Le Clerc, Prosper Marchand, etc., publiée par A. J. Q. Beuchot. Desoer, 1820-24. 16 v.   1110

Definitive edition.

— Pensées diverses sur la comète. Édition critique avec une introduction et des notes, publiée par A. Prat. Cornély, 1911-12. 2 v. (Société des textes français modernes). Reprint : Droz, 1939.   1111

Ascoli, Georges. Bayle et l'Avis aux réfugiés. RHL 20:517-45, 1913.   1112

Reopens question of B.'s authorship of *Avis*. After reëxamining all external evidence, finds Bastide (no. 1115) wrong in attributing it to Daniel de Larroque, in spite of Delvolvé's (no. 1129) demonstration from internal evidence that work is B.'s. *See* also no. 1126.

— Deux pamphlets inédits de Pierre Bayle contre le Maréchal de Luxembourg (1680). Rliv 2:76-109, 1914-17.   1113

Edited with introduction and notes.

Barnes, Annie. [Bayle]. *In her :* Jean Le Clerc (1657-1736) et la république des lettres. Droz, 1938. p. 228-37. *See* 2426, 2773, 2931.   1114

Section on B. set off by spaces; contains an account of human and personal aspects of B.-Le Clerc dispute, aspects previously neglected in favor of philosophical and theological issues involved.

Bastide, Charles. Bayle est-il l'auteur de l'Avis aux réfugiés? BSHP 56:544-58, 1907. Issued also separately : Fontenay-aux-Roses, Bellenand, 1908. 19 p.   1115

Attributes *Avis* to Daniel de Larroque, supposing Larroque sent it to B. who retouched it before publishing it. Cf. Ascoli (no. 1112).

Betz, Louis P. Pierre Bayle und die Nouvelles de la république des lettres (Erste populärwissenschaftliche Zeitschrift) 1684-1687. Zürich, Müller, 1896. 132 p.   1116

Five parts of this study deal with founding of B.'s periodical, its contents, the nature, method, and style of B.'s criticism, success of publication, and its significance and influence. B. given credit for being first to combine in one publication purposes of both learned and frivolous periodicals, for being first popularizer of literary and philosophical questions and first independent journalist, and for having gained cosmopolitan reading public. Bibliography, p. xv-xvi. Certain aspects of B.'s journalistic activities treated more thoroughly in later works of Reesink (no. 1153) and Lacoste (no. 1145).

Bolin, Wilhelm. Pierre Bayle, sein Leben und seine Schriften. Stuttgart, Frommans (Hauff), 1905. 111 p.   1117

Written as introduction to Feuerbach's work on B., v. V of *Sämmtliche Werke*, Stuttgart, 1905 (no. 1135). Based on Desmaizeaux's *Vie*, it remains best biographical study in German.

Bouvier, Emile. Contribution à l'étude des sources du Siècle de Louis XIV. RHL 45:364-71, 1938.   1118

Shows that a passage in *Siècle* is from B.'s *Dictionnaire*, article Jean de Launoy, note F.

Brunetière, Ferdinand. Études sur le XVIIᵉ siècle; la critique de Bayle. RDM 3rd per. 112:614-55, Aug. 1, 1892. *Also in his* : Études critiques sur l'histoire de la littérature française. *See* 1030. 5th ser., p. 111-82.   1119

Study of B.'s intellectual character, analysis of his ideas, and estimate of his influence. Still useful in spite of

contributions and rectifications of later studies.

Casati, Ennemond. Quelques correspondants français de Shaftesbury. RLC 11: 219-36, 1931. *See* 3005.   1120

One of correspondents was B. whose three letters to Shaftesbury as well as other sources are utilized by Casati in treating (p. 221-25) B.'s relations with Shaftesbury. Same subject taken up more fully in Courtines' book (no. 1122), p. 123-34.

Cazes, Albert. Pierre Bayle, sa vie, ses idées, son influence, son œuvre. Préfaces de Camille Pelletan et Deluns-Montaud. Dujarric, 1905. 264 p.   1121

Introduction contains biographical errors (see Haxo, no. 1137); much of it drawn from Lenient's study (no. 1147), sometimes without specific acknowledgement (see Smith, no. 1163). Selections are good. *See* no. 1137.

Review : T. Schoell in BSHP 57:359-75, 1908.

Courtines, Leo P. Some notes on the dissemination of Bayle's thought in Europe. RLC 17:700-05, 1937.   1122

In Germany, Italy, Switzerland, the Netherlands, Spain, and Sweden.

— Bayle's relations with England and the English. New York, Columbia Univ. Press, 1938. 253 p. (Diss., Columbia). *See* 3033.   1123

Treats in successive chapters B.'s knowledge of England, relations with French refugees there, influence on English periodicals and their interest in him, his ideas and works; relations with British learned society; with Locke, Shaftesbury, and other English liberals. Three appendices give English references found in *Œuvres diverses*, and articles and references to Englishmen in *Dictionnaire*. Bibliography, p. 231-44, including works by B., references to B. and his works in English periodicals, modern works on B., general works, and manuscripts of letters, most complete available up to 1938, but marred by several inaccuracies and some incomplete references. Index, p. 245-53.

Reviews : C. Becker in PhR 49:475-76, 1940; D. F. Bond in MP 36:322-25, 1938-39; E. von der Mühll in FR 13:232-34, 1939-40.

— Bayle, Hume and Berkeley. RLC 21: 416-28, 1947.   1124

Shows that " from both the point of view of documentation and ideas, Hume culled much useful material from Bayle" and that Berkeley also drew from B., but that, being a churchman, he could not cite him definitely as an authority.

Cowdrick, Ruth Elisabeth. The early reading of Pierre Bayle, its relation to his intellectual development up to the beginning of the publication of the Nouvelles de la République des lettres. Scottdale, Pa. Printed by Mennonite publishing house, [c1939]. 216 p. (Diss., Columbia). 1125

Purposes of this study on B. are " to trace the steps of his mental evolution more comprehensively and systematically than has been done before; to make apparent the connection between his mental development and reading; to bring new evidence to bear upon doubtful points and to clarify mental background against which his later work was to stand out " (p. 149). Study consists of 13 chapters, one each for books read by B. An appendix, p. 160-62, contains an unpublished letter of B; bibliography used in study given on p. 163-68; and a " list of writings mentioned in B.'s *Correspondance*, 1670-1684, and referred to in this study," on p. 169-216. Review : G. R. Havens in RR 34:79-80, 1943.

Damiron, Jean P. Mémoire sur Bayle et ses doctrines présenté à l'Académie dans la séance du 21 août 1847. AMPM 6:319-447, 1850. 1126

Long study including biographical sketch previously published as *Notice sur Bayle* in AMP 13:36-67, 1848, brief analysis of B.'s principal works and detailed summary and analysis of his *Système ou Cours de philosophie*. Interesting only as one of earlier efforts to reach conclusions about two problems in B. : authorship of the *Avis aux réfugiés*, and definition of his *esprit philosophique*. Regarding the first, Damiron concludes that it cannot be proved that B. wrote the *Avis*, but that it can be supposed that he shared to some extent ideas therein expressed. *See* no. 1112. As to the second, he finds B. not consistent skeptic, but free thinker who vacillates in his convictions, and that best way to characterize him is to call him " un incertain," term which, however, has found no acceptance.

Delaruelle, L. A propos d'un passage de

La Bruyère. RU 15²:18-21, June-Dec. 1906. 1127

Shows that La Bruyère's criticism of theatrical character of Catholic worship is found also in several places in B.'s *Critique générale de l'histoire du Calvinisme.*

Delvolvé, Jean. Le principe de la morale chez Pierre Bayle. BCP 4:299-335, 1902. 1128

Finds that principle of B.'s morality is a rational transposition of Calvinistic theological dogmas of faith and grace. The substance of study is reproduced in Delvolvé's book (no. 1129), sec. III, chaps. III-IV.

— Religion, critique et philosophie positive chez Pierre Bayle. Alcan, 1906. 445 p. 1129

Solid, scholarly study which still remains best and most authoritative general work on B.'s thought and critical method. Four sections of Part I and first section of Part II treat in chronological order ideas in various works of B. in relation to his life, times and to preceding philosophies. Second and last section of Part II devoted to B.'s " *doctrines positives.*" Delvolvé concludes that great originality of B. and principal interest of his work lie in critical method he applied to questions of religion, metaphysics, and morality. B.'s critical method influenced particularly Montesquieu; B.'s ideas show striking relations to Kant's thought. Bibliography includes a chronological list of B.'s works, principal editions of *Dictionnaire* published after B.'s death, *Œuvres diverses*, correspondence published after the *Œuvres diverses*, the collections of letters still in Mss., and main works on B. published from 19th century on. Reviews : L. D[auriac] in AnP 17:246-48, 1906; G. Lanson in RU 15²:421, June-Dec. 1906; T. Schoell in BSHP 57:359-85, 1908; anon. in RMM 15: supplement, March 1907, p. 3-5.

Denis, Jacques François. Bayle et Jurieu. MAC 1886, 54-132. Also issued separately : Thorin, 1886. 1130

Relying to large extent on Lenient's work (no. 1147), Denis first discusses B.'s battle for tolerance, his paradoxes of the erring conscience and of an atheistic society, and defines B.'s historical skepticism. Then he analyzes Jurieu's ideas and concludes that B. is champion of freedom of conscience against religious intolerance, and Jurieu, champion of political liberty against absolute power. Delvolvé says in his book (no. 1129) that this contrast is only superficially true.

Deschamps, Arsène. La genèse du scepticisme érudit chez Bayle. Liége, Vaillant-Carmanne, 1878. 235 p.   1131

B.'s skepticism has its roots in skepticism of Renaissance, intensified by that of his own times, and explained also by B.'s intellectual and moral character and by circumstances of his life. Some ideas of Deschamps rectified by more modern works. *Bibliographie bayliste*, p. 31-41; *Notice sur les ouvrages de Bayle*, p. 223-35.

Douen, O[rentin]. Un opuscule de Bayle. BSHP 26:94-95, 1877.   1132

Attributes to B. a *Requête présentée au roi de France par les protestants qui sont dans son royaume, que l'on a contraints ci-devant d'embrasser la religion romaine. Imprimée le 3 septembre 1697.*

Dubois, Lucien. Bayle et la tolérance. Chevalier-Marescq, 1902. 155 p. (Diss., Paris).
                    1133
Thèse de bachelier containing biographical sketch and exposition of principal arguments in favor of tolerance found in B.'s *Commentaire philosophique* and *Dictionnaire*. Useful but not important.

Faguet, Emile. Pierre Bayle. *In his :* Dix-huitième siècle; études littéraires. Société française d'imprimerie et de librairie, n.d. p. 1-30.   1134

Similarities and differences between B. and *philosophes* on basis of their ideas and character. Still useful, though some of Faguet's judgments have been rectified by later scholarship.

Feuerbach, Ludwig A. Pierre Bayle. Ein Beitrag zur Geschichte der Philosophie und Menschheit. Neu herausgegeben und biographisch eingeleitend von Wilhelm Bolin. *In his :* Sämtliche Werke, Stuttgart. Frommans (Hauff), 1905, v. V, 436 p. (of which the first 109 are taken up by Bolin's introduction).   1135

First appeared with different titles in 1838 and in 1844, and revised, improved and with above title in *Sämtliche Werke*, v. VI, 1848. Important as first 19th century book devoted to B.'s theological and philosophical significance. Feuerbach's main purpose is to show eloquently that B. represents culmination of tragic contradiction between faith and reason brought on by Christianity. B.'s faith,

he finds, is a sincere act of self-denial, a voluntary restriction of reason, involving no hypocrisy, because : " Bei dem Heuchler ist das Äussere im Widerspruch mit dem Inneren, das Innere die Verneinung des Äusseren; aber Bayle war in sich selbst im Widerspruch mit sich. Er heuchelte nicht den Glauben; er glaubte wirklich, aber er glaubte in Widerspruch mit sich, mit seiner Natur, seinem Geiste " (p. 272).

Groethuysen, Bernard. Bayle. Mesures 3:75-85, Jan. 15, 1937.   1136

Penetrating analysis of B.'s character and ideas, all the more effective for humorous slant.

Haxo, Henry E. Pierre Bayle and his biographers. MLN 37:55-56, 1922.   1137

Corrects several errors in biographical introduction of Cazes' selections from B. (no. 1121).

— Pierre Bayle and his literary taste. PMLA 38:823-58, 1923.   1138

Wishes to correct general opinion of critics that B. lacked literary taste and appreciation and was too loose and careless in style and composition. Concludes that B. was " no mean literary man and critic." *See* Smith, no. 1164; and Lacoste, no. 1145.

— Pierre Bayle et Voltaire avant les Lettres philosophiques. PMLA 46:461-97, 1931. See 3105.   1139

Attempts to show that B.'s influence is found in works Voltaire wrote before his trip to England, works in which he already appears as apostle of tolerance, enemy of fanaticism and traditional dogmas, and champion of natural and rational religion.

Hazard, Paul. Les rationaux. RLC 12: 677-711, 1932.   1140

Pages 693-702, devoted to important aspects of B.'s thought, reproduced as second part of chapter on B. in *La crise de la conscience européenne*, no. 1043, 1: 131-154. Work also contains, 1:206-15, excellent analysis of B.'s *Pensées diverses.*

Henriot, Emile. Bayle pacifiste. *In his :* Courrier littéraire. XVIIᵉ siècle. Éditions de la Nouvelle revue critique, 1933. p. 92-98 (Les essais critiques, 36). First appeared in Le temps, 1928.   1141

Appreciation inspired by Constantinescu Bagdat's *Études d'histoire pacifiste,*

v. III, devoted to B. Finds it surprising that study does not mention peace plan of Genevan Goudet who sought B.'s opinion before publishing it. B. had some of his friends read manuscript, but did not do so himself. Later called work visionary.

— Bayle critique et pamphlétaire. *In his:* Courrier littéraire. XVIIe siècle. Éditions de la Nouvelle revue critique, 1933. p. 99-106 (Les essais critiques, 36). First appeared in Le temps, 1929.   1142

Occasioned by publication of Lacoste's work (no. 1145). Interesting for suggestion that *Conversation du maréchal d'Hocquincourt avec le père Canaye,* attributed to St.-Evremond, might be by B., for it reminds one of B.'s *Harangue de M. le duc de Luxembourg à ses juges.* See next item for more detailed development of this hypothesis.

— La conversation du maréchal d'Hocquincourt avec le père Canaye. *In his:* Courrier littéraire. XVIIe siècle. Éditions de la Nouvelle revue critique, 1933, p. 107-13. (Les essais critiques, 36). First appeared in Le temps, 1929.   1143

Suggests that B. himself might have written *Conversation* which he published in *Le retour des pièces choisies ou bizarreries curieuses,* Emmerick, 1686, but which has been attributed to St. Evremond and by Voltaire to Charleval. Reasons: ironical devices in *Conversation* are like those in *Harangue de M. le duc de Luxembourg à ses juges;* if the conversation is supposed to have taken place in 1654, it is surprising that it was not published until 1686. In fact it cannot date as early as that, for there is an allusion to death of Mme de Monbazon who died in 1658.

Jeanmaire, Emile. Essai sur la critique religieuse de Bayle. Strasbourg, Silbermann, 1862. 103 p. (Diss., Strasbourg).   1144

Submitted for degree of Bachelor of Theology. Still interesting as work of a Protestant who, in spite of B.'s religious criticism, recognizes him as a Protestant who " avait la religion dans le cœur, dans la conscience," but whose " esprit était irréligieux." B., author further concludes, was not against religion itself, but against " le caractère absolu attribué aux formes de la religion " (p. 99, 100). Jeanmaire's conclusion that B. was a Protestant has been accepted by Schoell (no. 1160) and Serrurier (no. 1161). Few bibliographical

notes; no index; references to quotations rarely include page numbers.

Lacoste, Edmond. Bayle nouvelliste et critique littéraire, suivi d'une nouvelle édition des pamphlets de Bayle contre le maréchal de Luxembourg. *In:* MARB 24, fasc. 3, 1929. 274 p. and 92 p. *Also:* Picart, 1929.   1145

Takes up again a subject already treated in part by Betz (no. 1116), and more fully by Smith (no. 1164) and Haxo (no. 1138). Supersedes them because of complete and detailed manner in which are analyzed B.'s technique, activities, and value as literary critic. But his conclusions substantially same as Smith's and Haxo's. *Note bibliographique,* p. 259-62; *Addenda et Corrigenda,* p. 263; *Table des noms cités,* p. 265-72.

Pamphlets on Luxembourg had been edited by Ascoli from a different manuscript (no. 1113).

Review: A. E. A. Naughton in RR 22:55-56, 1931.

Lanson, Gustave. Bayle. *In his:* Origines et premières manifestations de l'esprit philosophique dans la littérature française de 1675 à 1748. RCC 16²:629-37; 738-52; 817-29, 1908.   1146

Place and importance of B.'s ideas in development of *esprit philosophique.*

Lenient, Charles. Étude sur Bayle. Joubert. 1855. 248 p. (Diss., Paris). Imprint covered by label: Paris, E. Thorin.   1147

Most detailed and methodical study of B.'s skepticism, core of it consisting of five chapters, one each on religious, theological, philosophical, and literary skepticism of B. Nature and purpose of B.'s skepticism are thus characterized: " Passer de la contradiction au doute, du doute à l'indifférence, de l'indifférence à la tolérance, tels sont les degrés par lesquels il prétend conduire l'âme humaine et la société toute entière au calme parfait " (p. 22). No table of contents, index, or page references to quotations.

Lévy-Bruhl, Lucien. Pierre Bayle. OC 12:653-63, 1898.   1148

Excellent definition of B.'s position on relationship of revelation and reason. Raises question whether B. is sincere in insisting on impossibility of reason's accepting dictates of religious faith. Concludes that B., by emphasizing helplessness of reason, really aims at showing incomprehensibility and absurdity of revelation. Essay reproduced with a few stylistic changes in his *History of modern philosophy in France*, (no. 1051) in the chapter on *Bayle and Fontenelle*, p. 107-38, and also in French in *Les tendances générales de Bayle et de Fontenelle*, RHph 1:49-68, 1927.

Lichtenstein, Erich. Gottscheds Ausgabe von Bayles Dictionnaire. Ein Beitrag zur Geschichte der Aufklärung. (Beiträge zur neueren Literaturgeschichte, Heft VIII). Heidelberg, Winter, 1915. 151 p. (Issued in part as diss., Heidelberg). 1149

Bulk of this thorough study of Gottsched's edition of B.'s *Dictionnaire* devoted to an analysis of notes which Gottsched added as editor of German translation. Notes are grouped under three chapters : *Theology and philosophy, Literature, Nationalism*. In first group B. is attacked and refuted by means of Leibniz's principles; in second, B. serves simply as occasion for Gottsched to express his literary ideas; in last group Gottsched takes every occasion to bring out virtues of Germans and criticize foreign, epecially French, evaluations of Germans.

Review : A. Streuber in LGRP 39: 359-60, Nov.-Dec. 1918.

Palante, Georges. Deux types d'immoralisme. RPFE 65:274-85, 1908. 1150

B. very briefly treated as originator of that type of immoralism which consists in maintaining that influence of morality is insignificant on conduct of individual, because individual always acts according to his temperament.

Pillon, François. L'évolution de l'idéalisme au XVIIIᵉ siècle. AnP 6 (1895) — v. 15 (1904) : L'idéalisme de Lanion et le scepticisme de Bayle. 6:121-94, 1895; La critique de Bayle. 7:121-88, 1896; La critique de Bayle : critique de l'atomisme épicurien. 8:84-167, 1897; La critique de Bayle : critique du panthéisme spinoziste. 9:87-143, 1898; Les remarques critiques de Bayle sur le spinozisme. 10:55-156, 1899; La critique de Bayle : critique du spiritualisme cartésien. 11:65-131, 1900; La critique de Bayle : critique du théisme cartésien. 12: 85-154, 1901; La critique de Bayle : critique des attributs métaphysiques de Dieu : immensité, unité. 13:29-96, 1902; 1903; La critique de Bayle : critique des attributs métaphysiques de Dieu : aséité ou existence nécessaire. 15:51-131, 1904. 1151

Not as much on B. as titles would indicate. His ideas discussed only to extent needed by Pillon for tracing evolution of idealism. In some articles B. makes only a brief appearance.

Ray, Jean. Du Dictionnaire de Bayle aux Lettres persanes. RPFE 135:72, 1945. 1152

Suggests that idea of *Lettres persanes* might have come from a passage in B.'s *Dictionnaire*.

Reesink, Hendrika J. [Bayle, Pierre]. Index analytique des Nouvelles de la république des lettres. *In her :* L'Angleterre et la littérature anglaise dans les trois plus anciens périodiques français de Hollande de 1684 à 1709. Zutphen, Thieme, 1931. Also Champion, 1931 (Bibliothèque de la Revue de littérature comparée, 67. p. 167-96). 1153

Analyses of B.'s reviews of English books in *Nouvelles de la république des lettres*.

Robinson, Howard. The great comet of 1680; a study in the history of rationalism. Northfield, Minnesota ,1916. 126 p. (Diss., Columbia). 1154

Chapter VII, p. 91-106, devoted to B.'s *Pensées diverses* (no. 1111). Contains account of its publication, analysis of contents, and consideration of importance as attack against cometary superstition.

— Bayle the sceptic. New York, Columbia univ. press, 1931. 334 p. 1155

Comprehensive treatment of B. meant for general English public. Biography and analysis of works woven together. Last two chapters survey broadly extent of B.'s influence in England, Germany, and France. Robinson overlooked Ascoli's article on question of B.'s authorship of *Avis aux réfugiés* (no. 1112). Had he known it, he might not have been inclined to accept belief that work probably not by B. Appendix contains bibliography of writings of B., of related works appearing in B.'s time, of works on B. published 1706 to 1789, and of principal modern studies on B. (but with important omissions).

Reviews : H. E. Haxo in MLN 47: 277-79; H. Peyre in MP 29:495-97, 1931-32.

— Bayle's profanation of sacred history. *In* EJHR, p. 145-62. 1156

B. handled sacred history in same manner as ordinary history, using same standards of historic truth. Substance of essay incorporated in Robinson's *Bayle the sceptic* (no. 1155), p. 155-70. Lenient had already devoted short section of his study, p. 174-81, to same subject.

Saigey, Edmond. La théologie de Bayle. NRT 5:1-22, 1860. 1157

After examining all passages in which B. speaks of Christian dogmas, Saigey concludes that B. cannot be sincere in recommending submission of reason to faith, for " il s'est efforcé de démontrer l'incompréhensibilité, l'absurdité du christianisme, et quand il a abattu et mis en morceaux la statue, il la rajuste, la replace sur son piédestal, se prosterne devant elle et l'adore " (p. 21).

Sainte-Beuve, Charles-Augustin. Du génie critique et de Bayle. RDM 4th ser. 4:543-61, Dec. 1, 1835. *Also in his :* Portraits littéraires, nouvelle édition, Garnier, 1862. 1:364-88. 1158

Still stands as very good definition of B.'s critical attitude and method.

Sayous, Pierre A. [Bayle]. *In his :* Histoire de la littérature française à l'étranger depuis le commencement du XVIIᵉ siècle. Paris and Geneva, Cherbuliez, 1853. 1:221-379. 1159

B.'s biography, analyses of his works, and an account of his controversies. Sayous is another early 19th century scholar who tries to show that B. is author of *Avis aux réfugiés. See no.* 1112.

Schoell, Th. Pierre Bayle, à propos de deux livres récents. BSHP 57:359-75, 1908. 1160

Most of article devoted to critical review of works of Delvolvé (nos. 1128-29) and Cazes (no. 1121), but some space given to studies of Betz (no. 1116), Dubois (no. 1133), Deschamps (no. 1131) and Lenient (no. 1147). Criticizes Delvolvé for making B. positivist philosopher and Cazes for conceiving B. as anticlerical free-thinker. Schoell believes B. in no way hostile to religion in its " pureté tolérante," and that he was " protestant d'esprit " if not " de cœur."

Serrurier, Cornelia. Pierre Bayle en Hollande; étude historique et critique. Apeldoorn, Dixon, 1913. 224 p. Also Lausanne, Imprimerie coopérative de la Concorde, 1913. 1161

After two introductory chapters, dealing with B.'s life up to his arrival in Holland and with religious and political conditions there, author takes up chronologically works of B., analyzing and summarizing his ideas. Refuses, with Delvolvé (no. 1129), to call B. skeptic in un-qualified sense, and takes issue with Cazes (no. 1121) who presents B. as skeptic in selections from *Pensées sur la comète.* Agrees with Schoell (no. 1160) in classifying B. among believers, and sees him as sincere though cold Calvinist. Real importance of B. for Serrurier lies not in his religious belief, but in being penetrating moralist and psychologist who probes deeply into motives behind men's actions, and it is from this point of view that his works are analyzed. Does not accept Delvolvé's demonstration of B.'s authorship of *Avis aux réfugiés,* concluding that, since there are no traces of duplicity and hypocrisy in B., it is not right to attribute work to him. Serrurier did not know Ascoli's carefully reasoned study (no. 1112) on this question published in same year as her work. Bibliography, p. 213-15. Index of proper names.

— Pierre Bayle. RH 2:1316-42, May, 1916. 1162

Lecture given at *Cercle français* of University of Amsterdam. Contains nothing that cannot be found in study she published earlier, except reference to Ascoli's article (no. 1112) on the *Avis aux réfugiés* which was published after her study. Still convinced problem of authorship not yet solved, though admits that Ascoli opened new perspectives on question.

Smith, Horatio E. Bayle and his biographers. MLN 27:158-59, 1912. 1163

Shows that in introduction to Cazes' selections (no. 1121), are many direct borrowings without specific acknowledgment from Lenient's study (no. 1147).

— The literary criticism of Pierre Bayle. Albany, Brandow, 1912. 135 p. (Diss., Johns Hopkins). 1164

Gathers and studies all passages in B.'s works concerning books and authors, fiction, poetry, drama, oratory, history, scholarship, style, ancients and moderns, and B.'s conception of function of critic. Concludes that " with Bayle literature is hardly a matter of art and that he is not a man of artistic discernment " (p. 113), and that he had " little enthusiasm for the beautiful, and little understanding of it " (p. 121). Bibliography, p. 133-35. Review : K. Holl in LGRP 34:151-52, May, 1913.

Souquet, Paul. Pierre Bayle, libre-penseur et politique (1647-1706). Rfr 18:97-124, 210-31, 1890. 1165

Souquet, developing an idea of Lenient (no. 1147), defines and explains "baylisme" as "un système de contradiction au service d'un système d'indifférence" (p. 226). One of important results of this system is B.'s doctrine that individual conscience is sovereign in sphere of religion, but that it must respect conscience of other men and submit to secular authority, doctrine by which B. intended to bring about peace and liberty and do away with "l'oppression et la guerre entre ces trois termes : le spirituel, le civil, l'individu" (p. 224).

Sugg, Elisabeth B. Pierre Bayle, ein Kritiker der Philosophie seiner Zeit. Leipzig, Meiner, 1930. 88 p. (Forschungen zur Geschichte der Philosophie und der Pädagogik, IV Band, Heft 3). (Diss., Cologne).   1166

Defines B.'s position on important problems of philosophy of his times, especially those raised by Cartesianism. Discussion of B.'s skepticism, his attitude toward the Cartesian order of evidence, mechanical concept of nature and of material and spiritual substances, criticism of biological mechanism, of antinomies of space and motion, significance of problem of reality, and B.'s opinion in dispute concerning body-soul problem. Bibliography, p. v-vi, lists only one French author, Pillon (no. 1151). Absence of Delvolvé (no. 1129) particularly surprising.

Bernard Le Bovier de Fontenelle*
(Nos. 1167-1203)

ALESSANDRO S. CRISAFULLI

* This bibliography does not include studies on Fontenelle found in histories of French literature, histories of philosophy and, with few exceptions, works of a general nature in which Fontenelle may be treated. It omits also any study not available for annotation and items which in the opinion of the compiler are of minor importance. All books, unless otherwise noted, are found in the Union Catalogue of the LC.

Best editions of works :

Œuvres de Monsieur de Fontenelle, Nouvelle édition. Les libraires associés, 1758-66. 11 v.   1167

— Œuvres. Nouvelle édition augmentée de plusieurs pièces relatives à l'auteur, mise pour la première fois par ordre des matières, et plus correcte que toutes les précédentes. Bastien, 1790-92. 8 v.   1168

— Œuvres de Fontenelle (éditées par G.-B. Depping). Belin, 1818. 3 v.   1169

Libraires associés (no. 1167) and Bastien editions (no 1168) equally good as far as text is concerned, but do not contain certain works attributed to F. These are found in present edition which also includes some inedited letters.

— Histoire des oracles. Édition critique publiée par Louis Maigron. Cornély, 1908. 217 p. (Société des textes français modernes). Reprint : Droz, 1934.   1170

Text is that of first edition of 1686 with variants from later editions. Introduction deals briefly with Van Dale's two dissertations, F.'s interesting adaptation, refutations of Baltus, and defense of F. by his friends. Commentary shows changes F. made in originally clumsy text and quotes important objections by Baltus.

— De l'origine des fables (1724). Édition critique avec une introduction, des notes, et un commentaire par J.-R. Carré. Alcan, 1932. 103 p. (On cover : Textes et traductions pour servir à l'histoire de la pensée moderne). (Diss., Paris).   1171

Introduction shows importance of this work derived from *Sur l'histoire* which was first published in 1758 but which Carré dates 1678 (cf. below, annotation of his study on F. (no. 1175)). Text that of first edition in *Œuvres* of 1724; but includes also those portions of *Sur l'histoire* not identical with *De l'origine*. Parts of two texts that coincide are distinguished from those which are entirely new by device of lines in left margin. Thorough commentary (longer than text) gives probable sources of F.'s ideas and shows their connection with his other works.

Boulan, Emile. Fontenelle. *In his :* Figures du dix-huitième siècle. Les sages : Fontenelle et Madame de Lambert. *See* 265, p. 3-110.   1172

Lengthy portrait of F. (p. 3-60), followed (p. 71-110) by four selections from his works, each presented with short introduction. Though drawn mostly from well-known materials, Boulan's portrait is interesting and different because of his stress on certain traits and because he gives to F.'s figure more relief by comparing and contrasting him with other French writers.

Breinbauer, Siglinde Anne. Bedingungssätze bei Fontenelle. Würzburg, Mayr, 1937. 89 p. (Diss., Munich). 1173

Shows extent to which F. tended toward hypothetical thinking and how through this tendency he revealed his whole individuality.

Brunetière, Ferdinand. Études sur le XVIIIe siècle; la formation de l'idée de progrès, RDM 3rd per. 113:881-920, Oct. 15, 1892. *Also in his :* Études critiques sur l'histoire de la littérature française. Hachette, 1893. 5th ser., p. 183-250. 1174

Pages (197-201, and 237-47) on F. show his belief in progress based on ideas of stability of laws of nature and solidarity of sciences. In formulating and propagating these ideas, F. contributed greatly to formation of idea of progress.

Carré, Jean-R. La philosophie de Fontenelle ou Le sourire de la raison. Alcan, 1932, 705 p. (Diss., Paris). (On cover : Bibliothèque de philosophie contemporaine). 1175

Utilizing every scrap of F.'s writings and all other available evidence, Carré skillfully weaves into a philosophical system F.'s ideas on man, society, nature, and God; indicates probable sources of his ideas and shows importance these ideas may have had in F.'s time. Remarkable fact about F.'s philosophy is that its fundamental principles go back probably to 1680, and are certainly in his possession by 1686. There is, therefore, no real evolution in his thought. This conclusion depends on fact that important ideas in *De l'origine des fables* (1724) are found in *Sur l'histoire* which Carré, from internal evidence, dates as far back as 1678. This would make F. founder of comparative method in history of religions. Index of authors and principal names. Bibliographical notes. Reviews : Anon. in RMM 39 : supplément, Oct.-Dec. 1932, p. 6-7; E. D. in RP ns 4:90-91, 1933; G. Lafeuille in RPFE 116:279-85, 1933.

Charma, Antoine. Biographie de Fontenelle. Extrait des Mémoires de l'Académie des sciences et belles-lettres de Caen. Caen, Hardel, 1846. 96 p. 1176

Drawing from Trublet's *Mémoires* and many other contemporary sources, Charma sketches life of F., dealing briefly with various aspects of his work. Most of material relegated to notes which, with bibliographical references, take up last half of book. But Charma's work has been superseded in all respects by studies of Laborde-Milaà (no. 1188), Maigron (no. 1194) and Carré (no. 1175).

Chaumeix, André. Un précurseur de la littérature scientifique (Fontenelle). Rheb 19^{10}:512-31, Oct. 22, 1910. 1177

Treatment of F. skeptic, popularizer of science, and precursor of modern science, inspired by books of Laborde-Milaà (no. 1188), Maigron (no. 1194), and Potez (no. 1197). Exaggerates F.'s ability to interpret scientific thought of his day.

Delavigne, Ferdinand. Études sur le XVIIIe siècle. Fontenelle. MAT 7th ser. 8:109-20, 1876. Reprinted : Toulouse, Douladoure, 1876. 12 p. 1178

Character sketch of F., emphasizing warmer and more generous side of man.

Doumic, René. Fontenelle. RDM 5th per. 77:444-55, Jan. 15, 1907. 1179

Inspired by publication of books of Laborde-Milaà (no. 1188) and Maigron (no. 1194), article contains good portrait of F. and good summary of his originality and significance.

Edsall, H. L. The idea of history and progress in Fontenelle and Voltaire. *In :* SFDY, p. 163-84. 1180

Concludes that F. must be considered as one source of Voltaire's philosophy of history, for he anticipated Voltaire in theory of a more social and psychological history and in idea of history as record of progress.

Egilsrud, Johan S. Le Dialogue des morts dans les littératures française, allemande et anglaise (1644-1789). L'entente linotypiste, 1934. 223 p. (Diss., Paris). 1181

Studies F.'s use of form of the *dialogue des morts* and influence on writers of this *genre* in France, Germany, and England.

Faguet, Emile. Fontenelle. *In his :* Dix-huitième siècle; études littéraires, 2e éd. Société française d'imprimerie et de librairie, n.d. p. 31-54. (Nouvelle bibliothèque littéraire). 1182

Contrast between literary and philosophic ideas and works of F. First characterized by wit and lack of feeling; second by intelligence and skepticism. But finds more feeling in F. than does Sainte-Beuve (no. 1201).

— Fontenelle. RDM 5th per. 56:541-49,
Apr. 1, 1910.   1183

Brings out Nietzsche's admiration for
F. and similarity of their ideas on questions of thought and action, and on value
of science and prejudices. Article reprinted as bulk of introduction to *Fontenelle; textes choisis et commentés par Émile
Faguet*. Plon, n.d. [1912]. (*Bibliothèque
française, XVIIIe siècle*).

Fernandez, Ramon. Fontenelle. *In his:*
Itinéraire français.   Éditions du Pavois,
1943. p. 381-94.   1184

Inspired by Rostand's essay on F.
(no. 1200), this appreciation stresses F.'s
rationalism, interpretation of history, art
as writer, and fact that with F. science
became part of humanism.

Flourens, Pierre. Fontenelle ou de la philosophie moderne relativement aux sciences
physiques. Paulin, 1847. 242 p. *See* 1201.
                                           1185

After briefly sketching contributions of
Descartes, Bacon, Galileo, and Newton
to methods and philosophy of modern
science, Flourens studies works of F. as
historian and philosopher of science. F.,
the "*grand esprit*," found in *Histoire de
l'Académie des sciences* and in *Éloges* where
he appears as continuator of Descartes
and historian of Newton. Appendix,
p. 149-240, contains important texts of
F. on science. Essential portion of work,
chapters IV-VII, had been published as
*Revue des éditions de l'Histoire de l'Aca-
démie des sciences par Fontenelle*, JS, 1846,
p. 193-201; 270-81; 329-40; 402-11.

Guyer, Foster E. C'est nous qui sommes
les anciens. MLN 36:257-64, 1921. 1186

The idea, frequent in 17th century,
that moderns are real ancients, expressed
by F. in *Digression sur les anciens et les
modernes* (1688) in a way so similar to
Pascal's in *Fragment d'une préface du
traité sur le vide* (between 1647-51) that
Guyer finds it highly probable that F.
knew Pascal's manuscript which, it is
known, was seen by acquaintances of F.

Hazard, Paul. Fontenelle. *In his:* La crise
de la conscience européenne. *See* 1043.
1:215-23.   1187

Lively analysis of ideas and significance
of the *Histoire des oracles*.

Laborde-Milaà, A. Fontenelle. Hachette,
1905. 175 p. (GEF)   1188

General study of F., containing character sketch, account of his most important
works, and estimate of his influence. But
its chief purpose is to show F.'s genius
as popularizer of knowledge. His importance lay in helping to establish idea
of progress on scientific basis and in
clearly formulating and propagating three
great ideas : (1) nature is subject to
laws; (2) all sciences are related and
are merely particular cases of a single
science; (3) this single science is the
coordination of all phenomena through
mathematical relationships. Literary and
philosophical aspects of F. have been
more thoroughly studied by Maigron
(no. 1194) and Carré (no. 1175) respectively, and his influence by both. No
exact references to passages quoted
from F., nor to authorities cited or
otherwise utilized, but bibliography given.

Reviews : P. Courteault in REH 71:
529-33, 1905; G. Lanson in RU 14²:
237-38, 1905; L. R[oustan] in Rcr ns
60:390-91, 1905.

Lagerborg, Rolf. Un écrit apocryphe de
Fontenelle. RHph 3:340-59, 1935.   1189

Analyzes *La république des philosophes
ou Histoire des Ajaoiens; ouvrage posthume
de M. de Fontenelle...* Geneva, [Amster-
dam], 1768. Finds it expresses ideas dear
to F. Raises question whether it may
not really be by him.

Lanson, Gustave. [Fontenelle]. *In his:*
Origines et premières manifestations de
l'esprit philosophique dans la littérature
française de 1675 à 1748. RCC 17:113-26;
145-57; 210-14, 1908-09. *See* 1047. 1190

F. as precursor of the *esprit philosophique*. Study of his ideas and influence
shows that he is first author who can be
called *philosophe* in sense of 18th century.

Le Breton, André. Vauvenargues et Fontenelle. JS ns 5e année : 550-58, 1907. *See*
2668.   1191

Vauvenargues an eloquent adversary of
F., not an unqualified admirer as both
Maigron (no. 1194) and Laborde-Milaà
(no. 1188) suggest. Although as *libre
esprit*, Vauvenargues did esteem F., the
philosophe, it is F. that Vauvenargues had
in mind in his portrait of *Isocrate ou le
bel-esprit moderne*. Moreover, Vauvenargues was led to misjudge Corneille
simply because F. had praised him.

Lenoir, Raymond. Fontenelle. *In his:* Les
historiens de l'esprit humain. Fontenelle,

Marivaux, Lord Bolingbroke, Vauvenargues, La Mettrie. Alcan, 1926. p. 1-33.
1192

Portrait of F. emphasizing his sense of mystery of all things, his conviction that human knowledge is uncertain and limited, and his cautious attitude and veiled wisdom which made him both revolutionary and conservative thinker. F.'s ideas are for most part paraphrased freely without mention of works from which they are taken; even the few direct quotations are given with no reference to their sources. Essay can be appreciated only by those already very familiar with F.'s works and ideas.

Lévy-Bruhl, Lucien. Fontenelle. OC 12: 705-13, 1898.
1193

F. one of first to express idea of scientific progress and of intellectual development of humanity according to laws. Article reprinted in L.-B.'s *History of modern philosophy in France* (no. 1051), in chapter on *Bayle and Fontenelle*, p. 107-38, and was also published in French as one part of *Les tendances générales de Bayle et de Fontenelle*, RHph 1:49-68, 1927.

Maigron, Louis. Fontenelle. l'homme, l'œuvre, l'influence. Plon, 1906. 432 p.
1194

Most comprehensive treatment of F. Revised biography, improving on Charma's (no. 1176). Excellent analysis and estimate of F.'s mediocre literary output and literary ideas; review of his most important philosophical and scientific works, still useful but largely superseded by Carré (no. 1175). Fine conclusion on F.'s influence in France. Maigron finds slow but sure evolution from F. *bel esprit* to serious F., which, according to Carré, is not true. No index, no bibliography, but bibliographical references in notes. Two portions of book, Ch. IV of Part I (with notes omitted) and Part V had appeared respectively as : *Caractère de Fontenelle*, RAu 23:233-46, 1906; and *L'influence de Fontenelle*, RHL 13:193-227, 1906.
Reviews : A. Laborde-Milaà in REH 72:639-42, 1906; A. Prat in Bcr 27:612-14, 1906; L. R[oustan] in Rcr ns 63:290-91, 1907; P. F. Willert in EHR 22:596-99, 1907 (Summary of contents).

Maugain, Gabriel. Fontenelle et l'Italie. RLC 3:541-603, 1923.
1195

F. was enthusiastic about Italian music, liked Tasso and Ariosto, praised Italian men of science. In Italy he served as guide for bucolic poets, was admired by savants, and was favorite of women who prided themselves on understanding astronomy.

Neumüller, Josef. Fontenelles Stil im Lichte des Satzverknüpfung. Murnau Obb., Fürst, 1933. 92 p. (Diss., Munich).
1196

Study shows what connectives F. preferred, to what extent he led way for his contemporaries in art of connecting clauses, and what place he occupies in development of French prose.

Potez, Henri. Un homme heureux : Fontenelle. MerF 76:38-54, Nov. 1, 1908.
1197

Lively, well-balanced interpretation of F., showing how the *bel esprit* finally gave way to the *grand esprit*. Article reprinted as introduction to volume of selections made by Potez and entitled : *Fontenelle*, Colin, 1909 *(Lectures littéraires; pages choisies des grands écrivains)*.

— Rabelais et Fontenelle. RER :362-67,6 1908.
1198

Explains why F. was both attracted and repelled by Rabelais.

Rödiger, Johannes. Darstellung der geographischen Naturbetrachtung bei Fontenelle, Pluche und Buffon in methodischer und stilistischer Hinsicht. Leipzig, Fischer, 1935. 130 p. (Diss., Leipzig). *See* 2624.
1199

F. studied as precursor of Pluche and Buffon in style and method of popularizing scientific knowledge.

Rostand, Jean. Fontenelle. *In his :* Hommes de vérité : Pasteur, Claude Bernard, Fontenelle, La Rochefoucauld. Stock, 1943. p. 125-75.
1200

Character sketch followed by exposition of F.'s thought. Of interest for emphasis on F.'s pessimism and value of his *prose de géomètre et de poète* (p. 173), for a *rapprochement* between F. and Renan showing former's influence on latter, and for statement that F. will always be needed as long as prejudice, pedantry, dogmatism, and fanaticism exist.

Sainte-Beuve, Charles-Augustin. Fontenelle, par M. Flourens. *In his :* Causeries du lundi, 3ᵉ édition. Garnier, 1858. 3: 314-35.
1201

Appreciation of F. inspired by Flourens' work (no. 1185). Sainte-Beuve shows, by study of Fontenelle's character and works, that there are two distinct Fontenelles, the *bel esprit*, and the *grand esprit*, and thus establishes one of most common conceptions of Fontenelle. Study dated Jan. 27, 1851.

— [Fontenelle]. *In his :* Nouveaux lundis. Calmann Lévy, 1868. 10:94-102.   1202

Written on occasion of publication of Flammarion's *La pluralité des mondes habités*, these pages point out great service Fontenelle performed for contemporaries with his timely *Entretiens sur la pluralité des mondes*, and praises his skill as popularizer. Study dated May 22, 1865.

Staubach, Charles N. Fontenelle in the writings of Feijóo. HR 8:46-56, 1940.   1203

Feijóo admired Fontenelle and borrowed scientific information and ideas from him, especially in his *Teatro crítico* and *Cartas eruditas*.

Julien Offray de La Mettrie

FRANCIS J. CROWLEY
(Nos. 1204-1217)

La Mettrie, Julien Offray de. Œuvres philosophiques de Mr de La Mettrie. Nouvelle édition, corrigée et augmentée. Amsterdam, 1774. 3 vols. (¹).   1204

L.'s propensity for alterations in his works with attendant capricious changing of titles makes his work a bibliographical nightmare, further complicated by attribution to him of controversial anonymous works. Several works not included in above edition should be mentioned here : Essai sur l'esprit et les beaux esprits. Amsterdam, Bernard, n.d. 42 p.
Lettre critique de M. de La Mettrie à Madame la marquise du Châtelet, in the : Histoire naturelle de l'âme, nouvelle édition, Oxford, 1747.
Vénus métaphysique ou Essai sur l'origine de l'âme humaine par L. M. Potsdam, 1751.
Essais sur le raisonnement dédiés à Messire de La Peyronnie, n.p. 1744.
Essai sur la liberté de produire ses sentiments, 1749.
Le petit homme à longue queue.

1. La Mettrie's works treating of medicine and medical disputes are in general left out of consideration here.

Published by Pierre Lemée : Une Œuvre inédite d'Offray de La Mettrie, Le petit homme à longue queue (1751), Baillière, 1934.

— L'homme machine; avec une introduction et des notes par Jules Assézat. Henry, 1865. 181 p.   1205

Edition which deserves commendation in its own right and entitles its editor to gratitude of scholarly world for first sympathetic treatment of L., hitherto subject of abuse and opprobrium.

— L'homme plante; republished with introduction and notes by Francis L. Rougier. New York, Columbia univ. (c1936), 153 p. (Publications of the Institute of French studies).   1206

Introduction contains sections on : L.'s reputation among contemporaries and in 19th century; his biography; his philosophy. Leans heavily on Lange (no. 1211) and Lemée (no. 1212). No index or bibliography. Notes on text rather inadequate.

Bergmann, Ernst. Die Satiren des Herrn Maschine; ein Beitrag zur Philosophie- und Kulturgeschichte des 18. Jahrhunderts. Leipzig, Wiegandt, 1913. 103 p.   1207

Painstaking study of four phases of quarrel with pious Leibnitzian, Dr. Albrecht von Haller, who was indignant over dedication to him of materialistic work by L. Adds important data to Poritzky (no. 1214).

Boissier, Raymond. La Mettrie, médecin, pamphlétaire et philosophe (1709-1751). Société d'édition, Les belles lettres, 1931. 182 p. (Diss., Paris).   1208

Poorly made book; lacks proportion. Many confusions and errors. No index. Useful only for situating L. in 18th century medical *milieux* and indicating trails he blazed in sciences.
Reviews : F. J. Crowley in FR 7: 326-28, 1933-34; A. E. A. Naughton in RR 22:338-39, 1931.

Hastings, Hester. Did La Mettrie write l'Homme plus que machine ? PMLA 51: 440-48, June 1936.   1209

Accepting traditional Luzac authorship, and arguments of Valkhoff (no. 1216), article supports this position by comparison of above work with known works of La Mettrie. Contradicts Poritzky's evidence (no. 1214). States Luzac had good reason to write work and it fits his beliefs and style. Claims it was included in only one edition of La Mettrie's works. Makes good case.

— La Mettrie as a degrader of man. *In her :* Man and beast in French thought of the eighteenth century. Baltimore, The Johns Hopkins press, 1936. p. 94-108. (The Johns Hopkins studies in Romance literatures and languages, no. 27). 1210

Discusses L.'s role in bridging gap between animal and man and shows that, in his own mind and despite charges of contemporaries, L. was not degrading man. Stress is on development of humanitarianism toward animals.

Lange, Frederick Albert. De La Mettrie. *In his :* History of materialism and criticism of its present importance. Authorized translation by E. C. Thomas. Third edition. London and New York, Harcourt, Brace, 1925. First Book, fourth section, Chapter II, p. 49-91. 1211

Study historically important as its author shares with Assézat (no. 1205) credit for rehabilitating L. and restoring him to position in history of thought to which his work entitles him. Sympathetic treatment and good notes.

Lemée, Pierre. Une figure peu connue; Offray de La Mettrie. ASSM 1923-1936. Médecin, philosophe, polémiste, 1923-24, p. 2-41, as separate : Saint-Servan, Haize, 1925. 52 p.; Le médecin et l'auteur médical, 1925, p. 53-82, as separate, Saint-Servan, Haize, 1927. 34 p.; Le philosophe, 1936, p. 78-134. Also as separates : Critique littéraire. Saint-Servan, Haize, 1929. 36 p. and, (no sub-title given) Saint-Servan, Hénon, 1936-37. 59 p. 1212

Series of articles or essays by enthusiast, far and away best informed *Lamettrien* of our day. Still in process of publication, and not readily obtainable, it is to be hoped that these articles will eventually be published in book form. Contain most up-to-date information on biography and bibliography, and are indispensable adjuncts to Poritzky (no. 1214), and Bergmann (no. 1207).

Lenoir, Raymond. La Mettrie. *In his :* Historiens de l'esprit humain; Fontenelle, Marivaux, Lord Bolingbroke, Vauvenargues, La Mettrie. Alcan, 1926. p. 131-72. 1213

Concise analysis of L.'s thought as outlined in *Histoire naturelle de l'âme.* Discusses influence of his ideas. Sympathetic treatment.

Poritzky, J. E. Julien Offray de Lamettrie, sein Leben und seine Werke. Berlin, Dummler, 1900. 356 p. 1214

Best full-length treatment of L. and his work. Well-organized, painstaking, scholarly study. A chapter on bibliographical idiosyncracies of works would have avoided some inaccuracies. Lacks index of persons and subjects. Superseded in some respects and brought up to date by Lemée's articles (no. 1212) and by Bergmann (no. 1207).

Rosenfield, Mrs. Leonora Cohen. From beast-machine to man-machine; animal soul in French letters from Descartes to La Mettrie. *See* 1070. 1215

Author's aim was to " ... examine the two-fold theme of the beast-machine and the animal-soul in French literature from Descartes to La Mettrie." Not very satisfactory treatment of subject, due in some measure to inexact use of terms (e.g., " literature ") and to inadequate background in 17th century. Good bibliography and index.

Valkhoff, P. Elie Luzac. Néo 4:10-21, 1918-19. 1216

Argues for Luzac's authorship of *l'Homme plus que machine,* against Poritzky(no. 1214), Bergmann (no. 1207), *et al.,* on basis of content and style. *See* no. 1209. Also attributes *Essai sur la liberté de produire ses sentiments* to Luzac. Evidence not conclusive.

Vartanian, Aram. Elie Luzac's refutation of La Mettrie. MLN 64:159-61, 1949. 1216A

Luzac admits authorship of *l'Homme plus que machine* in introduction to second edition of work, which was privately printed. (*See* nos. 1209, 1216).

Voltaire, François, etc. Voltaire's Poème sur la loi naturelle; a critical edition by Francis J. Crowley. Berkeley, Calif., Univ. of California press, 1938, p. 177-304. (*On cover :* Publications of the Univ. of California at Los Angeles, in languages and literatures, vol. I, no. 4). *See* 1607. 1217

Studies role played by L. in genesis of Voltaire's work, which was in part refutation of L.'s thought as expressed in *Anti-Sénèque ou Discours sur le bonheur.* Reviews : N. L. Torrey in RR 31: 181-83, 1940; P. Vernière in RHL 47: 372-73, 1947.

Etienne Bonnot de Condillac
(Nos. 1218-1261)

James R. Wadsworth

Condillac, Etienne Bonnot de. Cours d'étude pour l'instruction du prince de Parme. Parma, Bodoni, 1775. 13 v. 1218

Court of Spain opposed publication, and Bodoni secured permission only in 1782 to circulate his edition, after inserting corrections, extra pages, and new title page indicating place of publication as Deux-Ponts.

— Cours d'étude pour l'instruction du prince de Parme. Deux-Ponts, Bodoni, 1782. 13 v. 1219

Bodoni's corrected edition, really printed at Parma. Probably corrected by C.'s brother Mably. Includes *La grammaire, l'Art de penser, l'Art d'écrire, l'Art de raisonner*, and the *Histoire générale des hommes et des empires;* also *l'Étude de l'histoire*, written by Mably.

— Essai sur l'origine des connaissances humaines. Ed. by Raymond Lenoir. Colin, 1924. 225 p. 1220

Text established by comparing editions of 1746, 1792, and 1798. Biographical introduction gives substance of Lenoir's other studies on C., but through careless proofreading, some dates remain, obviously, incorrect. Bibliography incomplete.

— Lettre de M. L'abbé de Condillac à l'auteur des Lettres à un Américain. MerF, Apr., 1756. Part 2, p. 84-95. 1221

Objects vigorously to manner of criticism of his *Traité des animaux.*

— Œuvres de Condillac, revues, corrigées par l'auteur, imprimées sur ses manuscrits autographes, et augmentées de la Langue des calculs. Houel, An VI, 1798. 23 v. 1222

First complete edition based on C.'s own corrections. Includes *De l'étude de l'histoire*, written by Mably.

— Œuvres complètes. Brière, 1822. 16 v. 1223

Fine edition printed by Rignoux. Copies bearing name of Brière contain passages of *Cours d'étude* suppressed in Deux-Ponts edition but printed in Parma edition. Contains a *Notice sur la vie et les ouvrages de Condillac* by A. F. Théry, 1:i-lix. The *Notice* less valuable critically

and factually than for study of early 19th century reaction to C. Théry's opinions show influence of Bonald and Laromiguière. In false humility he combines praise for originality and consistency of C.'s theories with adverse criticism of much of his basic doctrine.

— Traité des sensations. Première partie, publiée d'après l'édition de 1798, augmentée de l'extrait raisonné, des variantes de l'édition de 1754, de notes historiques et explicatives, d'une introduction et d'éclaircissements, par François Picavet. Delagrave, 1885. 292 p. 6th edition, 1928. 1224

Best modern edition, with most complete introduction. Corrects errors of Cousin, Réthoré, and Robert and gives accurate interpretation and evaluation of C.'s position. Good sketch of history of Condillac-ism. Asserts that influence of C. and his school on formation of positivism has not been duly recognized. Notes offer significant comparisons with 19th century English, French and German philosophy and psychology. *Éclaircissements* reprint texts important for relations of Buffon, Diderot, and C.

— Traité des sensations. Première partie. Publiée avec une introduction par Georges Lyon, Alcan, 1886. 128 p. New ed., 1921. 1225

Introduction reasserts Laromiguière's forgotten statement that C.'s place in development of sensualism lies between Locke and La Mettrie. Concerning allegory of the statue, presents essential facts about C.'s rivals and precursors, and appendices give texts of possible sources.

— Traité des sensations. Première partie publiée avec une introduction, un extrait raisonné du Traité des sensations de Condillac et des notes par T. V. Charpentier. Hachette, 1886. 155 p. 1226

Introduction inadequate; biography reduced to minimum. However, does try to counteract anti-C. prejudices spread by Cousin and his disciples. Stresses pedagogical and philosophical value of historical volumes of *Cours d'étude.* Notes point out merits and defects of text from viewpoint of late 19th century psychology, offer frequent comparisons with theories of Taine, and indicate possible importance for work of Helmholtz.

— Condillac's Treatise on the sensations. Trans. by Geraldine Carr. Preface by H. Wildon Carr. Los Angeles, Univ. of

Southern California school of philosophy; London, Favil press, 1930. 250 p. 1227

Although preface does little more than emphasize need for this first version in English of a philosophical classic, translator, in her introduction on life and work of C., attempts to show how he reoriented philosophical inquiry in direction leading ultimately to idealistic position of modern French philosophy. Translation itself far more significant than either preface or introduction.

Adams, Lyell. Condillac and the principle of identity. NE 35:440-66, July, 1876. 1228

Cleverly written, with dual purpose of attacking Lewes (no. 1248) and explaining C.'s doctrine. Corrects interpretations of C. by Lewes, Stewart and Hamilton, and assigns him higher rank than they as a philosopher. Declares C. furnished original draft of the final form of empiricism.

Baguenault de Puchesse, Gustave. Condillac : sa vie, sa philosophie, son influence. Plon-Nourrit. 1910. 278 p. 1229

Most useful biography. Fairly detailed account of reactions of both 18th century and later critics to C.'s various works. Tends to overestimate importance of C.'s influence on his contemporaries; more accurate for 19th century attitude. Admits debt to Lebeau (no. 1243). Presentation of C.'s philosophy descriptive rather than critical.

Boyd, William. Étienne Bonnot de Condillac. *In his :* From Locke to Montessori. New York, Holt, 1914. p. 30-35. 1230

Although C. himself failed to realize educational applications of his own psychological doctrines, he made possible development of more fruitful conceptions of place of senses in intellectual life and, indirectly through Rousseau, his ideas have deeply influenced modern educational thought. Study too brief for thorough discussion.

Brockdorff, L. G. C. baron von. Wahrheit und Wahrscheinlichkeit bei Hobbes und Condillac. Kiehl, Lipsius & Tischer, 1937. Veröffentlichungen der Hobbes-Gesellschaft, v. 8, p. 3-13. 1231

Brief exposition of similarity of doctrines of C. and Locke; offers no conclusive proof of direct influence.

Capone Braga, Gaetano. Condillac. *In his :* La filosofia francese e italiana del settecento. Arezzo, Pagine critiche, 1920. v. 1, p. 100-60. 1232

While patriotic purpose of whole work is to put less stress upon French influence on Italian 18th century thought, it offers fairly good presentation and evaluation of C.'s essential doctrines. Most of discussion can be profitably read for comparative study of C., Bonnet, and French ideologists and, in v. 2, such Italians as Soave, Gioia, Ramognosi, etc.

Cousin, Victor. Condillac. *In his :* Philosophie sensualiste au dix-huitième siècle. Librairie nouvelle, 1856. p. 39-129. 1233

Substance of his lectures in 1819 designed to combat 18th century heritage of materialism, atheism, and revolutionary violence. Calls C. only real metaphysician of his time; admits his outstanding qualities of clearness, precision, logic, and intelligence, but brands him as narrow-minded, and ignorant of man, life, and society. Accuses C. of disregarding facts in order to support his theories, and of ignoring fundamental distinctions between good and evil. Highly prejudiced attack, but significant for history of 19th century reaction to C.

Damiron, Jean Philibert. Condillac. Son traité des systèmes. AMP 60:5-28; 61:5-31, 1862. *Also in his :* Mémoires pour servir à l'histoire de la philosophie au XVIIIe siècle. Ladrange, 1858-64. 3:226-81. 1234

Biographical half offers no new material, but at date of publication was more complete than contemporary studies, though now superseded by Baguenault de Puchesse (no. 1229). Adverse but well-founded criticism of *Traité des systèmes* as being negative and destructive work which was inaccurate, incomplete, and based on arbitrary choice of periods and philosophers. Damiron tempers blame with favorable general judgment of C.'s philosophy and life. Study is partially successful attempt to renew interest in C. (Copy at Michigan.)

Delbos, Victor. Condillac et les idéologues. *In his :* La philosophie française. 10th ed., Plon, 1921, p. 250-76. 1235

Posthumous reconstruction of author's Sorbonne lectures of 1910, 1914, and 1916. Chiefly analysis of *Essai sur l'or* and *Traité des sensations*, with brief indication of transformation of C.'s doctrines by Destutt de Tracy, Cabanis, and Maine de Biran. Deplores fact that no adequate book on C.'s philosophy has yet been written. Less important in itself than as example of 20th century academic approach by often-cited lecturer.

Dewaule, Léon. Condillac et la psychologie anglaise contemporaine. Alcan, 1892. 331 p. (Diss., Paris).   1236

Unconvincing attempt to rehabilitate C.'s reputation by establishing him as precursor of English associationists and evolutionists.   Detailed comparisons, principally with Bain, J. S. Mill, and Spencer, supply evidence of similarities rather than proofs of direct influence. Systematic in treatment of C.'s ideas, but fragmentary for any one English writer. Review : F. Picavet in Rph 39:215-19, 1895.

Havemann, Hans. Der erkenntnistheoretische Standpunkt Condillacs. Jena, Vopelius, 1912. 45 p. (Diss., Munich).   1237

Academic silhouette of C.'s theories projected against background of Descartes, Malebranche, Berkeley, Hobbes, and Locke, showing C.'s position between idealism and empiricism. Based mainly on Essai sur l'or and Traité des sensations. Youthful scholar attempts to correct Johnson, Erdmann and Réthoré (no. 1258). Routine type of German thesis, minus bibliography.   Of service primarily for historical study of German interpretations of C.

Kaye, F. B.   Mandeville on the origin of language. MLN 39:136-42, 1924.   1238

Points out possible indebtedness of C.'s theory of the origin of language to Mandeville's Fable of the bees, published in French translation six years before C.'s Essai sur l'or. Suggestive but not conclusive source study.

Küthmann, Alfred. Étienne Bonnot de Condillac. In his : Zur Geschichte des Determinismus. Leipzig, Quelle & Meyer, 1911. p. 38-61.   1239

Concise statement of C.'s nominalist doctrines and indication of 19th century critical attitudes toward them.   Grants historical value of C.'s work but stresses difference of modern views.   Disputes C.'s claim that perfection of science consists solely in perfection of language.

Lanson, Gustave. Les idées littéraires de Condillac. RSH 21:267-79, 1910. Also in his : Études d'histoire littéraire, Champion, 1929. p. 210-23.   1240

Based chiefly on the Art d'écrire, Ch. 5. C.'s literary theories make transition between doctrines of Boileau and Perrault, and those of Mme de Staël and the Idéologues.   C. was only 18th century writer who made real effort to formulate theory corresponding to actual state of French intelligence and taste.   Conclusion overestimates C.'s literary importance.

Laromiguière, Pierre. Paradoxes de Condillac ou réflexions sur la langue des calculs. Guilleminet, an XIII, 1805.   Also in his : Paradoxes de Condillac; discours sur la langue du raisonnement.   New ed., Brunot-Labbe, 1825. p. 1-167.   1241

Interpretation of La langue des calculs in attempt to decide whether C.'s logical doctrine is brilliant deduction of paradoxes or perfect model of reasoning. Laromiguière warns reader that when he seems most convinced, he himself is uncertain.   In spite of author's indecision, this is an important work, marking approaching trend away from C.

— Condillac.   Leçons 3, 5, 9, 10, in his : Leçons de philosophie.   Brunot-Labbe, 1815. 1:85-87; 119-44; 207-53.   1242

These Sorbonne lectures of 1811 especially significant as recording history of trend away from C.   Laromiguière explains and criticizes C.'s system of faculties, trying to prove that they do not originate in sensation.   Examines accusation of materialism and clears C. of charge.

Lebeau, Auguste.   Condillac économiste. Guillaumin, 1903. 458 p. (Diss., Law, Poitiers).   1243

Competent, detailed, and thoroughly documented study of Le commerce et le gouvernement in relation to historical background. Sketches C.'s life and philosophy, and economic doctrines of his contemporaries.   Proves C.'s economic reasoning based on facts, but shows his teachings mixture of truths and errors, essentially original, and differing from those of Physiocrats.   Believes that, with Quesnay, Turgot, and Adam Smith, C. created science of political economy. Appendix reproduces some rare criticism of C. by Baudeau.

Lenoir, Raymond.   Condillac.   Rph 95: 225-75, 1923.   1244

Although tending toward oversimplification of 18th century philosophical trends, study attempts rather successfully to create intellectual atmosphere of period. Stresses importance for C.'s intellectual evolution of St. Sulpice, Fontenelle, and Mme de Tencin's salon. Discussion of C.'s system superficial and inferior to rest of study. Concludes with good sketch of relationship of 19th century French thought to philosophy of C.

— Condillac. Alcan, 1924. 164 p. 1245

Lenoir's Rph study revised and expanded by including 90 pages summarizing C.'s works in chronological order, with a few notes giving comparisons to Fontenelle. Useful general introduction to C. Reviews : E. Bréhier in Rph 101:469-70, 1926; E. Seillière in Rcr 92:386-88, 1925.

Le Roy, Georges. La psychologie de Condillac. Boivin, 1937. 236 p. (Thèse compl., Lettres, Paris). *See* 3040. 1246

Stresses effect of Diderot's critical remarks and of Voltaire's interpretation of Newton, Locke, and Berkeley on composition of C.'s works. Asserts importance of Descartes and Leibnitz for C.'s logical method. Defines C.'s psychology as essentially panlogism. Adds little else to work of previous critics, whom author mostly scorns. Bibliography incomplete.
Review : G. R. Havens in PhR 47:554, 1938.

Lévy-Bruhl, Lucien. Condillac. OC 13: 258-66, 1899. *Also in his* : History of modern philosophy in France. Chicago, Open court publishing co., 1899. p. 271-87. 1247

Simple, clear statement of C.'s essential doctrines, based principally on *Traité des sensations.* Admits imperfections of C.'s solutions to problems he raised, but indicates fairly his importance for history of philosophy. More valuable to general student than specialist.

Lewes, George Henry. Condillac. *In his* : Biographical history of philosophy. New York, Appleton, 1863. 2:589-603. *Also in his* : History of philosophy from Thales to Comte. London, Longmans, Green, 3rd ed., 1867. 2:328-47. 1248

Although written century ago, study still of value as keen criticism of C.'s chief merits and weaknesses, which are explained by his use of verbal analysis rather than biological method, and by his failure to distinguish between sensation and ideation.

Macleod, H. D. Rise of the third school of economists. *In his* : The elements of economics. London, Longmans, Green; New York, Appleton, 1881. v. 1, p. 117-21. 1249

Discusses *Le commerce et le gouvernement,* concluding that C.'s is true conception of economics; after neglect of century, C. emerges as true founder of modern economics.

Madinier, Gabriel. Les orientations psychologiques et réflexives de la pensée de Condillac. *In his* : Conscience et mouvement. Alcan, 1938. p. 1-38. (Diss., Paris). 1250

Studies in strictly modern terms relations of C. to psychological problem of relationship between movement and thought. Shows C.'s development from *Essai sur l'or* through first and final editions of *Traité des sensations.* Maintains that C.'s work reveals tendencies which were fruitful orientations for successors rather than psychological system. Subsequent chapters trace evolution of C.'s doctrine through Laromiguière (no. 1241), Destutt de Tracy, Cabanis, and Maine de Biran to Bergson. Well developed and thorough. Essential for history of ideas.

Mallet, C. Condillac. *In* : Nouvelle biographie générale. Didot, 1855-70. v. 11, p. 429-59. 1251

Gives concise summaries of each work of C., followed by exposition of his psychological, philosophical, logical, and moral and economic doctrines. Claims that *L'étude de l'histoire,* usually ascribed to Mably, was really written by C. Useful as quick introduction to C.

Mann, James L. L'éducation selon la doctrine pédagogique de Condillac. Grenoble, Allier, 1903. 142 p. (Diss., Grenoble). 1252

Neither brilliant nor exhaustive, but still most detailed study of subject. References to United States schools and theories. First 85 pages mostly summary of C.'s *Motif des études* and *Discours préliminaire.* Stresses differences between pedagogical theories of Locke and C. Contends, without adequate discussion or proof, that Bacon was the real source of C.'s educational ideas.

Maynial, Edouard. Les grammairiens philosophes du XVIIIᵉ siècle; la grammaire de Condillac. RPL 4th ser. 19:317-20, March 7, 1903. 1253

Contends that C. exaggerated grammatical method of the Encyclopedists, enslaved genius of language to logic, and shared error of entire 18th century in treating grammar from philosophical rather than linguistic point of view.

Mondolfo, Rodolfo. Spazio e tempo nella psicologia di Condillac. Rfil 5:184-95, 1902.
1254

Minute and clear analysis of C.'s concept of space, which studies contradictions incurred in explanation of its origin. Particular attention given to senses of sight and touch in relation to idea of extension. Noteworthy is analogy between C.'s idea of extension and that of two modern associationists Bain and Spencer. Assertion that C. has utterly failed to explain origin of space closes first part of study. Second part treats C.'s concept of time briefly but adequately.

Pelikán, Ferdinand. La méthode de Condillac et de Descartes. TNC 3:43-48, 1937.
1255
Shows how C.'s method resembles that of Descartes while leading ultimately to " fictionalism " of Taine and Ribot.

Pion, Lucien. Condillac et sa philosophie. ADB ser. 3, 17:13-30, 1883.   1256
Pion's *Discours de réception* to *Académie delphinale* on Feb. 11, 1881. Begins with summary of C.'s influence in 18th century, describes its eclipse in first half of 19th. Presents readable analysis and estimate of C.'s work, without, however, any claim to originality.

Pra, Mario dal. Condillac. Milan, Bocca, 1942. 410 p.   1257
Interesting study, which expounds C.'s philosophy as spiritualism *(spiritualismo)* and panlogism, and initial idealism. Traces evolution of C.'s thought and aims to give unified and complete picture of this thought as reflected and modified in views of Carlini and Le Roy (no. 1246). Conclusion attempts to explain C.'s historical position by means of what Dal Pra calls spirituality of Age of Enlightenment.

Réthoré, François. Condillac ou l'empirisme et le rationalisme. Durand, 1864. 368 p.   1258
Defense of C., sensationalism, empiricism, and French philosophy, combined with violent attack on Cousin's eclecticism and German rationalism. Admits C.'s lack of physiological knowledge. Prejudice and patriotism of author confuse facts and issues. Of special interest to historian of 19th century philosophical trends as one of most important attempts to revive popularity of C.'s philosophy.

Saltykow, Wera. Die Philosophie Condillacs. Bern, Sturzenegger, 1901. 73 p. (Diss., Bern).   1259
Fairest and most complete general study on C. available in German. Leans heavily on Dewaule (no. 1236). Defends C. against Cousin's (no. 1233) objection to statue hypothesis. Stresses inconsistencies and contradictions of C., but points out his importance as precursor of modern experimental, comparative, and associationist psychology. No bibliography.

Schaupp, Zora. The naturalism of Condillac. Lincoln, Nebr., 1925. 123 p. (NSL 7).   1260
Competent and well-documented reevaluation of C.'s principal doctrines, focusing attention on naturalistic aspect of his philosophy as his most characteristic and original contribution. Objective yet sympathetic interpretation from viewpoint of 20th century psychology and philosophy. While not claiming to treat C.'s philosophy as whole, is best detailed study of subject available in English.

Strózewski, Stanislaus. Bonnets Psychologie in ihrem Verhältnis zu Condillacs Traité des sensations. Berlin, Rieger, 1905. 57 p. (Diss., Tübingen).   1261
Detailed comparison of C. and Bonnet. Supplements and largely supersedes study of Mülhaupt to whom Strózewski is evidently indebted, although he mentions him only in the conclusion. Last chapter presents adequate summary both of influence of C. on Bonnet and of basic differences in approach and results of each. No bibliography.

Jean Lerond d'Alembert
(Nos. 1262-1287)

Lester G. Crocker

BMF 3:61, 1900; 7:52, 1904; 8:67, 1905; 9:1, 1906; 10:113, 1907.   1262
Miscellany of brief mathematical references.

Alembert, Jean Lerond d'. Œuvres de d'Alembert. Didier, 1853, 326 p. (not 526 p. as LC card has it).   1263

Contents : *Discours préliminaire, Système du monde, Pensées, Portrait de Mme Geoffrin, Portrait de Mlle de Lespinasse.*

— Œuvres philosophiques, historiques et littéraires. Edited by J. F. Bastien. Bastien, 1805. 18 v. 1264

— Nouvelle édition augmentée. Belin, 1821. 5 v.

Standard edition, most complete; contains the literary works, and introductions to more important scientific works.

— Discours préliminaire de l'Encyclopédie. F. Picavet, ed. Colin, 1912. 250 p. 1265

Edition generally considered best.

— Élémens de musique, théorique et pratique, suivant les principes de M. Rameau, éclaircis, développés et simplifiés par M. d'Alembert. Lyon, Bruyset, 1779. 2nd edition. 236 p. 1266

— David, 1752 (first ed.).

— Mélanges de littérature, d'histoire et de philosophie. Berlin, 1753. 2 v. 1267

Same. Amsterdam, Chatelain, 1764-67. 5 v.

Early editions containing various of D'A.'s important works.

— Three unpublished letters. *In* : Hawkins, R. L. Newly discovered French letters of the seventeenth, eighteenth and nineteenth centuries. Cambridge, Harvard univ. press, 1933. p. 46-50. *See* 2233 1268

Three short letters, dealing with several of D'A.'s activities.

— Trois mois à la cour de Frédéric; lettres inédites de d'Alembert, publiées et annotées par Gaston Maugras. Calmann-Lévy, 1886. 91 p. 1269

Collection of letters written to Julie de Lespinasse from Prussian court; information on that court and on D'A.'s character and relations with Frederick II.

— Quatre lettres de Jean Lerond d'Alembert à Jean Baptiste de Boyer, Marquis d'Argens. [Dijon, Darantière, 1927]. 35 p. (61 copies). 1270

Second letter deals with abbé de Prades affair, others with D'A.'s relations with Frederick II.

— Œuvres et correspondances inédites de d'Alembert, publiées par Charles Henry. Perrin, 1887. 352 p. 1270A

Necessary supplement to previously published works.

Barni, Jules R. D'Alembert. *In his :* Histoire des idées morales et politiques en France au XVIIIᵉ siècle. Germer-Baillière, 1865-73. 3 v. 2:389-491. 1271

Chapter on D'A.'s life, noteworthy for fair appraisal of his character, followed by most complete study we have of his moral and political theories. Valuable contribution, since these are aspects of D'A.'s philosophy most neglected in other studies.

Bertrand, Joseph. D'Alembert. Hachette, 1889. 206 p. (GEF) 1272

Good introduction to D'A. Superficial, cursory, but interesting and readable. Bertrand surveys D.A.'s life, character, and friendships, his scientific and philosophical accomplishments, relations with academies, the *Encyclopédie*, and Frederick II. Sufficient attention paid to background material (18th century education, Jesuit-Jansenist quarrel, etc.). Philosophical ideas scarcely touched upon. Much material apparently based on Condorcet's *Éloge.*

Condorcet, A. N. de, *marquis.* Éloge de M. d'Alembert. *In* Œuvres, Arago-O'Connor edition. Didot, 1847-49, 3:51-110. 1273

Important contemporary document, by one of D'A.'s best friends. As is to be expected, certain phases of his life and personal relations (e.g., Julie de Lespinasse) are omitted and his character eulogized. Nevertheless, best brief analysis of his philosophy and scientific work, and possesses additional interest of expressing viewpoint of great contemporary.

Damiron, J. P. Mémoires pour servir à l'histoire de la philosophie au XVIIIᵉ siècle. *See* 1234. 2:1-143. 1274

Clear and thorough exposition of D'A.'s philosophy. Of particular interest is analysis of D'A.'s and Frederick the Great's intellectual relations, as seen in their correspondence. One must beware of division into D'A.'s " official " and " intimate " philosophy, which fails to take into account evolution of his thought.

Delbeke, François, *baron.* La franc-maçonnerie et la révolution française. Anvers, Les éditions lectura, 1938. 163 p. 1275

Ten unpublished letters (1765-1779), of considerable personal interest, of D'A. to Père Frisi, the Italian mathematician (D'A.'s pension, his recent publications, Beccaria). (p. 139-61).

Dupont-Châtelain, Marguerite. Les Encyclopédistes et les femmes. *See* 1303. 1276

Förster, Max. Beiträge zur Kenntnis des Characters und der Philosophie d'Alemberts. Hamburg, Groth, 1892. 96 p. (Diss., Jena). 1277

D'A.'s character studied through his relations with other men of his time, especially Rousseau. More interesting are the fifty pages devoted to his philosophy, scientific theories, and accomplishments. Discussion, while not so exhaustive or profound as Muller's (no. 1285), is more concentrated, and quite readable.

Frisi, Paolo. Elogio del Signor d'Alembert. Milan, Galeazzi, 1786. 81 p. 1278

Florid, bombastic eulogy of D'A.'s works, written by a friend of his, with special attention to mathematical publications. Occasionally interesting for comments of a contemporary.

Houssaye, Arsène. D'Alembert. *In his :* Galerie de portraits du XVIIIe siècle. 2nd ed. Lecou, 1854. 2:139-52. *See* 97. 1279

Bitter and unfounded attack on D'A.'s character and talents, interesting as contrast to estimates of other critics.

Kunz, Ludwig. Die Erkenntnistheorie d'Alemberts. AGP 20:96-126, 1907. 1280

Brief consideration of relation between d'A.'s metaphysics and English empiricists. While D'A.'s shortcomings are indicated, Kunz emphasizes that D'A.'s importance as link between empiricists and Comte has been underestimated. Outdated and surpassed by Muller's study (no. 1285).

Larivière, Charles. Catherine II et d'Alembert. *In his :* La France et la Russie au XVIIIe siècle. Le Soudier, 1909. p. 1-69. 1281

Keen, authoritative account of rise and fall of D'A.'s epistolary friendship with Catherine.

Lefebvre, E. D'Alembert. RQS 3rd ser. 30:460-84, Oct. 20, 1921. Reprinted : Louvain, Ceuterick, 1921. 29 p. 1282

Rather pretentious article, openly hos-

tile to " philosophic'" spirit. Description of D'A.'s studies at *Collège Mazarin* alone makes it worth mention.

Mallarmé, Camille. Un dramma di salotti del secolo XVIII. NA 262:471-87, 1928. 1283

Good account of three-cornered relationship between Mme du Deffand, Julie de Lespinasse, and D'A. Latter studied only in so far as he affected relations between the two women. Legend of his impotence, denied by Mme Dupont-Châtelain (no. 1303), accepted by Mallarmé, as well as by Houssaye (no. 1279).

Misch, Georg. Zur Entstehung des französischen Positivismus. Berlin, Reimer, 1900. 43 p. 1284

Misch studies mostly origins of Comte's positivism, viewed as culmination of three generations of thought, in the philosophical ideas of D'A. and Turgot. D'A.'s empiricism, materialistic viewpoint, and scientific positivism analyzed, forming interesting contrast with Barni's insistence on ultimate skeptical consequences of D'A.'s theories.

Muller, Maurice. Essai sur la philosophie de Jean d'Alembert. Payot, 1926. 309 p. (Diss., Paris). 1285

Exhaustive philosophical study. D'A.'s philosophical and scientific works analyzed not in themselves but rather as contributions to D'A.'s general philosophy. His logic, epistemology, metaphysics, esthetics, and ethics are examined. Somewhat diffuse. Mornet's review praises especially study of conflict within D'A. between rational skepticism and need for believing in the truths of science and intuitions of the heart.
Review : D. Mornet in RHL 35:272-73, 1928.

Pougens, Marie Charles Joseph de. Lettres philosophiques à Mme xxx sur divers sujets de morale et de littérature. Louis, 1826. 352 p. 1286

Pougens, a close friend of D'A. gives some intimate sketches and anecdotes, valuable for study of his life and character.

Sagnac, P. Les conflits de la science et de la religion au XVIIIe siècle : Dalembert et Buffon. Rfr 78:5-15, 1925. 1287

Some brief comments, based only on *Discours préliminaire*, and of little value.

The *Encyclopédie*
(Nos. 1288-1322)

LESTER G. CROCKER

Encyclopédie ou Dictionnaire raisonné des sciences, des arts et des métiers. Briasson, [etc.] 1751-65. 1288

Prospectus published in 1750. For *Suppléments, planches, tables,* later editions, etc., see BN and LC catalogues.

Ollivier, Remi. L'esprit de l'Encyclopédie, ou Choix des articles les plus agréables, les plus curieux et les plus piquants de ce grand Dictionnaire. Fauvelle et Sagnier, 1798-1808, 13 v. 1289

Albien, Paul. Das Pädagogische in der Encyclopédie von Diderot. Magdeburg-Alte Neustadt, Sorgler, 1908. 117 p. (Diss., Erlangen). 1290

Systematic survey. Analytic in method; broken down into 72 sections dealing with small aspects of educational theory and practice. At head of each, all pertinent articles listed; then summarized. Suggestive, rather than complete discussion.

Assézat, Jules. Notice préliminaire, *in* Diderot : Œuvres, edited by J. Assézat et M. Tourneux, 1875-77. 13:109-28. 1291

Brief *résumé* of history of *Encyclopédie*, reliable, but far from complete.

Barker, J. E. Diderot's treatment of the Christian religion in the Encyclopédie. New York, King's crown press, 1941. 143 p. 1292

Valuable both for technique of propaganda in *Encyclopédie* and for Diderot's thought. Thorough study of his attitudes toward Christianity and of thought content. Latter evaluated in light of, (1) sources, borrowing and originality and, (2) Diderot's other writings. Principal contribution lies in understanding and study of sources. Reviews : H. Dieckmann in RR 34: 174-77, 1943; G. R. Havens in MLN 57:398-99, 1942.

Belin, J. P. Le mouvement philosophique de 1748 à 1789. *See* 4, 1024. 1293

Contains brief history of *Encyclopédie*, especially in reference to polemics, opposition, and persecution.

Bredvold, L. I. A note on La Hontan and the Encyclopédie. MLN 47:508-09, 1932. 1294

La Hontan defended and attacked in *Encyclopédie.*

Brugmans, H. L. La Hollande du XVIIIe siècle dans l'Encyclopédie. RR 26:297-312, 1935. 1295

Clear analysis of geographic, political, economic, and intellectual information contained in *Encyclopédie*. Lacks general conclusions; limited interest.

Brunetière, Ferdinand. L'esprit nouveau. L'Encyclopédie. *In his :* Histoire de la littérature française classique. Delagrave, [1912]-17 3:[319]-420. 1296

Includes examination of doctrine of *Encyclopédie*, keenly critical, just. Emphasizes in competent fashion utilitarian character of 18th century thought.

Cazes, André. Grimm et les Encyclopédistes. Presses universitaires de France, 1933. 407 p. (Diss., Toulouse). 1297

Ch. V (p. 60-119) treats of Grimm's work as defender and propagandist of *Encyclopédie*, and of ideas in *Correspondance littéraire* which seconded work of Diderot. Discursive style, but valuable inquiry.
Cazes seems incorrectly to place Diderot's rupture with d'Alembert and with Rousseau after the revocation of the *privilège* (March 8, 1759).

Champion, Edme. Des mots équivoques, et en particulier du mot : " Encyclopédistes." Rfr 41:5-30, 1901. 1298

After analysis of various meanings and connotations of words *encyclopédiste* and *philosophe*, author gives series of penetrating remarks on various important questions (such as influence of *Encyclopédie*, opinions of men who edited it, especially in regard to despotism, religion, and freedom of the press). All this by way of criticism of Ducros' study of *Encyclopédistes* (no. 1302). Some may disagree with conclusion that word *philosophes* should be discarded and replaced by *cacouacs*.

Crane, R. S. and Arthur Friedman. Goldsmith and the Encyclopédie. TLS 32:331, May 11, 1933. 1299

Note on Goldsmith's unacknowledged pilferings from *Encyclopédie*, with references for further investigation.

Crocker, L. G. The problem of Malesherbes' intervention. MLQ 2:551-58, 1941. By L. G. Krakeur. 1300

Re-examination of seemingly incoherent evidence, with conclusion that Malesherbes did rescue mss., but in May 1759, not in 1752.

Documents nouveaux sur l'Encyclopédie. [Articles by Henri Berr and others]. Rsyn 15:5-30; Supplementary pages 31-110, 1938.
1301

Deliberations and expenses of associated *libraires.* Interesting details on organization and administration of work, and roles of D'Alembert and Formey.

Ducros, Louis. Les Encyclopédistes. Champion, 1900. 376 p.   1302

Essential work. *See* no. 1298.
Reviews : G. Lanson in RHL 9:149-54, 1902. Lanson's review an important article in itself.

Dupont-Châtelain, Marguerite. Les Encyclopédistes et les femmes. Daragon, 1911. 169 p.   1303

No new material, but delightful reading. Reliable in general, but recent discoveries make some of work out of date, especially chapter on Diderot. Author seems to have captured spirit of her " characters."

Duprat, Pascal. Les Encyclopédistes, leurs travaux, leur doctrine et leur influence. Lacroix, 1866, 196 p.   1304

Elementary and outdated but far from worthless survey of enterprise, its collaborators and principles, enemies, and influence.

Faguet, Emile. L'Encyclopédie. RDM 71st yr. 5th per. : 794-824, Feb. 15, 1901. 1305

Summarizes spirit of *Encyclopédie*, which he considers an excellent picture of France in 1750, and testament to thought of century (which, of course, it is only in part). Faguet believes that its spirit and definite intent were to destroy tradition, break with past, and initiate rationalistic, scientific revolution. He blames *Encyclopédie* for neglecting moral sciences, especially ethics.

Gaudin, Lois Frances (Strong). Les lettres anglaises dans l'Encyclopédie. New York, 1942. 256 p. (Diss., Columbia). *See* 2892.
1306

Excellent technical exercise, on subject of little import. Concludes treatment in *Encyclopédie* of English literature was fragmentary, capricious, mediocre, unoriginal, and behind vanguard of French thought. Since no systematic survey was attempted, this study could have been adequately treated in an article. Good indices help provide information of detailed nature.

Reviews : G. R. Havens in MLN 58: 303-04, 1943; H. M. Peyre in RR 34: 269-71, 1943.

Giraud, Victor. Les étapes du XVIIIe siècle. RDM 7 pér. 22:344-75; 23:882-917, 1924.
1307

Main outlines of history of 18th century thought are resumed, with some reference to *Encyclopédie*.

Gordon, D. H. and N. L. Torrey. The censoring of Diderot's Encyclopédie and the re-established text. *See* 365.   1308

Valuable for dispelling illusion that serious loss was suffered through Le Breton's deletions. Contains brief account of discovery of mysterious volume of censored proofs, summary of history of publication of *Encyclopédie*, appraisal of cuts and re-established text of deleted passages.

Hubert, René. Les sciences sociales dans l'Encyclopédie. Alcan, 1923. 368 p. (Diss., Paris).   1309

Intensive study of knowledge and opinions in *Encyclopédie* on what would now be called social sciences, namely : ancient and primitive civilizations, modern history, and especially, origins of political, religious, economic, and social institutions.

Review : R. Lenoir, cf. no. 1313.

— Rousseau et l'Encyclopédie. Gamber, [1928], 137 p. *See* 2084.   1310

Title deceptive. Only secondarily study of Rousseau's intellectual relations with *Encyclopédie* and its editors and of his contributions. Primarily attempt to trace history of Rousseau's political ideas.

— Introduction bibliographique à l'étude des sources de la science ethnographique dans l'Encyclopédie. RHph 1:160-72, 331-55, 1933.   1311

Very specialized but valuable study of 18th century erudition which formed base of *Encyclopédie*. Systematically catalogued list, with frequent brief comment. Valuable for study of sources.

Le Gras, Joseph. Diderot et l'Encyclopédie. 4th ed. Amiens, Malfère, 1928. 170 p.
1312

Essential work.
Review : D. Mornet in RHL 36:298-300, 1929.

Lenoir, Raymond. Les sciences sociales dans l'Encyclopédie. RSH 39:113-25, 1925.
1313
Not direct criticism of R. Hubert's study (1309). Attempt to formulate from it new set of conclusions regarding state of social sciences in second half of 18th century. Emphasizes insufficiencies of *philosophes.*

Lévi-Malvano, Ettore. Les éditions toscanes de l'Encyclopédie. RLC 3:213-56, 1923.
1314
History of *Encyclopédie* in Italy until 1780. A study of circumstances surrounding Tuscan editions and also of opinion concerning them. Erudite and thorough article.

Lombard, Alfred. L'abbé Dubos. Hachette, 1913. 616 p. Appendice I, Dubos et Jaucourt.
1315
Study of sources, containing list of passages in various articles of *Encyclopédie* taken from writings of Abbé Dubos.

Naves, Raymond. Voltaire et l'Encyclopédie. Éditions des presses modernes, [1938], 205 p. (Thèse complémentaire). *See* 1789.
1316
Thorough study of Voltaire's relations with the *Encyclopédie* and its editors—of his actual collaboration and development of his attitude toward enterprise. His encyclopedic articles analyzed and reciprocal influence of Voltaire and *Encyclopédie* noted. More weight might have been given to his adverse criticisms of *Encyclopédie.*
Reviews : G. R. Havens in MLN 54: 617-18, 1939; I. O. Wade in RR 31:78-81, 1940.

Oliver, A. R. The Encyclopedists as critics of Music. *See* 337.
1317
Definitive general study of the Encyclopedists and music—of their writings on theory of art as well as opera and other controversies. Emphasizes their positive contribution to music criticism, extent of their involvement with musical questions, and influence in France and abroad. Thorough erudition. Possibly some exaggerations in detail (e.g., in re-establishing Encyclopedists' musical competence, statement that Diderot's chief interest in mathematics was of musical nature).

Reviews : G. R. Havens in RR 40: 144-45, 1949; J. A. Westrup in FS 2: 368-69, 1948.

Powell, L. F. Johnson and the Encyclopédie. RES 2:335-37, 1926.
1318
Article *Anglois,* in *Supplément à l'Encyclopédie* (1776, 1:429 ff) is unacknowledged paraphrase of essay by Johnson, prefixed to his *Dictionary.*

Rocafort, Jacques. Les doctrines littéraires de l'Encyclopédie. Hachette, 1890, 338 p.
1319
Good survey of literary theory and criticism in *Encyclopédie* and *Supplément.* First part, concerning general theory, must be read with caution, as author's reasoning is at times superficial and conclusions disputable.

Rolland, Romain. Musiciens d'autrefois. *See* 349.
1320
In part, study of relations between Encyclopedists (Grimm, Diderot, Rousseau, and D'Alembert) and Gluck's operatic reform. Short summaries of musical abilities and accomplishments of each of these. Defense of their competence. Study of their ideas as an expression of musical aspirations of their time.

Van Roosbroeck, G. L. Who originated the plan of the Encyclopédie ? MP 27:382-84, 1929-30.
1321
After mentioning possibility that Abbé de Gua, and not Diderot, proposed the plan, Van Roosbroeck presents claim of a Dutch publisher, J. Néaulme, to its invention. No critical discussion, although Néaulme's claim may have been advertising scheme. Néaulme makes no mention of idea that constitutes essential originality of *Encyclopédie,* the assignment of work to specialists.

Zeller, Hugo. Die Grammatik in der grossen französischen Enzyklopädie. Weisswasser, Hampel, [1930], 61 p. (Diss. Heidelberg).
1322
Analysis, more than criticism, of various articles relating to grammatical subjects. Some effort made to study bases of grammatical knowledge of authors. General studies, such as those of terminology, orthography, and etymology supplemented with systematic view of ideas of two principal grammarians : Dumarsais and Beauzée. Concise but thorough. *See* no. 373.

Claude Helvétius
(Nos. 1323-1335)

WILLIAM C. HOLBROOK

Helvétius, Claude. Œuvres complètes.
Ed. L. Lefebvre de la Roche. Didot,
1795. 14 v.   1323
  Best edition.

— De l'esprit; De l'homme; notes, maximes
et pensées; Le bonheur; Lettres. Ed.
A. Keim. Mercure de France, 1909.
(Collection des plus belles pages). 337 p.
                                               1324
  Appendix contains documents, anec-
dotes, bibliography.

— Choix de textes et introductions. Ed.
J.-B. Séverac. Michaud, 1911. 222 p.
(Les grands philosophes français et étran-
gers).   1325

Angot de Rotours, *Baron J.* Le bon Helvétius et l'affaire " de l'Esprit " (avec
documents inédits). Rheb June, 1909:
186-214.   1326
  Good condensation of Keim's book
(no. 1332); shows that condemnation of
De l'esprit was not simply attempt to
discourage *Encyclopédistes,* but in part also
result of court jealousies.

Cherel, Albert. XVIIIᵉ siècle et romantisme.
RPL 71:533-37, 1933.   1327
  Excellent summary of H.'s theories;
indication of some aspects of his influence.

Cousin, Victor. Helvétius. *In his :* Cours
de l'histoire de la philosophie moderne.
1st ser., Ladrange, 1846. 3:163-214. *Also
in his :* La philosophie sensualiste au dix-
huitième siècle. 3rd ed., 1856. p. 130-81.
                                               1328
  Gives " analyse fidèle " of the four
Discours of *De l'esprit ;* condemns book
as mediocre.

Damiron, Jean. Mémoire sur Helvétius.
Durand, 1853. 183 p. *Also in :* AMP 1853,
v. 23 : p. 5-43; 24:5-57; 25:47-106, 345-72.
Also in his : Mémoires pour servir à l'histoire
de la philosophie au XVIIIᵉ siècle. *See* 1234.
                                               1329
  Kind to the man, severe toward his
writings : " ... si on le confondait avec
ses ouvrages... il faudrait... le condamner
avec une ferme sévérité." (From closing
paragraph of study).

Frauenglas, Edward. Diderot and Helvétius. RCC 38²:485-99, 1937.   1330

Good supplement to Keim's book
(no. 1332).

Grossman, Mordecai. The philosophy of
Helvétius, with special emphasis on the
educational implications of sensationalism.
New York, Teachers college, Columbia
university, 1926. 181 p. (Contributions
to Education, v. 120).   1331
  Objective statement of H.'s doctrine.
Bibliography worthless.

Keim, Albert. Helvétius, sa vie et son
œuvre, d'après ses ouvrages, des écrits divers
et des documents inédits. Alcan, 1907.
719 p. *See* 3051.   1332
  Most complete work on H. Starting
with notion that H. has been unknown
or misunderstood, Keim attempts his
rehabilitation. No bibliography, but in
Avant-propos mention of authors consulted; *Appendice* II, list of principal
editions of H.
  Reviews : J. de Gaultier in MerF 71:
307-09, 1908; D. Mornet in RHL 15:
362-65, 1908.

Lough, J. Helvétius and d'Holbach. MLR
33:360-84, 1938.   1333
  Purports to be first study of similarities
and differences between two; concludes
that their ideas were largely similar and
had little influence.

Morley, John. Helvétius. *In his :* Diderot
and the Encyclopædists. London, Macmillan, 1886. (First ed., 1878.) 2:123-54.
                                               1334
  Puts *De l'esprit* into intellectual atmosphere in which it was written and
published, exposes its fallacies, and, in
general, disapproves.

Plekhanov, Georgii V. Helvétius. *In his :*
Beiträge zur Geschichte des Materialismus.
Stuttgart, Dietz, 1896. p. 71-153. *Also
in his :* Essays in the history of materialism,
a translation of the foregoing, by Ralph
Fox. London, John Lane, 1934. p. 79-164.
                                               1335
  Solid work, still useful as supplement
to Keim (no. 1332).

Paul Henri Thiry, *baron* d'Holbach
(Nos. 1336-1355)

ANDREW R. MOREHOUSE

**Catalogue des livres de la bibliothèque
de feu M. le baron d'Holbach.** Bure,
Libraire de la Bibliothèque du Roi et de

l'Académie royale des inscriptions et belles-lettres. 1789. 1336

Contains some 3,000 titles of works in D'H.'s library on Theology, Jurisprudence, Philosophy, Arts, and Sciences, etc., especially rich in English sermons and deistic works. Statement in *Avertissement* not exaggerated : " Peu de Bibliothèques sont aussi bien composées que celle-ci, et réunissent un aussi bon choix de livres dans tous les genres..." (p. 111).

Avezac-Lavigne, C. Diderot et la société du Baron d'Holbach. 1875. 272 p. *See* 2327. 1337

D'H.'s appearance in title out of proportion to his appearance in book. He is shown almost incidentally as loyal and understanding friend in whose home ideas of Diderot and Encyclopedists blossomed. Rapid, sketchy, loosely arranged, but interesting account of social and intellectual life of *philosophes*, based on sources. No index, but detailed table of contents.

Cushing, Max Pearson. Baron d'Holbach; a study of eighteenth century radicalism in France. New York, 1914. 108 p. (Diss., Columbia). 1338

Although one of earliest modern studies and in detail superseded by later works, still valuable in concision and clarity for rapid introduction and orientation. Contains critical estimate of important works on D'H. and reference to 18th century criticism of his works. Chapters 2, 3 and bibliography give information concerning editions of D'H.'s works, their chronology, translations, locations, and refutations. Includes also list of his correspondence and number of unpublished letters.

— A forgotten philosopher. Monist 30:311-16, 1920. 1339

Brief but suggestive comments on D'H.'s influence on French revolution and modern thought.

Damiron, J. Ph. D'Holbach. *In his :* Mémoires pour servir à l'histoire de la philosophie au xviiie siècle. *See* 1234. p. 93-226. 1340

Detailed analysis and refutation of D'H.'s *Système de la nature* from point of view of his ideas on nature, man, society and God. Damiron passionate partisan of spiritualism against materialism : " ... je le dis d'avance, je condamnerai; mais je condamnerai les idées et non les hommes..." (p. xvii). Warns

reader against subversive ideas of D'H. Damiron's ideas hence highly colored, personal, and moralistic, but clear and often meaningful from point of view of spiritualism.

Delvaille, Jules. D'Holbach. *In his :* Essai sur l'histoire de l'idée de progrès jusqu'à la fin du xviiie siècle. *See* 1037. p. 651-59. 1341

D'H. identified as dynamic factor in evolution of idea of progress.

Genlis, Stéphanie F., etc., *comtesse de.* Les dîners du baron d'Holbach. 1822. 532 p. 1342

Cushing calls it piece of libellous fiction (no. 1338). For Mme de Genlis *philosophes* are band of conspirators formed to destroy institutions of France, and Voltaire chief of cabal, who supplied money and meeting place. Interesting as one of earliest post-revolutionary reactions against so-called sins of *philosophes*. Written in 1793 or 1794. First listed in Guérard, 1822.

Hubert, René. D'Holbach et ses amis. Delpuech, [c1928]. 224 p. 1343

Popular and readable summary of D'H.'s thought. Shows him as scientific humanitarian, with rich strain of materialistic fanaticism, whose spiritual progeny are *Messieurs* Homais (Flaubert, *Mme Bovary*) of 19th century. Scientific and positivistic assumptions of philosophers are well discussed in Chap. 6. Part 2 contains well-chosen excerpts from D'H.'s works. No index.
Reviews : D. Mornet in RHL 36:597-98, 1929; P. Masson-Oursel in MerF 213: 166, July 1, 1929.

Lalande, André. Quelques idées du baron d'Holbach. RPFE 33:601-21, 1892. 1344

Discusses striking similarities, often by comparing texts, between ideas of Herbert Spencer and those of D'H. despite former's disavowal of materialism as a philosophy. " Chez Spencer se retrouverait toute la philosophie du baron, plus l'idée centrale de l'évolution... et si son œuvre est moins détaillée que celle de M. Spencer, elle ne lui cède en rien pour la rigueur de la logique et l'unité de la conception." (p. 611].

Lange, F. A. The system of nature. *In his :* The history of materialism. *See* 1211. Sec. 2, p. 92-123. 1344A

In this section of his classic work, Lange discusses critically and authoritatively D'H.'s ideas in general and meaning, importance, and influence of his *Système de la nature* in particular. Shows weaknesses of Voltaire's refutation.

Lion, Henri. Essai sur les œuvres politiques et morales du baron d'Holbach. AnR 14:89-98, 265-80, 441-63, 1922.

— La politique naturelle de d'Holbach. *Idem* 15:209-19, 1923.

— L'éthocratie de d'Holbach. *Idem* 15:378-96, 1923.

— La morale universelle de d'Holbach. AHRF 1:42-63, 1924.

— Les idées politiques et morales de d'Holbach. *Idem* 1:356-70, 1924.   1345

Valuable series of articles, clear, succinct, meaningful, on D'H.'s philosophical, social, ethical, political, and economic ideas, as contained in *Système de la nature, Système social, Politique naturelle,* and *Ethocratie.* First three articles summarize his ideas; latter two discuss and evaluate them objectively.

Lough, J. Essai de bibliographie critique des publications du baron d'Holbach. RHL 46:215-34, 1939 and 47:314-18, 1947. 1346

Two important articles bringing into focus latest information concerning D'H. as author, translator, and adapter. Taking Barbier's conclusions in his *Dictionnaire des ouvrages anonymes* (1822-27, 2nd ed.) as point of departure, Lough completes and corrects conclusions of his predecessors in Holbachian studies. Shows among works attributed to D'H. those which are really his, those which belong to first half of century, and those which were translated and adapted from English works. Believes that Diderot's and Naigeon's role in composition and publication of D'H.'s works not very important.

Morley, John. D'Holbach's System of nature. *In his:* Diderot and the Encyclopedists. *See* 1334. 2:158-192.   1347

Critical appraisal of D'H.'s principal arguments as expounded in his *Système de la nature.* For its clarity, insight, and balanced judgment, Morley's discussion one of best in English.

Mornet, Daniel. Bibliographie d'un certain nombre d'ouvrages philosophiques du xviiie

siècle et particulièrement de d'Holbach (jusqu'en 1789). RHL 40:259-81, 1933.
1348

Article gives evidence of frequent publication and wide diffusion of D'H.'s works and attributions and of those of other *philosophes* before Revolution. Bibliography served Mornet in composition of his *Origines intellectuelles...* (*See* no. 45); cf. his note at head of article. J. Lough (*Supplément à la bibliographie des ouvrages du Baron d'Holbach* in RHL 43:287-88, 1936) adds a few titles.

— L'œuvre de d'Holbach et de ses collaborateurs. *In his:* Les origines intellectuelles de la Révolution française (1715-1787). *See* 45. p. 100-04.   1349

Succinct summary of D'H.'s ideas, their diffusion and influence in 18th century.

Naville, Pierre. Paul Thiry d'Holbach et la philosophie scientifique au xviiie siècle. Gallimard, [1943]. 471 p.   1350

Bibliography (p. 405-20) is most detailed and complete of contemporary studies. Gives sources for all attributions, and important information concerning each one of D'H.'s works. Bibliography of works about D'H. found in notes and in *Annexe* 9, p. 465.

Original, stimulating, enlightening, and powerful rehabilitation of D'H. by intelligent, though passionate partisan, who introduced behaviorism of American psychologist Watson into France. D'H. identified in Diderot's intellectual and spiritual *milieu,* and both become great generators of enlightenment and of authentic, materialistic truth for modern world. Most detailed and informative work on D'H.'s life and works. Contains number of documents never before published.

Plekhanov, G. C. D'Holbach. *In his:* Essays in the history of materialism. *See* 1335. p. 3-75.   1351

Study of materialism of D'H., Helvétius, and Karl Marx. Metaphysical materialism of former two analyzed, criticized, and contrasted with " superior ": dialectical materialism of latter, whose debt to Hegelian dialectics is also shown. Dialectical materialism held to be key that unlocks mystery of history, and communism the goal toward which history marches in its travail. Dogmatic and polemical in assumptions, discursive in style, but full of interesting flashes in interpretation of historical process. Written originally in 1896.

Röck, Hubert. Kritisches Verzeichnis der philosophischen Schriften Holbachs. AGP 30:270-90, 1916-17. 1352

Important article that discusses authenticity and dates of D'H.'s philosophical works, translations and adaptations, concluding with select list of titles.

Sée, Henri. Helvétius et d'Holbach. *In his :* Les idées politiques en France au XVIIIe siècle. *See* 104, p. 144-53. 1352A

— Helvétius et d'Holbach. *In his :* L'évolution de la pensée politique en France au XVIIIe siècle. *See* 1072, p. 217-24. 1353

Both books contain brief chapters on political ideas of Helvétius and D'H. with extracts illustrating Sée's generalizations. Scope of these works did not permit detailed treatment. Evidence and conclusions in both chapters similar : namely, that D'H. is not interested primarily in political forms, but in welfare and happiness of individual. D'H. identified in political current of his time, but for detailed treatment Lion's articles (no. 1345) should be consulted.

Wickwar, W. H. Helvétius and Holbach. *In :* Social and political ideas of some great French thinkers of the Age of Reason. Ed. by F. J. C. Hearnshaw. New York, Crofts, 1930. p. 195-216. 1354

France, not England, in persons of Helvétius and D'H. is cradle of 19th century utilitarianism. Discusses sources of D'H.'s political ideas and believes that " ... they were the forerunners of all of us who try to envisage social experience in a scientific... spirit..." (p. 215).

— Baron d'Holbach; a prelude to the French revolution. London, Allen, 1935. 253 p. *See* 3053. 1355

Bibliography in appendix subdivided into highly selected list of previous articles on D'H. and chronological list of D'H.'s publications with pertinent information concerning dates, translations, and attributions. List of D'H.'s articles in *Encyclopédie* is given. Notes often refer to valuable source material, but are difficult to use. For example, in reference to specific fact in appendix which contains 11 p., he merely says, " *Vide infra, Appendix C.*"

Book good, general treatment of main currents of D'H.'s thought in France and

abroad, judicious and unbiased, with biographical material based on newly found sources. Stresses D'H.'s utilitarianism and humanitarianism, and sees his atheism as important influence on 19th century secularism. Cross section of his thought given in well-translated excerpts. Largely superseded by Naville (no. 1350).

Reviews : A. J. Grant in SR 28:214-16, 1936; J. Lough in RHL 43:307-09, 1936.

Marie Jean Antoine Nicolas Caritat, *marquis* de Condorcet
(Nos. 1356-1444)

THOMAS E. OLIVER*

Condorcet, Marie, etc. Œuvres, publiées par A. C. O'Connor et F. Arago. Didot, 1847-49. 12 v. 1356

Carefully edited work, for which Arago deserves credit. He also wrote excellent biography of C. in vol. I, which was last one published and contains fairly detailed *Table alphabétique* and *Table chronologique* of C.'s works. This edition described in detail in Cahen (no. 1393, p. xvi-xviii). Contains everything found in 1804 edition, but still far from complete.

Review : In QR 87:1-44, 1850.

— Correspondance. *See :* Arago (1356, v. I), Charavay (1359), Doumic, (1407), Henry (1358), Lespinasse (271). 1357

Much work remains to be done upon C.'s *Correspondance*, in archives of *Institut de France*, and elsewhere.

— Correspondance inédite de Condorcet et de Turgot, 1770-1779. Publiée avec des notes et une introduction d'après les autographes de la collection Minoret et les manuscrits de l'Institut par Charles Henry. Charavay, 1883. 326 p. 1358

— Autographes et documents révolutionnaires : Condorcet-Barbaroux-Jourdan-Carnot. Edited by Etienne Charavay. Rfr 6:726-32, 1884. 1359

Contribution from C. is a letter of June, 1790, which gives admirable summary of his views on several important questions.

— Éloge de Blaise Pascal. *In :* Pascal, Blaise. Pensées de Pascal, avec les notes de Voltaire, une Préface et un Éloge de Blaise Pascal par Condorcet. London, (i.e., Paris or Avignon). 1785. v. I, p. 9-122. *Also in :*

* Deceased.

Condorcet, Marie, etc. Œuvres complètes
(1356) 4:375-476.   1360

Original edition of Pascal's *Pensées* as
chosen by C. was published in 1776; that
of 1778 is same.

— Esquisse d'un tableau historique des progrès de l'esprit humain. Boivin, [1933].
239 p.   Texte revu et présenté par
O. H. Prior. (Bibliothèque de philosophie).
                                     1361

Best edition so far; excellent introduction on C. and some discussion of
earlier editions of work.   Text not
annotated, however, and thus task of
critical, variorum edition still remains to
be done. Such edition must of course
be based upon study of all earlier editions,
and of *Fragments*. Attention must also
be paid to Cahen's : *Condorcet inédit ;
notes pour le Tableau des progrès de l'esprit
humain* (no. 1396).
Reviews : G. Lefebvre in AHRF 13:
280, 1936; F. L. Ryan in BA 8:44, Jan.,
1936; J. Thomas in Rcr ns. 100:495-96,
1933.

— Essai sur l'application de l'analyse à la
probabilité des décisions rendues à la pluralité des voix.   Imprimerie royale, 1785.
Discours préliminaire, p. i-cxci; Essai,
304 p.   1362 and 1363

Not in Arago (no. 1380).

— Un fragment inédit de Condorcet.   Ed.
by Léon Cahen. Rfr 42:115-31, 1902. 1364

Satirical work of C.'s youth, undated
but probably written between 1765 and
1770, showing him as strongly inclined
toward republican ideas far earlier than
generally believed. Memoir supposed to
be hitherto unpublished manuscript of
Machiavelli, who exhorts prince to place
consciences and intelligence of his subjects under control of clergy, whom he
must protect with all his power, etc.
Article closes with study of advantages
of spy system.

— Un fragment inédit de Condorcet.   Ed.
by Léon Cahen. RMM 22:581-94, 1914-15.
                                     1365
Interesting and important notes of C.
written for the *Esquisse*, and not included
in 1847 edition of the *Œuvres* (no. 1356).
Notes show clearly important aspects of
C.'s philosophical thought.   Cahen's
introductory remarks : p. 581-83.

— A letter from M. Condorcet, a member
of the National Convention, to a magistrate

of Swisserland [*sic*] respecting the massacres
of the Swiss guards on the 10th of August,
etc. New York, 1793. 12 p.   1366

Points out that keeping the Swiss
Guards in service had been unconstitu-
tional since adoption of constitution in
1791; says that their death was fault of
King.

— Une lettre de Condorcet à Diderot sur le
Parlement. Rfr 65:365-66, 1913.   1367

Letter from unedited manuscript collection of Noël Charavay. Undated, but
probably written in 1774. Refers to La
Barre affair and reveals C.'s already deep
animosity to Parlement for its many
injustices.

[—]. Lettres d'un bourgeois de New-Heaven
[*sic*] à un citoyen de Virginie, sur l'inutilité de
partager le pouvoir législatif entre plusieurs
corps. *In :* [Mazzei, Filippo]. Recherches
historiques et politiques sur les États-Unis
de l'Amérique septentrionale.   Froullé,
1788. v. 1, p. 267-371.   1368 and 1369

— Vie de Voltaire, par le marquis de Condorcet, suivie des Mémoires de Voltaire
écrits par lui-même. Kehl, Société litté-
raire-typographique, 1787. 374 p.   1370

This celebrated biography first prepared in 1784 by C. for Kehl edition of
Voltaire's works, and has been the basis
of many biographies of Voltaire ever
since. In Kehl octavo edition of Voltaire
it is found in v. 70, p. 1-180 (no. 1626).

— Voltaire. Œuvres complètes de Voltaire,
Edited by Beaumarchais, Condorcet and
Decroix. [Kehl]. Société littéraire-typo-
graphique, 1785-1789. 70 v. 8°, or 92 v. 12°.
                                     1371

Beaumarchais was financial backer of
edition, C. did editing and annotating,
and Decroix corrected proofs.   For full
account of edition, see Bengesco (no. 1618),
v. 4, p. 105-46. The *Vie de Voltaire*,
by C. (no. 1370) is in v. 70 of the octavo
ed., p. 1-180.

— Condorcet, par Ferdinand Buisson. Alcan,
1929. 139 p. (Réformateurs sociaux). 1372

Excellent anthology; excerpts chiefly
from *Esquisse* and his works on education.

Alengry, Franck. Condorcet guide de la
Révolution française, théoricien du droit
constitutionnel et précurseur de la science
sociale. Giard & Brière, 1903, 1904. 891 p.
(Diss., law, Toulouse).   1373

Still valuable work; well documented, uses much unedited material, especially in footnotes. Praise of C. exaggerated. Two-thirds of book devoted to C. as theorist of constitutional law; this emphasis shows that he was not active guide of Revolution. C.'s ideas on education receive scant treatment. Excellent summary of his influence after death (p. 338-54).

Reviews : A. Aulard in Rfr 46:71-74, 1904; R. Doumic in RDM 5th per. 23: 446-57, Sept. 15, 1904; A. Mathiez in Rcr ns 59:88-94, Jan. 30, 1905; H. Sée in RSH 9:115-18, 1904.

— Le sens des réalités chez Condorcet constitutionnaliste. RHP 1:605-14, 1937.   1374

Purpose of study is to show that C. had feeling for reality, and that his theories on constitutional law developed progressively, under influence of observation, meditation, experience and, at certain critical moments, under imperious impact of events. Alengry thus seeks to refute traditional conception of C.'s attitude, as expressed by Taine, Renan, Faguet, and others.

— Condorcet journaliste. Cpr 2:242-53, 1938.   1375

Article discusses C.'s best journalistic work, emphasizing his skill as educator of the people in political matters; praises his dignity, courage, sincerity, knowledge, unselfishness, and ironic wit.

Allison, J. M. Condorcet, a forgotten historian. In : Essays in honor of Albert Feuillerat, edited by Henri M. Peyre. New Haven, Yale univ. press; London, Milford, 1943. p. 183-94.   1376, 1377 and 1378

Admirable summary of significance of C. in his own time and since.

Antoine, Emile. Pèlerinage de Bourg-la-Reine. Les derniers jours de Condorcet. RO 1st sem., 1890, p. 124-54; Fête de Condorcet, RO 2nd sem., 1891, p. 67-90, 2nd sem., 1892, p. 99-108. Also printed, Châlon-sur-Saône, Marceau, 1890, 32 p.   1379

Contains procès-verbal of C.'s arrest, and of levée du corps; also death certificate which fixes date as 9 germinal an II (March 29, 1794). These documents and others reprinted as Annexe H, p. 358-69, in Robinet's Condorcet (no. 1437).

Arago, D. F. J. Biographie de Jean Antoine Nicolas Caritat de Condorcet. ASM 20:

i-cxiii, 1849. Also in : Œuvres de Condorcet (1356), v. 1, p. i-clxxxvi. Reprinted by Didot, 1849, 113 p. Also in : Arago, D. J. F. Œuvres complètes. Gide & Baudry; Leipzig, Weigel, 1854-1862. v. 2, p. 117-246.   1380

Based on information supplied by C.'s daughter, not complete or always accurate, and must be checked against later studies. Thus : it erroneously gives Apr. 8, 1794, as date of C.'s death, mistake frequently repeated since. Date is March 25, 1794, according to Robinet, (no. 1437, p. 329-32); Barroux (no. 1387) establishes correct date as March 29, 1794.

Archambault de Montfort, H[enri]. Les idées de Condorcet sur le suffrage. Société française d'imprimerie et de librairie. 1915. 218 p. (Diss., Poitiers).   1381

Essential study, broader in scope than title indicates, since it offers thorough, methodical assembling of most of C.'s ideas on nearly every phase of political science which he touched. Author believes many of C.'s theories on popular sovereignty were impractical of application because, as mathematician, he lived in world of abstractions, hostile to reality. Gives intelligent analysis and indictment of C.'s fundamental conceptions, from conservative point of view. Brief and badly made but still useful bibliography; no index. Book is rare in United States; copy at Princeton.

Aulard, [François Victor] Alphonse. Condorcet: L'éloquence parlementaire pendant la Révolution française; les orateurs de la Législative et de la Convention. Hachette, 1885-1886. v. 1 : p. 265-81.   1382

Believes that C. not good orator, but was admired and influential because of prestige given to his character and career.

— La constitution " girondine "; texte du projet et des articles votés. Rfr 34:503-54, 1898.   1383

This constitution, prepared by a committee of the Convention of which C. was chairman, never adopted. Jacobin party attacked it bitterly, and finally substituted shorter constitution, which however contained much of former one. C.'s indignation caused him to appeal, over heads of Convention, to French people to reject Jacobin constitution. For this action, C. was proscribed.

— Condorcet. In his : Histoire politique de la Révolution française; origines et dévelop-

pement de la démocratie et de la République. (1789-1804). Colin, 1901. 805 p.
1384

In this work, admirably documented, *Table alphabétique des noms de personnes*, p. 785-97, contains 62 references to C. References constitute excellent record of his activities. Aulard considers C. greatest thinker of his age.

Baldwin, S. E. The authorship of the Quatre lettres d'un bourgeois de New Heaven sur l'unité de la législation, published in Mazzei's Recherches historiques et politiques sur les États-Unis de l'Amérique septentrionale. NHS 6: 263-81, 1900.
1385

Article gives account of Mazzei's life, description of his work, and tells how C. happened to publish his : *Lettres d'un bourgeois de New Heaven* [sic] *à un citoyen de Virginie, sur l'inutilité de partager le pouvoir législatif entre plusieurs corps* (no. 1368).

Barni, Jules. Fragments inédits sur Condorcet. IGB 41:29-60, 1914.   1386

Fragments of course of lectures given by Barni in 1869 dealing with Malesherbes, Turgot, Necker, Mirabeau, and Condorcet as statesmen who were " promoteurs ou coopérateurs de la Révolution française." Above article contains what is left of lectures on Turgot and C. Three lectures on C. appear to be based on Arago (no. 1380). Barni refutes ably unjust condemnation of C. by Sainte-Beuve and Mme de Staël (p. 50-54).

Barroux, Marius. Jugement rectificatif de l'acte de décès de Condorcet, 12 ventôse an 3. Rfr 17:173-85, 1889.   1387

Article establishes fact that correct death-date is 9 *germinal an 2*, March 29, 1794. Date of April 8, as given in Arago's biography (no. 1380), incorrect, but has been perpetuated in many biographies.

— Acte de naissance de Condorcet. Rfr 18: 376, 1890.   1388

This birth certificate, copied from records at Ribemont and printed here in full, established C.'s birthday as Sept. 17, 1743, and that he was christened : Marie Jean Antoine Nicolas; Arago (no. 1380) omits the Marie.

Bigot, Henri. Les idées de Condorcet sur l'instruction publique. Lévrier, 1912. 186 p. (Diss., law, Poitiers).   1389

Good analysis, whose value is increased by several tabulations. Bigot expresses unbounded admiration for C. as educational theorist, declaring that this aspect of his genius is his chief title to fame and glory.

Bonald, Louis Gabriel Ambroise, *vicomte* **de.** Observations sur un ouvrage posthume de Condorcet intitulé : Esquisse d'un tableau des progrès de l'esprit humain. *In his :* Œuvres complètes, edited by J. P. Migne. Ateliers catholiques, 1864. v. 1, columns 722-42.   1390

Violent attack from this most extreme of reactionaries, of value only as revealing nature of prejudices against which C. had to contend.

Bouillier, Francisque. Projets divers de réorganisation des anciennes académies; Condorcet (papiers inédits)—Talleyrand—Mirabeau. AMP ns 15:636-73, 1881.   1391

Plan here outlined (p. 636-61), from C.'s *inédits* much the same as one he presented for organization of a national society of arts and letters in his report on public education made to Legislative Assembly.

Bury, John Bagnell. The French revolution : Condorcet. *In his :* The idea of progress; an inquiry into its origin and growth. *See* 1031. p. 202-16.   1392

Book considered by many scholars most widely historical and penetrating philosophic study of subject of progress in English. Bury believes that French revolutionaries in general made mistake of thinking that more legislation could create a new society at once. He thinks that C.'s ideas are found almost entirely in Turgot, but that they have new significance for C.

Cahen, Léon. Condorcet et la Révolution française. Alcan, 1904. 592 p. (Diss., Paris).   1393

Essential study. Was Cahen's major thesis for degree of *docteur-ès-lettres*. Reviews of such scholars as Aulard and Mathiez go far to establishing Cahen as leading authority on C. Book's main stress is, naturally, upon C.'s political connections with Revolution. However, his other activities are adequately discussed. Cahen has edited or described more of hitherto unedited writing of C. than any other scholar. In appendices to this main study are six such *inédits*, p. 549-73. On p. xiii of his Introduction,

Cahen mentions an inventory of still unedited material by C. in the *Bibliothèque de l'Institut*. This inventory, as yet unpublished, is available there to scholars. Cahen's bibliography, p. xi-xxxi, most extensive of all. He makes use of more unedited sources than any other writer; see his footnotes *passim*. In every respect this book is documented most thoroughly. Only valid criticism of study seems to be that subject and name index, p. 575-78, should have been greatly expanded.

Reviews : A. Aulard in Rfr 47:68-77, 1904; R. Doumic in RDM 5th ser. 23: 446-57, Sept. 15, 1904; A. Mathiez in Rcr ns 59:88-94, Jan. 30, 1905.

— Notes sur les manuscrits de Condorcet conservés à la Bibliothèque de l'Institut. AMP ns 61:779-85, 1904. 1394

Describes chaotic state in which C.'s papers reached *Institut*. As example of value of this unpublished material, Cahen gives brief summary and analysis of an essay on criminal law by C. found among these papers.

— La Société des amis des noirs et Condorcet. Rfr 50:481-511, 1906. 1395

Description of bundle of papers in library of the *Institut*, some entirely in C.'s handwriting, others with his comments, upon anti-slavery society of which he became leader.

— Condorcet inédit; notes pour le Tableau des progrès de l'esprit humain, Rfr 75:193-212, 1922. 1396

Notes are fragments, now in *Bibliothèque nationale*, and not in 1847-49 edition of C.'s *Œuvres* (no. 1356). Disconnected and hard to assign to places in the *Esquisse* where, however, they plainly belong. May possibly represent C.'s plan for a final revision of work.

Caillaud, Eugène. Les idées économiques de Condorcet. Poitiers, Bousrez, 1908. 189 p. (Diss., law, Poitiers). 1397

Appears to be only work devoted exclusively to this subject, though Alengry, (no. 1373, p. 638-728) gives much space to C. as financier and political economist. Considers C. faithful disciple of Turgot and, by his double belief in natural goodness of man, and limitless possibilities of perfectibility of human mind, precursor of socialism of Saint-Simon.

Charma, A[ntoine]. Condorcet, sa vie et ses œuvres. MAC 1863 : 259-338. 1398

Valuable study. Most original idea : that progress of C.'s political thought presents summary and prophecy of changing phases of political evolution of European states, especially greater ones. Robinet calls work important, and quotes from it in discussing C.'s religious ideas (no. 1437, p. 330).

Compayré, Gabriel. L'Assemblée législative et Condorcet. *In his :* Histoire critique des doctrines de l'éducation en France. 3rd ed., Hachette, 1881. v. 2, p. 273-90. 1399

Admirable summary, perhaps best in a few pages, of C.'s ideas on education, and of their influence.

Comte, Auguste. [Condorcet]. *In his :* Cours de philosophie positive. Bachelier, 1839. v. 4, p. 252-64. 1400

Not a book-chapter or a division of the text; primarily of interest as tracing a comparison between parts played respectively by Montesquieu and by C. in formation of social sciences.

— [Condorcet]. *In his :* Système de politique positive. Carilian-Goeury, 1851-56. v. 4, p. 109-19. (Appendice général). 1401

Essay written in 1822, while Comte was still disciple of Saint-Simon. Gives valuable criticism of the *Esquisse*, which Comte praises highly, but points out its failure to create a " *politique positive.*" Comte thinks that C. emphasized too strongly the philosophy of 18th century, which led him to condemn past instead of studying it with scientific impartiality.

Defourny, Maurice. La philosophie de l'histoire chez Condorcet. RNS 1904:157-75, 241-62. 1402

Written from clerical viewpoint, first article naturally critical of C. for his hostility to religion and priestly class of all times. Second article shows how C. received most of his ideas from Montesquieu, Rousseau, Quesnay, Turgot, and Physiocrats in France, and Bentham, Paine, Adam Smith, Price, and Priestley in England.

Delsaux, Hélène. Condorcet journaliste (1790-1794). Champion, 1931. 354 p. 1403

Valuable study, especially useful for selective bibliography of C.'s work (p. 295-300), and classified list of unedited material by him in *Bibliothèque de l'Institut de France*. Valuable feature of bibliography is list of journals upon which C. collaborated (p. 271-86).

Reviews : G. G. Andrews in AHR 30: 794-95, 1931-32; R. Durand in Rcr ns 99:174-75, 1932; Gaston-Martin [G. Martin] in Rfr 85:271-74, 1932; B. Iványi-Grünwald in Sz 67:233-34, 1933; A. Mathiez in ARF 9:182-83, 1932.

Delvaille, Jules. Condorcet. *In his :* Essai sur l'histoire de l'idée du progrès jusqu'à la fin du xviii⁰ siècle. *See* 1037, p. 670-707.
1404

Well-documented study, with copious bibliography and footnotes. Delvaille stresses fact that *Esquisse* was merely preface to immense work that C. was planning (p. 686). Believes that C.'s *Discours de réception* to Academy (Feb. 21, 1782) already contained many ideas later elaborated in *Esquisse.*

Denis, Hector. La dynamique sociale idéaliste de Godwin et de Condorcet. *In his :* Histoire des systèmes économiques et socialistes. Giard & Brière, 1904-1907. v. 2, p. 1-45.
1405

Treats connections between C.'s ideas (in *Esquisse*) concerning political justice and its influence on general virtue and happiness and those of William Godwin's *Of avarice and profusion.* P. 31-43 contain eminently just appreciation of *Esquisse* and statement that C.'s *Mémoires sur l'instruction publique* are in reality a true commentary on *Esquisse* and cannot be disassociated from it.

Dide, Auguste. Condorcet. Rfr 2:695-709, 745-54, 947-58, 1882.
1406

Concise, critical biography, based largely on that of Arago (no. 1356), and repeating some of its errors. Stresses C.'s admiration for United States and his prophetic vision of future of democracy there and in Europe.

Doumic, René. Lettres d'un philosophe et d'une femme sensible; Condorcet et Madame Suard. RDM 6th per. L'amitié tendre 5:302-25, Sept. 15, 1911; Les années de la vie commune, 5:835-60, Oct. 15, 1911; L'envers de la sensibilité, 7:57-81, Jan. 1, 1912. *See* 299.
1407

Important contribution to knowledge of C.'s life and character. Doumic does not edit the letters, but quotes from them liberally, adding his comments.

Dumesnil, Georges E. Condorcet. Condorcet et l'éducation des femmes. *In his :*

La pédagogie révolutionnaire. Delagrave, 1883, p. 107-48, 149-57.
1408

In first of these two chapters (p. 107-48), is an analysis of chief features of C.'s *Rapport et projet de décret sur l'organisation générale de l'instruction publique,* with occasional comparison with plans of Mirabeau and Talleyrand. In second (p. 149-57) is shown C.'s approval of co-education.

Fabre, Joseph. Condorcet. *In his :* Les pères de la Révolution (de Bayle à Condorcet). Alcan, 1910. p. 669-756.
1409

Fabre praises C. for his sociological even more than for his educational views, but warns against his excessively optimistic faith that education alone can produce higher moral and social values.

Finch, David. Condorcet. *In his :* La critique philosophique de Pascal au xviii⁰ siècle. Philadelphia, 1940. p. 53-73. (Diss., Pennsylvania). *See* 1757.
1410

Finch believes that C.'s criticism of Pascal's *Pensées* was a synthesis of what Voltaire, Diderot, and D'Alembert had already said.

Frayssinet, Marc. Le Rapporteur du Comité : Condorcet. *In his :* La république des Girondins. Toulouse, Société provinciale d'édition, 1903. p. 69-148.
1411

Interesting study, containing excellent summary of C.'s work, and well-balanced appraisal of his influence and value. Last chapter of section (p. 139-48) examines : *La Constitution girondine; le rapport de Condorcet.*

Gallois, L. C. A. G. Condorcet, rédacteur de La chronique du mois. *In his :* Histoire des journaux et des journalistes de la Révolution française. Société de l'industrie fraternelle, 1845-1846. v. 2, p. 97-112.
1412

Chronique du mois was considered C.'s favorite journal. Paper had 14 editors, each in charge of a department; C.'s was legislation and public education. Periodical published from December, 1791, to July, 1793.

Gidney, Lucy May. L'influence des États-Unis d'Amérique sur Brissot, Condorcet et Mme Roland. Rieder, 1930. 176 p. (Diss., Paris, Doctorat de l'Université).
1413

This thesis does not present any new or original views, or any unedited material but is, on the whole, conscientious piece of work. Author asserts that probably C. and Brissot borrowed from America their ideas on free public education; she has been criticized for advancing this opinion without documentary evidence in its support. Study exaggerates influence of American theories. Reviews : Gaston-Martin [G. Martin] in Rfr 84:363-66, 1931; P. Grunebaum Ballin in ARF 9:87, 1932.

Giraud, Victor. Pascal, Condorcet et l'Encyclopédie. RHL 13:110-11, 1906. 1414

The *Encyclopédie* not that of Diderot and d'Alembert, but the *Encyclopédie méthodique* published by Panckoucke in 1782-1792. This contained a long article by J. A. Naigeon on *Pascal (philosophie de)*, in v. 3, 1794, p. 855-947, in which he prints C.'s *Éloge* of Pascal (no. 1410). On p. 868, col. 2, of this printing of the *Éloge* is the passage which interested Giraud especially; in it C. described incident of accident to Pascal on Neuilly bridge.

Guillois, Antoine. La marquise de Condorcet, sa famille, son salon, ses amis, 1764-1822. *See* 205. 1415

Admirable, interesting book, showing high intellectual and moral character of Sophie de Condorcet, *née* de Grouchy. Explains importance of her salon as aid to her husband's career, and relations of Condorcets to their many friends. Chapter on *Proscription et mort de Condorcet, Ruine de Sophie*, p. 133-72, admirably written. Review : E. Charavay in Rfr 32:190-92, 1897.

Hansen, Millard. Condorcet's liberal philosophy of education. SAQ 36:385-99, 1937. 1416

Points out that 1935 platform of the National Education Association of the U. S. demanded chief principles that C. insisted upon. Good summary and analysis of C.'s ideas.

Haraszti, Zoltán. John Adams on Condorcet; his comments on The outline of the progress of the human mind now first published. MB 5:473-99, Dec., 1930. 1417

Interesting 7-page (p. 473-79) introductory notice by Haraszti. Remainder of paper consists of notes of John Adams, second President of the United States. Adams did not, in general, like C.'s ideas, in part because of latter's criticisms of his (Adams's) *Defense of the constitution*

of government of the United States of America (1787), as expressed in fourth of C.'s letters in the *Lettres d'un bourgeois de New Heaven* [*sic*], etc. (no. 1368).

[Henry, Charles]. Sur la vie et les écrits mathématiques de Jean-Antoine-Nicolas de Caritat, marquis de Condorcet. BMF 16: 271-91, 1883. 1418

P. 271-82 contain short biography of C., largely from mathematical angle. In fact, p. 276-78 discuss his *Essai sur l'application de l'analyse à la probabilité des décisions rendues à la pluralité des voix*, (1785). Then follows a complete list of C.'s mathematical works. Article has very brief notice by Max Henoch of Berlin in : JFM 16:24, 1884.

Hippeau, Célestin. L'instruction publique en France pendant la Révolution; Discours et rapports de Mirabeau, Talleyrand-Périgord, Condorcet, Lanthenas, Romme, Le Peletier-Saint-Fargeau, Calès, Lakanal, Daunou et Fourcroy. Didier, 1883. 2 v. 1419

These two volumes give complete picture of struggle to establish sound system of education for France. V. 2, p. 329-56, contains brief biographical notices of the legislators who helped this effort, with page references to their activity and quotations from their speeches. C.'s report is in v. 1, p. 185-389. Thorough subject index in v. 2.

Hoffman-Linke, Eva Elizabeth. Turgot und Condorcet. *In her :* Zwischen Nationalismus und Demokratie; Gestalten der französischen Vorrevolution. Munich and Berlin, Oldenburg, 1927. p. 196-227. (Beiheft 9 of the HZ) 1420

Excellent monograph. Influence of Turgot on C. in political, economic, and educational matters shown. These two were much alike in mind and temperament; C. attacked practical problems as Turgot would have done had conditions permitted. Author expresses deep admiration for C. and compares him with Lessing, noblest spirit of German enlightenment. Both were great liberals, far in advance of their time.

Laboulle, M. J. La mathématique sociale : Condorcet et ses prédécesseurs. RHL 46: 33-55, 1939. 1421

Important study. C. coined expression " mathématique sociale," explaining what it meant to him and how he intended to use it, in opening paragraphs of his

Tableau général de la science, qui a pour objet l'application du calcul aux sciences politiques et morales. Œuvres, ed. of 1847-49 (no. 1356), v. 1, p. 539-73; especially p. 540-41. Study discussed application of mathematics to social phenomena of all kinds that can be numerically measured. As in other aspects of his activity C. is here far ahead of his time; this article shows C.'s foresight in many other directions than in educational and constitutional theories, upon which his fame has hitherto chiefly rested.

Lacroix, S[ilvestre] F[rançois]. Notice historique sur la vie et les ouvrages de Condorcet. *In :* Magasin encyclopédique, ou Journal des sciences, des lettres et des arts, 1813, v. 6, p. 54-77. *Also in a reprint :* Sajou, 1813. 24 p.   1422

Lacroix, distinguished professor of mathematics, was a *protégé* and intimate friend of C. According to Henry (no. 1418, p. 273-74, n. 5), this *Notice* was intended for Michaud's *Biographie universelle,* but was not accepted. Important however because Lacroix is one of few biographers of C. who knew him intimately. This *Notice* frequently utilized by Robinet (1437) and other biographers.

La Fontainerie, François de. Condorcet (1743-1794) and his Report on public instruction. *In his :* French liberalism and education in the eighteenth century; the writings of La Chalotais, Turgot, Diderot and Condorcet on national education, translated and edited by F. de la Fontainerie. New York and London, McGraw-Hill, 1932. Introduction : p. 313-22; Report, p. 323-78. (Diss., Columbia).   1423

C. section based upon text as published by G. Compayré of : *Rapport et projet de décret sur l'organisation générale de l'instruction publique.* Author of this thesis would have given it much greater interest and value by an analysis of C.'s *Report,* and a comparison of it with other well-known ones. Limited bibliography. *See* no. 2324.

Lalande, J. J. L. Notice sur la vie et les ouvrages de Condorcet. MerF 19:141-62, Jan. 20, 1796.   1424

Lalande, famous astronomer, was friend, admirer, and patron of young C. His *Notice* has value of source-material, especially for earlier, scientific period of

C.'s life. Hence Alengry (no. 1373), Robinet (no. 1437), and others refer to it.

Lamartine, Alphonse de. [Portrait de Condorcet]. *In his :* Histoire des Girondins, Furne, 1848. v. 1, p. 183-84.   1425

Unjust criticism, ably answered by Arago, in supplementary pages to his biography of C. (no. 1380, p. clxxiii-clxxxvi).

Lecler, Joseph. Les idées religieuses de Condorcet; l'Église et l'état. Études 211: 35-53, 1932.   1426

Interesting article; intelligent, well-informed treatment of subject from clerical viewpoint. Concludes that C. remained to end bold intellectually, but timid in action, and that this double aspect of character explains both his limited influence on Revolution, and much wider influence on free thinkers of modern France.

Madlung, Ernst. Die kulturphilosophische Leistung Condorcets; ein Beitrag zur Geschichte der Philosophie der französischen Aufklärung. Weida i. Th., Thomas & Hubert, 1912. 81 p. (Diss., Jena). 1427

One of best of studies of *Esquisse.* Madlung feels that so-called *Fragments* of first, fourth, fifth, and tenth epochs of *Esquisse* should be studied in their proper connection with it; almost all unfavorable criticism of *Esquisse* has come from those who did not know or utilize these *Fragments.*

Maron, Eugène. Histoire littéraire de la Révolution; Constituante-Législative. Chamerot, 1856. 324 p.   1428

Scattered throughout the book are several interesting critical opinions on various aspects of C.'s work; perhaps most useful is a comparison between him and Sieyès.

Martin, Kingsley. Condorcet's theory of progress. *In his :* French liberal thought in the eighteenth century; a study of political ideas from Bayle to Condorcet. *See* 1055. p. 286-99.   1429

Excellent study. Introduction states keynote of book : all ideas of century are summarized and given life and religious power by their alliance with doctrine of progress, stated in comprehensive terms by Condorcet (p. 21).

Mathiez, Albert. La Constitution de 1793. RPar 35[4]:298-322, July 15, 1928. *Also, with*

some additions, in ARF ns 5:497-521, 1928. *Also in his :* Girondins et Montagnards. Firmin-Didot, 1930. p. 82-108.   1430

Study traces origin and history of this Constitution, so-called *Constitution girondine*, drafted by C. and his committee, and compares it with that ultimately voted by Jacobins.

Morley, John. Condorcet. FortR ns 7:16-40 [Jan. 1], 129-51 [Feb. 1], 1870. *Also in,* in substance, *his :* Critical miscellanies. London, Macmillan, 1886-1908.   v. 2, p. 163-255. *Also in :* The works of Lord Morley. London, Macmillan, 1921. v. 12 (Biographical studies), p. 27-130.   1431

Excellent appraisal.

Mornet, Daniel. Les origines intellectuelles de la Révolution française, 1715-1787. *See* 45, 1062.   1432

Closing date of book does not permit Mornet to give much attention to C., who had scarcely begun to be known. However, importance of this scholarly treatise lies in showing skeptical, intellectual atmosphere in which C. grew up; he carried its message into his active life. No better book for this purpose.

Natorp, Paul Gerhard. Condorcets Ideen zur Nationalerziehung; ein Schulgesetzentwurf vor hundert Jahren. MCG 3:128-46, 1894.   1433

High praise for C.'s educational plan; no closer analogy with ideas of Comenius can be found : national education for both sexes, abolition of class privilege in education. Education for all, and higher education for those worthy and capable of it. Also, education for laboring classes.

Niedlich, Joachim Kurd. Condorcets Esquisse d'un tableau historique und seine Stellung in der Geschichtsphilosophie. Sorau, Rauert & Pittius, 1907. 72 p. (Diss., Erlangen).   1434

Comments on this study made by Madlung (no. 1427, p. 75-76, footnote). Believes that C. has no faith whatever in miraculous utopia in this or any other world. To him, progress depends solely on human reason and human effort; no limit to this progress.

[Guillaume, James, Editor.] Procès-verbaux du Comité d'instruction publique de l'Assemblée législative, publiés et annotés par J. Guillaume. Imprimerie nationale, 1889. 540 p. (CDHF, v. 67).   1435

Procès-verbaux of the 107 sessions of Committee, of which C. was Chairman, p. 1-384.   Whole work edited and documented in most scholarly manner. It is, therefore, final, critical edition of work of C.'s committee.   C.'s famous report was result of deliberations of this Committee of the *Législative.*

— Procès-Verbaux du Comité d'instruction publique de la Convention nationale. Imprimerie nationale, 1891-1907. 5 v.   1436

On p. lxxvi of v. I are errata and addenda to *Procès-verbaux* of preceding Committee on education of the *Législative.* Deliberations of this new Committee began Oct. 15, 1792, and ended March 20, 1795, for total of 398 sessions. At first C.'s plan for national education was favored, but gradually opposition developed.   Decree for his arrest of July 8, 1793, and his flight, ended everything. Not until Oct. 25, 1795 did Convention approve C.'s plan, with certain modifications. History of debates on plan well summarized by Bigot (no. 1389, Ch. V).

Robinet, J. F. E. Condorcet, sa vie, son œuvre, 1743-1794. Librairies-imprimeries réunies, [1893]. 397 p.   1437

This, first larger biography of C., written by disciple of Comte. Work fairly well documented, but not as thoroughly as biographies of Alengry (no. 1373) and Cahen (no. 1393). However, Robinet has series of valuable annexes, p. 329-93, containing reprints of important documents. Robinet had access to C. papers in library of *Institut,* but did not utilize them as fully as later biographers.

Sagnac, Philippe. Condorcet et son Moniteur de 1788. RHM 15:348-51, 1911. 1438

This *Moniteur* a very rare pamphlet and almost unknown.   Critics not unanimous in attribution of this pamphlet to C., but Sagnac states that all of its ideas, especially those on municipal reform bear mark of C.

Sainte-Beuve, C. A. Condorcet. *In his :* Causeries du lundi. 3rd ed. Garnier, 1852-1862. v. 3, p. 336-59. *Also in his :* Galerie de portraits littéraires; écrivains politiques et philosophes. Garnier, 1893. p. 87-104.   1439.

Nominally a review of C.'s *Œuvres,* ed. of 1847-49 (no. 1356); strikes keynote of hostility to C. by characterizing Arago's *Éloge* of C. in this edition as being rather an *apologie.*   Sainte-Beuve approves

Arago in his favorable opinion of C. the savant, the geometrician, but finds fault with Arago's opinion of him as a literary man, politician, and moralist. Able comparison of C. with Turgot, in which latter has all the better of the parallel.

Sakmann, P. Condorcet und der demokratische Gedanke. PrJ 111:415-33, 1903. 1440

Competent and at times interesting analysis of C.'s doctrines; comparison of his ideas with those of Turgot, Voltaire, Rousseau, and Frederick II.

Schapiro, J. Salwyn. Condorcet and the rise of liberalism. New York, Harcourt, Brace [c1934] 311 p. 1441

Important and interesting book; certainly best so far published on C. in America. Excellent biography, unpretentious but sound and scholarly, provides understanding of background, or soil, from which C.'s ideas derived. C. here pictured as practicing liberal, who drew up concrete plans amounting in some cases to workable blueprints for human betterment in education, sociology, political science, and related fields, thus implementing admirably the often vague ideals of earlier *philosophes*. Modern liberals will generally applaud most of C.'s doctrines, as interpreted by Schapiro, except that many would not approve of C.'s preference for legislative representation on occupational basis.

Reviews : B. Drury in TBR, Dec. 2, 1934, p. 14, 34; H. A. L[arrabee] in Jph 32:103-04, 1935; G. Lefebvre in ARF 12:362-63, 1935; E. M. Sait in APSR 29:146-47, Feb., 1935; H. Sée in Rhist 178:120-21, 1936; [O. Starocel'skaja] in VKA 6:73-75, 1935.

Sée, Henri. Condorcet, ses idées et son rôle politique. RSH 10:22-33, Jan. 1905. 1442

Important study; probably best brief treatment of subject available. Begins with brief mention of Alengry (no. 1373), and Cahen (no. 1393); gives more unreserved praise to latter. Believes that C. was " le plus grand théoricien " of Revolution (p. 32).

Stern, Alfred. Condorcet und der girondistische Verfassungsentwurf von 1793. HZ 141:479-96, 1930. 1443

Thoughtful, scholarly study, containing much information not generally known, such as opinion on C. of Oelsner, a friend of Sieyès. Valuable analyses and appraisals of contributions of C. and of his

associates to the Constitution of 1793 (no. 1411), whose failure led to C.'s break with Jacobins, and therefore to his death.

Vial, Francisque. Condorcet et l'éducation démocratique. 3rd edition, Delaplane, [1913] 124 p. (First edition, 1903). 1444

Valuable book, offering competent classification and analysis of C.'s program for education. Vial, a specialist in field, does not allow his enthusiasm for C.'s many virtues to blind him to certain misconceptions on part of his subject. Vial's main criticism is that C. took too optimistic a view of human nature, and thus overestimated its capacity for betterment.

Gabriel Bonnot de Mably
(Nos. 1445-1456A)

ALESSANDRO S. CRISAFULLI

This bibliography does not include references to treatments of Mably in general works, or in special works covering his period or the fields of his interest. All books, except that of Rochery (no. 1454) are found in the Union Catalogue of the LC.

Mably, Gabriel Bonnot de (1709-1785). Collection complète des œuvres de l'abbé de Mably. Desbrière, 1794-95. 15 v. 1445

Prepared by Arnoux, edition contains M.'s posthumous works (v. 13-15) and is most complete. Following works, however, are not included in it or in any other edition of collected works : *Lettres à Madame la marquise de P. sur l'Opéra* (1740); *Parallèle des Romains et des Français* (1740), (rewritten with different point of view as *Observations sur les Romains*); *Observations sur les Grecs* (1749), (also repudiated and rewritten as *Observations sur l'histoire de la Grèce*); his known letters, some of which, however, may be found in J.-B. Champeval, *Lettres inédites de Maistre, Baluze et de Mably*, BSC 28:445-67, 1906.

Allix, Edgard. La philosophie politique et sociale de Mably. REH 65:1-18, 120-31, 1899. 1446

Though sensualist in philosophy, M. was rationalist in political and social science, for the society he conceives is creation of man's will. Therefore M. rejects Physiocrats' doctrine of a " natural order," Mandeville's idea that all things work for good of society, and Montesquieu's theory of climate. Allix also stresses practical sides of M.'s doctrine, thus correcting emphasis of other scholars on M., the uncompromising, visionary thinker.

Aulard, A. John Adams, Mably et la Révolution d'Amérique. Rfr 70:555-62, 1917.
1447

Adams' letter to Mably, originally published in Adams' *Défense des constitutions américaines* (1787) and reprinted in an appendix to Laboulaye's *Histoire des États-Unis*, v. 1, is again made available here. Adams' reflexions in English which precede the letter reprinted according to French translation by De La Croix in 1792.

Franck, A. Notice sur la vie et le système politique et social de Mably. AMP 14: 283-300, July-Dec., 1848. *Also* as an appendix *in his* Le communisme jugé par l'histoire, 2nd ed., Joubert, 1849. 98 p.
1448

Work of a conservative alarmed by political events of 1848. Is both analysis and criticism of M.'s socialistic ideas.

Guerrier, W. L'abbé de Mably moraliste et politique; étude sur la doctrine morale du jacobinisme puritain et sur le développement de l'esprit républicain au xviiie siècle. Vieweg, 1886, 208 p.
1449

Sketches moral theory of materialists and of Physiocrats and then shows in what points M.'s moral doctrine agreed or disagreed with them. Concludes that it results in communist utopia as means of conciliating personal interest and general happiness. M.'s political doctrine defined by contrast and comparison with that of Montesquieu and Rousseau and is found to fall between former's constitutional monarchy and latter's legislating democracy. Stresses utopian character of M.'s system, shows its contradictions and brings out his importance in French Revolution. Still remains valuable study, though some aspects treated by Guerrier have since received fuller treatment.

Mellis, Paul de. Le principe de la séparation des pouvoirs d'après l'abbé de Mably. Toulouse, Imprimerie Saint-Cyprien, 1907. 426 p. (Diss., Toulouse).
1450

After briefly reviewing M.'s conception of morality, his theory of passions, and idea of communism, author deals at length with following topics : governments based on indivisibility of political power : despotism, monarchy, aristocracy, direct or pure democracy, forms rejected by M.; government based on division of political powers, form advocated by M. because it establishes counter forces designed to maintain equality among citizens, this being M.'s basic intention; legislative, executive, and judicial powers; system of taxes and kind of army advocated by M. (questions previously treated by Mettrier); the ideas of Mably, Montesquieu, Rousseau and Physiocrats on separation of powers, showing that Mably much closer to Rousseau than to Montesquieu and completely opposed to Physiocrats; Mably's influence on constitutions of French Revolution, which is found to be profound and considerable. No bibliography; study apparently based entirely on Mably's works; if previous studies were utilized, they are not mentioned.

Mettrier, Henri. L'impôt et la milice dans J.-J. Rousseau et Mably. Larose, 1901. 248 p. (Diss., Paris).
1451

In accordance with their stress on moral function of state, both Rousseau and M. advocate system of heavy taxes on luxuries so as to encourage virtue. Both also agree in condemning offensive war and demanding for defense of state a citizen army patterned after Roman and Swiss military systems, idea accepted by the revolutionists. Bibliographical notes.

Michoud, L. Les théories sociales et politiques de Mably. Discours de réception à l'Académie delphinale. ADB 4th ser. 15:89-147, 1901.
1452

Places Mably's political and social ideas in their historical background, compares them to those of Mably's contemporaries, particularly Rousseau and Montesquieu, and traces his influence on certain men of the Revolution. *Réponse* to Michoud's *Discours*, p. 148-71, given by Paul Morillot who adds some interesting remarks on Mably.

Müller, Georg. Die Gesellschafts- und Staatslehren des Abbés Mably und ihr Einfluss auf das Werk der Konstituante. (Historische Studien, Heft 214), Berlin, Ebering, 1932. 123 p.
1453

Well-done study contains introduction, surveying previous scholarship on M., sketch of his life, work and personality (chap. I), analysis of his social and political doctrine (chaps. II-III), discussion of his sources and relation to his contemporaries, particularly the Physiocrats, Montesquieu and Rousseau (chap.

IV), thorough study of his influence on Constituent Assembly (chap. V), and conclusion, followed by notes and best bibliography on Mably to be found anywhere, for it lists also general works devoting space to him.

Rochery, Paul. Mably, ses théories sociales et politiques. Sandré, 1849.   1454

Résumé of M.'s ideas with an introduction in which the liberal Rochery highly praises the republican, socialistic and revolutionary M.

Sée, H. La doctrine politique et sociale de Mably. AHRF 1:135-48, 1924.   1455

Well-organized, clearly written essay. Author, drawing from Guerrier (no. 1449) and Lichtenberger (no. 1052), discusses M.'s ideas with reference to the French Revolution. M.'s socialism too utopian to have had any practical influence; but his conception of democracy (marked by supremacy of legislative power held by people's representatives), his recommendation for assembling of States General and for separation of legislative and executive powers, as well as other specific proposals, were prophetic of, and influential on, program of revolutionists.

Teyssendier de La Serve, Pierre. Mably et les Physiocrates. Poitiers, Société française d'imprimerie et de librairie, 1911. 163 p. (Diss., Poitiers).   1456

More complete treatment of subject touched upon or treated in part by other writers on M. Author contrasts in detail theories of M. and those of Physiocrats and, like Guerrier (no. 1449), places him midway between Montesquieu's constitutional monarchy and Rousseau's absolute democracy. Also stresses Mably's isolated position in his times. Short bibliography, p. v-vi.

Whitfield, Ernest A. Gabriel Bonnot de Mably. With an introduction by Harold J. Laski. London, Routledge, 1930. 311 p. (Diss., London).   1456A

Part I briefly treats M.'s life, work, and influence. Part II, core of study, a discussion of M.'s ideas on nature of man, moral conduct, basis of politics, origin and growth of society, history, equality, communism and property, riches and luxury, religion and toleration, liberty, law, education, international relations, reform, and organization of society. Part III consists of critical comments pointing out what is considered erroneous in M.'s ideas. Appendix contains bibliography (not as complete as Müller's no. 1453), long section of notes and index. Noteworthy is Whitfield's isolated position concerning Mably's influence on French Revolution, which he reduces to a minimum, and Mably's theory of separation of powers which, though not clearly expounded, is undoubtedly to be understood, he believes, as a three-fold division.

CHAPTER VI. CHARLES-LOUIS DE SECONDAT,
baron de LA BRÈDE ET DE MONTESQUIEU
(Nos. 1457-1613A)

DAVID C. CABEEN

The following abbreviations are used, in this chapter only : *Lois*, for *De l'esprit des lois*; *LP*, for *Lettres persanes*; *Romains*, for *Considérations sur les causes de la grandeur des Romains et de leur décadence*. The arrangement of items in this chapter follows that of *Montesquieu : a bibliography* (no. 1458), whose order was based on that of the cards on Montesquieu in the main catalogue of the New York Public Library.

Bibliography

Dangeau, Louis. *pseud.* of Louis Vian. Montesquieu, bibliographie de ses œuvres. Rouquette, 1874. 33 p.   1457

Principally of interest as establishing dates and other material facts concerning first and other important editions of those of M.'s works published before 1874. Lists some *inédit* material held at La Brède, and tells of efforts (notably those of Victor Cousin) to get it published.

Cabeen, David C. Montesquieu : a bibliography. BNYPL 51:359-83, 423-30, 513-25, 545-65, 593-616, June to Oct., 1947. Reprinted : New York, New York Public Library, 1947. 87 p.   1458

Has 650-odd titles by and about M., most of them evaluated and located at New York Public Library, Columbia, or occasionally other important libraries. The *Bibliography* has 8-page index, including reasonably complete subject lists : thus (see p. 82) *Esprit des lois : analyses of*, (48 references); *disorder of*, (16 references); *editions of*, (35 references); *epigraph of*, (5 references); *reputation and influence of*, (26 references); *sources*, (12 references); *theory on origin of title*, (1 reference). Naturally, analysis or identification of each item number would have added to usefulness of this index, but printing costs made such convenience impractical.
Review : J. C. Corson in MLR 44: 276-77, 1949.

Works by Montesquieu, each followed by the items devoted to it by title

Montesquieu, Charles, etc. Voyages de Montesquieu. Ed. by *Baron* Albert de Montesquieu. Bordeaux, Gounouilhou, 1894-96. 2 v.   1459

Largely made up of M.'s hasty notations and memorandums, probably never intended for publication. Of interest principally to students looking for germs of ideas developed in M.'s main books. Copious, reliable notes, and other editorial material by Céleste, Barckhausen, and Dezeimeris.
Reviews : E. Armstrong in EHR 11: 589-91, 1896; P. Bonnefon in RHL 2: 126-29, 1895; R. Doumic in RDM 4th per. 142:924-35, 1897 (1461); E. Faguet in RPL 4th ser. 3:151-54, Jan. 19, 1895; R. Marie in Rcr ns 40:515-16, Dec. 30, 1895 of v. I, and R. Rosières in Rcr ns 44:234-36, Oct. 18, 1897, of v. II; G. Monod in Rhist 59:129-30, Sept.-Dec., 1895; G. Picot in AMP 146 (ns 46): 42-51, 1896.

Bonnefon, Paul. Voyages de Montesquieu. RHL 2:126-29, 1895, review of v. I; 4:461-62, 1897, review of v. II.   1460

Review of v. I constitutes important article. Recalls that, on Jan. 25, 1889, members of Montesquieu family, gathered at La Brède to celebrate second decennial of his birth, decided to publish all of his *inédits*. Editing was entrusted to commission of three scholars of Bordeaux : Barckhausen, Dezeimeris, and Céleste. Review of v. II rather disappointing, since it does little more than summarize volume.

Doumic, René. Les Voyages de Montesquieu. RDM 4th per. 142:924-35, Aug. 15, 1897.   1461

Conscientious and on the whole successful effort to show how M.'s travels helped prepare him for *Romains* and *Lois*.

Montesquieu, Charles, etc. Deux opuscules de Montesquieu. Ed. by Jean Baptiste de Montesquieu. Bordeaux, Gounouilhou; Rouam, 1891. 81 p.   1462

First minor work is *Réflexions sur la monarchie universelle en Europe*, ten of whose twenty-five paragraphs have been incorporated into *Lois*. Remaining fifteen contain some of M.'s best political philosophy. Volume closes with article by R. Céleste on *Montesquieu à Bordeaux* which gives many dates and other details about M.'s life, family, and descendants not found elsewhere.

Reviews : P. Janet in JS Dec., 1892; 717-33; R. Mahrenholtz in ZFSL 13²: 165-66, 1891.

— Mélanges inédits de Montesquieu. Ed. by *Baron* Gaston de Montesquieu. Bordeaux, Gounouilhou; Rouam, 1892. 302 p.   1463

Thirty-one page *Introduction* by R. Céleste, Director of City Library of Bordeaux, gives valuable history of M.'s *inédits*. Sixteen pages of critical notes indicate literary and historical sources of many of M.'s ideas, and throw light on his methods of composition. Good analytical index.

Reviews : J. Franck in ZFSL 16²:38-63, 1894; P. Janet in JS, March, 1893:142-57; G. Lanson in RU 2¹:385-95, 1893. The last review is treated as an item (1464).

Lanson, Gustave. Mélanges inédits de Montesquieu. RU 2¹:385-95, 1893. *Also in his :* Hommes et livres. Lecène, Oudin, 1895. p. 169-83.   1464

Essential study. Description of content, with occasional analysis or criticism, of several of M.'s unpublished fragments. Lanson believes that many of M.'s examples and ideas tend to substitute physiology for psychology, and that this makes him precursor, and initiator of movement which permeates all 19th century literature (p. 394).

Montesquieu, Charles, etc. Œuvres complètes de Montesquieu. Ed. by Édouard Laboulaye. Garnier, 1875-79. 7 v. (Half-title : Chefs-d'œuvre de la littérature française, v. 40-45, 49).   1465

Unusually good edition mechanically : clear type, amply spaced, fine paper. Heavily documented with notes upon nearly every possible point of obscurity of bibliographical, historical, economic, political, and biographical nature. Editor includes and criticizes much of best comment on M. available to him. Edition far from complete, as M.'s *inédit* material

was not available till 1889. Not truly critical edition, in part because Laboulaye had little of our present body of scholarly research at his disposal. But is far superior to all other editions of M.

Reviews : F. Brunetière in RDM 33: 219-29, May 1, 1879; E. Caro in JS, 1878 : June, p. 328-37, July, p. 428-43; T[amizey] de L[arroque] in Rcr ns 1: 328-32, May 13, 1876, and ns 3:193-98, March 24, 1877.

— Le génie de Montesquieu. [Alexandre Deleyre, ed.] Amsterdam, Arkstée & Merkus, 1758. 436 p.   1466

Useful work, consisting of extracts from M., grouped into chapters, 29 in number, under such headings as *De la religion*, *De la république*, etc. Has index which is most valuable because in it (though not in text itself) subject headings of chapters are sub-divided. Thus, book is convenient medium for one seeking M.'s views on given subject, though it would be difficult to utilize in works of formal scholarship, since there is no indication of source of any of the extracts.

— Pensées choisies de Montesquieu tirées du Commonplace book de Thomas Jefferson. Introduction by Gilbert Chinard. Les belles lettres. 1925. 87 p. (Études françaises, Cahier 4).   1467

Important item : 22-page Introduction and notes indispensable as preliminary to study of M.'s influence on Jefferson, and on the leading authors of the United States Constitution, and for summary of opinions of several important modern historians on extent of this influence.

— Montesquieu : textes choisis et commentés par Fortunat Strowski. Plon-Nourrit, [c1912]. 308 p.   1468

Important book, whose title is far too modest to give idea of its value. Selections from M.'s work admirably chosen, and each section preceded by analysis and criticism, unsurpassed for clarity. Of the first-rate critics who have written on M., perhaps only Sainte-Beuve, Faguet, and Sorel equal Strowski in ease and charm of style, combined with sound content.

Reviews : H[enri] G[héon] in NRF 8: 1093-97, Dec. 1, 1912; K. Glaser in ZFSL 41²:56-57, 1913.

—Considérations sur les causes de la grandeur des Romains et de leur décadence. Avec commentaires & notes de Frédéric-le-Grand. J. Charvet, ed. Lemerre, 1876. 287 p.   1469

30-page Introduction gives best available account of history of Frederick's copy of *Romains*, bearing his manuscript notes. To modern reader these notes are more interesting when Frederick is expressing his shrewd, realistic views on war and statecraft than when he assumes the role of *philosophe* of period. Rare book; copy at Harvard.

— Considérations sur les causes de la grandeur des Romains et de leur décadence. 8th ed. Ed. by Camille Jullian. Hachette, [1923]. 304 p. 1470

Indispensable edition. Scholarly 38-page Introduction (signed in 1895) which is, perhaps, of greater historical than literary importance. Gives historical notes which (independently of M.'s own) indicate sources upon which Jullian believes that M. drew; passages of *Lois* which can be compared with others in *Romains*, and, finally, references to modern authors useful in study of. M.

— Correspondance de Montesquieu. Ed. by François Gebelin and André Morize. Champion, 1914. 2 v. 1471

Contains 679 letters, about 500 more than Laboulaye (no. 1465); two-thirds of them by M. himself, largely drafts. Much material on his life and times which is not in Laboulaye. Letters throw more light on publication and reception of M.'s books than on their composition. Introduction gives history of letters, and Guasco-Geoffrin affair. Unusually concise and acurate notes and index. Reviews : P. Bonnefon in RHL 21: 448-49, 1914; E. P. Dargan in MLN 30: 256-59, 1915; J. N. F. in EHR 30:376, 1915; K. Glaser in ZFSL 43²:162-64, 1915; L. R. in Rcr ns 79:146-48, March 6, 1915; F. Strowski in Corr 255 (ns 219): 434-48, May 10, 1914 (1472).

Strowski, Fortunat. La Correspondance de Montesquieu. Corr 255 (ns 219) : 434-48, May 10, 1914. 1472

Essential article in itself, though nominally review of M.'s *Correspondance* (no. 1471). Strowski draws from this *Correspondance* many salient points and interprets them most ably, showing their bearing on understanding of character and career of M. Thus he adds several illuminating brush strokes to known portrait of M.

Montesquieu, Charles Louis de. De l'esprit des lois. Texte établi et présenté par Jean Brèthe de La Gressaye. Tome premier (Books I-IX). Les belles lettres, 1950. (TF) 1472A

The complete edition will consist of three volumes as part of the *Œuvres complètes de Montesquieu* of which Carcassonne's edition of the *Lettres persanes* was the initial publication. This is the critical edition of the *Esprit des lois* so much needed and so long awaited. It features a long, scholarly introduction of 130 pages, *analyses* preceding the *Avertissement de l'auteur* and each book, and critical notes.

Extraits de l'Esprit des lois et des œuvres diverses. Ed. by Camille Jullian. 8th edition. Hachette, 1920. 351 p. 1473

Major contribution, on account of notes, which are of high scholarly value. Selections from *Lois* and of *LP* follow editions of 1758, with M.'s corrections, because they offer purest of texts. Jullian uses D'Alembert's *Éloge* (no. 1519) as being " ... fort beau, sincère de ton, exact dans les détails..." (p. iii).

Barckhausen, Henri Auguste. Un paragraphe de l'Esprit des lois. RLJ ns 11: 490-94, 1882. *Also in his :* Montesquieu, ses idées et ses œuvres d'après les papiers de La Brède (1523), p. 267-72. 1474

Important article. Author believes that key to understanding of M.'s doctrine of separation of powers is to be found in first paragraph of chapter *De la constitution de l'Angleterre* (Book XI, Ch. 6), namely that in each state there are three sorts of powers : legislative, executive for whatever depends on *droit des gens*, and executive for those which depend on the *droit civil*. Cf. John Locke, *Second Treatise of Civil Government*, Chap. XI.

— Le désordre de l'Esprit des lois. RDP 9:31-40, 1898. *Also in his :* Montesquieu, ses idées et ses œuvres d'après les papiers de La Brède. (1523), p. 253-66. 1475

Important article. By series of carefully reasoned analyses, based on many years of study, Barckhausen has been able to reduce *Lois* to compact plan, or diagram, occupying about half page (p. 39). Article one of most convincing of small number of attempts to show that " disorder " of *Lois* is merely superficial, or seeming. (*See also :* Lanson, no. 1580, and Oudin, no. 1496).

— Montesquieu, L'esprit des lois et les archives de La Brède. Bordeaux, Michel et Forgeot, 1904. 121 p. 1476

Has 41-page preface, now included, with misleading title *Préface à l'Esprit des lois*, in no. 1523, below, and 73 pages of M.'s notes for *Lois* not heretofore published. Some of this material appears in *Lois*, a few sentences in fact word for word, others in substance. Remainder, while interesting and in some cases important, is essential only for exhaustive, critical study of M.'s thought.

Reviews : P. Bonnefon in RHL 15:552, 1908; G. Picot in AMP 162 (ns 62): 430-37, 1904.

Bonno, Gabriel. Montesquieu's Esprit des lois (1748) and its significance for the modern world. FrAR 2:1-11, 1949.   1476A

Able re-appraisal of subject, in light of events of decade since author first considered it (no. 1530). He gives fresh and direct expression to generally accepted opinion with sentence " ... the very name of Montesquieu is the constitutional guarantee of political liberty by the separation and balance of powers " (p. 7).

Cabeen, D. C. The *esprit* of the Esprit des lois. PMLA 54:439-53, 1939.   1477

In part, attempt to decrease somewhat repetition of shallow Du Deffand epigram (" de l'esprit sur les lois ") (*See* no. 1504) by showing how small a portion of *Lois* really is devoted by M. to attempts at *esprit*. Bulk of article tries to establish by illustration and analysis that most of best of M.'s *esprit* is engendered by intellectual irritation.

Cestre, C. Les sources anglaises de l'Esprit des lois. RPB 12:145-58, 1909.   1478

Important study in itself, though nominally review of Dedieu's thesis (no. 1480). Cestre condemns Dedieu's failure to bring out originality of M.'s doctrine, which consisted in applying methods of observation and induction to political life. Closing paragraph of study forms fine eulogy of originality of M.'s part in creation of political science.

Condorcet, Marie Jean Antoine Nicolas Caritat, *marquis* de. Observations sur le vingt-neuvième livre de l'Esprit des lois. *In :* A. L. C. Destutt de Tracy, Commentaires sur l'Esprit des lois de Montesquieu (no. 1482), Desoer ed. p. 399-432; Delauney ed., p. 435-71; Duane ed. of 1811, p. 261-82, with the title : Observations on the twenty-ninth book of the Spirit of laws.   1479

Condorcet's purpose is, obviously, to find as much as possible to criticize; his tone is querulous, but his objections legitimate, though some of them seem of minor importance. One feels that M. might have answered that these points were mainly ones which could be omitted as being intermediate, and therefore taken for granted.

Dedieu, Joseph. Montesquieu et la tradition politique anglaise en France; les sources anglaises de l'Esprit des lois. Gabalda, 1909. 396 p. (Diss., Bordeaux). *See* 3056, 3101.   1480

Essential work, frequently referred to. Examines fully and minutely origin, growth, and decline of English influence on French political thought, from middle of 17th century, as reflected in M.'s work. Considers M. to have been popularizer rather than initiator. Shows how French loss of confidence in value of British parliamentarianism as foundation for liberty prepared success of Rousseau's ideas after 1760. Lacks bibliography of works consulted.

Reviews : H. Barckhausen in RHL 17: 405-08, 1910; C. Cestre in RPB 12:145-58, 1909 (1478); A. Girard in RHM 14:95-97, 1910; K. Glaser in ZFSL 36: 272-73, 1910.

Demiau de Crouzilhac, F. Recherches sur l'épigraphe de l'Esprit des lois. MAC, 1860, p. 303-13.   1481

Interesting article, within rather narrow field of its subject. Epigraph, (from Book II of Ovid's *Metamorphoses*) *Prolem sine matre creatam*, has given rise to many theories, several of which are discussed here. Author rejects Walckenaer's interpretation (no. 1612), which is generally accepted, namely, that book had no model (i.e., that it was original). Thesis of this article is that M. tried to get sponsor (a " mother ") for *Lois* and, failing in this, decided to launch book without one.

Destutt de Tracy, Antoine Louis Claude, comte. Commentaire sur l'Esprit des lois de Montesquieu. Desoer, 1819. 480 p. Delauney, 1819. 476 p.   1482

Essential study : perhaps still today most careful so far made of *Lois*. Author reasons clearly and honestly, and supports his points by lessons drawn from political developments since 1748. Though Tracy admires M., he is not awed by reputation of *Lois*, and several of his criticisms are telling. Principal weaknesses as guide and critic are a bent for somewhat dogmatic and too abstract theorizing, and a tendency to substitute his own thought for that of M. *See :* Janet, (no. 1573, p. 397); Sainte-Beuve, (no. 1593); Chinard, (no. 1483), and Oczapowski (no. 1588).

Chinard, Gilbert. Traduction et publication du Commentaire de Montesquieu. *In his :* Jefferson et les idéologues. Baltimore, Johns Hopkins press; Les presses universitaires de France. 1925. p. 31-96. (JHS, extra volume 1). 1483

This substantial book-chapter important on M., though he is studied here primarily through and in light of views expressed on him by Jefferson and by Destutt de Tracy (no. 1482). Chinard believes that essence of Tracy's book lies in showing that not Britain but the United States had *réalisé* separation of powers. Jefferson offered Duane, publisher of the translation and first version of *Commentaire*, his help in correcting proofs.

Dodds, Muriel. Les récits de voyages, sources de l'Esprit des lois de Montesquieu. Champion, 1929. 304 p. (Diss., Paris). 1484

Essential work : studies M.'s sources by countries; explains discrimination and integrity with which he used these sources, refuting Voltaire's criticism on this point. Part III groups in parallel columns ideas from *Lois* and passages from *récits* from which they might have been taken. Bibliography valuable, though carelessly made, since it omits initials or given names of one third of authors listed. No index.
Reviews : F. Desonay in RBP 8:1242-44, 1929; F. Gaiffe in RU 38²:53, 1929; A. Tilley in MLR 26:212-14, 1931; G. L. van Roosbroeck in RR 21:259-60, 1930.

Dufrenoy, Marie Louise. Les fondements statistiques de l'Esprit des lois. JSSP 89: 502-05, Nov.-Dec., 1948. 1485

Condensed, erudite study, which draws interesting parallels between M. and some of his predecessors : Oresme, Bodin, Melon, and makes comparison with Maupertuis. Article concludes that Montesquieu, while not statistician in any modern sense of word, yet " ... a vu dans l'infinie diversité des êtres et des choses un reflet de la diversité infinie des combinaisons possibles entre les phénomènes." (p. 504).

Dupin, Claude. Réflexions sur quelques parties d'un livre intitulé de l'Esprit des lois. Serpentin, 1749. 2 v. 1486

Book was published anonymously, and M. was not mentioned by name in it, but it is full of bitter criticism by its author, the *fermier général* Dupin, whose anger had been aroused by some remarks of M. on the occupation he followed. Dupin destroyed all but two copies, of which one was owned by a descendant, and the other by the Arsenal library. Vian (no. 1606, p. 357-60) quotes opinions on work by La Beaumelle, Delaporte, Maupertuis, Guasco and Chamfort, and then devotes six pages (360-66) to citations from book itself.

Fletcher, F. T. H. The poetics of L'Esprit des lois. MLR 33:317-26, 1942 1487

Maintains that some of M.'s prose is poetic in outlook and conception. Compares certain lines of the *Lois* with *Isaiah* and the free verse of Whitman (p. 318). Believes, with Lanson (no. 1580), Barckhausen (no. 1475) and Oudin (no. 1496), that if we view *Lois* as a whole, we shall discover beneath seeming disorder real unity.

Fontaine de la Roche, Abbé Jacques. Critique de l'Esprit des lois. Necc Oct. 9, p. 161-64; and Oct. 16, p. 165-67, 1749. Appears in substantially the same form, with the title Examen critique de l'Esprit des lois *in* Laboulaye (no. 1465), v. 6, p. 115-37. 1488

Attack on *Lois*, in this Jansenist periodical, made famous by M.'s answer, the brilliant *Défense de l'Esprit des lois*. Article attacks *Lois* in general and many of those of its ideas which touch religion and morals; attack which attempts to show that book tends to destroy Christianity, virtue, and State itself.

Gebelin, François. La publication de l'Esprit des lois. Rbib 34:125-58, 1924. 1489

Important bibliographical study. Gives detailed account of part played in publication by Guasco, Mussard, Jacob Vernet, the printer Barrillot, Helvétius, Saurin, Toussaint, and Mme de Tencin. Final third and more of article devoted to careful bibliographical description of several earlier editions of *Lois*.

Gérard-Varet, Louis. Montesquieu et le rôle social de la religion d'après l'Esprit des lois. RBE 11:123-45, 1901. 1490

Important article. Shows how much more realistic are M.'s ideas on religion than Bayle's. But shows also how some of M.'s limitations and those of his century in spiritual matters condemned him to "explications insuffisantes" (p. 142). Thinks that M. made possible, and even inevitable, a new science, the science of religions, in that he saw that they are social phenomena (p. 144).

Giraud, Victor. Sur l'Esprit des lois. *In his :* Moralistes français : Saint François de Sales — Molière — Pascal — Bossuet — Montesquieu — Maine de Biran — Joubert — Lamennais — Sainte-Beuve — Renan — Brunetière — Faguet.   Hachette, 1923. p. 93-104.   1491

Important study.   Advances convincingly several valuable ideas on *Lois.* Taking as theme M.'s own prediction that book would be " ... plus approuvé que lu...," Giraud asserts that the weakness and superficiality of most 18th century attacks on *Lois* show that critics had not even read it.   Also maintains that, of M.'s professed disciples and admirers in 18th century, only English and American publicists applied his principles seriously. Reasons : the book's spirit of moderation was not that of *philosophes ;* explains how this moderation was result of idea which dominated his whole work, that of universal *déterminisme.*

Helvétius, Claude Adrien. Lettres d'Helvétius à Montesquieu sur son manuscrit de l'Esprit des lois. Lettre d'Helvétius à M. Saurin sur le manuscrit de l'Esprit des lois. *In his :* Œuvres complètes, Lepetit, 1818. v. 3, p. 259-67.   1492

Important. Letter to M. justly famous and often referred to. Helvétius praises M.'s literary ability, but dislikes several things about *Lois,* especially M.'s indulgence toward aristocracy and English constitution. Letter to Saurin contains perhaps best and fairest criticism of M.'s tendency to tolerate special privilege.

Levin, Lawrence M. The political doctrine of Montesquieu's Esprit des lois; its classical background. New York, Institute of French studies, (c1936) 359 p. (Diss., Columbia).   1493

Essential work, which removes most serious obstacles to long-desired and needed scholarly edition of *Lois.* Footnotes contain wealth of information, and are best single available source of critical annotations and references for beginning

research student's card-file on M. Convenient subject index; Bibliography lists only works used in preparation of thesis, but is still most extensive one on M. up to 1936, in spite of a number of minor bibliographical inadequacies.

Review : E. Carcassonne in RHL 44: 283-85, 1937; F. T. H. Fletcher in MLR 32:629-30, 1937.

Maine, Sir Henry. " ... neither the institution of a Supreme Court, nor the entire structure of the Constitution of the United States were the least likely to occur to anybody's mind before the publication of the *Esprit des Lois.*" *In his :* Popular government, New York, Holt, 1886. p. 218.   1494

This statement is given, by exception, the status of an item because of importance of subject matter and because reputation of Maine in his field lends authority even to his undocumented opinions.

Martin, Kingsley. The British constitution; l'Esprit des lois. *In his :* French liberal thought in the eighteenth century. *See* 1055. p. 147-69.   1495

Essential study : contains very many ideas which invite and deserve quotation. Discussion of M. and the American Constitution (p. 165) especially original, and therefore controversial. Study maintains its high level of intelligence to end, which consists of brief and realistic characterization of M.'s published opinion on religion (p. 169, n. 1).

Masson, André. Naissance et fortune de l'Esprit des lois. RLH 1:701-10, Oct. 15, 1948.   1495A

Well-written literary article, with several interesting features : description of La Brède to-day; then, shows how various parties or elements have attempted to use prestige of *Lois* for their own ends, among such elements, surprisingly enough, the Germans in World War II.

Mirkine-Guetzévitch, Boris. Quelques réflexions sur l'Esprit des lois. RPP 51: June, 236-48; July, 28-37, 1949.   1495B

Important study, by one of leading political scientists of to-day, containing several original and penetrating ideas on *Lois,* and giving interesting interpretations of number of generally accepted opinions on book. Bulk of study devoted to problem of separation of powers, with special attention to its fortune in France in debates and constitutions of 1789, 1791, 1793, 1795, 1848, 1875, and 1946. Many of author's ideas on this subject seem to have been formulated with Great Britain in mind; they would apply less specifically to several other successful democracies.

Oudin, Ch. De l'unité de l'Esprit des lois de Montesquieu. Rousseau, 1910. 271 p. (Diss., Paris). 1496

Essential work. Attempts to discover logic which governed composition, arrangement, and order of *Lois*. Maintains that each of its parts can be understood only in connection with the others, and only if book is considered as work of jurisprudence. Thesis of unity of *Lois*, sustained by Lanson (no. 1580), and by Barckhausen (no. 1475), but contested by most critics, as listed by Levin (no. 1493, p. 4-9), here receives its most systematic, thorough, and convincing development and defense. Inadequate footnotes; no bibliography, no index. Rare book, privately owned.

Picard, Roger. Le deuxième centenaire de l'Esprit des lois. RLav 3:138-44, Oct., 1948. 1496A

Study proposes to deal with only single aspect of *Lois*, but one which " ... donne sa signification essentielle à la doctrine politique de Montesquieu : la condamnation du despotisme et l'organisation des libertés civiles." (p. 138.) Interesting account of printing of first edition, based largely on Gebelin (no. 1489). Sustains briefly but convincingly the thesis that the *Lois* is still worthy " ... de soutenir la foi politique des grandes nations et des hommes libres." (p. 144.)

Raynal, L. H. C. de. Le président de Montesquieu et l'Esprit des lois. *Reprinted from :* Cour de Cassation, Audience de rentrée du 3 novembre 1865. Cosse, Marchal, 1865. p. 11-55. 1497

Important study. This able, conservative lawyer, *bien pensant, fin lettré*, likes M. for his " ... mesure qui était le fond même de sa nature et le cachet de son génie " (p. 22) and for " ... cette aversion instinctive de tout ce qui est excessif ou précipité, violent ou chimérique..." (p. 50); believes that " ... il prendra son ascendant dans les temps calmes, sur les esprits éclairés et apaisés par l'expérience," (p. 51). Criticisms of weaknesses and omissions of *Lois* (p. 34-43) are less " literary " but more original than the eulogy of M. Rare book; copy at Univ. of Nebraska.

Sclopis di Salerano, Frederigo, *conte.* Recherches historiques et critiques sur l'Esprit des lois de Montesquieu. By Frédéric Sclopis. AST ser. 2, 17:165-271, 1858. 1498

Series of essays, philosophic in tone, concerned chiefly with sociological and legal aspects of the *Lois*. A first part consists of *Remarques de Monsieur de Monclar sur l'Esprit des lois*, (p. 174-207), which were probably not intended for publication, and are principally of interest as showing reactions of a highly literate member of *la vieille magistrature* toward M. Study contains comparisons of M. with D'Aguesseau, Helvétius, Rousseau, Vico, Thomasius, and Vernet. Conclusion seeks to apply M.'s principles to problems of society and government in mid-19th century Europe.

— Études sur Montesquieu. Considérations générales sur l'Esprit des lois. By Frédéric Sclopis. RLA 1870-71 : 497-526. 1499

Important study on account of number and value of its general critical ideas on M. Author thinks that few " ouvrages sérieux " on legislation appear without an appeal to M.'s authority (p. 497). Believes that M.'s work belongs in field of philosophy rather than in *droit public* or jurisprudence (p. 499). It is history considered from point of view of legislation. Some of M.'s predecessors were more learned than he, but had not his talent for observation, nor good fortune to be in touch with spirit of their times (p. 500).

Struck, Walter. Montesquieu als Politiker; eine Erläuterung zu den Büchern I-VIII und XI-XII des Geistes der Gesetze. Berlin, Eberling, 1933. 334 p. (HS, v. 228). 1500

Essential work. Makes acute analysis of Books I-VIII, and shows how they contrast with later ones, especially in that earlier books do not contain idea of representative institutions, whereas later ones, notably Book XI, develop this idea at great length. Struck tends to belittle originality of M.'s thinking, and attempts to portray him merely as brilliant popularizer of others, but does admit that M. exercised great political influence.
Review : W. Kalthoff in Archiv 167: 92-93, 1935.

Vellay, Charles. La genèse de l'Esprit des lois. Minerve 4:129-38, Jan. 15, 1920. 1501

Important and interesting study : advances thesis that seeds of *Lois* are found in following, which should be studied in order given : 1. *De la principale cause de la décadence de l'Espagne*, which became, 2. *Réflexions sur la monarchie universelle en Europe*, and finally, 3. *Considérations sur les richesses de l'Espagne*, which latter is printed in full on p. 139-53, following Vellay's article. All three of M.'s articles have been melted into text of *Lois*.

Voltaire, François-Marie Arouet. Lois (Esprit des). *In his :* Dictionnaire philosophique. Moland : v. 20, p. 1-15; Kehl : v. 41, p. 482-501. 1502

> For explanation of " Moland " and " Kehl " *see* nos. 1628, 1626.
> Most of Voltaire's points in this essay are well taken, especially his denunciation of M.'s defense of *vénalité des charges*. Critic also scores tellingly when he ridicules M.'s more extreme applications and illustrations of theory of influence of climate, and M.'s criticisms of Abbé Dubos. Ends with spirited defense of M. against " fanatics."

— Commentaires sur quelques principales maximes de l'Esprit des lois. Moland : v. 30, p. 405-64; Kehl : v. 29, p. 349-437. *Also in :* Bibliothèque de l'homme public, 1792, 3rd year, v. 4, p. 3-88. 1503

> Article probably of more interest for light it throws on Voltaire than as study of *Lois*. Critic has selected for comment many of the numerous passages which M. chose from his wide reading on account of their picturesque character, as being most likely to catch and hold interest of 18th century reading public. Voltaire seems to be attempting to convince his readers, and perhaps himself, that if M.'s illustrations and anecdotes are improbable, inaccurate or absurd, conclusions drawn from them are equally untrustworthy.

Du Deffand, Marie, etc. *marquise* [de l'esprit sur les lois]. 1504

> Wrote Voltaire : " Mme du Deffant a eu raison d'appeler son livre [i.e., the *Lois*] de l'esprit sur les lois : on ne peut mieux, ce me semble, le définir." (Moland : v. 37, p. 176; in slightly different wording : Kehl : v. 41, p. 500; Moland : v. 27. p. 14). This shallow epigram has been repeated by generations of critics (including even a few first-rate ones); it was best answered by La Harpe (no. 1579). For factual refutation based on statistical evidence, *see :* D. C. Cabeen, (no. 1477).

Barckhausen, Henri Auguste. L'Histoire de Louis XI par Montesquieu. RPB 1: 569-78, 1898. 1505

> Barckhausen does not believe that M. ever wrote *Histoire de Louis XI*, which legend alleges to have been burned by accident, and gives his reasons (p. 569-70). Says that M. was, however, much interested in Louis XI and prints here (p. 571-78) some of M.'s thoughts on this King which appeared in *Pensées et fragments inédits de Montesquieu* (no. 1515), v. I, p. 338-48. Barckhausen's introductory remarks, but without M.'s pages on Louis XI, reprinted in *Montesquieu, ses idées et ses œuvres d'après les papiers de La Brède* (no. 1523), p. 339-42.

Montesquieu, etc. Un carnet inédit; le Spicilège. Flammarion, [c1944]. 346 p. Introduction et notes par André Masson. 1506

> Last volume of known unedited M. material, though Barckhausen had published equivalent to five or six pages of its text in his editions of the *Pensées* (no. 1515), and the *Voyages* (no. 1459). This *Spicilège* was sort of hold-all note book, some 800 pages in length, in which M. collected newspaper clippings, literary opinions, and anecdotes; in short, anything which interested him. About 200 of 800 pages are in M.'s own handwriting. Masson presents evidence that M. used the *Spicilège* constantly while composing his major works. Edition has some 60 pages of excellent notes, and good index. Most valuable work for those doing research work on M.

Montesquieu, Charles, etc. Lettres persanes. Henri Barckhausen, ed. Imprimerie nationale, 1897. 418 p. 1507

> Barckhausen was named by *Garde des Sceaux* to prepare this edition for the Paris Exposition of 1900. Of folio size, is remarkable typographically. Text of *LP* as here established has been widely recognized as best. *Préface* has been reprinted elsewhere (no. 1523).

— Lettres persanes. R. L. Cru, ed., New York, Oxford univ. press, 1914. 312 p. 1508

> Prepared for American university students; contains about two-thirds of text as established by Barckhausen, but notes and comments are rather more complete. Cru points out several relationships between *Lois* and *LP*, and is especially

good in his account of sources of latter. Review : E. P. Dargan in MLN 30: 259-60, 1915.

— Lettres persanes. Grandeur et décadence des Romains. Dissertation sur la politique des Romains dans la religion. Émile Faguet, ed. Nelson [1915]. 541 p. (Edition Lutetia). 1509

Important edition, solely on account of Faguet's introduction of eight pages. In this brief space, critic presents, in clear and brilliant form, the following : summary of M.'s theory of intermediary powers and of separation of powers; analysis of M.'s literary style; contrast of *Lois* and *Contrat social;* and closing paragraph unsurpassed as brief statement of M.'s claim to greatness in French thought and letters.

— Lettres persanes. Élie Carcassonne, ed. Roches, 1929. 2 v. (TF). 1510

Important edition, which contains most scholarly comments of any on *LP*, and shows most fully relationships between them and *Lois*. Indicates most of sources of book's Oriental material, and points out number of similarities between *LP* and works of several of M.'s predecessors. Review : G. L. van Roosbroeck in RR 21:341-43, 1930.

Crisafulli, A. S. Parallels to ideas in the Lettres persanes. PMLA 52:773-77, 1937. 1511

Interesting study, by specialist on *LP*, showing moral and social ideas which M. had in common with Malebranche, Leibniz, and especially Shaftesbury. Concludes that first two almost certainly influenced M., but advises greater reserve in case of Shaftesbury.

Toldo, Pietro. Dell' Espion di Giovanni Paolo Marana e delle sue attinenze con le Lettres persanes del Montesquieu. GSLI 29:46-79, 1897. 1512

Important and interesting article. Claims for work of Marana three-fold importance : literary, historical, and philosophical. Believes that modest portion of glory of M. should be attributed to his Italian predecessor. Article discussed by Van Roosbroeck (no. 1514, p. 43, n. 1. and p. 46-51), and by Carcassonne (no. 1510, p. xix, n. 1).

Valéry, Paul. Préface aux Lettres persanes. *In his :* Variété II, 17th ed., Gallimard, (c1930). p. 53-73. *Also in :* Tableau de

la littérature française. Préface par André Gide. Gallimard, (c1939), p. 245-55, with the title : Montesquieu. 1513

Essential for its subject, to which it forms an introduction in most fundamental sense of word. Most of study devoted to analysis, brilliant and original, of state of society which favored production of work like *LP*, and of which it was so representative. This *Préface* was written for Terquem edition of *LP*, published in 1926, 295 p.

Van Roosbroeck, G. L. Persian letters before Montesquieu. New York, Institute of French studies, (c1932). 147 p. 1514

Essential study. Discusses pseudo-foreign letter in France, and gives as main reason for popularity of *genre* its usefulness as a disguised, and therefore relatively safe medium for social and political criticism. Discusses M.'s predecessors, and shows that he knew their work. Of them, J. F. Bernard here rated as ablest. Reviews : D. Mornet in RHL 40: 445-46, 1933; I. O. Wade in FR 6: 324-25, 1933.

Montesquieu, Charles, etc. Pensées et fragments inédits de Montesquieu. Bordeaux, Gounouilhou, 1899-1901. 2 v. 1515

Basic for any first-hand study of M.'s character and ideas. Many of these ideas, omitted by M. from his main works, are among most profound and brilliant he has written, not mere remarks. Notes give innumerable references to M.'s works and to his sources, established and possible; they form an invaluable body of information upon M. and his times. Preface, classification, and collation of *Pensées* by Barckhausen, who also did notes, assisted by Céleste and Dezeimeris. Reviews : P. Bonnefon in RHL 6:475-76, 1899; G. Picot in AMP 153 (ns 53) : 62-91, Jan., 1900. (1517).

Henriot, Emile. Les Pensées de Montesquieu. Temps, Feb. 28, 1939. p. 3. *Also in his :* Courrier littéraire, XVIIIe siècle. Renaissance du livre, 1945, v. I, p. 31-39. 1516

Important and interesting article. Demands reprinting in an *édition courante* of M.'s *Pensées*, saying that such an edition might bring him deserved recognition and place in first rank of French moralists, with La Bruyère and Vauvenargues. From obviously careful study of M.'s *Pensées*

Henriot draws portrait of character of their author which is one of best yet written.

Picot, Georges. Montesquieu; Pensées et fragments inédits. v. I. AMP 153 (ns 53): 62-91, Jan., 1900.   1517

Important article. While nominally review of *Pensées et fragments* (no. 1515) it is in fact series of short but sound and often brilliant affirmations of principles essential for political freedom, illustrated by quotations from M. Three pages (86-88) on necessity of independent, competent and honest judicial arm of government (especially supreme court) for the maintenance of democracy, constitute veritable breviary of political wisdom.

Montesquieu, Charles, etc. Cahiers (1716-1755). Bernard Grasset, ed. Grasset, (c1941). 305 p.   1518

Important edition, particularly valuable as presenting judicious selection, arranged by subject matter, from great mass of material contained in *Pensées et fragments*, (no. 1515], itself a first editing of the three volumes of *inédits* which M. called "*Mes pensées.*" Appendix reprints Céleste's *Histoire des manuscrits de Montesquieu*, from the *Mélanges inédits* (no. 1463). There is brief but valuable *Note bibliographique* on the *Cahiers* by André Masson; also explanations of book's 16 illustrations, and adequate table of contents.

Studies on Montesquieu

Alembert, Jean Lerond d'. Éloge de Montesquieu. *In his :* Œuvres philosophiques, historiques et littéraires. Bastien, 1805. v. 6, p. 243-301. *Also in :* Encyclopédie, ou Dictionnaire raisonné des sciences, des arts et des métiers. Briasson, 1751-65, v. 5, p. iij-xviij, and in many editions of M.'s Œuvres, and of the Lois.   1519

Carefully written, urbane composition, well balanced and well reasoned. Perhaps most interesting part is defense of structure of *Lois*, which affirms that the disorder is only seeming (p. 267-68). Is also spirited defense of book against ecclesiastical *insectes* who had criticized it (p. 272-77). *Éloge* vigorously attacked in Necc of Feb. 20, 1756, p. 33-34.

Alengry, Franck. Montesquieu. *In his :* Essai historique et critique sur la sociologie chez Auguste Comte. Alcan, 1900. p. 389-403.   1520

Important study. Alengry, translator of Durkheim's Latin thesis on M. (no. 1552) believes that this work established M. as one of Comte's most important precursors. Gives careful discussion of *lois positives* and *lois naturelles* or *lois psychologiques* and their importance in M.'s thought. P. 397-403 are occupied by interesting examination of : *Originalité respective de Comte et de Montesquieu.*

Baldensperger, Fernand. Un jugement diplomatique inédit sur Montesquieu en Angleterre. RLC 9:348-50, 1929.   1521

Begins by quoting M.'s letter of Feb. 12, 1730 (to Chauvelin or Fleury) from the *Correspondance* (no. 1471, v. 1, p. 280). *Inédit* is letter in which Comte de Broglie, Ambassador of France to London, answers inquiry on M. of Oct. 31, 1730. Glimpse of M. afforded by Broglie's letter most interesting and valuable, since it is opinion of obviously shrewd man of the world, speaking frankly and without diplomatic periphrase.

Barckhausen, Henri. Prévisions de Montesquieu. RPB 10:241-44, 1907. *Also in his :* Montesquieu, ses idées et ses œuvres d'après les papiers de La Brède, (1523), p. 142-46.   1522

Interesting article. Opens with sentence : " Les hommes intelligents savent voir; mais les hommes de génie prévoient." Among most striking examples are : M.'s prediction that enemy from which France (like Austria) had most to fear was Prussia; that House of Savoy would become masters of Italy, and that Russia, though trying to get rid of despotism, would be brought back to it.

— Montesquieu, ses idées et ses œuvres d'après les papiers de La Brède. Hachette, 1907. 344 p.   1523

Essential work. Omnibus book, containing most of its author's contributions on M., including prefaces to his editions of *LP* and *Romains*, his defense of order of *Lois* (*See* Lanson, no. 1580 and Oudin, no. 1496), prefaces to *Mélanges inédits, Voyages, Pensées et fragments*, etc. Though Barckhausen's admiration for M. perhaps not sufficiently tempered by critical attitude, *ensemble* of his work remains most considerable and substantial done on M. so far, and this book one of most essential of scholarly studies on M. No bibliography, but one hardly needed, as Barckhausen almost completely ignores other work on M. No index; footnotes meager but accurate.

Reviews : A. Aulard in Rfr 55:378-80, 1908; P. Bonnefon in RHL 15:552-53, 1908; E. Bouvy in RPB 10:573-76, 1907; L. R. in Rcr ns 65:433-36, May 28, 1908; T. de Visan in RP 13:82, 1908.

Barrière, Pierre. Un grand Provincial : Charles-Louis de Secondat, *baron* de La Brède et de Montesquieu. [Bordeaux], Delmas, [c1946]. 549 p. 1524

Useful and informative but not essential book. Tells all that is really worth knowing about M. in considerable detail. Author says he is not writing biography, but is trying to " ... tracer une vie, la vie d'une intelligence, d'une conscience..." (p. 2). Not primarily work of reference or academic scholarship (has no index or bibliography), nor really outstanding for analysis of political, literary, or other aspects on M.'s work. Treatment of different features of M.'s character and thought ranges from adequate to, in places, competent without however at any point being brilliantly illuminating or memorably penetrating.

Barthélemy Saint-Hilaire, Jules. Mémoire sur la science politique et particulièrement sur la politique de Platon, d'Aristote et de Montesquieu. AMP 14 (2nd ser 4):21-41, 149-65, 1848. *Also in* (without title) : Politique d'Aristote, 2nd ed., Dumont, 1848, p. lxxxv-cxii, and 3rd ed., Ladrange, 1874, p. lxxxi-cvii. 1525

Essential study; perhaps most severely critical of M. of any written on him from non-sectarian point of view. Author believes that M., drawing largely from Plato and Aristotle, has not always understood them. Admits, however, that to find anything greater in its field than *Lois*, one must go back to Plato and Aristotle.

Béchard, Ferdinand. La monarchie de Montesquieu et la république de Jean-Jacques. Corr 86 (ns 50):283-325, Jan., 25, 1872. 1526

Important study. Begins with survey of work of *philosophes*, of the Physiocrats, etc. Believes that influence of *Lois* was, unfortunately, neutralized by *Contrat social* (p. 291). Whole article reasoned and scholarly defense of M., closing with plea for his doctrines as preparation for representative monarchy, as against theories of Rousseau, an " eloquent sophist," whose teaching led France " ... *vers des révolutions sans issue* " (p. 325).

Bérard, Léon. Éloge de Montesquieu. RDM 8th ser. 48:825-35, Dec. 15, 1938. 1527

Important article. Bérard, François Mauriac, and Henry Bordeaux were official representatives of French Academy at dedication of a statue of M. at La Brède-en-Graves. Bérard made the formal address, printed as above. He believes that while M. has lost much of his following to-day, still he " ... reste un maître et un guide pour ceux qui ne désespéreront jamais de faire prévaloir dans la conduite des affaires humaines la primauté de l'expérience et de la raison " (p. 835).

Bersot, Ernest. Montesquieu. *In his :* Études sur le xvIIIe siècle. Durand, 1855. p. 297-357. 1528

Able and interesting study; expresses with force and clarity several original ideas. Admires M. because he had " ... peu espéré des hommes quand tout le monde espérait autour de lui " (p. 334). Of M.'s defense of the *vénalité des charges*, which some of his admirers have tried so hard to explain, Bersot says, " C'est à croire qu'il se moque, et qu'il est au fond républicain; il produit souvent cet effet " (p. 342).

Bonno, Gabriel. La constitution britannique devant l'opinion française de Montesquieu à Bonaparte. Champion, 1931. 317 p. *See also* 2888. 1529

Important and interesting work, *couronné par l'Académie française*. Delimits field of study as follows : Dedieu (no. 1480) examined English political tradition in France up to publication of *Lois;* this book proposes to study same subject for period between teachings of M. and coming to power of Bonaparte. Only Ch. I devoted exclusively to M.; begins with unusually clear exposition of doctrine of three powers, and its application in Britain in theory and practice. Summarizes criticisms of *Lois* of such writers as Véron de Forbonnais, Lavie, Réal, and Linguet.

Reviews : *See* 2888.

— Le modernisme de Montesquieu. FR 14: 288-93, Feb., 1941. 1530

Important and interesting article. Address inaugurating *Société Montesquieu*, delivered before 18th century group meeting (French V) at 1939 session of Modern Language Association of America.   Footnote on p. 288 enumerates objectives and lists officers of this *Société*. Address concerned largely with those of M.'s ideas which " ... demeurent encore... un précieux foyer d'idées-force " (p. 288). Author believes that many of M.'s pages appear to be commentary " ... écrit d'une encre encore fraîche en marge de l'actualité contemporaine " (p. 290). Years that have passed since this address was delivered have amply confirmed widsom of those of M.'s ideas which it cites, and soundness and insight of this article's comments upon them.

Brousson, Jean-Jacques. Montesquieu au château de La Brède. NL, Dec. 16, 1948. p. 1, 6.   1530A

Journalistic account of celebration at Bordeaux of 200th anniversary of publication of *Lois*. Announces forthcoming publication at Bordeaux of set of complete works of M., beginning with *LP*. Article interesting largely for air view of château of La Brède.

Brunet, Gustave. Bibliothèque de Montesquieu. *In his :* Fantaisies bibliographiques. Gay, 1864. p. 138-44. Also appeared, in substance, unsigned, in BDA 4:32-36, 1845.   1531

Important and interesting article. Brunet had seen an inventory of library at La Brède made soon after M.'s death; it had then 1556 volumes, most of which were already in château when M. inherited it. Brunet gives the number of volumes in each of following classifications : theology, jurisprudence, science and arts, *belles-lettres* and history; also titles and authors of most significant books. Concludes that M.'s library was collection of most important works of antiquity.

Brunetière, Ferdinand. Montesquieu. RDM 82:694-706, Aug. 1, 1887. *Also in his :* Études critiques sur l'histoire de la littérature française. Hachette, 1891, 4th ser., p. 243-65. *Also in his :* Questions de critique, Calmann-Lévy, 1897, p. 87-112.   1532

Essential article. While nominally a review of Janet (no. 1573), Sorel (no. 1598), and Zévort (no. 1613), this study is intended primarily to express rather fully Brunetière's views on M. These views are positive to point of dogmatism, and include more opinions unfavorable to M. than those of any other major critic. Thus : M. " ... est enfin un bel

esprit, et à certains égards... un bel esprit de province." Of famous *Invocation aux muses*, Brunetière says, " ... je n'y puis voir que l'affectation de bel esprit et le pédantisme d'un magistrat lettré. Montesquieu a trop d'esprit, plus encore d'envie d'en avoir, et cet esprit n'est pas toujours du bon aloi ni du meilleur goût " (p. 697).

Cairns, Huntington.   The separation of powers. *In his :* Law and the social sciences. New York, Harcourt, Brace, 1935. 240-58.   1533

Essential study. Contains only technical and carefully documented consideration of question of separation of powers as viewed by United States Supreme Court (beginning with 1825) which is treated in this bibliography. Footnotes numerous and specific, though in a few cases authors' initials omitted. Some earlier remarks on M. (p. 131-34), while not section of text, also well worth reading.

Carayon, Jean. Essai sur les rapports du pouvoir politique et du pouvoir religieux chez Montesquieu. Montbéliard, Imprimerie montbéliardise, 1903. 85 p.   1534

Dissertation for degree of *Bachelier en théologie* from *Faculté protestante de Paris*. Excellent study : well reasoned, soundly constructed, and interesting. Author believes that M. probably first to formulate theory that duty of political power is to guarantee liberty against all attacks, especially those which come from religious powers (p. 6). But, unlike some politicians, moralists, and sociologists who would destroy religion, M. proposes to use it as force for preservation of liberty (p. 7). Agrees with Sorel that M. preferred single, state church to competing sects (p. 55).

Carcassonne, Elie. Montesquieu et le problème de la constitution française au xviiie siècle. Les presses universitaires, [1927]. 736 p. (Diss., Paris).   1535

Essential work. Studies French conceptions of nature of their monarchy before M., how M. himself conceived it, and how much doctrines after him owed to their genesis and success to *Lois*. This thesis, by showing extent of influence of French political thought on M., implies that Dedieu (no. 1480) has rather overemphasized English influence on *Lois*.

Reviews : P. Dareste in RDF 4th ser. 7:504-08, 1928; F. Gaiffe in RU 37¹:245,

1928; A. Mathiez in ARF 4:509-13, 1927; 5:82-93, 191-92, 1928; R. Picard in RHES 15:388-90, 1927.

Caro, E. M. Publications nouvelles sur Montesquieu. JS, 1878, June, p. 325-37, July, p. 428-43. 1536

Reviews of Laboulaye (no. 1465) and Vian (no. 1606), which are worth attention in themselves, but whose purpose seems to be, in reality, to serve as pegs upon which Caro hangs wealth of anecdotes, facts, and opinions, all interesting and many important for understanding M.'s literary career and development. Most material of this study (except the review of Laboulaye) has been used, with only occasional and immaterial re-arrangements and modifications, in following, with title : *Montesquieu d'après une publication nouvelle*, AMP 110 (ns 10) : 501-26, 1878, and in his : *La fin du XVIIIe siècle, études et portraits*. 2nd ed., Hachette, 1881. v. 1, p. 20-59.

Carré de Malberg, Raymond. La théorie de Montesquieu sur les trois pouvoirs et leur séparation. *In his :* Contribution à la théorie générale de l'état. Recueil Sirey, 1920-22. v. 2, p. 1-142. 1537

Essential for its subject. Scholarly discussion by well-known Professor of Law at University of Strasbourg. Several important references to application of M.'s theories in United States, especially in footnotes. Expresses many interesting and forthright opinions on debatable and much-debated points, thus : " La séparation des pouvoirs, telle que l'a entendue Montesquieu, est irréalisable..." (p. 110). *See* Eisemann (no. 1555).

Cassin, René. Montesquieu et les droits individuels. AUP 19:3-11, Jan.-Mar., 1949. 1538

Speech delivered Dec. 20, 1948, at Sorbonne, at ceremony commemorating second centenary of publication of *Lois*. Hails M. as the Father of political liberalism. Emphasizes influence of M. on members of the *Constituante* and in debates leading to drafting of *Déclaration des droits de l'homme*. Brief, but fairly adequate summary, but contains nothing new or original.

Céleste, Raymond. Montesquieu. Légende. — Histoire. ADG 42:491-97, 1907. 1539

Focuses upon several anecdotes about M. searchlight of exact scholarship, which reduces them to myths, notably that of

supposed ransom from pirates by M. of one Robert, father of the young boatman at Marseilles. Concludes that " ... la critique des documents consultés s'impose à ceux qui ont le souci de la vérité." (p. 497).

Chaix-Ruy, Jules. Montesquieu et J. B. Vico. Rph 137:416-32, 1947. 1539A

Careful study, scholarly in method. Basing his claim on comparison between M.'s *Cahiers* and Vico's *Scienza nuova*, author, while carefully avoiding any finding of " influence profonde " of Vico on M., still sees " des préoccupations communes " and " un point de départ identique." (p. 418). Thinks that M. was too practical to develop, as Vico did " ... ces perspectives dramatiques d'une histoire saisie dans toute son ampleur..." (p. 432).

Cherel, Albert. Le lyrisme de Montesquieu. RPB [35]:49-60, 1932. *Also, in substance, in his :* De Télémaque à Candide. Gigord, 1933. p. 321-30. *Also :* RPL 71:99-103, Feb. 4, 1933. 1540

Finds M. completely at ease and therefore at his best in " idylle sociale ou politique " of Troglodyte story. His calm assurance in *Romains* give his style original accent of authority and enthusiasm (p. 56). Cherel believes that *Lois* has, through the medium of Algernon Sidney, inherited some of poetic power of " pamphlets bibliques " of Milton (p. 60). Reading M. aloud will bring out " ... le sens des sonorités magiques et des rythmes délicats et puissants..." (p. 60). Cover of RPB has good cut of library at La Brède.

Chevallier, J. J. De la distinction établie par Montesquieu entre la faculté de statuer et la faculté d'empêcher. *In :* Mélanges Maurice Hauriou. Recueil Sirey, 1929. p. 137-58. 1541

Article essential for clear understanding of certain terms useful in field of political science. Says that right to legislate and veto power were invented to preserve liberty, a fundamental preoccupation with M.; that he is originator of idea that the executive must possess veto power (p. 143). Traces history of subject in France, England, Germany, and other European countries. Concludes that the secret of eternal vitality of M.'s thought is found in fact that all of his studies began with man himself, rather than with theory.

Chinard, Gilbert. Montesquieu's historical pessimism. *In :* Studies in the history of culture : the discipline of the humanities. Menasha, Wis., Banta, 1942. p. 161-72.
                                                    1542
Important study; takes up main criticism of *philosophes*, as voiced by Helvétius, that *Lois* was not in harmony with doctrine of perfectibility (p. 163). Chinard believes that whole of M.'s work expresses " ... the very negation of the spirit of progress, enlightenment and the ' idealistic will ' by which most of his contemporaries were carried away " (p. 164). Closing paragraph is especially interesting in that it points out how M. " ... clearly indicated limitations which promoters of the League [of Nations] might well have kept in mind."

Comte, Auguste. [Montesquieu]. *In his :* Cours de philosophie positive. Bachelier, 1835-52. v. 4, Lesson 47, p. 243-63. 1543
Not division of text, but must be treated as item because Comte's opinions on M. as expressed in these pages are often quoted, always with respect, but frequently in disagreement. Comte believes M.'s work destined to establish social science. Also, that preliminary chapter of *Lois*, for first time in history of humanity, defines directly general idea of law (p. 243). Pages 252-63 devoted principally to comparison of M. with Condorcet; Comte believes that latter had advantage because in his time it was clear that humanity intended to cast off old social order for good.

Crane, R. S. Montesquieu and British thought. JPE 49:592-600, 1941.   1544
Important study; nominally review of Fletcher (1562). Crane criticizes Fletcher's estimate of influence of M. on Gibbon, Adam Smith, and Burke. Supporting his points, Crane shows sound knowledge and understanding of all three British writers, and of M. Article firmly reasoned, tightly knit, scholarly piece of work, which periodical rightly treats as independent study, rather than as book review.

Dareste de la Chavanne, A. E. C. L'histoire romaine dans Montesquieu. MLS 5:461-74, Apr., 1866. BN lists as a separate : Imprimerie impériale, 1866.   14 p. by C. Dareste.   1545
Interesting article; begins with survey of status of studies on Greece and Rome before M.   Gives definition of *esprit*

philosophique, from hostile viewpoint (p. 466). Believes that M., " ... philosophe et déiste, n'a jamais eu sur la religion et l'esprit religieux que des idées fausses " (p. 466), opinion written to introduce discussion of M.'s failure (from Dareste's viewpoint) to understand Roman religion.

Dargan, Edwin Preston. The æsthetic doctrine of Montesquieu; its application in his writings. Baltimore, Furst, 1907. 205 p. (Diss., Johns Hopkins).   1546
Important work. Exhaustive, logically arranged, rigorously documented study; remains definitive in its field, since the only really important *inédit* material in it by M. to appear after 1907 is the *Correspondance* (no. 1471). Of 205 letters by M. in latter work which Dargan could not have seen, only 24 bear on his subject, and these contain nothing to alter his findings.
Reviews : H. Barckhausen in RHL 17: 185-88, 1910; P. Sakmann in Archiv 122 (ns 22) : 185-86, 1909.

Davy, Georges. Pour le 250ᵉ anniversaire de Montesquieu : sur la méthode de Montesquieu. RMM 46: 571-86, 1939.   1547
Essential article; too closely packed with ideas to permit even summary. Believes that " fond original " of M.'s thought consists in understanding historical determinism " ... pour l'utiliser en vue de ses fins propres " (p. 583). Concludes that M.'s determinism not result of purely abstract deduction, but of interpretation of history by reason (p. 586).

Dedieu, Joseph. Montesquieu. Alcan, 1913. 358 p. (Les grands philosophes.)   1548
Essential work. Shows how historical method gradually gained ascendance over deductive method in guiding thought of M. Treatment of M.'s political, social, and economic ideas better than that of his religious ones. Book unusually good combination of attention to innumerable details with *vues d'ensemble* and conclusions, though there are some minor omissions and contradictions.
Reviews : E. P. Dargan in MLN 30: 253-56, 1915; J. Delvaille in Rph 79: 363-66, 1915; J. Frank in ZFSL 42²: 189-93, 1914; H. O. in RP 24:214-16, 1914; H. Sée in RSH 27:157-59, 1913.

— Montesquieu; l'homme et l'œuvre. Boivin, [c1943]. 202 p. (Le livre de l'étudiant).
                                                    1549

Useful work, well planned and adapted for its purpose : to supply readable, balanced, reliable, all-purpose book on its subject. Half of study (p. 5-99) is on *L'homme;* the remainder on *L'œuvre.* In latter half, chapter on *Le réformateur,* though without pretention to originality, deserves praise for its honesty and courage. Chapter on *L'écrivain* adds something of value to other treatments of M.'s writing. In his concluding three pages, Dedieu attributes to M. greater and more direct influence upon formation of Constitution of the United States than does any other authority.

Review : P. Jourda in RU 52:108-09, 1943.

Duhamel, Georges. Le magistrat frivole. *In his :* Les confessions sans pénitence, suivi de trois autres entretiens : Rousseau, Montesquieu, Descartes, Pascal. Plon, [c1941]. p. 51-59. 1550

Interesting and agreeably written *entretien,* devoted largely to *LP,* and important especially for its discussion of their humor. Good account of M.'s election to Academy, with emphasis upon psychological elements involved and, in this connection, with able defense of value to society of this and similar elective bodies.

Duprat, Pascal. Les idées économiques de Montesquieu. JE 18 : 13-37, 1870. 1551

Useful work, in that it groups M.'s economic ideas into their various classes, such as : property, agriculture and industry, commerce, currency, taxes, and population. Author hails Quesnay and (Adam) Smith as founders of political economy, but pays tribute to M. as last and most illustrious representative of economic ideas which governed world at time when political economy could hardly assume its rightful place.

Durkheim, Emile. Montesquieu : sa part dans la fondation des sciences politiques et de la science des sociétés. RHP 1:405-63, 1937. Translation by F. Alengry of doctoral dissertation : Quid Secundatus Politicae scientiae instituendae contulerit. Bordeaux, Gounouilhou, 1892. 76 p. 1552

Esential study. Thinks that M. established for first time main principles of political science; he did not formulate them in definite terms, but they are latent in his doctrines, especially " la notion de genre et la notion de loi " (p. 461). Former shows that not only government

but social life are not same in different societies. By " la notion de loi " Durkheim means that M. teaches that history depends not on external or accidental causes, but that there are laws which control it (p. 462).

Ehrlich, Eugen. Montesquieu and sociological jurisprudence. HLR 29:582-600, 1916. 1553

Interesting article which, in spite of its calmly judicial form and tone, is really warm eulogy of M. This eulogy, though not uncritical, remains under its moderate and unpretentious language one of finest ever written of him. Thus, to select one from among many highly quotable passages : " ... some twenty years before Blackstone... he [M.] perceived that the history of law... was a means to explain the structure of society by showing the progress of its institutions, and he guessed already the importance of historical continuity for understanding the present by the past " (p. 586).

Eichthal, Eugène d'. La séparation des pouvoirs politiques. *In his :* Souveraineté du peuple et du gouvernement. Alcan, 1895. p. 89-154. 1554

Important study, by well-informed specialist, who knows how to formulate ideas clearly and convincingly. Offers good definition of M.'s understanding of the three powers (p. 121). Believes that, in general and in many specific instances, M.'s treatment of principles of British constitution is " ... très éloigné de la réalité vivante des faits... " (p. 128). Eichthal, while not unfair, inclined to appraise value of M.'s ideas from a rather narrowly political-science point of view and therefore tends to allow minimum of importance to his originality and influence.

Eisemann, Charles. L'Esprit des lois et la séparation des pouvoirs. *In :* Mélanges R. Carré de Malberg. Recueil Sirey, 1933. p. 163-92. 1555

Much space and enormous footnotes devoted to discussion of Carré de Malberg's study of M.'s theories (no. 1537). Eisemann advances several challenging ideas of his own, and in closing says : " Montesquieu ne sépare pas Parlement et Gouvernement; l'indépendance qu'il leur confère est une indépendance, non de fait, mais purement juridique."

Faguet, Emile. Montesquieu. *In his :* Dix-huitième siècle; études littéraires. 28th ed.,

Société française d'imprimerie et de librairie, 1890. p. 139-97.   1556

Essential study. Sustains thesis that M. has several systems, little connected; that, though inventor in France of fatalistic sociology (Lanson's " *déterminisme historique* "), he is also firm believer in efficacy of legislation (Lanson's " *idéalisme social* "), and explains the paradox. Article one of best possible introductions to M.; equally but differently rewarding when read after careful study of M.'s own work and survey of other criticism of it. One of best ideas : how critical understanding of history evolves into prophecy (p. 168).

— La politique comparée de Montesquieu, Rousseau et Voltaire.   Société française d'imprimerie et de librairie, 1902. 297 p. *See* 1670 (Voltaire), 2065 (Rousseau). 1557

Essential study; summarizes positions of M., Rousseau, and Voltaire on French political and economic problems, representing M. as the liberal (and the real republican of his century), Rousseau as the high-priest of popular despotism, and Voltaire as the supporter of royal despotism. Faguet believes that essence of M.'s doctrine is advocacy of sort of corporative society made up of intermediate powers or bodies, which will serve as bulwark of liberty. Lanson's tightly-knit review, best of those listed below, gives admirable definition of patriotism as understood to-day, and in 18th century, with analysis of its expression in M. and in Voltaire, and of Faguet's presentation of subject (p. 246-47). Lanson has high praise for Faguet, but concludes, upon book as whole : " Trop d'abstractions donc, et trop d'actualité, pas assez de fonds historique..." (p. 248).
Reviews : C. Dejob in Rcr ns 54:78-80, July 28, 1902, and E. d'Eichthal 107-11, Aug. 11; J. Haas in ZFSL 25²:69-70, 1903; G. Lanson in RU 11²:244-48, 1902; H. Mazel in MerF 45:490-93, Feb., 1903; G. Monod in Rhist 80:119-24, 1902; E. Rigal in RLR 45 (5th ser. 5):331-32, 1902.

Fernandez, Ramon.   Montesquieu et la science des sociétés.   *In his* : Itinéraire français. Éditions du pavois, 1943. p. 312-27.   1558

Intelligent, brilliantly-written literary criticism, with several original ideas, some rather superficial, others penetrating and worth retaining.   Able and amusing

characterization of Usbek (of the *LP*), p. 320-21.

Ferri, Luigi. La filosofia politica in Montesquieu ed Aristotele. RIF 3¹:113-33, 1888. Summarized in RPFE 27:106-07, 1889.
                                    1559
Admirable study; one of best on its subject. Main similarities and differences between the two writers clearly and logically analyzed. Author believes that perhaps Aristotle's greatest superiority is that his understanding of constitutions was more exact and complete than that of M. But the latter, unlike his predecessor " ... ha il senso dell'avvenire, e ne annunzia l'aurora ! " (p. 131).

Flach, Jacques.   Platon et Montesquieu, théoriciens politiques. RPL 47:3-7 (Jan. 1), 36-42 (Jan. 9), 1909.   1560
Leçon d'ouverture at *Collège de France*, Dec. 9, 1908. Interesting study. Believes that link between M. and Plato was theory " ... de la séparation ou plus exactement de l'équilibre des pouvoirs " (p. 6). Makes no attempt to establish influence but draws many interesting parallels and contrasts between M. and Plato. Believes latter more modern, in that he is " ... communiste par une double tendance... " (p. 7). Credits M. with having raised law to dignity of a political science (p. 40).

Fletcher, F. T. H.   Montesquieu and penal law reform in England. UTQ 6:497-515, July, 1937.   1561
Excellent digest and interpretation of M.'s ideas on criminal law, and estimate of extent to which he influenced supporters of its reform in England. In defending M. from criticism by utilitarian philosopher Jeremy Bentham, Fletcher says : " Montesquieu never pretended to be a reformer; his aim was ever to discover the inward truth or spirit of existing laws and to describe it in historical terms " (p. 514).

— Montesquieu and English politics. (1750-1800). London, Arnold, [1939]. 286 p.
                                    1562
Essential work. To American readers at least title would describe book better if " political thought " replaced " politics." While work shows certain inadequacies of detail, as brought out in reviews, is on the whole an immensely valuable study of ideas dominating political and economic thinking of latter half

of 18th century. Book abounds in comparisons of M. with Adam Smith, Blackstone, Locke, Hume, Gibbon, and many others, all of which have been made before, perhaps best by Dedieu (no. 1480), but Fletcher usually adds something to findings of his predecessors. In general, the larger the question, the better the author treats it.

Reviews : D. C. Cabeen in MP 39: 104-05, Aug., 1941; R. S. Crane in JPE 49:592-600, 1941 (1544); M. Dodds in RR 32:214-17, 1941; H. J. Laski in NSN Dec. 9, 1939:862; C. Sprietsma in FR 14:153-55, Dec., 1940.

Flint, Robert. Montesquieu. *In his :* The philosophy of history in Europe. New York, Scribner, Welford and Armstrong, 1875. v. 1, p. 93-108. Second title page : The philosophy of history in France and Germany. 1563

Essential study; packed with lucidly worded, challenging ideas. Thus : maintains that M.'s chief weakness is inability to understand capacity of social phenomena for continuous development (p. 96); that he " ... paid little attention to the chronology of facts, which is, of course, the indispensable condition of their comparison...", and therefore that he did not discover general laws of facts, but only certain special reasons for them (p. 97). But, while denying soundness of M.'s approach to most problems, Flint admits that he was " ... endowed by nature with the highest form of historical genius " (p. 108).

George, William Henry. Montesquieu and De Tocqueville and corporative individualism. APSR 16:10-21, 1922. 1564

Interesting study. Advances idea that for M. class—such as aristocracy—is corporative element (p. 10), and that " ... a division of powers naturally presupposes a division of classes, for he had in mind England " (p. 11). Thinks that both M. and Tocqueville seek, through corporative, intermediate bodies, " ... to guard against the power of momentary and capricious will which is incompatible with stability and fundamental law " (p. 19). Main contribution of article is to express in language of modern political science certain familiar, accepted ideas on M. and Tocqueville.

Gurvitch, Georges. La sociologie juridique de Montesquieu. RMM 46:611-26, 1939. 1565

Essential item. Highly specialized study, much of it written in technical language of scholastic philosophy. Article cannot be summarized, or adequately characterized by quotations, because practically all of its key ideas resist separation from their context. At one point Gurvitch frees himself from his metaphysical vocabulary long enough to observe that the juridical sociology of M. merely studies conditions of the adaptation of the commands of the laws to the particular type of society which they are designed to govern (p. 624). Author believes that ablest of modern thinkers in field of sociology, such as Durkheim, Hauriou, and Max Weber are all, in different ways, indebted to profound views of M.

Hazard, Paul. Esquisses et portraits; Montesquieu. RDM 8th per. 65:225-34, Sept. 15, 1941. 1566

Penetrating study of mind, heart and soul of M. Author excels in fine portraiture and therein resembles portraitists of age he studies. M. emerges as person of flesh and blood, alive to world of things, ideas, and creatures.

Hémon, Félix. Cours de littérature. Delagrave, 1913. v. 15. Not paged continuously. Montesquieu, p. 1-53; Considérations sur les causes de la décadence des Romains [*sic*], p. 1-55; L'Esprit des lois, p. 1-71. 1567

Valuable book for the teacher, with several features useful in presentation of subject matter. Analysis of M.'s three main works, with judicious choice of opinions on him by such leading critics as Sainte-Beuve, Brunetière, Faguet and many others. Bibliography well selected for principal French books and book-chapters on M.; little from periodicals.

Holmes, Oliver Wendell. Montesquieu. *In his :* Collected legal papers. New York, Appleton, 1921. p. 250-65. 1568

Essential article; first published as critical and biographical introduction to reprint of *The spirit of laws*, New York, Appleton, 1900. Among many other valuable ideas, contains one of most acute criticisms of M. yet written, of type which could perhaps be ignored when coming from routine, conservative-minded person of less stature than Justice Holmes, (p. 251-53). Author believes idea of the threefold division of powers in England a fiction invented by M. (p. 263), but that *Lois* " ... probably has done as much to remodel the world as any product of the 18th century " (p. 264).

Hubert, René. La notion du devenir historique dans la philosophie de Montesquieu. RMM 46:587-610, 1939.   1569

Important study; opens by noting that Comte (1543), Sorel (1598), and Dedieu (1548) all affirm that idea of evolution, of progress, is absent from M.'s thought. Hubert believes that the "... question de devenir historique ne coïncide peut-être pas exactement avec celle du progrès " (p. 588), and that in M.'s time it was not the same as in 2nd half of his century. Author concludes that M. does hold definite theory of " *devenir historique*," but that this is not a theory of progress (p. 609); that is, M. was inclined to believe in progress of institutions and increase of human happiness indirectly, by means of increase of human knowledge (p. 610).

Ilbert, Sir Courtenay. Montesquieu. The Romanes lecture, delivered in the Sheldonian Theater, Oxford, June 4, 1904. Oxford, Clarendon press, 1904. 46 p.   1570

Essential article.   Contains many valuable ideas, some not found elsewhere, on M.'s contributions to theory of political science and jurisprudence.   Well documented with informative footnotes. One of conclusions explains relatively moderate interest in M. of past few decades : " His new ideas, his new methods, once so fresh, so attractive, so stimulating, have passed into and been merged in the common heritage of Western thought." (p. 46).

Jameson, R. P. Montesquieu et l'esclavage; étude sur les origines de l'opinion anti-esclavagiste en France au XVIIIᵉ siècle. Hachette, 1911. 371 p. *See* 3058.   1571

Conscientious, painstaking work. Foundation material, in part justifying subtitle, occupies 212 pages before M. is reached. Rigorous analysis of Book XV of *Lois (Comment les lois de l'esclavage civil ont du rapport avec la nature du climat)* will be useful in preparation of hoped-for definitive critical edition of this book.

Reviews : G. Audiat in RQH 90:333-34, 1911; H. Barckhausen in RHL 18:685-89, 1911; G. Chinard in MLN 26:227-29, 1911; R. Girard in RHM 16:219-20, 1911.

Janet, Paul. Comparaison des théories morales et sociales de Montesquieu et de Jean-

Jacques Rousseau. RPL Dec. 9, 1871, p. 556-61.   1572

Essential article, perhaps most interesting and important study of its subject yet made in periodical length. Need to attract and hold attention and carry conviction, while covering wide segments of several great subjects and authors, has often forced Janet in this study to substitute epigrams for the logical and scholarly though urbane exposition which he prefers. Closing lines show purpose of article : in presenting democratic M. and conservative Rousseau, Janet's object has been, he says, to " ... préparer... la fraternité des âmes en montrant la fraternité des esprits " (p. 561).

— Montesquieu. *In his :* Histoire de la science politique dans ses rapports avec la morale. 3rd ed., Alcan, 1887. v. 2, p. 303-405. 1573

Essential article.   Introductory discussion of ideas of Fénelon, Abbé de Saint-Pierre, D'Argenson, and Machiavelli, and their relationship to those of M. Study has not been surpassed for broad *vue d'ensemble* and clear, sane, moderate exposition, analysis and criticism of M.'s ideas, importance, and influence. Second part of article called, *Montesquieu et son école* (p. 399-405), and deals with Beccaria, Filangieri, Blackstone, Ferguson, and others.

Joël, Karl. Der Staatsaufklärer Montesquieu. *In his :* Wandlungen der Weltanschauung. Tübingen, Mohr, 1928-34. v. 2, p. 69-78.   1574

Important article because of its close, exacting reasoning, which grapples firmly with M.'s thought and extracts its essence. Thus, Joël believes that fundamental impulse of M. is individualism against absolutism, enlightenment against baroque spirit; that he is particularist and individualist much more than democrat and progressivist; that as political, religious, and moral relativist, he is enemy of every restricting absolutism; that, in a word, he is first of his century to overcome preceding one.

Klemperer, Victor. Montesquieu. Heidelberg, Winter, 1914-15. 2 v. Originally a Munich diss. : Heidelberg, Winter, 1914. 213 p.   1575

Essential study.   Vol. I treats M.'s work before *Lois;* Vol. II, *Lois.* Author talked with Barckhausen and had access to his material. Klemperer declares that he treats M. only as man and as poet, and does not consider his influence on posterity, since it is found everywhere, and therefore nowhere in particular. Keynote of book is that M. was at heart a poet, who tried to create a better world, rather than a scientific system or a textbook. Work certainly most interesting and probably most important written on M. in German. Main criticism of it, namely, that Klemperer is deficient in training for analysis of legal concepts, loses some validity in light of his approach, which is that of a German romantic.

Klimowsky, Ernst. Die englische Gewaltenteilungslehre bis zu Montesquieu. Berlin-Grunewald, Rothschild, 1927. 99 p. 1576

Important study. After careful survey of historical development of the division of powers in England until middle of 18th century, Klimowsky concludes that M., rather than Locke, or any other, was first to formulate theory that three powers are inherent in every state, and that political liberty can exist only when these three powers are kept separate. Author thinks that M. borrowed title. De l'esprit des lois from chapter heading of Jean Domat's Traité des lois (dated 1689), De la nature et de l'esprit des lois. (Œuvres complètes, Remy, 1828-30, v. I, Ch. XI, p. 36.)

Knust, Hermann. Montesquieu und die Verfassungen der Vereinigten Staaten von America. Munich and Berlin, Oldenbourg, 1922. 157 p. (HB, 48) (Diss., Greifswald). 1577

Essential study. Deals exclusively with origin and history of formal constitutional principle, namely, original organization of national power, which will mean, for purposes of this study, three-fold division of power. Author believes that M. was only possible source of idea of division of powers for makers of constitutions of various states. Also, that American federal constitution answers one of M.'s greatest questions, namely, on how liberty can be maintained in vast territory. Study concludes that this Constitution does apply effectively principles of M. on division of powers. Spurlin (no. 1599, p. 40) criticizes Knust because he has not " ... dealt with the larger implications created... by the fact of Jefferson's changing attitude toward Montesquieu."

Labat, Jacques-Nicolas. Le château de La Brède. SAA 1st ser. 3:175-89, 1834. 1578

Eulogy of M., followed by description of Château of La Brède and, most important, of library and contents. Says that at this time only about 4000 of M.'s volumes remained. Labat saw enough of M.'s manuscripts, letters, etc., to realize their interest and importance. This is the article referred to by George Saintsbury in his study on M. in the 11th edition of the Encyclopædia Britannica when he says that for many years M.'s inédits " ... were chiefly known by a paper contributed in 1834 to the Transactions of the Academy of Agen." (v. 18, p. 778).

La Harpe, Jean François de. Montesquieu. In his : Lycée, ou Cours de littérature ancienne et moderne. Mame and Delaunay-Valée, 1825. v. 15, Philosophie du dix-huitième siècle. v. 1, p. 37-64. 1579

Still of considerable interest. Devotes some space to defending M. against Voltaire who, he says, combats M. " ... comme il l'avait lu, très-étourdiment." (p. 42) Has admirable comment on Mme Du Deffand's epigram (" de l'esprit sur les lois "), namely, that he had known her well enough to be sure that she " ... n'était pas plus en état d'apprécier l'Esprit des lois que capable de le lire : elle ne pouvait que le parcourir pour en parler " (p. 48-49). This section of most unqualified eulogies of M. ever written.

Lanson, Gustave. L'influence de la philosophie cartésienne sur la littérature française. RMM 4:517-50, 1896. Also in his : Études d'histoire littéraire. Champion, 1929. p. 58-98. Section on M., p. 84-90. 1580

Essential study. In pages devoted to M. (p. 540-46), Lanson attempts to demonstrate that several of the faults usually ascribed to Lois (by himself among others, p. 540, n. 2) namely : its lack of order, of critical examination of sources, etc., are in effect results of exact application of Cartesian principles. Lanson thus reverses his position of first ten editions of his Histoire de la littérature française. Attempt deserves careful study, though it is more likely to arouse admiration for Lanson's ingenious, logical, and even brilliant reasoning than to carry conviction. Cf. 1475, 1493, 1496.

— Le déterminisme historique et l'idéalisme social dans l'Esprit des lois. RMM 23: 177-202, 1916. Also in his : Études d'histoire littéraire, Champion, 1929. p. 135-63. 1581

Essential, closely-reasoned study showing how M. solves conflict between
deterministic conception of history and
idealistic devotion to progress, and utilizes
his determinism to realization of his ideal,
and how, in dissolving contradiction
between the two, M. gains right to be
called founder of political science.

Lerminier, Eugène. Montesquieu. *In his:*
Introduction générale à l'histoire du droit.
2nd ed., Chamerot, 1835. p. 215-32. 1582

Excellent study, especially because it
emphasizes points upon which M. saw
further than his contemporaries. Among
these points were : his concern to judge
phenomena without preconceived opinions (p. 217) : knowledge of and interest
in Italian thought : Gravina, Machiavelli,
and probably Vico. Gives one of best
of the comparisons between latter and
M. (p. 220-23). Chapter closes with
enthusiastic and convincing eulogy of M.
as voicing best aspirations and ideals of
19th century.

Leroy, Maxime. Retour à Montesquieu.
Revue 7:408-19, Nov., 1948.   1582A
Believes that *Lois* is alive today because
of its advocacy of theory of political
liberty rather than that of separation of
powers, although latter theory was one
of main causes of high esteem in which
many in 18th century held book. Well-
reasoned article; brings out no new facts
or ideas, but gives intelligent and fresh
interpretation to several known and
accepted ones.

— Variations sur un centenaire; Montesquieu
social. RPP 51:16-21, 1949.   1582B
Believes that M., though no longer
important as apostle of liberalism, sur-
vives as precursor of social legislation.

Levi-Malvano, Ettore. Montesquieu e
Machiavelli. Champion, 1912. 144 p. *See*
3298.   1582C
Able study. Author convincingly
establishes influence of Machiavelli on M.,
but at same time affirms latter's essential
originality. Levi-Malvano is careful to
show how thoroughly M. detested certain
doctrines of his predecessor, such as his
apology for force, liking for absolutism,
and denial of principles of right and
justice.
Review : P. Courteault in RHB 5:285-
87, 1912.

Lévy-Bruhl, Lucien. Montesquieu. OC
13:28-35, 1899. *Also in his:* History of

modern philosophy in France. Chicago,
Open Court pub. co., 1899. p. 139-68. 1583
Valuable study. Defines contributions
to political science of Grotius, Puffendorf,
Hobbes, and Locke. Presents several
interesting ideas : " Montesquieu's originality consists in having fully perceived in
the various series of social phenomena
that solidarity by which each of these
contributes to limit the others, and is in
turn limited by them " (p. 31).

Loewenstein, Karl. The balance between
legislative and executive power : a study in
comparative constitutional law. CLR 5:
566-608, 1938.   1584

Whole study should be read as setting
for two pages (568-69) specifically devoted
to M. under title : *A realistic re-examination of Montesquieu's doctrine; separation
of powers and the constitution of the United
States.* Valuable footnotes, with copious
references to subject. Says that some
important New Deal legislation was
invalidated by arguments drawn from
M.'s theory of separation of powers, and
cites two cases (note 8).

Meinecke, Friedrich. Montesquieu. *In his:*
Die Entstehung des Historismus. Munich
and Berlin, Oldenbourg, 1936. v. 1., p. 125-
93.   1585
Important study. Believes that one of
M.'s material achievements was uniting
of two great intellectual movements of
preceding centuries, namely : of natural
law and rationalism on the one hand, and
of empiricism and realism on the other
(p. 137 ff). Meinecke considers that
political relativism of M. was preparatory
step toward *historismus* (p. 159).

Milsand, Joseph Antoine. Montesquieu et
sa philosophie politique. Rmod 35:197-224,
1865.   1586
Challenging article, by writer of considerable weight in his time in field of
philosophy. Most of his language in-
telligible to layman. Questions seriously
validity of M.'s conclusions because, as
typical representative of 18th century, M.
based his ideas on an arbitrary, external,
conception of life drawn from reason
rather than from experience or any real
knowledge of man's interior motives.
Able indictment of philosophy underlying
Lois; several of its points, however, owe
their impressiveness and vigor to same
oversimplification of which Milsand
accuses M.

Mondolfo, Rodolfo. La dottrina della proprietà nel Montesquieu. Rfil 11:129-35, 1908. 1587

Interesting study. Author has pointed out certain economic doctrines of M. which are so advanced that they would hardly be generally accepted today even in fairly liberal circles, and which show that M. was far less conservative in his economic than in his political thinking. Summarized by J. Pérés [sic] in RPF 66:223, 1908.

Morgan, Charles. The liberty of thought and the separation of powers ; a modern problem considered in the context of Montesquieu. Oxford, Clarendon press, 1948. 20 p. (The Zaharoff lecture, 1948.) 1587A

A very interesting, thoughtful analysis.

Oczapowski, Joseph. Montesquieu économiste. REP 5:1039-70, 1891. 1588

Essential contribution to study of M. as economist. Quotes and summarizes opinions on M. of several economists not mentioned elsewhere, and devotes much attention, especially in his last four pages, to Tracy's *Commentaire* (no. 1482), in which latter, according to Oczapowski, " ... voulait briller et montrer sa supériorité d'économiste," but in which he had " ... dévié de sa route, laquelle était simplement de commenter l'œuvre d'un homme de génie " (p. 1070).

Oudin, Ch. Le spinozisme de Montesquieu. Pichon, 1911. 163 p. 1589

Important study, frequently referred to. Oudin attempts to show that many of M.'s most important theories are derived from Spinoza. Thesis ably developed, but extent of Spinoza's influence considerably exaggerated. Book could not be located in any library in United States, but Catholic University of America owns microfilm copy.

Price, E. H. Montesquieu's historical conception of the fundamental law. RR 38:234-42, 1947. 1590

Interesting study, of value especially because it clarifies, by well-reasoned analysis, important point of M.'s doctrine. In establishing his main point, Price expresses this arresting opinion : " ... the *raison d'être* of the passages on England in the *Esprit des lois* was the desire to hold before French eyes a clear picture of political equilibrium conditioned, in France, on the correctional powers of the nobles of the robe." (p. 236).

Ratermanis, J. Essai sur le style de Montesquieu-historien. AUL 3rd ser. 7:225-48, 1935-37. 1591

Essential study. Seeks to show, by means of most careful and detailed analysis and comparison, that M.'s thought conforms to rhythm of his literary style, which in turn is dictated by his æsthetic and literary tastes and his temperament. Article most painstaking and systematic study yet made of M.'s style. Several of its conclusions are debatable, e.g., that M. " ... pense par saillies..." (p. 247).

Riaux, Francis-Marie. Montesquieu. By Fr. R. *In :* Dictionnaire des sciences philosophiques, Adolphe Franck, ed. Hachette, 1844-62. v. 4, p. 295-313. *Also in* the 2nd ed., 1875. v. 2, p. 1127-35. 1592

Study can still be read with profit, especially for brief but useful summary of status of political science when *Lois* appeared (p. 303-04), and for its competent conclusion.

Sainte-Beuve, C. A. Montesquieu. *In his :* Causeries du lundi. Garnier, v. 7, 1853. p. 33-66. 1593

Essential study, only really extensive one on M. by a critic of the very first rank as a literary artist. Familiar Sainte-Beuve " biography of the soul "; considers M. rather as personality and as writer than as historian or political scientist. Treats M. with more qualified admiration than does Faguet, but still with respect and understanding. His main criticism is that M. overestimates political capacity of humanity in average, and ascribes too little importance to element of chance. Little here not found elsewhere, but there are usual comparisons of M. with Bossuet and with Machiavelli, and the analyses of his style are in Sainte-Beuve's best vein. Article dated Oct. 18, 1852.

Saintsbury, George. Montesquieu. *In his :* French literature and its masters. Ed. by Huntington Cairns. New York, Knopf, 1946. p. 84-93. *See* 80. 1594

Important article; reprinting of author's essay on M. in 11th edition of *Encyclopædia Britannica*. 14th edition has much the same material, but abridged and of lessened interest. Most of article devoted to recounting M.'s life and to description of his work, in sober, unpretentious language. While M. is hardly the type to inspire a critic to write of him with the " gusto " which the Editor (p. vii) finds characteristic of Saintsbury, yet latter has compressed into his concluding lines a sentiment which is clearly a deeply felt, though measured and temperate admiration for M. and his work.

Schvarcz, Gyula. Montesquieu und die Verantwortlichkeit der Räthe des Monarchen in England, Aragonien, Ungarn, Siebenburgen und Schweden. (1189-1748). By Julius Schvarcz. Leipzig, Friedrich, 1892. 168 p.   1595

Frequently cited study. Author believes that M. had little conception of correct method of historical observation and of proper comparative evaluation of historical facts, opinions which he tries to prove by examples taken from histories of the countries named in title. From examination of M.'s life and writings, Schvarcz arrives at conclusion that M., though great as writer and interpreter of English constitution, has many shortcomings as political scientist.

Sclopis de Salerano, Federigo, *conte.* Montesquieu et Machiavel. By Frédéric Sclopis. RDF 2:15-28, 1856.   1596

Article examines three comparisons between M. and Machiavelli, those of : Macaulay, in article on Machiavelli in EdR 45:291-92, March, 1827, and reprinted in his *Critical, historical and miscellaneous essays*, New York, Armstrong, 1860, v. 1, p. 313-14; Venedy, (no. 1605) and P. S. Mancini, *Machiavelli e la sua dottrina politica*, Turin, 1852. Under title, *Machiavel, Montesquieu*, this study occupies p. 208-20 in 1498.

Shackleton, Robert. Montesquieu, Bolingbroke and the separation of powers. FS 3:25-38, Jan., 1949.   1597

Purpose of study is to examine sources of doctrine of separation of powers as expressed by M.; adequate on this subject, and on Bolingbroke, but author shows only limited acquaintance with other 20th century discussions of theme of his study.

Sorel, Albert. Montesquieu. Hachette, 1887. 176 p. (GEF)   1598

Essential study, which would probably be selection of most students of M. if they were asked to name their favorite work on him. Comments upon it, as they appear in reviews listed below and as found frequently throughout the body of work on M., range from commendatory to enthusiastic. Book is concise, accurate, scholarly, and penetrating, yet can be read

with as much ease and enjoyment as best of modern novelized biographies.

Reviews : F. Brunetière in RDM 82: 694-706, Aug. 1, 1887 (1532); M. Gaucher in RPL ser. 315:471-72, Oct. 8, 1887; F. Hémon in Rcr ns 25:149-51, 1888; P. Janet in JS, June, 1888 : 346-57; E. Schérer in his : *Études sur la littérature contemporaine*, 9:239-54; A. Tobler in Dlit 9:518-19, Apr. 7, 1888.

Spurlin, Paul M. Montesquieu in America, 1760-1801. University, La., Louisiana State univ. press, 1940. 302 p.   1599

Essential study; in its original form a Johns Hopkins Ph. D. thesis (1936) suggested and directed by Prof. Gilbert Chinard. Purposes and scope clearly stated in Introduction : " The present study is one of literary history, not political science... The immediate objective is to show the dissemination of Montesquieu's works in America " (p. 40), and in the Conclusion : " No attempt has been made... to study the ' influence ' of Montesquieu on American institutions "; the effort has been " ... to provide a more comprehensive basis for future opinions... as regards influence..." (p. 258). Within this carefully delimited field, author has unquestionably made more useful " contribution to knowledge " than if he had attempted to add to already considerable mass of controversial opinion on extent of M.'s influence in America. Reviews listed below, selected from larger number, agree that this study has covered the ground with method, thoroughness, and intelligence, although some of them would have liked to see it attempt wider range.

Reviews : K. C. Cole in MLQ 2:520-21, 1941; A. Guérard in BA 15:348, 1941; H. M. Jones in RR 32:312-13, 1941; C. F. Mullett in PSQ 56:479-80, 1941; R. R. Palmer in JMH 13:404-05, 1941; F. G. Wilson in APSR 35²:398, 1941; B. F. Wright in AHR 47:353-54, 1942.

Taine, Hippolyte. Montesquieu. *In his :* Essai sur Tite-Live. Hachette, 1874. p. 172-88.   1600

Important study. Forms second section of chapter on *Philosophie de l'histoire romaine dans les modernes,* of which eight pages on Machiavelli compose first part. Opens with brief summary of Saint-Évremond's and Bossuet's approach to Roman history. Next follows some fine general criticism of M., which applies especially to *Lois,* whose severity renders all the more impressive the high praise which Taine accords to the *Romains* (p. 173-80).

Taylor, O. R. Bernard Routh et la mort de Montesquieu. FS 3:101-21, 1949. **1600A**

Intelligent, well-documented study, which attempts to show that Voltaire's account of death of M. (*see* no. 1458, p. 70, item 578) is deliberately inexact, due to anticlerical bias.

Tchernoff, J. Montesquieu et J.-J. Rousseau. RDP 19:477-514, 1903, and 20:49-97, 1903. Also in a *tirage à part*, Chevalier-Marescq, 1903. 85 p. **1601**

Written largely to show exaggeration of two schools of thought on M. and Rousseau, namely : one contrasting M., the liberal-conservative, with Rousseau, the apostle of despotic, Jacobin *étatisme* (Taine *et al*); the other, in reaction against it, contending that Rousseau was the more conservative of the two. Tchernoff's citations (which are taken too exclusively from *Lois* and *Contrat social*), and his cautiously worded opinions, tend to show that differences between M. and Rousseau are due mainly to differences of inspiration of *Lois* and *Contrat social*. Review : F. M. Fling in AHR 10:888, 1905.

Tournyol du Clos, Jean. Les idées financières de Montesquieu. RSLF 10:220-41, 1912. **1602**

Important study within limits of its subject. Begins with the opinion that, on financial problems, M. showed " ... une faible compétence technique, une extrême modération, une prédilection pour l'agriculture." Emphasizes M.'s friendship with Melon, and similarity of their views. Bulk of article devoted to careful analysis of M.'s *Mémoires* to the Regent on the public debt.

Anon. Two forgotten jurists : Machiavelli and Montesquieu. SJ 65:798-99, Aug. 27, 1921. **1603**

Important article : tells how *London Times* exposed anti-Semitic *Protocols of the Elders of Sion* as a forgery, based on material taken from Joly's pamphlet, *Dialogue aux enfers entre Machiavel et Montesquieu*. Uses this as introduction to subject, which is a comparison, brief but one of clearest and most illuminating, between Machiavelli and M. Says that " ... the doctrine that the state is above moral law (i.e., Machiavelli's) and the doctrine that the state must develop its

laws in accordance with the moral law, to meet new economic conditions (i.e., M.'s) are the foundation of every modern tendency in jurisprudence " (p. 799).

Vaughan, Charles E. The eclipse of contract : Montesquieu. *In his :* Studies in the history of political philosophy before and after Rousseau. *See* 107, p. 253-302; 3077. **1604**

Essential study, perhaps most solid made in English of M.'s political thought. Title explained in *Introductory*. Pages on M. form second part of chapter whose first half is devoted to Vico. Thinks that, " Within the soul of Montesquieu there were... two men struggling for the mastery; the political philosopher and the practical reformer " (p. 255). Penetrating analysis of purpose and meaning of *Lois*, and its effects on ensuing political thinking.

Venedy, Jacob. Montesquieu. *In his :* Macchiavel, Montesquieu, Rousseau. Berlin, Duncker, 1850. p. 131-306. **1605**

Essential study. Venedy was active German intellectual revolutionary of 1848 who, after failure of revolution, continued struggle with his pen; thus, present work has as its purpose to advance political thinking in Germany by explaining doctrines of the three greatest theorists of the state in modern times. For Venedy, M., as leading advocate of constitutional monarchy, is not radical enough to erect system of government of definite theoretical and practical value.

Vian, Louis. Histoire de Montesquieu. 2nd ed. Didier, 1879. 411 p. **1606**

Essential work. Still most detailed, factual, personal biography of M. In it Vian assembled practically everything known about M. at time, and material is well arranged and interestingly treated. Second edition profited intelligently by severe criticism directed against first, of preceding year. There is analysis, criticism, and appraisal of M.'s individual works and of his place in literature and political science, etc. However, all of his " larger aspects," while their presentation is far from negligible in this book, have been better treated since by abler writers and thinkers than Vian. If, nevertheless, Vian's facts and opinions are considered as starting points, work can still render valuable service. Extensive but unreliable bibliography.

Reviews : E. de B[arthélemy] in BBB

1878:88; F. Brunetière in RDM 3rd ser. 33:219-29, May 1, 1879; E. Caro in JS, June, 1878: 325-37; same review in AMP 110(ns 10) : 501-26, 1878 (1536); R. Kerviler in Poly 23 (2nd ser. v. 8) : 344-46, 1878; G. Koerting in ZNSL 1²:104-06, 1879; T[amizey] de L[arroque] in Rcr 12 (ns 5) : 272-81, Apr. 27, 1878; [A. Laugel] in NNY 26:165-66, March 7, 1878.

Villegardelle, François. Histoire des idées sociales; Montesquieu. Rsoc 3: Feb., 8-9, March, 9-11, 1850.   1607

Important study, which advances some rather original ideas on M. Says that it is difficult from reading Lois to know just what kind of government M. really prefers. Shows by quotation from it, Book IV, Ch. 6 and 7 (Laboulaye, no. 1465, v. 3, p. 156-58) that M. favored " partage des terres," and that on this point, as on some others, he was more radical than the Socialists of middle 19th century (p. 10). Concludes one can find in M. arguments for almost any system of government and economics under which men have lived, or which has been proposed for them.

Villemain, Abel François. Eloge de Montesquieu. In his : Discours et mélanges littéraires. Didier, 1846, p. 55-102.   1608

Essential work, by far the best of the éloges of M., with possible exception of that of D'Alembert (no. 1519), to which it is superior in many ways. Éloge was awarded the French Academy Prix d'éloquence, when its author was only twenty-six. Many ideas invite quotation : e.g. when M. was writing on matters not worthy of his thought, he " ... se livrait à l'influence de son siècle, mais lorsqu'il avait rencontré un sujet égal à sa force... il redevenait simple et naturel... " (p. 74). Also : " Montesquieu corrige toujours par quelque vérité nouvelle une première pensée qui ne paraissait excessive que parce qu'on la voyait seule " (p. 90).

Voltaire, etc. Montesquieu. In his : Écrivains français du Siècle de Louis XIV. Moland, v. 14, p. 106-08.   1609

It is in this section that Voltaire made his much discussed charge that M., in order to remove objections to his admission to Academy, caused to be printed for the eyes of Cardinal Fleury a special edition of LP, " ... dans laquelle on retrancha ou on adoucit tout ce qui pouvait être condamné par un cardinal et par un ministre " (p. 107). Section contains

usual Voltaire-on-M. material : shrewd criticism and some commendation, sometimes grudging, sometimes generous.

— Remerciment sincère à un homme charitable. Moland, v. 23, p. 457-61; Kehl, v. 46, p. 6-12.   1610

Section has been reprinted in several editions of M.'s works. Note 1, p. 457, explains that this is reply to an article in Nouvelles ecclésiastiques of Apr. 24, 1750, on M.'s Défense de l'Esprit des lois. Whole tone of reply to " homme charitable " (i.e., the Nouvelliste) continues irony of title. Vian (no. 1606, p. 268) says of this Remerciment that in it Voltaire, under pretext of defending M., accuses him of lacking orderliness, making inaccurate quotations, and having written work merely pleasant to read.

— L'A, B. C, ou dialogues entre A, B, C; traduit de l'anglais de M. Huet. Premier dialogue. Sur Hobbes, Grotius et Montesquieu, Moland, v. 27, p. 311-36; Kehl, v. 36, p. 213-33.   1611

Most interesting passage is one which has become famous, though almost invariably in incorrect quotation. Voltaire wrote : " Il [M.] a partout fait souvenir les hommes qu'ils sont libres; il présente à la nature humaine ses titres qu'elle a perdus dans la plus grande partie de la terre..." (Moland, p. 322; Kehl, p. 227. Also in Moland, v. 24, p. 431; Kehl, v. 29, p. 207-08). Eulogy usually quoted : " Le genre humain avait perdu ses titres; M. de Montesquieu les a retrouvés et les lui a rendus." Destutt de Tracy closes his Commentaire sur l'Esprit des lois (no. 1482) with latter version, and Villemain uses it as the epigraph of his Éloge de Montesquieu (no. 1608).

Walckenaer, C. A. Montesquieu. In : L. G. Michaud, Biographie universelle. Desplaces, 1843-65. v. 29, p. 78-91.   1612

First-rate study, still interesting and well worth reading, and one of best biographical-critical on M. published up to its time. Among other ideas is theory on lost manuscript of Histoire de Louis XI (p. 90). Enumerates M.'s gifts for writing of history, and then advances several reasons why he could not have succeeded as historian. Closes with brilliant comparison between M. and Tacitus.

Zévort, Edgar. Montesquieu. Lecène and Oudin, 1887. 238 p. (CCP).   1613

Interesting and useful work for all students of M., though series for which it was written was intended primarily for French secondary schools. Book's principal value today lies in many human-interest touches, somewhat in manner of modern " book-chat " article, which serve to render its analytical and critical material easy to assimilate. Worth of these critical ideas lies not so much in their originality as in a sort of unpretentious, easily retained turn of expression.

Reviews : F. Brunetière in RDM 82: 694-706, Aug. 1, 1887 (1532); M. Gaucher in Rcr 3rd ser. 14:472, Oct. 8, 1887.

ADDENDUM

Barrière, P. Les éléments personnels et les éléments bordelais dans les Lettres persanes. RHL 51:17-36, 1951.   1613A

Underlines with examples the personal, domestic, and intellectual reminiscences in M.'s first important work. " Ces Asiatiques sont en réalité des Bordelais dont les usages, l'accent, la langue, les manies peuvent soulever tout autant l'ironie parisienne " (p. 19). Illuminating article with many plausible *rapprochements*. " Ce sont ces emprunts qui donnent aux *Lettres* leur réalité solide et leur sérieux " (p. 36).

CHAPTER VII. FRANÇOIS-MARIE AROUET DE VOLTAIRE
(Nos. 1614-1849)

GEORGE R. HAVENS

Bibliography

Whoever works with Voltaire must always be greatly in debt to the three indispensable bibliographies by Mary-Margaret H. Barr, which are briefly described below (nos. 1615, 1616, 1617). With their over 2000 titles of books and articles, they form both the necessary basis for, and a valuable supplement to, the present selective list. It is a pleasure also to acknowledge here the aid given by Mr. Joe B. Cox and by Mrs. Dorothy Rannebarger in the preparation of certain parts of this bibliography.

Quérard, J.-M. Notice des diverses éditions des ouvrages de Voltaire. *In his :* La France littéraire, see 51, v. 10, p. 276-436.　　1614

Bibliography of works by and concerning V.; now superseded by Bengesco (no. 1618) for works by V. himself, and by Mary-Margaret H. Barr (nos. 1615-17) for works about V. published after 1825.

Barr, Mary-Margaret H. A century of Voltaire study; a bibliography of writings on Voltaire, 1825-1925. New York, Institute of French studies, 1929. 123 p.
　　1615
Indispensable basic list of 1494 titles covering a century of V. studies. Reviews : G. R. Havens in MLN 45: 347, 1930; H. D. MacPherson in RR 21:256-57, 1930; D. Mornet in RHL 37: 623-24, 1930; Anon. in RLC 10:534-35, 1930.

— Bibliographical data on Voltaire from 1926 to 1930. MLN 48:292-307, 1933.　1616

This list supplements author's *Bibliography of writings on Voltaire, 1825-1925*, published in 1929 (no. 1615) and covers five years indicated. Brief comments on many titles.

— Bibliographical data on Voltaire from 1931 to 1940. MLN 56:563-82, 1941.　1617

This list brings the two previous bibliographies (nos. 1615-16) up to date through 1940.

Bengesco, Georges. Voltaire : Bibliographie de ses œuvres. Rouveyre and Blond (Vol. 1), Perrin (Vols. 2-4), 1882-90. 4 v.　1618

Essential instrument for work on V. Detailed study of publication of V.'s individual works and collected editions. Contains also *répertoire* of more than 10,000 letters in Moland edition (no. 1628) of V.'s correspondence, plus 100 letters not previously published in collected editions followed by indication of other letters published in various places but not in Moland. (Cf. 3:285-375). *See* 1619.

Reviews : F. Brunetière in RDM 59th yr. 3rd per. 96:208-20, Nov. 1, 1889; R. Mahrenholtz in ZFSL 12²:114-15, 1890; E. Ritter in ZFSL 14¹:211-19, 1892.

Crowley, Francis J. Corrections and additions to Bengesco's Bibliographie. MLN 50:440-41, 1935. *See* 1618.　1619

Lists 14 titles, with additions and corrections.

Flower, Desmond. Some aspects of the bibliography of Voltaire. Libr 5th ser. 1: 223-36, 1946-47.　1620

Additions or corrections to bibliography of *Œdipe, Lettre au Roi de Prusse, Histoire de Russie, Tancrède,* and *Prix de la justice*. Particularly interesting for announcement that author has embarked on " rather frightening task " (p. 223) of publishing a new bibliography of V., " a section at a time," to correct and supplement Bengesco (no. 1618).

Caussy, Fernand. Inventaire des manuscrits de la bibliothèque de Voltaire conservée à la Bibliothèque impériale publique de Saint-Pétersbourg (extrait des Nouvelles archives des Missions scientifiques et littéraires, nouv. série, fasc. 7). Imprimerie nationale, 1913. 96 p.　1621

Important list of V. MSS in State Public Library of Leningrad. Some inaccuracies of detail to be corrected only by work on the spot.

Morehouse, Andrew R. The Voltaire collection in the Rare book room. YLG 17:66-79, April, 1943. 1622

Yale University Library possesses in its Rare Book Room some 400 works by and about V., of which over 60 are first editions. An important bibliographical article.

Smith, Horatio. Voltaire : bibliographical notes. MLN 47:234-36, 1932. 1623

Locates at John Carter Brown Library in Providence, R. I., previously unknown edition of V.'s *Essay on the civil wars of France and on epic poetry*, printed in Dublin in 1728, with account of life of V., attributed to Swift.

Van Roosbroeck, Gustave L. Notes on Voltaire. MLN 39:1-10, 1924. 1624

Useful correction, for specialist, of details of dating V.'s letters, additions to his bibliography, etc.

— Additions and corrections to Voltaire's bibliography published in 1924. MLN 44: 328-30, 1929. 1625
Continuation of previous article.

Editions

Voltaire, François-Marie Arouet de. Œuvres complètes. [Kehl,] Imprimerie de la Société littéraire typographique, 1784 and 1785-89. 70 v. 8°, or 92 v. 12°. 1626

Famous " Kehl edition " published under direction of Beaumarchais. First posthumous edition of V.'s work, it is most complete of all 18th century collections and forms the basis of the great 19th century editions of Beuchot (no. 1627) and Moland (no. 1628) described below. Needless to say, however, it is not thoroughly scientific and has perpetuated textual errors. Review : G. Bengesco in no. 1618, 4:105-46.

— Œuvres. Ed. by Adrien Beuchot. Lefèvre, Didot, Werdet et Lequien fils, 1829 (v. 15 and others) -40. 72 v. 1627

Great " Beuchot edition." Since 1802, Beuchot had been occupied with research on V. which culminated in this remarkable work. " Nul n'avait mieux fait avant lui; nul n'a mieux fait depuis," observes Georges Bengesco (Voltaire : *Bibliographie*, (no. 1618) 4:181). Except for important additions to *Correspondance*, Louis Moland largely reprinted text,

Avertissements, and *Notes* of Beuchot. See no. 1628.
Review : G. Bengesco in no. 1618, 4:171-86.

— Œuvres complètes. Ed. by Louis Moland. Garnier, 1877-85. 52 v. 1628

This celebrated " Moland edition " is the indispensable general collection of V.'s works, constantly cited as standard. Confusingly enough, editor's name does not appear on title page. Based on great Beuchot edition (no. 1627) (1829-40, 72 v.), Moland supersedes his predecessor chiefly for the *Correspondance*, more complete (over 10,000 letters) and arranged throughout in chronological order (v. 33-50; v. 32, pp. 607-21; *Supplément*, end of v. 50; and *Appendice*, end of v. 52). Important biographical documents in v. 1. Unusually complete *Table générale* in v. 51-52. Several excellent critical editions in turn supersede Moland for certain individual works. (See below). Reviews : G. Bengesco in no. 1618, 4:196-203, 1890; F. Brunetière in RDM 50th yr. 3rd per. 38:457-68, Mar. 15, 1880; E. Ritter in ZFSL 14²:211, 1892.

— Supplément aux Œuvres de Voltaire : Œuvres inédites : Tome 1ᵉʳ, Mélanges historiques. Published by Fernand Caussy. Champion, 1914. 350 p. 1629

Caussy had planned publication of nine volumes of Supplement to V.'s works, three of *Mélanges* and six of *Correspondance*. These last would have brought together some 5,000 additional letters published in various periodicals since 1882, but not to be found in Moland edition (no. 1628). Unfortunately, only Volume 1 of this series was published. It contains, however, interesting MS material in form of notes for V.'s *Essai sur les mœurs* and *Siècle de Louis XIV*. Reviews : V. Pinot in RHL 24:512-15, 1917; P. Sakmann in ZFSL 43²:74-75, 1915.

Havens, George R. Selections from Voltaire. New York, Century, 1925; Revised ed., [1930]; Second revision, New York, Appleton-Century, 1940. xxviii, 439 p. 1630

Chronological presentation in single volume of selections from V.'s chief works arranged for class use or for general reader. Biographical and explanatory comments in relation to each work. *Appendix* gives briefly some of more significant studies on V. published between

1925 and 1940. Selective bibliography. Eight illustrations.

Review : Anon. in RLC 6:350, 1926.

Voltaire, François-Marie Arouet de. Candide, ou L'optimisme, édition critique. Ed. by André Morize. Hachette, 1913; Droz, 1931. 237 p.   1631

Authoritative critical edition of *Candide* with excellent *Notes* and *Introduction* written with that combination of scholarship and verve characteristic of best French tradition. Supersedes Moland (no. 1628) for V.'s best philosophical tale.

— Candide, ou L'optimisme. Ed. by George R. Havens. New York, Holt, [1934]. lxiii, 149, lxi p.   1632

Extensive *Introduction*, *Notes*, and *Vocabulary*. Based upon work of Morize (no. 1631), but adds material on composition and background of this novel, and on relations of author with Jean-Jacques Rousseau. Analysis of V.'s ironic prose style and bearing of his satire. New illustrations.

Review : B. M. Woodbridge in MLJ 20:250-51, 1935-36.

— Contes et Romans. Ed. by Philippe van Tieghem. Roches, 1930, 4 v. (TF).   1633

Excellent text of V.'s philosophical tales made available in convenient and attractive format for general reader. Introductions good, but somewhat too brief. Mornet's review, mentioned below, gives important hints on background of these *contes*, not treated by editor.

Review : D. Mornet in RHL 38:325-26, 1931.

— Correspondance de Voltaire (1726-1729). Ed. by Lucien Foulet. Hachette, 1913. 321 p. *See* 3081.   1634

Authoritative critical edition of V.'s *Correspondance* for brief, but important period of English journey. Reëstablishes authentic text of letters from original MSS where available. Illuminating Introduction and Notes. Supersedes Moland (no. 1628) for this three-year period.

Reviews : J. Acher in ZFSL 42²:169-88, 1914; C. C[harrot] in RHL 21:777-87, 1914; Anon. in MLN 29:64, 1914.

— Lettres d'Alsace à sa nièce madame Denis. Ed. by Georges Jean-Aubry. Gallimard, [1938]. 284 p.   1635

109 previously unknown letters of V

to his niece, Mme Denis, mostly from 1753 and 1754. Introduction and Notes on content, background, and dating. Source and present location of MSS not indicated. Valuable addition to our knowledge of period in V.'s life after break with Frederick and before settling of V. at Geneva.

Review : D. Mornet in RHL 46:252-53, 1939.

— Lettres inédites aux Tronchin, avec une introduction de Bernard Gagnebin. Geneva, Droz ; Lille, Giard, 1950. 3 v. (TLF).

1635A

Publication of 712 letters, plus two in Appendix, with Introduction by Conservator of Manuscripts at Library of Geneva. " La correspondance de Voltaire avec les Tronchin permet de mieux connaître le patriarche de Ferney dans son intimité, d'admirer sa vitalité et son ardeur à l'ouvrage, de louer son intelligence et sa vivacité " (p. XL). *See* no. 1635B.

— Correspondance avec les Tronchin. Edition critique établie et annotée par André Delattre. Mercure de France, 1950. 797 p.

1635B

Definitive publication, after more than a decade of work, of these 722 letters, plus several in Appendices. Most of these letters written between 1755 and 1766. Light on V.'s failure to understand vitality of Genevan Protestantism in midst of violent struggles of democratic opinion. Description of each manuscript. *See* no. 1635A.

Friedrich II, *der Grosse.* Briefwechsel Friedrichs des Grossen mit Voltaire. Ed. by Reinhold Koser and Hans Droysen. Leipzig, Hirzel, 1908-11. 3 v.   1636

As indicated by Tables in back of each volume, this edition gives 29 letters or pieces of verse by Frederick and 17 by Voltaire, which are not found in Moland (no. 1628). Text based on original MSS, though sometimes apparently on first, and not final drafts of letters. Complete study of all variants between this and the Moland text needed. Corrections and Notes in no. 1637, p. 60-78.

— Nachträge zu dem Briefwechsel Friedrichs des Grossen mit Maupertuis und Voltaire. Ed. by Hans Droysen, Fernand Caussy and Gustav Volz. Leipzig, Hirzel, 1917. 119 p.

(K. preussischen Staatsarchiven, v. 90). *See also* 2576. 1637

Letter 124-a by V. is Moland (no. 1628) item 1266 (35:419-22), but in this draft from Morrison Collection it is briefer and quite different. Eight other letters by or to V. not to be found in Moland.

Voltaire, François-Marie Arouet de. Dialogues et anecdotes philosophiques. Ed. by Raymond Naves. Garnier [1940]. 536 p. 1638

Useful presentation in single volume and in chronological order of a group of little-known pieces in which V.'s final ideas of life and conduct are given with his characteristic dramatic verve. Introduction, Notes, and *Rapprochements* by editor.

— Dictionnaire philosophique. Ed. by Julien Benda and Raymond Naves. Garnier, [1935-36]. 2 v. 1639

Valuable for its presentation in convenient format of original text of 1764, when *Dictionnaire philosophique* was still *portatif*, together with changes and additions introduced in 1765, 1767, 1769, 1770-72, and 1774. Review: D. Mornet in RHL 43:596-97, 1936.

White, Florence Donnell. Voltaire's Essay on epic poetry; a study and an edition. Albany, Brandow, 1915. 168 p. (Diss., Bryn Mawr). 1640

Introduction, original text, and notes. Important differences between first English edition of 1727 and French version of 1733. Evidence that V. may have had reading knowledge of English when he left France in 1726 (p. 15). Detailed study of V.'s slight mistakes in English of *Essay* (p. 20-26). His changing attitudes towards Homer and Milton.

Voltaire. L'ingénu, édition critique. Ed. by William R. Jones. Droz, 1936. lxxx, 142 p. 1641

Comprehensive Introduction on publication and background of this, which, with *Zadig*, *Micromégas*, and *Candide*, ranks as one of V.'s four greatest philosophic tales. Study of sources might be amplified in light of Rovillain's article (no. 1838). This edition of *L'ingénu* supersedes Moland (no. 1628). Reviews: F. J. Crowley in RR 29:

87-89, 1938; D. Mornet in RHL 43: 597-99, 1936.

— Lettres philosophiques, édition critique. Ed. by Gustave Lanson. 2nd ed. Hachette, 1915-17. 2 v. (TFM). *See* 3083. 1642

Authoritative edition which reëstablishes original text of first edition of 1734, thus superseding composite text of Moland (no. 1628) for this great early work. Since V. later modified and greatly amplified his ideas on many subjects, it is important to know what he thought and wrote about England and France in 1734 soon after the English journey. Detailed and carefully documented notes present in masterly fashion background of ideas in England and France out of which V.'s work sprang. Lacks literary Introduction similar to that in Morize's edition of *Candide* (no. 1631). *See* Lantoine (no. 1832). *See also* no. 2829. Review: D. Mornet in RHL 17:194-97, 1910.

— Lettres sur les Anglais. Ed. with Introduction and Notes by Arthur Wilson-Green. Cambridge univ. press (England), 1931. xxii, 192 p. 1643

Convenient compact edition for school or general public with brief Introduction and Notes based on authoritative critical edition of Lanson (no. 1642), but intentionally more elementary in character.

— Lettres philosophiques. Ed. by Raymond Naves. Garnier, [1938]. xvi, 304 p. 1644

Excellent brief Introduction and valuable Notes giving parallel passages from V.'s other works. Edition supplements without aiming to supersede Lanson's indispensable critical edition (no. 1642). Review: D. Mornet in RHL 46:253, 1939.

— Mérope, tragédie. Ed. by Thomas Edward Oliver. New York, Century, 1925. xlviii, 145 p. 1645

Contains scholarly Introduction tracing Merope theme from Euripides through Maffei, V., Alfieri, to Matthew Arnold. Cf. below, by same author, no. 1835, and reviews of this work by G. L. van Roosbroeck and H. C. Lancaster.

Wade, Ira O. Voltaire's Micromégas; a study in the fusion of science, myth., and art. Princeton, Princeton univ. press, 1950. 190 p. 1645A

Critical edition with introduction, text, and notes. Gives important evidence to show that *Micromégas*, though not published till 1752, was composed as early as 1739, probably with minor later revisions. Work significant, therefore, for evolution of Voltaire's thought in 1730s. Discussion of scientific background, style, and meaning of *Micromégas*.

Morize, André. L'apologie du luxe au 18e siècle et le Mondain de Voltaire : étude critique sur le Mondain et ses sources. Didier, 1909. 190 p.   1646

Excellent critical edition which ought to be reprinted. Essential study of important question of luxury in 18th century thought. Supersedes Moland (no. 1628) for this important and provocative little work. "La méthode de M. Morize est très sûre; son érudition précise et vaste" (Gustave Lanson, p. 188 of review cited below). *See below* no. 1648.
Reviews : Gustave Lanson in RHL 17: 188-89, 1910; P. Sakmann in ZFSL 41²: 58-60, 1913.

Voltaire. Voltaire's Poème sur la Loi naturelle; a critical edition. Ed. by Francis J. Crowley. Berkeley, Univ. of California press, 1938. 127 p. (numbered 177-304). *See* 1217.   1647

Text of this important philosophical poem, study of different editions, background of V.'s ideas, inception and composition of poem. Supersedes Moland (no. 1628).
Reviews : J. David in MLQ 2:133-34, 1941; H. Dieckmann in MLN 56:233-34, 1941; N. L. Torrey in RR 31:181-83, 1940; P. Vernière in RHL 47:372-73, 1947.

— Poèmes philosophiques (Le Mondain, Discours sur l'homme, Poème sur le désastre de Lisbonne). Ed. by Georges Ascoli. Centre de documentation universitaire [1936]. 207 p. (Mimeographed).   1648

Mimeographed studies of these important poems published in series of *Les cours de Sorbonne*. Not considered definitive by author (hence tentative form), but very valuable, detailed studies, nevertheless. Supplements in some ways Morize's authoritative edition of *Le mondain* (no. 1646) and goes far beyond Moland (no. 1628), which it supersedes for the three poems studied. Reader should be on guard against numerous

typographical errors due to tentative form of publication.

— Sémiramis, tragédie. Édition critique publiée par Jean-Jacques Olivier. Droz, 1946. 95 p.   1649

Good Introduction and Bibliography, but lacks extensive, penetrating commentary of great critical editions of Lanson (no. 1642), Morize (no. 1646), Foulet (no. 1634), Ascoli (no. 1653), etc. Would have been well to reprint V.'s illuminating *Dissertation sur la tragédie ancienne et moderne*. Reader should correct misprint of Count de Lauragnais instead of Lauraguais, man who freed French drama from nuisance of spectators on stage (p. XLIV).

— Siècle de Louis XIV. Ed. by Émile Bourgeois. 5th ed. Hachette, 1906. 802 p.   1650

Comprehensive Introduction showing changes in V.'s plan over period of twenty years. Starting with desire simply to depict reign of Louis XIV and to contrast it favorably with that of his successor, V., under influence of Mme du Châtelet and coming to throne of Frederick, decided to make a "philosophical" history in which errors and intolerance of Louis XIV would stand out in conclusion. Thus work fits into framework of *Essai sur les mœurs* as example of human stupidity mitigated occasionally by leadership of great men. Breadth and excellence of V.'s first-hand sources, oral, printed, and manuscript. Scientific aim and method, though not completely realized due to philosophical *parti pris*. Great work, nevertheless. Editor gives *Table* of numerous letters in which V. discusses matters relative to *Siècle de Louis XIV*. Index to *Siècle* at end. Very valuable edition and text.

— Le temple du goût, édition critique. Ed. by E. Carcassonne. Droz, 1938. 197 p. (TFM).   1651

Excellent critical edition with Introduction showing essentially intuitive quality of V.'s classical taste. Supersedes Moland (no. 1628).
Reviews : G. R. Havens in RR 31: 77-78, 1940; A. Schinz in MLN 54:301-02, 1939.

— Traité de métaphysique (1734). Ed. by [Mrs.] H. Temple Patterson. Manchester, Manchester univ. press, 1937. 76 p. 1652

Critical edition of this posthumous work of V. " reproduced from Kehl text (no. 1626), with Preface, Notes, and Variants." Author holds that *Traité* more than mere introduction to *Éléments de Newton;* has close connections with *Lettres philosophiques, Dictionnaire philosophique, Discours sur l'homme, Le philosophe ignorant,* and *Correspondance* of 1733-38 (p. vii-viii). Supersedes Moland (no. 1628).

Voltaire. Zadig, ou La destinée, édition critique. Ed. by Georges Ascoli. Hachette, 1929. 2 v. (TFM). *See* 695.　　1653

Illuminating Introduction and Notes showing in detail background of ideas and circumstances out of which came V.'s first great philosophical tale. Supersedes Moland (no. 1628).
Review : G. L. van Roosbroeck in MP 29:125-27, 1931-32.

General Biography or Criticism

Aldington, Richard. Voltaire. London, Routledge, 1925. 278 p. (Republic of letters series).　　1654

No claim to originality in retelling facts of V.'s life, though these facts are well and briefly narrated. In general, penetrating analysis of V.'s literary work, especially his poetry and historical writings. Omits V.'s attack on war and rather undervalues serious side of his thought. Author quite evidently was writing from the calm peace and seeming security of 1925.

Ascoli, Georges. Voltaire. *In:* Bédier et Hazard, Histoire de la littérature française illustrée. *See* 60, 2:71-77, 103-08, or revised edition (1949), 2:57-65, 101-07.
　　1655

Excellent compact discussion based upon authoritative modern sources.

— Voltaire. RCC 25^1:673-87; 25^2:16-27, 128-44, 275-87, 302-15, 417-28, 616-30; 26^1: 262-73, 501-14, 703-21; 26^2:153-67, 373-84, 619-26, 627-39, 1924-25. *See* 3086, 3087.
　　1656

Series of 14 articles, impartial, authoritative, carefully documented, among best of all *études d'ensemble* of V. See especially II-III, *L'état d'esprit philosophique de Voltaire avant le séjour en Angleterre;* VI-VII, *L'Œuvre poétique;* and XIII, *L'art du conteur.*

Bellessort, André. Essai sur Voltaire. Perrin, 1926. 389 p. (Also in Rheb 34; Jan.-April, 1925).　　1657

Vivid, generally impartial, yet sympathetic discussion of V.'s life and work. Occasional statements of alleged facts need careful checking, which is difficult, since few documentary references are given.
Reviews : G. Ascoli in RHL 34:603-04, 1927; H. Bidou in APL, Aug. 2, 1925, p. 116-17.

Bertaut, Jules. Voltaire. Michaud [1910]. 192 p. (La vie anecdotique series).　　1658

Vivid narrative of V.'s life accompanied by numerous anecdotes. No discussion of his literary work. Not always accurate and needs to be checked carefully with original sources.

Brailsford, Henry N. Voltaire. New York, Holt; London, Butterworth, 1935. 256 p.
　　1659

In this lively little volume, well-known liberal thinker presents in brief compass vivid picture of V. the reformer and forerunner of Revolution. Unrestrained in his praise of V. Minimizes his faults. Good introduction to V. if taken with a few grains of realistic salt.

Brandes, Georg. Voltaire. Translated by Otto Kruger and Pierce Butler. New York, Boni, 1930. 2 v.　　1660

Detailed study of life and works of V. by great Danish critic. Translation from German or Danish not always accurate and apparently not checked with original French of citations from V.'s works. Occasional " howlers " in consequence as well as errors of detail. For example, we read that Rousseau has written V., " ... a letter for which he deserves his own prescription of *exposure in the rain and a diet of raw meat...*" (II, p. 94). Original is as follows : " Il m'a écrit une lettre pour laquelle il faut le baigner, et lui donner des bouillons rafraîchissants," (Moland, 40:437). Not always in touch with latest scholarship, and important statements given without proof. Yet valuable for broad picture of V. and his works.
Reviews : G. R. Havens in YR ns 20: 851-53, 1930-31; J. Orrick in Symp 2: 270-73, 1931; G. L. Van Roosbroeck in RR 22:334-36, 1931.

Brunetière, Ferdinand. Voltaire. *In his:* Études critiques sur l'histoire de la littérature française. 1:263-347, 1880; 3:259-90, 5th ed., 1904; 4:267-324, 4th ed., 1904.
　　1661

First study is biographical. Evaluates unfavorably V.'s personality. Second, inspired by Maugras' *Voltaire et Rousseau* (no. 1719), rightly censures Maugras' extreme position in favor of V., though Brunetière in turn is extreme in other direction. Third study praises highly Bengesco's bibliographical work on V. (no. 1618) and reacts against idea of Morley (no. 1676) that English journey "made" V. Underlines importance of formative French influences, Bayle, etc. Valuable corrective study. Author dogmatic and conservative, but always suggestive and not to be ignored, even by those who disagree with him. Characteristically Brunetière prefers Bossuet to V. Third division of last article inspired by Faguet's study (no. 1671).

— Voltaire, Introduction by Joseph Bédier. RDM 5th per. 60:5-33 (Nov. 1), 324-42 (Nov. 15), 606-37 (Dec. 1), 1910.   1662

Chapters, dealing with V.'s life up to 1754, were intended to form part of a projected volume for *Grands écrivains français* series. Hostile, but interesting. Author again emphasizes importance of French influence on V. (Bayle, Fontenelle, etc.), in contrast to influence attributed to English journey. (Cf. Morley, no. 1676).

Celarié, Henriette. Monsieur de Voltaire, sa famille et ses amis. Colin, 1928. 237 p.   1663

Lively, popular narrative of various aspects of V.'s life, from love affair with "Pimpette" Du Noyer in Holland to last days in Paris. His various lodgings in Paris, "L'ardente Émilie," Mme Denis, Mlle Corneille, and Mme de Villette.

Champion, Edme. Voltaire : Études critiques (1892). Colin, 3rd ed., 1921. viii, 306 p.   1664

Important book. With wealth of quotations from V.'s works, author demolishes many hostile opinions or misinterpretations. Collection of separate essays rather than succession of unified chapters. Each chapter suggestive rather than complete and final study. Should inspire further research in many cases. Courage of V. in combatting real dangers; V. and Pascal; *La Pucelle* first of all satire of Chapelain; date of *Le sermon des cinquante*; V. and the Revolution; these are some of subjects treated. Appendix : *Avis aux futurs éditeurs de Voltaire*, containing notes on corrections to be made in text of V.'s complete works.

Review : E. Welvert in Rcr 89:428-30, 1922.

Condorcet, Marie-Jean-Antoine-Nicolas de Caritat, marquis de. Vie de Voltaire (pub. in Vol. 70 of the Kehl octavo ed. of Voltaire in 1789. 256 p. Reprinted in Moland, 1:187-292).   1665

Written by 18th century disciple of V., one of two literary editors of Kehl edition of V.'s works (no. 1626), published by Beaumarchais. Tends to be over-admiring and uncritical. Valuable contemporary source, nevertheless.

Cresson, André. Voltaire, sa vie, son œuvre, avec un exposé de sa philosophie. Presses universitaires de France, 1948. 139 p. 1665A

Brief, popular *exposé*. Extracts at end are hardly extensive enough to be of much consequence. Exposition of V.'s philosophy offers useful introduction in small space. Conclusion : " Voltaire n'est donc nullement athée. Mais il n'en est pas moins impie. La religion est faite d'émotion et de confiance. Son théisme est fait de raisonnements abstraits et d'ironies grimaçantes. C'est ce qui a tant irrité contre lui les fervents du romantisme, un Chateaubriand, un Lamartine, un A. de Musset " (p. 89).

Crouslé, Léon. La vie et les œuvres de Voltaire. Champion, 1899. 2 v.   1666

One of best known of several long onslaughts against ideas and personality of V. Fails to take into consideration gross abuses which called forth V.'s angry attacks. Sees in him only negative side of critic and satirist. Overlooks his continued and courageous warfare for justice and the liberty of human spirit. Worth taking account of, however, as representative of viewpoint unyieldingly hostile.

Reviews : H. Chantavoine in Corr 197: 178-86, Oct. 10, 1899; T. Delmont in RLille 22 (ns 8):193-416, 1903-04.

Desnoiresterres, Gustave. Voltaire et la société au XVIIIe siècle. 2nd ed., Didier, 1869-76. 8 v. (Vol. 3, 1869, vol. 1, 1871).   1667

This eight-volume biography one of indispensable basic works for any detailed study of V.'s life and literary activity. Not a discussion of his ideas, however. Later biographers have all drawn extensively from Desnoiresterres' work, with or without acknowledgement. In addition to series title given above, each volume also bears a distinguishing sub-title. Review : E. Caro in JS 1874:810-23.

[Du Vernet, Abbé Théophile]. La vie de Voltaire. Geneva, 1786. 355 p. (Posthumous ed. " très augmentée," 1797). **1668**

Projected as early as autumn of 1771 (Moland (no. 1628), 47:437) and based in part upon information obtained from V. himself (*ibid.*, 48:6, 37, 49, 195, 423, 434), and from his friend, Thieriot (*ibid.*, 48:6). Of latter, V. says : " Il est très-vrai que, dans ma seconde retraite à la Bastille, il me pourvut de livres anglais " (*ibid.*). V. soon became alarmed at Du Vernet's zeal, however, and sought to restrain him (*ibid.*, 48:64). Du Vernet's work interesting and anecdotic, but uncritical and filled with errors. To be accepted with reserve. A contemporary notice by Meister in Grimm, *Correspondance littéraire* (no. 2357), 14:437, 1786.

Faguet, Emile. Voltaire. RCC 8²:289-96; 385-94; 454-62; 481-91; 9¹:1-11; 97-106; 337-47; 481-89; 584-93; 776-82; 9²:8-16; 145-54; 258-66; 289-98; 385-93; 529-37, May 3, 1900, — May 30, 1901. **1669**

Important series of 16 articles, dealing chiefly with V.'s literary and poetic ideas. V.'s criticism of Shakespeare. Extended discussion of *La Henriade*. V.'s conception of free will in second of the *Discours sur l'homme*.
Reviews : G. Monod in Rhist 80:119-24, 1902 ; E. Rigal in RLR, 5ᵉ série, 45:331-32, 1902.

— La politique comparée de Montesquieu, Rousseau et Voltaire. *See* 1557 (Montesquieu), 2065 (Rousseau). **1670**

Interprets Montesquieu as real liberal of his century, Rousseau as an advocate of tyranny dominated by masses of the people, and V. as exponent of concentration of powers in beneficent despotism. Insufficient emphasis upon V.'s attacks on tyranny and his attempt to deal practically with the situation in France as he saw it at the time.
Most penetrating review by Lanson (RU 11²:244-48, 1902).

— Voltaire. *In his* : Le dix-huitième siècle, études littéraires. Boivin, n.d. (Preface dated 1890). p. 199-288. **1671**

Author has little sympathy for V. the man. Admires negative side of his ideas, not positive. " Ce grand esprit, c'est un

chaos d'idées claires " (p. 226). Exaggerates V.'s supposed inability to appreciate mystery of life (cf. *Le philosophe ignorant*). Dogmatic in believing V. incapable of understanding liberty (p. 287) (Cf. *Dictionnaire philosophique*, Articles : *Liberté*, *Liberté de penser*, and *Liberté d'imprimer*). But this study is important if read critically. Lanson (nos. 1672, 1673), as usual, preserves better balance. Article discussed by F. Brunetière (no. 1661).

Francis, Louis. La vie privée de Voltaire. Hachette, 1948. (Collection Les vies privées). **1671A**

Brief and rapidly-moving biography from purely personal side with little or no attention to literary works or ideas. Well told, favorable, yet impartial. Numerous side lights on many controversial points. Filled with interesting details, but written only for general public and documentation unfortunately omitted, making it difficult to check. Written by experienced novelist, but happily not a *vie romancée*.

Lanson, Gustave. Voltaire. 2nd ed. Hachette, 1910. 224 p. (GEF). **1672**

Probably best brief survey of V.'s life and work in any language. Accurate, intelligent, succinct, written with verve worthy of V. himself. No doubt best book for general reader or student to begin his acquaintance with V.
Reviews : P. B[onnefon] in RHL 14:565-67, 1907 ; A. Chameix in Jdéb 13²:1028-30, Nov. 29, 1906 ; P. Sakmann in ZFSL 32²:58-63, 1908.

— Histoire de la littérature française. 23rd ed. Hachette [1928 ?]. *See* 70. **1673**

See particularly p. 648-52, 688-708, 755-72. Brilliant pages by master of French literature, able to appreciate such diverse men of genius as V. and Rousseau. " I! n'est pas nécessaire que leur guerre se continue dans nos esprits," says Lanson (p. 792, n.). Cf. also interesting, frank modifications of opinion in footnotes, showing rare intellectual honesty. Whole represents remarkable discussion in small space. Cf. also v. 2 of Lanson's *Histoire illustrée de la littérature française* (Same text, but accompanied by beautiful illustrations.)

Mahrenholtz, Richard. Voltaire's Leben und Werke. Oppeln, Franck, 1885. 2 v. **1674**

Leading German authority endeavors to correct element of bias in favor of V. which he finds at times in Desnoiresterres (no. 1667), as for example in discussion of V.'s relations with Frederick the Great. Goes beyond Desnoiresterres in treatment of V.'s thought and literary work as well as his life.
Review : W. Knörich in ZFSL 8²: 150-52, 1886.

— Zur Korrespondenz Voltaires. ZFSL 4¹: 248-80, 1882.   1675

Important summary of V.'s character, opinions, and activities as revealed by his correspondence. Article evoked by publication of Moland edition (no. 1628).

Morley, John. Voltaire [1872], London, Macmillan, 1913. 365 p. (First printed in this form in 1885).   1676

Penetrating interpretation by vigorous, first-rate mind, awake to V.'s great virtues, yet not blind to his defects. Some dates and details need to be checked in light of subsequent modern research. Inclined somewhat to exaggerate effect of English influence on V. (Cf. Brunetière, no. 1661). Still probably best over-all book in English on V.
Reviews : Bl 111:270-90, 1872, (reprinted in LA 113:131-46, 1872); FM ns 5:678-91, 1872.

Naves, Raymond. Voltaire, L'homme et l'œuvre. Boivin, 1942. 176 p. (Collection : Le livre de l'étudiant).   1677

Excellent little book, well-informed and of balanced judgment. Good treatment of V.'s background. Essential unity of his thought. Analysis of V.'s style and effective irony. V. abandoned uncertainties of metaphysics, but believed in action to ameliorate human conditions. Did not lack courage, as has been claimed. If he had, he needed only to have remained silent. Took grave risks, which is sometimes forgotten today. Worked for immediate and practical reforms. Believed in liberty and constantly attacked oppression. Slight errors in statement (p. 38) that *Épître à Uranie* was printed in 1732, when it still circulated only in MS, and in arguing from *après coup* conclusion of *Espérance* at end of *Poem on Lisbon* (p. 153). (Cf. nos. 1828, 1829). Useful evaluations in brief bibliography up to outbreak of War in 1939.
Review : P. Jourda in RU 52:109, 1943.

Nourrisson, J. F. Voltaire et le voltairianisme. Lethielleux, 1896. 671 p.   1678

One of most extensive and violent diatribes against V.'s character and all his works. Dogmatic. Numerous quotations, but considered out of their context. Little discussion of significance of V.'s major works. For an unfavorable estimate of V., Brunetière (1661-62) is abler and more convincing.

Noyes, Alfred. Voltaire. New York, Sheed and Ward, 1936. 643 p.   1679

Very personal interpretation of "moral" and " Christian " V. which does credit to author's independence and courage. Author insufficiently informed, however, about recent scholarship, which does not fully support his view. Morley (no. 1676) is sounder. Work admirable, nevertheless, in appreciation of V.'s poetic and prose style. Good also in explaining moral basis of V.'s revolt against many tenets of orthodoxy. Third edition, London, Faber and Faber, 1939. " Text... unaltered from... second edition which the former publishers withdrew from circulation, by order of the Supreme Congregation of the Holy See, in June, 1938." (p. xi-xii).
Reviews : E. Boyd in SRL 14²⁰:7, Sept. 12, 1936; A. Guérard in HTB, Oct. 4, 1936, p. 1-2.

Oulmont, Charles. Voltaire en robe de chambre. Calmann-Lévy, 1936. 224 p.
1680

Valuable familiar study of V.'s personality with some previously unpublished material. Explains many of V.'s mercurial changes and his lack of physical courage by excessive nervous temperament. Author at times uncritical in attitude.

Pellissier, Georges. Voltaire philosophe. Colin, 1908. 304 p.   1681

Good treatment of V.'s ideas.
Reviews : P. Sakmann in ZFSL 35²: 213-16, 1909-10; A. Schinz in MLN 24: 183-84, 1909.

Robertson, J.M. Voltaire. London, Watts, 1922. 122 p.   1682

Brief discussion of V.'s life and work. Sees in V. a militant freethinker, badly needed in his own age, and in ours.

Saintsbury, George. Voltaire. *In his :* French literature and its masters. *See* 1594. p. 94-118, 322-23.   1683

Reprinted from *Encyclopædia Britannica*, 11th ed. Important article by able critic. Full of penetrating evaluations and comments. Endeavors to hold even balance between praise and blame, but finds V.'s personality basically unsympathetic. Shows independence by putting *La Pucelle* above *La Henriade*. V.'s " peculiar quality " is " ironic style without exaggeration " (p. 114). In evaluating V.'s trickery, makes insufficient allowance for tyranny against which he fought. Some errors of detail. Remains, however, vigorous, able, and stimulating article. Supplementary recent bibliography, supplied by editor, is rather undiscriminating.

Sakmann, Paul. Voltaire's Geistesart und Gedankenwelt. Stuttgart, Frommann, 1910. 383 p. 1684

Thorough-going study of V.'s thought by long-time specialist in subject. Does not consider V. ridiculous figure sometimes portrayed by Faguet (no. 1671). His philosophy not frivolous. Lessing also too severe in his criticism of V.'s tragedies. References not given, since book written for general public, but can be found in specialized articles by same author listed at beginning of volume.
Review : W. Martini in ZFSL 36²: 273-76, 1910.

Sée, Henri. Les idées politiques de Voltaire. Rhist 98:255-93, 1908. 1685

V. believed that politics should be submitted to laws of reason and be guided by lessons of history. Attacked divine right of kings and elaborated doctrine of rights of man. Urged tolerance and emancipation from ecclesiastical authority. Vague on form of government. Seems to prefer limited monarchy. Democracy favored only for smaller countries. (Reader should note similarity with Montesquieu here and make necessary allowance for effect of slow and sparse methods of travel and communication in 18th century). V. thinks absolute monarchy can be beneficent. Does not dream of overturning existing social order, but works for practical and immediately realizable reforms. Contrast Faguet (no. 1670).

Strauss, David F. Voltaire; six conférences. Translated into French from the German by Louis Narval. Reinwald, 1876. 392 p. 1686

The German theologian, well known for his rationalistic *Life of Jesus*, finds in V. a sympathetic figure. Sees in V.

a man born for action who broke or weakened many chains binding humanity. From what now seems comparatively peaceful 19th century, Strauss thought mankind had progressed beyond much of V.'s thought. Such optimism may appear questionable in our savage modern world. In some details, Strauss's work naturally needs to be checked with more recent scholarship *Épître à Uranie*, for example, was not printed in 1732, though it did circulate in MS.

[Hall, Evelyn Beatrice]. The life of Voltaire. By S. G. Tallentyre [*pseud.*]... London, Smith, Elder, 1903. 2 v. 4th ed. : New York, Putnam, n.d., one v. 584 p. 1687

Vividly written " life " based on older biographies and to great extent on V.'s correspondence. Precedes Lanson's excellent little work (no. 1672) in *Grands écrivains* series. Author more appreciative than critical. Some factual material to be corrected in light of modern scholarship. Brailsford enthusiastically considers this " by far the best life in English " (no. 1659, p. 253). The scholar will probably still prefer Morley (no. 1676).

Specialized biographical Studies

Allizé, Fabrice. Voltaire à la Haye en 1713. RPar 29⁶:321-43, Nov. 15, 1922. 1688

Detailed account of V.'s love affair at age of 19 with Olympe (" Pimpette ") Du Noyer at The Hague. Author in error, however, when he says (p. 329) that the 14 letters of V. published in 1720 by mother of Olympe are not found in his collected correspondence. They are contained in Moland (no. 1628, 33:9-28), though omitted from Kehl edition (no. 1626) (cf. Moland, 33:9, n. 1).

Bachman, Albert. Censorship in France from 1715 to 1750; Voltaire's opposition. *See* 357. 1689

See especially p. 91-125. Illuminating discussion of V.'s " obstinate and cleverly elusive campaign against the censors " (p. 125).

Baldensperger, Fernand. Les prémices d'une douteuse amitié : Voltaire et Frédéric II de 1740 à 1742. RLC 10:230-61, 1930. 1690

Carefully documented article showing impartially and realistically grave defects of both protagonists.

Beaune, Henri. Voltaire au collège : sa famille, ses études, ses premiers amis : Lettres et documents inédits. Amyot, 1867. clxxxvii, 143 p.   1691

Only the 187 p. (clxxxvii) of Introduction remain important, since these treat of V.'s early years. To be compared with more complete study of same period by Pierron (no. 1724). Nos. VIII and IX of the *Lettres inédites* are not in Moland (no. 1628). No. IX was published by Bengesco, *Bibliographie*, (no. 1618), 3: 350-51. On No. VIII, cf. *ibid.*, 3:260, 374.

Beaunier, André. Voltaire en Prusse. RDM 6th per. 25:216-27, Jan. 1, 1915.   1692

Based on Descharmes' new edition of V.'s *Mémoires*. Author believes V. did not take his diplomatic negotiations with Frederick the Great seriously. But this appears to be an *après coup* interpretation on part of V. Contrast Doumic (no. 1710).

Bengesco, Georges. Voltaire et la Hollande (1713-1743), RPar 19¹:794-820, Feb. 15, 1912.   1693

V.'s several journeys to Holland, in 1713, 1722, 1737, 1740, and 1743. Mlle du Noyer, Mme de Rupelmonde, relations with publishers, the *Anti-Machiavel* of Frederick, diplomatic negotiations for French government. More scholarly than Allizé's article. (*See* no. 1688). Author cites his authorities.

Bonnefon, Paul. Une inimitié littéraire au xvIIIe siècle, d'après des documents inédits; Voltaire et Jean-Baptiste Rousseau. RHL 9 : 547-95, 1902.   1694

New details on well-known hostility of V. and Jean-Baptiste Rousseau based on previously unpublished letters.

— A propos des restes de Voltaire. RPL 5th ser. 7:208-12, Feb. 16, 1907.   1695

Detailed story of V.'s burial in 1778 at Abbaye de Scellières and later removal of body to Panthéon at Paris in 1791 during Revolution.

Brown, Harcourt. Voltaire and the Royal Society of London. UTQ 13:25-42, 1943-44. *See* 3095.   1696

Excellent article. V.'s first superficial knowledge of Royal Society broadened during Cirey period. Successive revisions of last of 24 *Lettres philosophiques*, the one dealing with the Royal Society. V.'s election to that body in 1743. Article adds important material to Lanson's

detailed commentary on famous *Lettres* (no. 1642).

Campardon, Emile. Voltaire : Documents inédits recueillis aux archives nationales. Le moniteur du bibliophile, 1880. 190 p.   1697

Publication of numerous documents on 18th century attempts to suppress works by or about V. Note particularly those relating to *La Ligue, Les lettres philosophiques, Candide,* and the *Histoire universelle.* Light on controversies with Jore, Desfontaines, Travenol, etc.

Caussy, Fernand. La mission diplomatique de Voltaire (1743-45), d'après des documents inédits. GR 65:547-63, Feb. 10, 1911.   1698

Outmaneuvered in his candidacy for French Academy, V. openly reveals his pique and boasts of his intimacy with King of Prussia. Maurepas decides to appease V. and try to make use of his acquaintance with Frederick by sending the Frenchman on diplomatic mission to Berlin. Details of his attempt to sound out intentions of Frederick. Learned that King of Prussia no longer considered himself ally of Louis XV, disliked King of England, and planned to open campaign in spring with 40,000 men. Advantageous personal offers for V. to leave France and settle at court of Frederick, but Mme du Châtelet for the present keeps V. at home. Cf. Beaunier (no. 1692) and Doumic (1710).

— Lettres inédites de Voltaire au libraire Lambert. RHL 16:798-819, 1909.   1699

V. himself was instigator of some of pirated editions of his works. Motivated by desire to make slight corrections, improvements, or additions, but above all by wish to reach largest possible number of readers (p. 798).

— Lettres inédites de Thieriot à Voltaire. RHL 15:131-61, 340-51, 705-21, 1908; 16: 160-80, 1909.   1700

Important series of letters from V.'s intimate friend and agent, Thieriot. Gives details on V.'s life not elsewhere available.

— Voltaire gentilhomme ordinaire. MerF 107:133-40, Jan. 1, 1914.   1701

Important article giving details on V.'s life as *gentilhomme ordinaire de la chambre du Roi.* V.'s pride in his title.

— Voltaire seigneur de village. Hachette, 1912. 355 p. 1702

Carefully documented study. Pictures condition of peasants in *pays de Gex* under *ancien régime*. V.'s disputes with *Président de Brosses*, his controversies over taxation, establishment of port of Versoix, trade relations with Geneva and with France. Adds much to our knowledge of V.'s non-literary activity during his final years. Daniel Mornet comments in his review (p. 456): " Un volume qui par sa seule richesse et sa seule précision serait un modèle d'étude biographique." Review : D. Mornet in RHL 20:456-57, 1913.

Chaponnière, Paul. Voltaire chez les calvinistes. Geneva, Journal de Genève, 1932. 182 p. *Also :* Perrin, 1936. 265 p. 1703

Beautifully illustrated and printed. Lively narrative of pros and cons of V.'s relations with people and disputes of Geneva. For less smiling portrayal, see F. Baldensperger, *Voltaire et la diplomatie française dans les " Affaires de Genève,"* RLC 11:581-606, 1931. Reviews : D. Mornet in RHL 43:305-06, 1936; F. Ruchon in AJJR 20:274-75, 1931; Anon in RLC 12:436-37, 1932.

Chardonchamp, Guy [*pseud.*] La famille de Voltaire : les Arouet, avec tableau généalogique. Champion, 1911. 70 p. 1704

Careful study of V.'s family and antecedents.

Colini, Côme-Alexandre. Mon séjour auprès de Voltaire. Colin, 1807. 373 p. 1705

Another of V.'s secretaries speaks. Valuable first-hand testimony, generally favorable to V. Author not free from bias, however, and must be checked with other testimony wherever possible.

Coquerel, Athanase. Jean Calas et sa famille. Cherbuliez, 1858. 527 p. 1706

Old, but still best study of a most controversial subject. Conclusions perhaps unjustly open to doubt simply because author was Protestant pastor. This whole difficult and important question of the Calas case needs to be reviewed with complete objectivity in light of modern scholarship.

Cornou, François. Trente années de luttes contre Voltaire et les philosophes du XVIIIe

siècle; Elie Fréron (1718-1776). Champion, 1922. 477 p. *See 2793.* 1707

Most complete pro-Fréron study. Needs objective reëxamination to remove bias in either direction.

Crist, Clifford M. Some judgments of Voltaire by contemporaries. MLN 50: 439-40, 1935. 1708

Discovery of small fourteen-page pamphlet entitled, *Dialogue entre Voltaire et Rousseau, après leur passage du Styx,* published in Geneva in 1778. V. and Rousseau depicted as reconciled after their death. Interesting brief word-portrait of V.

Desnoiresterres, Gustave. Iconographie voltairienne. Didier, 1879. 158 p. 1709

Valuable reproduction of paintings, engravings, sketches, and statues portraying V., along with text by well-informed and leading V. specialist of older generation.

Doumic, René. La carrière diplomatique de Voltaire. RDM 68th yr. 4th per. 149: 453-66, Sept. 15, 1898. 1710

Based on Albert de Broglie, *Voltaire avant et pendant la guerre de sept ans,* Calmann-Lévy, 1898. Judicious discussion of V.'s qualities and shortcomings as diplomat. His abilities too much neglected, in author's opinion, by government of France. Considers V. unpatriotic, but overlooks V.'s preference for peace over dynastic wars of inefficient French government, which was unrepresentative of interests of French people. Cf. Beaunier (no. 1692) and Caussy (no. 1698).

Galland, Elie. L'affaire Sirven, étude historique d'après les documents originaux. Mazamet, [1911]. 542 p. 1711

Impartial and thorough study which leaves no doubt of Sirven's innocence. Similar modern study of Calas case much to be desired. Cf. Coquerel, no. 1706. Review : G. Lanson in RHL 18:452, 1911.

Grafigny, Françoise, etc. Lettres de Mme de Grafigny suivies de celles de Mme de Staal, etc., sur leur séjour auprès de Voltaire. Ed. by Eugène Asse. Charpentier, 1883. 504 p. 1712

Valuable first-hand account of life of V. and Mme du Châtelet at Cirey in 1738, though some allowance must be made for fact that these letters were written by disgruntled observer.

Haupt, Herman. Voltaire in Frankfurt 1753; mit Benutzung von ungedruckten Akten und Briefen des Dichters. ZFSL 27¹:160-87, 1904; 30¹:87-117, 1906; 34¹: 159-211, 1909.   1713

Extensive study of V. in Frankfort and his relations with Frederick the Great, based on some unpublished material. Tends to be less severe toward Frederick.

Henriot, Emile. Voltaire et Frédéric II. Hachette, 1927. 127 p. (Récits d'autrefois series). (*Also in* Rheb 35¹²:131-53, 299-325, 441-53, 1926).   1714

Presents impartially controversial subject in brief narrative. Important additional considerations on significant issues in review by Mornet, below. " C'est un excellent petit livre " (Mornet, p. 301). Review : D. Mornet in RHL 36:301-02, 1929.

Kozminski, Léon. Voltaire financier. Presses universitaires, 1929. 338 p. (Diss., Paris).   1715

Good, if not profound study of V.'s entire life from financial point of view. Does not go into background of financial standards of time by which alone V.'s practices might be fairly judged. " Un bon ouvrage... La documentation est bonne... Conclusions... judicieuses " (Mornet, p. 111). Review : D. Mornet in RHL 37:111-12, 1930.

Lachèvre, Frédéric, ed. Voltaire mourant, etc. Champion, 1908. 208 p.   1716

Account of V.'s death written by a priest for his superior. Not narrative of eyewitness, however, and accuracy of this unsympathetic view not proved. Reviews : P. B[onnefon] in RHL 15: 761, 1908; P. Sakmann in ZFSL 33²: 206-07, 1908.

Levin, Lawrence M. A note on the Arouet > Voltaire problem. SP 34:52-54, 1937.   1717

Finds interesting coincidence in juxtaposition of *Volaterrae* and *Arretium* which, author believes, may have influenced V. in his change of name from Arouet.

Longchamp, S. G., and J. L. Wagnière. Mémoires sur Voltaire et sur ses ouvrages. André, 1826. 2 v.   1718

Valuable first-hand testimony from two of V.'s secretaries. Occasionally subject

to error or bias. Alfred Noyes (no. 1679) inclined particularly to discredit Longchamp. Review : C. A. Sainte-Beuve in *Premiers lundis*, 2nd ed., Michel Lévy, 1875 (3 v.), 1:95-100.

Maugras, Gaston. Querelles de philosophes : Voltaire et Jean-Jacques Rousseau. 2nd ed. Calmann-Lévy, 1886. 607 p. 1719

Detailed study, but badly vitiated by author's strong prejudice in favor of V. and against Rousseau. *See* no. 1962. Review : F. Brunetière in RDM 56th yr. 3rd per. 76:208-25, July 1, 1886.

Maurel, André. La marquise du Châtelet, amie de Voltaire. Hachette, 1930. 239 p.   1720

Vivid evocation of " la divine Émilie " in her relations to Voltaire. No exact references to sources, and bibliography carelessly given. Imaginative interpretation of thoughts and works put into mouth of characters sometimes suggests fashion of *vie romancée*. Accurate and sound in main, however. Supplemented by Wade's penetrating study of Mme du Châtelet's ideas, *Voltaire and Mme du Châtelet* (no. 1811).

Nicolardot, Louis. Ménages et finances de Voltaire (1854). 3rd ed., Dentu, 1887. 2 v.   1721

Detailed, but violently hostile study of V.'s life from financial point of view. Useful, but allowance must be made for strong prejudice. Review : L. Ulbach, *Écrivains et hommes de lettres*, Librairie internationale, 2ᵉ ed., 1863, p. 45-78.

Omont, Henri. Projet de saisie des papiers de Voltaire au début du règne de Louis XVI. RHL 12:282-92, 1905.   1722

Publication of documents proving intention of government to confiscate V.'s papers in event of his death in 1774. Shows tangible character of hostility with which he was threatened, even in remote Ferney. Project later abandoned and forgotten, fortunately.

Perey, Lucien [*pseud.* for Herpin, Clara Adèle Luce] and Gaston Maugras. La vie intime de Voltaire aux Délices et à Ferney. Calmann-Lévy, 1885. 546 p. 1723

Vivid and useful picture of intimate side of V.'s later years. Draws on some previously unpublished letters. Often careless and inaccurate, however, in details.

Pierron, Alexis. Voltaire et ses maîtres. Didier, 1866. 354 p.   1724

More complete than similar book of following year by Beaune, *Voltaire au collège* (no. 1691). Important for V.'s studies under Jesuits at *Collège Louis-le-Grand.* Points out shortcomings of V.'s knowledge of Latin and particularly of Greek.

Prod'homme, J.-G. Voltaire raconté par ceux qui l'ont vu. Stock, 1929. 286 p.   1725

Useful collection of documents dealing with V.'s life up to his arrival at Geneva in 1754, omitting period of his stay in England from 1726 to 1729. Review : D. Mornet in RHL 37:624, 1930.

Sainte-Beuve, Charles-Augustin. Lettres de Mme de Grafigny, ou Voltaire à Cirey. Causeries du lundi, 3rd ed. (n.d.). 2:208-25. 1726

Vivid portrayal of life of V. and Mme du Châtelet at Cirey, based on well-known letters of Mme de Grafigny. Article is dated June 17, 1850.

— Mme du Châtelet, suite de Voltaire à Cirey. Causeries du lundi, 3rd ed. (n.d.). 2:266-85.   1727

Excellent account of relations of V. and Mme du Châtelet. Effect on V. of her death in 1749. Article dated July 8, 1850.

— Voltaire et le Président de Brosses. Causeries du lundi, 3rd ed. (n.d.). 7:105-26. 1728

Narrative of one of ugly episodes of V.'s life, his petty quarrel with De Brosses, former proprietor of Tournay, over 14 measures of firewood worth mere 280 livres. Out of vengeance, V. used his influence to exclude De Brosses from French Academy, threatening to resign if his intrigues were not successful. After V.'s death, his niece and heir, Mme Denis, had to pay son of De Brosses some 40,000 francs for damage V. had done to estate of Tournay, thus showing that V. had not maintained the property in accordance with his contract. Article dated Nov. 8, 1852.

— Lettres inédites de Voltaire. Causeries du lundi, 2nd ed. Garnier, 1869. 13:1-38. 1729

In two articles, author gives keen analysis of V.'s life and character without exaggerating either his qualities or his faults. Full of penetrating suggestions which are worth re-reading. Letter on p. 14, formerly dated 1724, is indeed of early April, 1726, as Sainte-Beuve first thought without quite having courage of his convictions (cf. Foulet, *Correspondance,* 1634, p. 6-7). Brief reflections on reasons for V.'s hostility to J.-J. Rousseau. Articles dated Oct. 20 and 27, 1856.

— Correspondance de Voltaire avec la duchesse de Saxe-Gotha. Causeries du lundi. Garnier, 1862. 15:219-23.   1730

Only a few pages on V. Rest of article and one following deal with J.-J. Rousseau. Shows V.'s wit and easy grace which lend interest and distinction even to correspondence devoted wholly to courtly compliments addressed to a German princess. Article dated July 15, 1861.

Sieveking, A. Forbes. Some little-known portraits of Voltaire. Conn 78:153-59, July, 1927.   1731

Reproductions of eight portraits of V., one attributed to Curtius being especially lifelike and expressive. Descriptive text accompanying plates.

Stern, Jean. Belle et Bonne, une fervente amie de Voltaire (1757-1822). Hachette [c1938]. 254 p.   1732

Story of Mme de Villette. First part to p. 89 deals with V.'s last years and death. Summarizes various accounts, discounting legends. Quotes documents.

Valkhoff, J., and J. Fransen. Voltaire en Hollande. RH 1:734-54, 1915; 2:1071-1110, 1916.   1733-1734

Uncompleted (?) study (two installments only ?), but covers V.'s several journeys to Holland, his love for " Pimpette " du Noyer, his relations with Dutch scholars, publication of Frederick's *Anti-Machiavel,* V.'s diplomatic mission, and his numerous disputes with Dutch publishers.

Vézinet, François. Autour de Voltaire, avec quelques inédits. Champion, 1925. 143 p. 1735

Five articles, of which last deals with Rousseau. Subjects treated : 1. Some of V.'s lawsuits; 2. Repercussion of execution of La Barre on V.; 3. Simon Bigex and Father Adam at Ferney; 4. V.'s generosity to the Crassy family. V. is revealed realistically with his faults and his virtues. Documents largely speak for themselves. Reviews : G. Chinard in MLN 41: 352, 1926; D. G. Larg in MLR 21:451-53, 1926; D. Mornet in RHL 34:605, 1927.

Vial, Fernand. Vauvenargues et Voltaire. RR 33:41-57, 1942. *See* 2705.   1736

Vauvenargues influenced Voltaire in matters of literary criticism. Similarity in taste. Respect of Voltaire for his younger contemporary.

Wade, Ira O. Voltaire's name. PMLA 44: 546-64, 1929.   1737

Thorough-going survey of many different theories for explaining V.'s change of name from Arouet to Voltaire. Author suggests that this change may have come, not from anagram of *Arouet le jeune*, as has often been maintained, but from inverting syllables of Airvault, a village in Poitou where some of V.'s relatives owned property. Plausible theory.

Watts, George B. Notes on Voltaire. MLN 41:118-22, 1926.   1738

Correction of dates and details regarding *Mahomet*. V.'s return from Brussels to Paris established as about November 18, 1742. This leads to conclusion that letters in the Moland edition (no. 1628) for this period need rearrangement in order to follow chronology.

Studies of Style, Ideas,
Sources, or Influence

Anon. Deux lettres inédites de Voltaire à Wagnière. Les livres dont Voltaire se servait pour écrire. ICC 18:254-56, April 25, 1885.   1739

In two letters of May 7 and 10, 1778, V. instructs his secretary, Wagnière, to send him from Ferney several books which he uses in his writing : *Grammaire de Port-Royal*, that by Restaut, *Synonymes* of Girard, *Tropes* of Dumarsais, *Remarques* of Vaugelas, *Le petit Dictionnaire des proverbes*, " un livre en deux volumes sur l'orthographe française, qui doit être sur le bureau de la bibliothèque," two books on Italian, etc. (cf. nos. 399, 1808). Amid " le brillant fracas de Paris," V., three weeks before his death, misses Wagnière and his home at Ferney. " On me tue et vous êtes absent ! "

Arrom, José Juan. Voltaire y la literatura dramática cubana. RR 34:228-34, 1943.   1740

Brief exploratory article showing that popularity of *Zaïre, Mahomet,* etc., in Cuba continued from 1800 to 1874. Attitude of José María Heredia toward Shakespeare seems to reflect language and tone of V.

Barr, Mary-Margaret H. Voltaire in America, 1744-1800. Baltimore, Johns Hopkins press, 1941.   150 p.   (Johns Hopkins studies in Romance literatures and languages, 39).   1741

American and foreign editions of V. in library and booksellers' catalogues, newspaper and magazine discussion of V., opposition of clergy, attitude of Paine, Franklin, and Jefferson. Survey limited to New England and Middle Atlantic states. Important state of Virginia, as well as city of Charleston, S. C., so strongly under French influence, still invite study.
Reviews : D. F. Bond in MLQ 3: 144-46, 1942; J. L. Brown in CathHR 27:517-18, 1941-42; M. Kraus in AHR 47:944-45, 1941-42.

Becker, Carl. Brunetière's Kampf gegen Voltaire. ZFSL 42²:229-41, 1914.   1742

Important article by well-known American historian. Sketches in detail Brunetière's opposition to V. Brunetière was subjective, not objective, an inherently pessimistic, Jansenistic spirit, while V., in spite of *Candide*, was practical optimist, true in this respect to his early Jesuit training.

— The heavenly city of the eighteenth-century philosophers. *See* 1023.   1743

Has no book-chapter on V., but is included here because of its brilliant exposition of 18th century as age of " naïve faith in the authority of nature and reason..." (p. 30). " Climates of opinion." History is " ... only a pack of tricks we play upon the dead..." (p. 43), said V. Point of view to be reckoned with, but needs correction in light of realistic modest ignorance of—for example—V.'s *Philosophe ignorant*. Insufficient recognition on part of author of positive achievement of *philosophes* in behalf of civilization and real dangers which they risked by their boldness.

Black, John Bennett. Voltaire. *In his :* The art of history; a study of four great historians of the eighteenth century. London, Methuen; New York, Crofts, 1926. p. 29-75. 1744

Excellent discussion of V. as historian. Without ignoring his faults, author does justice to his virtues. V. gathered great amount of accurate information, simplified and popularized it. Sought to present record of ideas rather than dramatic portraits, particularly in *Siècle de Louis XIV* and *Essai sur les mœurs*. Curious sameness of presentation due to his belief in identity of human nature throughout all ages. Yet author believes balance of good points greatly in V.'s favor.

Boswell, James. Boswell with Rousseau and Voltaire, 1764. *In :* Private papers of James Boswell, ed. by Geoffrey Scott. Mount Vernon, N.Y., Rudge, 1929. 4:129-52. *See* 1958. 1745-1748

Unpublished letter of Boswell to Temple of Dec. 28, 1764, giving firsthand details on V.'s knowledge of English, his deism, and doubts concerning immortality. Similar views on soul in brief letter of V. to Boswell of Feb. 11, 1765. Very important direct testimony of V. himself, unwarped by restraining thought of censor or of public opinion. Review : A. Schinz in RPar 1933[3]:299-325, (May 15), 630-667, (June 1).

Bréhier, Emile. Les théories de la société : Voltaire. *In his :* Histoire de la philosophie. Tome 2, fasc. 2, 1ᵉ Partie, Le dix-huitième siècle. Alcan, 1930. p. 455-65. 1749

V.'s thought not mere " chaos d'idées claires " (Faguet, no. 1671). If not system, he had principles. V. pessimistic in sense of not believing in rapid progress; he held men to be fixed in their diversity and complexity. Review : D. Mornet in RHL 38:323-25, 1931.

Brunetière, Ferdinand. Voltaire. RDM 59th yr. 3rd per. 96:208-20, Nov. 1, 1889. *See* no. 1661. 1750

Important article suggested by publication of Bengesco's *Bibliographie* (no. 1618). Believes influence of French background on V. greater than that of England. Bayle, the *Épître à Uranie*. (Cf. I. O. Wade, no. 1847). V.'s attack on Pascal. Reasons for relative prudence of V. up to 1750. Discussion of *Le sermon des cinquante*. Brunetière, perhaps overpatriotically, tends to minimize English influence, but valuable corrective to ex-

aggeration on other side by John Morley (cf. no. 1676).

Carré, Jean-Raoul. Consistance de Voltaire : le philosophe. RCC 39[2]:97-108, 193-211, 289-307, 531-52, 606-25, 1938. *Also in,* with less detail, a separate : Boivin, 1938. 107 p. 1751

Able discussion of essential unity of V.'s ideas. For V.'s realistic attitude toward progress, see author's final pages.

— Réflexions sur l'Anti-Pascal de Voltaire. Alcan, 1935. 120 p. 1752

Presentation of Pascal versus V. with strong preference for philosophy of latter. Cf. Finch (no. 1757), Morehouse (no. 1786), and Waterman (no. 1814).

Chinard, Gilbert. Notes de John Adams sur Voltaire et Rousseau. MLN 46:26-31, 1931. 1753

Generally hostile notes on *Philosophie de l'histoire* and *Traité sur la tolérance*, written in 1801 and influenced in part by disillusioning experience of French Revolution and rise of Napoleon as dictator.

Clark, Harry Hayden. Thomas Paine's relation to Voltaire and Rousseau. RAA 9:305-18, 393-405, 1931-32. *See* 2053. 1754

First section of article devoted to parallels in thought between V. and Paine. Not attempt to show direct sources, but similar intellectual atmosphere.

Edsall, H. Linn. The idea of history and progress in Fontenelle and Voltaire. *See* 1180. 1755

Shows probable influence of Fontenelle's *De l'origine des fables, Sur l'histoire, Histoire de l'Académie des sciences,* and *Éloge de Leibnitz,* on development of V.'s conception of history.

Fellows, Otis. Voltaire in liberated France. RR 37:168-76, 1946. 1756

Excellent article on V. as viewed in France in 1945 after liberation from the Germans. Shows living quality of V.'s thought during reaction from oppression.

Finch, David. La critique philosophique de Pascal au xviiiᵉ siècle. *See* 1410. 1757

Rapid survey of V.'s attacks on Pascal, along with those of other leading French writers of 18th century. Written after work of J.-R. Carré (no. 1752), but before more detailed study of V.'s earlier attitude toward Pascal by Miss Waterman (no. 1814).

Gaffiot, Maurice. La théorie du luxe dans l'œuvre de Voltaire. RHES 14:320-43, 1926.
1758

Author sees V. examining luxury as historian with full appreciation of its relativistic character, " qui varie suivant les temps comme suivant les personnes " (p. 330). This is careful, objective study with emphasis on *Essai sur les mœurs* and *Dictionnaire philosophique*. *Le Mondain* is of course studied, but author seems to have overlooked indispensable critical edition published by André Morize in 1909 (no. 1646) with its detailed discussion of luxury.

Grubbs, Henry A. Voltaire and rime. *See* 406.
1759

V. a poor rimer.

Guéhenno, Jean. Voltaire. *In :* Tableau de la littérature française : xviiᵉ-xviiiᵉ siècles. Gallimard [1939], p. 257-74.
1760

Several pages of contrast between V. and Pascal, in favor of former. Those who reproach V. with having donned mask are just the ones who belong to party of repression which makes such prudence necessary. Author says his heart draws him to Rousseau, but his intelligence to V. Rousseau's respect for opinion of populace is attractive, but dangerous; it can cause revolutions to stay in fixed groove; while spirit of V. sends them constantly forward toward new goals.

Havens, George R. The Nature doctrine of Voltaire. PMLA 40:852-62, 1925.
1761

Chronological survey of V.'s appeal to nature and to natural law. Like Rousseau in his opposition to doctrine of Original Sin, V. too believes that " l'homme n'est point né méchant " (p. 859).

— Voltaire's marginal comments upon Pope's Essay on Man. MLN 43:429-39, 1928.
1762

Marginal comments of V. found in his private library at Leningrad and studied with brief discussion of his attitude toward ideas of Alexander Pope.

— Voltaire's marginalia on the pages of Rousseau. Columbus, The Ohio state university, 1933. 199 p.
1763

Facsimile, bibliography, and detailed discussion of V.'s marginal comments on

Rousseau as found in Leningrad, thus putting into striking juxtaposition these two great 18th-century rivals. Contrasts and agreements in their ideas.

Reviews : D. Mornet in RHL 41: 135-36, 1934; A. Schinz in AJJR 22: 259-61, 1933.

— Les notes marginales de Voltaire sur Rousseau. RHL 40:434-40, 1933.
1764

Brief *résumé* of most characteristic and piquant of V.'s marginal notes on Rousseau translated from *South Atlantic quarterly* (October, 1932), for benefit of French readers. For more detailed study of the subject, cf. monograph by same author (no. 1763).

— Voltaire, Rousseau, and the Lettre sur la Providence. PMLA 59:109-30, 1944. *See* 2176.
1765

Detailed history of complex story of composition and publication of this important letter of Rousseau criticizing V.'s position in *Poème sur le désastre de Lisbonne*. Throws light upon relations of V. and Rousseau before and after the break of 1760. Corrects Desnoiresterres (no. 1667) and Maugras (no. 1719).

— Voltaire and English critics of Shakespeare. LHM 15:177-86, 1944. (Reprinted as Franco-American pamphlet, 2nd series, No. 16, New York, American society French Legion of honor, Summer, 1944, 12 p.).
1766

Popular in form of presentation, but documented by translated quotations from V., his contemporaries and predecessors. Shows similarity of V.'s criticism of Shakespeare to views of leading English critics of time. V. not hostile to Shakespeare merely because he was a Frenchman. Contrast Lounsbury (no. 3114).

— Voltaire today. LHM 18:380-90, Winter, 1947-48.
1767

Discussion in popular form of value of V.'s thought in chaotic modern world. Religious liberty, political liberty, and problem of war represent three characteristic and important areas of V.'s activity.

— and **Norman L. Torrey.** Voltaire's books : a selected list. MP 27:1-22, 1929.
1768

Selection of about 400 titles owned by V., chosen from among total of some 2500 to 3000, while we await publication of complete catalogue of V.'s books which has been promised by the State Public Library at Leningrad. Valuable partial indication of books V. owned, furnishing some direct testimony on sources of his ideas.

— and **Norman L. Torrey.** The private library of Voltaire at Leningrad, PMLA 43:990-1009, 1928. *See* 3108.   1769

History of Voltaire Library bought by Catherine the Great after its owner's death and arranged at Saint-Petersburg in 1779 by V.'s secretary, Wagnière. Brief survey of contents of Library and of some of V.'s characteristic marginal notes.

Hazard, Paul. Voltaire et la pensée philosophique de la Renaissance italienne. MélAL, p. 473-78. *See* no. 3307.   1770

V. was little influenced by Renaissance. " Avec Voltaire commence une ère nouvelle : celle de la prépondérance de la pensée anglaise " (p. 478).

— Voltaire et Spinoza. MP 38:351-64, 1940-41.   1771

V. did not study Spinoza profoundly. Rejected him as irritating ally of atheistic D'Holbach. V. neither atheist nor pantheist, but deist. Did, however, have merit of exploring Spinoza's thought even though he did not understand it clearly or accept it.

Hertz, Eduard. Voltaire und die französische Strafrechtspflege. Stuttgart, Enke, 1887. 530 p.   1772

Hertz states that he writes as jurist, not as historian of literature. Relies almost entirely on Hettner (no. 68) and Desnoiresterres (no. 1667). Might have evaluated Beccaria better in relation to his time. Yet a valuable study which fills a gap.
Review : R. Mahrenholtz in ZFSL 9²: 267-68, 1887; 12¹:134, 1890.

Kellenberger, Hunter. Voltaire's treatment of the miracle of Christ's temptation in the wilderness. MLN 51:17-21. 1936.   1773

Though it was joined to list of other miracles discussed by English deist Woolston, V. probably drew on French sources for his treatment of this miracle.

Kinne, Burdette. Voltaire never said it ! MLN 58:534-35, 1943.   1774

Shows that V. was never known to have used oft-quoted phrase : " I disapprove of what you say, but I will defend to the death your right to say it." Phrase due to S. G. Tallentyre [Mrs. Evelyn Hall], who inadvertently put it into quotation marks, believing she was expressing " the spirit of Voltaire." Another popular legend disappears !

Korff, H. A. Voltaire im literarischen Deutschland des XVIII. Jahrhunderts, ein Beitrag zur Geschichte des deutschen Geistes von Gottsched bis Goethe. Heidelberg, Winter, 1918. 2 v.   1775

Extensive work which puts emphasis on German literature rather than on V. Author best in treatment of Wieland, Herder, and Schiller (Klemperer, p. 229, 238).
Reviews : V. Klemperer in ZFSL 46: 229-38, 1920-23; J. H. Scholte in Neo 5:281-86, 1919-20.

Lanson, Gustave. Esquisse d'une histoire de la tragédie française. *See* 536.   1776

P. 138-53 of second edition offer valuable sketch, in form of notes, of V.'s contributions to French tragedy and his attitude toward Shakespeare. P. 165-73 contain important details of *mise-en-scène*, costume, and declamation.

Lenient, C. F. Voltaire auteur comique. *In his :* La comédie en France au XVIIIᵉ siècle. *See* 540, 2:44-80.   1777

Chap. 17 treats *L'indiscret, La fête de Bélébat, L'enfant prodigue, Nanine* and *L'Écossaise.* V.'s failure as writer of comedies due to his inability to efface his personality behind those of his characters (p. 45). " Il fait de ses personnages comiques de simples pantins " (*ibid.*).

Libby, Mrs. Margaret (Sherwood). The attitude of Voltaire to magic and the sciences. New York, Columbia univ. press, 1935. 299 p. (Diss., Columbia).   1778

Shows V.'s best scientific work was in field of Newtonian physics. After 1740, V. did not greatly add to his scientific ideas and did not go far with new developments in geology, biology, and anthropology.
Review : G. R. Havens in PhR 46: 232-33, 1937.

Lion, Henri. Les tragédies et les théories dramatiques de Voltaire. Hachette, 1895. 477 p. (Diss., Paris).   1779

Basic general study of this important subject.

Review : G. Pellissier in *Études de littérature contemporaine*, Perrin, 1898. 1:353-62.

Lovejoy, Arthur O. Optimism and romanticism. PMLA 42:921-45, 1927.   1780

Important article with significant bearing on V.'s reaction to gloomy and fatalistic 18th century so-called "Optimism." "Vous criez 'Tout est bien' d'une voix lamentable ! " (p. 923); Moland, no. 1628, 9:474, *Poème sur le désastre de Lisbonne*, line 122).

Lowenstein, Robert. Voltaire as an historian of seventeenth-century French drama. Baltimore, Johns Hopkins press, 1935. 195 p. (Diss., Johns Hopkins).   1781

V. possessed little first-hand knowledge of early French dramatists of 17th century. His chief source, even for his *Commentaire sur Corneille*, is *Histoire du Théâtre français* of the Frères Parfaict. Orthodox in his literary opinions, he did not question much of what he read on subject of drama. Frequently inaccurate in information he does give. Yet he crystallized 18th century tradition and made his opinions typical of his time. This severe judgment formed in light of very recent scholarship. Question might be asked : Did any one in V.'s time know more ?

Reviews : E. P. Dargan in MP 34:436-38, 1936-37; R. Naves in RHL 43:443-45, 1936; N. L. Torrey in MLN 51:477-78, 1936; F. Vial in FR 14:151-53, 1940-41.

McGhee, Dorothy M. Voltairian narrative devices as considered in the author's Contes philosophiques. Menasha, Wisconsin, Banta, 1933. 192 p. (Diss., Ohio State).   1782

Valuable study of background and structure of V.'s philosophical prose tales. Interesting graphic diagrams showing rise and fall of action in stories, which reader should of course take only as suggestive, not interpreting them too literally as conscious literary devices of author.

Reviews : H. B. in MLR 30:415-16, 1935; R. Naves in RHL 41:614-15, 1934.

Maestro, Marcello T. Voltaire and Beccaria as reformers of criminal law. New York, Columbia univ. press, 1942. 177 p. *See* 3308.   1783

Influence of Beccaria in systematizing V.'s ideas on complete reform of criminal law. *Relation de la mort du chevalier de La Barre* and *Commentaire sur le livre des délits et des peines* particularly testify to Beccaria's influence.

Reviews : T. I. Cook in MLQ 5:107-09, 1944; A. R. Morehouse in RR 35:171-75, 1944.

Mahrenholtz, Richard. Herr F. Brunetière als Voltairekritiker. ZFLS 12¹:134-36, 1890.   1784

Unfavorable review of Brunetière's hostile treatment of V. in article in RDM, Nov. 1, 1889 (no. 1750).

Miller, Jean W. Voltaire's introduction of the spelling *ai* in such words as *français*. RR 14:316-18, 1923.   1785

V. is said to have first introduced this spelling in 1736 ed. of *Zaïre*. It had been suggested as early as 1675 by Nicolas Berain. Note, however, that already in 1734 the Jore ed. of *Lettres philosophiques* printed *Français*, *Anglais* (Lanson ed., (no. 1642) I, p. xlix). V.'s most complete discussion of subject is in article on letter *A* (1770) in *Dictionnaire philosophique*. He notes *a* also beginning to be used in imperfects. " Ne faut-il pas écrire comme on parle autant qu'on le peut? " D'Alembert preferred *è*, but V. argued for *ai* as better indicating etymology.

Morehouse, Andrew R. A few remarks on one or two aspects of the Pascal-Voltaire controversy. EssAF, p. 149-62.   1786

Excellent article, noteworthy for sympathetic attitude toward both Pascal and V. Cf. Carré (no. 1752), Finch (no. 1757), and Waterman (no. 1814).

— Voltaire and Jean Meslier. New Haven, Yale univ. press, 1936. 158 p.   1787

Important study of an obscure and difficult subject. Shows manner in which V. used Meslier's work. In contrast to Morley (no. 1676), author finds V.'s mind open to sense of mystery of the universe. Contrast Faguet also (no. 1671). In this attitude, V. was essentially different from Meslier.

Reviews : E. P. Dargan in MP 34: 436-38, 1936-37; D. Mornet in RHL 43: 594-95, 1936; I. O. Wade in RR 28: 285-89, 1937.

Naves, Raymond. Le goût de Voltaire. Garnier [1938]. 566 p. (Diss., Paris). 1788

Thorough-going study of V.'s taste in its relation to that of his time. V.'s reading and influence of his personal contacts surveyed in detail. V. and Shakespeare.

Review : G. R. Havens in RR 31:77-78, 1940.

— Voltaire et l'Encyclopédie. *See* 1316. 1789

Studies the limited, but gracious co-öperation of V. with *Encyclopédie*. His *Dictionnaire philosophique* and *Questions sur l'Encyclopédie* are outgrowths of earlier collaboration. Details of relations between V. and Diderot.

— Voltaire éditeur de Rousseau. RHL 44: 245-47, 1937. 1790

In 1766, under date of 1765, V. published his *Recueil nécessaire*, containing, among other things, extract from Rousseau's *Vicaire savoyard*. V. naturally selected a part he approved of : namely, Rousseau's criticism of revealed religions. V. introduced three slight changes in accordance with his views.

Oake, Roger B. Political elements in criticism of Voltaire in England, 1732-47. MLN 57:348-54, 1942. 1791

V. " was,... in one case unwillingly, in another wittingly, involved in English politics after his return to France " (p. 348).

Philips, Edith. Le Quaker vu par Voltaire. RHL 39:161-77, 1932. 1792

Important and interesting subject well treated in brief compass. For fuller discussion, see author's book (no. 1793).

— The Good Quaker in French legend. Philadelphia, Univ. of Pennsylvania press, 1932. 235 p. 1793

Good study of interesting subject. Chap. II, p. 43-67, deals with " The Quaker seen by Voltaire." Many other references also to V. (*see* Index). Extensive bibliography. " Quakerism seemed to the Deists to be the form which popular religion ought to take... Here, in Quakerism, was a ' natural ' religion ready made " (p. 200). Note that Benjamin Franklin's prestige in Paris (1776-85) benefited by fact that he was mistakenly thought in many quarters to be Quaker (cf. p. 92). Cf. 1792.

Reviews : L. Cons in RLC 14:591-93, 1934; A. Schinz in RHL 40: 447-48, 1933.

Pommier, Jean. Le cycle de Chactas. RLC 18:604-29, 1938. 1794

Last half of article discusses probable influence of V.'s *L'ingénu, Candide*, and even his *Siècle de Louis XIV* on the Chactas of *Les Natchez*. Author believes first sketches of character of Chactas were made before Chateaubriand's departure for America in 1791.

Price, Erwin H. The opinions of Voltaire concerning Montesquieu's theories of Roman greatness. PQ 16:287-95, 1937. 1795

V. thought Montesquieu had generally been too much influenced by Stoics. V. believed Roman greatness due rather to inherent qualities than to conscious planning.

— Voltaire and Montesquieu's three principles of government. PMLA 57:1046-52, 1942. 1796

V. criticizes Montesquieu as " too theoretical " (p. 1052). Article is a sound and factual study of contrasts between two points of view.

Rockett, K. An optimistic streak in Voltaire's thought. MLR 39:24-27, 1944. 1797

Author argues for an instinctive optimism in V. struggling against pessimism. In discussing conclusion of important *Poème sur le désastre de Lisbonne*, however, author, like Alfred Noyes, overlooks *après coup* nature of these lines added to avoid trouble with censor or public. *See* nos. 1679, 1828, 1829.

Rowbotham, Arnold H. Voltaire, sinophile. PMLA 47:1050-65, 1932. 1798

V. built up a legend of China on basis of narratives of Jesuit missionaries, ignoring other sources. An ideal of Utopia, centering on Confucius and spirit of tolerance.

Russell, Trusten W. Voltaire, Dryden and heroic tragedy. New York, Columbia univ. press, 1946, 178 p. (Diss., Columbia). *See* 3117. 1799

Careful study of background of English-French literary relations. Author finds Dryden's influence on V. greater than Shakespeare's.

Salvio, Alfonso de. Voltaire and Spain. Hisp 7:69-110, 157-64, 1924. *See* 3317. 1800

Finds V.'s treatment of Spain and Spanish literature prejudiced and ill-informed. Emphasis on Inquisition and cruelty to natives of New World. V. knew little Spanish.

Schilling, Bernard N. The English case against Voltaire: 1789-1800. JHI 4:193-216, 1943.   1801

English conservative view of religion, and particularly Christianity, as necessary support of government, fitted in readily with conception of an anti-religious V., cause of French Revolution. Apotheosis of V. in 1791, pause of his sarcophagus overnight on ruins of Bastille, various tributes to his triumph over tyranny, all appeared to support this English attitude as expressed by Burke and many others. Barruel's *Memoirs illustrating the history of Jacobinism*, published in 1797, came as final manifestation of this generally-accepted interpretation.

Sturm, Paul J. Joubert and Voltaire: a study in reaction. *In:* SFDY, p. 185-220.   1802

Evolution of Joubert from admiration of V. to bitter hostility, tempered, nevertheless, by inability to escape charm of V.'s style and genius.

Torrey, Norman L. The spirit of Voltaire. New York, Columbia univ. press, 1938. 314 p.   1803

Not intended to be full-length portrait or biography. Sympathetic interpretation of V.'s personality and thought. Less sympathetic to Rousseau. Distinguishes between what V. really thought and what he could with fair safety put before general public. V. " could have purchased complete personal integrity only at the price of martyrdom " (p. 139). Well informed and well written book.

Reviews: E. P. Dargan in MP 37: 217-18, 1939-40; G. R. Havens in PhR 49:375-76, 1940; D. Mornet in RHL 45:532-33, 1938; E. Philips in RR 31: 178-81, 1940; I. O. Wade in MLN 54:383-84, 1939.

— Voltaire and the English deists. New Haven, Yale univ. press, 1930. 224 p. *See* 3123.   1804

Authoritative study of difficult subject checked by work in private library of V. at Leningrad. Author finds two periods of " pronounced English influence on Voltaire: First, the Mme du Châtelet period of metaphysical research; and secondly, the later period of borrowings of method and material for the antibiblical attacks of the last fifteen years of his life " (p. 200). Cf. also Wade's important book on *Voltaire and Mme du Châtelet*, 1941 (no. 1811).

Reviews: F. Baldensperger in RLC 11: 568-72, 1931; L. Bredvold in MLN 46: 419-20, 1931; E. P. Dargan in MP 29: 120-25, 1931; G. R. Havens in YR ns 20:851-53, 1930-31.

— Voltaire's reaction to Diderot. PMLA 50:1107-43, 1935. *See* no: 2342.   1805

Substantial article based, not only on usual sources of V.'s and Diderot's complete works, but also on V.'s books in Leningrad Public Library with their bookmarks and occasional marginal comments. Shows V. admired Diderot in spite of essential differences in their thought.

Trahard, Pierre. La sensibilité dans le théâtre de Voltaire. *In his:* Les maîtres de la sensibilité française au XVIIIe siècle (1715-1789). *See* 832. 1:237-59.   1806

Useful corrective to too-current idea that V. was all reason and skepticism. Author expresses with vividness and verve the warmth and *sensibilité* of V.'s personality.

Reviews: G. R. Havens in MLN 47: 534-36, 1932; 49:268-69, 1934; M. E. I. Robertson in MLR 27:347-50, 1932; 29:97-99, 1934; 30:272, 1935.

Trudel, Marcel. L'influence de Voltaire au Canada. Montreal, Fides, 1945. 2 v. (Diss., Laval).   1807

Detailed and documented study of more than century and half of Voltairianism in Canada. Author, however, is unwaveringly hostile and, in considering V.'s faults, has no word for the abuses of intolerance and persecution which called forth his bitter attacks.

Review: G. R. Havens in BA 21:60-61, 1947.

Vernier, Léon. Étude sur Voltaire grammairien et la grammaire au XVIIIe siècle. *See* 399.   1808

Cf. evaluation by Schutz, no. 399. " Une thèse... fort intéressante, et qui n'est pas à refaire " (Maurice Souriau, review, below, p. 105). Cf. no. 1739.

Reviews: G. Paris in Rom 19:365, 1890; M. Souriau in RHL 28:105-31, 279-88, 423-49, 1921.

Wade, Ira O. Voltaire and Malesherbes. FR 8:357-69, 455-80, 1935.   1809

Important unpublished letters of Malesherbes, *Directeur de la librairie*, to V. Refutation of some of Brunetière's strictures against V. Circumstances of publication of several of V.'s histories and of *La Pucelle.*

— A favorite metaphor of Voltaire. RR 26: 330-34, 1935.   1810

The metaphor is the well-known passage in *Zadig* and elsewhere in which V. defends the passions as "the winds which fill the sails of the vessel." Wade finds substantially the same figure, not only in Pope's *Essay on man,* as pointed out by Ascoli, but also in Fontenelle's *Dialogues des morts,* Montaigne, Plutarch, Charron, Nicole, the *Spectator,* etc. It appears strange that Ascoli should have emphasized Du Resnel's diffuse translation instead of Pope's succint lines. Although this figure, defending passions as powerful sources of good, as well as of evil, is obviously old one, and V. was very probably familiar with it in his French predecessors, possible influence of Pope still seems to this reviewer not to be ruled out in view of V.'s intimate acquaintance with English author and his recent free imitation of *Essay on man* in his own *Discours sur l'homme.*

— Voltaire and Mme du Châtelet; an essay on the intellectual activity at Cirey. Princeton univ. press, 1941.   xiv, 241 p. *See* 3125.   1811

Important and objective study of V.'s relations in ideas to Mme du Châtelet. Cirey was not mere romantic interlude in V.'s career, but period of intense intellectual activity. Influence of French and English deists continues without break in continuity. Much of V.'s Biblical criticism published after 1760 was prepared for, and even written in first draft, during Cirey period. To be compared with Torrey's *Voltaire and the English deists* (no. 1804). Reviews : H. Brown in MLQ 3:340-44, 1942; G. R. Havens in RR 33:80-82, 1942; J. Lough in MLR 37:225-27, 1942; E. Malakis in MLN 57:238-39, 1942; N. L. Torrey, AHR 47:584-85, 1941-42.

— Studies on Voltaire, with some unpublished papers by Madame du Châtelet. Princeton, Princeton univ. press, 1947. 244 p. *See* 400, 3126.   1812

Further exploration of V.'s active years at Cirey. (Cf. same author's *Voltaire et Madame du Châtelet,* no. 1811.) Discusses: 1) Genesis of *L'ingénu;* 2) V. and Mandeville; 3) A note on genesis of *Le mondain;* 4) *Traité de métaphysique;* and 5) Some aspects of Newtonian study at Cirey.

Shows importance of *Le traité de métaphysique de Newton, Dictionnaire philosophique,* and *Philosophe ignorant* (p. 113). Reviews : G. R. Havens in RR 39: 164-67, 1948; E. Malakis in MLN 62: 497-98, 1947; D. Mornet in RHL 48: 271-73, 1948.

— and **Norman L. Torrey.** Voltaire and Polier de Bottens. RR 31:147-55, 1940.
                                                 1813

Important article which shows V. inspiring, then extensively revising article written by Lausanne pastor, Polier de Bottens, for 1764 ed. of *Dictionnaire philosophique* and also published, in different form, in *Encyclopédie.* "When one considers how little was left of the original contribution one must conclude that Voltaire editor was really publishing his own work" (p. 155).

Waterman, Mina. Voltaire, Pascal and human destiny. New York, King's crown press, 1942. 130 p. (Diss., Columbia.) 1814

Excellent, objective study. V. not without his faults, but was "intent upon liberating human beings from a tradition which forced them to keep their hearts and minds fixed upon the punishments and rewards of the next life rather than upon the amelioration of their lot in this one" (p. 105). Cf. Carré (no. 1752), Finch (no. 1757), and Morehouse (no. 1786).
Reviews : A. Guérard in RR 33:393, 1942; G. R. Havens in PhR 52:526, 1943; R. B. Oake in MLQ 4:502-03, 1943.

— Voltaire and Firmin Abauzit. RR 33: 236-49, 1942.   1815

Shows that V. was telling simple truth when he claimed to have used extracts from Abauzit for article *Apocalypse* in 1764 ed. of *Dictionnaire philosophique.* V.'s article, however, "is sparkling and incisive, bearing none of the marks of pedantry so often characteristic of Abauzit. Yet his debt to the author of the *Discours* is manifest" (p. 249).

Studies of individual Works

Besterman, Theodore. The Beaumarchais transcripts of Voltaire's correspondence. TLS 48:272, April 23, 1949.   1815A

Errors and omissions in collected editions of V.'s correspondence, based on preliminary study of Beaumarchais transcripts made in preparation of Kehl edition (no. 1626) and now in hands of author. About 2800 of 4700 Kehl letters still represented in these copies, which are judged accurate, though not accurately printed. Author planning new edition of immense V. correspondence. Important communication. *See* no. 1819.

Bonno, Gabriel. Un texte inédit de l'abbé Leblanc sur les Lettres philosophiques de Voltaire. MLN 55:503-05, 1940.　　1816

Interesting comments, generally hostile, on first edition of V.'s piquant work on England. Underlines danger of author's again being sent to Bastille. Letters on Quakers are " très plaisamment écrites " (p. 504).

Brunetière, Ferdinand. Une nouvelle édition de la correspondance de Voltaire, RDM 50th yr. 3rd per. 38:457-68, Mar. 15, 1880.　　1817

Discussion of Moland's (no. 1628) important contribution to publication of collected correspondence of V. New letters, lost letters, problems of dating letters, chronology of *Sermon des cinquante* and of Rousseau's *Émile*, the personality of V.

Caussy, Fernand. Voltaire et l'affaire des Lettres philosophiques. RPL 5th ser. 10:25-28, 56-59, July 4 and 11, 1908.　　1818

V.'s correspondence and disavowal of responsibility for publication of *Lettres philosophiques*.

Charrot, Charles. Quelques notes sur la Correspondance de Voltaire, RHL 19:170-200, 653-92, 1912; 20:167-93, 679-709, 1913.　　1819

Most important series of articles showing by internal evidence numerous errors in standard Moland edition (no. 1628) of V.'s correspondence. These errors are due largely to lack of scientific attitude on part of 18th century editors who first determined text which has been perpetuated in later editions. Hence need now of recourse to original MSS whenever possible. This suggests importance of a critical edition of the correspondence, immense though the task would be. (*See* no. 1815A) Present-day reader now has before him a text which in many instances reveals omissions, changes, errors, or even *résumés* of what V. actually wrote. Charrot's articles least complete in study of Volumes 37, 38, and 39 of Moland (cf. RHL 19:171, n.). See also *Additions et corrections* (*ibid.*, 20:704-09).

Crist, Clifford M. The Dictionnaire philosophique portatif and the early French deists. Brooklyn, Clark, 1934. 66 p. (Diss., Princeton.)　　1820

Compact tabulation of similarities in ideas between first edition of *Dictionnaire philosophique* and several early French deists. Fact that references, but not quotations, are generally given, makes this little book difficult to use without extensive labor of looking up relevant passages for oneself.

— Voltaire, Barcochébas and the early French deists. FR 6:483-89, 1932-33.　　1821

Subject of false Messiah, Barcochébas, which is most fully discussed by V. in article *Messie* of original 1764 edition of *Dictionnaire philosophique*, is thought by author to have been " inspired by Meslier, possibly recalled to V.'s mind by Dumarsais," and documented from Bayle's *Dictionnaire historique et critique*. Hardly appears certain, however, that Bayle is necessarily the source. (Cf. Wade and Torrey, no. 1813, p. 154.)

Crowley, Francis J. New Voltaire-Gabriel Cramer letters. RR 30:39-51, 133-50, 1939.　　1822

More than 100 new items added to V.'s correspondence. Though mostly notes of only a few lines, many are significant for author's personality or literary work from 1755 on.

Delattre, André. Les lettres de Voltaire des manuscrits Tronchin. MLN 58:441-47, 1943.　　1823

Bibliothèque publique et universitaire de Genève possesses collection of 597 MSS of V. letters of which 572 are to Tronchin family. Only 267 of these Tronchin letters have been previously published. 112 of those in MSS are in Moland edition of V.'s collected works (no. 1628). Numerous inaccuracies with which they have been reproduced. It has been announced elsewhere that Delattre is about to bring out a Répertoire of V. letters published in many different periodicals since 1885, date of last volume of Moland. *See also* no. 1635B.

Feugère, A. La Lettre à d'Alembert; la querelle de Rousseau et de Voltaire. RCC 36[1]:114-31, 1934-35.　　1824

Points out contrasts in character of Rousseau and V. which made it impossible for latter to understand Jean-Jacques.

Their relations, at first outwardly cordial, then embittered by *Lettre à d'Alembert* (of 1758), became openly and violently hostile with Rousseau's sudden outburst in his letter of June 17, 1760. Brief account of their further unhappy relations. *See* no. 1765.

Groos, René. Le siècle de Louis XIV de Voltaire. MerF 212:587-94, June 15, 1929.
1825

Brief appreciation of main characteristics of V.'s *Louis XIV*. " Et s'il se trompe quelquefois sur les causes, il n'erre guère quant aux faits... Voltaire sait recouper les témoignages, il sait douter lorsqu'ils se contredisent, peser les autorités et balancer les raisons " (p. 593).

Havens, George R. The composition of Voltaire's Candide. MLN 47:225-34, 1932.
1826

Refutation of popular legend that *Candide* was composed in three days, though it may have been written in three weeks. Other details on inception of *Candide*, possibly inspired in part by suggestion of Frederick the Great.

— The beginning of Voltaire's Poème sur le désastre de Lisbonne. MLN 62:465-67, 1947.
1827

Brief article which shows that first two lines of V.'s famous poem are incorrectly printed in standard Beuchot (no. 1627) and Moland editions (no. 1628) of the *Œuvres complètes*. Second line should read : " fléaux " instead of repetitious " mortels."

— Voltaire's pessimistic revision of the conclusion of his Poème sur le désastre de Lisbonne, MLN 44:489-92, 1929.
1828

Shows that V.'s half-optimistic conclusion with its emphasis on Hope cannot be taken at face value (*See* 1829). Albert Schinz (*Voltaire reread*, MLN 45:120, 1930) proposes a better reading for one of V.'s unpublished revisions of a phrase in his conclusion.

— The conclusion of Voltaire's Poème sur le désastre de Lisbonne, MLN 56:422-26, 1941.
1829

Article completes nos. 1828 and 1830 by same author. Shows Morley's (no. 1676) pessimistic interpretation of poem to be supported by evidence of V.'s correspondence in contrast to over-optimistic interpretation of Alfred Noyes (no. 1679), who errs in taking text at its face value. Important for realistic evaluation of V.'s ideas.

— Twelve new letters of Voltaire to Gabriel Cramer, RR 31:341-54, 1940.
1830

Letters from MSS Coindet in *Bibliothèque de Genève*. Interesting especially for light thrown on V.'s reasons for toning down conclusion of his *Poème sur le désastre de Lisbonne. See* nos. 1828, 1829.

— Voltaire's letters to Pierre Pictet and his family, RR 32:244-58, 1941.
1831

Eighteen letters from MSS Constant in *Bibliothèque de Genève*. Nine were previously unpublished, others had appeared with errors or omissions. Here we see V.'s letters reëstablished in their original form. All given with annotations which explain allusions and justify dating. Some refer to Lisbon earthquake. *See* nos. 1828, 1829, 1830.

Lantoine, Albert. Les Lettres philosophiques de Voltaire. Malfère, 1931. 191 p. (GEL) *See* 3113.
1832

Generally sound and vivid discussion. Occasional errors in proper names, particularly English. Unfortunately inclined to depreciate Lanson's essential edition of this important work. *See* nos. 1642, 2889.

McKee, Kenneth N. Voltaire's Brutus during the French Revolution. MLN 56: 100-06, 1941.
1833

V.'s *Brutus* had only flash of popularity during Revolution, contrary to sweeping statements of Moland (no. 1628). Was " discarded from active repertories " (p. 105) after fall of Robespierre. Napoleon never permitted it to be performed in public and play apparently has never been revived since.

Mornet, Daniel. Les imitations du Candide de Voltaire au XVIIIᵉ siècle. MélGL, p. 298-303.
1834

Study of eight avowed or evident imitations of *Candide* in 18th century. V.'s novel vied for popularity with Rousseau's *Nouvelle Héloïse*. But imitators of *Candide* were basically optimistic in contrast to V. They were influenced, however, by his ideal of tolerance, humanitarian instincts, and hostility to war.

Jeffreys, George. The Merope of George Jeffreys as a source of Voltaire's Mérope, by Thomas E. Oliver. [Urbana.] The University of Illinois, 1927. 111 p. (Half-title : University of Illinois studies in language and literature, v. 12, no. 4) *See* 3116.   1835

Thorough study, but has tendency to overemphasize importance of Jeffreys's *Merope* without due attention to possible French influences and to V.'s ability to introduce independently minor changes in Maffei theme.

Reviews : H. C. Lancaster in MLN 43:561-62, 1928; G. L. van Roosbroeck in RR 21:257-59, 1930.

Price, William Raleigh. The symbolism of Voltaire's novels with special reference to Zadig. New York, Columbia Univ. press, 1911. 269 p.   1836

Overdoes evidence in favor of symbolistic interpretation of V.'s names, characters, and incidents in *Zadig.* Interesting hypotheses, but to be accepted with caution. Severely satirized by Ascoli in his critical edition of *Zadig* (no. 1653), v. I, p. xxxix-xli.

Review : P. Toldo in ZFSL 39²:208-12, 1912.

Ritter, Eugène. Le Sermon des cinquante [par Voltaire]. RHL 7:315, 1900.   1837

Important page which confirms, by testimony of La Beaumelle, idea that *Sermon des cinquante,* published in August, 1762, had been composed some ten years earlier at Berlin, as Grimm had previously stated. Thus, this work was not, as Brunetière thought, a hurried reply to Rousseau's *Vicaire savoyard.* Cf. I. O. Wade, *Voltaire and Mme du Châtelet* (no. 1811, p. 141), who puts composition as possibly in 1749, certainly in 1752, and believes that it circulated in MS by 1759 or 1760 (p. 139).

Rovillain, Eugène E. L'ingénu de Voltaire; quelques influences probables. PMLA 44:537-45, 1929.   1838

Interesting parallels between *L'ingénu* and Lesage's *Aventures du chevalier de Beauchêne,* Prévost's *Cléveland, Delisle de La Drèvetière,* and Pascal's *Provinciales.*

— Sur le Zadig de Voltaire; quelques influences probables. PMLA 43:447-55, 1928.   1839

Intention to indicate interesting *rapprochements* rather than positive *sources.* Valuable hints on V.'s intellectual background some of which probably did determine content of *Zadig.*

— Sur le Zadig de Voltaire; quelques autres influences. PMLA 46:533-39, June, 1931.   1840

Continuation of previous article. *See* no. 1839.

Souriau, Maurice. La langue de Voltaire, dans sa correspondance. *See* 398.   1841

Important study of V.'s use of obsolete, neologistic, or other unusual words. Points out a few singularities in grammar of V. He wrote rapidly and sometimes carelessly. Cases noted, however, are given as exceptions out of great mass of his letters. Question arises : Would these conclusions be affected by establishment of a critical text of the *Correspondance* ? (Cf. article by Charrot, no. 1819.)

Tannery, Jean. L'édition originale de Candide. BBB ns 12:7-15, 1933; 13:62-70, 1934; 17:246-51, 337-39, 1938.   1842

Original edition of *Candide* probably not, he believes, Cramer edition (299 p.) of Geneva, 1759, as stated by Morize (no. 1631), but Paris edition of Lambert (237 p.) published about two weeks before. Cf. Vandérem (no. 1846) and Torrey (no. 1844).

Torrey, Norman L. The date of composition of Candide and Voltaire's corrections. MLN 44:445-47, 1929.   1843

Wagnière, V.'s secretary, testified that he made first MS copy of *Candide* in July, 1758, at Schwetzingen for Elector of Palatinate, Charles-Theodore.

— The first edition of Candide. MLN 48: 307-10, 1933.   1844

Adduces three undated notes of V., previously published in the periodical, *Le nain jaune,* in support of the Lambert, Paris, edition as first. Cf. Jean Tannery (no. 1842) and Fernand Vandérem (no. 1846). Cramer edition, Geneva, 1759, however, "remains the most important as the basis for the author's subsequent augmentations and revisions " (p. 310). Further details on this question in *The bibliopolist, a bibliographic catalogue,* published by Maurice Sloog (French book corporation), New York, 29 West 56th Street, May, 1946, p. 1-3.

— Voltaire's composition of Les adieux du vieillard. RR 30:361-68, 1939.   1845

Interesting evidence of " la difficulté vaincue " in various " états " of poem written during last weeks of V.'s life. Two pages of MS facsimiles.

Vandérem, Fernand. Précisions et conclusions sur l'originale de Candide. BBB ns 17:289-93, 340-44, 433-36, 1938.   1846

Author agrees with Jean Tannery (1842) that Lambert's Paris edition, not Geneva edition of Cramer, is true original so far as our present knowledge goes, though it is possible that an earlier copy of Cramer edition, " sans cartons ni suppression " (p. 344), may yet be discovered, in which case it would be the original. Until then, Lambert edition should be regarded provisionally as original. Cf. Torrey (1844). Bengesco simply followed Beuchot in classification of editions called original. Beuchot, for his part, in his MS Catalog at BN, gave no proof for his classifications, which may be correct, but must in each case be subject to further check. They are in no sense conclusive as they stand.

Wade, Ira O. The Épître à Uranie, PMLA 47:1066-1112, 1932.   1847

Careful study of numerous MS copies of this important deistic *Épître*, which antedates the English journey. Relation of this early poem to background of French ideas. Cf. divergent attitudes of Morley (no. 1676) and Brunetière (nos. 1661, 1750) to the question of the importance of the English influence on V.

— Poems attributed to Voltaire. MP 34:63-73, 1936-37.   1848

Preliminary survey of V.'s poetic output from 1714 to 1732 in effort to determine authenticity of certain disputed poems not included in Moland (no. 1628), thus giving more complete picture of young V.

— Some forgotten letters of Voltaire. MLN 47:211-25, 1932.   1849

Fourteen letters of V. and part of another, not previously published in Moland (no. 1628) or elsewhere. They come from Beuchot papers, but were not utilized in his edition (no. 1627). Several long and interesting letters to Malesherbes and Grimm.

NOTE

For further information on Voltaire's relations with England, see also Chapter XI, nos. 3081-3127.

CHAPTER VIII. JEAN-JACQUES ROUSSEAU

(Nos. 1850-2202B)

PAUL M. SPURLIN

This Rousseau bibliography, first undertaken by the late Professor Albert Schinz, was left largely uncompleted at the time of his death. Coming late and unexpectedly to the formidable task, the present compiler was happily able to profit by using Schinz's valuable work as a point of departure. The degree of this indebtedness is more accurately indicated in the annotation of Schinz's well-known *État présent des travaux sur J.-J. Rousseau.* In a selective bibliography such as this, many significant items of detail—books and articles—have of necessity been omitted. For such items up to the year 1940, Schinz's book should be consulted. The extensive bibliographical apparatus of the *Annales de la Société Jean-Jacques Rousseau,* published from 1905 on, offers a rich mine of further information.

The late start, the pressure of unavoidable rival responsibilities, and the enormous scope of the bibliography dealing with Rousseau have forced the compiler to have recourse to several friends for indispensable help in completing the task in time for the printer. To George R. Havens he expresses his gratitude for generous guidance and unstinting help in making a great number of evaluations, to David C. Cabeen his appreciation for assistance and for numerous annotations of titles, and to William T. Bandy, A. S. Crisafulli, and Norman L. Torrey, his thanks for their evaluation of certain entries. In spite of such aid, it has been necessary to leave a few titles unevaluated and merely listed. In a number of other instances, evaluations have been made less extensive and thoroughgoing than ideally might be wished.

Bibliography

Quérard, J.-M. Notice des diverses éditions des ouvrages de J.-J. Rousseau. *In his :* La France littéraire, see 51, v. 8, p. 192-231.
1850

Bibliography of works by and on R. Its *Notice des principaux écrits relatifs à la personne et aux ouvrages de J.-J. Rousseau* (p. 207-31) by A.-A. Barbier, originally printed in the *Annales encyclo-*

pédiques of 1818, with subsequent additions.
Review : A. Schinz in EprR, p. 149-50.

Lanson, Gustave. Manuel bibliographique de la littérature française moderne : XVIe, XVIIe, XVIIIe et XIXe siècles. Nouvelle édition revue et corrigée. Hachette, 1931. 1851

R. titles on pp. 778-806 and in *Supplément,* p. 1646-50. Selective. *Index général* must also be consulted. Covers through year 1920.

Giraud, Jeanne. Manuel de bibliographie littéraire pour les XVIe, XVIIe et XVIIIe siècles français, 1921-1935. *See* 30B. 1852

R. titles on pp. 257-75. Important list which supplements R. entries in Lanson's *Manuel bibliographique* (no. 1851), to which it adds, according to Schinz's calculation, 675 titles. Begins with 1921, where Lanson stops, and goes through 1935.

Rousseau, J.-J. Catalogue général des livres imprimés de la Bibliothèque nationale. Imprimerie nationale, 1939. v. 157, p. 410-535. 1853

This important and extensive R. bibliography is introduced by a *Cadre de classement,* an *Index alphabétique des titres,* and an *Index alphabétique des éditeurs, traducteurs, annotateurs.*
Review : P. E. Schazmann in AJJR 29:292-93, 1941-42.

— Catalogue des ouvrages de Jean-Jacques Rousseau conservés dans les grandes bibliothèques de Paris, par E.-G. Ledos, conservateur-adjoint. Champion, 1912. 60 p.
1854

Important list, as of 1912, of rare editions of R. found in great libraries of Paris. Essential research tool.
Review : A. François in AJJR 9:127, 1913.

Aubert, Fernand. Catalogue des manuscrits de Rousseau à Genève. AJJR 24:179-250, 1935. 1855

Catalogue of MSS available in one of great centers of study of R.

Ducros, Louis. Jean-Jacques Rousseau. *See* 1911.   1856

Excellent bibliography appears as footnote at head of each chapter.

Dufour, Théophile André. Recherches bibliographiques sur les œuvres imprimées de J.-J. Rousseau, suivies de l'inventaire des papiers de Rousseau conservés à la Bibliothèque de Neuchâtel. Giraud-Badin, 1925. 2 v. (I, 273 p.; II, 297 p.).   1857

Indispensable research tool. In addition to descriptions of printed editions of R.'s works, this work is particularly important because it lists R. manuscripts at Library of Neuchâtel. Also lists books belonging to R. Introduction by Pierre-Paul Plan. *See also* Sénelier, no. 2202B.
Reviews : E. Magne in MerF 181:439-41, 1925; D. Mornet in AJJR 17:261-64, 1926; A. Schinz in EprR 100, 152, 154 and in MLN 41: 424-26, 1926.

Annales de la Société Jean-Jacques Rousseau. Geneva, Jullien, 1905-.   1858

Indispensable bibliographical tool and repository for articles and sometimes lengthy studies on R. At end of each volume is an annual bibliography by countries, characterized by Albert Schinz as " fort complète," much of which is reviewed critically. Volumes also contain *Revue des bibliographies* and *Chronique.* Very valuable likewise are occasional bibliographies on special subjects, e.g. A. Riza, *J.-J. Rousseau dans la littérature turque (1839-1930).*
Volume 17 (1926) has a *Table générale des tomes I à XV* (1905-1923) which includes *Mémoires et documents, Illustrations,* and *Index des noms propres.*
For brief details concerning *Annales,* Rousseau Society and its activities, see A. Schinz, *État présent des travaux sur J.-J. Rousseau,* no. 1859, p. 59-61.

Schinz, Albert. État présent des travaux sur J.-J. Rousseau. New York, Modern language association of America, 1941. 411 p.   1859

Indispensable bibliographical tool. Traces history of Rousseauistic literature, enumerates and discusses important books and articles dealing with R. and his writings, indicates status of studies on his principal works, discusses problems relating to him, and suggests problems to be studied. Articles devoted to R.

bibliography published previously by author in MP and MLN were " absorbed " in present volume.
Mine of information, book is, however, not *sans reproche.* User must be constantly on his guard against misspelled names, partial or incorrect titles, wrong dates, inaccurate bibliographical data. Absence of an Index also reduces book's effectiveness. Reader should likewise be wary of Schinz's tendency toward Rousseauistic bias. At same time, the compiler of the present bibliography is deeply indebted to Schinz's long years of work and profound knowledge of R., and he has frequently found that a quotation from his book offered a succinct and accurate evaluation of title under consideration. Basically, moreover, items in the present bibliography follow recommendations of Schinz. In this Rousseau section of *A critical bibliography of French literature* important references in *État présent des travaux sur J.-J. Rousseau* are indexed among reviews under abbreviation EprR.
Reviews : F. Baldensperger in MLF 27:167-70, Dec., 1942; R. Bray in AJJR 29:295-99, 1941-42; J. David in MLQ 3:463-65, 1942; H. A. Larrabee in Jph 40:27-28, 1943; H. Peyre in Ren 1:159-61, 1943; R. Picard in FR 17:121-23, 1943-44; N. L. Torrey in RR 33:393-96, 1942; F. Vial in Th 18:543-44, 1943.

Courtois, Louis-J. *See* 1909, p. 298-342.   1860

Schiff, Mario. Éditions et traductions italiennes des œuvres de Jean-Jacques Rousseau. Rbib 17:183-216, 1907; 18:9-39, 1908. (Extracted and reprinted, Champion, 1908. 71 p.)   1861

Concrete evidence of vogue of R. in Italian translation.
Review : A. François in AJJR 5:311, 1909.

Schinz, Albert. La collection Jean-Jacques Rousseau de la Bibliothèque de J. Pierpont Morgan... Lettres, notes manuscrites et éditions (avec trois fac-similés) Northampton, Mass., Smith college, 1925. 59 p. (SSML, v. 7, no. 1)   1862

See also complement in AJJR 17:322-24, 1926.
Review : L.-J. Courtois in AJJR 17: 247, 1926.

Warner, James H. A bibliography of eighteenth-century English editions of J.-J. Rousseau, with notes on the early diffusion of his writings. PQ 13:225-47, 1934. Addenda to the Bibliography of eighteenth-century English editions of J.-J. Rousseau. PQ 19:237-43, 1940. 1863

Title indicates scope of this valuable article with its supplement.
Review : A. Schinz in AJJR 23:208-09, 1934.

Editions

Rousseau, Jean-Jacques. Collection complète des œuvres de J. J. Rousseau, citoyen de Genève. Ed. by P. A. Du Peyrou. Geneva, 1782. 24 v. 1864

See Dufour (no. 1857), II, 25-27.

Supplément à la Collection des œuvres de J. J. Rousseau, citoyen de Genève. Ed. by P. A. Du Peyrou. Geneva, 1783-84. 6 v. 1865

See Dufour (no. 1857), II, 25-27.

— Œuvres complètes de J. J. Rousseau, mises dans un nouvel ordre, avec des notes historiques et des éclaircissements; par V. D. Musset-Pathay. Dupont, 1823-26. 25 v. 1866

Basic 19th century edition in so far as there is one. Has *Table générale*.

— Œuvres complètes. Édition de Ch. Lahure, Hachette, 1865. 13 v. 1867

Vaughan, in his edition of *Contrat social* (no. 1877, p. 167), says that this edition is " ... full of inaccuracies, which often affect not only the style, but the sense." Hachette edition remains, nevertheless, because of its accessibility and cheapness, in spite of bad paper and small type, the regularly cited " Vulgate " of R. Needs to be supplanted by a really good general edition, comparable to the " Moland " of Voltaire (no. 1628).

— Œuvres et correspondance inédites de J. J. Rousseau; publiées par M. G. Streckeisen-Moultou. Lévy, 1861. 484 p. 1868

Some minor writings and pieces not found in collected editions of R.

— The works of Jean Jacques Rousseau. Translated from the French. Edinburgh, 1773-74. 10 v. 1869

See Dufour (no. 1857), II, 17, and Warner (no. 1863), in PQ 13:239, 1934 and *ibid.*, 19:240, 1940.

— Vie et Œuvres de J. J. Rousseau, avec des notes explicatives, par Albert Schinz.

Boston, New York, Heath, 1921. 382 p. 1870

Good anthology for undergraduates.
Reviews : A. François in AJJR 14:275, 1922; G. R. Havens in MLN 38:174-75, 1923; C. E. Young in MLJ 6:481-82, 1921-22.

— Morceaux choisis, avec une introduction et des notes par Daniel Mornet. 9th ed., Didier; Toulouse, Privat, (1910) 1933. 375 p. 1871

Good student anthology. Abundant documentary illustrations.
Reviews : A. François in AJJR 7:157-58, 1911; L. R. in Rcr 73:410, 1912.

— Les confessions. Édition intégrale, publiée sur le texte autographe conservé à la Bibliothèque de Genève, accompagnée de variantes extraites du manuscrit de la Chambre des Députés, de notes et d'un index, par Ad. Van Bever et suivies des Rêveries du promeneur solitaire. Crès, 1913. 3 v. (First edition, Crès, 1912, 2 v.) 1872

Valuable for text, notes, and index.
Reviews : J. de Gourmont in MerF 107:805, Feb., 16, 1914; E. Ritter in AJJR 10:203-05, 1914-15; A. Schinz in EprR, p. 161.

— The confessions of J. J. Rousseau in an anonymous English edition first published in two parts in 1783 and 1790, now revised and completed by A. S. B. Glover, with an introduction by Havelock Ellis. London, Nonesuch press, 1938. 2 v. 1873

A. Schinz, in EprR, p. 161, calls this " ... l'édition classique anglaise..."

— Extraits des œuvres autobiographiques. Notice et annotations par Alexis François. Delagrave, 1936. 126 p. 1874

Scholarly if short anthology.
Review : P.-E. Schazmann in AJJR 25:298-99, 1936.

— Du contrat social; édition comprenant avec le texte définitif les versions primitives de l'ouvrage collationnées sur les manuscrits autographes de Genève et de Neuchâtel; une introduction et des notes par Edmond Dreyfus-Brisac. Alcan, 1896. 424 p. 1875

" Après une remarquable introduction sur la genèse, les principales idées et le but du *Contrat social*, M. Dreyfus-Brisac donne le texte de l'édition publiée à Amsterdam, en 1762, en l'accompagnant de nombreuses citations empruntées aux écrivains qui paraissent avoir inspiré

Rousseau. Puis viennent en appendice : la reproduction intégrale du manuscrit de Genève,... document capital pour l'histoire des idées de Rousseau; les passages des manuscrits de Neuchâtel et ceux des divers écrits de Rousseau qui sont à rapprocher du *Contrat*, soit pour l'éclaircir, soit pour en fixer les origines ; les textes relatifs à la condamnation du *Contrat* par les magistrats de Genève." Champion. p. 87-88. " ... très utile et excellent travail..." Lanson, review, below, p. 282.

Reviews : R. Allier in Renc, 589, 1896; E. Champion in Rfr 30:87-88, 1896; G. Lanson in RU²:281-82, 1896; R. Radouant in RHL 5:484-87, 1898; A. Schinz in EprR, 221.

— Du contrat social. Ed. by Georges Beaulavon. Société nouvelle de librairie et d'édition, 1903. 336 p. 1876

Serious students' edition. Has informative preface, revised in 1914 edition, dealing with R.'s moral preoccupations, his search for a government in conformity with his view of nature of man, and sources and influences of *Contrat social*. Received with reservations by leading French critics.

See also Hubert (no. 2084), and Schinz, (no. 2191).

Reviews (of various editions) : L. Brunel in RHL 11:517-21, 1904; A. Espinas in RIE 46:374-76, 1903; E. Faguet in Rlat 3:145-50, 1904; R. Hubert in RDS 2:325-26, 1914; G. Lanson in RU 12²: 420-21, 1903; P. E. Schazmann in AJJR 27:317, 1938; A. Schinz in EprR, p. 218-19, 238-49, *passim;* G. Truc in RHL 22:616-17, 1915.

— Du contrat social; ou, Principes du droit politique. Ed. by C. E. Vaughan. Manchester, The University press; London, New York, Longmans, Green, 1918. 184 p. 1877

Considered by Schinz best edition for class use in any language. Introduction and notes in English.

Reviews : C. Bémont in Rhist 132: 335-36, 1919; L.-J. Courtois in AJJR 12: 167-68, 1918-19; A. Schinz in EprR, 97, 217.

— Du contrat social, texte original publié avec introduction, notes et commentaire par Maurice Halbwachs. Aubier, 1943. 462 p. 1878

Has important introduction and chapter by chapter commentary on treatise. Also *Indications bibliographiques*.

Review : A. de Maday in AJJR 30: 202-07, 1943-45.

— Du contrat social, précédé d'un essai sur la politique de Rousseau, par Bertrand de Jouvenel, accompagné des notes de Voltaire et d'autres contemporains de l'auteur. Geneva, Éditions du cheval ailé, 1947. 398 p. 1879

M. de Jouvenel agrees that R.'s diagnosis of society's ills was correct, but believes that weakness of character prevented him from accepting heroic remedies that situation demanded. Strictly logical interpretation presents a completely non-revolutionary R., but R. cannot be comprehended on strictly logical plane. Vaughan's interpretation (no. 1882) not superseded and Dreyfus-Brisac edition (no. 1875) remains the most useful.

Review : N. L. Torrey in RR 39:323-26, 1948.

— The social contract. (Everyman's library). London, Dent; New York, Dutton (1913), 1935. 287 p. 1880

English translation by G. D. H. Cole. Highly recommended by Schinz in R. essay in *Encyclopædia of the social sciences* [XIII (1935)]. The *Discourses* are also included.

— Social contract; essays by Locke, Hume, and Rousseau. With an Introduction by Sir Ernest Barker. New York and London, Oxford univ. press, 1948. 307 p. 1881

Contains excellent translation of R.'s *Contrat social* (p. 167-307) made especially for this volume by Gerard Hopkins.

— The political writings of Jean Jacques Rousseau, ed. from the original manuscripts and authentic editions, with introductions and notes by C. E. Vaughan. Cambridge, Eng., The University press, 1915. 2 v. (I, 516; II, 577). 1882

Definitive and indispensable. " I have attempted," wrote Vaughan of this work, " three things in the following volumes : to collect all the political writings of Rousseau in one body; to present a correct text of what he wrote; and to define his place in the history of political thought." I, p. vii. Book has Introduction of 117 pages. Several appendices of which one is on Rousseau and his enemies.

Reviews : S. C. Chew in APSR 10: 591-93, 1916; L.-J. Courtois in AJJR

11:238-41, 1916-17; A. Schinz in EprR 215-18, 240, 249-51 and in PhR 26: 214-27, 1917.

— Correspondance générale de J.-J. Rousseau. Ed. by Théophile Dufour [and Pierre-Paul Plan]. Colin, 1924-34. 20 v.   1883

Its publication epoch-making; crowned by French Academy. Indispensable for any objective and scholarly investigation on R. Volumes have name indexes.

Reviews in AJJR as follows : G. Ascoli, 16:282-87, 1924-25 (vols. 1-2), 17:254-56, 1926 (vols. 3-6); P. Kohler, 20:224-34, 1931 (vols. 7-10); L.-J. Courtois, 19: 247-49, 1929-30 (vols. 11-14), 20:256-59, 1931 (vols. 15-16), 21:283-85, 1932 (vols. 17-18); L. Rácz, 22:270-71, 1933 (vol. 19); B. Bouvier and L.-J. Courtois, 23:210-12, 1934 (vol. 20). See also H. Ellis in Atl 36:366-70, 1935; A. Schinz in EprR, 99, 155-57.

— Lettres à M. de Malesherbes. Préface et notes par Gustave Rudler. London, Scholartis press, 1928. 62 p.   1884

Edition of R.'s four letters to Malesherbes. These letters " in which he tries so sincerely to understand himself," wrote N. L. Torrey, (RR 29:189,1938) " must be classified among the world's greatest epistles." Text of letters is that of Dufour edition of Correspondance générale (no. 1883), but regularized. See Bisson, no. 2038.

Reviews : Anon. in TLS, p. 350, May 10, 1928; E. Langenbach in AJJR 18:347, 1927-28.

Hendel, Charles W. Citizen of Geneva; selections from the letters of Jean-Jacques Rousseau. New York, London, Oxford Univ. press, 1937. 405 p.   1885

Compiler's intention " to provide in one volume of translations an anthology, a gleaning of the best letters " in twenty-volume Dufour edition of R.'s Correspondance générale (no. 1883). Letters preceded by good biographical sketch of 123 pages. Has Index of letters and Index of persons.

" The reader will find in this anthology an authentic Rousseau, as human as he is lovable." Torrey, review, below, p. 189.

Reviews : E. N. Curtis in AHR 44: 194-95, 1938-39; A. Guérard in NNY 146:160-61, Feb. 5, 1938; E. Malakis in MLN 53: 476-77, 1938; A. Schinz in AJJR 26:330-32, 1937; N. L. Torrey in RR 29:188-90, 1938.

Rousseau, Jean-Jacques. Discours sur les sciences et les arts. Édition critique avec une Introduction et un Commentaire, par George R. Havens. New York, Modern language association of America; London, Oxford Univ. press, 1946. 278 p.   1886

Critical edition of R.'s first important philosophical work. Consists of Introduction, text of original edition published at Geneva in 1750, and Commentaire. Appendice contains Essai de classement des premières éditions of this work. Abundant cross-references and good Index.

In addition to treating its inspiration and sources and indicating its meaningful truths, author studies influence on R. himself of this prize-winning essay and of polemics which followed its publication. Objective and definitive.

Reviews : O. Fellows in RR 38:277-79, 1947; F. T. H. Fletcher in MLR 42: 269-70, 1947; Al(exis) F(rançois) in AJJR 31:262-64, 1946-49 ; A. C. Keller in MLQ 11:125-26, 1950 ; D. Mornet in RHL 49:178-79, 1949 ; R. Shackleton in FS 4:161-64, 1950 ; P. M. Spurlin in MLN 63:423-25, 1948; I. O. Wade in FR 21: 509-11, 1947-48. (cf. reply by Havens, ibid., 22:58-59).

— Essay by Jean-Jacques Rousseau, which obtained the prize of the Academy of Dijon, in 1750. In the question, Whether the reestablishment of the arts and sciences have tended to purify the manners ? Tr. from the French Geneva ed. Brussels, printed at the British press, 1818. (In Smithers, Henry. The cultivation of the arts and sciences. Brussels, 1818).   1887

On various early English translations of R.'s First discourse (editions of 1751, 1752, 1760, and 1767), cf. Havens (no. 1886), p. 255.

— Discours sur l'origine et les fondements de l'inégalité parmi les hommes, with an introduction by F. C. Green. Cambridge [Eng.] University press, 1941. 21-142 p. (Reprinted in 1944, and 1947.)   1888

Contains text and R.'s extensive notes. Introduction of 20 p. No notes by editor.

Review : F. J. Crowley in MLF 27:146, Sept., 1942.

— A discourse upon the origin and foundation of the inequality among mankind. By John James Rousseau. London, Dodsley, 1761. 260 p.   1889

First published translation in English. See J. H. Warner (no. 1863), p. 236.

— Émile; ou, De l'éducation. Nouvelle édition, avec une introduction, une bibliographie, des notes, et un index analytique par François et Pierre Richard. Garnier, [1939] 664 p.   1890

Edition evaluated by A. Schinz in EprR, p. 254.

— La profession de foi du vicaire savoyard. Édition critique d'après les manuscrits de Genève, Neuchâtel et Paris, avec une introduction et un commentaire historiques, par Pierre-Maurice Masson. Hachette, 1914. 608 p.   1891

Authoritative edition, done with all of Masson's characteristic intelligence and thoroughness. *See* nos. 1790, 2202A.
Reviews : G. Lanson in RHL 24: 321-22, 1917; E. Ritter in AJJR 11:242-43, 1916-17; A. Schinz in EprR, p. 265 ff.

— La profession de foi du vicaire savoyard, publiée avec une introduction, des notes et des illustrations par Georges Beaulavon. Hachette, [1937]. 203 p.   1892

Beaulavon adopted text of Masson edition (no. 1891) and says that latter is " ... rigoureusement conforme à l'édition originale de 1762." (p. 72). Characterized by Schinz as " une édition pour classes." EprR, p. 268. *See* no. 2202A.
Reviews : H. R. in AJJR 25:301-02, 1936 (unimportant); A. Schinz in EprR, p. 101-02, 268, 277.

— Émile. (Everyman's library). London, Dent; New York, Dutton, (1911) 1933. 444 p.   1893

English translation by Barbara Foxley. Recommended by Schinz in R. essay in *Encyclopædia of the social sciences* [XIII (1935)] as best in this language.

— L'état de guerre and Projet de paix perpétuelle; two essays by Jean-Jacques Rousseau; with introduction and notes by S. G. Patterson... foreword by G. H. Putnam. New York and London, Putnam, 1920. 90 p.   1894

Review : A. Schinz in MLN 36:245-47, 1921.

— Les institutions chymiques de Jean-Jacques Rousseau, publiées et annotées par Maurice Gautier. AJJR 12:1-164, 1918-19; 13:1-178, 1920-21.   1895

For information concerning MS here published, which R. had confided to Paul Moultou in 1778, and which was discovered by Théophile Dufour (no. 1857), see *Introduction*, p. vii-xxiii.

Review : E. Carcassonne in RHL 29: 377-78, 1922.

— Lettre à M. d'Alembert sur les spectacles, publiée avec une introduction, un sommaire, des appendices et des notes historiques et grammaticales par L. Brunel. Hachette, 1896. 223 p.   1896

Characterized by Schinz as " excellente." EprR, p. 190.

— Lettre à M. d'Alembert sur les spectacles. Ed. by M. Fuchs. Geneva, Droz, 1949. xlviii, 208 p. (TLF)   1897

Useful edition with Introduction, but hardly of scope of critical edition, as it is called.
Review : G. R. Havens in RR 40:292-96, 1949; F. Vial in FR 23:57, 1949.

— La nouvelle Héloïse. Nouv. éd. publiée d'après les manuscrits et les éditions originales avec des variantes, une introduction, des notices et des notes par Daniel Mornet. Hachette, 1925. 4 v. *See* 701.   1898

Authoritative critical edition of R.'s influential and widely-read novel. First volume devoted entirely to comprehensive Introduction.
Reviews : G. Ascoli in RSH 43:150-53, June, 1927; P. Chaponnière in AJJR 17: 252-54, 1926; D. Mornet in RHL 34: 604-05, 1927; A. Schinz in MLN 41: 431-34, 1926, and in EprR, p. 196-215, *passim*.

— Eloisa; a series of original letters. Translated from the French of J. J. Rousseau, to which are added the adventures of Lord B— at Rome, being the sequel of Eloisa. London, printed for John Harding, 1810. 3 v.   1899

English edition of *Nouvelle Héloïse*, first translated in 1761 (*see* Warner, no. 2200).

— Les rêveries du promeneur solitaire. Édition critique par Marcel Raymond. Lille, Giard; Geneva, Droz, 1948. 225 p. (TLF)   1900

Introduction, text, appendix, notes, and *Bibliographie sommaire* of R.'s delightful, final autobiographical work.
Review : F. Vial in RR 40:296-98, 1949.

— Les rêveries du promeneur solitaire. Édition critique publiée d'après les manuscrits autographes par John S. Spink. Didier, 1948. 245 p. (TFM)   1900A

In 55-page Introduction, is detailed

discussion of manuscripts and dates of composition of each *Rêverie* (Cf. Monglond, no. 2180). R. made notes on playing cards. Facsimiles. More discussion of style and content in edition by Marcel Raymond (no. 1900), published in same year in TLF series by E. Droz. Review : N. Suckling in FS 4:165-66, 1950.

— The reveries of a solitary. Translated with an introduction by John Gould Fletcher. New York, Brentano, [1927]. 196 p.   1901

Main points of Fletcher's introduction (p. 1-28) : that R. erred in confusing values of society with values of truth, since he supposed, like Plato, " that a human society based on justice and truth could exist;" and that he blundered in romantically idealizing small city-states of antiquity, in setting their government up as a model. Holds R. responsible, therefore, for " purely commercial plutocracy which calls itself democracy in all the Western nations." Fletcher considers R., whom he calls a mystic and a kind of hermit, of interest only as the " solitary, the man born out of his time, the tragic prophet who saw with clearsighted pessimism that nothing could save European culture, and still more, religion, upon which all culture rests, except a complete ' return to nature.' " Reviews : J. M. Murry in MC 7: 78-82, Jan., 1928; A. L. Sells in AJJR 18:344-47, 1927-28.

General Biography or Criticism

Andersson, Paul. Jean-Jacques Rousseau, der Philosoph, der Erzieher, der Mensch, im Gericht seiner französischen Ankläger (1906-1925). Bochum, Fretlöh, 1930. 97 p. (Diss. Cologne).   1902

Study of chief adversaries of R. in period 1906-25, principally of Jules Lemaître, Pierre Lasserre, and Ernest Seillière, and critical examination of R. in light of their attacks. *See also* Dumur (no. 1973), and Rowbotham (no. 1941). Reviews : W. Müller in AJJR 20:219-20, 1931; A. Schinz in EprR, 62 n.

Beaudouin, Henri. La vie et les œuvres de Jean-Jacques Rousseau. Lamulle et Poisson, 1891. 2 v. (I, 585; II, 627).   1903

Important as marking real advance in R. studies. Morin (no. 1930) had worked on same documents utilized by Musset-Pathay in 1820's. Beaudouin incorporates results of intervening research and discussion. Unmarked by originality,

however, and information frequently unreliable. Has index of authors cited. Reviews : E. Lintilhac in Rcr 33:75-79, Jan. 25, 1892; A. Schinz in EprR 55, 127-28; H. W. in BU 56:659-61, Oct.-Dec., 1892.

Bouvier, Bernard. Jean-Jacques Rousseau, conférences prononcées dans l'Aula de l'Université de Genève à l'occasion du deuxième centenaire de la naissance de J.-J. Rousseau. Geneva, Jullien, 1912. 401 p.   1904

" ... un volume d'ensemble sur Rousseau... un livre chaleureux autant qu'il est solide... On n'a rien écrit sur Rousseau qui témoigne d'une impartialité plus sûre que ces conférences prononcées par un Genevois pour des Genevois." Mornet, review, below, p. 722. Reviews : E. Faguet in APL 62¹:76-79, 1914; D. Mornet in RHL 20:722, 1913; G. Rudler in RCLN 8:129-30, June 15, 1913.

Brédif, Léon. Du caractère intellectuel et moral de J.-J. Rousseau étudié dans sa vie et ses écrits. Hachette, 1906. 414 p.   1905

Procedure and plan of book clarified by author in MerF 67:380, 1907 : " Les quatre premiers chapitres sont le développement de l'*Émile*, miroir concentrique des *idées* maîtresses de Rousseau en éducation, philosophie, morale, politique, idées issues de son *caractère*. A partir du chapitre 5ᵉ, l'auteur étudie plus spécialement *l'homme* dans sa psychologie parfois déconcertante; il met au point ses qualités diverses : orgueil, bonté, reconnaissance, amitié, sentiment religieux, etc. Il le considère dans ses relations sociales, recherche son caractère dans ses écrits, dont le fond est toujours la personnalité de Rousseau, héros de ses ouvrages... et dans ses dispositions dominantes, l'impressionnabilité effective et l'imagination. Le chapitre 10ᵉ entre dans le détail du mécanisme de son cerveau et des effets divers de son *tempérament*.   Il prépare ainsi le chapitre 11ᵉ où est examiné le problème délicat de la sincérité de Jean-Jacques, et le 12ᵉ (*conscience, affections pathologiques, conclusion*, p. 393.) " Reviews : F. Baldensperger in Rcr 63: 129-30, 1907; G. Lanson in RU 16¹: 173, 1907; D. Mornet in RHL 14:744-46, 1907; L. Pinvert in AJJR 3:269-70, 1907; A. Schinz in EprR, p. 133-34.

Brockerhoff, Ferdinand. Jean Jacques Rousseau; sein Leben und seine Werke. Leipzig, Wigand, 1863-74. 3 v.   1906

" Le texte très serré fourmille de notes excellentes — jusqu'en 1874." Schinz, p. 127.

Review : A. Schinz in EprR, 48-49, 127.

Carré, J.-R. Le secret de Jean-Jacques Rousseau. RHL 49:130-54, 220-34, 1949.
1906A

R.'s " secret " is his conception of happiness and his lifelong search for it. " Le repos dans le silence des passions, c'était peut-être le rêve de toujours du passionné Rousseau " (p. 139). Excellent appraisal of *Nouvelle Héloïse* and of R.'s other major works, culminating in *Rêveries*.

Chaponnière, Paul. Jean-Jacques Rousseau. *In :* Grands hommes de la Suisse. Zurich, Editions Atlantis, Lausanne, Payot, 1945. (In German translation also). p. 146-57.
1907

Admirably succinct presentation of R.'s life and writings in which author points out what R. owes to Geneva and what he has contributed to life and literature.

Review : P. Chaix in AJJR 30:221, 1943-45.

Chuquet, Arthur. J.-J. Rousseau. Hachette, (1893) fifth ed. 1919. 201 p.
1908

" La collection [GEF] dans laquelle a paru cette étude en garantit l'excellence; quelque substantielles que soient ces deux cents pages, elles ne peuvent donner cependant qu'une vue très succincte d'un écrivain de l'importance de Rousseau;..." Schinz, p. 128-29.

Review : A. Schinz in EprR, p. 128-29, 232.

Courtois, Louis-J. Chronologie critique de la vie et des œuvres de Jean-Jacques Rousseau. AJJR 15:364 p., 1923. (Extracted and reprinted, Geneva, Jullien, 1924. 364 p.).
1909

Indispensable research aid. Meticulously documented day by day reconstruction of R.'s life and activity. In addition, book contains *Remarques critiques sur la correspondance générale de Rousseau telle qu'elle est contenue dans les éditions Hachette* (no. 1867) *et Streckeisen-Moultou* (no. 1868), *Bibliographie des ouvrages imprimés et des documents manuscrits utilisés dans la Chronologie et les Remarques, Index des ouvrages et fragments de Jean-Jacques Rousseau,* and *Index des noms propres.*

For methodology, see author's *Considérations sur la chronologie de la vie et des*

œuvres de Jean-Jacques Rousseau, IGB 45: 143-72, 1922-23.

Reviews : E. Carcassonne in RHL 32: 470-71, 1925; P. Chaponnière in BU, Jan.-June, 255, 1925; K. R. Gallas in Neo 11:57-58, 1925-26; L. Roustan in Rcr 92:124-26, Mar. 15, 1925; A. Schinz in EprR 98-99, 303 ff.

Cresson, André. J.-J. Rousseau; sa vie, son œuvre, avec un exposé de sa philosophie. Alcan, 1940. 148 p.
1910

Purpose of collection in which this book appears is to give to a large public knowledge of great philosophical doctrines. Book consists of biographical sketch (p. 1-38), exposition of R.'s philosophy (p. 39-92), and selections from his writings, mostly from *Contrat social* (p. 95-143). Completed by chronological list of R.'s works (p. 93-94) and selected bibliography dealing with his philosophical thought. Author points out various facets of R.'s philosophy, analyzes *Profession de foi du vicaire savoyard,* and shows how its principles illuminate his political and educational doctrines. Author's conclusion : R.'s philosophy was certainly imperfect, but important because of its influence.

Review : P. E. Schazmann in AJJR 29:291-92, 1941-42.

Ducros, Louis. Jean-Jacques Rousseau. Fontemoing, Boccard, 1908-1918. 3 v. V. I, De Genève à l'Hermitage (1712-1757). Fontemoing, 1908, 418 p. V. II, De Montmorency au Val de Travers (1757-1765) Boccard, 1917. 331 p. V. III, De l'Ile de Saint-Pierre à Ermenonville (1765-1778). Boccard, 1918. 424 p.
1911

Extensive and important study of R.'s life, personality, and work. Not to be neglected. In general, fair and impartial, avoiding extremes of praise or blame.

Reviews : (V. I) E. Champion in Rfr 57:72-73, 1909; D. Mornet in RHL 17: 419-23, 1910; E. Ritter in AJJR 6:315-17, 1910; L. Roustan in Rcr 68:180-82, 1909. (V. II) E. Ritter in AJJR 12:173-77, 1918-19. (V. III) H. Buffenoir in Rcr 87:212-16, 1920; (3 volumes) A. Schinz in EprR, p. 134-37.

Faguet, Emile. Jean-Jacques Rousseau. *In his :* Dix-huitième siècle : études littéraires. Société française d'imprimerie et de librairie, (of 1890) 13th ed. n.d. 327-407.
1912

Essay on R.'s life, writings, and " system." Views in section on *Contrat social* perhaps of special interest. Held

this work to be contradictory to general ideas of R.
Review : G. Monod in Rhist 43:417-21, 1890.

— Vie de Rousseau. Société française d'imprimerie et de librairie, [1911]. 417 p. 1913

" C'est le vrai livre pour ceux qui lisent et qui ne font pas métier d'érudition." Mornet, review, below, p. 216.
Reviews : B. Bouvier in AJJR 8:335-40, 1912; D. Mornet in RHL 19:215-17, 1912; A. Schinz in EprR, p. 282, 327.

[**Aimery de Pierrebourg, Marguerite**, *baronne.*] Jean-Jacques Rousseau et les femmes. Fayard, [1934]. 411 p. Author's pseud., Claude Ferval, at head of title. 1914
Utilizes Dufour edition of *Correspondance* (no. 1883). Excellent general biography.
Reviews : E. Henriot in *Le Temps*, July 3, 1934 ; A. Schinz in EprR, p. 143-44 ; J. Violette in AJJR 23:214-15, 1934.

Feugère, Anatole. Jean-Jacques Rousseau. RCC 34:223-36, 429-42, 638-54, Dec.-Mar. 1932-33; 66-83, 273-88, 558-72, 708-27, Apr.-July, 1933. 1915
Lecture course, characterized by Schinz as " ... la dernière étude compréhensive sur Rousseau..." EprR, p. 89. Publication not completed by RCC.
Reviews : F. Ruchon in AJJR 22:278-80, 1933; A. Schinz in EprR, p. 89-90.

Gauss, Christian. Jean-Jacques Rousseau. Encyclopedia Americana, 23:723-25, 1938. 1916
Concise essay on R.'s life, basic views, and significance. Bibliographical recommendations.
Review : P.-E. Schazmann in AJJR 29:299-300, 1941-42.

Gehrig, Hermann. Jean Jacques Rousseau; sein Leben und seine Schriften. Neuwied and Leipzig, Heuser, 1900-01. 3 v. 1917
Review : R. Mahrenholtz in ZFSL 11:149-50, 1889. (Review of an earlier edition.)

Geiger, Ludwig. Jean Jacques Rousseau, sein Leben und seine Werke. Leipzig, Quelle and Meyer, 1907. 131 p. 1918
Study characterized by Schinz as " excellent." EprR, p. 134.
Reviews : P. A. Becker in ZOG 59: 239-42, 1908; J. Dresch in RG 4:340, 1908; E. Ritter in AJJR 4:284-85, 1908.

Gerin, René. Jean-Jacques Rousseau. Rieder, 1930. 80 p. LX pl. 1919
Brief and commendable presentation of R.'s life and writings which Courtois calls a " tour de force " and an " excellent manuel." Book is not, however, entirely free from errors. Sixty pages of fine, interesting iconography follow text.
Reviews : L.-J. Courtois in AJJR 19: 260, 1929-30; F. Gaiffe in RU 42:49, Jan. 1933; D. Mornet in RHL 38:642, 1931; A. Schinz in EprR, p. 101, 299.

Gran, Gerhard von der Lippe. Jean Jacques Rousseau. Christiana, Aschehoug, 1910. 304 p. American edition : Jean Jacques Rousseau... trans. by Marcia H. Janson. New York, Scribner, 1912. 393 p. Published in England also, according to AJJR 9:99, 1913. 1920
Excellent life with shrewd evaluation of truth and falsity in *Confessions*. With R.'s almost complete lack of family training and moral stamina, author considers it remarkable that R. did not go to complete ruin. Saved by his pride, ambition, and fantasy (Amer. ed., p. 153). Corrects Lemaître (no. 1926) on essential sincerity of R.'s reform (p. 374-77) even though it was not complete. Book stops with *First discourse* and its consequences. " Even as early as about the year 1750 Rousseau was, in all essentials, the man he continued to be for the remainder of his life " (p. 392).
Review (of the 1910 edition) : A. Mercier in AJJR 7:184-85, 1911; (of the American edition), A. Schinz in EprR, p. 177.

Hendel, Charles W., *see* no. 1885. 1921

Josephson, Matthew. Jean-Jacques Rousseau. New York, Harcourt, Brace, [c1931]. 546 p. English edition, Gollancz, 1932. 562 p. 1922
Full-length biography based on best modern sources. Appreciative of R.'s original personality, but not blind to his weaknesses. Some discussion of his ideas, but main emphasis on the " life " in narrower sense.
Reviews : K. Anthony in NR 69:353-54, Feb. 10, 1932; G. R. Havens in SRL 8:487, Jan. 30, 1932; A. Schinz in AJJR 21:275-82, 1932; same in FR 5:408-14, 1931-32; same in EprR, p. 115; same in YR 21:623-24, 1931-32.

Lanson, Gustave. Jean-Jacques Rousseau. *In his :* Histoire de la littérature française,

18e édition. Hachette, (1894) 1924. 773-803. *See* no. 70. 1923

Gives brief biographical sketch, discusses unity of R.'s work, sources of his ideas, doctrines, and influence. Valuable and broad-minded treatment.

Text of this and subsequent editions essentially that of 12th edition (1912). Appendices of various editions, however, should be consulted. Text likewise that of author's *Histoire illustrée de la littérature française* (no. 71).

— Rousseau. *In :* La grande encyclopédie 28:1060-70, 1900. 1924

Excellent account of R.'s life, writings, and aims. *See also* Lanson, no. 1923.
Review : A. Schinz in EprR, p. 129, 373.

Laski, Harold J. A portrait of Jean Jacques Rousseau. YR 17:702-19, 1927-28. 1925
Stimulating and appreciative essay on R., " plebeian " and " citizen of Geneva," his significance to his own day and today.
Review : A. Schinz in AJJR 18:354-55, 1927-28.

Lemaître, Jules. Jean-Jacques Rousseau. Calmann-Lévy, 1907. 360 p. Tr. into English by Jeanne Mairet, Madame Charles Bigot. New York, McClure, 1907. 365 p. 1926

Important biography, inclined toward hostility.
Reviews : B. Bouvier in AJJR 4:304-09, 1908; L. Dumur in MerF 67:577-600, June 15, 1907; E. Faguet in APL 48:247-49, Apr. 21, 1907; G. Renard in GR 43:55-75, Apr. 10, 1907; E. Rod in RDM 5th per. 39:129-63, May 1, 1907; A. Schinz in Bookman 26:85-89, Sept. 1907; same in EprR, p. 64, 120, 132.

Mahrenholtz, Richard. Jean-Jacques Rousseau. Leben, Geistesentwickelung und Hauptwerke. Leipzig, Renger, 1889. 176 p. 1927
" ... demeure, croyons-nous, le meilleur ouvrage d'ensemble en Allemagne." Schinz, EprR, p. 127.
Review : A. Schinz in EprR, p. 127, 284 n.

Masson, Pierre-Maurice. La religion de J.-J. Rousseau. 2. éd. Hachette, 1916. 3 v. 1928
Remarkable study of R.'s intellectual and emotional life in connection with development and expression of his religious ideas. Believes R., though finally

Protestant, contributed to Catholic revival in France after Revolution. Supersedes all previous studies of subject. Extensive bibliography. *See* no. 2202A.
Reviews : I. Babbitt in MP 15:121-26, 1917-18; A. Cahen in RDS 2:163-70, 1916-17; G. Lanson in RHL 24:322-27, 1917; E. Ritter in AJJR 11:243-46, 1916-17; A. Schinz in EprR, p. 92, 265-66.

Maury, Fernand. Jean-Jacques Rousseau. *In :* Petit de Julleville, Histoire de la langue et de la littérature françaises des origines à 1900. Colin, (1896-99) 1922?-26. v. 6, p. 252-305. *See* no. 77. 1929

Conspectus of life and writings. *Bibliographie*, p. 314-15.

Morin, G. H. Essai sur la vie et le caractère de J.-J. Rousseau. Ledoyen, 1851. 604 p. 1930

" ... livre injustement négligé de nos jours... un des commentaires les plus minutieux et les plus consciencieux sur les points controversés de la vie de Rousseau." Schinz, EprR, p. 26, 121.
Review : A. Schinz in EprR, p. 26, 121, 338, 349.

Morley, John. Rousseau and his era. London, Macmillan, (1873) 1923. 2 v. 1931

Title as originally published : *Rousseau.* " L'ouvrage... demeure, en Angleterre, le meilleur travail d'ensemble, quand même il peut sembler aujourd'hui écrit dans un esprit un peu vieillot et arriéré en érudition." (Schinz, review below.)
Review : A. Schinz in EprR, p. 121-24.

Mornet, Daniel. Jean-Jacques Rousseau. *In :* Bédier and Hazard, Histoire de la littérature française illustrée. *See* 60, 2:117-30. 1932

Treats of R. as *philosophe*, novelist, and theorist on education; discusses his religion, politics, and *Confessions*.
Review : L.-J. Courtois in AJJR 17:231, 1926.

— Rousseau, l'homme et l'œuvre. Boivin, 1950. 187 p. (Collection : Connaissance des lettres ; ancienne collection, Le livre de l'étudiant). 1932A

Excellent brief discussion of R.'s life and works by a master of the subject. Factual, balanced, objective, free from polemics. " Le dessein de ce petit livre... est seulement de rassembler toutes les certitudes qu'un lecteur ou un critique ne saurait contredire sans tomber dans le paradoxe ou la fantaisie pure " (p. 7).

Mowat, Robert B. Jean-Jacques Rousseau. Bristol, Arrowsmith, 1938. 368 p.   1933

This biography, which reviewer below calls " la plus copieuse, en langue anglaise, depuis celle de John Morley en 1873," utilizes R.'s *Correspondance générale* edited by Dufour, (no. 1883). Review : L. Ledermann in AJJR 30: 193, 1943-45.

Musset, Victor Donatien de, called **Musset-Pathay.** Histoire de la vie et des ouvrages de J.-J. Rousseau. Dupont, (1821, 2 v.) 1827. 473 p.   1934

" Le premier ouvrage qui compte et qui, aujourd'hui encore, doit être consulté par quiconque s'occupe de Rousseau... Étude consciencieuse..." Schinz, EprR, p. 120. Review : A. Schinz in EprR, p. 104, 120, 348.

Nourrisson, Jean Félix. J.-J. Rousseau et le Rousseauisme. Fontemoing, 1903. 507 p.   1935

" Cette histoire de Rousseau et du Rousseauisme ne prétend pas... apporter des documents nouveaux. Elle s'efforce seulement d'être une synthèse des travaux déjà parus. M. Nourrisson semble avoir suffisamment connu les études de langue française... Je n'ai pas vu la moindre allusion aux travaux critiques allemands dont quelques-uns... sont loin de s'accorder avec ses conclusions personnelles. En définitive, si l'on y cherche autre chose que les idées philosophiques et politiques de l'auteur, le livre peut rester comme un répertoire commode de toutes les contradictions maladives où se sont embarrassées la vie de Rousseau et parfois ses ouvrages." Mornet, *infra*, p. 352. Reviews : G. Lanson in RU 12²:62, 1903; D. Mornet in RHL 10:351-52, 1903; G. Picot in AMP 159 (ns 59), 755-56, 1903; F. Pillon in Rph 58:307-09: 1904; A. Schinz in EprR, p. 120, 131-32, 399.

Proal, Louis. La psychologie de Jean-Jacques Rousseau. New ed. Alcan, (1923) 1930. 463 p.   1936

" Tel qu'il est, cet ouvrage, d'une lecture attachante, a rassemblé en une belle gerbe quantité de matériaux précieux pour l'édification d'une psychologie définitive de Jean-Jacques." Claparède, review below, p. 303.

Reviews : E. Bréhier in RIE 79:59, 1925; H. Buffenoir in Rcr 90:433-34, 1923; E. Claparède in AJJR 16:302-03, 1924-25; S. Moreau-Rendu in RP 31: 348-50, 1924; A. Schinz in EprR, p. 99, 357, 387.

Revue de métaphysique et de morale (Bicentenary number). 20:265-482, 1912.   1937

Les idées philosophiques et religieuses :
Boutroux, E. Remarques sur la philosophie de Rousseau   p. 265-74
Höffding, H. Rousseau et la religion   p. 275-93
Parodi, D. La philosophie religieuse de J.-J. Rousseau   p. 295-320
Les idées politiques et sociales :
Bosanquet, B. Les idées politiques de Rousseau   p. 321-40
Bouglé, C. Rousseau et le socialisme   p. 341-52
Bourguin, M. Les deux tendances de Rousseau   p. 353-69
Jaurès, J. Les idées politiques et sociales de J.-J. Rousseau   p. 371-81
Stammler, R. Notion et portée de la Volonté générale chez Jean-Jacques Rousseau   p. 383-89
Les idées pédagogiques :
Claparède, E. J.-J. Rousseau et la conception fonctionnelle de l'enfance p. 391-416
Influences et variétés :
Lévy-Bruhl, L. Quelques mots sur la querelle de Hume et de Rousseau (*See* no.1991)   p. 417-28
Delbos, V. Rousseau et Kant   p. 429-39
Benrubi, J. Goethe et Schiller, continuateurs de Rousseau   p. 441-60
Dwelshauvers, G. Rousseau et Tolstoï   p. 461-82
Reviews : A. François in AJJR 9:139-41, 1913; A. Schinz in EprR, p. 75.

J.-J. Rousseau jugé par les Français d'aujourd'hui. Perrin, 1890. 575 p.   1938
Introduction par John Grand-Carteret   iii-xx
Poésies par MM. Chantavoine, Grandmougin, Clovis Hugues, Eugène Manuel, Marc Bonnefoy   xxiii-xxx
L'homme
I.   Défense de Rousseau con-

Reviews : R. Mahrenholtz in ZFSL 12²:
117-20, 1890; H. Pergameni in RBelgique
66:190-92, 1890; A. Schinz in EprR,
p. 54-55.

**J.-J. Rousseau jugé par les Genevois
d'aujourd'hui; conférences faites à Genève** par J. Braillard, H. F. Amiel, A. Oltramare, J. Hornung, A. Bouvier and Marc-
Monnier. Geneva, Sandoz, 1879. 295 p.
1939

Oltramare, A. Les idées de
J.-J. Rousseau sur l'éduca-
tion   p. 67-133
Hornung, J. Les idées poli-
tiques de J.-J. Rousseau   p. 135-95
Bouvier, A. Les idées religieuses de J.-J. Rousseau p. 197-261
Marc-Monnier. J.-J. Rous-
seau et les étrangers   p. 263-95
Review : A. Schinz in EprR, p. 44-45,
202, 271-72, 279.

**Jean-Jacques Rousseau; leçons faites à
l'Ecole des hautes études sociales, par**
MM. F. Baldensperger, G. Beaulavon,
I. Benrubi, C. Bouglé, A. Cahen, V. Delbos,
G. Dwelshauvers, G. Gastinel, D. Mornet,
D. Parodi, F. Vial. Alcan, 1912. 303 p.
                                      1940

Préface, par G. Lanson   iii-xii
I.   La vie, par A. Cahen   p.   1
II.   Le Rousseauisme avant Rous-
        seau, par D. Mornet   p. 47
III.   Jean-Jacques Rousseau et la
        philosophie encyclopédiste,
        par G. Gastinel   p. 67
IV.   Rousseau éducateur, par F.
        Vial   p. 89
V.   La philosophie religieuse de
        J.-J. Rousseau, par D. Pa-
        rodi   p. 121
VI.   La doctrine politique du
        Contrat social, par G.
        Beaulavon   p. 155
VII.   Rousseau et le socialisme,
        par C. Bouglé   p. 171
VIII.   Rousseau et Kant, par V.
        Delbos   p. 187
IX.   Rousseau et les grands repré-
        sentants de la pensée alle-
        mande, par I. Benrubi   p. 201
X.   Rousseau et Tolstoï, par
        G. Dwelshauvers   p. 251
XI.   Rousseau et le romantisme,
        par F. Baldensperger   p. 279
Reviews : L. Pinvert in AJJR 9:108-09,
1913; A. Schinz in EprR, p. 75, 261 n.

Rowbotham, Arnold H. Rousseau and his
critics. Srev 38:385-97, 1930.   1941

  Good summary of R. criticism. See
also Andersson, no. 1902, and Dumur,
no. 1973.
  Review : A. Schinz in AJJR 19:246,
1929-30.

Saint-Pierre, Jacques-Henri-Bernardin
de. La vie et les ouvrages de Jean-Jacques
Rousseau; édition critique publiée avec de
nombreux fragments inédits, par Maurice
Souriau. Cornély, 1907. 190 p.   1942

  Important edition of projected and
uncompleted biography of R. by his
friend and disciple.
  Reviews : A. François in AJJR 4:315-
20, 1908; A. Schinz in MLN 23:260-61,
1908.

Schinz, Albert. Jean-Jacques Rousseau.
ESS 13:445-47, 1935.   1943

  Concise essay on R. and writings.
Bibliographical recommendations.
  Review : L.-J. Courtois in AJJR 23:
210, 1934.

— La pensée de Jean-Jacques Rousseau.
Northampton, Mass., Smith college, 1929.
2 v. (Smith college fiftieth anniversary
publications, no. 9). Also : Alcan, 1929.
521 p. See 3075.   1944

  Author's most important contribution
to study of R.'s ideas, summarizing nearly
lifetime of work and containing gist of
number of Schinz's previous articles. Cf.
Schinz's EprR, 140-42, 184-85, 186-87,
194, 208, 240-41, 277-80, 357-58, 375-76.
Numerous reviews indicate importance of
this work and offer at same time somewhat differing viewpoints.
  Reviews : G. Ascoli in Rcr 98:557-58,
1931; L.-J. Courtois in JGen Jan. 3,
1930; E. P. Dargan in MP 28:117-20,
1930-31; V. L. Dedeck-Héry in RR 24:
167-70, 1933; P. Kohler in AJJR 19:
268-87, 1929-30; A. O. Lovejoy in MLN
46:41-46, 1931; F. M. in RP 30 ns 1:
195-98, Mar.-Apr., 1930; E. Magne in
MerF 223:421-24, Oct. 15, 1930; J. E.
Morel in RHM 5:289-302, 1930; D. Mornet in RHL 37:233-37, 1930; H. de
Ziégler in BU, Oct., 1930, p. 528-29;
Anon. in RMM 37, 1930, Supplement to
Jan.-Mar. number, p. 7-9.

Seillière, Ernest Antoine Aimé Léon,
baron. Jean-Jacques Rousseau. Garnier,
1921. 458 p.   1945

  With Irving Babbitt, Paul Elmer More,
and Lasserre, Seillière is vigorous preacher
against what he considers harmful influence of R. on modern world.
  Reviews : H. Buffenoir in Rfr 75:42-47,
1922; A. François in AJJR 14:278-80,
1922; G. M. in RIE 78:190, 1924;
A. Schinz in EprR, p. 65, 88.

Smith, Horatio E. Rousseau. In his :
Masters of French literature. New York,
Scribner, 1937. p. 163-217.   1946

  Fine and very readable essay for general
reader.
  Reviews : L. Cons in RR 28:290-93,

1937; A. Schinz in AJJR 26:328-30, 1937; C. H. C. Wright in MLN 53:472-73, 1938.

[Staël-Holstein, Anne Louise Germaine (Necker) *baronne* de]. Lettres sur les ouvrages et le caractère de J.-J. Rousseau. Dernière éd., augm. d'une lettre de Mme la comtesse Alexandre de Vassy, et d'une réponse de Mme la baronne de Staël. [n.p.] (1788) 1789. 92 p. 1947

Early study of R.'s work and personality by a near-contemporary. Revealing both for influence of R. and development of Mme de Staël. *See* Schinz, EprR, p. 8.

Tiersot, Julien. J.-J. Rousseau. *See* 355. 1948

Reviews : E. Faguet in APL 59:254-55, 1912; A. François in AJJR 9:134-35, 1913; L. Roustan in Rcr 75:374-75, 1913; mention by A. Schinz in EprR, p. 292-94, 325.

Vallette, Gaspard. Jean-Jacques Rousseau, genevois. Plon-Nourrit; Geneva, Jullien, 1911. 454 p. 1949

" Le but du livre est de ' montrer comment et combien Rousseau est Genevois, et combien il le restera toujours dans sa vie, dans son caractère, dans sa pensée et dans son œuvre,' et qu'on ne peut expliquer Rousseau ' sans connaître la Genève de son temps.' Il y a une excellente bibliographie au bas des pages; le tout est d'une documentation très sûre, et souvent minutieuse. Un livre qu'aucun étudiant de Rousseau n'a le droit d'ignorer..." Schinz, EprR, p. 137-38. Reviews : C. Borgeaud in AJJR 8: 354-65, 1912; D. Mornet in RHL 19: 217-18, 1912; M. Rouff in Rfr 61:177-80, 1911; L. Roustan in Rcr 71:353-55, 1911; G. Rudler in RU 20:324-26, Nov. 15, 1911; A. Schinz in EprR, p. 71-72, 137-38.

Vulliamy, Colwyn E. Rousseau. London, Bles, 1931. 294 p. 1950

" ... an essentially sane book, extremely readable, and well documented." B. Dobrée, *infra*, p. 300. Reviews : B. Dobrée in Spect 147:299-300, Sept. 5, 1931; A. P. Nicholson in SatR 152:59, July 11, 1931; A. L. Sells in AJJR 20:246-48, 1931.

Wright, Ernest H. The meaning of Rousseau. London, Oxford univ. press, Milford, 1929. 168 p. 1951

One of best evaluations of R.'s thought in light of his intentions at time. Shows real meaning of his theory of " the natural goodness of man " and that it was not ridiculous as he conceived it, though it has often been made to seem so by modern hostile interpreters. An admirable antidote to Irving Babbitt (no. 2029). *See :* Ellis (no. 2169), Havens (no. 2077), Lovejoy (no. 2179), Moreau-Rendu (no. 2115), and Schinz (no. 2139). Reviews : G. Ascoli in Rcr 98:555-56, 1931; H. J. Laski in TT 10:938, Aug. 2, 1929; D. Mornet in RHL 37:107-09, 1930; A. Schinz in EprR, p. 138-39; H. Sée in Rhist 162:165-66, 1929; A. L. Sells in AJJR 19:235-36, 1929-30; R. Shafer in Bookman 71:503-12, Aug., 1930.

Specialized Biographical Studies

Aurenche, Louis. Jean-Jacques Rousseau chez Monsieur de Mably. Société française d'éditions littéraires et techniques, [1934.] 146 p. 1952

" Dans cet excellent ouvrage d'une sûre érudition, M. Aurenche nous fait connaître le résultat de ses recherches sur la famille de Mably, sur le préceptorat de Jean-Jacques auprès des enfants du Grand Prévôt, sur ses relations lyonnaises." Ruchon, review below, p. 212. *See also* Grosclaude (no. 1983). Reviews : F. Ruchon in AJJR 23:212-14, 1934; A. Schinz in EprR, p. 315-16.

Allen, Isabel Wait. Thérèse Le Vasseur. Cleveland, Ohio, 1933. (Unpublished diss., Western Reserve University). 557 p. 1952A

This sizable study available by interlibrary loan. Is included here, not only because possible duplication of doctoral labor may be avoided by calling attention to it but also because it is a good *étude d'ensemble*. In reality, and inevitably, it is more a life of R. than of Thérèse, though writer seems to have tapped, for all practical purposes, available sources of information concerning Thérèse, whom she considers to have had the mentality of a seven-year old. It was R. who made all decisions. *See* Martin-Decaen (no. 1994), and Wille (no. 2026).

Bandy, W. T. Rousseau's flight from England. RR 39:107-21, 1948. 1953

New facts on R.'s last weeks in England and on pension received from George III. Six letters from Hume to Davenport, written in April and May, 1767. Text of article of May 12, 1767, in *London chronicle*, which decided R.'s departure. *See also :* Courtois, 1972, Lévy-Bruhl, 1991, Guillemin, 1985, Peoples, 1998, Pottle, 2004, Roddier, 2012.

Beaulavon, Georges. A propos du portrait de Jean-Jacques Rousseau par Jean Houël. AJJR 25:219-50, 1936.   1954

" ... c'est un modèle de ce que doivent être des travaux iconographiques." Schinz, EprR, p. 299.

Benedetto, L.-F.   Madame de Warens d'après de nouveaux documents. Plon-Nourrit, 1914.   328 p.   (Under title of Madame de Warens, la " maman " de Rousseau, Florence, 1921.   328 p.)   1955

Uses documents in Turin archives (1726-30) not found in Mugnier's book (no. 1997). Contains discussion of R.'s stay at Turin, and of mysterious mission of Madame de Warens to Paris. Has reproduction of an authentic portrait of her. Benedetto's article, *Madame de Warens espionne de la maison de Savoie*, in RDS 1:366-95, 1913, is taken from this book. *See also :* Mugnier (no. 1997). Reviews : E. Ritter in AJJR 10:206-12, 1914-15; A. Schinz in EprR, p. 97.

Berthoud, Fritz.   J.-J. Rousseau au Val de Travers, 1762-1765.   Fischbacher, 1881. 410 p.   1956

This item and the next are important for knowledge of R.'s exile in Switzerland in three-year period following condemnation of *Émile*. " ... livres classiques, mais depuis longtemps épuisés... [qui] gardent leur valeur malgré de nouvelles recherches sur maint point." Schinz (EprR, p. 340). Reviews : A. Le Roy in RPL 19²:173-77, Feb. 11, 1882; A. Schinz in EprR, p. 340.

— J.-J. Rousseau et le pasteur de Montmollin, 1762-1765; suite et complément de " J. J. Rousseau au Val de Travers." Fleurier, 1884. 373 p.   1957

Extensive study of important and even crucial episode in R.'s career. Review : A. Schinz in EprR, p. 340.

Boswell, James.   Boswell with Rousseau and Voltaire, 1764. *See* 1748.   1958

Contains Boswell's letter to William Johnson Temple telling of his visit to R. at Môtiers, *Dialogue with Rousseau*, anecdotes of R., and facsimile of letter

from R. to Boswell, dated Môtiers, May 30, 1765. On Boswell papers and Boswell's visit to R., *see* Schinz (no. 2016). *See also* Charly Guyot, *De Rousseau à Mirabeau ; pèlerins de Môtiers et prophètes de 89.* Neuchâtel, Attinger, 1936.

Bouchardy, François.   Note sur Condillac et Rousseau. MélBB, p. 17-31.   1959

Cautious article devoted to problem of Condillac's influence on R. Documented by parallel texts from writings of both. Important especially for *Second discours* and *Essai sur l'origine des langues*.

Bouvier, Bernard.   Mélanges d'histoire littéraire et de philologie offerts à Bernard Bouvier...   Geneva, Société anonyme des éditions Sonor, 1920.   360 p.   1960

For annotations of two of four studies of this volume dealing with R. *See :* Bouchardy (no. 1959) and Oltramare (no. 2123). Reviews : A. François in AJJR 13: 261-62, 1920-21; A. Schinz in EprR, p. 345.

Bouvier, C.   La bibliothèque des Charmettes. Chambéry, Gentil, 1914.   44 p.   1961

Information on library of M. de Conzié, books which R. used. Review : A. Schinz in EprR, p. 148, 315.

Brunetière, F.   Voltaire et J.-J. Rousseau. *In his :* Études critiques sur l'histoire de la littérature française. Hachette, 1-8 series, 1896-1907. 3:259-90, 1898.   1962

Stimulating pages on contrasts between Voltaire and R. Also appeal for equity towards latter. Essay is a corrective to Maugras (nos. 1719, 2108).

— La folie de J.-J. Rousseau. *In his :* Études critiques sur l'histoire de la littérature française. Hachette, 1896-1907, 4:325-55. 1963

Exposition of relationship in R. between literary genius and " folie," origin of which author attributes to R.'s " sensibilité." Review : L. Claretie in Rcr 33:30-32, Jan. 11, 1892.

Buffenoir, Hippolyte.   La comtesse d'Houdetot, une amie de J.-J. Rousseau. *See* 259. 1964

" Le travail de M. Buffenoir sur la comtesse d'Houdetot est peut-être le meilleur que nous ayons sur cette amie de Rousseau, et l'auteur montre très bien que c'est à Rousseau qu'elle doit surtout sa renommée." Chuquet, *infra*, p. 213. In Lanson's opinion, Buffenoir's " ... chapitre qui doit exciter le plus vivement la curiosité, est le plus faiblement et vaguement traité : celui des relations de la comtesse avec Jean-Jacques." *Infra*, p. 261. Book supplemented by no. 1965. Reviews : A. Chuquet in AMP 181: 213, 1914; C. François in RHM 3:520-21, 1901-02; G. Lanson in RU 10²:261-63, 1901; A. Schinz in EprR, p. 58, 337.

— La comtesse d'Houdetot, sa famille, ses amis, avec neuf portraits et illustrations. *See* 260.   1965

For R. consult Chapter IV. Numerous letters of R. to Countess are here published for first time. Book supplements his earlier work, no. 1964. Reviews : G. Lanson in RU 14²:239, 1905; E. Ritter in ZFSL 29²:258-61, 1906; A. Schinz in EprR, p. 58, 204, 337.

— La maréchale de Luxembourg (1707-1787); souvenirs, documents, témoignages. *See* 284.   1966

" M. Buffenoir... se devait, après la peinture fidèle et gracieuse de Mme d'Houdetot, de donner, sur un tableau d'ensemble, dont la poésie voile l'érudition—le récit touchant de l'amitié qui unit Rousseau et les Luxembourg. Ces trois chapitres, IV, V et VI ne fournissent pas de faits inédits, mais ils situent en leur vraie place ceux qui étaient dispersés." Courtois. *infra*, p. 293. Reviews : L.-J. Courtois in AJJR 16: 293-94, 1924-25; K. R. Gallas in Neo 9:297-98, 1924; D. Mornet in RHL 33:123-24, 1926; A. Schinz in EprR, p. 338.

— Les portraits de Jean-Jacques Rousseau; étude historique et iconographique; souvenirs, documents, témoignages. Leroux, 1913. 271 p.   1967

Reviews : A. Chuquet in AMP 181: 213-14, 1914; A. François in AJJR 10: 213-22, 1914-15.

— Le prestige de Jean-Jacques Rousseau; souvenirs, documents, anecdotes. Émile-Paul, 1909. 476 p.   1968

Reviews : F. Baldensperger in Rcr 68: 491, 1909; A. François in AJJR 6:327-29, 1910; E. Ritter in ZFSL 35²:218, March 26, 1910.

— Le tombeau de Jean-Jacques Rousseau à

Ermenonville. RDS [4]:173-96, 335-60, 1917.   1969

Study deals with iconographic records and with writings about Ermenonville and its distinguished visitors. *See :* Martin-Decaen (no. 1994). Review : A. François in AJJR 12:181, 1918-19.

Cabanès, Augustin. J.-J. Rousseau. *In his :* Grands névropathes, malades immortels. Michel, [1930-c31]. 2 v. 2:37-70.   1970

" Ce que nous nous sommes attaché, avant tout, à établir, dans ce travail exclusivement voué à l'étude de la névrose de Rousseau, en laissant de côté ses autres manifestations pathologiques, c'est que sa constitution, nettement psychopathique, fut un terrain éminemment propice à l'éclosion du délire que de nombreuses causes occasionnelles favorisèrent. Si ce délire n'éclata qu'après la quarantaine, on peut dire qu'il existait en germe depuis l'enfance.
" Ses troubles psychasthéniques, ses tendances hypocondriaques, sa timidité excessive, ses scrupules poussés jusqu'à la minutie, sa sensibilité hyperesthésiée, son émotivité morbide l'annonçaient, en rendaient l'échéance fatale." p. 70. Review : A. Schinz in EprR, p. 360-61.

Chaponnière, Paul. Voltaire chez les Calvinistes. *See* 1703.   1971

Courtois, Louis J. Le séjour de Jean-Jacques Rousseau en Angleterre (1766-1767); lettres et documents inédits. AJJR 6:1-313, 1910. *Also :* Lausanne, Pache-Varidel and Bron, 1911. 315 p. (Diss., Geneva). *See* 3070.   1972

Most extensive study of subject, still valid except for occasional details of later scholarship. *See* Bandy (no. 1953). Reviews : D. Mornet in RHL 19:215, 1912; A. Schinz in EprR, p. 343.

Dumur, Louis. Les détracteurs de Jean-Jacques. MerF 67:577-600, June 15, 1907.   1973

Spirited defense of R. against such opponents as Lasserre, Lemaître, and Maurras. " Une des meilleures contre-attaques qui aient jamais été faites," wrote Schinz, review below, p. 68. *See* Andersson (no. 1902), and Rowbotham (no. 1941). Review : A. Schinz in EprR, p. 68-69.

Ellis, (Miss) M. B. Jean-Jacques Rousseau : biographical problems (1732-1742). RR 38:117-32, 1947.   1974

Offers solutions to certain obscure points in R.'s life in decade prior to his final departure from Savoy. Deals with date and circumstances of R.'s " mysterious trip " to Besançon, his desire for contemplative life, significance of *Projet pour l'éducation de M. de Sainte-Marie*, and his movements in 1741.

Elosu, Suzanne. La maladie de Jean-Jacques Rousseau. Fischbacher, 1929. 158 p.   1975

In *résumé* of this book under same title (BSHM 23:349-56, 1929), author, a physician, explains thus method used in dealing with the malady : " Pour tenter d'élucider la question, il ne restait qu'un procédé : en essayant de se dégager des conclusions déjà émises, remonter à l'origine, interroger le malade lui-même dans ses écrits autobiographiques, prendre une observation aussi complète que possible." (p. 352). Conclusion of *résumé* : " Rousseau ne fut donc pas un fou, mais un malade urinaire tourmenté par la plus douloureuse des infirmités [*See* Allen, 1952A] et dont le génie sombra, vers la fin de sa vie, dans un délire toxique urémique circonstantiel. La distinction est d'importance, parce qu'elle permet de comprendre les apparentes contradictions de l'homme à la fois le plus grand et le plus misérable de son siècle." (p. 356).

Reviews : E. Henriot in Temps, July 2, 1929; R. de Saussure in AJJR 19:255-56, 1929-30; J. Séval in Cméd 36:194, 1929; P. Voivenel in MerF 214:183-85, Aug. 15, 1929.

Faguet, Emile. Les amies de Rousseau. Société française d'imprimerie et de librairie, 1912. 425 p.   1976

Author calls this book an appendix to his *Vie de Rousseau* and also a study in literary history. Among others, essays on, and R.'s relations with Mesdames de Warens, Larnage, Epinay, D'Houdetot, Verdelin, Luxembourg, Créqui, and Boufflers. Reasons to explain R.'s attraction for women set forth in concluding pages.

Reviews : B. Bouvier in AJJR 9:120-22, 1913; C. Dejob in Rcr 74:66-67, July 27, 1912.

— Rousseau artiste. Société française d'imprimerie et de librairie, [1912]. 394 p. 1977

" ... il examine comment la sensibilité et l'imagination de Rousseau influèrent sur sa manière de composer, de conter, de peindre son propre caractère, ceux de son entourage et des personnages qu'il a inventés; il étudie en lui l'orateur, le directeur, l'argumentateur, et enfin le rattache à son école." Dejob, review below, p. 187-88.

Reviews : C. Dejob in Rcr 75:187-89, Mar. 8, 1913; D. Mornet in RHL 20: 723-24, 1913.

Foster, Elizabeth A. Le dernier séjour de J.-J. Rousseau à Paris, 1770-1778. Northampton, Mass., 1921. 184 p. (SSML v. 2, nos. 2-3, Jan.-Apr., 1921). (Diss., Smith College).   1978

Shows that final eight years of R.'s life, in spite of his exaggerated fears of plot against him, were not in general somber. R. was not the unsociable being usually depicted, but lived tranquil life, on whole, and even made new acquaintances. Important background for the *Dialogues* and *Rêveries*.

Reviews : L.-J. Courtois in AJJR 14: 275-76, 1922; D. Mornet in RHL 29:370-72, 1922; L. Roustan in Rcr ns 89:289-90, 1922; A. Schinz in EprR, p. 162, 164, n., 345.

François, Alexis. J.-J. Rousseau et leurs Excellences. Lausanne, Éditions SPES, 1924. 109 p.   1979

" Entendons : ' Comment Leurs Excellences du sénat de Berne ont chassé J.-J. Rousseau d'Yverdon, où il s'était réfugié après l'affaire de l'*Émile*, et condamné eux-mêmes l'*Émile*.' C'est le commentaire d'une page des *Confessions*. M. A. François l'a fait avec son habituelle et minutieuse précision... Nous apprenons à y mieux connaître des amis de Rousseau, notamment Daniel Roguin... Tscharner, Tissot et d'autres, et ses ennemis Bonnet, Haller, etc." Mornet, *infra*, p. 122-23.

Reviews : D. Mornet in RHL 33: 122-23, 1926; E. Ritter in RHV 33:29-30, 1925; A. Schinz in MLN 41:428-29, 1926, and in EprR, p. 99-100.

Gallas, K. R. Autour de Marc-Michel Rey et de Rousseau. AJJR 17:73-90, 1926.   1980

" Les travaux de M. Gallas sur Marc-Michel Rey... remettent en lumière la touchante physionomie de ces amis fidèles, que la défiance de Rousseau finit par écarter." E. Carcassonne in RHL 35:595, 1928. *See* Schinz, no. 2018.

Girardin, Fernand. Iconographie de Jean-Jacques Rousseau; portraits, scènes, habitations, souvenirs. Morel (Eggimann), 1909. 344 p.   1981

Basic study of Rousseau iconography. Reviews : P. Bonnefon in RHL 15:760, 1908; L. Pinvert in AJJR 5:297-99, 1909.

— Iconographie des œuvres de Jean-Jacques Rousseau, pour faire suite à l'Iconographie de Jean-Jacques Rousseau, suivie d'un addendum à cette iconographie. Morel (Eggimann), [1910.] 262 p. 1982

Essential supplement to preceding title. Review : L. Pinvert in AJJR 7:168-70, 1911.

Grosclaude, Pierre. Jean-Jacques Rousseau à Lyon. AnL, Nouv. sér. II. Droit, lettres.—fasc. 43). Lyon, Rey; Paris, Alcan, 1933. 125 p. (Diss., Paris). 1983

" … résume ce qu'on savait, y compris le séjour de 1770; bonne bibliographie et appendice intéressant sur la question du *Devin* (qu'est-ce qui appartient à Rousseau ?)." Schinz, review below. *See also* Aurenche, no. 1952.

Reviews : L.-J. Courtois in AJJR 22: 273, 1933; E. Magne in MerF 254:574-75, 1934; A. Schinz in EprR, p. 316.

Guillemin, Henri. Les affaires de l'Ermitage (1756-1757); examen critique des documents. AJJR 29:59-258, 1941-42. 1984

Detailed critique of R.'s *Confessions*, *Mémoires* of Mme d'Epinay, Diderot's testimony regarding R., actions of Saint-Lambert and of Grimm. Reëstablishes chronology of R.'s stay at Hermitage in 1756 and 1757 (cf. Courtois, no. 1909). Finds errors and falsifications on all sides, but those of R. of less consequence and for most part unintentional. Important study which must be essential basis for any further investigation of many difficult and controversial problems involved. But *see* Ritter, no. 2011.

— " Cette affaire infernale," l'affaire J.-J. Rousseau-Hume 1766. Plon, [1942]. 353 p. 1985

Vivid, but partisan study of subject, favoring entirely R. *See also* Bandy (no. 1953), Lévy-Bruhl (no. 1991), Peoples (no. 1998), Pottle (no. 2004), Roddier (no. 2012).

Reviews : P. Kohler in AJJR 29:300-15, 1941-42; B. Lalande in RHph ns 12:85-86, 1944.

— Un homme, deux ombres (Jean-Jacques—Julie—Sophie). Geneva, Éditions du milieu du monde, 1943. 323 p. 1986

Method, purpose, and general result of Guillemin's version of oft-told story of

R.'s love affair with Mme d'Houdetot are evident in last paragraph of *Avant-propos* : " Il fallait donc, avant toutes choses, aller aux sources, revoir tous les documents, ceux de Paris et ceux de Suisse, étudier les lettres même, en recourant le plus possible aux originaux autographes, établir une chronologie précise enfin et sûre. Au terme d'une pareille enquête beaucoup de choses apparaissent différentes de ce qu'on les avait crues d'abord, sur la foi des livres." Guillemin's interpretation of this ugly episode leads him to this conclusion concerning rôles of R. and his enemies : " Entre Grimm et Diderot d'une part, et Rousseau de l'autre, tous trois successivement, sous nos yeux, coupables en effet d'insincérité, on notera pourtant cette différence : Rousseau ment pour se couvrir, parce qu'il a peur—peur de Saint-Lambert, peur de l'opinion, peur de Dieu; Grimm et Diderot mentent contre quelqu'un, contre un homme qui les gêne et qu'ils ont résolu de perdre. Rousseau est un malheureux, si l'on veut même un misérable, empêtré dans une tentation du cœur et des sens, et qui patauge honteusement dans le bourbier où il s'est fourré; Grimm et Diderot sont les spadassins d'une cause qui les tient au ventre, et ils mènent une chasse à l'homme." (p. 312). *See* Ritter, no. 2011.

Review : C. Guyot in AJJR 30:216-20, 1943-45.

Hervier, Marcel. Jean-Jacques Rousseau. *In his :* Les écrivains français jugés par leurs contemporains. V. II, Le dix-huitième siècle. *See* 67. Rousseau, p. 140-202. 1987

Valuable collection of contemporary opinions. Review : A. Schinz in EprR, p. 104.

Jansen, Albert. Jean-Jacques Rousseau als Botaniker. Berlin, Reimer, 1884. 482 p. 1988

Review : Schinz, EprR, p. 291.

— Jean-Jacques Rousseau als Musiker. *See* 325. 1989

Review : A. Schinz in EprR, p. 291.

Lacassagne, Alexandre. La mort de Jean-Jacques Rousseau. MAL 3rd ser. 13: 273-323, 1913. Extracted and reprinted: Lyon, Rey, 1913. 57 p. *See also his :* Les dernières années et la mort de Jean-Jacques Rousseau. AAcr 28:721-80, 1913. Extracted and reprinted : Lyon, Rey, 1913. 64 p. 1990

" Étude psychologico-médicale, pour conclure, après examen de toutes les opinions émises sur la question, à la mort naturelle par urémie, suivie de chute accidentelle. L'auteur expose et écarte l'hypothèse " [assassination with hammer by Thérèse Levasseur] " du docteur Julien Raspail, chez qui il a examiné le masque mortuaire de Rousseau." Pinvert, *infra*. Death mask by Houdon reproduced here.

Reviews : J. Flach in AMP 181 (ns 81): 616-17, 1914; L. Pinvert in AJJR 10:225, 1914-15; A. Schinz in EprR, p. 347, 349-50.

Lévy-Bruhl, L.   Quelques mots sur la querelle de Hume et de Rousseau. RMM 20:417-28, 1912.   1991

Except for one unpublished letter (from Mme de Saint-Maur to Hume), this is mere recapitulation, completely superseded by more recent studies. *See also* Bandy (no. 1953), Guillemin (no. 1985), Peoples (no. 1998), Pottle (no. 2004), Roddier, (no. 2012).

Macdonald, *Mrs*. Frederika (Richardson). Jean Jacques Rousseau, a new criticism. New York, Putnam; London, Chapman and Hall, 1906. 2 v.   1992

Presentation of new material derived from minute study of the MSS of the novel of Mme d'Epinay, showing especially changes and intercalations done by hand or on advice of Diderot. Work corrects many false notions of R. current during 19th century, but, because of unwarranted hypotheses and misinterpretations, adds many others. More objective study of same documents needed. *See* Torrey, no. 2021.

Reviews : G. Charlier in RBelgique 2nd ser. 57:150-63, 260-72, 1909; L. Maury in RPL July 3, 1909, p. 26-30; E. Rod in RDM 413:129-63, May 1, 1907; A. Schinz in EprR, p. 166-67, 327; G. Vallette in AJJR 3:256-67, 1907.

— La légende de Jean-Jacques Rousseau rectifiée d'après une nouvelle critique et des documents nouveaux. (Traduit de l'anglais par Georges Roth). Hachette, 1909. 297 p.   1993

Translation, in condensed form, of preceding book.

Reviews : J. de Gourmont in MerF 81:683-84, Oct. 16, 1909; L. Maury in RPL July 3, 1909, p. 26-30 ; D. Mornet in RHL 17:417-19, 1910 ; L. Roustan in Rcr 68:182-83, 1909; G. Rudler in RU 19¹:348-50, 1910.

Martin-Decaen, André. Le dernier ami de J.-J. Rousseau : le marquis René de Girardin, 1735-1808. Perrin, 1912. 251 p.   1994

Author has made use of Girardin family archives. Chapters 5, 6, 7 and 8 are devoted to R. They deal, respectively, with *Rousseau à Ermenonville, La mort de Rousseau, L'héritage de Rousseau, La veuve de Jean-Jacques*, and *Les pèlerins de l'Ile des peupliers et la gloire d'Ermenonville*. Chapter 7 is extracted from the author's article in the RPar, 1995; see also Allen, no. 1952A. In connection with materials presented in chapter 8, see Buffenoir, no. 1969.

Reviews : E. Faguet in APL 60:93-95, Feb. 2, 1913; J. de Gourmont in MerF 100:610-11, Dec. 1, 1912; L. Pinvert in AJJR 9:128-29, 1913; L. Roustan in Rcr 75:373-74, 1913.

— Marie-Thérèse Levasseur, " veuve de J.-J. Rousseau." RPar 18:368-96, Sept. 15, 1911.   1995

See above, no. 1994.

Moebius, Paul Julius.   J. J. Rousseau's Krankheitsgeschichte. Leipzig, Vogel, 1889. 192 p.   1996

" ... livre... qui continue à faire autorité." Schinz, p. 49. *See also :* F. Brunetière, no. 1963.

Review : A. Schinz in EprR, p. 49, 349, 357.

Mugnier, François. Madame de Warens et J.-J. Rousseau; étude historique et critique. Calmann-Lévy, 1891. 443 p. 1997

" ... contribution originale aux études rousseauistes, et qui demeure de premier ordre..." Schinz. *See also*, Benedetto, no. 1955.

Reviews : A. Chuquet in Rcr 33:510-12, June 27, 1892; A. François in AJJR 1: 307-08, 1905; E. Ritter in ZFSL 14²: 14-19, 1892; A. Schinz in EprR, p. 56.

Peoples Margaret H.   La querelle Rousseau-Hume. AJJR 18:1-331, 1927-28. *See* 3073.   1998

Well-documented and comprehensive study which, although not perhaps entirely convincing as interpretation of Hume's motives and of R.'s behavior, still must be regarded as most reliable work on subject to date. Regrettable that text was not more carefully edited. *See :* Bandy (no. 1953), Guillemin (no. 1985), Lévy-Bruhl (no. 1991), Pottle (no. 2004), Roddier, (no. 2012).

Review : E. Carcassonne in RHL 38: 454-55, 1931.

Pittard, Mme Hélène (Dufour). Jean-Jacques Rousseau et Madame de Warens, by Noëlle Roger, *pseud.* RDM 7th per. 23:639-59, Oct. 1, 1924.   1999

New light on their relations by daughter of Théophile Dufour, editor of *Correspondance générale* (no. 1883) of R. Publication of *Correspondance* enabled her to correct *Confessions* on certain points of the relationship. Shows that autobiography seeks to protect Mme de Warens, whose liaison with Wintzenried, " le chevalier de Courtilles," precipitated break.
Review : A. Schinz in EprR, p. 144.

— Jean-Jacques, le promeneur solitaire. Flammarion, [c1933]. 388 p. Author's *pseud.*, Noëlle Roger, at head of title. 2000

Biography of R. by daughter of Théophile Dufour. Grounded in *Confessions* and *Correspondance générale* (no. 1883). *Épilogue* treats of *La création du faux Jean-Jacques* (p. 283-320). " Ce serait faire injure à Mme Noëlle Roger de dire que son livre est une vie romancée, c'est plus et mieux que cela. Ce n'est pas non plus un livre pour ' spécialistes,' bardé de notes et de références, et pourtant il témoigne d'une profonde connaissance de l'œuvre et de la bibliographie de Rousseau." Ruchon, review below, p. 277.
Reviews : E. Magne in MerF 254:571-73, Sept. 15, 1934; A. Rheinwald in JGen Dec. 27, 1933; F. Ruchon in AJJR 22: 277-78, 1933; A. Schinz in EprR, p. 144.

Plan, Pierre-Paul. J.-J. Rousseau et Malesherbes; documents inédits. MerF 97: 5-38, May 1, 1912.   2001

Author reproduces a *dossier*, consisting of 40 pieces in the *Bibliothèque nationale*, " ... formé par Malesherbes, alors Inspecteur général de la Librairie de France... relatif aux opérations de son service au sujet de quatre ouvrages de Rousseau : le *Discours sur l'origine de l'inégalité*, la *Lettre à d'Alembert*, la *Lettre à M. de Voltaire* et *Émile*. Il est constitué par des lettres de différents libraires, de d'Alembert, de Jean-Jacques Rousseau, de la duchesse de Luxembourg et par les minutes autographes de lettres de Malesherbes." p. 6.

— ed. J.-J. Rousseau raconté par les gazettes de son temps, 3e éd. Mercure de France, 1912. 323 p.   2002

" ... j'ai demandé à plusieurs gazettes du temps les anecdotes, les comptes-rendus, les faits-divers, les commérages, les ' échos,' dirait-on aujourd'hui, relatifs à la personne et aux œuvres de Jean-Jacques Rousseau, durant la période qui a suivi l'apparition d'*Émile* jusqu'à celle des *Confessions*, et je les reproduis dans l'ordre où ils ont atteint leur premier public..." p. 7.
Reviews : A. François in AJJR 9:132-33, 1913; A. Schinz in MLN 28:231, 1913.

Pochon, Alfred. J.-J. Rousseau, musicien, et la critique; essai de mise au point. *See* 340.   2003

Œuvres musicales de J. J. Rousseau : p. 51-53.
Review : G. Wissler in AJJR 28:147-48, 1939-40.

Pottle, F. A. The part played by Horace Walpole and James Boswell in the quarrel between Rousseau and Hume. PQ 4:351-63, 1925.   2004

Suggests Walpole and Boswell as possible authors of various gibes at R., published pseudonymously in *Saint James Chronicle*. Attribution questioned, in part, by Peoples, no. 1998. *See :* Bandy (no. 1953), Guillemin (no. 1985), Lévy-Bruhl (no. 1991), Peoples (no. 1998), Roddier (no. 2012).
Review : A. Schinz in AJJR 17:249-50, 1926.

Pougin, Arthur. Jean-Jacques Rousseau, musicien. Fischbacher, 1901. 141 p. 2005

For scope of book, *see* A. Schinz, EprR, p. 291-92.
Reviews : H. Bourgin in RHM 3:55, 1901-02; G. Lanson in RU 10:362, Apr. 15, 1901; A. Schinz in EprR, p. 291-92.

Raymond, Marcel. J.-J. Rousseau : deux aspects de sa vie intérieure (intermittences et permanence du moi). AJJR 29:5-57, 1941-42.   2006

Interesting study of high-lights of *Confessions*. R. " ... s'enflamme, s'exalte, se perd de vue jusqu'à ' devenir un autre '; puis il retombe sur soi et ' s'anéantit ' " (p. 12-13). Analogy with Proust's " intermittences du cœur " (p. 33). Profundity of R.'s psychology, which goes beyond psychological theory of his time. (p. 52).

Régis, Emmanuel. Étude médicale sur

228 CRITICAL BIBLIOGRAPHY OF FRENCH LITERATURE

J.-J. Rousseau. Cméd 7:65-76, 132-401, 173-77, 194-206, 353-71, 391-99, 1900.
2007

Purpose of this study is to justify his diagnosis that R. was " neurasthénique artério-scléreux." Says that R. was descended " ... d'arthritiques et de nerveux." (p. 71), that his neurasthenia was mental in type and " ... a touché presque à la folie." (p. 76) R.'s onanism, as in cases of many other " névropathes " and " dégénérés à tous les degrés " was symptom rather than cause. (p. 176) Agrees with signers of R.'s autopsy that his death " ... s'est faite par le cerveau." (p. 206). P. 353-71 discuss what he calls R.'s delusion of persecution. Concludes that, in general, doctors pity and admire R. as they have Molière (p. 399).

Rey, Auguste. Le château de La Chevrette et Madame d'Epinay. Plon-Nourrit, 1904. 283 p.
2008

See below, no. 2009.
Reviews : in AJJR 1:308-09, 1905; A. Schinz in EprR, p. 336.

— Jean-Jacques Rousseau dans la vallée de Montmorency. Plon-Nourrit, 1909. 294 p.
2009

" En écrivant jadis Le Château de la Chevrette et Mme d'Epinay, j'en avais à peu près écarté l'hôte et l'ami le plus illustre... Je consacre aujourd'hui à Jean-Jacques un volume, où je le rétablis dans la place qu'il mérite, parmi la société de Mme d'Epinay et de célèbres entours." Avant-propos, IV. Both of these books by Rey are characterized by Schinz as of capital importance.
Reviews : F. Baldensperger in Rcr 69: 115-16, Feb. 10, 1910; D. Mornet in RHL 17:879-80, 1910; E. Ritter in AJJR 6:340, 1910; A. Schinz in EprR, p. 66, 336.

Ritter, Eugène. La famille et la jeunesse de J.-J. Rousseau. Hachette, 1896. 305 p. This edition superseded by one in the AJJR 16:3-250, 1924-25.
2010

Indispensable work on subject.
Reviews : E. Carcassonne in RHL 36: 477-78, 1929 (new edition); G. Lanson in RU 2:281, 1896; S. Rocheblave in RIE 32:587-89, 1896; J. Texte in RHL 3: 453-55, 1896.

— J.-J. Rousseau et Madame d'Houdetot. AJJR 2:1-136, 1906.
2011

" ... étude minutieuse, impartiale et qu'on peut considérer comme définitive..." Schinz. See no. 2021.
Reviews : A. Luchaire in AMP 167:248, 1907; A. Schinz in EprR, p. 337.

Roddier, Henri. La querelle Rousseau-Hume. RLC 18:452-77, 1938. See 3074.
2012

Author has read The letters of David Hume (edited by J. Y. T. Greig, Oxford, Clarendon press, 1932, 2 v.) and does recognize the obvious deficiencies of Musset-Pathay and Plan. But, while claiming objectivity, he fails completely to understand Hume, referring to him as a " provincial dédaigné à Londres," and he ends with a psychological over-subtle and withal sentimental, apology for R. See also, by same author, A propos de la querelle Rousseau-Hume ; précisions chronologiques. RHL 46 :211-14, 1939, and : Bandy (no. 1953), Guillemin (no. 1985), Lévy-Bruhl (no. 1991), Peoples (no. 1998), Pottle (no. 2004).
Reviews : A. Schinz in AJJR 28:137-38, 1939-40, and EprR, p. 343-44.

Roger, Noëlle. See Pittard, nos. 1999, 2000.
2013

Sainte-Beuve, C. A. Mme de La Tour-Franqueville et Jean-Jacques Rousseau. In his : Causeries du lundi, v. 2, p. 63-84. 2014

Portrait of R. in relation to his correspondence with Mme de La Tour-Franqueville, published in 1803. " Cette Correspondance... montre Jean-Jacques au naturel depuis le lendemain de la Nouvelle Héloïse jusqu'au moment où sa raison s'altéra irrémédiablement " (p. 63). (Dated Apr. 29, 1850).

Schaad, Herbert W. Der Ausbruch der Geisteskrankheit Jean-Jacques Rousseaus und ihre Anzeichen in seinen letzten Werken und Briefen. Erlangen, Junge, 1928. 122 p. (Diss., Erlangen). 2015

" Une des études récentes les plus attentives sur la mentalité de Rousseau..." Schinz.
Reviews : R. de Saussure in AJJR 19: 219-20, 1929-30; A. Schinz in EprR, p. 361.

Schinz, Albert. Documents nouveaux sur Rousseau et Voltaire; les Boswell papers. RPar 40:299-325 (May 15), 630-67 (June 1), 1933. 2016

Account of significance of Boswell's long letter of 1764 (see nos. 1748, 1958) narrating colorful details of his visits to R. and to Voltaire.

Reviews : L.-J. Courtois in AJJR 22:283-84, 1933; E. Henriot in Temps, June 6, 1933.

— L'idylle des Charmettes. RFrance 14:239-62, Nov. 15, 1934. 2017

Detailed analysis of this article, important for its treatment of controversial point of R. biography and as regards credibility of the *Confessions*, given in review below. *See also* Schinz's EprR, p. 313-14.
Review : F. Ruchon in AJJR 23:224-27, 1934.

— Jean-Jacques Rousseau et le libraire-imprimeur Marc-Michel Rey; les relations personnelles. AJJR 10:1-134, 1914-15. (Also published separately at Geneva, Jullien, 1916. 134 p.). 2018

For supplementary material, see EprR, p. 179-80, 326, and Gallas, no. 1980.

— La querelle Rousseau-Hume; un document inédit. AJJR 17:13-46, 1926. 2019

" M. Schinz étudie une lettre de Hume à la présidente Durey de Meinières (ex-Mme Belot, née Guichard), tirée de la Bibliothèque Pierpont-Morgan à New York : c'est un premier récit apologétique de la fameuse querelle, qui, s'il ne nous apprend rien d'essentiellement nouveau, montre tout le prix qu'attachait l'auteur à l'opinion parisienne." E. Carcassonne in RHL 35:595, 1928. Schinz's study is followed by a *Liste des articles en prose et en vers relatifs à la querelle entre Rousseau et Hume, et trouvés dans le St. James's Chronicle, avril à décembre 1766*, contributed by F. A. Pottle, p. 48-51. *See also* p. 249-50. *See* Bandy (no. 1953), Guillemin (no. 1985), Lévy-Bruhl (no. 1991), Peoples (no. 1998), Pottle (no. 2004), Roddier (no. 2012).

Sells, Arthur L. The early life and adventures of Jean Jacques Rousseau, 1712-1740, from the latest sources. Cambridge, Eng., Heffer, 1929. 148 p. 2020

Good account of youth of R. for general reader.
Reviews : L.-J. Courtois in AJJR 19:233-35, 1929-30; F. C. Roe in MLR 28:267-68, 1933.

Torrey, Norman L. Rousseau's quarrel with Grimm and Diderot. EssAF, p. 163-82. 2021

Agrees basically with facts brought out by E. Ritter in his study, *J.-J. Rousseau et Madame d'Houdetot* (no. 2011), but

with more severity in judgment of R. Believes with Ritter that what Pierre-Paul Plan in the *Correspondance générale* (no. 1883) has called " Lettre fausse " is entirely authentic letter, in spite of a slight and unintentional error in dating. Believes also that Mme d'Epinay's *Mémoires*, although novelized, partly rewritten in consultation with Diderot, and although often confused as to exact dates, are nevertheless much more worthy of credence in essentials than has been maintained by Mrs. Macdonald (no. 1992). Presents evidence to show that Mme d'Epinay went to consult Dr. Tronchin at Geneva on illness due to cancer, not because of concealed pregnancy as hinted by R. Concludes with reflections on contrast between " two fundamentally opposing systems, one Encyclopedic and deterministic, by which men's acts are judged by their effects on their fellowmen, the other individualistic and romantic, by which the consciousness of good intentions is the ethical criterion. In the eighteenth century, Diderot was the leading proponent of the one approach, Rousseau of the other " (p. 181). Important study of a controversial subject in which it is still difficult to avoid a subjective attitude on either side. *See* Texte, no. 2415.
Reviews : W. M. Frohock in RR 36: 148-52, 1945 ; H. Kellenberger in MLQ 5:488, 1944.

Trintzius, René. La vie privée de J.-J. Rousseau. Hachette, 1938. 252 p. 2022

Popular but sound.
Review : P. E. Schazmann in AJJR 27:317, 1938.

Variot, G. L'abandon des enfants de Jean-Jacques Rousseau et le fonctionnement de l'Hôpital des Enfants trouvés à cette époque. BHM 19:63-83, 1925. 2023

Significant article in which writer reproduces contemporary documents to identify R.'s eldest son.
Reviews : L.-J. Courtois in AJJR 17: 288-89, 1926; E. Henriot in *Le Temps*, July 14, 1925; A. Schinz in EprR, p. 324.

Vitry, Paul. Les monuments à J.-J. Rousseau de Houdon à Bartholomé. GBA 54 (4th per. 8):96-117, Aug., 1912. 2024

Characterized by Schinz as " ... un travail fort important." *See his* EprR, p. 297.

Wilde, Norman. On the conversion of Rousseau. IJE 26:54-71, 1915. 2025

Insists that gap between his imagination and conduct is central fact in R.'s life. Concludes that he underwent no moral conversion but did experience character growth. Cf. Lanson, *Histoire de la littérature française*, 790: "... il a fallu que Rousseau fût supérieurement moral, pour n'avoir pas mal fini, après ses commencements."

Wille, Hanns Julius. Träume und Tränen; das Leben der Therese Levasseur mit Jean Jacques Rousseau. Leipzig, Günther, 1937, 579 p.   2026

"... vie romancée de Rousseau, avec Thérèse comme figure centrale." Schinz, *infra*, p. 318. The author utilizes the *Correspondance générale* (no. 1883).
Reviews : P. E. Schazmann in AJJR 26:324-25, 1937; A. Schinz in EprR, p. 318-20.

Studies of Style, Ideas, Sources, or Influence

Annales de la Société Jean-Jacques Rousseau. Vol. 8 (1912). (Bi-centenary year).   2027

Lanson, G. L'unité de la pensée de Jean-Jacques Rousseau	p. 1-31
Mornet, D. L'influence de J.-J. Rousseau au xviiie siècle	p. 33-67
Höffding, H. Rousseau et le xixe siècle	p. 69-98
Benrubi, I. Rousseau et le mouvement philosophique et pédagogique en Allemagne	p. 99-130
Gosse, E. Rousseau en Angleterre au xixe siècle	p. 131-60
Reynold, G. de. J.-J. Rousseau et la Suisse : Rousseau et les écrivains du dix-huitième siècle helvétique	p. 161-204
Seippel, P. La personnalité religieuse de J.-J. Rousseau	p. 205-31
Favre, L. Le manuscrit Favre de l'*Émile*	p. 233-315

Reviews : D. Mornet in RHL 20:721, 1913; A. Schinz in EprR, p. 75.

Aron, A. W. The mature Goethe and Rousseau. JEGP 35:170-82, 1936.   2028

Presents evidence to show that, contrary to commonly accepted viewpoints, Goethe's admiration for R. did not wane after *Werther* but continued to end of his life. Reconsideration of Goethe-R. relationship for interpretation of Goethe's later works is indicated. *See* Benrubi (no. 1937), Schmidt (no. 2140).

Babbitt, Irving. Rousseau and romanticism. Boston and New York, Houghton Mifflin, (1919) 1935. 426 p.   2029

" A highly unromantic treatment of the subject. A brilliant and suggestive but intensely partisan attack on romanticism by the late leader of the ' new humanist ' school." H. N. Fairchild in PMLA 55:58, 1940.
Reviews : F. Baldensperger in Rcr 87: 8-10, Jan. 1, 1920; E. P. Dargan in MP 18:162-71, July 1920; A. O. Lovejoy in MLN 35:302-08, 1920 (*see also* polemic between Babbitt and Lovejoy, *ibid*. 37: 257-74, 1922); W. A. Nitze in The Dial 68:131-36, 1920; J. G. Robertson in MLR 15:198-200, 1920; A. Schinz in EprR 110 and in JPh 17:20-27, 1920 (*see also* Babbitt's reply, *ibid*., 186-91).

Barras, Moses. The stage controversy in France from Corneille to Rousseau. *See* 512.   2030

Consult particularly his chapter XII (p. 253-301) for a discussion of R.'s *Lettre à d'Alembert* and the polemic which followed. *See also* Bourquin (no. 2041), and Moffat (no. 2111).
Reviews : P. Jourda in Rcr 100:150-51, 1933; J. O'Brien in RR 24:245-47, 1933; A. Schinz in AJJR 22:252-55, 1933.

Baumecker, Gottfried. Schiller und Rousseau. *In his* : Schiller und die französische Revolution. Berlin, Junker and Dünnhaupt, 1939. p. 7-20.   2031-2034

Author treats of young Schiller and R., dealing exclusively with *Die Räuber* and *Fiesco*. Shows that Schiller's insistence on mighty, heaven-storming action by heroes of his first two dramas decidedly not in harmony with R.'s *Discours sur la vertu la plus nécessaire aux héros*. References to previous articles on Schiller and R. noted, p. 11-12. *See also* Benrubi (no. 1937), and Claretie (no. 1938).

Benrubi, Isaac. L'idéal moral chez Rousseau, Mme de Staël et Amiel. Alcan, 1940. 334 p. (Reprinted from AJJR 27:7-287, 1938.) (*See also* : Benrubi, Isaac. J. J. Rousseaus ethisches Ideal. Langensalza, Beyer, 1904. 141 p. Diss., Jena.)   2035

In *First discourse*, R. combats for moral ideal rather than against sciences and arts (p. 17). Moral ideal predominant throughout his work. R. opposed only to " le faux savoir, la demi-culture " (p. 106). R. did not advocate return to mythical state of nature, but attacked false emphasis on unmoral " civilization." (*See* Havens, no. 1886). Important monograph on essential unity of R.'s work, and his influence on Mme de Staël and Amiel. Reviews : E. Bréhier in RMM 47:420-21, 1940 ; R. Lenoir in Rsyn, 60:170-72, 1945 ; H. Reverdin in AJJR 30:187-91, 1943-45.

— Pestalozzi und Rousseau. DV 11:294-328, 1933.   2036

    Shows differences and comparisons in their pedagogical views. Review : W. Müller in AJJR 22:249-50, 1933.

— Rousseau et le mouvement philosophique et pédagogique en Allemagne. AJJR 8:99-130, 1912.   2037

    Sees R. as a dominant influence in enriching inner life of Germany. Kant, Herder, Fichte, Pestalozzi, Basedow, Hegel, Schelling, Schopenhauer, and others. Not all resemblances, however, as author admits, can be traced to R., and article is somewhat " dated " by relative optimism of 1912, preceding two world wars.

Bisson, L. A. Rousseau and the Romantic experience. MLR 37:37-49, 1942. (French trans., AJJR 30:27-45, 1943-45).   2038

    Article devoted to study of R.'s letters to Malesherbes. Author proposes to show that " they are documents of the first importance to the study of the birth, growth and fruition of the Romantic experience and of its historic manifestation in the Romantic movement." p. 49. *See* Rudler, no. 1884.

Bosanquet, Bernard. Les idées politiques de Rousseau. RMM 20:321-40, 1912. 2039

    Of importance for *First* and *Second* discourses and *Social contract*. Author's purpose is to show their meaning and significance. Penetrating and sagacious. *See also* no. 2040.

— The philosophical theory of the state. 4th ed., London, Macmillan, (1899) 1923. 320 p.   2040

    Capital study, which includes sections on *Problem of the Contrat social, Meaning of the General Will of Rousseau*, and *Rousseau's literary influence in Germany*. (*See also* no. 2039). Reviews : S. W. Dyde in PhR 9:198-206, 1900, and 20:559-62, 1911.

Bourquin, Louis. La controverse sur la comédie au XVIIIe siècle et la Lettre à d'Alembert sur les spectacles. RHL 26: 43-86, 555-76, 1919; 27:548-70, 1920; 28:549-74, 1921.   2041

    Important study, but unfinished, because of author's death in First World War; does not reach the *Lettre à d'Alembert*. *See* Barras (no. 2030), and Moffat (no. 2111). Reviews : A. François in AJJR 13:251-52, 1920-21; A. Schinz in EprR, p. 192.

Buchner, Margaret L. A contribution to the study of the descriptive technique of Jean-Jacques Rousseau. Baltimore, Johns Hopkins press; London, Oxford univ. press, Milford, 1937. 184 p. (JHS, v. 30) (Diss., Johns Hopkins)   2042

    R. more interested in " l'état d'âme " than in details of external description. Foreshadows " le paysage intérieur " of Lamartine. But, we may also ask, did R.'s near-sightedness contribute to vagueness with which he described external world? Contrast Bernardin de Saint-Pierre's use of color and exact details. R.'s emphasis upon musical prose. Supplements Mornet (no. 2120), and Rice (no. 2131). Reviews : G. R. Havens in RR 29: 89-90, 1938; D. Mornet in RHL 45: 104-05, 1938; A. Schinz in AJJR 26: 326-27, 1937, and MLN 53:309-10, 1938.

Buck, Rudolf. Rousseau und die deutsche Romantik. Berlin, Junker and Dünnhaupt, 1939. 146 p.   2043

    From author's conclusion : " Certainly Rousseau is of importance for German Romanticism. But his influence was almost stronger in an indirect way, i.e. through his influence on the general spirit of the times out of which Romanticism grew, than through direct influence. The Romanticists... benefited by him, although he himself was more in the background than in the center of the picture. It cannot be overemphasized how very little the Romanticists mentioned Rousseau's name." p. 140. But note R.'s importance for the great figures, Goethe and Schiller, of *Sturm und Drang* period. Reviews : P.-E. Schazmann in AJJR 28:138-39, 1939-40; H. M. Wolff in Grev 15:152-53, 1940.

Cassirer, Ernst. Kant and Rousseau. *In his :* Rousseau, Kant, Goethe. Trans. from the German by James Gutmann, Paul Oskar Kristeller, and John Herman Randall,

Jr. Princeton, Princeton univ. press, 1945. 1-80. 2044

Study of R.'s influence on Kant. *See also* V. Delbos, Rousseau et Kant, 1940. Reviews : P. Armstrong in AJJR 30: 201, 1943-45; J. Barzun in Rrel 10:325-26, 1945-46; J. V. Flynn in CathHR 31:364-65, 1945-46; P. Gleis in Th 20: 729-33, 1945; B. R. Redman in SRL 28:39-40, June 9, 1945.

— Das Problem Jean Jacques Rousseau. AGP 41:177-213, 479-513, 1932. 2045

Cassirer " ... développe ici une thèse, en faveur de l'unité de la pensée de Rousseau, que l'on retrouvera dans sa communication à la *Société française de philosophie*... et la discussion qui l'a suivie : Rousseau serait avant tout un rationaliste qui, bien loin d'être l'initia-teur du sentimentalisme, a toujours au contraire résisté à ce mouvement." E. Bréhier in Rph 117:478, 1934. *See also* Cassirer (no. 2046), Lanson (no. 2091) and Derathé, (no. 2202A). Reviews : W. Müller in AJJR 21:264-65, 1932; A. Schinz in EprR, p. 376.

— *et al.* L'unité dans l'œuvre de Jean-Jacques Rousseau. BSFP 32:45-85, 1932. 2046

Interesting exchange of ideas on one of most mooted and important problems in R. scholarship, raised by a communi-cation on subject delivered by Ernst Cassirer before *Société française de philo-sophie*, Feb. 27, 1932. V. Basch, C. Bouglé, E. Gilson and R. Lenoir were participants in discussion. In addition to Cassirer, no. 2045, *see*, among others, Lanson, 2091, Schinz, 1944, and Wright, 1951. Reviews : L.-J. Courtois in AJJR 21: 291, 1932; A. Schinz in EprR, p. 376-77.

Champion, Edme. J.-J. Rousseau et la révolution française. Colin, 1909. 276 p. 2047

" En ce petit volume bien documenté... M. Edme Champion étudie l'influence exercée par Rousseau sur la Révolution. L'auteur s'insurge contre le jugement de ceux qui, incarnant en un seul homme une révolution pareille, montrent en Rousseau, mal lu, mal interprété, le pré-curseur des terroristes et le mauvais génie de la Révolution... M. Edme Champion veut ' écarter de cet homme paisible l'auréole sanglante de l'enveloppe,' sans autre souci que d'être exact, de voir clair, d'atteindre et de garder la juste mesure. Il nous semble qu'il y a réussi." Vallette,

infra, p. 330. *See* Dide (no. 2058), Mornet (no. 2117), Peyre (no. 2126). Reviews : A. Aulard in Rfr 58:171-72, 1910; R. Girard in RSH 22:106-09, 1911; W. E. Lingelbach in AHR 15:914-15, 1909-10; A. Schinz in EprR, p. 225, 231, 233; G. Vallette in AJJR 6:330-32, 1910.

Chinard, Gilbert. Influence des récits de voyages sur la philosophie de J.-J. Rousseau. PMLA 26:476-95, 1911. 2048

Holds that R.'s ideas concerning man's primitive goodness were influenced by memories of readings in accounts of America given by travelers and mission-aries. Article summed up in his book, *l'Amérique et le rêve exotique dans la littérature française au XVIIe et au XVIIIe siècle* (no. 789), 341-65.

— Un continuateur des missionnaires jésuites, Jean-Jacques Rousseau. *In his :* l'Amérique et le rêve exotique dans la littérature fran-çaise au XVIIe et au XVIIIe siècle. (789), p. 341-65. 2049

Study, with particular reference to *Discours sur l'inégalité*, of R.'s indebted-ness to printed accounts of missionaries and travelers in America. *See* no. 2048. Reviews : F. Baldensperger in Rcr 77: 492-93, June 20, 1914; C. Cestre in RIE 67:315-17, 1914; A. François in AJJR 10:223, 1914-15; A. Tilley in MLR 9: 284-85, 1914.

Choulguine, Alexandre. Les origines de l'esprit national moderne et Jean-Jacques Rousseau. AJJR 26:7-283, 1937. 2050

Important study of development of patriotic feeling, particularly in France. Rather neglects Mably and Encyclope-dists, however. Review : E. Carcassonne in RHL 46: 254-55, 1939.

Ciancio, Maria E. La critica delle idee del Rousseau in alcuni pedagogisti italiani del Risorgimento. RivP 17:772-82, 1924. 2051

Article devoted mainly to consideration of attitudes towards R. of Capponi, Lambruschini, and Rosmini. Concludes, while recognizing his varying fortunes among Italian writers on pedagogy in the *Risorgimento*, that ideas of R. were influential.

Claparède, Ed. J.-J. Rousseau et la concep-tion fonctionnelle de l'enfance. RMM 20: 391-416, 1912. 2052

Considered by Schinz to be " ... la tentative la plus importante d'estimer la signification d'*Émile* dans l'histoire des idées." EprR, p. 260.

Reviews : R. Cousinet in EdM 7:381-82, 1912; A. Schinz in EprR, p. 259-60.

Clark, Harry H. Thomas Paine's relation to Voltaire and Rousseau. See 1754. 2053

Although Paine did not speak or understand spoken French there is no evidence that he did not read French (p. 308). Parallels between his ideas and those of Voltaire and R. may be due to reading of originals, of translations, or to conversation with Frenchmen or others who knew French thought. Because of lack of positive evidence, however, article makes no claim to prove definite influence. In religion, Paine has some affinities with R., but is more rationalistic, less emotional. In political field, both admire the state of nature in contrast to artificialities of civilization. Both have confidence in inherent rightness of mass of people.

Review : A. L. Sells in AJJR 21:291-92, 1932.

Cobban, Alfred. Rousseau and the modern state. London, Allen and Unwin 1934. 288 p. 2054

" Dr. Cobban attempts a thorough analysis of Rousseau's political ideas and arrives at the conclusion that his political theory starts with the individual and ends with the individual." SatR 157:899, July 28, 1934. Book contains appendices devoted to comte d'Antraigues and extracts from his manuscripts.

Reviews : P. Léon in AJJR 23:190-99, 1934; H. Sée in Rhist 177:158-59, 1936; Anon in SatR 157:899, July 28, 1934.

Compayré, Gabriel. J.-J. Rousseau et l'éducation de la nature. Delaplane, 1901. 112 p. *Also :* Jean Jacques Rousseau and education from nature. tr. by R. P. Jago New York, Crowell, 1907. 120 p. Translated into Spanish : Buenos Aires, Estab. tip. el Comercio, 1905. 103 p. 2055

Study of R.'s theories of education by well-known authority on subject.

Review (of original) : A. Schinz in EprR, p. 259.

Cornelissen, Anthony J. M. Calvijn en Rousseau; een vergelijkende Studie van beider Staatsleer. Nijmegen-Utrecht, Dekker, van de Vegt, 1931. 314 p. 2056

Comparative study of political theories of Calvin and R. Careful analysis of book made by Boasson in review below.

Reviews : J. J. Boasson in AJJR 21:

255-60, 1932; E. Wolf in HZ 148:355-58, 1933.

Culcasi, Carlo. Gli influssi italiani nell'opera di G. G. Rousseau. Rome, Società editrice Dante Alighieri, [1907]. 264 p. 2057

Author proposes to show R.'s great debt to Italy and to Italian writers, e.g., impact on R. of Petrarch, Tasso, Metastasio, Machiavelli.

Reviews : A. Schinz in EprR, p. 202; J. Volmar in AJJR 4:329-32, 1908.

Dide, Auguste. J.-J. Rousseau; le protestantisme et la révolution française. Flammarion [1910]. 312 p. 2058

Attack on Calvinism and R.'s Genevan heritage as though they were exclusive sources of intolerance and persecution. Consistently hostile interpretation of R. Last chapter deals with R. and Revolution. Although constructive side of Revolution, believes Dide, did not spring primarily from books (p. 278, 284), evil aspects of Revolution, says author, were encouraged by R. " On peut affirmer que de Rousseau est sorti Robespierre " (p. 287). Bouvier comments : " C'est une œuvre de dénigrement systématique " (*infra*, p. 162). Mornet says : " C'est un sermon et une diatribe, non une démonstration " (*infra*, p. 219). *See also* Champion (no. 2047), Mornet (no. 2117), Peyre (no. 2126).

Reviews : G. [*sic*] Baldensperger in ZFSL 38²:53-60, Oct. 1, 1912; J. Benrubi in RSH 22:377, 1911; B. Bouvier in AJJR 7:162-65, 1911; D. Mornet in RHL 19:218-19, 1912; A. Schinz in EprR, p. 72, 225, 230-32, 244.

Duguit, Léon. Jean-Jacques Rousseau, Kant et Hegel. RDP 35:173-211; 325-377, 1918. (Extracted and reprinted, Giard et Brière, 1918. 94 p.) 2059

Incisive exposition of absolutist doctrine in R.'s *Contrat social* and in Kantian and Hegelian philosophies.

Durkheim, Emile. La pédagogie de Rousseau. RMM 26:153-80, 1919. 2060

" Ce sont en réalité des notes seulement que Durkheim (mort en 1917) avait laissées d'un cours de quatre leçons; mais des notes capitales." Schinz, EprR, p. 263.

Review : A. Schinz in EprR, p. 188-89, 263-64.

Eckstein, Walter. Rousseau and Spinoza : their political theories and their conception of ethical freedom. JHI 5:259-91, 1944. 2061

Evidence that R. read Spinoza. Similarities in their ideas of social contract, state of nature, origin of civil society, relation between individual and state, and in their central emphasis on ethical freedom. Their common stoic background, mentioned by author, may have had more influence than he suggests. Article seeks to explain " the apparent inconsistency between Rousseau, the champion of liberty, and Rousseau, the advocate of state authority " (p. 288). Author does not believe R. an advocate of totalitarianism.

Ellis, Havelock. Rousseau today. Atl 109: 784-94, 1912.   2062

Article written on occasion of bicentenary of R.'s birth. Was incorporated as chapter 5 of book below (no. 2063) and consequently is not to be confused, as is sometimes the case, with the book's chapter 7, also entitled *Rousseau today*. Author's review of *Correspondance générale* (no. 1883) in *American mercury* 36: 366-70, 1935, was basis for latter chapter. Review : A. Schinz in AJJR 9:103-05, 1913.

— [Rousseau.] *In his :* From Rousseau to Proust. Boston and New York, Houghton, Mifflin, 1935. p. 19-145.   2063

Reviews : A. Schinz in AJJR 24:268-73, 1935; also in EprR, p. 358-59; also in RHL 43:309-12, 1936.

Etienne, Servais. Le genre romanesque en France depuis l'apparition de la " Nouvelle Héloïse " jusqu'aux approches de la révolution. *See* 716, 903.   2064

From *Avant-propos :* " ... je me suis proposé l'étude du genre romanesque en me confinant à l'intérieur même du genre; je n'ai pas dû me préoccuper des romans qui ont déterminé dans le développement général de la littérature une transformation qui s'est propagée à d'autres genres et sur les époques ultérieures. ... J'ai accordé une grande attention aux œuvres de second et de dernier ordre." (p. 5-6.) Says Mornet : " Sur Richardson, sur Rousseau,... les jugements pénétrants et les justes formules abondent. Pourtant, je ne crois pas que son livre soit vraiment une étude du genre romanesque en France, de 1750 à la Révolution." (Mornet, *infra*, p. 90.) Reviews : G. Cohen in RBP 3:884-88, 1924; A. François in AJJR 15:368, 1923; D. Mornet in RHL 30:90-92, 1923; A. Schinz in EprR, p. 98, 214, 406.

Faguet, Emile. La politique comparée de Montesquieu, Rousseau et Voltaire. *See* 1557 (Montesquieu); 1670 (Voltaire). 2065

Faguet, perhaps most zealous, outspoken, and uncompromising liberal among French 19th century critics and essayists, and warm admirer of Montesquieu, denounces R.'s political theories as leading, inevitably, to popular despotism which will suppress all liberty in favor of a sort of " volonté générale," interpreted and represented by a minority group of fanatical theorists like the Jacobins. (p. 69-72) Faguet concludes, pessimistically, that future belongs to R. because his " pensée directrice " will triumph, as being " ... la plus vulgaire." (p. 293) *See* Schinz, EprR, p. 230, 237, 244.

— Rousseau contre Molière. Société française d'imprimerie et de librairie, [1912.] 343 p.   2066

" J'examinerai cette question dans l'ordre suivant : jugement de Rousseau sur la comédie de Molière *Le misanthrope ;* autres pièces de Molière blâmées par Rousseau; silence peut-être significatif de Rousseau sur d'autres pièces de Molière; griefs généraux de Rousseau contre Molière; idées générales de Molière et de Rousseau." p. 1.
Reviews : B. Bouvier in AJJR 9:113-15, 1913; C. Dejob in Rcr 73:390-92, May 18, 1912.

— Rousseau penseur. Société française d'imprimerie et de librairie, 1912. 408 p. 2067

Penetrating study of R., whose aim and scope author defines as follows : " Quant à ceux de ses sentiments et de ses idées qui vivent encore parmi nous de telle sorte qu'ils se traduisent à chaque instant en écrits, en paroles et en actes, c'est à quoi j'apporterai toute l'attention dont je suis capable." (p. 1-2.) Among others, there are chapters devoted to R.'s ethics, his literary, religious, pedagogical, sociological, and political ideas.
Reviews : B. Bouvier in AJJR 9:115-20, 1913; C. Dejob in Rcr 74:431-33, Nov. 20, 1912; D. Mornet in RCLN 8:80-81, 1913; A. Schinz in EprR, p. 373.

— Le sentiment de la nature chez J.-J. Rousseau. RCC 17²:481-89, 577-86, 673-81, 1909.   2068

" ... une rapide récapitulation..." Schinz, EprR, p. 180.

Fester, Richard. Rousseau und die deutsche Geschichtsphilosophie : ein Beitrag zur

Geschichte des deutschen Idealismus. Stuttgart, Göschen, 1890. 340 p. 2069

Scholarly study. " It presents an important chapter in the evolution of the thought of the eighteenth century into that of the nineteenth." F. C. French, *infra*.

Chapters on R. and the German *Aufklärung*—Herder, Kant, Schiller, Fichte, Schelling, Friedrich Schlegel, Schopenhauer and Herbart, Krause, Hegel and Schelling's positive philosophy, and Wilhelm von Humboldt. Has Appendix on *The idea of perpetual peace in the 18th century*.

Reviews : F. C. French in PhR 2:628, 1893; L. Herr in Rcr 33:32-35, Jan. 11, 1892; R. Mahrenholtz in ZFSL 13²:74-75, 1891.

François, Alexis. Les provincialismes suisses-romands et savoyards de Jean-Jacques Rousseau. AJJR 3:1-67, 1907. 2070

Interesting evidence of continuance of Swiss linguistic influence on R. in spite of his long sojourn in France.

Reviews : H. Chatelain in RU 18²: 63-64, 1909; J. Désormaux in Rsav 49:63-66, 1908.

Gillot, Hubert. La pensée de Jean-Jacques Rousseau. Courville, 1934. 87 p. (Extrait du Bulletin de la Faculté des lettres de Strasbourg, 1932-1933-1934) 2071

Lectures mainly on *La nouvelle Héloïse*, especially in its idyllic, religious, and sentimental aspects, with final lecture on *Rêveries*. A presentation rather than scholarly study.

Reviews : F. Ruchon in AJJR 23: 215-16, 1934; E. Seillière in AMP 95: 581-82, Nov.-Dec., 1935.

Gilson, Etienne. La méthode de M. de Wolmar. *In his :* Les idées et les lettres. Vrin, 1932. p. 275-98. 2072

Wolmar brings his wife and Saint-Preux together with aim of making latter forget his love for former Julie d'Etange in midst of the new family environment in which matronly Mme de Wolmar now lives. Meillerie evokes powerful memories in Saint-Preux because of physical associations built up by his previous stay there, but not in Julie, who has never been there before. R., believes Gilson, here attempts to apply principles of his *Morale sensitive, ou le Matérialisme du sage*, never written, but described in the *Confessions*, as R. conceived the work in embryo.

Reviews : L.-J. Courtois in AJJR 21: 287-88, 1932; D. Mornet in RHL 41: 139-40, 1934.

Gosse, Edmund. J. J. Rousseau in England in the nineteenth century. FortR [98]:22-38, July, 1912. Translated : Rousseau en Angleterre au xixᵉ siècle. AJJR 8:131-60, 1912. 2073

Burke's opposition to R. provoked by Revolution. Godwin a devotee of R. Revival of enthusiasm for R. with rise of Byron and Shelley. Hostility of Walter Scott influential. Walter Savage Landor praises R. in 1828. Ruskin's affinities with R. Decline of R.'s vogue in England until John Morley's book (no. 1931) in 1873. Admiration of George Eliot for R., however. But Morley did not arouse general interest in study of R. in England. Mrs. Frederika Macdonald (no. 1992), with her exaggerated enthusiasm, closes period and begins 20th century.

Review : H. D. Davray in MerF 98: 427-32, July 16, 1912.

Graves, Frank P. Rousseau and naturalism in education. *In his :* Great educators of three centuries; their work and its influence on modern education. New York, Macmillan, 1938. p. 77-111. 2074

" une petite étude fidèle, de la vie, pensée et influence de Rousseau, surtout relativement à l'*Émile*, lequel est bien résumé en douze pages." Schinz, *below*.

Review : A. Schinz in AJJR 9:102, 1913.

Gueroult, M. Nature humaine et état de nature chez Rousseau, Kant et Fichte. RPFE 131:379-97, Dec., 1941. 2075

Contradictions in R., which confused the criticism of Kant and Fichte. By natural man, did R. mean man as he is, realistic man, or man as he ought to be, ideal man ? In the two *Discourses*, believes Gueroult, he meant ideal man; in *Contrat social*, realistic man. Hence the difficulties and confusions in understanding his thought.

Havens, George R. Rousseau's doctrine of goodness according to nature. PMLA 44: 1239-45, 1929. 2076

Short but critical explanation of this doctrine provoked by objections in article (no. 2148) of Jeannette Tresnon to Havens's interpretation of R.'s theory of man's natural goodness.

— La théorie de la bonté naturelle de l'homme chez J.-J. Rousseau. RHL 31:629-42, 1924; 32:24-37, 212-25, 1925. 2077

R.'s idea of " natural goodness " to be understood as reaction against discouraging theological doctrine of " natural perversity," in vogue at time. In *Émile*, R. makes an important distinction between *bonté* (mere aspiration toward goodness) and *vertu* (which implies strength and victory). R. aims at creating a society favorable to goodness. His ideas must be understood in the light of texts and background of their time. Following nature is following conscience, for R. (cf. *Émile*). Summarized here are the following articles by same author : *The theory of " Natural goodness " in Rousseau's Nouvelle Héloïse*, MLN 36:385-94, 1921, and *The theory of " Natural goodness " in Rousseau's Confessions*, MLN 38:257-66, 1923. *See* Ellis (no. 2169), Lovejoy (no. 2179), Moreau-Rendu (no. 2115), Schinz (no. 2139), and Wright (no. 1951).
Review : L. Pinvert in AJJR 17:282-83, 1926.

— Voltaire's marginalia on the pages of Rousseau; a comparative study of ideas. Columbus, O., The Ohio state university, 1933. 199 p. 2078

For a brief, popular presentation of the book, see Havens's *Voltaire's marginal comments on Rousseau* in SAQ 31:408-16, 1932, or his *Les notes marginales de Voltaire sur Rousseau* in RHL 40:434-40, 1933.
Reviews : G. Mongredien in NL, March 17, 1934; A. Schinz in AJJR 22: 259-61, 1933.

Hellweg, Martin. Der Begriff des Gewissens bei Jean Jacques Rousseau; Beitrag zu einer Kritik der politischen Demokratie. Marburg/Lahn, Ebel, 1936. 125 p. (MBRP, v. 20) 2079

Paul Léon, in review below, calls this monograph on the idea of conscience in R.'s writings " ... une étude importante qui marque un nouveau point acquis dans l'interprétation de Rousseau." (p. 322)
Review : P. L. Léon in AJJR 26:317-23, 1937.

Hendel, Charles W. Jean-Jacques Rousseau, moralist. London and New York, Oxford univ. press, 1934 2 v. 2080

" My object has been to determine what the ideas of Rousseau really were. I have tried to seize hold of them in their first formation, and to follow, step by step, their own argument in his thought." (I, p. vii.) Of this fine study, Larrabee, in review below, says : " Nowhere else in English does Rousseau speak for himself so extensively or so intelligibly." (p. 110.)
Reviews : G. Ascoli in Rcr 102:162-63, 1935; M. Josephson in SRL 11:59, Aug. 18, 1934; H. A. Larrabee in IJE 45:110-12, 1934-35; A. Schinz in AJJR 23:201-07, 1934; E. Vivas in NNY 139: 334-35, 1934.

Höffding, Harald. Jean-Jacques Rousseau et sa philosophie. Tr. d'après la 2ᵉ édition danoise avec un avant-propos par Jacques de Coussange. Alcan, 1912. 164 p. First edition : Jean Jacques Rousseau og hans Filosofi. 1896. Rousseau und seine Philosophie. Stuttgart, Frommann, 1897. 158 p. Jean Jacques Rousseau and his philosophy. Translated from the second Danish edition by William Richards... and Leo Saidla... with a new preface by the author. New Haven, Yale univ. press; London, Milford, Oxford univ. press, 1930. 165 p. 2081

Important study in brief compass.
Reviews, (of the French edition) : V. Delbos in RU 22²:61-62, 1913; E. Faguet in APL 61:92-93, 1913; D. Mornet in RCLN 8:79-80, 1913; F. Pillon in AnP 23:276-78, 1912; A. Schinz in EprR, p. 129-30; C. Werner in AJJR 9:123-25, 1913. (Of the English edition) : Anon in TLS, March 5, 1931, p. 172; F. C. Roe in MLR 28:267-69, 1933.

— Rousseau et le xixᵉ siècle. (Trans. from the Danish). AJJR 8:69-98, 1912. 2082

Obvious direct influence of R. on French literature : Chateaubriand, Mme de Staël, Lamartine, Lamennais, George Sand, etc. In England, Southey, Wordsworth, and Byron. Great influence in Germany. Similarities with Carlyle, Kierkegaard, and Nietzsche even though former derives from Goethe and two latter would have denied affinities. Influence of R. on Tolstoy. Divergences. Influence on modern psychology. R.'s criticism of modern civilization has relation to socialism. Conflicting tendencies in *Contrat social* which R. said he himself couldn't understand. R. not lacking in historical sense and insisted on constitutions being based on background and experience of nations. By word *nature*, R. " entendait justement tout ce qu'il y a d'original, de spontané, de naïf dans la vie émotionnelle " (p. 76).

Hubert, René. Rousseau et l'école positiviste. APD 2:407-27, 1932. 2083

Deals particularly with antagonism towards R. of Comte, Durkheim, and Duguit. Author's purpose in this discerning and substantial article is to vindicate R.'s thought against attacks of members of French positivistic school. Review : P. Léon in AJJR 23:183-85, 1934.

— Rousseau et l'Encyclopédie; essai sur la formation des idées politiques de Rousseau (1742-1756). *See* 1310. 2084

Important for development of R.'s political ideas. Author believes in essential unity of R.'s thought. *See also* Beaulavon (no. 1876), and Schinz (no. 2191). Reviews : E. Carcassonne in RHL 38: 627-29, 1931 ; F.Pillionel in AJJR 18:369-70, 1927-28; H. Sée in Rhist 162:166-67, 1929.

Izoulet, J. B. J. De J. J. Russeo (J.-J. Rousseau) utrum misopolis fuerit an philopolis ex Genavensi codice cum ceteris Russei operibus collato quæritur. Alcan, 1894. 79 p. (Diss., Paris). 2085

Thesis characterized by Schinz as " excellente " (*infra* p. 183). Especially important for problems presented by the *Social contract* and the *Second discourse*. Object of thesis, wrote author, was to show that R. " ... a certainement esquissé une psychogenèse sociale." (*La cité moderne*, Alcan, 1896, p. 584.) Review : A. Schinz in EprR, p. 183, 233.

Janet, Paul. Comparaison des théories morales et sociales de Montesquieu et de Jean-Jacques Rousseau. *See* 1572. 2086

Janet studies Locke's ideas as reflected in work of Montesquieu and of R. Latter's principal borrowing from Locke was idea of equality. Janet believes that R.'s " gloire " is to have " ... élucidé... le droit et l'autorité de la volonté générale..." (p. 557) Janet thinks that R., had he lived to see Revolution, would not have belonged to the " ... parti démagogique et révolutionnaire." (p. 561).

Keller, Abraham C. Plutarch and Rousseau's First *discours*. PMLA 54:212-22, 1939. 2087

Judicious, compact article which, after citing R.'s own testimony regarding his lifelong enthusiasm for Plutarch, indicates important similarities in viewpoint between two authors. Avoids error of concentrating on a supposed single source and does not fail to point out that in many instances Plutarch's influence came to R. through Montaigne. On central question of arts and sciences, Plutarch and R. not in complete accord. Indeed, R. warps a passage of Plutarch to twist it to his purpose. Here it was Montaigne who offered R. the forthright support he sought. *See also* Oltramare (no. 2123).

Klein, Timotheus. Wieland und Rousseau. SVL 3:425-80, 1903; 4:129-74, 1904. (Diss., Munich) *See* 3195. 2088

A study of R.'s influence on Wieland.

Kritschewsky, S. B. J. J. Rousseau und Saint-Just; ein Beitrag zur Entwicklungsgeschichte der socialpolitischen Ideen der Montagnards. Bern, Wyss, 1895. 63 p. 2089

Interesting essay, with special reference to Saint-Just and his *Fragments des institutions républicaines*, on influence of ideas *versus* actual conditions. Considers that R.'s importance for French Revolution was that his political and social doctrines furnished theoretical formulas and justification for practical efforts and aims of the revolutionaries but does not believe they constituted motivating or driving force. Lack of success of Saint-Just and other disciples of R. in carrying out his political and social teachings during the Revolution shows, in author's opinion, ineffectiveness of theory when confronted with historical developments.

Lanson, Gustave. Deux phrases artistiques du xviiie siècle. In his : l'Art de la prose, 6e édition. Librairie des annales politiques et littéraires, (2e éd. 1909) p. 198-204. 2090

A few suggestive remarks on R.'s *phrase musicale*. Real power of his prose style is in its rhythm. *See* Wartburg, no. 2157.

— L'unité de la pensée de Jean-Jacques Rousseau. AJJR 8:1-31, 1912. 2091

Capital study of an important problem in R. scholarship. Believes that after 1752 the thought of the " vrai " R. followed certain constant directions, was not contradictory. *See also* his *Histoire de la littérature française*, p. 780-86. Review : A. Schinz in EprR, p. 33-34, 129, 373-74.

Lasserre, Pierre. Le romantisme français; essai sur la révolution dans les sentiments

et dans les idées au XIXᵉ siècle. Société
du Mercure de France, 1908. p. 9-547.
La ruine de l'individu (J.-J. Rousseau)
p. 9-74.   2092

Like Irving Babbitt in the U. S.,
Lasserre finds in R. point of departure
for our modern faults.
Reviews : J. Bainville in MerF 66:661-
76, Apr. 15, 1907; F. Baldensperger in
Rcr 41 (ns 63-64) : 456-58, 1907; R. Dou-
mic in RDM 5th per 38:924-35, Apr. 15,
1907; L. Dumur in MerF 67:577-600,
June 15, 1907; D. Parodi in Rmois 3:
719-27, Jan.-June, 1907, answered by
P. Lasserre in Rmois 4:355-66, July-Dec.,
1907; L. Pinvert in AJJR 4:301-04, 1908;
H. Potez in RHL 16:404-09, 1909;
A. Schinz in EprR, p. 62-63.

Lecoq, John P. Rousseau's system of
education in the light of modern research.
EF 9:289-98, March, 1945.   2093

Good article. Stresses need of fairness
in judging and of a real understanding
of R.'s purpose in *Émile*. " Rightly
considered and objectively studied, the
educational system of Rousseau still has
a real intrinsic value... Rousseau may,
with profit, be studied anew." p. 298.

Léon, Paul. L'idée de volonté générale chez
J.-J. Rousseau et ses antécédents historiques. APD 6:148-200, 1936.   2094

Important study, well presented.
Review : A. Cobban in AJJR 25:287-
92, 1936.

— Rousseau et les fondements de l'état moderne. APD 4:197-238, 1934. Reprinted,
Recueil Sirey, 1934.   2095

" ... une étude sur Rousseau et l'idée
du droit naturel, qui est la première partie
d'un ouvrage à paraître... A l'occasion
de la publication des travaux de
C. W. Hendel et de A. Cobban,
entr'autres, M. Paul Léon tente de dégager le sens de la pensée de Rousseau
'par rapport aux problèmes fonda-
mentaux de la politique et de la sociologie.' " Borgeaud, review *below*, p. 222.
Review : M. A. Borgeaud in AJJR 23:
222-24, 1934.

Lévy-Bruhl, Lucien. L'influence de Jean-
Jacques Rousseau en Allemagne. AESP
2:325-58, 1887.   2096

Synthesis of R.'s influence on German
writers, particularly of the *Sturm und
Drang* period. For supplementary

material, *see* EprR, p. 48-49. *See also*
Benrubi, no. 1940.

Lichtenberger, André. Rousseau—sa critique de la société. Rousseau—ses projets
de réforme. *In his :* Le socialisme au
XVIIIᵉ siècle : étude sur les idées socialistes
dans les écrivains français du XVIIIᵉ siècle
avant la Révolution. *See* 147, p. 128-51;
152-79. *See* 1052.   2097

Complementary chapters in which
author studies R.'s ideas on property and
society. Considers R. most important
figure in book. Second chapter particularly
important for R.'s views on property.
Concludes that however bold in theory,
R. was, practically, a conservative as
regards property; that far from being a
revolutionist himself, R. inadvertently
became the father, nevertheless, of many
subversive doctrines because of the
violence of his language and of subsequent
utilization by others of isolated passages
in his writings without regard to context
or restrictions.
Reviews : F.-A. Aulard in Rfr 29:89-91,
1895; F. P. in Rph 42:310-11, 1896.

Liepe, Wolfgang. Der junge Schiller und
Rousseau; eine Nachprüfung der Rousseau-
legende um den Räuberdichter. ZDP 51:
299-328, 1926.   2098

See EprR, p. 102-03.
Review : W. Müller in AJJR 19:220-
21, 1929-30.

— Friedrich Schiller und die Kulturphilo-
sophie des 18. Jahrhunderts; zur Deutung
der Jungfrau von Orleans. Grev 16:97-107,
1941.   2099

See EprR, p. 102-03.

— Kulturproblem und Totalitätsideal; zur
Entwicklung der Problemstellung von Rousseau zu Schiller. ZDK 41:738-50, 1927.
                                   2100

See EprR, p. 102-03.

Lovejoy, Arthur O. Monboddo and Rousseau. MP 30:275-96, 1932-33.   2101

Scotchman Monboddo and R. agree in
animality and undesirability of earliest
state of nature. Agree in relationship
between man and higher apes and hence
in kind of evolutionism. Certain that
Monboddo had read R.'s *Discours sur
l'inégalité* before writing his book, though
former implies that he hit on his ideas
independently. Developed his ideas
further than R., though R.'s " priority
in the enunciation of all of them renders

Monboddo's originality in these points somewhat questionable " (p. 295).
Reviews : A. Schinz in AJJR 23:177-80, 1934, and *ibid.*, 25:285-86, 1936.

McNeil, Gordon H. The cult of Rousseau and the French revolution. [n. p., 1945]. p. 197-212. Reprinted from JHI 6:197-212, Apr., 1945. (Part of a Diss., Chicago.) 2102

Distinguishes between cult and influence. Two phases : one literary, other political. First based on *Nouvelle Héloïse* and *Émile ;* second came only with French Revolution, which first brought *Contrat social* into popularity. It was a legendary R. who was popular. R. was adopted as symbol even by opposing factions who saw different things in his works and personality. Article constitutes brief and interesting summary based on unpublished U. of Chicago dissertation. Need of more detailed analysis of R.'s ideas in their relation, or non-relation, to French Revolution.

Maritain, Jacques. Trois réformateurs : Luther—Descartes—Rousseau. Plon, 1925. 284 p. Translation : London, Sheed and Ward, 1928. 234 p.   2103

See Schinz, *infra.*
Reviews : L. Pinvert in AJJR 17:268-70, 1926; A. Schinz in EprR, p. 88.

Markovitch, Milan I. Jean-Jacques Rousseau et Tolstoï. Champion, 1928. 419 p. (Diss., Paris).   2104

Study of R.'s influence on Tolstoy. Some Slavic bibliography and Index of names. " L'ouvrage... est... le plus étendu et le plus systématique qui ait été consacré jusqu'à présent à ce sujet..." Benrubi, review *below*, p. 372. *See also* Dwelshauvers, nos. 1937 and 1940.
Reviews : I. Benrubi in AJJR 18:371-74, 1927-28; J. Patouillet in Rcr 96:278-81, June, 1929; A. Schinz in MLN 44:550-52, 1929; H. Tronchon in RU 40²:249-50, Oct. 1931.

Martin, Kingsley. Democracy. *In his :* French liberal thought in the eighteenth century. *See* 1055. p. 192-219. 2105

Whole chapter (VIII) devoted to R., with several sub-headings containing his name. R. " was a genius whose real influence cannot be traced with precision because it pervaded all the thought that followed him " (p. 219).
Review : A. L. S. in AJJR 19:231-33, 1929-30.

Masson, Paul-Marie. Les idées de Rousseau sur la musique. Rmus 8:1-17, (June 15), 23-32 (July-Aug.), 1912. 2106

Characterized by Schinz, review below, as an " excellent article " on subject. *See* no. 325.
Reviews : A. François in AJJR 9:149, 1913; A. Schinz in EprR, p. 292.

Masson, Pierre-Maurice. Rousseau contre Helvétius. RHL 18:103-24, 1911. 2107

Important article. Additions and corrections to article of Schinz, *La Profession de foi du vicaire savoyard et le livre De l'esprit* (RHL 17:225-61, 1910) (no. 2190). Gives complete text of R.'s critical marginal notes on Helvétius, previously published only in part in R.'s collected works. R. wrote an early draft of *Émile* before reading Helvétius. Did not at beginning write *Profession de foi* to refute Helvétius, but added his passages of refutation later.
Review : L. Pinvert in AJJR 8:344-45, 1912.

Maugras, Gaston. Querelles de philosophes; Voltaire et J.-J. Rousseau. *See* 1719. 2108

Only extensive and detailed study of relations between Voltaire and R. Untrustworthy, however, because of author's attitude, constantly favorable to Voltaire and hostile to R. For correction of some points in connection with their relations up to 1764, *see* Havens's article, no. 2176. *See also* Brunetière, no. 1962.
Reviews : C. R. in BU 35:666-68, July-Sept. 1887; A. Schinz in EprR, p. 46.

Merlant, Joachim. Rousseau et le Werthérisme. *In his :* Le roman personnel de Rousseau à Fromentin. *See* 725. p. 32-53. 2109

R. serves as point of departure and basis of comparison throughout. Importance of R.'s emphasis upon subjective study of personality. Goethe, Restif de La Bretonne, Sénancour, Chateaubriand, Mme de Staël, Benjamin Constant, Sainte-Beuve, and Musset. Fromentin's *Dominique.* Autobiographical novel in form conceived by R. has disappeared, but only after enriching whole field of literature.
Reviews : F. Baldensperger in Rcr ns 60:117-18, 1905; G. Lanson in RU 14²:46-47, 1905; L. Pinvert in AJJR 2:281-82, 1906; A. Schinz in EprR, p. 66.

Meynier, Albert. Jean-Jacques Rousseau

révolutionnaire. Schleicher, [1910?] 254 p.
                                              2110

" En 1909 M. Edme Champion a publié un livre intitulé : *Jean-Jacques Rousseau et la Révolution française;* le but de l'auteur était de montrer ce qui, dans la Révolution, ne dérive pas de Rousseau. L'objet de M. Albert Meynier est au contraire de rechercher ce qui procède de lui. *Jean-Jacques Rousseau révolutionnaire* est la rédaction, la mise au point d'un cours libre professé... à... Toulouse... mais on sent dès les premières lignes, et plus encore par l'excellence de la composition, que ce ' petit livre,' comme dit l'auteur, a été plus assidûment préparé et plus longuement mûri que bien des gros volumes. La forme en est très accessible, et l'érudition aimable." (Monin, review *below*, p. 644.) *See,* on this important and controversial subject of R. and the Revolution, Champion (no. 2047), Kritschewsky (no. 2089), Mornet (no. 45), and Peyre (no. 2126).

Reviews : E. Barthélemy in MerF 100: 365-67, Nov., 1912; B. Bouvier in AJJR 9:129-31, 1913; H. Monin in RHRF 3: 644-45, 1912; L. Roustan in Rcr 75:372-73, 1913; A. Schinz in EprR, p. 225; Anon in GR 73:216, March 10, 1913.

Moffat, Margaret M. Rousseau et la querelle du théâtre au XVIIIe siècle. Boccard, 1930. 424 p.   2111

" L'ouvrage prend la suite des articles que M. Bourquin a publiés dans la *Revue d'histoire littéraire* sur *La controverse sur la comédie au XVIIIe siècle et La lettre à d'Alembert...* (no. 2041). En continuant et achevant les études de M. Bourquin, Mlle Moffat n'a pas seulement achevé l'histoire d'un des épisodes de la guerre philosophique, elle a achevé un commentaire désormais indispensable de l'une des grandes œuvres de la littérature française." (Daniel Mornet in RHL 38:114-15, 1931.) *See also* Barras (no. 2030), Bourquin (no. 2041), Von der Mühll (no. 2153).

Reviews : P. Chaponnière in AJJR 19: 261-62, 1929-30; F. Gaiffe in RU 40²: 427, 1931; D. Mornet, *supra.*

Monglond, André. Le préromantisme français. *See* 818.   2112

Review : B. Bouvier in AJJR 20:235-40, 1931; RLC 11:327-28, 1931.

Monod, Albert. J.-J. Rousseau. *In his :* De Pascal à Chateaubriand; les défenseurs français du Christianisme de 1670 à 1802. Alcan, 1916. p. 402-24. (Diss., Paris). 2113

Chapter IX (p. 402-24) devoted to R. He was first man of genius in 18th century to defend religion. But, in appealing to the inner light, ignoring original sin, and attacking miracles, R. shocked orthodox believers, both Catholic and Protestant. At same time, he alienated his former philosophic friends. R., however, greatly stimulated apologists of Christianity. He gave to the word *divine,* not a supernatural, but an ethical meaning.

Reviews : A. François in AJJR 11:246, 1916-17 (paragraph only); G. Lanson in RR 9:236-38, 1918; A. Schinz in EprR, p. 95.

More, Paul Elmer. Rousseau. *In his :* Shelburne essays. Sixth series. New York and London, Putnam, 1909. 214-41. 2114

Summary : the " dæmonic personality " of R. imposed his private emotions upon the modern world in the form of a new and havoc-working religion. R. fathered romanticism and " a morbid individualism that seeks to hide itself under the cloak of a collective ideal." (p. 237). From English sources came the " dynamic derivation " of his thought.

Reviews : A. Schinz in EprR, p. 110 and in AJJR 10:200-02, 1914-15.

Moreau-Rendu, S. L'idée de bonté naturelle chez J.-J. Rousseau. Rivière, 1929. 337 p.
                                              2115

Only extensive book on this basic aspect of R.'s thought. Unacquainted with previous studies of Havens, no. 2077, in RHL. *See also* Ellis (no. 2169), Lovejoy (no. 2179), Schinz (no. 2139), and Wright (no. 1951).

Reviews : N. H. Crowell in PhR 41: 91-92, 1932; F. Grandjean in AJJR 19: 262-66, 1929-30; H. Guillemin in AJJR 29:328-29, 1941-42.

Mornet, Daniel. Les enseignements des bibliothèques privées (1750-1780). RHL 17:449-96, 1910.   2116

Significant findings concerning diffusion of R.'s writings in pre-Revolutionary France, based upon analysis of 500 catalogs of books in private libraries.

Reviews : A. François in AJJR 7:177, 1911; D. Williams in EHR 48:416, 1933.

— L'influence de J.-J. Rousseau au XVIIIe siècle. AJJR 8:33-67, 1912.   2117

Largely synthesis of author's previous

studies and of work by Edme Champion, no. 2047. " Tous les sujets que choisit Rousseau sont exactement des sujets d'actualité " (p. 33). " Rousseauism " before R. In 500 private libraries of 18th century, before the French Revolution (*see* no. 2116), 185 copies of *Nouvelle Héloïse* to one of *Contrat social* (p. 44). " Jean-Jacques n'a pas créé le goût du sentiment; mais il l'a fait tyrannique " (p. 52). Influence on Romanticism and on foreign countries. Both hated and admired by opposing parties of Revolution. " Au total Rousseau fut au xviiie siècle un puissant libérateur d'instincts " (p. 65). Article stops with 1789. Does not deal in detail with R.'s possible influence on French Revolution. *See* Peyre, no. 2126.

— Le romantisme en France au xviiie siècle. Hachette, 1912. 286 p.   2118

Capital study extending to 1789. While emphasizing fully R.'s great importance to French romanticism, here defined essentially as " le goût profond de la nature," author points to other forces which also contributed heavily to its development. " Ce livre se donne pour une simple mise au point de travaux antérieurs... Et pourtant son livre reste avant tout une contribution originale." (Monglond, review below, p. 207-08.) Table of references, but no index. Reproductions of sixteen interesting engravings.

Reviews : P. Brun in RIE 66:371-72, 1913; A. François in AJJR 9:131-32, 1913; A. Monglond in RHL 20:204-08, 1913.

— Le Rousseauisme avant Rousseau. Jean-Jacques Rousseau. Leçons faites à l'École des hautes études sociales. Bibliothèque générale des sciences sociales. Alcan, 1912. p. 47-66.   2119

Mme de Staël's assertion that R. " ... n'a rien inventé de nouveau " finds corroboration in this essay by Mornet, which contains views expounded by him in various other writings. Defining Rousseauism as essentially " l'exaltation de la sensibilité," author, by careful documentation, demonstrates that ground was prepared in France long before 1761 for success and influence of *Nouvelle Héloïse*.

— Le sentiment de la nature en France de J.-J. Rousseau à Bernardin de Saint-Pierre; essai sur les rapports de la littérature et des

mœurs. Hachette, 1907. 572 p. (Diss., Paris).   2120

" ... l'idée centrale du travail, celle qui semble avoir servi de point de départ à l'auteur, c'est celle-ci : quelle est la part réelle de Rousseau dans ce magnifique éveil du sentiment de la nature dont témoignent, au xviiie siècle, les mœurs et les arts, notamment la littérature ? Cette part... ce qui appartient en propre à l'auteur de la *Nouvelle Héloïse*... c'est l'entrée en rapport de la nature avec la vie morale... c'est, on peut dire, l'enlacement définitif de la nature et de l'âme, d'où naît une forme nouvelle de la sensibilité." (A. François, review *below*, p. 311.) This classic study abundantly documented, equipped with very detailed *Table des matières*, and four valuable indexes.

Reviews : F. Baldensperger in Rcr 65: 447-49, June 11, 1908; E. Faguet in Rlat 7:534-44, 1908; A. François in AJJR 4: 310-14, 1908; J. Haas in ZFSL 35:216-17, Mar. 26, 1910; G. Lanson in RHL 15: 168-70, 1908.

Ogden, Henry V. S. The antithesis of nature and art, and Rousseau's rejection of the theory of natural rights. APSR 32:643-54, 1938.   2121

Important article, especially as regards *Second discourse*. " It is the purpose of this paper to point out that Rousseau did reject the doctrine of natural rights decisively, and to show how he came to do so." (p. 643-44.)

Review : A. Schinz in AJJR 27:309-10, 1938.

Oliver, Alfred R. The Encyclopedists as critics of music. *See* 337.   2122

Considerable information on R. as " chief authority on music " in the *Encyclopédie* and as critic of music. *See also* Reichenburg, no. 2129.

Reviews : H. G. F. in Mlet 29:295-96, 1948; D. J. Grout in MQ 34:127-29, 1948; G. R. Havens in RR 40:144-45, 1949; J. A. Westrup in FS 2:368-69, 1948.

Oltramare, André. Plutarque dans Rousseau. MélBB, p. 185-96.   2123

Study of influence of Plutarch on R., and particularly as regards genesis of first *Discours*. Not Diderot but Plutarch. *See :* Havens (no. 1886), and Keller (no. 2087).

Osborn, Annie M. Rousseau and Burke; a study of the idea of liberty in eighteenth-century political thought. London, New

York, Oxford University press, 1940. 272 p. (Diss., Columbia). 2124

Study and comparison of political philosophies of the two men. Good treatment of respective political backgrounds. Among the chapters : *The foundations of the modern state, The general will, The British constitution.* Reviews : E. E. Kellett in NSN 20:46, July 13, 1940; L. Ledermann in AJJR 30:194-99, 1943-45; B. E. Lippincott in APSR 35:969-71, 1941; M. B. M. in Jph 38:109-10, 1941; H. V. S. Ogden in AHR 46:899-900, 1940-41; J. S. Schapiro in PSQ 56:445-47, 1941.

Parodi, D. La philosophie religieuse de J.-J. Rousseau. RMM 20:295-320, 1912. 2125

Valuable brief article, published also under *J.-J. Rousseau; leçons faites à l'École des hautes études sociales,* 1912, p. 121-54. For more complete study of subject, cf. Masson, no. 1928. Review : Anon in AJJR 19:267, 1929-30; A. Schinz in EprR, p. 272.

Peyre, Henri. The influence of eighteenth century ideas on the French Revolution. JHI 10:63-87, 1949. 2126

Important article suggestive of many topics for further study. Differs with Mornet as to importance of ideas in shaping Revolution. Many passages on influence of Rousseau and other 18th century thinkers. *See* Champion (no. 2047), Dide (no. 2058), Mornet (nos. 2117, 45, 1062, 1432, 2766).

Pinot, Virgile. Rousseau en Suède; les causes de son succès et de son influence. RDS 2:389-96, 1914. 2127

Nouvelle Héloïse, never translated into Swedish in 18th century, was most read novel in Sweden in this period. *Profession de foi du vicaire savoyard* was influential. R.'s influence on Oxenstiern. Swedish adversaries of R., etc.

Pons, Jacques. L'éducation en Angleterre entre 1750 et 1800; aperçu sur l'influence pédagogique de J.-J. Rousseau en Angleterre. Leroux, 1919. 266 p. (Diss., Paris). 2128

Author finds that R.'s influence was felt in enthusiasm for education in period studied, in pedagogy of new school of educators, where it was mingled with that of Locke, in textbooks of science, and in education of women. Only rarely, however, did authors of moral tales for children follow fundamental principles of school of R., namely, that mind and heart of the student should be studied, that education should be an experimental science. Classified bibliography of sources used found on p. 253-62. Review : A. Schinz in EprR, p. 265.

Reichenburg, Louisette E. Contribution à l'histoire de la " querelle des Bouffons," guerre de brochures suscitées par le Petit prophète de Grimm et par la Lettre sur la musique française de Rousseau. Philadelphia, 1937. 136 p. (Diss., Pennsylvania). 2129

Good study of this significant episode in R.'s early literary life. *See also* Oliver, no. 2122. Reviews : P. E. Schazmann in AJJR 26:337-38, 1937; A. Schinz in EprR, p. 293, 325.

Reichenburg, Marguerite. Essai sur les lectures de Rousseau. Geneva, Jullien, (Philadelphia, 1932) 1934. 209 p. (Diss., Pennsylvania). 2130

Valuable indication of R.'s reading. Contains rather large number of errors of detail. This study printed in part in AJJR 21 (1932). Author appears in Schinz's EprR as Richebourg. *See also* P. Léon, *Additions et corrections au répertoire des lectures de J.-J. Rousseau.* AJJR 23:243-50, 1934. Reviews : G. Ascoli in Rcr 102:163-64, 1935; [P. Léon] in AJJR 23:234-42, 1934; D. Mornet in RHL 42:284-85, 1935; A. Schinz in EprR, p. 148-49; G. L. Van Roosbroeck in RR 26:61-62, 1935.

Rice, Richard A. Rousseau and the poetry of nature in eighteenth century France. Northampton, Mass., Smith college, 1925. 96 p. (SSML, v. 6, no. 3 and 4). 2131

R.'s treatment of natural scenery, his background and influence, with particular reference to *Nouvelle Héloïse.* Reviews : G. Chinard in MLN 41:418-19, 1926; A. Schinz in AJJR 17:248-49, 1926, in EprR, p. 113, 383, in RHL 33:459-61, 1926.

Rod, Edouard. L'affaire J.-J. Rousseau. Perrin, 1906. 359 p. 2132

" Ce que M. Edouard Rod appelle ' l'Affaire Jean-Jacques Rousseau '... c'est l'ensemble des dissensions qui se produisirent à Genève de 1762 à 1766, à propos de la condamnation de Jean-Jacques Rousseau, comme auteur du *Contrat social* et de l'*Émile,* par le Petit

Conseil de la République de Genève."
(Faguet, *infra*, p. 385.) *See also* Rovillain,
no. 2134.

Reviews : E. Faguet in Rlat 5:385-401,
1906; G. Lanson in RU 15²:35-36, 1906;
A. Schinz in MLN 22:252-56, 1907.

Roddier, Henri. J.-J. Rousseau en Angleterre au xviiiᵉ siècle : l'œuvre et l'homme.
Boivin, [1950]. 435 p. (Paris diss.)   2132A

" ... vaste travail d'ensemble mené à
bonne fin, au cours de treize années, par
M. Roddier. Son ouvrage, de première
main, repose entièrement sur des dépouil-
lements originaux. C'est une mine et
c'est une somme." Carré, review below,
p. 464. See also Bandy (no. 1953), Lévy-
Bruhl (no. 1991), Peoples (no. 1998),
Pons (no. 2128), Pottle (no. 2004),
Roddier (no. 2012), Sewall (nos. 2192-
95), Warner (nos. 1863, 2156, 2200-02).
Publication date of Roddier's book pre-
cluded cross-referring these studies to it.
Review : J.-M. Carré in RLC 24:
464-67, 1950.

Roshem, Julien. Rousseau et l'hygiène de
la première enfance. RPL [50²]:53-57,
July 13, 1912.   2133

A physician's study of the *Émile*,
restricted to alimentation and clothing.
Conclusion : " Seul Rousseau révolu-
tionna les mœurs; des progrès aujour-
d'hui obtenus, il est le premier auteur.
L'opinion courante est juste, qui attribue
à l'*Émile* la renaissance de l'allaitement
maternel." p. 57.

Rovillain, Eugène E. L'Angleterre et les
troubles de Genève en 1766-1767, d'après
les papiers du comte de Shelburne. ZSG
7:164-203, 1927.   2134

" Nous avons jugé qu'un article qui
donnerait des extraits [from the *Shelburne
papers* in the William L. Clements
Library], rendrait quelque service à ceux
qu'intéresse la période troublée, mais
féconde en idées libérales, qui suivit à
Genève la condamnation de Rousseau et
de ses deux grandes œuvres, l'*Émile* et le
Contrat social." (p. 165) In Courtois'
opinion, these papers " ... constituent un
chapitre nouveau de l'*Affaire Rousseau*..."
(infra.) See Rod, no. 2132.
Review : L.-J. Courtois in AJJR 18:
408, 1927-28.

Sabine, George H. The rediscovery of the
community : Rousseau. *In his :* A history
of political theory. New York, Holt, (1937)
1938. 575-96.   2135

On the whole, deals severely with R.
To be compared with more favorable
treatment by C. E. Vaughan (no. 1882).
Reviews : H. Janzen in APSR 31:959-
60, 1937; H. J. Laski in NSN 14:1030,
Dec. 11 1937; H. W. Schneider in Jph
34:527-29, 1937.

Schiefenbusch, Erna. L'influence de Jean-
Jacques Rousseau sur les beaux-arts en
France. Trans. from the German by Elie
Moroy. AJJR 19:1-212, 1929-30.   2136

Study limited to 18th century. Chapters
on : *Les beaux-arts jugés par Rousseau, le
Rousseauisme dans la théorie de l'art, le
Rousseauisme dans les beaux-arts. Bibliographie* and *Index des noms propres.* " ... sur
l'évolution du goût et des théories esthétiques, et sur la pratique des ' arts
majeurs ' dans leur relation avec Rousseau, l'ouvrage est instructif, plein de
choses, et fait d'original." (Carcassonne,
infra, p. 141-42.)
Review : H. Carcassonne in RHL 41:
141-42, 1934.

Schinz, Albert. Les dangers du cliché littéraire : le Dr. Johnson et Jean-Jacques
Rousseau. MLN 57:573-80, 1942.   2137

Danger lies in perpetuation of notion,
made popular by Johnson's well-known
quip on R., as reported by Boswell, that
Johnson and R. had nothing in common.
Author cites, to contrary, parallels in
their philosophies.

— La pensée religieuse de Rousseau et ses
récents interprètes. Alcan, 1927. 52 p.
Also in : SSML, v. X, no. 1.   2138

Underlines R.'s Protestantism and
insistence on reason in contrast to the
Catholicism of Masson's famous interpretation (no. 1928). Discussion of Abbé
Bremond, Victor Giraud, and Maritain,
among others, in a similar connection.
Reviews : G. Berguer in AJJR 18:376-
77, 1927-28; E. Magne in MerF 223:424,
Oct. 15, 1930.

— La théorie de la bonté naturelle de l'homme
chez Rousseau. RDS 1:434-47, 1913. 2139

Pioneer study of this basic aspect of
R.'s thought. Concentrates on *First* and
Second discourses. Concise summaries of
this article given by author in EprR 187-
88 and in his *La pensée de Jean-Jacques
Rousseau,* p. 177-79. *See also* Havens
(no. 2077), Ellis (no. 2169), Lovejoy
(no. 2179), Moreau-Rendu (no. 2115),
and Wright (no. 1951).

Review : A. François in AJJR 10:233, 1914-15.

Schmidt, Erich. Richardson, Rousseau und Goethe; ein Beitrag zur Geschichte des Romans im 18. Jahrhundert. Jena, Frommann (1875); Biedermann, 1924. 331 p. *See* 3076, 3206.   2140

Epoch-making study of relationship between *Clarissa Harlowe*, the *Nouvelle Héloïse*, and *Werther*. Deals not only with Rousseau's influence on Goethe but also with points wherein the two authors resemble each other. Parts of book outmoded by later scholarship. *See* Aron (no. 2028), Benrubi (no. 1937).
Reviews : C. J. in Rcr 156-59, Sept. 1875 ; W. Müller in AJJR 16:267-68, 1924-25 ; A. Schinz in EprR, p. 49, 202, 204.

Sée, Henri. Jean-Jacques Rousseau. *In his :* Les idées politiques en France au XVIIIe siècle. Hachette, 1920. 105-36.   2141

Brief *mise au point* of leading political and social ideas of R., consisting largely of an arrangement of pertinent quotations from his writings.
Reviews : F. M. Fling in AHR 26: 507-09, 1920-21; A. Schinz in EprR, p. 225; W. J. Shepard in APSR 15:441-42, 1921.

Spell, Jefferson R. Rousseau in the Spanish world before 1833; a study in Franco-Spanish literary relations. Austin, Univ. of Texas press, 1938. 325 p.   2142

Important monograph on R.'s influence. Incorporates author's previous study on *Pygmalion in Spain.* For an *analyse d'ouvrage* by Paul Hazard, *see : RLC* 20:255-56, 1940.
Reviews : E. H. Hespelt in RR 31: 82-84, 1940; A. Schinz in AJJR 27:310-13, 1938, and in EprR, p. 294.

Spink, John S. Jean-Jacques Rousseau et Genève; essai sur les idées politiques et religieuses de Rousseau dans leur relation avec la pensée genevoise au XVIIIe siècle, pour servir d'introduction aux Lettres écrites de la montagne. Boivin, 1934. 324 p. (Diss., Paris).   2143

Important for background of the *Lettres de la montagne*, the *Affaire de Genève*, and especially for understanding the *Social contract.*
Reviews : A. Cahen in RU¹ 44:442, May 1935; P. C. in JGen Aug. 6, 1934; D. Mornet in RHL 42:280-81, 1935;

P.-E. Schazmann in AJJR 23:219-20, 1934; A. Schinz in EprR, p. 41, 101, 219-20, 251-52, 342 and in RR 28:46-53, 1937; H. Sée in Rhist 180:122-23, 1937; J. S. Wood in RCC 35²:765-68, July 30, 1934.

Spurlin, Paul M. Rousseau in America 1760-1809. FrAR 1:8-16, 1948.   2144

Presentation of some findings of research made to determine extent of American acquaintance with R.'s writings in formative and early period, opinions of colonists and later Americans concerning his ideas and theories, and use made of them.

Texte, Joseph. Jean-Jacques Rousseau et les origines du cosmopolitisme littéraire; étude sur les relations littéraires de la France et de l'Angleterre au XVIIIe siècle. *See* 740, 831, 2912. English tr. by J. W. Matthews. London, Duckworth; New York, Macmillan, 1899. 393 p.   2145

Epoch-making study having as thesis that literary cosmopolitanism was born in 18th century " de l'union féconde du génie anglais avec le génie de Jean-Jacques." p. xvi. According to Texte, " montrer en Rousseau l'homme qui a le plus fait pour nous inspirer le goût et le besoin des littératures du Nord,—c'est tout l'objet de ce livre." p. xi.
Chapters on consequences to French literature of Revocation of Edict of Nantes, and of the French Revolution, on the popularizers of English thought : Muralt, Prévost, Voltaire, on Samuel Richardson, etc. No Index.
Reviews : L. P. Betz in ZFSL 18²: 153-82, 1896; E. Faguet in RPL [32²]: 167-70, Aug. 10, 1895; S. Rocheblave in RIE 30:412-15, 1895; A. Schinz in EprR 58-59, 213-14; M. Souriau in RHL 3:128-31, 1896 (see reply of Texte o, *ibid.*, 286-91); L. Stephen in *Studies of a biographer* 4:247-79, 1902; E. M. de Vogüé in RDM 130:676-91, Aug. 1, 1895.

Trahard, Pierre. Les maîtres de la sensibilité française au XVIIIe siècle. *See* 832, v. 3.   2146

Of twelve chapters in this volume, eleven devoted to R. Able treatment of R.'s " sensibilité." " J'ignore, en définitive, si je crois comprendre Rousseau, parce que je l'aime, ou si je l'aime, parce que je crois le comprendre " (p. 258). Has extensive *Bibliographie sur J.-J. Rousseau,* p. 279-309.
Reviews : G. Ascoli in Rcr 100:329-32,

1933; G. R. Havens in MLN 49:268-69, 1934; M. E. I. Robertson in MLR 29: 97-99, 1934; F. Ruchon in AJJR 21: 289-91, 1932; A. Schinz in EprR, p. 142-43, 376.

— La sensibilité révolutionnaire (1789-1794). *See* 690. 2147

Discusses role of emotion during Revolution and, in chapter 2 particularly, traces its relation to preceding century with some brief and passing references to Rousseau.
Reviews : M. Bardon in RCC 38:94-96, Apr. 15, 1937; A. Schinz in RR 29:288-90, 1938, and in EprR, p. 11; J. Thomas in RHL 44:564-66, 1937.

Tresnon, Jeannette. The paradox of Rousseau. PMLA 43:1010-25, 1928. 2148

Attack on Havens's interpretation of R.'s idea of natural goodness. For Havens's reply, *see* no. 2076.
Review : A. Schinz in AJJR 18:356-57, 1927-28.

Vaughan, Charles E. Studies in the history of political philosophy before and after Rousseau. *See* 107. *See also* 1064, 3077. 2149

" Anyone who wishes to study the development of the doctrine of social contract, from the dogmatic individualism and legalism of its beginnings to the social theory of revived Hellenism into which it dissolved in the days of Hegel and his successors, a socialism made practicable by democratic nationalism, cannot do better than turn to these pages." Catlin, review *below*, p. 90.
Reviews : G. E. G. Catlin in PhR 36: 89-90, 1927; R. M. MacIver in AHR 45:860-62, 1939-40; A. Schinz in AJJR 28:139, 1939-40.

Vauquelin, Robert. Les origines de la psychologie pédagogique de Rousseau à Kant. Alcan, 1934. 194 p. 2150

Reviews : P. Bovet in AJJR 23:220, 1934; A. Schinz in EprR, p. 260-61; Z. Tourneur in MerF 263:601-02, Nov. 1, 1935.

Vial, Francisque. La doctrine d'éducation de J.-J. Rousseau. Delagrave, 1920. 208 p. 2151

Reviews : E. Claparède in AJJR 13: 251, 1920-21; A. Schinz in EprR, p. 86, 98, 188-89, 261-63.

Villey, Pierre. L'influence de Montaigne sur les idées pédagogiques de Locke et de Rousseau. Hachette, 1911. 270 p. 2152

Important study of Montaigne's influence on R.'s *First* and *Second discourses* and on *Émile*.
Reviews : A. François in AJJR 8:341-42, 1912; D. Mornet in RHL 19:220, 1912; J. Plattard in RER 9:333-35, 1911.

Von der Mühll, Emanuel. Rousseau et les réformateurs du théâtre. MLN 55:161-69, 1940. 2153

Points out closeness of R.'s and Diderot's ideas on theatre and emphasizes influence exerted by R., in *Lettre à d'Alembert*, on reformers of theatre in 18th century France and on *drame sérieux*. Corrects an interpretation of Moffat, no. 2111.
Review : A. Schinz in AJJR 28:141, 1939-40.

Vreeland, Williamson Updike. Étude sur les rapports littéraires entre Genève et l'Angleterre jusqu'à la publication de la Nouvelle Héloïse. Geneva, Kündig, 1901. (Diss., Geneva). *See* 2814. 2154

First part deals with *Les Anglais à Genève et les Genevois en Angleterre jusqu'au milieu du XVIIIe siècle*. Second part treats of *La nouvelle Héloïse et Clarisse Harlowe*. Lanson expresses himself thus in review below : " La partie de cette étude qui concerne les relations de Genève et de l'Angleterre est instructive et neuve... la partie proprement littéraire est plus faible." There are findings of importance to problem of English influence.
Review : G. Lanson in RU 10²:472, 1901.

Vuy, Jules. Origine des idées politiques de Rousseau. 2nd ed. Geneva, Trembley, (1878) 1889. 258 p. 2155

Old study but important subject. Rather extensively treated.
Reviews : J. F. Nourrisson in AMP 110:904-09, 1878; A. Rivier in RBelgique 28:434-37, 1878.

Warner, James H. The basis of J.-J. Rousseau's contemporaneous reputation in England. MLN 55:270-80, 1940. 2156

Concludes that his reputation rested upon his emotional and sentimental appeal, an appeal heightened by sentimental and social forces at work in latter half of 18th century.

Review : A. Schinz in AJJR 28:142, 1939-40, and in EprR, p. 214.

Wartburg, W. von. Rousseau's style. *In his :* Évolution et structure de la langue française. Leipzig and Berlin, Teubner; Cambridge, Heffer, 1934. p. 199-203. 2157

R.'s style " est le reflet de son âme " (p. 199). He mingles impressions from different senses such as sight and touch. Likewise, " pour lui l'impression morale est inséparable de l'impression visuelle " (p. 200). Familiar and popular expressions. New use of vocabulary. Music of his prose. Analysis of his rhythm. Variety of his style. R. says : " Mon style inégal et naturel, tantôt rapide et tantôt diffus, tantôt sage et tantôt fou, tantôt grave et tantôt gai fera lui-même partie de mon histoire " (p. 203). Cf. G. Lanson, *L'art de la prose,* no. 2090, p. 198-204.
Review (brief comment) : A. Schinz in EprR, p. 382.

Williams, David. The influence of Rousseau on political opinion, 1760-95. EHR 48: 414-30, 1933. 2158

Interesting *mise au point* of question of influence of *Social contract* in France. Influence considered slight indeed until Revolution. Writer takes into consideration evidence provided by Mornet, no. 2116, in his investigation of private libraries.
Review : P. Léon in AJJR 23:175-77, 1934.

Windenberger, J. L. Essai sur le système de politique étrangère de J.-J. Rousseau : la république confédérative des petits états. Picard, 1900. 308 p. 2159

" M. Windenberger begins his work with a review of the system of Rousseau as applied to a single state, but follows the enquiry a stage farther. Assuming the existence of a social contract, how shall the small state, which was Rousseau's ideal, maintain itself in the presence of powerful and aggressive neighbors ? ... Windenberger's book presents a careful and complete study of the international politics of Rousseau, but all that is new in his discussion might easily have been stated with greater brevity. The last 50 pages of the book contain interesting extracts from the Geneva manuscript of the *Contrat social,* and unpublished manuscripts in the Neuchâtel library." Merriam, review *below,* p. 386.

Reviews : A. Bertrand in RIE 40:562-64, 1900; J. B. in EHR 19:404-05, 1904; A. Lichtenberger in Renc, Dec. 22, 1900, p. 1056; C. E. Merriam in AHR 6:385-86, 1900-01.

Wyneken, Friedrich A. Rousseaus Einfluss auf Klinger. Berkeley, Univ. of California press, 1912. 85 p. (Diss., California) (CPMP, v. 3, no. 1). 2160

" Contribution à l'étude de l'influence de Rousseau sur les écrivains allemands de la période du *Sturm und Drang.*" A. François in AJJR 9:102, 1913.

Xylander, Oskar. Heinrich von Kleist und J. J. Rousseau. Berlin, Ebering, 1937. 389 p. (Diss. Munich). 2161

" He has exercised discriminating judgment in the difficult question of literary influence, in pointing out differences as well as similarities between Rousseau and Kleist, and in differentiating between mere kinship of spirit and actual influence... the treatise as a whole is a commendable contribution." Blankenagel, review *below,* p. 306-07.
Review : J. C. Blankenagel in MLN 54:306-07, 1939.

Studies of Individual Works

Ayers, Eleanor H. Histoire de l'impression et de la publication de la Lettre à d'Alembert de J.-J. Rousseau. PMLA 37:527-65, 1922. 2162

Reviews : A. François in AJJR 15:369-70, 1923; A. Schinz in EprR, p. 189-90.

Battaglia, Otto Forst de. Un peu de lumière sur les Considérations. AJJR 17:97-119, 1926. 2163

R.'s *Considérations sur le gouvernement de Pologne* was first published, with alterations and omissions, by Wielhorski in 1782. Original and only authentic text still awaits its editor.
Reviews : E. Carcassonne in RHL 35: 595-96, 1928; A. Schinz in EprR, p. 251.

Claparède, E. Rousseau et l'origine du langage. AJJR 24:95-119, 1935. 2164

" Une étude intéressante et originale à propos de l'*Essai sur l'origine du langage.* ... L'auteur voit en Rousseau un précurseur de Jespersen... et de Ch. Bally... Il s'agit de la place accordée au sentiment et à la passion dans l'origine du langage." Schinz, EprR, p. 294-95.
Review : E. Carcassonne in RHL 44: 562, 1937.

Crocker, Lester G. Diderot's influence on Rousseau's First *Discours*, by L. G. Krakeur. PMLA 52:398-404, 1937. *See* 2329.
2165

Additional evidence on behalf of R.'s originality in this *Discourse*. *See also* Havens, no. 2174.
Reviews : A. Schinz in AJJR 26:327, 1937, and in EprR, p. 171-72.

Dedeck-Héry, Ernestine. Jean-Jacques Rousseau et le projet de constitution pour la Corse; histoire des pourparlers de J.-J. Rousseau avec ses correspondants corses et des répercussions de ces pourparlers dans le monde des lettres. Philadelphia, 1932. 112 p. (Diss., Pennsylvania).
2166

Reviews : L.-J. Courtois in AJJR 21:274-75, 1932; A. Schinz in EprR 250; H. Sée in RHM 9 (ns 3):457-58, 1934; J. Thomas in Rcr 100:494-95, 1933.

Delaruelle, L. Les sources principales de J.-J. Rousseau dans le Premier discours à l'Académie de Dijon. RHL 19:245-71, 1912.
2167

See also author's *Encore les sources de Rousseau dans le Premier discours, ibid.*, 20:424, 1913.
Basic general study of sources of R.'s *First discourse*. *See* Havens, no. 1886, Introduction, p. 61-82, for more recent *étude d'ensemble*.

Dufour, Théophile. La première rédaction des Confessions (Livres I-IV); publiée d'après le manuscrit autographe. AJJR 4:xvi, 1-276, 1908. (Extracted and published at Geneva, Jullien, 1909. 276 p.). 2168

Important early text of first half of *Confessions*. Beginning shows by direct reference significant influence of Montaigne, reference later eliminated.
See Schinz, EprR, p. 159.
Review : D. Mornet in RHL 17:415-17, 1910.

Ellis, (Miss) M. B. Julie or La Nouvelle Héloïse : a synthesis of Rousseau's thought (1749-1759). Toronto, Univ. of Toronto press, 1949. 209 p. 2169

Important recent study. With abundant citations, aims to demonstrate complete unity of R.'s thought up to and including *Nouvelle Héloïse*. Tends to challenge in part all previous interpretations of R. and in some respects will undoubtedly be itself challenged. Ignores Wright's important book (no. 1951) and its bearing on subject. Sound in holding that for R. following

nature is not following passion, but conscience (cf. Havens, no. 2077). Appears questionable in neglecting fact that social prejudice prevents Julie and Saint-Preux from legitimate marriage and, through her father, forces her into marriage with Wolmar, which indeed brings about her redemption, but is nevertheless first accepted as *pis-aller*. Rejects conventional interpretation of *Nouvelle Héloïse* as book which starts as novel of passion and ends with glorification of marriage. Does not discuss whether course of R.'s novel was affected by abortive conclusion of his *affaire* with Mme d'Houdetot, as most previous students of R. have thought. In spite of possible objections, book remains significant contribution to understanding of R.'s thought.
Reviews : P. Kohler in RHL 50:326-28, 1950 ; R. Shackleton in FS 4:161-62, 1950 ; Anon in TLS, Sept. 25, 1949, p. 622.

Ferrero, Guglielmo. Genève et le Contrat social. AJJR 23: 137-52, 1934. 2170

Population of Geneva in 18th century was divided into five classes : 1) *citoyens*, 2) *bourgeois*, 3) *habitants*, 4) *natifs*, and 5) *sujets*. Territory was governed by first two classes, *citoyens* and *bourgeois* only, never comprising more than 1600 people. Hence Geneva was aristocratic republic, more so even than Venice in some respects. *Contrat social* was modeled on Genevan republic. Should have been supplemented by theory of universal suffrage, but R. did not dare go so far. Explosive character of his work was concealed by its timidities and contradictions. Most people saw in it what they wanted to see. Genevan oligarchy alone perceived its dangerous character. Explosion occurred after 1789.

Feugère, Anatole. Pourquoi Rousseau a remanié la Préface de la Lettre à d'Alembert. AJJR 20:127-62, 1931. 2170A

Defends R. against Diderot. R., at bottom, put himself in wrong by *manner* of his protest to public.
Review : E. Carcassonne in RHL 41: 143, 1934.

François, Alexis. Matériaux pour la correspondance de J.-J. Rousseau. Hachette, 1923. 152 p. 2171

" La *Correspondance générale* (no. 1883) semble ignorer les lettres et documents publiés par A. François, *Matériaux*,

numéros 24, 43, 69, 83, 94, 95, 97, 103, 106." L.-J. Courtois in AJJR 19:249 n., 1929-30.
Reviews : G. Ascoli in AJJR 16:282, 1924-25; K. R. Gallas in Neo 9:135, 1923-24; D. Mornet in RHL 31:699-700, 1924.

Françon, Marcel. La publication de l'Émile. FR 21:272-73, 1947-48.   2172
Shows that original edition of *Émile* was published in France and not in Holland.

Guillemin, Henri. Sur quelques inédits de J.-J. Rousseau. RPar [53²]:100-07, Sept., 1946.   2173
Three brief passages, previously unpublished, from Archives of Neuchâtel, accompanied by commentary. The first two contain advice to young men; the third contains R.'s comment on the alleged " plot " of Diderot and his friends. Comment dates apparently from about 1770. Guillemin discusses hostility of Diderot, Voltaire and Grimm toward R., whom they regarded as renegade philosopher and defender of Christianity. Author thinks that R. was justified in remaining preoccupied for so long with their dangerous and persistent attacks.

Havens, George R.   Diderot and the composition of Rousseau's First Discourse. RR 30:369-81, 1939.   2174
Evidence in favor of view that Diderot did not dictate to R. negative position adopted in *First discourse*, but that this attitude was natural development of R.'s own thought and character. See Havens's critical edition, *Jean-Jacques Rousseau : Discours sur les sciences et les arts* (no. 1886), Introduction, 5-23. *See also* Crocker, no. 2165.
Review : P.-E. Schazmann in AJJR 28:141, 1939-40.

— The sources of Rousseau's Edouard Bomston. MP 17:13-27; July, 1919. 2175
The " Englishman " of *Nouvelle Héloïse* was, as writer endeavors to show, composite : a character called into being because of R.'s admiration for English people as he knew them and because of prevailing Anglomania, creation revealing influence of both Prévost's *Cléveland* and Muralt's *Lettres sur les Anglois et sur les François*, and a sublimation of R. See Schinz's reply to this article in MLN 35:184-85, 1920, and Havens's reply to Schinz, *ibid.*, 375-76.

— Voltaire, Rousseau, and the Lettre sur la Providence. *See* 1765.   2176
Important as objective study of relations between Voltaire and R. up to and including 1764, superseding Maugras (no. 2108) for period covered.

Istel, Edgar.   Jean-Jacques Rousseau als Komponist seiner lyrischen Scene Pygmalion. Leipzig, Breitkopf and Härtel, 1901. 90 p. (Diss., Leipzig).   2177
See also author's summary, *La partition originale du Pygmalion de J.-J. Rousseau* in AJJR 1:141-77, 1905, Appendix of which contains reproduction of original score.
Review : A. Schinz in EprR, p. 293-94.

Lanson, G.   Quelques documents inédits sur la condamnation et la censure de l'Émile et sur la condamnation des Lettres écrites de la montagne. AJJR 1:95-136, 1905. 2178
Documents from *Archives nationales* and *Collection Joly de Fleury* in *Bibliothèque nationale* of interest for history of condemnation of these two works by Parlement de Paris. For complementary material, consult P.-M. Bondois : *Documents relatifs à la condamnation de l'Émile.* RHL 45:232, 1938. *See also* A. Schinz, EprR, p. 254-55.

Lovejoy, Arthur O.   The supposed primitivism of Rousseau's Discourse on inequality. MP 21:165-86, 1923-24.   2179
" Le titre indique la thèse.   Article pensé." Schinz, *infra*, p. 279. *See also* Havens (no. 2077), Moreau-Rendu (no. 2115), Schinz (no. 2139), Wright (no. 1951).
Review : A. Schinz in AJJR 16:279-80, 1924-25. *See also* EprR, p. 185.

Monglond, André.   Les deux dernières années de Rousseau et les Rêveries du promeneur solitaire.   *In his :* Vies préromantiques.   Éditions des presses françaises, 1925. p. 15-89.   2180
Dating of *Rêveries du promeneur solitaire.* Differs in details, however, from critical edition of Spink, no. 1900A.
Reviews : F. Ruchon in AJJR 17:270-72, 1926; A. Schinz in EprR, p. 346.

Morel, Jean. Recherches sur les sources du Discours de l'inégalité. AJJR 5:119-98, 1909. (Extracted and reprinted, Lausanne, Pache-Varidel et Bron, 1910. 82 p.). 2181
Carefully documented study on formation of this *Discourse*, with no claim to

being definitive. Influence of intellectual climate in which R. worked, as well as of books, examined. Sections devoted to Diderot, Condillac, Grotius, and Puffendorf, and to scientific information of *Discourse.*

Reviews : D. Mornet in RHL 17:874-76, 1910; G. Rudler in RU 19²:315-16, 1910; A. Schinz in EprR, p. 85, 181.

Mornet, Daniel. La nouvelle Héloïse de J.-J. Rousseau; étude et analyse. Mellottée, 1928. 340 p.   2181A

Excellent, brief presentation of essentials by editor of definitive edition of this novel (no. 1898).

Reviews : L. Cons in MLN 43:560-61, 1928; E. Magne in MerF 213:411-12, July 15, 1929; B. M. Woodbridge in BA 4:264-65, 1930; H. Z. in AJJR 18:360-61, 1927-28.

Osmont, Robert. Contribution à l'étude psychologique des *Rêveries du promeneur solitaire.* AJJR 23:[7]-135, 1934.   2182

" ... ce que M. Osmont a cherché, en dénombrant les timbres et les rythmes, c'est à définir l'accent d'une joie ou d'une souffrance intime, à montrer comment les ondulations d'une phrase enregistrent les frémissements les plus fugitifs du cœur. Par là, il fait œuvre de psychologue et d'esthéticien, il contribue à éclairer, non seulement le cas de Jean-Jacques, mais le problème général de la traduction artistique des sentiments." (Carcassonne, review *below,* p. 562.) Osmont's study followed by *Notes complémentaires sur quelques manuscrits de la Bibliothèque de Neuchâtel,* p. 121 ff.

Reviews : E. Carcassonne in RHL 44: 562, 1937; A. Schinz in EprR, p. 163 n.

Ravier, André. L'éducation de l'homme nouveau; essai historique et critique sur le livre de l'Émile de J.-J. Rousseau. Lyon, Bosc and Riou, 1941. 2 v. (Diss., Grenoble).   2183

Detailed study of history and doctrine of *Émile.* " ... une recherche historique de la genèse de l'*Émile*, un exposé critique du Traité lui-même, une rapide discussion enfin sur la valeur de ce message, telles sont les trois étapes de cette étude." (I, p. 7) In spite of challenging content and profound influence of R.'s book on modern education, Ravier finds in it one serious defect : its failure to develop will. Insufficient recognition of existence of sin. R. lacked feeling of humility. " Sa religion, qui montait vers Dieu et son

Christ, est retombée sur elle-même et s'est enclose dans un égotisme douloureux." II, p. 500).

Reviews : F. Bouchardy in AJJR 29: 323-28, 1941-42; P. Bovet, *ibid.,* 316-23; M. Françon in MP 46:138-42, 1948; A. Schinz in EprR, p. 264-65.

— L'unité de l'homme d'après le livre de l'*Émile.* AJJR 26:285-302, 1937.   2184

Pierre-Maurice Masson found fundamental contradiction between *la Profession de foi du vicaire savoyard* and rest of *Émile.* Ravier explains this on basis that first three books represent a " pre-education," before awakening of the passions which, owing to an internal conflict in man, require help of religion to conquer and lead through to virtue. Man's unity a goal to be attained through aid from above. *Vicaire savoyard* therefore an essential part of R.'s system.

Review : E. Carcassonne in RHL 46: 255, 1939.

Sainte-Beuve, C. A. Les Confessions de J.-J. Rousseau. *In his :* Causeries du lundi, v. 3, p. 78-97.   2185

Excellent analysis of originality of style of *Confessions :* naturalness, realism, occasional archaisms, and charm. (Dated Nov. 4, 1850).

[Saint-Pierre, Charles Irénée Castel, *abbé* **de.]** A lasting peace through the federation of Europe; and The state of war, by Jean Jacques Rousseau; trans. by C. E. Vaughan. London, Constable, 1917. 128 p.   2186

Title indicates its present-day interest. Note R.'s interesting comment upon Abbé de Saint-Pierre's project : " Qu'on ne dise donc point que, si son système n'a pas été adopté, c'est qu'il n'étoit pas bon; qu'on dise au contraire qu'il étoit trop bon pour être adopté " (Hachette, no. 1867:5:335).

Review : A. Schinz in EprR, p. 252-53.

— A project of perpetual peace, Rousseau's essay, trans. by Edith M. Nuttall, and printed in French and English, with an introduction by G. Lowes Dickinson. London, Cobden-Sanderson, 1927. 141 p.   2187

See preceding comment.

Schinz, Albert. Histoire de l'impression et de la publication du Discours sur l'inégalité, de J.-J. Rousseau. PMLA 28:253-90, 1913.   2188

Correspondence of R. with publisher,

Marc-Michel Rey, concerning *Second Discourse*, details of its printing, distribution, first editions.

— La notion de vertu dans le Premier Discours de J.-J. Rousseau. MerF 97:532-55, June 1, 1912.   2189

Study of meanings which R. attaches to word "virtue" in this *Discourse*. Finds three different concepts used : *vertu-sagesse*, *vertu-innocence*, and *vertu-renoncement*, the last considered by writer to be central in R.'s thought in this work. As a corrective to Schinz's interpretation, *see* A. O. Lovejoy in MLN 46:42-44, 1931.
Review : A. François in AJJR 9:156, 1913.

— La Profession de foi du vicaire savoyard et le livre De l'esprit. RHL 17:225-61, 1910.   2190

Detailed study of R.'s refutation of Helvétius in relation to *Vicaire savoyard*. Article corrected in some respects by Pierre-Maurice Masson, no. 2107. Cf. also latter's article in RHL 19:642-46, 1912.
Review : L. Pinvert in AJJR 7:181-83, 1911. See EprR, p. 274.

— La question du Contrat social; nouvelle contribution sur les rapports de J.-J. Rousseau avec les Encyclopédistes. Colin, 1913. 49 p.   Extract from RHL 19:741-90, 1912.   2191

Argues that *MS de Genève* gives a form of *Contrat social* anterior to *Second Discourse*.   Written, therefore, under strong influence of Diderot and Encyclopedists, hence apparent contradictions of final form.   For convincing rebuttals, *see* above, Beaulavon (no. 1876), and Hubert (no. 2084).
Reviews : G. Beaulavon in RHL 20: 585-601, 1913 (Answer by A. Schinz in RHL 21:194-98, 1914); P.-M. Masson in AJJR 9:49-56, 61, 1913; L. Pinvert in AJJR 9:156-57, 1913.

Sewall, Richard B.   An early manuscript translation of Rousseau's Second *Discours*. MLN 57:271-73, 1942.   2192

Unpublished translation, dated 1756 and now in Yale University Library, was made by John Farrington, London merchant.   Writer believes it to be first translation into English of this *Discourse*. Has important implications concerning knowledge of this work in England prior

to its first published translation, dated 1761.

— Rousseau's First discourse in England. PMLA 52:908-11, 1937.   2193

Periodical references, not noted by Warner (no. 2202), aid in dating four English translations of the *First Discourse* and indicate a wider circulation than has been thought, and " a livelier sympathy " (p. 909).   *See* Schinz, EprR, p. 182-83.

— Rousseau's Second discourse in England from 1755 to 1762. PQ 17:97-114, 1938.   2194

Evidence to show that reception of *Second discourse*, like the *First*, was somewhat more favorable in England than thought by Warner (no. 2202). Adam Smith, Goldsmith, Burke, and Dr. Johnson among first to feel impact, or to criticize, R.'s thought.
Review : A. Schinz in AJJR 27:306, 1938.

— Rousseau's Second discourse in England and Scotland from 1762 to 1772. PQ 18: 225-42, 1939.   2195

New material on periodical reception of translation of R.'s *Second discourse*. Opinions of Boswell, Wodhull, Dr. John Gregory, and James Beattie, more liberal than those of Dr. Johnson and Burke. Supplements author's previous article (no. 2194) and Warner (no. 2202).
Review : A. Schinz in AJJR 28:140-41, 1939-40.

Spink, J. S.   La première rédaction des Lettres écrites de la montagne, publiée d'après le manuscrit autographe.   AJJR 20:9-125, 1931, and 21:9-156, 1932.   2196

Important publication from original manuscript at Neuchâtel. Shows painful labor by which R., here as elsewhere, after numerous revisions, little by little attained final form of his writings.   R. simplified his sentences and suppressed many passages of pure eloquence in favor of a more factual presentation; while defending himself boldly and firmly, R. softened many attacks which he considered too violent or too provocative.
Reviews : E. Carcassonne in RHL 41: 142-43, 1934; D. Mornet in RHL 42: 280-81, 1935; A. Schinz in EprR, p. 251.

Tisserand, Roger.   Au temps de l'Encyclopédie; l'Académie de Dijon de 1740 à 1793. Vesoul, Imprimerie nouvelle; Boivin, 1936. 683p.   (Diss., Paris).   2197

Contains valuable brief account of history of *First* and *Second discourses* in their relation to Academy of Dijon.
See p. 550-56.
Reviews : G. Lefebvre in ARF 17:251-52, 1940; E. Magne in MerF 280:551-56, Dec. 15, 1937; A. Schinz in MLN 52: 286-87, 1937.

— Les concurrents de J.-J. Rousseau à l'Académie de Dijon pour le prix de 1754. Vesoul, Imprimerie nouvelle; Boivin, 1936. 219 p. (Diss., Paris). **2198**

Detailed account of prize contest for which R. submitted his *Discours sur l'inégalité*, with texts of ten of competing MSS. Unfortunately, R.'s own MS disappeared mysteriously late in 19th century. Further information on prize contest of 1750.
Reviews : G. Lefebvre in ARF 17: 251-52, 1940; E. Magne in MerF 280: 556-57, Dec. 15, 1937; P.-E. Schazmann in AJJR 25:303, 1936; A. Schinz in EprR, p. 178-79 and in MLN 52:287-88, 1937.

Van Tieghem, Philippe. La nouvelle Héloïse de Jean-Jacques Rousseau, avec un index de tous les noms cités. Malfère, 1929. 144 p. **2199**

" Excellente étude... présentant sous une forme commode et concise les derniers résultats de la critique rousseauiste... de ce texte classique." F. Ruchon, *infra*, p. 288-89.
Reviews : G. Ascoli in Rcr 100:327-28, 1933; E. Carcassonne in RHL 37:620-21, 1930; F. Ruchon in AJJR 19:288-89, 1929-30; A. Schinz in BA 4:265, 1930.

Warner, James H. Eighteenth-century English reactions to the Nouvelle Héloïse. PMLA 52:803-19, 1937. **2200**

First translation by William Kenrick appeared promptly in 1761. Article points out aspects of its inaccuracy and inferiority to original. Numerous unfavorable opinions on novel in spite of its vogue.
Review : A. Schinz in AJJR 26:332-34, 1937.

— Émile in eighteenth-century England. PMLA 59:773-91, 1944. **2201**

Both *Émile* and *Nouvelle Héloïse* issued in English eight times. *Émile*, like *Nouvelle Héloïse*, also translated by William Kenrick, who endeavored to " improve " upon original. Comparison of Kenrick and Nugent translations. Some favorable comments on *Émile*, but prevailing comment hostile or severely critical. British readers generally failed to grasp central significance of R.'s " emphasis on education as an inner development rather than an injection from outside " (p. 791).

— The reaction in eighteenth-century England to Rousseau's two *Discours*. PMLA 48:471-87, 1933. **2202**

" ... the English exhibited curiosity over both the *Discours sur les sciences* (1750) and the *Discours sur l'inégalité* (1755) ; but, with few exceptions, they did not approve the content of either " (p. 487). *See also* Sewall, nos. 2192-95.
Review : A. Schinz in AJJR 22:267-68, 1933.

ADDENDA

Derathé, Robert. Le rationalisme de J.-J. Rousseau. Presses universitaires de France, 1948. 201 p. **2202A**

Significant study emphasizing the role and fundamental importance of reason in R.'s thought and doctrine. Rejects Masson's interpretation stressing predominance of feeling (nos. 1891, 1928). *See also* Beaulavon, no. 1892. Appendix on *Les interprètes néo-kantiens* : " Le problème Jean-Jacques Rousseau ", par Ernst Cassirer, p. 181-91. *See no.* 2045.

Sénelier, Jean. Bibliographie générale des œuvres de Jean-Jacques Rousseau. Edition " Encyclopédie Française ", 1950. 282 p. **2202B**

Elaborate and indispensable bibliography. Corrects and complements Dufour (no. 1857) and extends research to date of publication. Chronological presentation. Notes on R.'s life. Description and location of MSS. Dissemination of R.'s writings by countries. Index.

CHAPTER IX. DENIS DIDEROT
(Nos. 2203-2343)

HERBERT DIECKMANN and NORMAN L. TORREY

Bibliography

See : Diderot, Œuvres, Assézat-Tourneux ed., (no. 2209) v. 20; Billy, A., (no. 2255); Busnelli, M. D., (no. 2328) ; Johannson (no. 2250); Thomas, J. (no. 2282) ; also Mornet, D. (no. 2278). 2203

Leyds, J. J. C. Principaux écrits relatifs à la personne et aux œuvres, au temps et à l'influence de Diderot. Compilation critique et chronologique. Garnier, and Amsterdam, Binger 1887. 39 p. 2204

Still valuable critical bibliography of works around and about D.

Delamarche, Léon. Les bibliophiles et Diderot. CLF 3:714-15, 1925. 2205

Article gives summary of two articles by Delamarche in the *Éclair*, (May 14, 1923, and May 26, 1924) on first editions of D., especially on scarcely known 1753 edition of the *Interprétation de la nature*, of which author possesses D.'s own copy. This copy contains numerous *cartons* giving additions which form 1754 edition, long considered the original.

Dieckmann, Herbert. Stand und Probleme der Diderot-Forschung. Ein Beitrag zur Diderot-Kritik. Bonn, Cohen, 1931. 40 p. 2206

Selective bibliography of D.'s works and comments on critical studies of D.

— Bibliographical data on Diderot. *In :* Studies in honor of Frederick W. Shipley. St. Louis, 1942. p. 181-220. (Washington univ. studies. New series. Language and literature, no. 14). 2207

Not complete, but most comprehensive critical bibliography of D. to date.

Editions

Complete works (selective and chronological)

Diderot, Denis. Œuvres. Publiées sur les manuscrits de l'auteur, par Jacques-André Naigeon. Desray, Déterville, an VI [1798] 15 v. 2208

Incomplete. Important for text, preface, and introductions.

— Œuvres complètes. Revues sur les éditions originales, notices, notes, table analytique, par J. Assézat et M. Tourneux. Garnier, 1875-77. 20 v. 2209

Most complete of all editions, but does not contain all of D.'s works, and text of those it contains not critical. Errors of chronology. General index incomplete and insufficient. Most of sections comprising D.'s contributions to *Encyclopédie* unreliable, since passages and whole articles belonging to other authors are attributed to D. See Textual Criticism below.

— Correspondance littéraire, philosophique et critique, par Grimm, Diderot, Raynal, Meister, etc. Revue sur les textes originaux par Maurice Tourneux. Garnier, 1877-82. 16 v. 2210

Contains D. material not in A.-T. edition (no. 2209). *See* no. 2357.

Selected Works
(selective and chronological)

— Diderot's thoughts on art and style. With some of his shorter essays, selected and translated by Beatrix L. Tollemache. London, Remington, 1893. 291 p. 2211

Extracts from D.'s theoretical writings on art and from his *Salons* in translation. Partial translation of *Lettre sur les aveugles* and *Lettre sur les sourds et muets.* Translation of *Entretien d'un père avec ses enfants, Regrets sur ma vieille robe de chambre, Éloge de Richardson.* Translations good but rather free.

— Diderot's early philosophical works, translated and edited by Margaret Jourdain. Chicago and London, Open court, 1916. 245 p. 2212

Only readily available translation of D.'s early philosophical works.

— Dialogues. With a Foreword by Sir Edmund Gosse and an Introduction by Francis Birrell. New York, Brentano, [1927]. 196 p. 2213

Selections *(D'Alembert's dream, Supplement to the Voyage of Bougainville, Regrets for an old dressing-gown, Conversation of a philosopher with the Maréchale de... On women)* give excellent introduction to D. for English readers. Birrell's appreciation good on artistic side, weak on philosophic.

— Œuvres. Texte établi et annoté par André Billy. NRF (Bibl. de la Pléiade), 1935. 1005 p. 2213A

Good introduction, good selections, good text, good, but insufficient notes ; no *Salons*, no *Correspondance*.

— Diderot, interpreter of nature; selected writings, translated by Jean Stewart and Jonathan Kemp. Edited, with an Introduction, by Jonathan Kemp. London, Lawrence and Wishart, [1937] ; New York, International Publishers, 1938. 358 p. (Introd., 1-34). 2214

Good selection of D.'s philosophical dialogues and other writings. (From *The indiscreet toys*, from *The interpretation of nature, D'Alembert's dream, Philosophic principles on matter and motion*, from *Elements of physiology, Supplement to Bougainville's voyage, Conversation between the abbé Barthélemy and Diderot, Discourse of a philosopher to a king, Conversation of a philosopher with the Maréchale de..., Rameau's nephew.)* Good translation. Diderot is conceived of as ancestor of " modern dialectical materialism and the new humanism of Marxism." (p. 2) Notes consequently refer mostly to modern materialistic writers. Though many points are open to discussion, no other commented edition of D.'s writings has notes as complete, serious, and stimulating.
Review : M. F. Ashley-Montagu in Isis 29:435-36, 1938.

Luc, Jean. Diderot. Éditions sociales internationales, 1938. 330 p. 2215

Contains extracts from philosophical works, p. 183-330.
Stimulating discussion of D.'s philosophy from Marxist point of view.

Single Editions
(selective and chronological)

— The paradox of acting. Translated with annotations from Diderot's Paradoxe sur le comédien, by Walter Herries Pollock; with a preface by Henry Irving. London, Chatto and Windus, 1883. 108 p. 2216

Fair preface with quotations from other actors. Good historical notes.

— Entretien entre D'Alembert et Diderot. Rêve de d'Alembert. Suite de l'Entretien. Introduction et Notes de Gilbert Maire... (Collection des chefs-d'œuvre méconnus). Bossard, 1921. 193 p. 2217

Convenient separate edition with explanatory notes which contain some factual information but are worthless as interpretation. Introduction may be disregarded.

— Paradoxe sur le comédien, présenté par Jacques Copeau. Plon, 1929. 113 p. (Les conversations, 3.) 2218

Introduction, *Réflexions d'un comédien sur le Paradoxe de Diderot*, p. 1-24, a re-arrangement and amplification of an article in Runiv 33:641-50, June 15, 1928; contains valuable but somewhat confused reflexions on art and process of impersonation, giving pertinent criticism of D.'s paradoxical ideas.

— Lettre sur le commerce de la librairie, commentée par Bernard Grasset. Grasset, 1937. 171 p. (Introd., 1-34; Text, 37-171). 2219

Republishes uncritical text of A.-T. edition (no. 2209) (see below, Brunel, no. 2244). Introduction and comment present in modern form problem of literary rights.

Loy, J. Robert. Diderot's determined fatalist : a critical appreciation of Jacques le fataliste. New York, King's crown press, 1950. 234 p. 2219A

Author attempts to show that D. gave his novel a deliberate structure by interweaving three major themes. He defends the characters and the realism of the novel against previous criticism. Stimulating discussion of D.'s " fatalism " in relation to his ethical thought. Should have been classified under Studies of single works, no. 2289B.

Works not in Assézat edition (no. 2209), or presenting a more critical text

Diderot. Sept lettres à l'Impératrice Catherine II, publiées sous les auspices de la société impériale pour l'histoire de la Russie, par J. Grot. Saint-Pétersbourg, 1881. 2219B

Contains remarks on D.'s stay in Russia and his *Plan d'une université*.

Henry, Charles. Histoire des sciences; introduction à la chymie, manuscrit inédit de Diderot. Rsc July 26, 1884, p. 97-108.

2220

Consists of notes by Henry on the *Cours de chymie* of Rouelle, " inédit, rédigé par Diderot." If these notes are compared with a letter in same volume of this periodical, (Aug. 9, p. 184-85) by E. Grimaux entitled, *Le cours de chymie de Rouelle*, it will be evident that the *Introduction* is not an original work, but re-arrangement and elaboration of notes taken from Rouelle's lectures, and that only the style seems to be D.'s own.

Diderot, Denis. Le neveu de Rameau : satyre, publiée pour la première fois sur le manuscrit original autographe, avec une introduction et des notes, par Georges Monval, accompagnée d'une notice sur les premières éditions de l'ouvrage et de la vie de Jean-François Rameau, par Er. Thoinan [*pseud.*]. Plon-Nourrit, 1891, 232 p.   2221

Most valuable French edition to date.

Le neveu de Rameau. Edition critique avec notes et lexique, par Jean Fabre. Geneva, Droz ; Lille, Giard, 1950.   329 p.

2221A

Glossary, appendices and critical bibliography very useful.   Notes extensive and thorough, but rather overelaborate.   Critical interpretation of genesis and significance of the work and its place in history of D.'s intellectual activity is open to question. Does not supersede Schlösser (no. 2341).
Reviews : G. T. Clapton in FS 4:265-67, 1950 ; N. L. Torrey in RR 41:299-302, 1950.

— Fragments inédits de Diderot, publiés par Maurice Tourneux. RHL 1:164-74, 1894.

2222

Pages written for the *Correspondance littéraire* (no. 2210) : reviews of books, letter defining " plaisir, allégresse, joie," interpretation of passage of Livy, fragment on *anticomanie*.

Tourneux, Maurice. Diderot et Catherine II. Calmann Lévy, 1899. 601 p.   2223

Gives excellent account, based on reliable documents, of D.'s relation to Catherine II and his stay in Russia. Contains number of important un-

published pages of D., among others, *Sur ma manière de travailler* and *Mélanges philosophiques, historiques*, etc., written for Catherine's benefit.   Appendices important for D.'s political thought.
Review : G. Lanson in RHL 6:637-41, 1899.

Diderot, Denis. Un factum inconnu de Diderot. Publié par Maurice Tourneux. BBB 1901:349-85.   2224

Concerns Luneau de Boisgermain's attack on publishers of *Encyclopédie*.

— Paradoxe sur le comédien. Édition critique par Ernest Dupuy.   Société française d'imprimerie et de librairie, 1902.   178 p.   2225

Indispensable.   Publishes manuscript of *Paradoxe* in Naigeon's handwriting, consisting of first redaction of *Paradoxe* called *Observations sur une brochure intitulée : Garrick ou les acteurs anglais*, and additions to it, written on margin. Dupuy believed these additions to be work of Naigeon.   Publication started memorable controversy about textual criticism of D.'s works and role of Naigeon as editor. On this *see :* Bédier (no. 2242), Faguet (no. 2246), and on its methodological significance, A. Morize, *Problems and methods of literary history*, New York, Ginn, (c1922). p. 158-69.

[—] Dialogue philosophique inédit; Diderot et l'abbé Barthélemy. Rmond 135:257-75, Apr. 1, 1920. [Edited by Albert Cim]. Reprinted : Messein, 1921. 64 p.   2226

Interesting pages in which D. discusses his " esprit de contradiction."   Editor does not prove authenticity of work, which to some Diderot scholars appears highly doubtful.

— Observations sur l'instruction de S. M. I. aux Députés pour la confection des lois (1774).   Œuvre inédite publiée avec une introduction par Paul Ledieu.   RHES 8: 271-412, 1920. Also, as separate : Rivière, 1921.   140 p.   2227

Tourneux published a fragment of this work with title : *Diderot législateur; un mémoire inédit*, in Nrev 12:33-51, Sept.-Oct., 1881, and also in : *Diderot et Catherine II* (no. 2223), App. D. Introduction, p. 1-8. Catherine II's text is printed at the top of the pages, D.'s comments at the bottom.   Valuable and interesting material on D.'s social and political ideas which has quite consistently escaped attention of scholars.

— Le bréviaire des jeunes mariées. Lettre inédite de Diderot à sa fille. Préface d'Albert Cim. Messein, 1922. (Préface, 7-16; Lettre, 19-29). 2228

Letter written by D. to his daughter four days after her marriage, containing advice for conduct in marriage. Letter already published by F. Strowski in *Le Temps*, Dec. 21, 1913.

Van Roosbroeck, G. L. Diderot's earliest publication. MLN 39: 504-05, 1924. 2229

" Epître à M. B. ..." [Boisard?] published in *Le perroquet*, 1741, p. 78.

Charlier, G., and L. Herman. Diderot, annotateur de Perse. RHL 35:39-63, 1928. 2229A

A study of a MS. (No. 2321, Bibl. Royale de Belgique) in which D. wrote his note, and observations on Persius in connection with Abbé Le Monnier's French translation. Conclusions on D.'s latinity somewhat narrow and unjust.

Diderot, Denis. Lettres à Sophie Volland. Texte, en grande partie inédit, publié pour la première fois d'après les manuscrits originaux, avec une introduction, des variantes et des notes, par André Babelon. Gallimard, [1930]. 3 v. 2230-2231

For corrections and critical observations, see L. G. Crocker, no. 2287. Reviews : F. Birrell in Criterion 12: 632-41, 1932-33; H. Dieckmann in ZFSL 55:343-46, 1932.

— Correspondance inédite, publiée d'après les manuscrits originaux, avec des introductions et des notes, par André Babelon. Gallimard, [1931]. 2 v. 2232

For corrections and critical observations, see L. G. Crocker, no. 2287. See also no. 2375. Reviews : H. Dieckmann in LGRP 53: 401-06, 1932; E. Magne in MerF 235: 408-10, 1932.

[—] ... to Monsieur Suard... to Mme Necker. *In :* Hawkins, R. L. Newly discovered French letters of the seventeenth, eighteenth and nineteenth centuries. Cambridge, Harvard univ. press, 1933. p. 50-54. (Half-title : Harvard studies in Romance languages... vol. IX). 2233

Bonno, Gabriel. Un article inédit de Diderot sur Colbert. PMLA 49:1101-06, 1934. 2234

Attribution somewhat doubtful.

Diderot, Denis. Supplément au Voyage de Bougainville, publié d'après le manuscrit de Léningrad, avec une introduction et des notes par Gilbert Chinard. Droz, 1935. 211 p. 2235

Reprint of text of A.-T. edition (no. 2209) with variants (of Leningrad manuscript) discovered and published by J. V. Johannson (no. 2250). Valuable notes containing especially extracts from Bougainville's *Voyage autour du monde*. Introduction places *Supplément* among currents of primitivism and theories of physical love in 18th century and earlier. Indispensable for study of D.'s ethics. Reviews : H. Dieckmann in RFor 50: 241-48, 1936; N. L. Torrey in MLN 51: 469-71, 1936.

— Pages inédites contre un tyran. Éd. par Franco Venturi. G.L.M. 1937. [38 p.]. 2236

Pamphlet against Frederick II's refutation of D'Holbach's *Essai sur les préjugés*. Venturi's title, *Pages inédites contre un tyran*, and his introduction imply greater political zeal on part of D. than this writing warrants.

Works containing uncollected letters or passages of Diderot, (arranged in alphabetical order)

See : Busnelli, no. 2328; Cru, no. 2330; Hermand, no. 2302; Ledieu, no. 2258; Nicolini, no. 2253. For a list of single *lettres inédites*, see Dieckmann, no. 2206, p. 14, n. 3.

Condorcet, Marie... etc. Récit de Diderot. *In his :* Mémoires sur le règne de Louis XVI. Ponthieu, 1824. v. I, p. 155-57. 2236A

On virtue and happiness.

Diderot. [Mme d'Epinay]. *In:* Mémoires de Madame d'Epinay, ed. by Paul Boiteau. Charpentier, 1865. 2:101-11. 2237

Consists of conversation between D. and Grimm about Madame d'Epinay; reported and written by D.

Haussonville, Gabriel, comte d'. Diderot. *In his :* Le salon de madame Necker. *See* 294, v. I, p. 162-77. 2238

Several letters from D. to Mme Necker. Fragments of a conversation between D., Mme Necker, and Naigeon. Important for D.'s philosophical and ethical views.

— Copie des tablettes de Diderot. *In :* Maugras, Gaston. Une femme du monde au XVIIIᵉ siècle; la jeunesse de madame d'Epinay, by Lucien Perey [*pseud.*] and Gaston Maugras. 7th ed., Calmann Lévy, 1898. p. 537-39. 2239

These three pages contain D.'s *Tablettes*, or accusations, against J.-J. Rousseau, which are also published in D.'s *Correspondance littéraire* (no. 2210), v. 16. See 2374.

Tronchin, Henry. Le conseiller François Tronchin et ses amis : Voltaire, Diderot, Grimm... d'après des documents inédits. Plon-Nourrit, 1895. 399 p.   2240

Contains several letters from D. to Fr. Tronchin concerning dramatic projects and technique, also acquisition of art collections for Catherine II.

Textual Criticism

See : Busnelli, no. 2328; Cru, no. 2330; Delamarche, no. 2205 ; Hermand, no. 2302 ; Naigeon, no. 2264.

Babelon, André. On possède enfin les manuscrits de Diderot. RDM 7th per. 50:99-103, March 1, 1929.   2241

Some information concerning D.'s manuscrits in *stock Vandeul.*

Bédier, Joseph. Le Paradoxe sur le comédien est-il de Diderot ? *In his :* Études critiques. Colin, 1903. p. 83-112.   2242

Proves that the *Paradoxe sur le comédien* is not by Naigeon, as Dupuy (no. 2225) and others have asserted. Masterpiece of textual criticism, results of which have since been confirmed by a passage in *Correspondance inédite* (no. 2232), 1:217.

Brummer, Rudolf. Studien zur französischen Aufklärungsliteratur im Anschluss an J. A. Naigeon. Breslau, Priebatsch, 1932. 338 p. (*See* Appendix 1 of Naigeon's ed. of Diderot's works, no. 2208).   2243

Together with studies of Tourneux (no. 2254) and Johansson (no. 2250), the most important contribution to textual criticism of D.'s works. Careful and exhaustive analysis of Naigeon's role as editor of D.'s manuscrits, refuting all charges against Naigeon's trustworthiness. Reviews : H. Dieckmann in ZFSL 58: 372-75, 1934; D. Mornet in RHL 40:597-98, 1933; F. Schalk in Archiv 165:276-77, 1934.

Brunel, Lucien. Observations critiques et littéraires sur un opuscule de Diderot (Lettre sur le commerce de la librairie). RHL 10:1-24, 1903. *See* no. 2219.   2244

Indispensable material for critical edition of *Lettre sur le commerce de la librairie.* Literary observations weak.

Dieckmann, Herbert. J.-A. Naigeon's analysis of Diderot's Rêve de d'Alembert. MLN 53:479-86, 1938.   2245

Contribution to textual criticism of the *Rêve de d'Alembert* and the *Éléments de physiologie.*

Faguet, Emile. Diderot et Naigeon. Rlat 1:705-54, 1902.   2246

Excellent presentation of controversy over authorship of D.'s *Paradoxe sur le comédien*, prior to Bédier's solution of the problem (no. 2242).

Fellows, Otis E., and **Norman L. Torrey,** *editors.* Diderot studies. Syracuse, Syracuse univ. press, 1949. 191 p.   2247

Seven significant studies by as many different authors, the product of graduate seminars at Columbia University under direction of the two editors. These essays illustrate present trends in D. criticism, with emphasis on his theories of narrative fiction and poetry. Note especially *Diderot et le symbole littéraire, Notes on Diderot's fortunes in Russia,* and *Jean-François Rameau and Diderot's Neveu,* the latter a searching study of relation between D.'s unique character creation and real nephew of Rameau. Review : J. Doolittle in FR 24:64-67, 1950.

Gillot, Hubert. Denis Diderot. L'homme; ses idées philosophiques, esthétiques et littéraires. Courville, 1937. 336 p. App. II : Inventaire des papiers de Diderot. Liste des pièces et papiers se trouvant à l'Abbaye de Septfontaines compris dans un inventaire du 29 Juin 1913 et décrits comme suit dans un acte du 14 oct. 1913, communiquée par M. Benoit, notaire à Andelot (Haute-Marne), qui nous a autorisé à la publier.

                                            2248

Appendix II gives inventory of D. manuscrits still in hands of his descendants. *See* no. 2275.

Glotz, René. Conjectures sur un vers de Molière. Remarques et conjectures sur quelques passages de Diderot. RHL 42: 551-60, 1935.   2249

Contains jottings on textual criticism of : *Le rêve de d'Alembert, Additions aux Pensées philosophiques, Satire I, sur les caractères et les mots de caractères, de profession,* etc. *Paradoxe sur le comédien, Essai sur les femmes, Les Eleuthéromanes.* Useful, but rather sketchy.

Hermand, Pierre. Sur le texte de Diderot et sur les sources de quelques passages de ses œuvres. RHL 22:361-70, 1915. 2249A

Of particular importance for the sources of the articles of the *Encyclopédie*.

Johansson, J. Viktor. Études sur Denis Diderot. Recherches sur un volume-manuscrit conservé à la bibliothèque publique de l'État à Leningrad. Champion, 1927. 209 p. 2250

Scholarly study of history of editing and publication of D.'s manuscripts, a textual description, with variants, of Leningrad MS 17 (which Tourneux had been unable to find during his researches in Russia) containing the *Supplément au voyage de Bougainville* and other dialogues; Appendix : the use by Raynal and D. of Franklin's *Speech of Polly Baker*. Reviews : R. Brummer in ZFSL 55: 110-16, 1931-32; D. Mornet in RHL 35: 286-87, 1928.

Muller, Daniel. La véritable édition originale de deux contes de Diderot. BBB June 1, 1928:261-68. 2251

The contes are : *Deux amis de Bourbonne* and *Entretien d'un père avec ses enfants*. Published first in German : *Moralische Erzählungen und Idyllen von Diderot und Gessner*. Zurich, 1772.

Naigeon, [Jacques-André]. Diderot. *In :* Encyclopédie méthodique. [v. 50]. Philosophie ancienne et moderne. Panckoucke, 1792. 2:153-228. 2252

First extensive study on D. by his friend and disciple. Still valuable for textual criticism, biographical details, and observations on D.'s thought.

Nicolini, Fausto. Lumières nouvelles sur quelques ouvrages de Diderot, d'après la correspondance inédite de l'abbé Galiani. Eit ns 2:87-103, 161-73, 209-19, 1932. 2253

First two sections correct text and chronology of some of D.'s " petits papiers." Third section contains some *lettres inédites* of D. to Abbé Galiani. No mention of D.'s acquaintance with Vico's ideas.

Tourneux, Maurice. Les manuscrits de Diderot conservés en Russie. AMS 3rd ser. 12:439-74, 1885. Reprinted : Imprimerie nationale, 1885. 40 p. 2254

Indispensable for scholarly research. *See also* Johansson, no. 2250.

Biography

Also to be consulted, the *Mémoires* and *Correspondances* of persons who knew Diderot, as e.g. D'Argenson, Mme d'Epinay, Galiani, Marmontel, Morellet, Mme Necker, Rousseau, Suard, Voltaire. *See also* Garat : *Lettre aux auteurs du Journal de Paris sur la Notice qu'ils ont donnée de la Vie de Sénèque.* MerF Feb. 15, 1779, p. 172-80.

Billy, André. Diderot. Éditions de France, 1932. 616 p. 2255

Novelized biography, based on first-hand documents. Uncritical but extensive bibliography. The essential biography to date. (Extracts in *Œuvres libres*, v. 85 and 128, give substantially identical text). Reviews : E. Magne in MerF 235: 404-08, 1932; A. E. A. Naughton in RR 23:260-61, 1932.

Havens, George R. The dates of Diderot's birth and death. MLN 55:31-35, 1940. 2256

Final solution of problem.

— The chronology of Diderot's journey to Langres in 1759. MLN 59:33-37, 1944. 2257

In addition to precise indications on D.'s journey, article corrects date of death of D.'s father and establishes correct date of three letters of D. (Letters to Sophie Volland of August 17 and 23, 1759; letter to Monsieur Caroillon of September, 1759).

Ledieu, Paul. Diderot et Sophie Volland. Publications du Centre [c1925]. 172 p. 2258

Delightful treatment, slightly novelized, of D.'s relations with Sophie Volland, using some of material later published by Babelon (no. 2231). Review : D. Mornet in RHL 33:458-59, 1926.

Lortel, J. Une rectification : un amour inconnu de Diderot. RHL 23:482-503, 1916. 2259

Well-documented study of D.'s relations with Mme de Maux. Partially obsolete since publication of letters to Grimm in *Correspondance inédite* (no. 2232).

Marcel, Louis. Le frère de Diderot. Champion, 1913. 215 p. 2260

Useful documents buried beneath weight of polemics, which sometimes falsify author's judgment. For a complete list of Marcel's books see : Jean Thomas, *Diderot* (no. 2282), p. 169. Review : C. Urbain in RHL 22:607-09, 1915.

— La mort de Diderot, d'après des documents inédits. Champion, 1925. 54 p.   2261

— La sœur de Diderot, Denise Diderot. Langres, Au Musée, 1925. 48 p.   2262

Printing of a lecture.

Massiet Du Biest, Jean. La fille de Diderot. Extrait de sa correspondance inédite avec son mari et avec Jacques-Henri Meister, de Zurich. Tours, chez l'auteur, aux Archives départementales d'Indre-et-Loire. 1949. 231 p.   2262A

This work, which has its place beside publications of the Chanoine Marcel (nos. 2260-2262), contains great wealth of hitherto unknown material on D.'s daughter, his son-in-law, and the *milieu langrois*. It also has some new information on D. himself, which does not essentially modify our knowledge of his life and character, but adds to it a few interesting and charming traits.

Massiet du Biest's book suffers somewhat from poor organization and lack of knowledge of D.'s life and work. Most serious shortcoming, however, is that author has paid no attention to material of the *fonds Vandeul* which is not in the *Archives nationales de la Haute-Marne*. Is possible that he had no access to it; he mentions, however, several times that he has consulted the Baron Le Vavasseur. Massiet du Biest affirms with surprising definiteness that part of material is lost. Statement is incorrect, at least in this form. Great number of letters of Madame de Vandeul and of her husband are still in existence. Above all, Meister's letters, without which history of his relationship with Madame de Vandeul cannot be written, were neither destroyed nor lost, as author repeatedly affirms.

— Lettres inédites de Naigeon à Mr. et Mme de Vandeul (1786-1787) concernant un projet d'édition des œuvres de Diderot et opinion de ceux-ci sur le même sujet, d'après leur correspondance inédite (1784-1812). BSHL 12:1-12, Jan. 1, 1948. 2262B

Documents of the *Archives de la Haute-Marne* published in this article are one of most important sources of textual criticism of D.'s work.

Meister, Jacques-Henri. A la mémoire de Diderot. First separate edition : Aux mânes de Diderot. London, 1788. *Also in* the A.-T. edition (no. 2209), i:xiii-xix.   2263

This interpretation of D.'s genius and personality published two years after his death is first literary portrait of him, and one of finest ever written. Meister's sympathetic and revealing pages offer excellent introduction to study of D.

Naigeon, Jacques-André. Mémoires historiques et philosophiques sur la vie et les ouvrages de D. Diderot. Brière, 1821 [1823]. 432 p.   2264

Naigeon's atheistic zeal and pedantic mind are serious handicaps in an evaluation of D. However, his long personal acquaintance with D. and his knowledge of author's works and manuscripts make work an important source for studies on D.

Pellisson, Maurice. Diderot et sa fille. Rped ns 63:205-17, 1913.   2265

Sympathetic, understanding article on D. as educator of his daughter; corrects many current mistakes (Faguet, [no. 2274], Compayré, *Histoire critique des doctrines de l'éducation en France*, 3ᵉ éd., Hachette, 1881, 2 v.) and gives essential complement to D.'s theories on education.

Salesses, R. Diderot et l'université, ou les conséquences d'une mystification. RU 44:322-33, 1935.   2266

Disproves Marcel's thesis that D. was student under Jesuits at Louis-le-Grand.

— Les mystères de la jeunesse de Diderot, ou l'aventure théologique. MerF 280:498-514, Dec. 15, 1937.   2267

Emphasizes, probably exaggerates, importance of D.'s early theological studies in formation of his mind.

Vandeul, Madame Marie-Angélique. Mémoires pour servir à l'histoire de la vie et des ouvrages de Diderot. *In :* Allgemeine Zeitschrift von Deutschen für Deutsche. Ed. by F. W. Schelling. Nuremberg, 1813. 1:2. *Also :* Sautelet, 1830, and A.-T. ed. (2209), I:xxix-lxii.   2268

This biographical sketch written by D.'s daughter is source for many later biographies. Has been corrected in many respects, and is valuable today chiefly as personal document.

Critical Studies of Diderot's Works

General Studies

Barbey d'Aurevilly, Jules Amédée. Goethe et Diderot. Dentu, 1880. 290 p.   2269

Not, as title suggests, a comparative study. Some good pages on D. as art critic.

Bersot, Ernest. Études sur la philosophie du XVIII⁰ siècle : Diderot. 1851. 108 p. (*Also in :* Études sur le XVIII⁰ siècle, 2:147-296).   2270

Bersot was first to refute argument that D.'s works are only improvisations. He made a serious and scholarly study of main themes of D.'s works and their coherent treatment, stressed role of experiment and observation as opposed to rationalism in D.'s thought and interpreted him on basis of specific problems of his period, no longer in a timeless, unhistorical way.

Caro, Elme M. Diderot inédit. *In his :* La fin du dix-huitième siècle; études et portraits. See 96, I:155-354.   2271

First serious study of transformism in D.'s works. Recognition of importance of *Réfutation d'Helvétius*.

Dieckmann, Herbert. Zur Interpretation Diderots. RFor 53: 47-82, 1939.   2272

Author devises a method for interpretation of D.'s contradictory ideas. Interprets these contradictions as a dialectical movement and tries to establish unity of D.'s thought.

Ducros, Louis. Diderot, l'homme et l'écrivain. Perrin, 1894. 344 p.   2273

Most comprehensive study of D. in French. Ducros attempts to interpret D.'s ideas as expression of his personality, but commits the error of using as categories for this interpretation D.'s judgments of himself. Good pages on his philosophy and ethics; unsatisfactory on esthetics and novels or tales.

Faguet, Emile. Diderot. *In his :* Dix-huitième siècle. Boivin, [193-] p. 289-333.   2274

General understanding of D. quite inadequate. Some good observations on D.'s style and theory of drama.

Gillot, Hubert. Denis Diderot. L'homme; ses idées philosophiques, esthétiques, littéraires. Courville, 1937. 336 p.   2275

Painstaking but diffuse. Good collection of D.'s literary and artistic criticism. Philosophic sections least satisfactory. Index inadequate. Valuable appendices. *See* no. 2248.

Luppol, Ivan Kapitonovitch. Diderot. Traduit du russe par Y. et V. Feldman. Éditions sociales internationales, 1936. 404 p.   2276

One of most sympathetic, penetrating, and philosophic works written on D. Particularly good on Darwinian aspects of D.'s thought and relation of his philosophy to other 18th century thinkers. Marxist point of view sometimes too narrow, e.g., in opposition of collectivism to individualism, of political and economic man to D.'s conception of psychosomatic unity of man, in judgments on his political ideas. Highly controversial but stimulating presentation of D.'s esthetics.
Review : L. G. Crocker in RR 28: 77-79, 1937. See also J. Thomas, no. 2282, p. 172-73.

Morley, John. Diderot and the Encyclopædists. *See* no. 1334.   2277

Excellent in its day. Still good reading for D.'s relation to broader aspects of enlightenment.

Mornet, Daniel. Diderot, l'homme et l'œuvre. Boivin, [1941]. 208 p.   2278

Good introduction to and exposition of D.'s thought. Discussion of points where D.'s ideas and those of 18th century coincide is more pertinent than analysis of D.'s individuality. Categories used for interpretation and judgment often seem too conventional. Nevertheless an outstanding contribution by one of leading representatives of French academic criticism.
Review : H. Dieckmann in RR 38:360-62, 1947.

Rosenkranz, Karl. Diderots Leben und Werke. Leipzig, Brockhaus, 1866. 2 v. 2279

First penetrating and serious discussion of D. as philosopher. Unsurpassed in general history of ideas, but reads too much system into D. Somewhat colored by Hegelianism. Still indispensable for scholarly research.

Sainte-Beuve, Charles-Augustin. Diderot. Mémoires, correspondance et ouvrages inédits. *In his :* Premiers lundis, Garnier, s.d. 1:372-93.   2280

— Diderot. *In his :* Portraits littéraires. Garnier, s.d. 1:239-64.   2281

These works present best introduction to D.'s personality and thought. Full of excellent insights and written with a fine understanding of D.'s individuality.

Thomas, Jean. L'humanisme de Diderot. Société d'édition les belles lettres, 1932. 185 p. (2nd ed., rev. et augm., *ibid.*, 1938, 183 p.).   2282

Excellent introduction to D., man and philosopher. Succinct, scholarly, readable. Stresses esthetic trends of his nature and shows that they increase as he matures; they cross, modify, and outweigh scientific and moral trends. Unity toward which D. strives amid all his contradictions not a purely naturalistic or scientific conception of man and of the world, but a new humanism, the comprehension of man in his complexity, of which reason and its disciplines are only part, and the exaltation of the intensity and the expressivity of life. Appendix offers excellent account of studies on D. and trends in D. criticism.
Review : M. Bonnafous in Rech 2: 622-23, 1932-33; D. Mornet in RHL 40:446-47, 1933.

Trahard, Pierre. La sensibilité de Diderot. *In his :* Les maîtres de la sensibilité française au xviiie siècle. *See* 832. 2:49-286.   2283

Thorough, sympathetic attempt to establish unity of D.'s emotional nature. Good pages on D.'s artistic sensitivity. Concept of *sensibilité* not precise.

Venturi, Franco. Jeunesse de Diderot (1713 à 1753). Traduit de l'italien par Juliette Bertrand. [Skira], 1939. 417 p. *See* 3049.   2284

Indispensable for knowledge of historical and social background of D.'s early works, and for newly discovered documents. Philosophically naïve. Attempt to construe unity of D.'s thought from political, pre-Marxist nature of his ideas seems erroneous.
Review : D. Mornet in RHL 46:129-31, 1939.

Vexler, Felix. Diderot and the Leçons de clavecin. *In :* Todd memorial volumes. New York, Columbia univ. press, 1930. 2:231-49.   2285

Concludes plausibly but much too casually that not only the form of this work but the ideas are to be attributed

to D. rather than to Bemetzrieder. Analysis of development of D.'s ideas on music confused. *See* no. 341.

Studies of single works

Bastier, Paul. Le Paradoxe sur le comédien. Talma, Tieck et Roetscher pour et contre Diderot. RLC 12:871-75, 1932.   2286

Supersedes his article : *A propos du Paradoxe : Talma plagiaire de Diderot*, RHL 11:108-09, 1904. Gives two opposing opinions of Talma on D. German scholars' reactions to Talma are in reality reactions to D. *See also :* E. Delacroix, *Journal*, ed. by A. Joubin. Plon, 1932. 1:170-74.

Crocker, L. G. La Correspondance de Diderot; son intérêt documentaire, psychologique, et littéraire. By L. G. Krakeur. New York, Kingsley press, 1939. 120 p.   2287

An attempt to relate the *Correspondance*, especially recently published portions, to whole of D.
Review : H. Dieckmann in MLN 55: 472-73, 1940.

Dieckmann, Herbert. Théophile Bordeu und Diderots Rêve de d'Alembert. RFor 52:55-122, 1938.   2288

Investigation into relations between natural sciences in 18th century and D.'s philosophy. Determines role of Bordeu in the *Rêve.*

Dussane, Mme Béatrix. Le comédien sans paradoxe. Plon, [1933]. 285 p. (*See* p. 3-23).   2289

Observations of several actors on D.'s theory.

Mornet, Daniel. La véritable signification du Neveu de Rameau. RDM 7th per. 40:881-908, Aug. 15, 1927.   2290

An interpretation of the *Neveu de Rameau* as dialogue between D. and his *alter ego;* between sentimental moralist and materialistic determinist. Approach and conclusions similar to those of Carl Becker : *The dilemma of Diderot*, PhR 24:54-71, 1915. Seems to overstress the " dilemma," as Becker does, and to neglect artistic significance of the work. *See* Schlösser, no. 2341.

Venturi, Franco. Addition aux Pensées philosophiques. RHL 45:23-42, 289-308, 1938.   2291

Shows, by parallel texts, how the *Objections diverses contre les écrits de différents théologiens* furnish both plan and essential material for the *Addition.*

Villey, Pierre. A propos de la Lettre sur les aveugles. RDS 1:410-433, 1913. 2292

Penetrating study and evaluation by an eminent scholar. Somewhat unjust on subject of D.'s atheism. Commends D.'s psychological insights.

Critical studies of Diderot's thought

(*See also* Belin, no. 360), and Folkierski, no. 1040)

Philosophy and Science

Barker, Joseph E. Diderot's treatment of the Christian religion in the Encyclopédie. *See* 1292. 2293

Penetrating study of manner in which D., in spite of his many censors, succeeded in presenting a liberal interpretation of Christian religion, mingled with irony.

Reviews : H. Dieckmann in RR 34: 174-77, 1943; G. R. Havens in MLN 57:398-99, 1942; H. A. L[arrabee] in Jph 38:528-29, Sept. 11, 1941.

Carpentier, J. Diderot et la science de son temps. Rmois 16:537-52, Nov. 10, 1913. 2294

Good introduction to D.'s relation to scientific trends of his time.

Crocker, L. G. Diderot and the idea of progress. By L. G. Krakeur. RR 29:151-59, 1938. 2295

Analysis of passages in which D. expresses pessimistic view of possibility of progress.

— and R. L. Krueger. The mathematical writings of Diderot. By L. G. Krakeur and R. L. Krueger. Isis 33:219-32, 1941. 2296

Proves D.'s interest and competence in mathematics.

Dieckmann, Herbert. Diderots Naturempfinden und Lebensgefühl. Istanbul, 1937. Publ. de la Faculté des lettres de l'université d'Istanbul, 2:57-83. 2296A

Analysis of the different aspects of D.'s feeling for nature.

Doublet, Suzanne-Madeleine, *née* Lévèque.** La médecine dans les œuvres de Diderot. Bordeaux. Cadoret, 1934. 107 p. (Diss., Bordeaux). 2297

Supersedes Tribouillet, P., *Diderot et la médecine.* Lyon, 1921. Good summary of D.'s interest in medicine and of his ideas on general problems such as pathology, therapeutics, and hydropathy. Merely factual with no hint of philosophical implications. Very few references to problems of history of medicine.

Groethuysen, B. La pensée de Diderot. Grev 82:322-41, Nov. 25, 1913. 2298

Very stimulating study not of content but of method and movement of D.'s thought. Independence, freedom of mind, and experimental, factual method are combined in D.'s art of interpretation, which is neither philosophic deduction nor scientific objectivation. Excellent pages on relation between thought and verbal expression and on imagination in D.

Janet, Paul. La philosophie de Diderot. Le dernier mot d'un matérialiste. Ncent 9: 695-708, Apr., 1881. 2299

Aspects of D.'s materialism in relation to Leibniz and Maupertuis. Relevant only as starting point of new study on this topic.

Lovejoy, Arthur. Some eighteenth century evolutionists. PSM 65:238-51, 323-40, 1904. 2300

For D., see p. 323-27. Very brief discussion of D., but important one for his sources and development of transformism or evolutionism during 18th century. Cf. : *Buffon and the problem of species.* PSM 79:464-73, 554-67, 1911.

Paitre, Fernand. Diderot biologiste. Lyon, Storck, 1904. 106 p. 2301

Still only study of its kind; the plan (a history of D.'s scientific ideas, their origin and development; relation between science and philosophy; nature, range, and influence of D.'s physiological and biological knowledge) is good, but organization and execution are poor. Neither correctly evaluates part and significance of philosophy in D.'s biological ideas, nor influence of Maupertuis (Leibniz) and Robinet. Wild claims for D. as precursor of modern ideas. Factual material very useful.

Ethics

Hermand, Pierre. Les idées morales de Diderot. Les presses universitaires de France, 1923. 299 p. 2302

Comprehensive and scholarly treatment of D.'s ethics; good *exposé* of all questions involved, some uncertainty of method in presentation. Excellent and exemplary in the differentiation of D.'s ideas corresponding to various periods of his life, prevalence of his interests, differences of purpose. Valuable introduction on : *La conscience morale française vers 1740*, and Appendices on textual criticism. Review : D. Mornet in RHL 32:611-13, 1925.

Hubert, René. La morale de Diderot. RDS 2:329-40, 1914; 3:29-42, 1916.   2303

Useful as short summary.

Aesthetics

(*See: Journal des Goncourt*, published in 1886 ; *see also* Folkierski, no. 1040).

Belaval, Yvon. L'esthétique sans paradoxe de Diderot. Gallimard, 1950. 310 p.
2303A

Discursive review of D.'s esthetic ideas with special emphasis on his interest in the theater and the drama. The general headings are : *La Vocation théâtrale* ; *L'Imitation de la nature* ; and *Le Paradoxe sur le comédien*. Useful for its abundant quotations, but marred by lack of understanding of function of paradox in D.'s thought and by philosophic terminology which does not fit ideas. Sympathetic, but somewhat uncritical.

Brunetière, Ferdinand. Les Salons de Diderot. *In his :* Études critiques, 4th ed. 1893. 2:295-321.   2304

Violent attack on D. as art critic. For historical significance, see excellent remarks of J. Thomas, no. 2282, Ch. I.

Diderot, Denis. Fragments inédits d'un projet de Dictionnaire des peintres. Éd. par Franco Venturi. Hip 6:321-27, 1938.
2305

Short notes on painters collected from Leningrad manuscripts. Presumably D.'s direct impressions from the paintings.

Dieckmann, Herbert. Diderot's conception of genius. JHI 2:151-82, 1941.   2306

D.'s contribution to transforming of conception of genius, and role of this idea in D.'s various works.

Dresdner, Albert. Diderots Kunstkritik. *In his :* Die Entstehung der Kunstkritik im

Zusammenhang mit der Geschichte des europäischen Kunstlebens. Munich, Bruckmann, 1915. p. 235-84.   2307

Best exposition to date of D.'s art criticism and its historical origins. Very useful distinction between D.'s esthetic theories and his criteria in applied art criticism. Main themes of latter carefully analyzed.
Review : W. Weisbach in PrJ 165:145-49, 1916.

Eloesser, Arthur. Diderot. *In his :* Das bürgerliche Drama; seine Geschichte im 18. und 19. Jahrhundert. Berlin, Hertz, 1898. p. 67-76.   2308

Concise and penetrating analysis of D.'s dramatic principles and of the structure of his own dramas. Conclusions somewhat too negative.

Fontaine, André. Les doctrines d'art en France, peintres, amateurs, critiques, de Poussin à Diderot. Laurens, 1909. 316 p.   2309

Indispensable for background and general aspects of D.'s art criticism, but inferior to Dresdner (no. 2307). D.'s dependence upon classical art theories widely overrated and individuality and originality of his art criticism underestimated and misjudged.

Gilman, Margaret. The poet according to Diderot. RR 37:37-54, 1946.   2310

Careful and understanding analysis of D.'s conception of qualities constituting the poetic character and creative process. Gives parallels between D.'s ideas and those of English romanticists and Baudelaire.

Guggenheim, Susanna. Drammi e teorie drammatiche del Diderot, e loro fortuna in Italia. Eit 3:27-35, 155-69, 1921.   2311

Traces influence of D.'s theories on some minor Italian critics and dramatists.

Hunt, H. J. Logic and linguistics; Diderot as " grammairien-philosophe." MLR 33: 215-33, 1938.   2312

D. caught in linguistic prejudices of his age; better as literary critic than as esthetician. Comparisons with Baudelaire and Swift.

Jullien, Adolphe. Diderot. *In his :* La ville et la cour au xviiie siècle. Rouveyre, 1881. p. 153-66. In the Appendix : Diderot musicien, p. 193-204.   2313

D.'s stand in the *Querelle des bouffons* contrasted with his own principles on music. Appendix gives evaluation of D.'s pamphlets on *Querelle*.

Mayoux, J. J. Diderot and the technique of modern literature. MLR 31:518-31, 1936. 2314

Not a study of style and structure of D.'s novels, but analysis of D.'s " surprising excursions toward the future," in both biological and esthetic speculations. Towards Freud and Proust.

Pommier, Jean. Les Salons de Diderot et leur influence au XIXe siècle : Baudelaire et le Salon de 1846. RCC 37^2:289-306, 437-52, May 30, June 15, 1936. 2315

Shows a definite relationship between Baudelaire's and D.'s *Salons.* Cf. also *Un plagiat de Baudelaire.* BLS, May-June, 1937.

— Études sur Diderot. RHph 10:153-80, 1942. 2316

Notes in depth on *Rameau's nephew*, D.'s ethics, his early disagreements with Rousseau and fragments of letters probably addressed to Mme de Maux. Valuable leads for new insights.

Sainte-Beuve, C. A. Diderot. *In his :* Causeries du lundi. Garnier, n.d., 3:293-313. 2317

Mostly on D.'s art criticism. Sympathetic and pertinent observations. Excellent evaluation of literary elements of D.'s art criticism.

Spitzer, Leo. The style of Diderot. *In his :* Linguistics and literary history; essays in stylistics. Princeton, Princeton univ. press, 1948. p. 135-91. 2318

Beginning with examination of D.'s style in the *Encyclopédie,* article *Jouissance,* which Naigeon had pointed to as stylistically superior, Spitzer shows D.'s " sensitivity to the acoustic as such by his translation of feelings into rhythm..." (p. 173) and suggests that the tendency toward mobility and " self-potentiation " (p. 135) was essence of both the style and the man.

Steel, Eric M. Diderot's imagery; a study of literary personality. New York, The corporate press, 1941. 269 p. (Diss., Columbia). 2319

Starting from the assumption that images an author uses reveal his personal-

ity, taste, his intentions, and interests, Steel classifies and studies D.'s images. Revelatory significance of images seems exaggerated, but study is one of the few works that make real contribution to our knowledge of D.'s art and style.
Review : H. Dieckmann in RR 35:345-48, 1944.

Thomas, Jean. Diderot et Baudelaire. Hip 6:328-42, 1938. 2320

Study not of influence of D. upon Baudelaire, but of affinities between esthetic ideas of both authors. Pertinent remarks on modernity of D.'s thought; slightly underestimates importance of D.'s taste for classicism.

Vexler, Felix. Studies in Diderot's æsthetic naturalism. New York, Columbia univ. press, 1922. 115 p. *See* 3050. 2321

Chiefly exposition of D.'s dramatic theories. View of dualism between naturalistic and idealistic-classicist elements too narrow and too rigid. Social and revolutionary aspects of D.'s dramatic theories over-emphasized. Good pages on *Paradoxe sur le comédien.*
Review : D. Mornet in RHL 32:609-10, 1925.

Walker, Eleanor M. Towards an understanding of Diderot's esthetic theory. RR 35:277-87, 1944. 2322

Excellent study on relation of D.'s esthetics to his general philosophy. Clearly demonstrates limitations of historical interpretation of D.'s esthetic ideas.

Education
(*See also* Pellisson, no. 2265)

Codignola, Ernesto. Diderot e le origini dell' utilitarismo pedagogico in Francia : il piano di una Università russa. RivP 1917, p. 380-407. 2323

Competent article on utilitarianism of D.'s educational theories.

La Fontainerie, François de. Diderot (1713-1784) and his plan for a Russian university. *In his :* French liberalism and education in the 18th century; the writings of La Chalotais, Turgot, Diderot and Condorcet on national education. *See* 1423, p. 187-310. 2324

Weak general introduction on D. (p. 187-98), and a translation of the *Plan d'une université* (p. 199-310).

Mesrobian, Avédik. Les conceptions pédagogiques de Diderot. Molouan, [1913]. 168 p. (Diss., Paris).   2325

Fundamental investigation of relation between D.'s educational ideas and his philosophy. Excellent treatment of relation between determinism and pedagogy. D.'s place in modern educational theory.

Politics

(*See also* Kingsley Martin, no. 1055)

Oestreicher, Jean. La pensée politique et économique de Diderot. Vincennes, Rosay, 1936. 80 p. (Diss., Paris).   2326

Attempt to show that D.'s ideas on politics and economics are as original and important as his ideas in other fields. Results unsatisfactory. Investigation consists mainly in accumulating quotations, historical importance of which is overstressed. No comparison of D.'s ideas with those of Montesquieu, Voltaire, Turgot, or Rousseau.

Comparative Literary Relationships
(*See also* Chapter XI)

Avezac-Lavigne, Charles. Diderot et la société du baron d'Holbach. *See* 1337.   2327

Good presentation of only *salon* which D. frequented and which influenced his thought. No longer up to date, since important new material on question has been published in Babelon's edition of D.'s letters, nos. 2231-32.

Busnelli, Manlio D. Diderot et l'Italie; reflets de vie et de culture italiennes dans la pensée de Diderot, avec des documents inédits et un essai bibliographique sur la fortune du grand encyclopédiste en Italie. Champion, 1925. 305 p. (Diss., Grenoble). *See* 3294.   2328

Exhaustive and scholarly study. Results generally negative except in sections on Italian music and Goldoni. Good chapter on general sources, especially for the *Encyclopédie*.
Reviews : C. de Lollis in Cult 5:560-62, 1925-26; G. Maugain in Rcr 93:404-06, 1926; C. Pellegrini in Leo 2:42-43, 1926.

Crocker, L. G. Diderot's influence on Rousseau's first *Discours*. *See* 2165.   2329

An attempt to solve problem by relating theme to general body of D.'s and Rousseau's thought. *See also* Havens, no. 2174 and no. 2338.

Cru, R. Loyalty. Diderot as a disciple of English thought. New York, Columbia univ. press, 1913. 498 p. *See* 3044.   2330

Thesis that D. is a disciple of English thought somewhat exaggerated, especially in regard to Shaftesbury and Bacon. Good chapters on D.'s dramatic theories, novels, and critical principles. Contains valuable material on sources of D.'s articles in the *Encyclopédie*.
Review : G. Lanson in RHL 21:443-45, 1914.

Curtius, Ernst Robert. Diderot und Horaz. *In his :* Europäische Literatur und lateinisches Mittelalter. Bern, Francke, 1948. 556-64.   2331

Shows that D.'s epigraphs from Horace's satires are important keys to understanding of his works, especially the *Neveu de Rameau,* as *Satyre seconde.* Both Horace's conception of satire and context reveal that D.'s main intent was to satirize human pantomime and to show that only the philosopher is free.

Dickenmann, Rudolf. Beiträge zum Thema Diderot und Lessing. Zurich, Leemann, 1915. 56 p. (Diss., Zurich).   2332

Useful and critical dissertation.

Dieckmann, Herbert. Goethe und Diderot. DV 10:478-503, 1932.   2333

Analysis of Goethe's contacts with D.'s thought, and evaluation of D.'s influence on Goethe.

— The influence of Francis Bacon on Diderot's Interprétation de la nature. RR 34:303-30, 1943.   2334

Determines instances of real influence and separates them from those showing only parallelism of thought and outlook.

Eggert, Charles Augustus. Goethe and Diderot on actors and acting. MLN 11: col. 205-220, 1896. (Practically same as : Goethe und Diderot; über Schauspieler und die Kunst des Schauspielers. Euph 4:301-17, 1897).   2335

Shows some similarities between D.'s and Goethe's conception of good actor. Author's assumption of influence questionable.

Eggli, Edmond. Diderot et Schiller. RLC 1:68-127, 1921.   2336

Very complete study.

Hankiss, Johann. Diderot und Herder.

Archiv. (Sonderheft) 140 ns 40:59-74, 1920.
2337

Fair study of D.'s influence on Herder. Little on their intellectual kinship. Parallel passages unconvincing.

Havens, George R. Diderot and the composition of Rousseau's First discourse. *See* 2174. 2338

Careful and objective analysis of relevant documents. *See also* Havens, 1886, Crocker, 2165, 2329.

Jacoby, Daniel. Diderot in Leipzig. Euph 6:645-49, 1899. 2339

Extracts from a letter of liberal Swiss theologian Zollikofer to Chr. Garve. D. called on Zollikofer in Leipzig and discussed philosophy, atheism, and literature with him. Interesting description of D.

Koscziusko, Jacques. Diderot et Hagedorn. RLC 16:635-69, 1936. 2340

Shows that D. used French translation of Hagedorn's *Betrachtungen über die Malerei* as starting-point and occasionally the source of his *Pensées détachées sur la peinture...* Confrontation of texts rudimentary and general conclusions meager.

Schlösser, Rudolf. Rameau's Neffe. Studien und Untersuchungen zur Einführung in Goethes Uebersetzung des Diderotschen Dialogs. Berlin, Duncker, 1900. 292 p.
2341

Most successful attempt to determine various stages of composition of *Neveu de Rameau* and to interpret its essential unity of form and content. Thorough study of Goethe's translation of *Neveu de Rameau* and of his annotations. Indispensable for further research.
Reviews : O. Harnack in ZDA 45, ns 33:324-27, 1901; G. Witkowski in Dlit 22:917-21, 1901.

Torrey, Norman L. Voltaire's reaction to Diderot. PMLA 50:1107-43, 1935. *See* 1805. 2342

Study based chiefly on Voltaire's comments in margin of D.'s works.

Tronchon, Henri. Goethe, Herder et Diderot. *In :* Goethe; études publiées pour le centenaire de sa mort par l'Université de Strasbourg. PFS 57:113-26, 1932. 2343

Short, insufficient on Goethe and D., good on affinities between Herder and D. List of Herder's statements on D.

CHAPTER X. MISCELLANEOUS PROSE
(Nos. 2344-2884)

Gabriel Bonno, Jean David, Jean Dufrenoy, Otis E. Fellows, Francis W. Gravit, Anne C. Jones, Hunter Kellenberger, J. Robert Loy, Dorothy M. McGhee, Robert B. Michell, Andrew R. Morehouse, Clifford H. Prator, Donald S. Schier, Edward D. Seeber, Joseph R. Smiley, Fernand Vial

Jean-Baptiste Du Bos
(Nos. 2344-2356)
JOSEPH R. SMILEY

Du Bos, Jean-Baptiste. Histoire de la ligue faite à Cambray, entre Jules II, pape, Maximilien I. empereur, Louis XII. roy de France, Ferdinand V. roy d'Aragon et tous les princes d'Italie, contre la république de Venise. Delaulne, 1709. 2 v. 2344

Best edition is 4th ed., *revue, corrigée et augmentée par l'auteur.* Chaubert, 1729. 2 v.

— Réflexions critiques sur la poésie et sur la peinture. Mariette, 1719. 2 v. 2345

Published in 3 volumes in 1733 by Mariette, volume III containing reflections on declamation, music, and theater of Ancients. These were formerly parts of Sections XLII and XLIII of volume I of first edition, and are here developed. Edition of 1740, also by Mariette, is first to bear author's name. Most readily accessible edition now that of 1770, Pissot. D.'s great word on esthetics.

— Histoire critique de l'établissement de la monarchie françoise dans les Gaules. Osmont, 1734. 3 v. 2346

Generally considered D.'s most significant historical work, it created a new method of writing history based on research and remained definitive during 19th century. Best edition is second, Didot, 1742, 2 v. Chapters rearranged and new material added by author.

Braunschvig, Marcel. L'abbé Du Bos; rénovateur de la critique au XVIIIᵉ siècle. Toulouse, Brun, 1904. 86 p. (Diss., Paris). 2347

Situates *Réflexions critiques* between 17th century rationalism and 19th century impressionism. Elaborates two principal aspects of D.'s criticism : psychological

(effect of work of art on spectator, reader, or hearer), and scientific (how work of art is created). Concludes with life of D. and bibliography of works only.

Geffroy, A. Les conquêtes germaniques; l'école romaniste et la théorie des races. RDM 2nd per. 106:280-316, July 15, 1873. 2348

Excellent comparison of ideas of D. and Montesquieu on establishment of monarchy in Gaul. D.'s *Monarchie françoise* weak in premises, according to Montesquieu : based on transformation of Roman element under Christian influence. Montesquieu contended another element present as result of Germanic invasion. Geffroy's charge : " ... Du Bos ... prétendait plier l'histoire à ses idées préconçues."

Gigas, Emile. Choix de la correspondance inédite de Pierre Bayle. Copenhagen, Gad, 1890. 728 p. 2349

Contains 12 letters from D. to Bayle, dated December 19, 1695, to June 4, 1706. D. sends literary and personal news of Paris. Interesting for his acquaintance with men like Boileau and Perrault.

Leysaht, Konrad. Dubos et Lessing. Greifswald, Kunike, 1874. 30 p. (Diss., Rostock). Also published in German as : Dubos und Lessing, Rostock, 1883. 2350

Reproduces texts of D. and Lessing, but draws no precise consequences. Obviously close relation between *Laokoon* and *Réflexions.*

Lombard, Alfred. La querelle des anciens et des modernes; l'abbé Du Bos. Neuchâtel, Attinger, 1908. 59 p. 2351

Brief treatment of D.'s position in the Quarrel. His role in early esthetics of

266

18th century. Excellent bibliography of works of D.
> Review : H. Heiss in ZFSL 36²:266-69, 1910.

— L'abbé Du Bos; un initiateur de la pensée moderne. Hachette, 1913. 614 p. 2352
> Indispensable critical work on D.; treats fully all aspects of life and works. Supersedes all previous studies; exhaustive bibliography.
> Reviews : G. Lanson in RHL 21:441-43, 191 ; A. Schinz in MP 14:689-700, 1916-17.

— La correspondance de l'abbé Du Bos. Hachette, 1913. 90 p. (Diss., Paris). 2353
> Lists chronologically all known letters of D. Of those previously published, only headings are given; full text of letters appearing for first time.

— Notes sur l'abbé Du Bos. RHL 15:65-75, 1908. 2354
> Interesting treatment of D.'s diplomatic activities as background for his major historical works. Offers D.'s lack of *esprit d'intrigue* as explanation for his slow progress in diplomatic career.

— L'abbé Du Bos et l'origine de l'école romaniste. RHL 16:677-90, 1909. 2355
> D. first realized projection of Roman history into history of Middle Ages. Genesis of his *Monarchie françoise*.

Peteut, Paul. Jean-Baptiste Du Bos; contribution à l'histoire des doctrines esthétiques en France. Tramelan, Zachmann-Vuille, 1902. 98 p. (Diss., Berne). 2356
> Elementary analysis of *Réflexions critiques* and attempted rehabilitation of D.'s reputation. Especially concerned with D.'s influence in Germany : Bodmer, Breitinger, Schlegel, Lessing.

Friedrich Melchior, *baron* de Grimm
(Nos. 2357-2417)
Robert B. Michell

Grimm, Friedrich-Melchior, baron de. Correspondance littéraire, philosophique et critique, par Grimm, Diderot, Raynal, Meister, etc., revue sur les textes originaux ... notices, notes, table générale, par Maurice Tourneux. Garnier, 1877-82. 16 v. 2357
> Standard version of *Correspondance littéraire*. Contains, besides what is found in earlier editions, " les fragments supprimés en 1813 par la censure " and " les

parties inédites conservées à la Bibliothèque ducale de Gotha et à l'Arsenal à Paris." By way of introduction, there is included Meister's brief biography of G. and G.'s *Mémoire historique* on his relations with Catherine II of Russia. Volume I and part of Volume II are devoted to *Nouvelles littéraires* of Abbé Raynal, starting-point of the *Correspondance* idea.

— Correspondance inédite (1794-1801) du baron Grimm au comte de Findlater (éd. A. Cazes), Les presses universitaires de France, 1934. 302 p. (58 letters). 2358
> Important for activities of Grimm after the Revolution had driven him from France.
> Review : D. Mornet in˙RHL 42:281-83, 1935.

— Mémoire historique sur l'origine et les suites de mon attachement pour l'impératrice Catherine II. *In :* Correspondance littéraire. No. 2357, 1:17-63. 2359
> " Une sorte d'autobiographie " (Scherer). Appeal to Tsar Paul on behalf of G.'s *protégés*, the De Bueil family.

— Opuscules et lettres de Grimm. *In :* Correspondance littéraire, No. 2357, 16:247-502. 2360
> Here are reprinted most of G.'s minor works and most important of his letters, which are not readily available in other publications.

— Lettres de M. Grimm à l'auteur du Mercure sur la littérature allemande. MerF. Oct., 1750, p. 14-25, and Feb. 1715, p. 10-33. *Also in :* Correspondance littéraire, No. 2357, 16:269-87. 2361
> These two letters form chief basis for regarding G. as a propagandist for German literature.

— Projet de souscription pour une estampe tragique et morale, 1765. *In :* Correspondance littéraire, No. 2357, 16:352-63. 2362
> G.'s effort to raise money for Calas family by sale of a print by Carmontelle. *See* no. 2412.

— Du poème lyrique. *In :* Encyclopédie ou Dictionnaire raisonné, etc. Briasson, 1751-65. 12:823-36. *Reprinted in :* Correspondance littéraire, No. 2357, 16:363-405. 2363
> G.'s only contribution to *Encyclopédie*. Discussion of nature and history of

opera, with special reference to different development of opera in Italy and France.

— Préface du Journal étranger, 1754. *In :* Correspondance littéraire, No. 2357, 16:336-47.   2364

G.'s only contribution to this comparative literature publication, of which he had been asked to become editor. Appeal for European collaboration in advancing cause of enlightenment.

— Une correspondance inédite de Grimm avec Wagnière (éd. Paul Bonnefon). RHL 3:481-535, 1896.   2365

G. seeks information about Voltaire and his library, recently acquired by Catherine II. Wagnière was Voltaire's secretary.

Bechtolsheim, Katherina von (née Bueil). Baron Grimm. *In :* Erinnerungen einer Urgrossmutter (ed. Oberndorff). Berlin, Fontane, 1902. p. 51-72, and in Appendix.
2366
Contains valuable information concerning G.'s last years in exile with his adopted family, that of comte de Bueil.

Buffenoir, Hippolyte. Melchior Grimm et les ennemis de J.-J. Rousseau. Rfr 78:125-32, 1925.   2367

Violent attack on G., " ce Tartuffe d'un nouveau genre ", for his conduct toward Rousseau. Article based on A. Jay, no. 2387.

Carlez, Jules. Grimm et la musique de son temps. Caen, Le Blanc-Hardel, 1872, 41 p. (Extract from MAC).   2368
Attempt to estimate G.'s competence in field of music.

Cazes, André. Grimm et les encyclopédistes, Presses universitaires de France, 1933. 407 p.   2369
Most recent lengthy discussion of G. Mornet, in review below, calls this thesis " un travail médiocre " and criticizes it severely for its inaccuracies and *lacunae*, indicating many problems in connection with G. which have either been entirely overlooked or treated inadequately. Though Cazes's volume adds nothing particularly new to our knowledge of G., it is, nevertheless, of some value for its lengthy, if somewhat unsatisfactory, bibliography.
Review : D. Mornet in RHL 42:281-83, 1935.

Charavay, Etienne. Grimm et la cour de Saxe-Gotha. RDH 5:8-76, 1878.   2370
Interesting as revelation of G.'s relations with one of his most faithful correspondents in Germany.

Charlier, Gustave. Mme d'Epinay et J.-J. Rousseau. *In his :* De Ronsard à Victor Hugo ; problèmes d'histoire littéraire, Brussels, Editions de la Revue de l'université de Bruxelles, 1931, p. 193-220.   2371
Charlier traces long controversy between partisans of Rousseau and those of Mme d'Epinay over veracity of *Confessions* and *Mémoires.* Devotes particular attention to book of Mrs. Mac-Donald (no. 1992), pivot of modern discussion of subject. While accepting some of Mrs. MacDonald's conclusions, he finds that too often she allows her prejudices and imagination to lead her astray into hypotheses which have little or no basis in fact. *See* no. 2415.

Cocteau, Jean. Jean-Jacques Rousseau. RPar 45:742-61, 1938; 46:54-79, 1939. 2372
Rousseau's persecution mania was justified by real treachery of Diderot and G., according to Cocteau. In support of this theory a certain amount of evidence is advanced.

Danzel, Theodor W. Letters of Grimm to Gottsched. *In his :* Gottsched und seine Zeit. 2nd ed., Leipzig, Dyk, 1855. 343-54.   2373
Contains six letters of Grimm to Gottsched, revealing Grimm's youthful attitude toward great German literary master of time.

Diderot, Denis. Copie des Tablettes de Diderot. *In :* Correspondance littéraire, No. 2357, 16:218-22.   2374
Essential document in break between Rousseau and his friends, as it lists the " sept scéleratesses," which, according to Diderot, have alienated all Rousseau's friends. *See* no. 2239.

— Correspondance inédite, publiée ... par André Babelon. *See* no. 2232, 1:19-183.
2375
Eighty letters addressed to G. Introduction deals with relations of Diderot, G., and Mme d'Epinay.

Ducros, Louis. Grimm et Mme d'Epinay. *In his :* Diderot, l'homme et l'écrivain. *See* no. 2273, p. 28-44.   2376

Devoted to relations between G. and Mme d'Epinay.

— Jean-Jacques Rousseau : De Genève à l'Ermitage (1712-1757). *See* no. 1911, p. 323-418. 2376A

— De l'Ile de Saint-Pierre à Ermenonville (1765-1778). *See* 1911, p. 66-85. 2377

First of these two chapters discusses Rousseau's quarrel with his friends and so-called " complot " against him. Second is an attempt to refute arguments of Mrs. MacDonald (no. 1992). Both chapters have strong anti-Rousseau bias.

Epinay, Louise Florence, etc. Memoirs and Correspondence of Madame d'Epinay. Translated, with an Introduction, by E. G. Allingham. London, Routledge, 1930. 315 p. 2378

Abridgment of Brunet edition of 1818. Introduction defends Mme d'Epinay from " calumnies " of Rousseau, and especially of Rousseau's champion, Mrs. MacDonald (no. 1992).

Ewen, Frederic. Criticism of English literature in Grimm's Correspondance littéraire, SP 33:397-404, 1936. 2379

Brief evaluation of attitude of Raynal and especially of G. toward English literature. In general, G.'s much vaunted good critical sense not much in evidence in his treatment of English literature. He fails to grasp adequately important role England was playing in changing French literary ideas.

Georges, Karl A. Friedrich Melchior Grimm als Kritiker der zeitgenössischen Literatur in seiner Correspondance littéraire (1753-1770) Leipzig, Bär & Hermann, 1904. 81 p. (Inaug.-diss., Leipzig). 2380

Very brief summary of G.'s criticism of contemporary writers, mainly French. Discussion too brief to have much critical value. Rather good bibliography, especially of German works on G.

[Hall, Evelyn Beatrice]. Grimm the journalist. *In her :* The friends of Voltaire, by S. G. Tallentyre [*pseud*]. New York, Putnam, and London, Smith, Elder, 1907. p. 150-75. 2381

Interesting little essay, offering, along with Sainte-Beuve's essay (no. 2405), best general introduction to G. and his *Correspondance littéraire* (ed. Taschereau).

Author reveals herself as strongly sympathetic toward G.

Haussonville, [Gabriel] Othénin. Le salon de Mme Necker, RDM 3e pér. 38:63-106, March 1, 1880. 2382

G. is discussed (p. 78-87) as member of Mme Necker's salon.

Herpin, Clara Adèle Luce (Lucien Perey, *pseud*.), et **Gaston Maugras.** Une femme du monde au XVIIIe siècle; dernières années de Mme d'Epinay; son salon et ses amis, d'après des lettres et des documents inédits. *See* 234. 2383

New documents utilized by Perey and Maugras are incorporated in narrative of Mme d'Epinay's life, based on earlier edition of *Mémoires*, the result being, according to authors, " une biographie complète." Authors declare their belief in absolute veracity of these *Mémoires* in all essential points.

— Mme d'Epinay à Genève. BU 3rd per. 21:327-45, 551-71, 1884; 22:128-38, 1884. 2384

Account of visit of Mme d'Epinay to Geneva, visit which was closely connected with Rousseau's quarrel with his friends. *See* no. 2021.

Hillebrand, Karl. Katharina II und Grimm. DR 25:377-405, 1880. 2385

Analysis of correspondence between Catherine II and G., in effort to understand tastes and ideas of the two personalities concerned.

Hunter, Alfred C. Les opinions du baron Grimm sur le roman anglais. RLC 12:390-400, 1932. 2386

G. admires English novel for its realism. This realism presents broad picture of humanity and possesses certain poetic quality, by which G. probably means that it is imaginative and not merely reproduction of reality.

Jay, Antoine. Mémoires et correspondance de Madame d'Epinay. *In his :* Œuvres, Sauvignat, 1839. 4:313-72. 2387

Slashing attack on character of G. in connection with his treatment of Rousseau in Hermitage episode.

[Jeffrey, Francis]. Review of the Correspondance littéraire (no. 2357). EdR 21:263-99, July, 1813. 2388

This review goes far beyond scope of

ordinary review. Is really pleasantly written essay, in course of which G.'s attitude to writers of his age is discussed. General tone very favorable to G.

Jones, Anne Cutting. Frederick-Melchior Grimm as a critic of eighteenth century French drama, Bryn Mawr, 1926. 69 p. (Diss., Bryn Mawr). 2389

G.'s ideas on drama reveal him as very frank and relatively sane critic. His taste for sentimental in drama is corrected by his good sense. His dramatic views much like those of Diderot, but seem to have developed independently of Diderot's "organized theory." This does not, however, prevent their having been influenced by personal discussion between the two friends.

— In defence of Melchior Grimm. PMLA 43:210-19, 1928. 2390

Reply to Reynaud's claim, in no. 2401, that G. was propagandist for German literature in France. If G. had any influence in attracting greater attention to German literature, it was unconscious : his primary interest was in literary criticism with special relation to French literature.

Koch, A. Baron Melchior von Grimm und seine Pariser Briefe. ZFSL 7:219-25, 1885. 2391

Brief sketch of general character of *Correspondance littéraire* (no. 2357).

MacDonald, Mrs. Frederika. Jean-Jacques Rousseau : a new criticism. *See* 1992. 2392

Very important book, which has stirred much controversy among Rousseau critics. The "new criticism" in question is author's attempt to prove by "historical evidence" role played by G. and Diderot in a deliberate effort to blacken character of Rousseau. The "historical evidence" is largely drawn from G.'s *Correspondance* and *Mémoires* of Mme d'Epinay. Review : G. V[allette] in AJJR 3:256-67, 1907.

— A woman of the world in the France of Voltaire. *In her :* Studies in the France of Voltaire and Rousseau, London, Unicorn, 1895, p. 61-108. 2393

Little essay on Mme d'Epinay, which, of course, includes discussion of G.

Mahrenholtz, Richard. Bemerkungen über die Correspondance philosophique, litté-

raire et critique [1747-1793]. ZFSL 11²:90-104, 1889. 2394

Historical sketch of *Correspondance littéraire* (no. 2357) with particular stress on G.'s contribution to the work.

— Friedrich-Melchior Grimm, der Vermittler des deutschen Geistes in Frankreich, Archiv 82:291-302, 1889. 2395

G. is considered as sort of precursor of Mme de Staël in making known German literature to the French. Mahrenholtz's arguments based essentially on G.'s two letters to *Mercure français* (1750-1751) in which he admits inferiority of German literature, but expresses his faith in a coming renaissance, prophecy soon to be fulfilled by appearance of Lessing and Goethe.

Marmontel, Jean François. Mémoires d'un père pour servir à l'instruction de ses enfants. 1800-1805, 6 v. 2396

Book VIII, v. 2, gives Marmontel's version of the Hermitage episode, which probably reflects viewpoint of Diderot.

Meister, Jakob Heinrich. Le baron de Grimm. *In :* Grimm's Correspondance littéraire, No. 2357, 1:3-13. 2397

Written in 1808. " C'est ce document ... qui a fourni depuis soixante ans les éléments de toutes les biographies de Grimm." (No. 2357, I:iii-xiii.)

Morsch, H. Goethe's Festspiel : des Epimenides Erwachen. GJa 14:212-44, 1893. 2398

Discusses Goethe's general attitude toward *Correspondance littéraire* (no. 2357). Author (p. 221 ff) points out role of *Correspondance* in composition of *Epimenides Erwachen*.

Perey. *See* Herpin, no. 2383. 2398A

Reichenburg, Louisette E. Contribution à l'histoire de la Querelle des bouffons, guerre de brochures suscitée par Le petit Prophète de Grimm et par la Lettre sur la musique française de Rousseau. *See* 2129. 2399

Thorough-going discussion of famous musical controversy of second half of 18th century over respective merits of French and Italian music. In this controversy G. played an important part. Author of this thesis has collected a formidable bibliography of subject. (34 p.).

Reynaud, Louis. Les débuts du germanisme en France. MerF 147:386-407, 1921. 2400

G. discussed as one of first to introduce German literature to France. *See* no. 2390.

— Les lettres de Grimm au Mercure de France. *In his :* L'influence allemande en France au xviiie et au xixe siècle. Hachette, 1922. p. 16-18. 2401

Reynaud seems to have been responsible for idea of G. as propagandist for German literature, view rejected by most other critics. *See* Jones, no. 2390.

Ritter, Eugène. J.-J. Rousseau et Mme d'Houdetot. *See* 2011. 2402

Careful and very impartial analysis of Rousseau's quarrel with his friends in last months of his Ermitage sojourn. Torrey (no. 2021) calls this study " the high point of Rousseau apologetics from the scholarly point of view." *See also* no. 2415.

Pittard, Mme Hélène (Dufour). J.-J. Rousseau et les drames de l'Ermitage, par Noëlle Roger (*pseud*). RDM 7th per. 27:650-69, June 1, 1925. 2403

Re-examination of quarrel between Rousseau and his friends, in light of newly published correspondence of Rousseau and of so-called new criticism of Mrs. MacDonald (no. 1992). Rousseau presented as innocent victim of machinations of G. and Diderot, who used Mme d'Epinay as their tool.

Rubensohn, Georg. Die Correspondance littéraire unter Friedrich-Melchior Grimm und Heinrich Meister (1753-1793). Berlin, Ebering, 1917. 173 p. (Diss., Berlin). 2404

Overly-ambitious attempt to set forth systematically in brief compass the critical attitude of chief authors of *Correspondance littéraire* (no. 2357) toward great questions—philosophical, religious, social, political, artistic, and literary— which interested cultured society for whom G. and his continuators wrote.

Sainte-Beuve, Charles-Augustin. Grimm, sa Correspondance littéraire (éd. Taschereau). *In his :* Causeries du lundi, Garnier, 1851-1862, 7:287-328. 2405

Excellent introduction to G. Sainte-Beuve reverses an earlier opinion, and shows himself highly appreciative of G., both as man and as critic. Essays dated January 10 and 17, 1852.

— Mémoires et Correspondance de Mme d'Epinay. *In his :* Causeries du lundi, Garnier, 1851-1862, 2:187-207. 2406

Extremely sympathetic character sketch of Mme d'Epinay and fine tribute to her lover, G., as man and as critic, " un des critiques les plus distingués, les plus fermes à la fois et les plus fins qu'ait produits la littérature française." Essay dated June 10, 1850.

Saint-Marc-Girardin (Marc Girardin, *known as*). La rupture de Rousseau avec Mme d'Epinay, Grimm et Diderot. *In his :* Jean-Jacques Rousseau : sa vie et ses ouvrages. Charpentier, 1875, 1:273-321. 2407

Author sides with G. in his quarrel with Rousseau.

Scherer, Edmond. Madame d'Epinay. *See* 235. 2408

Scherer refuses to accept Rousseau's version in the *Confessions* of his quarrel with Mme d'Epinay's group, and criticizes Boiteau, editor of Mme d'Epinay's *Mémoires* (no. 2237), for so doing.

— Melchior Grimm. L'homme de lettres— le factotum—le diplomate—avec un appendice sur la Correspondance secrète de Métra. Calmann Lévy, 1887. 477 p. *See* 3257. 2409

Most complete discussion of G. so far. G.'s biography is brought into line with latest documents and his ideas on various subjects carefully analyzed. Picture of G. presented by Scherer on the whole distinctly attractive one.

— Notes et additions. *In his :* Melchior Grimm (no. 2409). p. 373-458. 2410

These *Notes et additions* are really bibliography, which is quite complete up to 1887 ; it is combined with running commentary, year by year, of events of G.'s life. This material is thus not presented in form easy to consult.

Schinz, Albert. Jean-Jacques Rousseau. NNY 107:725-27, Dec. 14, 1918. 2411.

Defense of Rousseau against aspersions cast on his character by many critics from Sainte-Beuve down. Defense based especially on arguments of Mrs. MacDonald (no. 1992).

Smiley, Joseph P. The subscribers of Grimm's Correspondance littéraire. MLN 62:44-46, 1947. 2412

Supposedly new list of subscribers to *Correspondance littéraire* (no. 2357) offered by Mrs. MacDonald (no. 1992) in her book on Rousseau is probably merely list of subscribers to fund raised by G. for benefit of Calas family (no. 2362). Original manuscript of G.'s list of subscribers mentioned by Buisson in his first edition of *Correspondance* has apparently been lost.

— Grimm's alleged authorship of certain articles on the theater in Paris. MLN 63:248-51, 1948. 2413

Certain scholars have regarded G. as author of four articles on Parisian drama in *Beiträge zur Historie und Aufnahme des Theaters*, short-lived review published at Stuttgart in 1750. According to Smiley, it is possible, but extremely improbable, that G. wrote these articles, which express ideas on French drama widely at variance with his later views.

— Diderot's relations with Grimm. Urbana, Univ. of Illinois press, 1950. 127 p. 2413A

First detailed study of subject. Important influence of Grimm on Diderot's dramatic work and theories, and on gene is of *Salons*. Grimm also stimulated lively interest in *Encyclopédie*. Extensive bibliography.

Streckeisen-Moultou, Georges. J.-J. Rousseau, ses amis et ses ennemis. Lévy, 1865. 2 v. 2414

Introduction by Jules Levallois (p. iii-lii) discusses Rousseau's quarrel with his friends.

Torrey, Norman L. Rousseau's quarrel with Grimm and Diderot. *See* 2021. 2415

" A few critical notes and commentaries " on famous quarrel of Rousseau with his friends. All evidence uncovered by more recent research carefully and impartially re-examined. Conclusion seems to be that there was no plot against Rousseau by the Encyclopedists, and that if blame is to be attached to any one, it must fall upon Rousseau, who allowed his imagination to run away with his sense of proportion. G. appears incidentally in discussion of facts of the quarrel.

Ustéri, Paul. La Correspondance littéraire de Grimm. RHL 14:712, 1909. 2416

Three letters of Meister to Gessner and Escher, fellow citizens of Zurich, concerning *Correspondance littéraire* (no. 2357). Meister justifies subscription price in view of risks involved in undertaking.

Vaissière, Pierre de. Grimm et la Révolution française, d'après des documents inédits. RQH 83:492-515, 1908. 2417

G.'s experiences with Revolutionary authorities in connection with sequestration of his property. His grievance against his friends for not sufficiently protecting his interests seems to have had no basis in fact.

Suard, *see* nos. 2797-2802

Jean François de La Harpe
(Nos. 2418-2424)
DOROTHY M. McGHEE

La Harpe, Jean François de. Œuvres. Verdière, 1821. 16 v. 2418

— Lycée, ou Cours de littérature ancienne et moderne. Depelafol, 1825. 16 v. 2419

Bonnefon, Paul. Une aventure de la jeunesse de La Harpe : l'affaire des couplets. RHL 18:354-63. 1911. 2420

Schoolboy anecdote of some defamatory couplets against his teachers. Illustrates early ability at insinuatingly clever writing.

Peignot, Gabriel. Recherches historiques, littéraires et bibliographiques sur la vie et les ouvrages de M. de La Harpe. Dijon, Frantin, 1820. 159 p. 2421

Valuable anecdotal material, arranged chronologically, illustrates this complex literary figure. Study inclines toward approval of L.'s seeming disdain for some of his contemporaries, notably Diderot.

Pitou, Alexis. Les trois textes de la Mélanie de La Harpe. RHL 16:540-53. 1909. 2422

Commentary proves of value in comparing texts. L.'s insistence upon glory.

Préaudeau, Louis de. La Harpe et son bonnet rouge. Rheb 20th yr 9:532-56, Sept., 1911. 2423

Subtle evocation of L.'s faculty for evasion. Interesting portrait of a man disliked by many, who succeeded in making himself indispensable.

Sainte-Beuve, Charles-Augustin. La Harpe. *In his :* Causeries du lundi. Garnier, n. d. 5:103-44. 2424

Corroborative of a frequent judgment on L.—his prideful ineptitude mingled with audacity. Concedes, however, his important literary contribution as critic of moderation and insight. Essays dated November 10 and 17, 1851.

Jean Le Clerc
(Nos. 2425-2431)

HUNTER KELLENBERGER

Le Clerc, Jean. Parrhasiana, ou Pensées diverses sur des matières de critique, d'histoire, de morale et de politique, avec la défense de divers ouvrages de Mr. L. C. par Théodore Parrhase (*pseud.*). Amsterdam, chez les héritiers de A. Schelte, 1699-1701. 2 v.   2425

Furnishes reasonably complete *résumé* of L.'s ideas and most convenient introduction to his thought. Contains data on life. For his voluminous works on theology, philosophy, apologetics, criticism, and history, his important translations of the Bible into Latin with commentaries, and his editions of ancient and modern works, see A. Barnes (no. 2426), p. 263-66 and, more completely, E. & E. Haag (no. 2428), v. 6, p. 467-70.

Barnes, Annie. Jean Le Clerc (1657-1736) et la république des lettres. Droz, 1938. 280 p. *See also* 1114.   2426

Excellent and thorough account of L.'s life and his personal contacts throughout western Europe. Wide use of his unpublished correspondence. Six letters from Burnet published entire. Main aspects of L.'s intellectual activity indicated but more thorough study and appraisal still needed. Useful summary of Protestant theological disputes (1650-1700) in Geneva, France, and Holland. Good bibliography (q. v.), p. 261-71. Index of names.
Reviews : H. Bibas in MLR 34:610-12, 1939; D. F. Bond in MP 37:213-14, 1939-40; D. Mornet in RHL 46:131-32, 1939; E. Philips in RR 30:202-04, 1939.

Casati, E. Hérauts et commentateurs de Shaftesbury en France. RLC 14:615-45, 1934. *See* 3006.   2427

Additional evidence of important role played by L. in propagating English thought on Continent. Was chief of those to introduce Shaftesbury.

Haag, Eugène and Emile. [Jean Le Clerc]. *In their :* La France protestante. 1st ed., Cherbuliez, 1846-58. v. 6, p. 464-70. 2428

Account of L.'s life, with detailed bibliography of his works.

Monod, Albert. Jean Leclerc et Richard Simon. *In his :* De Pascal à Chateaubriand; les défenseurs français du Christianisme de 1670 à 1802. Alcan, 1916. p. 44-60. *See also :* p. 160-61, 204, *passim.* (Diss., Paris).
2429

Thorough and carefully documented study. In spite of some errors of detail, is invaluable for information about complex and often neglected field. Affords best available explanation of L.'s theological and apologetic writings. *See* especially p. 46-50 (*la critique*), p. 160-61 (on free will), p. 186-87 (on incredulity). Detailed bibliography of works published in defense of Christianity. Index.

Reesink, H. J. [Jean Le Clerc]. *In her :* L'Angleterre et la littérature anglaise dans les trois plus anciens périodiques français de Hollande de 1684 à 1709. *See* 1153.
2430

Fundamental work, showing that these journals (Bayle's *Nouvelles de la république des lettres*, L.'s *Bibliothèque universelle*, and Basnage's *Histoire des ouvrages des savans*) devoted great attention to English books and events as early as 1680's. List of all articles in these journals on English subjects, with brief analyses and commentaries. Bibliography. Excellent indices.
See also Bonno, no. 2889, which has much material on Le Clerc and supplements Reesink for the later period.

Sandys, John E. [Le Clerc as editor]. *In his :* History of classical scholarship. Cambridge (Eng.), University press, 1908. v. 2. p. 441-43.   2431

These pages consider L. as scholar and editor of classic texts, in this work which is still only comprehensive treatment of its subject.

Guillaume Thomas Raynal
(Nos. 2432-2455)

ROBERT B. MICHELL

Feugère, Anatole. Bibliographie critique de l'abbé Raynal. Angoulême, Imprimerie ouvrière, 1922. 98 p. (Thèse complémentaire, Paris).   2432

Excellent work, companion volume to author's exhaustive monograph on R. (no. 2445); may be said to be definitive. Completely supersedes all previous bibliographies dealing with R. Nothing essential seems to have been omitted, up to 1922, date of publication.

Raynal, Guillaume Thomas. Histoire philosophique et politique des établissements et du commerce des Européens dans les deux Indes.   2433

Feugère, in his excellent bibliography of R. (no. 2432) distinguishes four main editions of this famous work :
(1) Amsterdam, 1770, 6 v.
(2) The Hague, Gosse, 1774, 7 v. " Voici enfin l'œuvre tel qu'il est sorti des mains de l'auteur " (Avertissement).
(3) Geneva, Pellet, 1780, 5 v. This is first edition to bear R.'s name on title-page.
(4) Paris, Costes, 1820-21, 12 v. with additional atlas volume. " Nouvelle édition corrigée et augmentée d'après les manuscrits autographes de l'auteur." Biographical introduction by Antoine Jay. Supplementary volume by Peuchet brings colonial situation up to date.
There are many reprints, legal and pirated, of these four main editions, and numerous translations. All these are carefully noted in Feugère's bibliography. Feugère lists also some 25 editions of *Extraits*, and admits that his list is probably far from complete. All this testifies to the great popularity, in its own time, of a work which is now almost completely forgotten.

— Révolution de l'Amérique.   London, Davis, 1781.   183 p.   2434

Extract from *Histoire philosophique*, dealing with American Revolution. Work seems to have been popular, for it had a number of editions in French and English translations. It was this pamphlet that called forth Thomas Paine's letter to R. on real facts of the Revolution (no. 2449).

Bird, C. W. Une source de la Chaumière indienne. RHL 45:520-26. 1938.   2435

Source is P. Sonnerat's *Voyage aux Indes orientales et à la Chine* (dated 1782). Bernardin de Saint-Pierre used this source for his story rather than R.'s *Histoire des deux Indes*.

Chinard, Gilbert. [Raynal]. *In his :* L'Amérique et le rêve exotique dans la littérature française au XVIIe et au XVIIIe siècle. *See* 789. p. 389-98.   2436

Excellent brief estimate of importance of Raynal's *Histoire des deux Indes*.

Combes de Patris, B. Un économiste ignoré : l'abbé Raynal. REH 78:695-708, 1912.   2437

Attempts to show that R., as " un historien austère," was listened to and admired in his century.

Couderc, Camille. L'abbé Raynal et son projet d'histoire de la révocation de l'Édit de Nantes. BSHP 38:592-608, 638-63, 1889.   2438

Published also as separate pamphlet : *Agence centrale de la Société*, 1890, 44 p.

Fabre, Joseph. L'abbé Raynal. *In his :* Les pères de la Révolution (de Bayle à Condorcet). *See* 1409, p. 513-30.   2439

Helpful summary of R.'s subversive ideas.

Feugère, Anatole. L'abbé Raynal et les Pays-Bas. RBelgique 3rd ser. 44:491-505, 558-65. 1912.   2440

Discussion of l'*Histoire du Stadhoudérat* (dated 1747) and l'*Histoire du Parlement d'Angleterre* (dated 1748), semi-official pamphlets in support of policy of French ministry toward Holland and England.

— Un homme de lettres au XVIIIe siècle; l'abbé Raynal. RPL 50²:440-45, Oct. 5, 1912; 50²:467-71, Oct. 12, 1912.   2441

R.'s social and literary career before *Histoire des Indes*. Summary of chaps. I-III of Feugère's *L'abbé Raynal* (no. 2445).

— La doctrine révolutionnaire de Raynal et de Diderot, d'après l'Histoire des Indes. MerF 102:498-517, Apr. 1, 1913.   2442

Abridgment of Chapter 7 of Feugère's work on R. (no. 2445), setting forth " les idées philosophiques et politiques de l'*Histoire des Indes*."

— Raynal, Diderot et quelques autres historiens des Deux Indes. RHL 20:343-78, 1913; 22:408-52, 1915.   2443

These two articles correspond substantially to Ch. V and VI of author's volume on R. (no. 2445), with addition of considerable illustrative material.

— L'abbé Raynal et la Révolution française; documents inédits. AnR 6:309-44, 1913.   2444

Résumé of chapters 9-11 of author's *L'abbé Raynal* (no. 2445).

— Un précurseur de la Révolution; l'abbé Raynal (1713-1796); documents inédits. Angoulême, Imprimerie ouvrière, 1922. 459 p.   2445

Most complete treatment of R. and his work which has so far appeared, incorporating results of all investigations prior to 1922. Good index. Bibliography published separately in companion volume of same date (no. 2432). Review : P. de L. in Rcr ns. 90:134-35, 1923.

Irvine, Dallas D. The Abbé Raynal and British humanitarianism. JMH 3:564-77, 1931. 2446

Role of R.'s *Histoire des deux Indes* in developing British humanitarian feeling in late 18th century, with special reference to oppression of backward peoples, especially natives of India and negro slaves of America.

Jay, Antoine. Précis historique sur la vie et les ouvrages de l'abbé Raynal. Sauvaignat, 1839. 4:203-58. 2447

Reprint of Jay's introduction to fourth edition (dated 1820) of R.'s *Histoire des deux Indes*, under title *Une Notice biographique et des considérations sur les écrits de Raynal.*

Morley, John. Raynal's History of the Indies. *In his :* Diderot and the Encyclopaedists. *See* 1334, 2:204-31. 2448

Rather old but very penetrating study of R.'s importance. Best general introduction to the work of R.

Paine, Thomas. A letter addressed to the abbé Raynal on the affairs of North America. In which the mistakes of the Abbé's account of the Revolution of America are corrected and cleared up. Philadelphia, Aitken, 1782. 78 p. 2449

Paine's reply to R. is found in several English editions and French translations, so that it would seem to have attained a certain currency among both English and French readers.

Rocquain, Félix. Progrès des idées révolutionnaires attesté par le livre de Raynal sur le Commerce et l'établissement des Européens dans les deux Indes. *In his :* L'esprit révolutionnaire avant la Révolution. *See* 1069, p. 389-91. 2450

Revolutionary ideas of l'*Histoire des deux Indes.*

Sainte-Beuve, Charles-Augustin. [L'abbé Raynal]. *In his :* Nouveaux Lundis. Lévy, 1864-1870. 11:312-30. 2451

Concerned mainly with R.'s famous letter to Constituent Assembly (of 1791), in which he apparently disavowed many of radical ideals associated with his name in popular mind.

Salone, Emile Auguste. Guillaume Raynal, historien du Canada; étude critique, Guilmoto, 1906. 90 p. 2452

Thesis, dealing with only small section of R.'s broad subject, namely, his discussion of French colonies in Canada, which he judges with excessive severity.

Scherer, Edmond. L'abbé Raynal. *In his :* Études sur la littérature au XVIIIᵉ siècle. Calmann Lévy, 1891. p. 269-91. 2453

One of first attempts (dated 1886) to rescue R. from oblivion into which he had fallen. Interesting brief sketch of R.'s life, with excellent estimate of qualities and defects of l'*Histoire des deux Indes.* Along with Morley's chapter (no. 2448), forms best introduction to R.

Sypher, Wylie. Thomas Anburey on the Indian; his plagiarism from Raynal. FAR 2:272-75, 1937-38. 2454

Shows that Lieut. Anburey's idealization of American Indian in Letter 8 is taken almost verbatim from the Justamond (dated 1785) translation of R.'s *Histoire des Indes,* 7:153-160.

Vermale, F. Un entretien avec l'abbé Raynal. RHL 37:77-80, 1930. 2455

Meeting of R. with Dr. Fleury.

Charles Irénée Castel, *abbé* de Saint-Pierre (Nos. 2456-2469)

OTIS E. FELLOWS

Andréadès, Andréas M. Les idées financières de l'abbé de Saint-Pierre. RSLF 10:621-63, 1912. 2456

Examining S.-P.'s ideas on finance under headings of *Dépenses publiques* (p. 625-34), *Impôts* (p. 634-50), *Emprunts* (p. 650-58), and *Statistique* (p. 658-61), article concludes that some of concepts are new and most of them " justes " (p. 662). Critic correct in claiming to be first to study " l'ensemble de son œuvre financière " (p. 624), but admits inadequacy of present study.

Derocque, Gilberte. Le projet de paix perpétuelle de l'abbé de Saint-Pierre comparé au pacte de la Société des nations. Rousseau, 1929. 203 p. (Diss., Paris). 2457

Comparative study of many of more important peace schemes of modern times with particular emphasis on contribution of S.-P. Useful, though in those parts relative to French thought largely superseded by Souleyman (no. 2469).

Drouet, Joseph. L'abbé de Saint-Pierre; l'homme et l'œuvre. Champion, 1912. 397 p. (Diss., Paris).   2458

Based in part on hitherto unpublished documents, this stylistically undistinguished book is most complete *ouvrage d'ensemble* on S.-P. to date. Though main body of study emphasizes visionary contributions of S.-P., *Préface* and *Conclusion* portray him as " réalisateur " (p. 8, 346) rather than inventor. Weakest parts of book are those dealing with S.-P. as historian and economist. Includes index and useful bibliography of S.-P.'s published and unpublished works although, among other *lacunae,* no mention of Rousseau manuscripts at Neuchâtel. (Cf. Théophile Dufour, no. 1857. See v. 2, p. 112, 120, 158-59, 190, 288).
Reviews : E. Depitre in RHDE 5:395-97, 1913; G. Desdevises du Dezert in RQH 93:325-26, 1913; K. Glaser in ZFSL 41²:48-52, 1913; H. Hauser in Rhist 113:97, 1913; C. G. Picavet in Rcr ns. 74:449-52, Dec. 7, 1912.

Faguet, Emile. L'abbé de Saint-Pierre. RDM 82 yr. 6th per. 10:559-72, Aug. 1, 1912.   2459
Of interest to reader wishing brief, lucid *résumé* of Drouet's dissertation (no. 2458) as well as Faguet's own lively and sympathetic interpretation of S.-P.'s role in history of ideas.

Gorceix, Septime. Du nouveau sur un vieux projet de paix perpétuelle. MerF 251:522-37, May 1, 1934.   2460
Based on reports of official censors designated to examine S.-P.'s efforts to have L'*abrégé du projet de paix perpétuelle* published in France, this article valuable as first, and, to date, only attempt to study position taken by royal government in opposition to the Abbé's peace plan.

Goumy, Edouard. Étude sur la vie et les écrits de l'abbé de Saint-Pierre. Bourdier, 1859. 332 p. (Diss., Paris).   2461
In conjunction with G. Molinari's L'*abbé de Saint-Pierre, membre exclu de*

l'*Académie française*; *sa vie et ses œuvres* (Guillaumin, 1857), largely responsible for initiating 19th century revival of interest in the *Abbé.* Book remains model of urbanity and sprightliness in treatment, as well as essential reference work for S.-P. scholars, though some of its original and independent judgments should be accepted with caution. Widely quoted.

Harsin, Paul. L'abbé de Saint-Pierre économiste d'après de nouveaux documents inédits. RHES 20:186-218, 1932.   2462
Essential article. Indicates hitherto unknown facts about S.-P. as well as MSS overlooked by Drouet (no. 2458) and others, thus convincingly demonstrating that a definitive study on S.-P. as economist has yet to be written.

Mann, Fritz Karl. L'abbé de Saint-Pierre, financier de la Régence d'après des documents inédits. RHDE 3-4:313-20, 1910.   2463
Calls attention to fact that Paultre, Molinari, Ringier (no. 2464), Goumy (no. 2461), Siégler-Pascal (no. 2468), and Beaurepaire have either overlooked or misinterpreted S.-P.'s first tax project, *Mémoire sur l'établissement de la taille proportionelle*; examines differences between this first *mémoire* and second, *Projet de taille tarifée.* Though in certain respects a " réhabilitation " (p. 313) of S.-P., study declares documents on finance prove S.-P. incapable of using any but means or expediencies of his age, and that " ... il n'était, dans toutes ses intentions, qu'un enfant de l'ancien régime " (p. 313).

Ringier, J. Ernst. Der abbé de Saint-Pierre; ein Nationalökonom des XVIII. Jahrhunderts. Karlsruhe, Braun, 1905. 136 p.   2464
Compact book which holds that all aspects of S.-P.'s intellectual activity may fall under " die drei Kategorien der Moral, der Volkswirtschaft und der Politik " (p. 135). S.-P. is studied as enlightened mercantilist who, moreover, should rank as one of great moral economists of all time. Though somewhat outmoded by subsequent studies in French, remains best general work in German, and is particularly helpful as antidote for some of Goumy's (no. 2461) independent judgments.

Sainte-Beuve, Charles Augustin. L'abbé

de Saint-Pierre. *In his:* Causeries du lundi. Garnier, n. d., 15:246-74. 2465

With studies by Molinari and Goumy as double point of departure, critic writes urbane and piquant essay in which he depicts S.-P. as belonging to 17th century and succeeding period of transition rather than to 18th. Despite pervasive tone of condescension, may still be read with profit. Essays dated August 5 and 12, 1861.

Sarolea, Charles. The abbé de St. Pierre. Crev 146:179-85, 1934. 2466

Defending thesis that S.-P. " incarnates the reforming spirit of his age " (p. 181), and calling *Treatise on perpetual peace* work of extreme realist rather than of dreamer or utopian, critic overstates his case. Nevertheless, this provocative essay represents a good digest for English-speaking readers on Abbé and his projects.

Seroux d'Agincourt, Camille. Exposé des projets de paix perpétuelle de l'abbé de Saint-Pierre (et de Henri IV), de Bentham et de Kant. Jouve, 1905. 514 p. 2467

Clear, well-written examination of S.-P.'s, Bentham's and Kant's projects of enduring peace, their strong points and weaknesses, their similarities and differences. Not completely overshadowed by subsequent studies. Bibliography, helpful table of contents, no index.

Siégler-Pascal, S. Un contemporain égaré au XVIIIe siècle; les projets de l'abbé de Saint-Pierre, 1658-1743. Rousseau, 1900. 288 p. 2468

Devoid of index or bibliography, but with helpfully detailed table of contents, this book attempts to give S.-P. " sa véritable figure " (p. 1) by brushing aside all that is " suranné dans son œuvre " (p. 7) and emphasizing " les conceptions utiles et originales et dont l'intérêt est encore actuel " (p. 7). Though largely superseded by Drouet (no. 2458), and limited to S.-P.'s selected works, *Les rêves d'un homme de bien*, Duchesne, 1775, it remains informative analysis and discussion of S.-P.'s more familiar principles. Reviews : H. Hauser in Rhist 73:321-22, 1900; A. Le Glay in Renc [10]:399-400, 1900.

Souleyman, Elizabeth V. [Saint-Pierre]. *In her:* The vision of world peace in seventeenth and eighteenth-century France. New York, Putnam, [c1941]. (Diss., Columbia). 2469

Section entitled, *L'abbé de Saint-Pierre*, as indicated in Index, occupies p. 77-91 of chapter on *Early eighteenth-century projects*, p. 76-99. Well-documented volume skillfully handled, important commentary on French peace plans of some 36 writers whose contributions are grouped both chronologically and according to nature of their views. Clear, concise presentation of S.-P.'s pacifist ideals concludes with the statement, " His carefully elaborated project was realistic and utilitarian..." (p. 99). Easily consulted book with excellent bibliography and index. Reviews : (Unsigned) in NYT, Feb. 23, 1941, p. 3; S. J. Hemleben in Th 17:170-71, 1942; J. R. Pennock in FI 98:784, Dec., 1941.

Anne Robert Jacques Turgot, *baron* de l'Aulne (Nos. 2470-2498)

J. Robert Loy

Turgot, Anne Robert Jacques, *baron* de l'Aulne. Œuvres de Turgot et documents le concernant, avec biographie et notes par Gustave Schelle. Alcan, 1913-23. 5 v. 2470

Most complete collection of T.'s works, along with most detailed and complete running commentary on his life. Supersedes all the biographies, (Say [no. 2493], Mastier, Foncin, Batbie, Tissot) and earlier collections of his works (Daire). Schelle had access to family documents in the Château of Lantheuil. He combines enthusiasm for his subject with close and valid documentation. Review : Anon in PSQ 30:192-93, 1915 (book note).

— The life and writings of Turgot, edited by W. Walker Stephens. London. Longmans, Green. 1895. 331 p. 2471

Important English edition of better-known pieces of T., with introductory sketch that completes and complements (from point of view of T. as figure in political life) the essay by Morley (no. 2489).

Adams, John. A defence of the constitution of the government of the United States of America against the attack of M. Turgot in his letter to Dr. Price. London, Stockdale, 1794. 3 v. 2472

Very interesting document in which Adams situates U. S. government historically in three volumes of analysis of types of government from ancient times. Actual answers to T. as to democracy in

America and bi-cameral government are limited to v. 1, p. 3, 5, 108 and 123.

Alengry, Franck.   Turgot (1727-1781) homme privé — homme d'état.   Charles-Lavauzelle, 1942.   155 p.   2473

Excellent, well-documented general study which presupposes previous knowledge of his life.   In terse style, Alengry makes first attempt at complete psychological study of T., and sees historical events in terms of T.'s individual heart and character.   Most recent on whole man and is greatly enriched by information from the *Journal* of the abbé de Véri, close friend of Maurepas, and by the Lantheuil documents made available by Schelle (no. 2470).

Barrault, H. E.   L'évolutionisme sociologique chez Turgot.   Nrev 4th ser. 91:161-72, Sept-Oct., 1927.   2474

Valid article emphasizing T. sociologist rather than politician and economist, and establishing him, not so much as accidental forerunner of Auguste Comte but as conscious and complete precursor of the ideas of social evolution.   At times this insistence seems exaggerated, since much the same might be said of all of the *philosophes.*

Bérard-Varagnac, Emile.   Turgot, penseur et écrivain.   JE 4th ser. 43:352-56, 1888.   2475

Very short article which catches spirit of T. and gives critical estimate of two of his foremost biographers, Neymarck (no. 2490) and Léon Say (no. 2493).

Bonnefon, Paul.   Turgot et Devaines d'après des lettres inédites.   RHL 8:577-621, 1901.   2476

Interesting revelations on details of friendship between T. and Jean Devaines as well as justifying texts since published in Schelle's *Œuvres de Turgot* (no. 2470). Incidental mention of other contemporary figures.

Carré, Henri.   Turgot et le rappel des Parlements.   AMP 58:442-58, 1902, and Rfr 22:193-208, 1902.   2477

Well-documented, soberly written article, important for unorthodox position taken in regard to T.'s feeling for recall of the parlements dismissed by Maupeou. Carré puts T. in 1774 and his philosophic friends in camp of Maurepas and Miromesnil.

Condorcet, J. A. *marquis* de.   Vie de Monsieur Turgot.   London, 1786.   299 p.   2478

Although superseded in great part by later documents, work important for its 18th century estimate of T. and because it is one of first sources for subsequent studies.   Some interesting mathematical formulations of T.'s economic theories.

Dakin, Douglas.   Turgot and the *ancien régime* in France.   London, Methuen, 1939. 360 p.   2479

Best work in English on subject, admirably filling up *lacuna* which heretofore obtained; well-written, indexed, and copiously annotated.   Dakin considers Schelle (no. 2494) most complete treatment in French, unlikely to be superseded.   Best existing bibliography (particularly for Mss and articles of T. in 18th-century publications) on works, life, articles about, and general historical background at end of book.

Dupont de Nemours, P. S.   Mémoires sur la vie et les ouvrages de M. Turgot.   Philadelphia, n. p., 1782.   268 p.   2480

Important 18th-century estimate of life, personality, and aims of T. by man closest to him in life.   Although obviously prejudiced in some details, book is important as initial work to which all subsequent biographers and students of T. have returned.

Ellwood, Charles.   Turgot, une philosophie sociale méconnue du XVIIIᵉ siècle.   RIS 43:113-22, 1935.   2481

Good, short, recent appraisal as to T.'s place in history of sociology.   Analogies and comparisons are made to other social thinkers, especially Montesquieu and Comte.

Feilbogen, S.   Smith und Turgot; ein Beitrag zur Geschichte und Theorie der Nationalökonomie.   Vienna, Hölder, 1892. 170 p.   (Diss., Vienna).   2482

Only complete study of important points of similarity and divergence between T. and Adam Smith in light of general national economy.   Valuable chapter on Smith as a Physiocrat.

Fengler, Otto.   Die Wirtschaftspolitik Turgots und seiner Zeitgenossen im Lichte der Wirtschaft des Ancien régime.   Leipzig, Deichert, 1912.   141 p.   2483

Well-documented, sober development of a basic problem through its background to the effect of T.'s theory of individual freedom and into aftermath of Necker and Mirabeau. Good general bibliography of problem at beginning of work.

Ferry, François de. Les idées et l'œuvre de Turgot en matière de droit public. Rousseau, 1911. 126 p. (Diss., Paris). 2484

Repetition of former works in so far as life and times are concerned. Some good concluding chapters on T. and on problems of freedom—economic, political, religious, and personal. Bibliography of titles on T. and on historical and economic points which touch him appears at beginning of the thesis.

Hervé, Georges. Turgot ethnographe et linguiste. Rsc 5th ser. 48:67-75, 1910. 2485

Excellent short article on details of sides of T. which are usually mentioned only in passing if at all. Hervé shows that both his ethnological and linguistic intuitions have since been borne out by later specialists.

Lavergne, Léonce. Turgot. In his: Les économistes français du XVIIIe siècle. Guillaumin, 1870. p. 218-78. 2486

Good general essay, situating T. in his times.

Lodge, Eleanor C. Sully, Colbert, and Turgot; a chapter in French economic history. London, Methuen, 1931. 263 p. 2487

Valuable work of comparison in which T. and his last-effort policies which did not avert the Revolution are put into an economic synthesis with earlier administrations and crises in French economic life.

Martin, Paul. Les idées de Turgot sur la décentralisation administrative. Jouve, 1917. 226 p. 2488

Adequate treatment of T.'s part in larger problem of the Revolution and national decentralization. Background well prepared; little or no repetition of T.'s life and thought. Valuable bibliography, particularly for general background books on T.'s predecessors and contemporaries.

Morley, John. Turgot. In his: Critical miscellanies. London, Macmillan, 1886. v. II, p. 40-162. 2489

Excellent short essay, obviously incomplete, on the man and his works. Morley, in highly readable style, fits T. into general society of the *philosophes* with a certain common background, faith, and experience.

Neymarck, Alfred. Turgot et ses doctrines. Guillaumin, 1885. 2 v. 2490

Remains most complete study of T., man, economist, politician, philosopher, and man of letters. Very clearly paragraphed and indexed. Treatment of T.'s economic policies extremely clear, and picture of him in general frame of philosophic century is best available. At end of Vol. II are valuable *pièces justificatives*, letters, and reproductions of state economic ledgers. Some details superseded by later discoveries (cf. Schelle, nos. 2470, 2494).

Oncken, August. Turgot und der Zusammenbruch der Physiokratie. In his: Geschichte der Nationalökonomie. HLS 1 Ab., 2 Band, 1 Teil: 435-81, 1902. 2491

Best historico-critical study in German of works of T. Study valuable for its wealth of careful detail, despite obviously antipathetic tone toward T. and toward his importance in economic history.

Renan, Ernest. Turgot. RPar 8th year 4:1-11, July-Aug., 1901. 2492

Article which is repetitive factually, and important only for faith shown by Renan in his conclusion in men of T.'s stamp.

Say, Léon. Turgot. Hachette, 1887. 208 p. (GEF). Translated into English by Melville B. Anderson. Chicago, McClurg, 1888. 231 p. 2493

Valuable short general work *d'ensemble*, well-written by a perceptive authority. Most of factual knowledge has been superseded by Schelle (no. 2494). Obviously somewhat of a popularization, but is referred to by all subsequent scholars. Reviews : E. Bérard-Varagnac in JE 4th ser. 43:352-56, 1888.

Schelle, Gustave. Turgot. Alcan, 1909. 267 p. 2494

Average, readable life of T. important for opening *état présent* of editions of T.'s works and studies of his life. It was this earlier work which led to Schelle's more complete editing of works and life in 1913 (*see* 2470). Several typographical errors.

Ségur, Pierre Marie Henri, *marquis* **de.** Au couchant de la monarchie, (v. II) Louis XVI et Turgot. *See* 105.   2495

Information on T. mostly repetition of other studies, but situation of Louis and T. historically and treatment of relations between them is valuable and interesting. Book seems sometimes over-simplified. Cf. also : Pierre Lafue, *Louis XVI; l'échec de la révolution royale.* Hachette, 1942. p. 95-104.

Shepherd, Robert P. Turgot and the six edicts. New York, 1903. 214 p.   2496

Most complete handling of background, texts, and effects of famous six edicts just before T.'s resignation. Book particularly useful for complete bibliography (as of 1903) on works and articles about T. and his *milieu.*

Tangorra, V. Le teorie finanziarie di Turgot. GE 2nd ser. 17:309-33, (Oct.) 1898.   2497

Only extensive article in Italian on T. If the exposition of his economic ideas seems superficial and simplified in places, it has the great value of being extremely clear overall.

Weulersse, Léon. Les physiocrates sous le ministère de Turgot. RHES 13:314-37, 1925.   2498

Valuable, well-documented article on *rapports* between the school of thought itself and actual application made by one of its members, T.; traces physiocratic ideas in government from accession of Louis XVI to advent of Necker, concluding that if the party *per se* was destroyed, it was not before several valid principles were instilled into French economic tradition.

Quesnay and the Physiocrats
(Nos. 2499-2514)

EDWARD D. SEEBER

Daire, Eugène. Physiocrates : Quesnay, Dupont de Nemours, Mercier de La Rivière, l'abbé Baudeau, Le Trosne, avec une introduction sur la doctrine des physiocrates, des commentaires et des notices historiques. Guillaumin, 1846. 2 parts, 425 and 601 p.   2499

Earliest extensive presentation of physiocratic doctrine; texts and prefaces on lives and works of authors cited in title. Weak in historical background; displays

physiocracy exclusively as science of wealth. (Cf. criticism by H. Passy, *De l'école des physiocrates,* in JE 17:229-43, 1847).

Collection des économistes et des réformateurs sociaux de la France. Paul Geuthner (and others), 1910-38. 15 v. 2500

Texts of Dupont de Nemours, Mercier de La Rivière, Baudeau, Morelly, etc., presented by various editors (Dubois, Depitre, Dolléans, etc.), with useful prefaces containing bibliographical and other material.

Beer, Max. An inquiry into Physiocracy. London, Allen and Unwin [1939]. 196 p.   2501

Penetrating study of doctrinal sources and rise of physiocracy. Two chapters on Q.

G. S. The physiocrats. *In :* Palgrave's dictionary of political economy, ed. by Henry Higgs. London, New York, Macmillan, 1925-26. v. 3. p. 103-08.   2502

Article useful chiefly for its bibliography.

Higgs, Henry. The physiocrats; six lectures on the French *économistes* of the 18th century. London New York, Macmillan, 1897. 158 p.   2503

Succinct account of rise of the school, its doctrines, activities, opponents, and influence. Offers nothing new beyond earlier French works.

Reviews : W. J. Ashley in AHR 2:725-26, 1896-97; C. Gide in EJ 7:245-48, 1897; S. J. M. in JPE 5:540-41, 1896-97.

Ware, Norman J. The physiocrats; a study in economic rationalization. AER 21:607-19, 1931.   2504

Emphasizes class point of view, emerging from French bureaucracy, of physiocrats, and interprets in this light their doctrines of free trade, single tax, and sole productivity of agriculture. *See* Neill, no. 2513.

Weulersse, Georges. Le mouvement physiocratique en France (de 1756 à 1770). Alcan, 1910. 2 v. (Diss., Paris). *See* no. 1080.   2505

Long the authoritative work on physiocracy despite limitations imposed by period covered. Rather overstresses notion that physiocratic thought is essentially capitalistic. Good indexes and bibliography.

Reviews : C. Gide in REP 26:244-45, 1912; H. Higgs in EJ 21:436-38, 1911; J. Hollander in AHR 17:657-58, 1911-12; A. S. Johnson in JPE 19:891-93, 1911.

Jefferson, Thomas. The correspondence of Jefferson and Du Pont de Nemours, with an introduction on Jefferson and the physiocrats, by Gilbert Chinard. Baltimore, Johns Hopkins press; Paris, Les belles lettres, 1931. 293 p. 2506

114 page introduction gives an account of striking parallelism, as well as divergencies, between Jeffersonian and physiocratic doctrines. Jefferson's conclusions " ... were probably derived, by the use of ordinary common sense and judgment, from a body of very simple principles generally recognized at the time by all liberal thinkers in all the countries of Europe " (p. xii). Analytical index. Reviews : L. Gottschalk in JPE 39:831-33, 1931; T. J. Wertenbaker in AHR 37:357-59, 1931-32.

Schelle, Gustave. Du Pont de Nemours et l'école physiocratique. Guillaumin, 1888. 456 p. 2507

One of best of older works on contributions of numerous physiocrats to economic thought and reforms. Good treatment of history and importance of several contemporary journals. Helpful analytical index.

Rossi, Joseph. The abbé Galiani in France. New York, Publications of the Institute of French studies, 1930. 63 p. 2508

Succinct account of Galiani's sojourn in France (1759-69), his relations with important writers, and disagreements with the physiocrats on questions of prices, wealth, free-trade, etc. Summary bibliography; index lacking.

Brocard, Lucien. Les doctrines économiques et sociales du marquis de Mirabeau dans *L'ami des hommes*. Giard et Brière, 1902. 394 p. 2509

Intensive study of Mirabeau's ideas and reform activities prior to his alliance with the physiocrats. Weak in its account of later parts of *L'ami des hommes*, which show growing knowledge of economic theory. Bibliography and index lacking. Reviews : C. Gide in REP 16:962-63, 1902; H. Higgs in EJ 12:242-44, 1902.

Ripert, Henri. Le marquis de Mirabeau (L'ami des hommes), ses théories politiques et économiques. Rousseau, 1901. 460 p. (Diss., Paris). 2510

Maintains that Mirabeau, in his early period, showed great potential power as social reformer, but that, once under spell of physiocratic ideals and formulas, he lost his verve, originality, and usefulness.

Mazure, Auguste. Les idées de l'abbé Morellet, membre de l'Académie française, 1727-1819. Société du Recueil Sirey, 1910. 199 p. (Diss., Lille). 2511

Substantial study of the philosopher's life, and opinions on liberty, government, patriotism, and economics. Bibliography; index lacking.

Quesnay, François. Œuvres économiques et philosophiques de F. Quesnay, fondateur du système physiocratique; accompagnées des éloges et d'autres travaux biographiques sur Quesnay par différents auteurs; publiées avec une introduction et des notes par Auguste Oncken. Francfort s/M, Baer, 1888. 814 p. 2512

Good study on Q. but inadequate in treatment of origins and ultimate development of physiocratic doctrine.

Neill, Thomas P. Quesnay and physiocracy. JHI 9:153-73, 1948. 2513

Reiterates charge of Ware (no. 2504), that physiocratic theories have commonly been misinterpreted; sees a tendency " to identify physiocracy with one or the other of the prevailing systems " (of Descartes, Locke, Newton, etc.), and a failure to relate it to medieval economic thought. Invites a more systematic study of the scope of physiocratic principles and of the role of Q.'s disciples.

Schelle, Gustave. Le docteur Quesnay, chirurgien, médecin de madame de Pompadour et de Louis XV, physiocrate. Alcan, 1907. 402 p. 2514

Comprehensive biography, with account of Q.'s published and unpublished works on economic theory. Important complement to Schelle's earlier studies. Bibliography and index lacking. Review : A. Deschamps in REP 21:398-400, 1907.

The Literature of Travel
(Nos. 2515-2575)

JEAN DAVID

Cox, Edward Godfrey. A reference guide to the literature of travel. Seattle, Univ. of Washington, 1935-38, 2 v. (Univ. of

Washington publications in language and literature, v. 9 and 10.)   2515

Lists travel publications until 1800 printed in Great Britain; especially useful for translations into English of writings of French travelers, in which it is rather complete. Many receive ample notices.
Review : G. B. Parks in MLN 52:310, 1937.

Atkinson, Geoffroy. Les relations de voyages du xviie siècle et l'évolution des idées; contribution à l'étude de la formation de l'esprit du xviiie siècle. *See* 1020.   2516

Important introduction. Shows concisely how social ideas of 18th century had already appeared in real travels of 17th century (cf. especially p. 185).
Reviews : G. Ascoli in RHL 32:478-81, 1925; A. Le Duc in RR 16:189-91, 1925.

— The extraordinary voyage in French literature from 1700 to 1720. *See* 1019.   2517

Good study of sources utilized by writers of extraordinary voyages. Shows F. Leguat was not a real traveler, but one imagined by Misson.
Review : G. Chinard in MLN 37:496-98, 1922.

Bamboat, Zénobie. Les voyageurs français dans l'Inde aux xviie et xviiie siècles. Société de l'histoire des colonies françaises, 1933. 197 p. (Diss., Paris).   2518

Judgment of A. Martineau in preface seems a just one : " ... ouvrage sobre, clair, précis et exact." Believes that Western powers were harmful to India. Reserved in judgments even when travelers like Sonnerat were hostile to the country.

Bougainville, Louis Antoine de. Voyage autour du monde, par la frégate La Boudeuse et la flûte L'Étoile en 1766-1769. Saillant & Nyon, 1771. 417 p.   2519

English translation made in 1772. First French expedition around world. Among its objectives was collection of all kinds of curiosities of natural history. Cox (no. 2515), I, p. 55.

Bourgoing, Jean-François de. Nouveau voyage en Espagne ou tableau de l'état actuel de cette monarchie ... depuis 1782 jusqu'à présent. Regnault, 1789, 3 v., carte.   2520

Twice in Spain from 1777 to 1785 and from 1792 to 1793, Cox (no. 2515), I, 158.

First time as secretary of embassy; second as *chargé d'affaires;* one of best works on above country.

Boucher de La Richarderie, Gilles. Notice complète et raisonnée de tous les voyages anciens et modernes... Treuttel and Wurtz, 1806. 6 v.   2520A

Valuable, almost indispensable work, Cox (no. 2515), II, 534.

Chappe d'Auteroche, abbé Jean. Voyage en Californie pour l'observation du passage de Vénus sur le disque du soleil le 3 juin 1769..., Jombert, 1772. 172 p.   2521

Contains best account of Mexico City before Humboldt; Pinkerton quoted by Cox, (no. 2515), II, 240.

Brissot de Warville, Jacques-Pierre. Nouveau voyage dans les États-Unis. Buisson, 1791. 3 v.   2522

Author founded in 1788 in France *Société des amis des noirs.* Made above trip to United States to investigate slavery system. Gives long account of B. Franklin and personal details on Washington, Cox (no. 2515), II, 165.

Chantreau, P. N. Voyage philosophique, politique et littéraire fait en Russie dans les années 1788 et 1789. Briand, 1794. 2 v.   2523

" Replete with curious and original information," (Cox no. 2515, I, 198); on other hand, according to BioM. v. 8, p. 46 : supposedly translated from Dutch, not real travel, numerous errors. However, translated into German and English. Same author. *Voyage dans les trois royaumes d'Angleterre, d'Écosse et d'Irlande.* Briand, 1792. 3 v.
Extended account of London.

Charlevoix, Pierre François Xavier de, S. J. Histoire du Paraguay. Desaint, 1757. 6 v.   2524

Most complete and satisfactory work on Paraguay and only one in which vast system of Jesuits is fully developed, position of author affording him peculiar opportunities for its examination, quoted by Cox (no. 2515), II, 282.

Chappe d'Auteroche, abbé Jean. Voyage en Sibérie fait par ordre du roi en 1761. Debure, 1768. 4 v.   2525

Some criticisms of Russia drew sharp retort from Empress Catherine II. Splendid and accurate engravings. Excellent descriptions of manners and character. Description of Kamtchatka in last volume, Cox (no. 2515), I, 351-52.

Chastellux, François Jean, marquis de. Voyages de M. le marquis de Chastellux dans l'Amérique septentrionale, dans les années 1780, 1781 & 1782. Prault, 1786. 2 v. 2526

Author traveled through Virginia, Pennsylvania, Connecticut, Massachusetts, and New Hampshire, kept a diary of his expeditions. Some important observations, mingled with trifling incidents. (Cox, no. 2515, II, p. 159).

Chinard, Gilbert. L'Amérique et le rêve exotique dans la littérature française au XVIIe et au XVIIIe siècle. See 789. 2527

Retraces appeal of vast open spaces and of men newly discovered in them to all classes of travellers, through all literary forms. Book shows vast erudition and has strong literary appeal.

— Influence des récits de voyages sur la philosophie de J.-J. Rousseau. See 2048. 2528

Concludes Rousseau was not a revolutionary, but that he popularized further the concept of " good savage."

Courte de La Blanchardière, René. Nouveau voyage fait au Pérou. Delaguette, 1751. 216 p. 2529

Observations and descriptions sensible, pertinent, and entertaining, Cox, (no. 2515), II, 274.

David, Jean. La danse et la musique chez les Indiens d'Amérique au XVIIIe siècle d'après les voyageurs français en Amérique. CF 30:340-54, 1943. 2530

Taste for Indian dancing and music first found in French literature before Romantics, in the travellers. Bibliography.

Delanglez, Jean, S. J. The French Jesuits in lower Louisiana (1700-1763). Washington, D. C. The Catholic university of America, 1935. 547 p. 2531

Completes previous study of Rochemonteix. French, U. S., Canadian, Italian archives consulted. Thorough work. Bibliography.

Diderot, Denis. Supplément au voyage de Bougainville ... avec une introduction et des notes par Gilbert Chinard. See 2235. 2532

Editor shows how attraction of new lands shifted, in course of 17th century, from America to Austral lands, and how Diderot used Bougainville to make most hedonistic plea of 18th century.

Du Halde, Jean-Baptiste. Description géographique, historique, chronologique, politique et physique de l'Empire de la Chine et de la Tartarie chinoise. Lemercier, 1735. 4 v. 2533

First volume and a half deals with China; Du Halde collected letters of Jesuits residing in China, added from other printed works. Some have considered author uncritical in choice of material; others have regarded work as best history to date, Cox (no. 2515), I, 335.

Fleuriot, Jean-Marie-Jérôme, marquis de Langle. Voyage en Espagne, 5th ed. Lucet, 1796. 263 p. 2534

Very sarcastic in its criticisms of Spanish ways. English translation entitled : " A sentimental journey through Spain, translated from the Paris edition, that was burnt by the common hangman," Cox (no. 2515), I, 155.

Frézier, Amédée François, Relation du voyage de la mer du Sud aux côtes du Chily et du Pérou. Nyon, 1716. 300 p. 2535

" Engineer in Ordinary " to the French King, sailed from Saint Malo November 23, 1711. Most navigators with him, and himself from St. Malo, hence islands named " Malouines." One of most valuable of early records on Falkland Islands. Useful in its day and later times to navigators doubling Cape Horn, Cox (no. 2515), II, 267.

Garnier, Charles G. T. Voyages imaginaires, songes, visions et romans cabalistiques. See 697. 2536

See Gove (no. 2538) for contents and discussion. Essential book for study of imaginary travel.

Gaubil, Antoine, S. J. Observations mathématiques, astronomiques, ... tirées des anciens livres chinois ou faites nouvellement aux Indes et à la Chine par les Pères de la Compagnie de Jésus. Rollin, 1729-1732. 3 v. 2537

Versed in Chinese and Manchu languages. Translator from and into those languages and Latin. BioM. v. 16, p. 558b, probably alludes to above work : " Son premier travail fut un traité historique de l'astronomie chinoise," where it is shown that opinion based on astronomical observations that world is very old is relatively new in China.

Gove, Philip Babcock. The imaginary voyage in prose fiction. *See* 699.   2538

More repertory than book. Numerous entries. Thorough. Occasional bibliographical discussions. Touches upon Prévost's *Cléveland* and Voltaire's *Candide*.
Review : E. Bernbaum in MLN 59:139, 1944.

Guys, Pierre Augustin. Voyage littéraire de la Grèce, etc. Duchesne, 1771. 2 v.
2539

Possessed admirable knowledge of Greek antiquity, familiarity with modern Greek and Turkish languages, included specimens of song from both those peoples. " He may be said to have been the first folklorist who directed his attention towards the Orient," Cox (no. 2515), I, 231, quoting Iorga (no. 2541).

Hennepin, Louis. Voyage ou nouvelle découverte d'un très grand pays de l'Amérique entre le Nouveau Mexique et la mer glaciale... Amsterdam, Braakman, 1704. 604 p.   2540

Gren. v. 19, 1069a : A Belgian missionary (1640-1705) companion of La Salle and his historian. Cox (no. 2515), II, 84 : Explored upper reaches of Mississippi and may have touched site of future city of Minneapolis. Truth of some of his claims has been contested.

Iorga, Nicolas. Les voyageurs français dans l'Orient européen; voyageurs au xviiie siècle. RCC 28²:354-65; 663-72; 1927.
2541

Short items. Mostly presentation of facts. A few conclusions which cause one to regret discussion not more elaborate.

Kerguelen-Trémarec, Yves-Joseph. Relation de deux voyages dans les mers australes et des Indes faits en 1771, 1772, 1773 et 1774. Knapen, 1782. 247 p.   2542

Decree of French government Dec. 21st, 1924, placed islands Kerguélen, Crozet, St. Paul, Amsterdam, Adélie Land under Madagascar government.

Labat, J. B. Nouveau voyage aux isles de l'Amérique contenant l'histoire naturelle de ces pays ... le commerce et les manufactures

qui y sont établies et les moyens de les augmenter. Cavelier, 1722. 6 v.   2543

His most famous work. Details of all islands visited, notably of Martinique and Guadeloupe. For some islands only source of information for that time, Cox (no. 2515), II, 235.

— Voyage du chevalier des Marchais en Guinée, isles voisines et à Cayenne. Osmont, 1730. 4 v.   2544

Labat (1663-1738) missionary in West Indies in 1693; Gren. v. 21, 682 a. Des Marchais in slave trade; gave his papers to Labat, BioM. v. 23, 11b. Labat made several voyages to Africa and America. Able draughtsman, good geometrician, excellent navigator, spoke most languages encountered on West Coast of Africa. Exact account, Cox (no. 2515), I, 381.

La Billardière, Jacques Julien Houtou de. Relation du voyage à la recherche de La Pérouse fait par ordre de l'Assemblée constituante pendant les années 1791, 1792... Jansen, an VIII [1799]. 2 v.   2545

In command of the two vessels of expedition. A naturalist. Trip unsuccessful in its search, but of considerable importance. First scientific description of New Zealand flax; brought back New Zealand plants. Describes visit expedition made to Tasmania, New Caledonia, Solomons, etc. Cox (no. 2515), I, 68.

La Condamine, Charles Marie de. Relation abrégée d'un voyage fait dans l'intérieur de l'Amérique méridionale. Depuis la côte de la mer du Sud jusqu'à celle du Brésil et de la Guyane en descendant la rivière des Amazones. Pissot, 1745. 216 p.
2546

Paris Academy of Sciences conducted two researches in geodetic measurement to determine configuration of the earth by measuring a degree of longitude, one in Lapland, carried on by Maupertuis and others in 1736, the other executed by La Condamine at the equator on high Andean plateau, Cox (no. 2515), II, 272.

Lafitau, Joseph François, S. J. Mœurs des sauvages américains comparées aux mœurs des premiers temps. Saugrain, 1724. 2 v.   2547

First traveler to establish parallel indicated in title, BioM. 22:488 gives very exact and elaborate details on Indian customs, manners, religion; lived long time among Iroquois.

Lahontan, L. A., *baron* **de.** Dialogues curieux etc. and Mémoires de l'Amérique septentrionale. Gilbert Chinard ed. Baltimore, Johns Hopkins press, and Paris, Margraff, 1931. 268 p. 2548

Shows Lahontan as one of first travelers to criticize passionately European civilization.

— Nouveaux voyages de M. le baron de Lahontan dans l'Amérique septentrionale. The Hague, L'Honoré, 1703. 2 v. 2549

Lahontan went to Canada at 16, commanded various forts there. Journeyed to western extremity of Great Lakes, Mississippi, Minnesota. Truth of some parts called questionable, Cox (no. 2515), II, 88.

La Pérouse, Jean François de Galaup, *comte* **de.** Voyage autour du monde. Imprimerie de la République, an V. (1797). 4 v. 2550

Relations of peculiarities of Northwest Coast natives of America especially valuable. Visited among others Sandwich, Tonga, Norfolk islands, and Botany Bay, whence account sent, Cox (no. 2515), I, 67.

La Rochefoucauld-Liancourt, François Alexandre Frédéric, *duc* **de.** Voyage dans les États-Unis d'Amérique fait en 1795, 1796 et 1797. Du Pont, an VII [1799]. 8 v. 2551

Interested in social welfare, particularly agricultural economy, gave Arthur Young facilities to study farming methods on his estates in France. Exiled. Description of Senecas and other Indians in vicinity of Buffalo. Fair picture of America at time as to agriculture, national and domestic habits, Cox (no. 2515), II, 175.

La Roque, Jean de. Voyage de l'Arabie heureuse par l'Océan oriental et le détroit de la mer Rouge, 1708-1710. Huguier and Cailleau, 1715. 403 p. 2552

London translation, 1742, contains added matter; particularly full respecting history of coffee in Asia and Europe, Cox (no. 2515), I, 222. Cf. also BioM. v. 38, 572.

— Voyage de Syrie et du Mont Liban. Cailleau, 1722. 2 v. 2552A

Le Gentil de la Galaisière, G. J. H. J. B. Voyage dans les mers de l'Inde fait par ordre du Roi à l'occasion du passage de Vénus sur le disque du soleil le 6 juin 1761, etc. Imprimerie royale, 1779-1781. 2 v. 2553

Pondichéry captured by English when he arrived; actually observed Venus there in 1769. Between two dates travelled in Madagascar, Coromandel coast, Philippines. Above work contains : observations on tides, monsoon, etc. Study of lanes to India, of Indian manners. Added much to knowledge of country, BioM. 23, 563-65.

Levaillant, François. Voyage ... dans l'intérieur de l'Afrique par le Cap de Bonne-Espérance, dans les années 1780-1785... Leroy, 1790. 2 v. 2554

Interesting as account of South Africa at a time when little was known regarding its natural history and Dutch settlers. Less valuable for geographical information than for natural history of those regions, Cox (no. 2515), I, 389.

Lesseps, J. B. B. de. Journal historique du voyage de M. de Lesseps ... employé dans l'expédition de M. le comte de La Pérouse ... au port de Saint-Pierre et Saint Paul du Kamtschatka. Imprimerie royale, 1790. 2 v. 2555

Sent by Louis XVI to explore more accurately Northeastern coast of Siberia. Left at Petropavlovsk to carry despatches overland across Siberia to France. Narrative gives lively picture of inhabitants of northern parts of Asiatic and European Russia. Cox (no. 2515), I, 353.

Le Page du Pratz, [Antoine Simon]. Histoire de la Louisiane. De Bure, 1758. 3 v. 2556

Le Page du Pratz travelled in Western Missouri and in Arkansas. Was an employee of French *Compagnie occidentale* at New Orleans. Arrived at Louisiana in 1718 and lived there ten years as official physician. Gives minute description of various Indian tribes, especially Natchez.

Lichtenberger, André. Le socialisme au XVIIIe siècle. *See* 147, 1052. 2557

Important discussion of influence of utopias and real travels on formation of socialism. Says " communists " of time looked to Jesuit state of Paraguay, advocates of benevolent despotism to Peru.

Lucas, Paul. Voyage du sieur Paul Lucas fait par ordre du Roy dans la Grèce, l'Asie mineure, la Macédoine et l'Afrique. Simart, 1712. 2 v.   2558

This French traveler later became member of African association to further British trade.

— Troisième voyage ... fait en 1714 ... dans la Turquie, l'Asie, la Syrie, la Palestine, la Haute et la Basse-Égypte... Rouen, Machuel, 1719. 3 v.   2558A

At early age went to Turkey for jewelry trade. Cf. trans. in BioM. 25: 345B. His travels often reprinted. Exaggerated ; but is learned on countries visited and for long time only source of information on certain parts of Greece and Asia Minor.

Mahé de La Bourdonnais, Bertrand-François. Mémoires historiques de Mahé de La Bourdonnais gouverneur des îles de France et de Bourbon, recueillis et publiés par son petit-fils. Pélicier and Chalet, 1827. 367 p.   2559

Born St. Malo 1699. Worked also in India for *La compagnie des Indes*, BioM. v. 26, p. 157-64.

Martineau, Alfred. Histoire des colonies françaises et de l'expansion de la France dans le monde. At head of title : Gabriel Hanoteaux. Alfred Martineau. Plon, 1929. 7 v.   2560

Essential work.

Martino, Pierre. L'Orient dans la littérature française au xviie et au xviiie siècle. *See* 1055A.   2561

Leaves out question of contacts of travellers with Orient in Eastern European countries. Lanson says : " ... a mieux montré le progrès de la connaissance de l'Orient que l'usage qui a été fait de cette connaissance."
Review : G. Lanson in RHL 13:545-47, 1906.

Michaux, François André. Voyage à l'ouest des monts Alleghany, dans les états de l'Ohio etc. ..., 1804, Levrault, Schoell. 312 p.   2562
Travels to the West... etc., in the year 1802. London, Crosby, 1805. *Also in* R. G. Thwaites : *Early western travels,* 1748-1846, Cleveland, 1904, v. 3.
Rarely was an outlander's description received as graciously as was that of André Michaux the younger.

[**Pauw, Cornelius de.**] Recherches philosophiques sur les Américains ou, Mémoires

intéressants pour servir à l'histoire de l'espèce humaine. Berlin, Decker, 1770, 2 v.   2563

Not relation of travel. Very eloquent representative of those who thought colonizing America not worth while : costly enterprise, unhealthy climate. BioM, v. 33, 228a : work eagerly read throughout Europe.

Pernety, Antoine Joseph. Histoire d'un voyage aux isles Malouines, fait en 1763 et 1764, avec des observations sur le détroit de Magellan et sur les Patagons. Saillant and Nyon, 1770. 2 v.   2564

Expedition under command of Bougainville for purpose of colonizing Falklands for France.

Poivre, Pierre. Œuvres complètes. Fuchs, 1797. 310 p. Comprises : Observations sur les mœurs et les arts des peuples de l'Afrique, de l'Asie et de l'Amérique, 1772; Discours ... à son arrivée à l'Isle de France; Extrait du voyage fait en 1769 et 1770 aux Isles Philippines et Moluques, etc.   2565

Cox (no. 2515), I, 82, on *Observations :* " curious and interesting little book." Poivre a missionary versed in handicrafts and botany. At 20 left for China and Cochinchina where he learned languages thereof. Back in France 1745, presented project for commerce with latter country to French East India Co. Sent back to carry it out, BioM., v. 35, 161-62.

Pons, E. Le " voyage," genre littéraire au xviiie siècle : indications bibliographiques et critiques. BLS Jan., p. 97-101; Feb., p. 144-49; Mar., 201-07, 1926.   2566

Leaves out real travels to countries outside of Europe. Brief and penetrating studies and notices. Detailed on Gulliver and Robinson.

Prémare, Joseph Henri de, S. J. Lettres inédites ... sur le monothéisme des Chinois, publiées avec la plupart des textes originaux... Duprat, 1861. 55 p.   2567

One of most learned missionaries of 18th century in Chinese language and history. Prominent in school which saw occidental influences in sacred books of China and gave rise to controversy between Jesuits and Dominicans, BioM. v. 36, p. 39-44.

Prévost, Antoine, François, *called* **Prévost d'Exiles.** Histoire générale des voyages. Didot, 1746-1789. 80 v.   2568

Widely used by Encyclopedists although seldom quoted.

Rochon, Alexis Marie de. Voyage à Madagascar et aux Indes orientales. 1791. 322 p. 2569

Member of several academies of Europe, Cox (no. 2515), I, 392. Astronomer and navigator, member of Academy of Sciences; cf. BioM. for translations. Too favorable an idea of natives, BioM. v. 38; invented a micrometer using crystal he had brought from trip to Madagascar, p. 339 b.

Saint-Pierre, Jacques-Henri-Bernardin de. Voyage à l'isle de France, à l'isle de Bourbon, au cap de Bonne-Espérance, etc., Merlin, 1773. 2 v. 2570

Interesting information on manners and customs of both natives, whites, natural history of places visited. More important for affirmation of "noble savage," Cox (no. 2515), I, 385.

Sonnerat, Pierre de. Voyage à la Nouvelle Guinée. Ruault, 1776. 206 p. 2571

Book translated into German in 1777. Sonnerat did not actually go to New Guinea, but to Poulo-Gheby, a small island 126 degrees east of Paris, a few minutes north of Equator. Curious details on Manila and Philippines, BioM. v. 43, 88b.

— Voyages aux Indes orientales et à la Chine, faits par ordre de Louis XVI, depuis 1774 jusqu'en 1781. Dentu, 1806. 4 v. 2572

Book translated into German in 1783. Author born in Lyon in 1745; went into naval administration. First volumes give thorough survey of India, last ones of China, of which country they present unfavorable picture. Sonnerat transplanted plants from China to islands of France and Bourbon; e. g., cocoa. BioM. v. 39, p. 611.

Volney, C. F. C., *comte* **de.** Tableau du climat et du sol des États-Unis d'Amérique... Courcier, Dentu. 1803. 2 v. 2573

View of soil and climate of United States of America ... translated with occasional remarks by C. B. Brown. Philadelphia & Baltimore, Conrad. 1804. 446 p.

Most significant regional work of period.

— Voyage en Syrie et en Égypte... 1783-1785. 2 ed. Desenne, 1787. 2 v. 2574

One of most exact and valuable works of kind ever published, Cox (no. 2515), I, 235. Volney a member of the States General and later of Constituent Assembly.

Von der Mühll, Emanuel. Denis Veiras et son histoire des Sévarambes, 1677-1679. Droz, 1938. 292 p. (Diss., Johns Hopkins). 2575

Veiras belongs to 18th century because he believes that all classes should participate in government and defense of the country; to 17th century in that he favors paternalism, and bases his laws not on a doctrine of equality but on reason and logical deduction; thinks that only when masses are rich and happy can a nation be powerful and stable. Many-sided and well-documented study.

Pierre Louis Moreau de Maupertuis
(Nos. 2576-2596)

JEAN DUFRENOY

Friedrich II, *der Grosse.* Nachträge zu dem Briefwechsel Friedrichs des Grossen mit Maupertuis und Voltaire. Ed. by Hans Droysen, Fernand Caussy and Gustav Berthold Volz. *See* 1637, p. 1-78. 2576

Contains several letters of interest, most important of which is, perhaps, one describing and characterizing La Condamine (no. 2546), (p. 13-30) and explaining why M. went to Lapland rather than to Peru.

Abelé, Jean. Introduction à la notion d'action et au principe de l'action stationnaire. RQS 119:25-42, Jan. 20, 1948. 2577

Shows that principle of least action was first enunciated by M. in 1744 as result of a metaphysical law, according to which nature acts through simplest ways; like Descartes in relation to principle of invariance, M. and his contemporaries saw in principle of least action an evidence of wisdom of the Creator.

Arcy, Chevalier [Patrice] d'. Réplique à un mémoire de M. de Maupertuis sur le principe de moindre action inséré dans les Mémoires de l'Académie royale de Berlin de l'année 1752. MAS 1752. p. 503-19. 2578

Irrelevant criticism of M.'s principle of least action.

Brunet, Pierre. Maupertuis. Blanchard, 1929. 2 v. 2579

Important study. Vol. I (*Étude biographique*, 199 p.) retraces life of M. Vol. 2, (*L'œuvre et sa place dans la pensée scientifique et philosophique du 18ᵉ siècle*, 487 p.) appraises his contributions to mathematics, astronomy, cosmography, mechanics, physics, biology and, last but not least, philosophy, and notably relation of his concepts to those of Berkeley, Leibniz, and Montesquieu.

— La notion d'évolution dans la science moderne avant Lamarck. Archeion 19:21-43, 1937. 2580

Most theories published by M. in his *Essai sur la formation des corps organisés* had already been advanced in 1751 under pseudonym of Bauman in *Dissertatio inauguralis metaphysica de universali naturae systemate*, (Erlangen), in which M. presented, in new guise, the material he had already published in *Vénus physique* (of 1745). Since it is most improbable that M. had at that time any knowledge of Maillet's writings, M. may be credited with having introduced the scientific notion of evolution into biological sciences.

— Étude historique sur le principe de moindre action. Hermann, 1938. 113 p. (PAHS). 2581

In M.'s mind, principle of least action embodied necessary notion of " minimum," making possible in single general mathematical formula the expression of providential design of Universe (p. 20). If practically nothing remains today of that notion, still M. must be credited with having originated research on subject. (p. 22).

Bürckhardt, Fr. Maupertuis. BJ 1910 : 29-53. 2582

Address delivered in Basel on Nov. 15, 1908, in connection with celebration in honor of Bernoulli brothers. Account of M.'s life mainly taken from Du Bois-Reymond (no. 2584). Emphasis placed on relationship between M. and Jean Bernoulli, to whom M. made a bequest in his holograph testament, French text of which is reproduced on p. 49. Article ends with reproduction of Latin epitaph on M.'s tomb.

Damiron, [Jean Philibert]. Maupertuis. *In his :* Mémoires pour servir à l'histoire de la philosophie au xviiiᵉ siècle. Ladrange, 1858-64. v. 3. p. 1-149. *See* 1234. 2583

Study based on an examination of the letter of Frederick available in Feuillet de Conches collection, and shows M.'s activity as President of Berlin Academy and as, virtually, Frederick's state secretary to Department of Letters and Sciences.

Du Bois-Reymond, Emil. Maupertuis; Rede zur Feier des Geburtstages Friedrichs II und des Geburtstages seiner Majestät des Kaisers in der Akademie der Wissenschaften zur Berlin am 28 Januar 1892. Leipzig, Von Veit, 1893. 92 p. 2584

Shows that shape of the earth, as explained by M. and La Condamine, was still matter of dispute at time of publication of Bernardin de Saint-Pierre's *Paul et Virginie*, (dated 1787). Law of Least Action, in which M. generalized Law of Rest which he had formulated in 1740, met with violent opposition. Maintains that this Law of Least Action represents foundations on which, through mathematical developments of Lagrange, Hamilton, and Helmholtz, principles of dynamics and notably of electrodynamics are based.

Dufrenoy, J[ean] and M. L. Un bicentenaire oublié : La Vénus physique, 1746, ou Maupertuis, précurseur de la pathologie comparée. RPC 48:107-15, March-April, 1948. 2585

Study shows that M. believed that all varieties of living beings are potentially present in Nature, and may come into being either by chance, or by human art. He therefore postulated possibility of selection and breeding of better strains, and even believed in eugenics. Enunciated statistical laws of heredity, following his studies on hereditary transmission of polydactylism in human families; after Bodin and Boyle, he was much interested in hereditary transmission of skin color among men, also in that of gigantism, and advocated research in institutes of comparative pathology. Bibliography of 27 titles.

Fee, Jerome. Maupertuis, and the principle of least action. SM 52:496-503, 1941. 2586

Author thinks it rare to find a modern author who recognizes importance of M.'s analysis; one of few who have done so is Richtmeyer, who writes in his Introduction to modern physics : " Nearly two centuries ago, by a line of reasoning which would have done credit to the Greeks, Maupertuis proposed the law of least action." (p. 503).

Glass, Bentley. Maupertuis and the beginnings of genetics. QRB 22:196-210, Sept., 1947.   2587

Scholarly discussion of M.'s theory of heredity and evolution shows him seeking for a real truth, that was to be captured by Charles Darwin who, it would seem, had " never heard of him." (p. 208). Later scientists or philosophers did not appear either to be fully aware of the fact that M. " ... not only deserves to be ranked as greater than his contemporaries in biology, but stands out as one of the greatest figures in the history of science ..." (p. 209).

[Grandjean de Fouchy, Jean Paul]. Éloge de M. de Maupertuis. MAS 1759, p. 259-76.   2588

Grandjean de Fouchy was *Secrétaire perpétuel de l'Académie des sciences de Paris;* this *Eloge* was read in the *assemblée publique de cette Académie le 16 Avril, 1760.* Printed version was corrected by La Condamine. This is a sober, factual biography of M. with estimate of his work and character in same vein.

Gueroult, Martial. Note sur le principe de la moindre action chez Maupertuis. *In his :* Dynamique et métaphysique leibniziennes. Les belles lettres, 1934. PFS v. 68, p. 215-35.   2589

Believes that, to establish his principle of least action, M. had first to do away with physical and metaphysical theories of Leibniz, through convergent use of Huyghens's objections to Leibniz's system, of Newton's physical theories and of Malebranche's contribution to science and metaphysics; it is therefore inconceivable that M. could have derived his notion of the principle of least action from Leibniz. (p. 235).

Hervé, Georges. Maupertuis génétiste. Ranth 22:217-30, 1912.   2590

M. should be credited, not only with having formulated, before Buffon and Diderot, concept of transformation, but also with having clearly expressed notion of transformation by mutations.

La Beaumelle, L. Angliviel de. Vie de Maupertuis, ouvrage posthume, suivi de lettres inédites de Frédéric le Grand et de Maupertuis, avec des notes et un appendice. Ledoyen, 1856. 494 p.   2591-2592

First 216 pages retrace chronologically events of M.'s life, from his birthday, (Sept. 28, 1698) to his death, (July 27, 1759), as recorded by La Beaumelle in the manuscript he had prepared but had been unable to publish before his death in 1773. Completed, with critical notes, by Maurice Angliviel. P. 225-453 print letters between M. and King of Prussia.

Landrieu, Marcel. Lamarck et ses précurseurs. Ranth 16:152-69, 1906.   2593

Vénus physique was violently discussed as soon as it was published, notably in *Antivénus physique ou Critique de la dissertation sur l'origine de l'homme,* (Paris, 1746, 2 v.), attributed to Basset des Rosiers. Nevertheless, *Vénus physique* was re-edited six times in four years. *Le système de la nature,* first published in Latin, and used by Diderot as basis of his *Pensées sur l'interprétation de la nature* (dated 1754) was printed twice in French. But these publications had been almost forgotten when, toward the end of the 19th century, they were found to have expressed, more than a century before, what was being heralded as the discovery of the laws of heredity.

Le Sueur, Abbé A. Maupertuis et ses correspondants; lettres inédites du grand Frédéric, du prince Henri de Prusse, de La Beaumelle, du président Hénault, du comte de Tressan, d'Euler, de Kaestner, de Koenig, de Haller, de Condillac, de l'abbé d'Olivet, du Maréchal d'Écosse, ... etc. Picard, 1897, 448 p.   2594

Preface of 83 pages retraces history of letters written to M., which are published on p. 84-442, with explanatory notes. These letters made more useful by Index of names; they represent a most valuable source of information for history of the decade from 1750 to 1760, and show importance of role played by M. during this decade.

Lewin, Marcus. Ueber die Prinzipien von Hamilton und Maupertuis. Leipzig, Teubner, 1898. 49 p. (Diss., Heidelberg). 2595

Discussion, in mathematical terms, of physical significance of the principle of least action, namely as to involvement of " forces " vs. " time ", with a short historical comment on changes in original meaning of " least action " as understood by M., through mathematical developments made by Lagrange and then by Hamilton.

Tressan, Louis Elisabeth de La Vergne de Broussin, *comte de.* Éloge de M. Moreau de Maupertuis. *In his :* Œuvres choisies, Desray, 1791.   v. 12, p. 309-41.   2596

This *Éloge* of M. by Tressan, who was his friend and colleague, briefly summarizes main events of M.'s life, and discusses importance of his discoveries on 18th century scientific and philosophic world. Mentions La Condamine in connection with travels involved in proving that earth is flattened at poles.

Georges Louis Leclerc, *comte* de Buffon
(Nos. 2597-2629)

Donald S. Schier

Badey, Lucien. Buffon, précurseur de la science démographique. Agéo 38:206-20, 1929.   2597

Careful examination of B.'s statistical studies of populations of Burgundy and France, which are to be found in seventh of the *Époques de la nature.* Badey finds that B. was too hasty in assuming that demographic statistics for Burgundy were necessarily representative of all of France. Author calls B.'s studies " vigoureuses esquisses " (p. 220) but inadequate, since idea of population density was unknown in 18th century.

Bouchard, Marcel. Un épisode de la vie de Buffon. AEst 4th ser. 2:21-42, 197-212, 1934.   2598

Primary source of article is hitherto unpublished documents in *Archives de la Côte-d'Or.* Shows how B.'s activities at Montbard foreshadow those of greater scope in the *Jardin du Roi.* Author points out [as have Edouard Estaunié (no. 2602) and W. F. Falls (no. 2605)] that B. never lost sight of his own interests. He sold some of his own land to the province as site for nursery he was to manage (p. 29); made no great effort to carry out charitable intentions of the Crown in ordering founding of nursery (p. 203-4); for years his management consisted in drawing a salary (p. 206); and in the end he tried to buy back the nursery for far less than it was worth and so lost it all (p. 209). Author shows B. to have had " le sens pratique d'un Bourguignon avisé " (p. 211).

Brunetière, Ferdinand. Buffon. *In his :* Nouvelles questions de critique, Calmann Lévy, 1898, p. 127-51.   2599

Written September 15, 1888, for centenary of death of B., attempts his

rehabilitation as a writer.   Author holds that neglect into which B. has fallen due to hostility of lesser Encyclopedists : D'Alembert, Marmontel, etc.   Considers B. greater writer than Diderot (p. 128) and, with Voltaire and Montesquieu, greatest of century.   Article not without interest, but clearly hagiographical.

Condorcet, Antoine-Nicolas de. Éloge de Buffon. *In :* Œuvres complètes de Buffon (éd. Achille Comte), Société des publications illustrées, 1851, I, p. I-X.   2600

Despite formal praise of academic eulogy, Condorcet allows reader to acquire some misgivings about B.'s scientific reliability. Author several times (p. iii, v) comes back to B.'s weakness for generalizing, points out that " l'*Histoire naturelle* a eu parmi les savans des censeurs sévères " (p. v), and in the end compares B. not with Newton or Haller but with Aristotle and Pliny.   Mention (p. viii) of B.'s success in dealing with government officials concludes with the barbed remark that " ... aucun des moyens de contribuer aux progrès de la science ...   n'avait été négligé." (Cf. Falls, W. F., no. 2605).   Impression is left that Condorcet's own opinion of B.'s scientific achievement was not high, although he was willing to give B. full praise as a writer.

Daudin, Henri. Les naturalistes français et les " méthodes " : Buffon, Daubenton et la classification. *In his :* De Linné à Jussieu; méthodes de la classification et l'idée de série en botanique et en zoologie (1740-1790). Alcan, [1927?], p. 117-44.   2601

Author denies (p. 135) that B.'s dislike of Linnaean system stopped its progress in France.   Shows B.'s objections to Linnaeus were partly founded on misunderstanding (p. 126), and partly on scientific caution. Chapter thoroughly documented and treatment of this subject appears authoritative.

Estaunié, Edouard. La vraie figure de Buffon. Rheb [33]:5-27, 1924.   2602

Essentially, this essay attempts to destroy legend that B. was remote from ordinary concerns.   Shows him making money from his *forges* at Montbard, (this is denied by Germain Martin in no. 2618, p. 10), as the administrator of *Jardin du Roi,* questioning his servants about local gossip, and as *bon vivant.* Originally read before Academy of Dijon, article well documented from B.'s letters,

Humbert-Bazile (no. 2615), and Hérault de Séchelles (no. 2611). Article should be read in connection with Falls, W. F., no. 2605.

Faguet, Emile. Buffon. *In his :* Dix-huitième siècle, Boivin, n. d., p. 425-87.   2603

B. presented as type of serene genius above concern for other than purely scientific problems. This view should be corrected by comparison with that given by Edouard Estaunié, no. 2602, and W. F. Falls, no. 2605. The defense of B.'s theory of reproduction is not helped by Faguet's error in saying that, like B., almost all scientists of time believed in spontaneous generation (p. 433). Sections III (*Le moraliste*) and IV (*L'écrivain(* (p. 460-482) are the most rewarding parts of this essay.

Falls, W[illiam] F[ranklin]. Deux lettres inédites de Buffon. MLN 47:170-72, 1932.
2604

Two letters addressed to Jean-Baptiste Guillaumont and have to do with quarries found in 1779 beneath *Jardin du Roi.* Originals in library of *Muséum d'histoire naturelle* in Paris.

— Buffon et l'agrandissement du Jardin du Roi à Paris. Philadelphia, 1933. Reprinted from Archives du Muséum, 6e série, X, 131-200. 69 p. (Diss., Pennsylvania).
2605

First part of this work (p. 135-60) discusses in detail how B. acquired land for growth of *Jardin du Roi.* Second (p. 183-98) shows that B., except for Revolution, would have made a large profit from repayment of money lent to the government for purchase of this land. Book is two separate essays, not a unit. Documentation adequate, but conclusion to second part appears timid. Part two agrees with, but enlarges upon an article by Edouard Estaunié, no. 2602. Book is the only extended discussion of B. as administrator. Well printed, and reproductions of plans for growth of *Jardin* (p. 162-81) are good. Index lacking, and bibliography must be supplemented by footnotes.

Flourens, P[ierre]. Buffon; histoire de ses travaux et de ses idées. Paulin, 1845, 368 p.   2606

Extended discussion of B.'s ideas by practicing naturalist. Still of considerable interest is chapter on B.'s method (p. 1-24), but most of rest of Flourens's criticism outdated, since it appeared fifteen years before Darwin's *Origin of species.* Book described by Sainte-Beuve as an " excellent écrit" (no. 2626, p. 347), and by Brunetière as " médiocre" (no. 2599, p. 132).
Review : F. Hoefer in NRE 1:481-94, Aug., 1846.

— Des manuscrits de Buffon. Garnier, 1860. 298 p.   2607

Essential collection of documents for student of B.'s style and methods of composition. Flourens reproduces (p. 126-77) first draft of various passages of *Époques de la Nature* for comparison with final version. Author discusses how B. managed his collaborators, especially Bexon, who not infrequently corrected the master (p. 51-62). Other collaborators are adequately dealt with : Daubenton (p. 181-94); Guéneau de Montbeillard (p. 194-218); Emmanuel Baillon, André Thouin etc. (p. 229-35). Interesting are the *Pièces justificatives* (p. 254-70) showing on facing pages citations from some of B.'s hypotheses on origin of earth, objections of Sorbonne, and relevant texts from Scriptures. These are followed by *Explications et réponses* of Bexon.

Giard, Alfred. Buffon. *In his :* Controverses transformistes, Masson, 1904. p. 10-12.   2608

Author says B. was held back in his thinking about evolution by fear of Sorbonne (p. 11). Discussion makes no attempt at thoroughness, and is at best a sketch of an interpretation of B.'s evolutionary thought.

Haussonville, [Gabriel Paul Othenin de Cléron], comte d'. Buffon. *In his :* Le Salon de Madame Necker. *See* 294, v. I, p. 304-34.   2609

Throws some light on B.'s relations with Madame Necker, which began five years after death of Countess de Buffon, i.e., in 1774. Author quotes from hitherto unpublished correspondence found at Coppet. Although some of this material is trivial (there are several versions of Latin epigrams which B. composed for his own statue in the *Jardin du Roi* and for a portrait of Madame Necker, p. 316-19), account of B.'s last illness and death and of his fervency in accepting consolations of the Church are of great interest because of his earlier *démêlés* with Sorbonne and anti-religious statements attributed to him by Hérault de Séchelles, no. 2611.

Hazard, Paul. Buffon. *In his :* La pensée européenne au XVIIIe siècle. *See* 1044, v. I, p. 189-95.   2610

In six pages Hazard sets forth B.'s place in scientific thought. He considers B. not greatest scientist of his time, but most representative (p. 189). No attempt made to summarize B.'s ideas; he here becomes a symbol of scientific spirit. These few pages serve to locate B. in context of his time, and make good starting point for study of B.'s work.

Hérault de Séchelles, Marie Jean. Voyage à Montbard. Librairie des bibliophiles, 1890, 17, 51 p.   2611

This malicious piece of journalism is one of very few contemporary accounts of B. the man. Author most impressed by B.'s vanity. (Cf. Marmontel, *Mémoires*, Firmin-Didot, 1891, p. 313). Séchelles gives an account of typical day in B.'s life which has been used by almost all later writers. Is significant that despite this uncharitable account of B., his family remained on good terms with author (p. xv). Book sprinkled with praise for B. (p. 16-17, 43-44). Value of this book as source is dubious, but book itself cannot be overlooked.

Herring, Margaret. Un résumé de quelques années de la vie de Buffon. Lettre inédite. MLN 49:317-20, 1934.   2612

Letter addressed, says Miss Herring, to Jean Jallabert of Geneva, and dated April 4, 1744. Is preserved in Simon Gratz collection of Pennsylvania Historical Society. While it adds nothing new to our knowledge of B., it does mention troubles between him and his father, and gives first-hand account of multiplicity of B.'s tasks at time of writing.

Hervé, Georges. Buffon et son œuvre ethnologique. Ranth 28:195-218, 1918; 30:1-19, 1920.   2613

Articles are lectures given at *École d'anthropologie* in 1915-16 on *Les origines françaises de l'ethnologie.* Credits B. with having first discovered " les rapports ethniques " (28:197). Author carefully examines B.'s contributions to this field. Points out that while B. is often wrong, he is never negligible. Considers B. incomparable for richness and profundity of his ideas. (30:19).

Höhne, Ernst. Der Stil Buffons. Marburg, Schaaf, 1914. 80 p. (Diss., Marburg). 2614

Discusses details of B.'s stylistic technique : sources of B.'s comparisons (p. 28-33); his use of antithesis (p. 38-39); of colors, tastes, and tactile impressions (p. 46-49). Gives numerous examples of metaphor, metonymy, oxymoron, etc., in B.'s work (p. 67-74). Book has no particular thesis, and as examination of B.'s style it is lost in mass of pedantic detail. Author does not rise to consideration of æsthetics. Index lacking, brief bibliography (p. 79-80).

Humbert-Bazile. Buffon, sa famille, ses collaborateurs et ses familiers. Renouard, 1863, 15, 428 p.   2615

Although book contains *mémoires* of Humbert-Bazile, B.'s secretary, it also contains source-material relating to B.'s family and associates. Editor, Nadault de Buffon, has added to secretary's conventional remarks letters and documents concerning Bexon, Verniquet, Père Ignace, etc., which make this book, with B.'s *Correspondance*, indispensable for study of B.'s life.

Krantz, Emile. Buffon. *In his :* Essai sur l'esthétique de Descartes. Germer Baillière, 1882, p. 342-59.   2616

Chapter a gloss of *Discours sur le style*, which author considers highest development of classical literary doctrine. To Krantz, B. is a Cartesian reasoner rather than empirical scientist ; hence B.'s *Discours* extends Descartes' explanation of the origin of thought to the expression of thought (i.e. style). In keeping with his argument Krantz would change B.'s definition to read " Le style—mais le style général—c'est l'homme—mais l'homme essentiel et abstrait." (p. 359). Closely reasoned criticism intended to show Descartes' metaphysics as the source of classical æsthetics.

Malesherbes, Chrétien Guillaume de Lamoignon de. Observations de Lamoignon-Malesherbes sur l'histoire naturelle générale et particulière de Buffon et Daubenton. Pougens, An VI (1798), 2 v. 2617

Work of minister of Louis XVI was published posthumously. Is sharply critical of B., especially as to B.'s method (I, 1-220), and the *Théorie de la terre.* Is closely reasoned, and defense of Tournefort and Linnæus appears sound. As example of sober contemporary criticism of B. work cannot be neglected. Does not, however, take up B.'s zoology, and of course many of author's criticisms, like theories of B., are now outdated.

Martin, Germain. Buffon, maître de forges. Le Puy, Marchessou, 1898. 12 p. 2618

Seven of these twelve pages devoted to reproduction of a description of B.'s *forge* by Gabriel Jars, who saw it in 1768-9. Author quotes B. as saying he made no profit from enterprise. (p. 10). Contrary maintained by Edouard Estaunié, no. 2602.

Mornet, Daniel. [Buffon]. *In his :* Les sciences de la nature en France au XVIIIe siècle, See 868, p. 10-290. 2619

About one-fifth of book concerns B. directly. An excellent discussion of him as scientist. Apparently a contradiction in Mornet's saying (p. 199) " Buffon n'hésita pas, quelquefois, à plier ses idées aux exigences de l'expression," and later that, as to whether he did or not, " Il serait périlleux d'en juger." (p. 207). There is good criticism of belletristic side of B., p. 198-212, as well as selected bibliography, p. 249-77, covering book as a whole.

Nordenskiöld, Erik. Buffon. *In his :* The history of biology. New York, Knopf, 1928. p. 219-29. 2620

Considers B. important in history of science not for any discovery, but for his attempt to base a natural history of creation " on law-bound evolution " (p. 224). Indicates influence of B. on Cuvier, Bichat, and Lamarck. Holds that B.'s championing of theories of reproduction resembling spontaneous generation was by way of " explaining the origin of life without the assumption of a supernatural act of creation." (p. 228). Treatment of B. as scientist brief and favorable because general. Makes no criticism of B.'s method; discussion confined to B. as maker of hypotheses.

Nourrison, [Jean Félix]. La philosophie de Buffon. AMP 119 (ns 19):378-88, 683-95, 1883. 2621

Interesting, but not of primary importance. Begins with brief but able summary of spirit of 18th century, from hostile viewpoint. Contrasts B. and Condillac, to former's advantage. In general, a eulogy of B.'s conception of nature, and of its interpretation and expression in his philosophy.

Panckoucke, Charles Joseph. De l'homme et de la reproduction des différens individus. 1761 [No publisher given]. 214 p. 2622

Well-known publisher here takes up cudgels to defend B.'s theory of reproduction against Haller. Although *moule intérieur*, as well as debate it brought about, is now outdated, book should be consulted by historians of biology.

Perrier, Edmond. Buffon. *In his :* La philosophie zoologique avant Darwin. 2nd ed. Alcan, 1896, p. 56-72. 2623

Holds that B. rejected classifications of Linnæus because he believed that a scientist accepting them and theories of mutation would take man to be " pour le moins un cousin des singes, et Buffon recule devant l'énormité de cette conclusion." (p. 59). Author exaggerates (p. 68) clarity of B.'s ideas on evolution, but shows how he helped prepare way for Darwinism.

Rödiger, Johannes. Darstellung der geographischen Naturbetrachtung bei Fontenelle, Pluche und Buffon in methodischer und stilistischer Hinsicht. See 1199. 2624

Thesis is that scientific popularizations began with Fontenelle's *Entretiens ;* that form and matter of such popularizations became more clear-cut and effective in Pluche's *Spectacle de la nature* and reached their final form in B.'s *Théorie de la terre* and *Époques de la nature.* (p. 108). Devotes considerable attention to problems of style in Pluche (p. 31-45) and B. (p. 63-96). Some sections unreadable (for example, that on geographical vocabulary in Pluche and B., p. 72-88) and in general book should be consulted rather than read. Useful *Geographisches Namenverzeichnis* (p. 118-128) as well as brief bibliography (p. vii-viii).

Roule, Louis. Buffon et la description de la nature. Flammarion, n. d. [1924]. 248 p. 2625

First chapters a biography of B. which adds nothing new to our knowledge of him. P. 99-245 contain chronological presentation of his methods and ideas. Essentially " popular " book, but good one of its kind—systematic, sober, and accurate. Does not exaggerate B.'s importance for the present but clearly shows his great stature in his own time. Of interest particularly is discussion (p. 219-22) of B.'s debt to Leibniz, Descartes, and the English philosophers, and (p. 227-9) of his influence on Diderot.

Sainte-Beuve, Charles-Augustin. Buffon. *In his :* Causeries du lundi. Garnier, 4th ed., n. d. 4:347-68; 10:55-73; 14:320-37.
2626

Dates of these three essays are respectively 1851, 1854, and 1860. Second, in which are discussed reasons for widely differing judgments of B. by Cuvier and G. Saint-Hilaire, and the third, on B.'s personality and literary style as they appear in his letters, are incisive and useful. Sainte-Beuve's warning against applying the *genre-Michelet* to B. (10:71 n.) has not been sufficiently taken to heart by such later writers as Brunetière (no. 2599). All three essays primarily biographical and literary, and their temperateness is an antidote to exaggerated praise of B.'s admirers such as Faguet (no. 2603) and Dimier.

Sauter, Eugen. Herder und Buffon. Rixheim, Sutter, 1910. 94 p. (Diss., Basel).
2627

Author holds Herder was deeply indebted to B. and often quoted him, especially in first ten books of the *Ideen zur Philosophie der Geschichte der Menschheit,* usually without indicating source. Conscientious study of " influence " soberly and critically done. Of interest especially in that it considers B.'s philosophical importance rather than his scientific work. Brief bibliography but no index.

Strohl, Jean. Buffon. NRF 44:837-51, 1935.
2628

Author considers not B. but Réaumur most representative scientist of 18th century (p. 841). Finds B. lacking in long patience necessary for scientific work, but grants him even greater gift— literary skill by which he accomplished " ... la réintégration de la découverte dans le patrimoine intellectuel de l'humanité... " (p. 851). Judicious article, and one of very few on B. in recent years.

Villemain, [Abel François]. Buffon. *In his :* Cours de littérature française; tableau de la littérature au XVIIIe siècle. *See* 82, v. II, p. 180-217.
2629

Florid essay still interesting despite superficiality. Villemain devotes four pages to discussion of Aristotle and Pliny, to latter of whom he compares B. Remainder devoted to exposition of B.'s work. Negligible as assessment of B.'s

scientific contribution, it is a good example of official criticism of B. as a writer.

Charles Bonnet
(Nos. 2630-2648)

Donald S. Schier

Bonnet, Georges. Charles Bonnet (1720-1793). Lac, 1929. 319 p. (Diss., Paris).
2630

Mostly deals with B. as a philosopher. Second half a reconstruction of what B.'s philosophical system might have been, had he gathered its scattered bits together. Since B.'s worth is acknowledged to lie in his scientific discoveries, and, from standpoint of influence, in his psychological theories, the interest of this book is at best secondary. Treatment of some matters, especially of influences on B. (p. 87-103) is sketchy. Has bibliography of B.'s works (p. 14-16); list of his mss. (p. 16-20); and list of critical works on B. (p. 22-25).

Claparède, Ed[ouard]. La psychologie animale de Charles Bonnet. Geneva, Georg, 1909. 95 p.
2631

Deals with B.'s ideas on animal psychology from scientific point of view. Sees in B. an empirical psychologist, and praises him for having linked psychological to physiological. Discusses a part of B.'s psychological theories mostly unstudied by Speck (no. 2642) and Offner (no. 2637). Sound work which treats B.'s ideas in light of theories current in 1909. Brief bibliography, p. 9-10, and other bibliographical data in footnotes. Portrait of B.

Daudin, Henri. Les théories philosophiques de la série chez les modernes : Leibniz et Ch. Bonnet. *In his :* De Linné à Jussieu; méthodes de la classification et de l'idée de série en botanique et en zoologie (1740-1790). *See* 2601, p. 92-105.
2632

Author holds that B. took over idea of " chain of being " from Leibniz, but that this borrowing was limited to theoretical formulation of concept (p. 99). B.'s definition of " superiority " as greater or less degree of similarity between a given species and man is thought by author to be an application of B.'s metaphysics to natural history. Reliable and interesting discussion of thought of B. and Leibniz on this question. Annotated bibliography, p. 235-62.

Flournoy, Th. Le cas de Charles Bonnet.
Aps 1:1-23, 1901-02.   2633

Title of essay misleading; author deals
not with B. himself but with a case of
visual hallucination which B. observed in
his maternal grandfather. Bibliographical note about this case on p. 351.

Fritzsche, Oskar William. Die pädago-
gisch-didaktischen Theorien Charles Bonnets. Langensalza, Beyer, 1905. 120 p.
(Diss., Leipzig).   2634

For most part a summing-up of the
psychological theories of B. in so far as
they influence what he says about
education. Not essential book for understanding B., although of interest in
history of educational thought, especially
p. 77-93 *(Natur, Idealmensch)*, which
contrast with Rousseau's position B.'s
insistence that moral character grows out
of intellectual.

Isenberg, Karl. Der Einfluss der Philosophie Charles Bonnets auf Friedrich Heinrich Jacobi. Borna-Leipzig, Noske, 1906,
65 p. (Diss., Tübingen).   2635

Author holds B.'s chief contributions
to Jacobi's thought were clarification of
problems and means to reconcile rationalism and sensualism *(Rationalismus und
Sensualismus zu vereinigen.* p. viii).
Denies that Jacobi ever adopted B.'s
physiological psychology (p. 63). Shows
that B.'s influence on Jacobi waned as
Jacobi in his later years tended to
withdraw from pure science. Useful
study, painstakingly done.

Lemoine, Albert. Charles Bonnet de Genève, philosophe et naturaliste. Durand,
1850. 232 p. (Diss., Paris).   2636

Discusses B. from philosophical point
of view, comparing his work with that of
Locke, Condillac, and Leibniz. A work
of technical philosophy. Studies by J.
Speck (no. 2642), Offner (no. 2637) and
Claparède (no. 2631) deal better with B.'s
psychology from scientific point of view.
Index, table of contents, and bibliography
lacking.

Offner, Max. Die Psychologie Charles
Bonnet's. *In :* Schriften der Gesellschaft
für psychologische Forschung. 1.
Sammlung, p. 555-722. Leipzig, 1893,
v. 5.   2637

Best and fullest treatment of B.'s
psychological work. Offner begins with
very useful bibliographical essay (p. 555-

574). Four chapters on aspects of B.'s
psychological theory. Author here displays considerable capacity for synthesis.
Of interest especially are Offner's comments defining B.'s influence on German
psychologists in general (p. 716); on Jean
Paul (p. 717); and on J. Chr. Hennings
(p. 718); these should, however, be
completed through reading of studies by
Speck (no. 2642), Strózewski (no. 2643),
Schubert (no. 2641), and Isenberg (no.
2635). Author finds B.'s greatest contribution was his thorough-going attempt
to put psychology on physiological basis.

Perrier, Edmond. C. Bonnet. *In his :*
La philosophie zoologique avant Darwin.
See 2623, p. 39-47.   2638

Discusses primarily B.'s efforts to
establish chain of being running from
" subtle matter " to man, and his
theories of reproduction. Defines B.'s
philosophical efforts as " une alliance
singulière d'un raisonnement rigoureux,
s'appuyant sur des faits mal connus, trop
peu nombreux, avec les affirmations bibliques prises au pied de la lettre " (p. 47).
Does not discuss B.'s psychology, which
was very influential in Germany, and only
mentions in passing his lasting scientific
discoveries.

Sayous, [Pierre] André. Charles Bonnet,
sa vie et ses travaux. RDM 2nd per.
12:49-81, Oct. 1, 1855.   2639

Interesting as being one of few primarily literary essays on B. Sayous here
makes use of letters of B. for an account of
his life and short discussion of some of his
work. Of little worth for historian of
science, this essay might well be used as
introduction to B. by general reader.
Author's summary of relations, scant as
they were, between Voltaire and B.
(p. 63-65), deserves notice.

— **[Pierre], A[ndré].** Charles Bonnet. *In
his :* Le dix-huitième siècle à l'étranger.
Amyot, 1861, I, p. 157-205.   2640

Reworking of RDM, 2nd per. 12:49-81,
Oct. 1, 1855. Lacks pages given in
article to B.'s meeting with Voltaire, but
p. 170-73, dealing with B.'s likeness to
Rousseau in educational thought have
been added.

Schubert, Anna. Die Psychologie von
Bonnet und Tetens mit besonderer Berücksichtigung des methodischen Verfahrens
derselben. Zurich, Meier, 1909. 122 p.
(Diss., Zurich).   2641

Essentially a more detailed study of ground previously covered by J. Speck (no. 2642). Author holds that while both Tetens and B. were empiricists (p. 21), Tetens tried to make study of psychology independent of that of physiology (p. 119). Agrees with Speck that influence of B. (and Tetens) was cut short in Germany by work of Kant and resultant rejection of empiricism.

Speck, Johannes. Bonnets Einwirkung auf die deutsche Psychologie des vorigen Jahrhunderts. AGP 10:504-19, 1897. 11:58-72; 181-211, 1898. 2642

Discusses B.'s considerable influence on Irwing, Platner, Haller, Tetens, etc. *See* no. 2641. Author holds that B.'s theories on nature of thought-processes, memory, soul, and especially his argument for immortality were very influential; but this influence was cut short by Kant and consequent swing of German thought from empiricism to idealism.

Strózewski, Stanislaus. Bonnets Psychologie in ihrem Verhältnis zu Condillacs Traité des sensations. *See* 1261. 2643

Points out a fact generally passed over, *viz.*, indebtedness of both B. and Condillac to Locke and English empiricism (p. 50). Holds that in fact Condillac and B. agreed on most main points (p. 52) but does not answer question as to whether B. followed in Condillac's footsteps knowingly or unknowingly (p. 55). Argues that greatest difference between Condillac and B. is that former is mostly deductive thinker, latter inductive. Interesting study showing many problems about which Genevan apologist and Parisian philosopher saw eye to eye.

[Trembley, J.] Mémoire pour servir à l'histoire de la vie et des ouvrages de M. Charles Bonnet. Berne, Société typographique, 1794. 128 p. 2644

Chronological treatment of B.'s life and principal works. Book a eulogy, not a criticism of B., but of interest since author was obviously a friend. Contains occasional personal notes, such as fact that B.'s favorite author was Sallust (p. 117), but, by and large, discussion of B., except for main events of his life such as his marriage, limited to summaries of his books and articles.

— Ueber Carl Bonnet. Halle, Waisenhaus, 1795, 152 p. 2645

Anonymous translation. Translator says he expects book to be of interest in Germany because B. has had a " sehr heilsamen Einfluss " (p. vii) on German science.

Viatte, Auguste. Quelques épisodes de la propagande " illuminée " au XVIIIᵉ siècle. RLC 4:653-70, 1924. 2646

Selection from correspondence of B. with Jean-Gaspard Lavater covering (with some gaps) years 1765-1789. Letters interesting for light they throw on Lavater's attempt to convert Moses Mendelssohn through arguments found in B.'s *Palingénésie*. They also show B.'s skepticism about soothsayers and mesmerism, which he owed to his Calvinistic orthodoxy; here apologist was far more skeptical than inventor of " physiognomy."

Whitman, C[harles] O[tis]. Bonnet's theory of evolution. *In :* Wood's Hole, Mass. Marine biological laboratory. Biological lectures delivered at the Marine biological laboratory at Wood's Hole in the Summer session of 1894. Boston, Ginn, 1896. Eleventh lecture, p. 225-40. 2647

Evolution as understood by B. has, in author's view, no relation to concept conveyed by that term in modern times. Lecture is a refutation of Huxley who considered genetics of his time in harmony with B.'s theory of development. Whitman holds that B.'s later views had nothing in common with modern theory, and that confusion has arisen from the acceptance of B.'s vocabulary without account being taken of his apologetical intentions.

— The Palingenesia and Germ doctrine of Bonnet. *In :* Wood's Hole, Mass. Marine biological laboratory. Biological lectures delivered at the Marine biological laboratory at Wood's Hole in the Summer session of 1894. *See* 2647. Twelfth lecture, p. 241-72. 2648

Whitman here holds that B.'s views chiefly interesting as being antithesis of modern theory. Author says of B. : " Often his words counterfeit the language of modern evolution; but what monstrous travesties they disclose on closer examination " (p. 256-7). Whitman concludes : " The old evolution was the greatest error that ever obstructed the progress of our knowledge of development." (p. 272).

Luc de Clapiers, *marquis* de Vauvenargues
(Nos. 2649-2710)

FERNAND VIAL

Vauvenargues. 1st edition; Introduction à la connaissance de l'esprit humain, suivie de réflexions et de maximes. Briasson, 1746. 384 p. (Anonymous). 2649

Reviews: JS 139:226-40, 1746. (Anonymous). Mémoires pour l'histoire des sciences et beaux-arts (Journal de Trévoux), May, 1746, p. 1139; January, 1747, 74-83 (Anonymous); MerF, March, 1746, 130-33. (Anonymous.)

— Œuvres de Vauvenargues, édition nouvelle, précédée de l'éloge de Vauvenargues et accompagnée de notes et commentaires, par D. L. Gilbert. Furne, 1857. 500 p. 2649A

— Œuvres posthumes et Œuvres inédites de Vauvenargues, avec notes et commentaires par D. L. Gilbert. Furne, 1857. 370 p. 2650

Old, but still best edition of V.'s works. Particularly valuable since most of manuscripts examined by Gilbert were lost in incendiary fire of Louvre Library, in 1870. New material includes very important correspondence with Mirabeau. Exacting critical apparatus includes variants of previous editions, and notes of Suard, Fortia, Voltaire.
Review: F. T. Perrens in RDM 2ᵉ pér. 12:232-40, Nov. 1, 1857. " Ces deux volumes resteront longtemps, sinon toujours, le dernier mot de la critique... " (p. 240). Detailed description of the edition.

— Œuvres de Vauvenargues, publiées avec une introduction et des notices, par Pierre Varillon. Cité des livres, 1929. 3 v. 2651

Follows texts established by Gilbert (no. 2650). Excellent physical presentation, easily readable, but not erudite. Not suitable for research purposes.

— Œuvres choisies de Vauvenargues. Avec une introduction par H. Gaillard de Champris. Aubier, 1942. 360 p. 2652

Excellent introduction making use of latest research, particularly Vial (no. 2704). Complete bibliography, reproducing Vial's, with addition of latest items from Saintville (nos. 2693-2699).

Ascoli, G. Vauvenargues. RCC 24²:827-38, 1923. 2653

Penetrating and reliable presentation

of V.'s aspirations, and rapid analysis of his ideas. Thinks of V. as a " saint laïque."

Barni, Jules. Vauvenargues; l'homme, sa vie. *In his*: Les moralistes français au dix-huitième siècle. Baillère, 1873. p. 1-70. 2654

Biography of V. necessarily sketchy and valueless. Good critical presentation of V.'s determinism, and of his attempt to reconcile free will with complete dependency upon God. Explains V.'s *vertu* by courage and humanity. Many deficiencies : neglects V.'s religious ethics, and metaphysics.

Borel, Antoine. Essai sur Vauvenargues. Neuchâtel, Guinchard, 1913. 123 p. (Diss., Zurich). 2655

Useful, but somewhat arbitrary synthesis. Many affirmations unsupported by documentary evidence. Explains V.'s ideas by his love of glory and by tragic conflict between V.'s aspirations and meager opportunities he had to realize them. Uneven style; unpleasant reading.

Bréhier, Emile. Vauvenargues. *In his*: Histoire de la philosophie. Alcan, 1927-32, 2, 11:426-31. 2656

Solid; condensed. Insists on importance of V.'s thought, frequently underestimated.

Brunetière, Ferdinand. L'erreur du dix-huitième siècle. RDM 5ᵉ pér. 10:634-59, Aug. 1, 1902. 2657

V. one of first moralists responsible for error of 18th century which was to believe that " la question morale est une question sociale."

Gaillard de Champris, Henry. Vauvenargues directeur de conscience. AMPR 96:842-61, 1936. 2658

Studies V.'s relationship with De Seytres and chevalier de Mirabeau. Seductiveness of V.'s method : liberal and energetic. Exact and pleasing presentation.

— Vauvenargues. RCC 38¹:481-96; 620-36; 38²:51-65; 749-62, 1937. 2659

Substantial discussion of V.'s religious attitude wherein author disagrees with Lanson's interpretation (no. 2667). Excellent study of V.'s failures in love and of qualities he brought to his friendships. Abundant quotations. Unfortunately

Saintville's latest researches (nos. 2693-2699) seem to have been ignored.

Cavallucci, Giacomo. Vauvenargues dégagé de la légende. Naples, Pironti, 1939. 418 p.   2660

Thorough, judicious, critical examination of all original documents and studies pertaining to V.'s life with stated purpose of weeding out doubtful or biased testimonies in order to restore an historical V. as revealed by most authenticated documents objectively interpreted. Many points are thus clarified, with good distinction of what is hypothetical, probable, and definitely established. Same method applied, but with less success, to V.'s thought. Ineffective chapter on V.'s readings and intellectual formation. Appreciation of V.'s religious ideas contradicted by Vial (no. 2704). Inconclusive comparison with Vigny; competent, but incomplete comparison with Nietzsche. Bibliography is most extensive to date and includes secondary items not listed by Lanson (no. 2667), Vial (no. 2704), and Wallas (no. 2709).

Feugère, A. Rousseau et son temps : la littérature du sentiment au XVIII⁰ siècle : Vauvenargues, réfutation vivante de La Rochefoucauld. RCC 36²:162-76, 1935.   2661

Optimism of V., suffering, unknown, contrasted with pessimism of La Rochefoucauld. Optimism of V. founded on rehabilitation of sentiment and passion. Authoritative and learned deductions.

Giraud, Victor. La vie secrète de Vauvenargues. RDM 8ᵉ pér. 3:457-68, May 15, 1931.   2662

Inspired by renewal of popularity enjoyed by V. Based mostly on Lanson, no. 2667.

Gosse, Edmund. Vauvenargues and the sentiment of "la gloire," FortR 109 (ns 103):511-23, 1918. *Also in*, with the title of " Vauvenargues," *his :* Three French moralists. London, Heinemann, [1918], p. 97-132.   2663

Enthusiastic and slightly *romancée* biography, containing some rather rash affirmations. Exclusively study of personal and theoretical ethics of V. Emphasizes differences between V.'s ethics and those of 18th century, and in so doing differs sharply with La Harpe's ideas on this subject (no. 2666).

Guérin, Joseph. Un ami de Vauvenargues. NRM 8:470-83, 1925.

— Les ambitions de Vauvenargues. *Ibid.* 4:217-24, 1927.   2664

Interesting revelations on most intimate friend of V. and confidant of his financial difficulties, the *président* de Saint-Vincens. Factual details on V.'s desire to enter diplomacy.

Heilman, Ella. Vauvenargues als Moralphilosoph und Kritiker. Leipzig, Nuschke, 1906. 58 p.   2665

Interesting comparison between V. and 18th century moralists. Emphasis on solidity of V.'s literary criticism.

La Harpe, Jean de. Philosophie du dix-huitième siècle. *In his :* Lycée : ou Cours de littérature ancienne et moderne. *See* 2419, v. 15, I, p. 194-234.   2666

V. seeks to establish ethics on basis of certitude. His metaphysics weak. Critical analysis of some of V.'s ethical principles. La Harpe strives, unsuccessfully, to present V. as orthodox believer. Opposes V.'s idealism to Helvétius' sensationalism; " amour de nous-même " to " amour propre." Judgments not free from bias.

Lanson, Gustave. Le marquis de Vauvenargues. Hachette, 1930. 221 p.   2667

Interprets V. the man through his works. Psychological and factual biography which clarifies many points hitherto obscure. Lanson has uncovered new documents, particularly in Archives of War Department in Paris, dealing with V.'s military activities. Gives new interpretation of already known sources. General survey of V.'s ideas, not too deep, but keen and comprehensive, with interesting, if subjective, indications of possible further studies. Splendidly methodical and authoritative, *à la Lanson*. *See* no. 2659.

Review : G. Saintville in RCC 33¹:92-96, 1931-32. " ... entreprise infiniment riche et féconde et, conduite avec une pareille autorité, toute nouvelle..." (p. 94.)

Le Breton, André. Vauvenargues et Fontenelle. *See* 1191.   2668

Proves by conclusive arguments that original for portrait of Isocrate (in *Œuvres de Vauvenargues*, no. 2650, p. 355), was Fontenelle, rather than unknown Rémond de Saint-Mard, as Suard (no. 2701) and Gilbert (no. 2650) contend.

— Le souvenir de Vauvenargues. RDM
6ᵉ pér. 50:429-47, Mar. 15, 1919.   2669

Influence of V.'s thought, courage, energy, stoicism on psychology of soldier of World War I. Usefulness and actuality of V.'s works.

Lenoir, Raymond. Vauvenargues. *In his :* Les historiens de l'esprit humain. Alcan, 1926. p. 89-130.   2670

Many inaccuracies in biographical data. Some grievous : " Assez peu sensible à la beauté de l'action " (p. 99). Fanciful interpretations, frequently unfavorable. Summary of V.'s ideas mostly in V.'s own words but without quotation marks : uninformed reader does not know what is V.'s and what is Lenoir's. No commentary, nor effort to connect various aspects of V.'s philosophy.

Lods, Armand. Les éditions originales des œuvres de Vauvenargues. ICC 97:527-28, 1934.   2671

Self-explanatory title. Indispensable factual information.

Maccall, William. Vauvenargues. *In his :* Foreign biographies. London, Tingsley, 1873, 1:99-113.   2672

Interesting general considerations but completely obsolete biography.

Marmontel, J. F. Mémoires, I, 3:133-35; 163-65; Nouveaux contes moraux, l'erreur d'un bon père, V. 3:119-62 *passim. In his :* Œuvres complètes. *See* 332.   2673

Invaluable information on Vauvenargues's virtue, fortitude in suffering, his conversations with Voltaire witnessed by Marmontel. Compares Vauvenargues to Fénelon. Scene at Voltaire's bedside with Vauvenargues, Cideville, and Marmontel.

Merlant, Joachim. De Montaigne à Vauvenargues. Société française d'imprimerie et de librairie, 1914. 420 p. A chapter of the book : L'âme selon Vauvenargues, previously published in RPL 51²:788-91; 815-19, 1913.   2674

V. has rehabilitated human nature, against Pascal and La Rochefoucauld. Good analysis of V.'s practical psychology. But Merlant has not observed ferments of action latent in V.'s soul, point stressed by Lanson (no. 2667) and developed by Vial (no. 2704).

Morlais, abbé Mathurin. Étude sur le

Traité du libre arbitre de Vauvenargues. Thorin, 1881.   187 p. (Diss., Rennes).   2675

Heavy, but seemingly effective, refutation of V.'s determinism, by metaphysical arguments, and defense of thomistic doctrine of free-will. Strictly philosophical treatise on obscure problems.

Morley, John. Vauvenargues. *In his :* Critical miscellanies. *See* 1431, v. 2, p. 1-40.   2676

Short but keen appreciation of V.'s literary and moral position. Excellent study of V.'s religious attitude as compared with that of his century.

Mornet, Daniel. La pensée française au xviiiᵉ siècle. *See* 1061.   2677

Erudite criticism *(passim)* of V., and references to his works and his position in development of French literary thought.

Mouan, J. L. G. Quelques mots sur un exemplaire de la première édition des œuvres de Vauvenargues, avec notes manuscrites aux marges. Aix, Tavernier et Illy, 1856.   16 p.   2678

Very important monograph. Establishes for first time, even before Gilbert edition (no. 2650), that some of marginal notes in Aix edition of V.'s works are in Voltaire's handwriting. For details of controversy between Mouan and Gilbert on anteriority of this discovery, *see :* Saintville : Le *Vauvenargues annoté,* no. 2697.

Nebel, Carl. Vauvenargues' Moralphilosophie. Leipzig, Naumann, 1901.   70 p.   2679

General and superficial study of V.'s philosophical, political, social, and religious ideas.

Nisard, Désiré. Pertes dans la philosophie morale. *In his :* Histoire de la littérature française. 3rd ed., Didot, 1863.   4:301-22.   2680

V. does not have authority of first-class moralist because he has no principles, and admits legitimacy of passion in moral life. Inferior to La Bruyère as psychological portraitist. More original as literary critic or rather as " spéculatif littéraire." Highly controversial and debatable judgments.

Norman, Sybil M. Vauvenargues d'après sa correspondance. Toulouse, Privat, 1929. 118 p. (Diss., Toulouse).   2681

Useful moral biography, with superficial analysis of V.'s emotions as revealed in his correspondence. No new factual information, nor original appreciations. Poorly documented and not free from inaccuracies. Bibliography wholly inadequate.

Paléologue, Maurice. Vauvenargues. Hachette, 1890. 153 p. (GEF).   2682

One of earliest of V.'s biographers; has not had benefit of recent research, which frequently contradicts him. Biography drawn almost exclusively from V.'s correspondence, or inferred from his works. Has established definitely some traits of V.'s character. Good analysis of points that V. has in common with his century, and of those in which he is an " isolé." Fac-simile of a letter of V. to Voltaire concerning *Sémiramis*.
Reviews : A. Delboulle in Rcr ns 29:253, 1890 : " M. Maurice Paléologue s'est attaché particulièrement à mettre en lumière la vertu de Vauvenargues. ... Bon résumé, élégamment écrit;" A. Tobler in Dlit 11:508, 1890.

Pellisson, Maurice. La rénovation des idées morales au XVIIIᵉ siècle : Vauvenargues. Grev, Nov. 15, 1904:350-75.   2683

Interesting parallel between V. and Fontenelle and Spinoza. Sound appreciation of V.'s culture. Unity of V.'s thought, particularly in his practical and theoretical ethics, which are intimately connected.

— Les hommes de lettres au XVIIIᵉ siècle. *See* 369, 44, 237, 239.   2684

V. named, and quoted, on lack of prestige of men of letters in 18th century.

Prévost-Paradol, L. A. P. Études sur les moralistes français. Hachette, 1865. 2nd ed. p. 213-36.   2685

Short, but brilliant and extremely sympathetic study of V.'s psychology. Important considerations on V.'s determinism, more readable than Morlais (no. 2675). Elegant style; sound criticism.

Rabow, Hans. Die zehn Schaffensjahre des Vauvenargues, 1737-1747. Berlin, Ebering, 1932. 262 p.   2686

Valuable study of V.'s relationship with Mirabeau and Saint-Vincens during last ten years of his life, based mostly on correspondence. Finds in V. " inquiétude," activity and resignation. Sound analysis of V.'s psychological tendencies.

Review : Fritz Schalk in Archiv 165: 104-06, 1934.

Read, Herbert. Vauvenargues. *In his :* The sense of glory, essays in criticism. Cambridge, University press, 1929. p. 101-22.   2687

Shows V. seeking glory successively in army, diplomacy, and finally in literature. Compares V.'s conception of glory with Traherne's. Interesting, and frequently keen analysis.
Review : G. Lanson in RHL 38:133-34, 1931.

Reinhardt (Dr.). Vauvenargues; examen critique de son influence sur la littérature française et de ses critiques sur le rapport de la grammaire. Gotha, 1863. 7 p. 2688

Does not justify at all its ambitious title. Explains, and justifies V.'s grammatical errors noticed by various editors.

Richard, Pierre. La vie de Vauvenargues. Gallimard, 1930. 256 p.   2689

Lively, frequently lyrical, enthusiastic *biographie romancée*, with all defects of *genre ;* many fanciful constructions around well-established facts. Entertaining and touching if not scholarly. Important as proof of V.'s popularity during and after World War I.
Review : J.-J. Brousson in NL, March 29, 1930, p. 3.

Rocheblave, Samuel. Vauvenargues ou la symphonie inachevée. Je sers, 1934. 198 p.   2690

Very idealized presentation of V. in poetic style suggested by title. Many inaccuracies of fact handed down from V.'s previous biographers. Touching and in part convincing. Unity of V.'s thought, and desire to create a system.
Review : G. Saintville in RCC 36¹:91-96, 1934.

Rouville, Marguerite de. De levenskunst van Vauvenargues. Leiden, Sijthoff, 1920. 107 p.   2691

Biography of V. His relations with Mirabeau, Saint-Vincens, Voltaire, Amelot.

Sainte-Beuve. Vauvenargues. *In his :* Causeries du lundi. Garnier, n. d. 3rd ed. 3:123-43; 14:1-55.   2692

Admirable study and appreciation of V.'s morality, natural virtue, his efforts to rehabilitate human nature. V. " a l'âme antique." Purity of V.'s style. His religious spirit.

Second study, written after Gilbert edition (no. 2650), happily supplements previous study, and corrects it in some points where correspondence with Mirabeau, revealed by Gilbert, warrants new deductions. Sainte-Beuve discovers ambition and thirst for action in V.'s soul. Essays dated Nov. 18, 1850, and Aug. 24, 31, and Sept. 7, 1857.

Saintville, G. Quelques notes sur Vauvenargues. Vrin, 1931. 27 p. 2693

Remarkable document on V.'s military career happily completing Lanson's investigation (no. 2667) of same point.

— Sur une comparaison de Vauvenargues et Pascal par Voltaire. RHL 38:593-98, 1931. 2694

Reproduction of various drafts of a famous page of Voltaire, with interesting variants. Considerations on Voltaire's intentions and on approximate date of composition.

— Autour de la mort de Vauvenargues. Vrin, 1932. 31 p. 2695

V.'s will published with notes and comments. Finally sets at rest legend of a V. dying in utter poverty.

— Recherches sur la famille de Vauvenargues. Vrin, 1932. 46 p. 2696

New information on V.'s two brothers and three sisters, especially on his sister Carmélite.

Review : D. Mornet in RHL 40:300, 1933. " Publication très scrupuleuse, très savante."

— Le Vauvenargues annoté de la bibliothèque Méjanes. Giraud-Badin, 1933. 26 p. 2697

Important document on controversy between Mouan (no. 2678) and Gilbert (no. 2650), each claiming to have been first to discover that marginalia in first edition of V.'s works in the Aix library were by Voltaire.

— L'étude de Vauvenargues. RCC 36¹:91-96, 1934. 2698

Excellent *État présent des études sur Vauvenargues* written apropos of works of Rocheblave, no. 2690, and Zyromski, no. 2710. Review of previous studies on V. and their weak points.

— Stendhal et Vauvenargues. Au divan, 1938. 55 p. 2699

Publication of many passages of V. copied by Stendhal in his notebook, or used in his *Pensées-filosofia.*

These short monographes of Saintville, based on documents from archives and on most scrupulous and erudite research, are latest and most reliable sources of information. They have revealed many unknown points of V.'s biography and have clarified others hitherto hopelessly confused.

Souchon, Paul. Vauvenargues, philosophe de la gloire. Tallandier, 1947. 252 p. 2700

Sound and warm biographical study utilizing Saintville (nos. 2693-2699) to a considerable extent. Somewhat weakened by improbable thesis, namely : that V. is true son of Provence; also weakened by vain attempts to restore V. to his native province. Superior knowledge of contemporary background. Division of material too minute; chronological order not readily apparent.

Review : F. Vial in RR 39:162-64, 1948.

Suard, J. B. De Vauvenargues. *In his :* Mélanges de littérature. Dentu, 1803. 1:299-313. 2701

One of earliest tributes to V.; gives valuable information on V.'s culture. Appreciates V.'s literary criticism and his optimism in regard to human nature.

Trahard, Pierre. Vauvenargues, ou les lettres de noblesse de la sensibilité. *In his :* Les maîtres de la sensibilité française au XVIIIe siècle. *See* 832, v. 2, p. 29-48. 2702

Excellent and erudite analysis of role of sentiment and passion in philosophy of V.

Van Raalte, L. Publications récentes sur Vauvenargues. Neo 20:256-61, 1934-35. 2703

Publication of five studies and two books on V. between 1928 and 1934 attests increased popularity of this author. Judicious comments on works of Richard (no. 2689), Lanson (no. 2667), Saintville (nos. 2693-2699).

Vial, Fernand. Une philosophie et une morale du sentiment : Luc de Clapiers, marquis de Vauvenargues. Droz, 1938. 304 p. 2704

Attempt to integrate V.'s philosophical and moral ideas into broad and comprehensive system. Lofty sentimentalism which has inspired V.'s private life and has been source of his aspirations, appears also to form basis of V.'s ethics and metaphysics. All apparent discrepancies and contradictions, his practical optimism, and intellectual pessimism, which have baffled V.'s commentators, easily reconciled in this profoundly human and adaptable system.

Reviews : E. Eggli in MLR 35:253-57, 1940. " ... cet ouvrage est actuellement le commentaire le plus détaillé que nous ayons de cette œuvre ... analyses pénétrantes, ... indications utiles ... sur les sources de Vauvenargues..." (p. 257); B. A. Morrissette in MLN 55:312-14, 1940 (disagrees completely with Vial's thesis); A. Schinz in FR 13:62-64, 1939-40.

— Vauvenargues et Voltaire. *See* 1736. 2705

Several instances of V.'s influence on Voltaire : Voltaire was led by V.'s advice to modify his opinion of Corneille, Racine, Pascal.

Villemain, A. F. Vauvenargues. *In his :* Cours de littérature française : tableau de la littérature au XVIIIe siècle. *See* 82, v. 2, p. 1-16. 2706

On theme, V. as disciple of 18th century, which is only partly accurate, Villemain, like Vinet, repeats errors of all ultraconservative critics.

Vinet, Alexandre. Vauvenargues. *In his :* Histoire de la littérature française au dix-huitième siècle. Chez les éditeurs, 1853. 1:275-313. 2707

V. is " un astre égaré dans l'époque qui le vit naître." Conclusion based on attentive study of V.'s works, but disproved by recent commentators.

Voltaire. Éloge funèbre des officiers qui sont morts dans la guerre de 1741, 23:249-62; Discours de réception à l'Académie française, 23:205-17; Relation de la mort du chevalier de la Barre, 25:501-16; Commentaires sur Corneille, 31:171-600; 32:1-375 *passim;* Note sur une pensée de Vauvenargues, 31:41-42; Correspondance, 36:203-447, *passim* (1743-1749). *In his :* Œuvres complètes, ed. Moland, *See* 1628. 2708

Eloquent and touching testimony of Voltaire's veneration for V. Also examples of high esteem of Voltaire for V.'s literary taste which prompted him to seek V.'s advice and to follow it. V.'s influence on Voltaire attested by Raymond Naves in : Le goût de Voltaire, no. 1788, p. 364.

Wallas, May. Luc de Clapiers, Marquis de Vauvenargues. Cambridge, University press, 1928. 308 p. 2709

Still best informed *ouvrage d'ensemble* on V.'s biography. Occasionally corrected, on minor points, by latest researches of Saintville (nos. 2693-2699). Sound treatment of V.'s ethics in spite of pretentious phraseology. Places V. accurately between 17th and 18th centuries, and finds him related to both.

Reviews : G. Ascoli in Rcr ns 97:506-07, 1930 : " Excellente étude, attentive, complète, précise "; G. Lanson in RHL 36:293-97, 1929 : " Actuellement le meilleur et le plus sûr guide."

Zyromski, Ernest. Le lyrisme de Vauvenargues. Feu 19:509-14, 1925. 2710

Outline, and rough draft of work " de synthèse et d'édification," which death did not allow Zyromski to write.

Antoine Rivarol
(Nos. 2711-2736)

ANDREW R. MOREHOUSE

La fiche bibliographique française. Sept. 5, 1923. 2711

Gives complete bibliography of works by R., dates and places of publication, publishers, etc., and list of works about R.

Rivarol, Antoine. Œuvres choisies. Ed. M. de Lescure. Librairie des bibliophiles, 1880. 2 v. 2712

Vol. 1 contains *De l'universalité de la langue française, Discours sur l'homme intellectuel et moral, Maximes et pensées, Anecdotes et bon mots.* Vol. 2 made up completely of articles from *Journal politique national,* 1st and 2nd series.

— Œuvres complètes de Rivarol, précédées d'une notice sur sa vie. Collin, 1808. 5 v. 2713

" ... Une édition où manque à peu près un tiers de ses *Œuvres,* où se rencontrent ... des libelles dirigés contre lui, et où lui sont attribuées des pages qu'il n'a pas écrites..." (Le Breton, no. 2730, p. v). Contains, among other works, *De l'universalité de la langue française* (Vol. 2); *Prospectus d'un nouveau dictionnaire de la langue française; De l'homme intellectuel et moral* (another title : De la nature du langage en général) (Vol. 1); *Première lettre écrite à Mr. Necker, sur son livre de l'importance des opinions religieuses; Se-*

*conde lettre à Mr. Necker sur la morale;
Lettre à M. le Président de***, sur le globe
aérostatique...; Sur Florian; Lettre sur
l'ouvrage de Mme de Staël, intitulé : De
l'influence des passions...; Songe d'Athalie;
Essai sur l'amitié; Traduction en prose et
en vers de quelques fragments de l'Énéide*
(Vol. 2); *De la vie et des poèmes du Dante;
L'Enfer, poème du Dante (avec des notes
sur chaque chant); Récit du portier du
Sieur Pierre-Augustin Caron de Beaumarchais; Le chou et le navet* (Vol. 3);
Extraits du Journal politique-national
(Vol. 4); *Le petit almanach de nos grands
hommes; De la vie politique, de la fuite et de
la capture de M. La Fayette; Portrait du
duc d'Orléans et de Mme de Genlis; Pensées, traits et bon mots* (Vol. 5).
For works not by R. in *Œuvres complètes,* see Le Breton, no. 2730, p. 375-82.

— De l'universalité de la langue française.
1st ed. Berlin, 1784; 2nd ed. Paris, 1785,
which differs textually from the 1st edition;
3rd ed. corrected by Rivarol, Hambourg,
1797. BN has all three editions. Text of
3rd ed. corresponds with that of Œuvres
complètes, 1808. 2714-2715

Modern editions :
Discours sur l'universalité de la langue
française. Éd. crit. par Marcel Hervier. Delagrave, 1929. 144 p.
De l'universalité de la langue française.
Texte établi et commenté par Th.
Suran. Didier, 1930. 384 p.
Discours sur l'universalité de la langue
française. Aux dépens de la société
des bibliophiles havrais. Firmin-
Didot, 1934.
Discours sur l'universalité de la langue
française. Avec une notice biographique, une notice historique et littéraire,
des notes explicatives, des jugements,
un questionnaire sur le discours et des
sujets de devoirs, par Maurice Faver-
geat. Larousse, 1936. 76 p.
De l'universalité de la langue française;
ed. by W. W. Comfort... Boston,
New York, Ginn, [1919]. 62 p.

— Œuvres de Rivarol. Études sur sa vie et
son esprit par Sainte-Beuve, Arsène Houssaye, Armand Malitourne. Didier, 1852.
319 p. 2716

Introduction by above-named writers.
Includes series of extracts taken from his
important works on metaphysics, ethics,
political science, and from his *Discours
sur l'universalité de la langue française.*
Contains some of his poetry, essay on
Dante, and *Le dernier jour de la royauté.*

— Mémoires de Rivarol, avec des notes et des
éclaircissements historiques... Baudoin,
1824. 386 p. 2717

Misnamed. *Mémoires* are merely an
incomplete collection of his articles in
Journal politique national, which had
already been printed in Vol. 4 of *Œuvres
complètes* (no. 2713), and of which
Mémoires are exact reproduction. Cf.,
however, Le Breton, no. 2730, p. 362.

— Pensées inédites de Rivarol, suivies de deux
discours sur la philosophie moderne et sur
la souveraineté du peuple. Boudon, 1836.
237 p. 2718

Edited by Claude-François, R.'s
brother. "En général, Claude-François
en a retranché toutes les hardiesses qui
alarmaient sa concience de pur royaliste
ou de chrétien." (Le Breton, no. 2730,
p. 370). Text very suspect.

— Littérature : Universalité de la langue
française; Voltaire et Fontenelle; Petit
almanach de nos grands hommes; Mme de
Staël; Le génie et le talent. Politique :
Journal politique national; Actes des apô-
tres; Petit dictionnaire de la Révolution.
Philosophie : Lettres à M. Necker; Discours
préliminaire à un dictionnaire de la langue
française. Fragments et pensées littéraires, politiques et philosophiques. Lettres. Rivaroliana. Appendice : documents,
bibliographie... Mercure de France, 1906.
434 p. (Collection des plus belles pages).
2719

Review : E. Faguet. Rivarol. Rev
61:38-43, March 1, 1906 : " Je ne saurais
reprocher à ce volume que d'être un peu
trop volumineux. Il est de quatre cent
trente pages très petit texte. C'est beaucoup trop de Rivarol. Le Rivarol des
gens de goût tient en deux cents pages
texte moyen et je lui fais peut-être encore
la part trop grande ... *Basta la metà.*"
(p. 38).

— Discours sur l'universalité de la langue
française. Ed. by Marcel Hervier. *See*
380. 2720

Review : U. T. Holmes in BA 5:198,
1931 : "... first critical edition ever
published of the prize discourse... edition
is admirably done and both author and
editor should give much pleasure to the
reader."

Barbey d'Aurevilly, Jules Amédée. Rivarol. *In his :* Les critiques, ou les juges
jugés. Frinzine, 1885. p. 245-72. (Les
œuvres et les hommes, 1860-1895. v. 6).
2721

Judgments based on Sainte-Beuve's (no. 2734) and Lescure's (no. 2731) studies. Richly colored portrait. Barbey considers R. most gifted man of 18th century, on a par with Voltaire, Buffon, Montesquieu. As a conversationalist he was incomparable : " Ni avant, ni après Rivarol on n'entendit et on ne vit de conversation semblable à la sienne " (p. 249). He was a born journalist in whom journalism rose to heights of history : " Jamais impersonnalité plus détachée et plus haute, jamais sang-froid plus saisissant et plus tuant ne sont tombés d'une plume, depuis Tacite." (p. 263).

Bourget, Paul. Rivarol. *In his :* Études et portraits. Lemerre, 1889-1906, 1:39-57.
2722

Psychological study which Le Breton calls a " fine et pénétrante étude." R. emerges " un homme supérieur .... capable d'égaler Montesquieu et s'amusant au rôle de persifleur .... La pensée chez lui est d'un philosophe de premier ordre; l'esprit est d'un incorrigible railleur... " (*passim*, p. 44, 47, 49).

Brunetière, Ferdinand. Rivarol. *In his :* Histoire et littérature. Calmann Lévy, 1886-1896. 2:271-98. 2723

Succinct and penetrating essay on R.'s life and works, occasioned by Lescure's *Rivarol et la société française pendant la Révolution*, no. 2731. Brunetière denies R. place among moralists because of his limitations. He moralized about *men* rather than about *man*, about society rather than nature. And he disagrees with Lescure (no. 2731) and Sainte-Beuve (no. 2734), who believe that R. would have been a great writer if Revolution and early death had not intervened.

Faguet, Emile. Rivarol. Rev 61:38-43, March 1, 1906. 2724

Identifies R. primarily as " un narrateur, polémiste et moraliste." As political thinker and critic he is relatively weak. *Discours sur l'universalité de la langue française* has no scientific value but stands out as work of art (p. 39). R. as brilliant moralist as La Rochefoucauld, with broader base of experience. His maxims are proverbs of *gens d'esprit*.

Dimier, Louis. Rivarol. *In his :* Les maîtres de la contre-révolution au dix-neuvième siècle. Nouvelle librairie nationale, 1917. p. 78-97. 2725

Dimier, historian and critic of French painting, and member of the *Action française*, gives succinct description of R. as counter-revolutionary, with illustrative citations taken primarily from R.'s *Journal politique national*. " En lui [Rivarol] ... se rend sensible comme en nul autre, la perpétuité de l'esprit français." (p. 80-81).

Gass, K. E. Antoine de Rivarol (1753-1801) und der Ausgang der französischen Aufklärung. Hagen, Baake, 1938. 274 p.
2726

With certain reservations (notably, failure to discuss role that Diderot, Vauvenargues and Rousseau played in development of R.'s thought and, in R.'s attack on Condillac, exaggerating triumph of metaphysics over sensualism), Dieckmann believes Gass' book to be one of most original contributions to our knowledge of R. " Quiconque désormais lira Rivarol, devra recourir à ce livre pour trouver les sommets de sa pensée analysés, étudiés sous leurs rapports différents " (review below p. 186).
Review : H. Dieckmann in RR 31:183-87, 1940.

Gourmont, Remy de. Rivarol. *In his :* Promenades littéraires, 3ᵉ série. Mercure de France, 8th ed. 1919. p. 95-165. 2727

Full-length critical study founded on Le Breton's biography, no. 2730, containing penetrating comments on R.'s ideas, particularly political ideas (" la philosophie politique est dans Rivarol. M. Taine explique la Révolution. Rivarol la fait comprendre." p. 135), and sprinkled with apt quotations. Gourmont concludes that Rivarol... " était un grand et bel esprit dont la floraison était éclatante et la maturité un peu tourmentée." (p. 97). In same volume is interesting article on Champcenetz, R.'s early literary collaborator, whom R. called his " clair de lune." (p. 166-87).

Henriot, Emile. Rivarol, traducteur de Dante. Temps, August 31, 1926. 2728

Discusses R.'s theories of translation, and by comparison of his version of Francesca da Rimini incident in Canto V of the *Inferno* with other French translations, shows his superiority and faults. *See also :* Le Breton's excellent comments on Rivarol as a translator, no. 2730, p. 114-21; and Sainte-Beuve no. 2734 p. 169-70.

Latzarus, Louis. La vie paresseuse de Rivarol. Plon-Nourrit, 1926, 259 p.

2729

Valuable for rapid introduction to R.'s life and works. Popular, readable, lively, dramatic distillation of source biographies of Lescure (no. 2731) and Le Breton (no. 2730). No references or authorities cited. No index.

Review : A. Bellessort in Jdeb, Aug. 11, 1926, p. 3.

Le Breton, André. Rivarol, sa vie, ses idées, son talent d'après des documents nouveaux. Hachette, 1895. 388 p. 2730

Bibliography (p. 355-84) contains chronological list of all R.'s works published in his lifetime and after his death, scattered and incomplete works printed in contemporary biographies, correspondence, false attributions, and lost works. For each title valuable, pertinent information is given. Preface contains critical appraisal of important works about R. Le Breton's work is indispensable.

Although written with impassioned zeal in favor of R., is best, most complete, and authoritative work concerning his life, works, and art. Uses new and original documents and succeeds in penetrating his mind and spirit. Gives valuable information concerning moral and intellectual *milieu* of Revolution. R. shown as " ... un homme de tradition et de progrès ... un grand amoureux du verbe... " and most intelligent of the counter-revolutionaries.

Reviews : R. Doumic, Chamfort and Rivarol. *In his : Études sur la littérature française*, 1st ser. 2nd ed., Perrin, 1896. p. 155-79; R. de Gourmont. *Rivarol. In his : Promenades littéraires*, 3rd ser., Mercure de France, 8th ed., 1919. p. 95-165; G. Pellissier. *Deux moralistes à la fin du XVIIIᵉ siècle : Chamfort et Rivarol. In his : Études sur la littérature contemporaine*, Perrin, 1898. p. 339-52.

Lescure, M. F. A. de. Rivarol et la société française pendant la révolution et l'émigration (1753-1801). Plon. 1883. 516 p.

2731

" M. de Lescure laissait dans l'ombre bien des points de la biographie de Rivarol, et y mêlait des traits empruntés à la légende; il ne nous révélait qu'à demi l'homme et ne nous faisait point du tout connaître le penseur." (Le Breton, no. 2730, p. II). Still useful, however, especially for pictures of French society

just before and after its collapse, and in which R. played role of pamphleteer and fearless *émigré*. Lescure an amateur with tendency to prolixity. Many of his digressions interesting and enlightening. No index but detailed table of contents. Valuable bibliographical notes at bottom of pages.

Reviews : P. Bourget *in his : Études et portraits*, Lemerre, 1889-1906, 1:39-57; F. Brunetière *in his : Histoire et littérature*, Calmann Lévy, 1896, 2:271-98; W. F. Rae in TB 89:513-27, 1890.

Poulet-Malassis, Auguste. Écrits et pamphlets de Rivarol... Lemerre, 1877. 143 p.

2732-2733

" Comble quelques-unes des lacunes de l'édition des *Œuvres complètes*, mais où il y a du faux Rivarol " (Le Breton, no. 2730, p. V). Contains *Dialogue entre Fontenelle et Voltaire* (1785), *Lettre sur la capture de M. l'abbé Maury à Péronne* (1789), *Conseils donnés à S. M. Louis XVI en 1791...*, *Réponse de M. le baron de Grimm ... à la lettre de M. Chassebœuf de Volney* (1792), *Lettre à la noblesse française...* (1792). Bibliography.

Sainte-Beuve, C.-A. Rivarol. *In his : Causeries du lundi*, 3ᵉ ed. Garnier, [1857-62], 5:62-84. 2734

In broad outline, enlightening introduction to R.'s character and thought. He identifies R. as best critic and, before Burke, best political writer of end of century. He was moved at times by deep religious insight. Potentially great writer, the spirit of the age stifled stirrings of gifted mind. For minor errors concerning R.'s origins and early years, consult Le Breton, no. 2730. Essay dated Oct. 27, 1851.

— Chênedollé : relations avec Rivarol. *In his : Chateaubriand et son groupe littéraire.* Calmann Lévy, 1889. 2:156-80. 2735

Sainte-Beuve quotes at length from Chênedollé's *Ma première visite à Rivarol*, which contains vivid and authentic account of R.'s prowess as conversationalist and critic, a critic, among others, of Voltaire, Buffon, Montesquieu, Rousseau, and Pascal. To which Sainte-Beuve adds his customary penetrating comments. Chênedollé text somewhat suspect. (Cf. p. 157, Note 1).

Saintsbury, George. Chamfort and Rivarol. *In his : Miscellaneous essays.* New York, Scribner, 1892. p. 42-80. 2736

Valuable critical appraisal of R. as writer of maxims. His other works only briefly referred to. It was R.'s misfortune to have been born in age destitute of literary forms and ideas. Forty years later he might have been a rival to Mérimée or Sainte-Beuve by his power of style and faculty of appreciation. And so he remains frustrated as one who merely had "unexampled powers of malign epigram" and who lacked sincerity.

Anne Thérèse de Marguenat de Courcelles, marquise de Lambert
(Nos. 2737-2760)

ANNE C. JONES

Lambert, Anne Thérèse. Réflexions nouvelles sur les femmes. np., nd. 34 p.   2737

Edition which Madame de L. tried to suppress. "Je crus les anéantir en achetant toute l'édition; cela n'a fait qu'augmenter la curiosité. Le manuscrit sur les Femmes est si défiguré, qu'on ne sait ce que c'est; on a ôté le commencement et la fin, qui apprenaient pourquoi il avait été fait."
Œuvres de Madame la marquise de Lambert, Ganeau, 1761. 2:212.

— Discours sur la différence qu'il y a de la réputation à la considération. (*In :* Montesquieu, [Charles Louis de Secondat, *baron* de.]. Deux opuscules de Montesquieu. *See* 1462, p. 57-62.)   2738

— Avis d'une mère à son fils et à sa fille. Ganeau, 1728. 212 p.   2739

First edition of *Avis* which had been circulated in manuscript form since 1703 or before.

Ascoli, Georges. Essai sur l'histoire des idées féministes en France du XVIᵉ siècle à la Révolution. RSH 13:25-57; 161-84, 1906.   2740

Very little material on Madame de L. but interesting bibliography on feminist movement.

Boulan, Emile. Figures du dix-huitième siècle : les sages : Fontenelle et Madame de Lambert. *See* 265.   2741

Points out close friendship between Madame de L. and Fontenelle and shows them both as moderns who have broken with 17th century tradition.

Broglie, Emmanuel de. Les mardis et les mercredis de la marquise de Lambert. Corr 179:140-62; 319-45, 1895.   2742

Lively and interesting picture of Madame de L.'s salon. Article can be read with pleasure for atmosphere of 18th century. List of guests can not be relied upon, however. For example, Broglie states, without giving proof, that Dancourt, Lesage, and Watteau frequented the salon.

Brunetière, Ferdinand. Les salons : Madame de Lambert. *In his :* Histoire de la littérature française classique; le dix-huitième siècle. *See* 1296, v. 3, p. 102-09.   2743

Superficial judgment of Madame de L.'s salon. Considers it little more than center of literary and scientific *préciosité.*

Carré, J. R. La philosophie de Fontenelle ou le sourire de la raison. *See* 1175, p. 517-28.   2744

Friendship of Fontenelle and Mme de L. well handled in excellent chapter.

Cherel, Albert. Fénelon au XVIIIᵉ siècle en France. Hachette, 1917. p. 19-20; 316-18; 342-43.   2745

Interesting comparison of Fénelon's ideas on education of girls with those of Madame de L. Fénelon's influence on Madame de L. and their correspondence.

Cougny, Edme. Montesquieu et Madame de Lambert : petite question de propriété littéraire. MSSO 11:235-52, 1878. Separate, Versailles, Aubert, 1877. 22 p. (Copy at Harvard).   2746

Cougny tries to show that Montesquieu borrowed from Madame de L.'s *Discours sur la différence qu'il y a de la considération à la réputation* for his *Réflexions sur la considération et la réputation.* (Montesquieu, *Œuvres,* Laboulaye ed., 7:70-75). Cougny could not have known of M.'s letter (*Pensées et fragments inédits de Montesquieu,* 1899, 1:62-63) which says that article published in Madame de L.'s *Œuvres* was his own, found among her papers after her death in 1733.

Dauvergne, Robert. La marquise de Lambert à l'Hôtel de Nevers (1698-1733). Albin Michel, 1947. 40 p.   2746A

Reconstruction with plans of Mme de L.'s home, rue Colbert. Inventory of rooms, furniture, pictures, library, *objets d'art,* clothing. Interesting documentary material for any study of 18th century life. Excellent bibliography and notes on Mme de L.'s family history.

Droz, François Xavier Joseph. Compte rendu des œuvres complètes de Madame de Lambert. FJE 2:1-4, Aug. 11, 1813. 2747

Article, signed " T." is one which Sainte-Beuve refutes : " L'excellent M. Droz, jugeant les écrits de Madame de Lambert, était frappé de ce qu'une telle morale, qui prêche ouvertement l'ambition, renferme de dangereux et même d'absurde..." (*Causeries du lundi*, 4th ed., v. 4, p. 221). Interesting as showing a critical point of view toward Mme de L. before Sainte-Beuve's article.

Dubled, Victor. Le salon de la marquise de Lambert. *In his :* La société française du XVIe siècle au XXe siècle. *See* 184, p. 165-205. 2748

Madame de L. as a feminist. Comparison of her salon with Rambouillet. Author has used Broglie's article (no. 2742) extensively.

Giraud, Charles. Le salon de Madame de Lambert. JS p. 112-27, Feb. 1880. 2749

Very interesting comparison of salon of Madame de L. with those of the Duchesse du Maine at Sceaux and of the Maréchale de Villars at Vaux-Villars. One of best articles on Madame de L.

Gréard, Octave. Mme de Lambert. *In his :* L'éducation des femmes par les femmes. Hachette, 1889, p. 169-216. 2750

Madame de L. as a feminist. Her ideas on education of women.

Lescure, [M. F. A.] de. Étude biographique et littéraire sur la marquise de Lambert. (*In :* Lambert, Anne Thérèse, etc. Œuvres morales de la Marquise de Lambert. Librairie des bibliophiles, 1883. p. i-xlviii). 2751

— Le couvent de Fontenelle; la marquise de Lambert. *In his :* La société française au dix-huitième siècle; les femmes philosophes. *See* 1731, p. 9-45. 2752

Considers Madame de L. as one of first *philosophes*. Interesting point of view rather sentimentally treated. Many details from Giraud's article (no. 2749).

Loménie, Louis de. De l'influence des salons littéraires sur la littérature du dix-huitième siècle. RCL 1:37-39, Dec. 26, 1863; 57-58, Jan. 2, 1864; 125-28, Feb. 13, 1864; 369-73, June 11, 1864. 2753

General article on Madame de L., with specific attention to Quarrel of ancients and moderns.

Mason, Amelia Ruth (Gere). An antichamber of the Académie française. *In her :* The women of the French salons. *See* 190, p. 135-45. 2754

Material largely from Sainte-Beuve (no. 2758). Places Salon in Hôtel Lambert, Ile Saint-Louis, instead of Hôtel Mazarin.

Picard, Roger. Deux grands bureaux d'esprit. *In his :* Les salons littéraires et la société française, 1610-1789. *See* 194, p. 180-87. 2755

Attempts to present Madame de L. in lively, casual manner. Result is careless and inaccurate. Picard assumes that Fénelon frequented the Salon, that there was a secret marriage between Madame de L. and Sainte-Aulaire, and states that famous reconciliation of Ancients and Moderns took place in her home. Fénelon, in exile from 1697 on, corresponded infrequently with Madame de L. D'Argenson only hints at a " tendresse constante et presque platonicienne." For dinner party given in honor of Madame Dacier and La Motte see *Œuvres de Madame de Staal*, Renouard, 1821, 1:294.

Reynold, Gonzague de. Madame de Lambert et son salon. *In :* Centre international de synthèse, Paris. L'hôtel de Nevers et le centre international de synthèse. Allocutions ... à l'inauguration officielle du Centre. Renaissance du livre, 1929. p. 27-38. *Also in his :* Le XVIIe siècle. Montreal, Éditions de l'arbre, [c1944]. p. 273-78. 2756

Madame de L. reveals new tendencies while remaining faithful to tradition. Gives to woman intellectual role in society. Good article. *See* no. 266.

Roustan, Mario. Les philosophes et les salons. *In his :* Les philosophes et la société française au XVIIIe siècle. *See* 1071, p. 241-64. 2757

Importance of women in 18th century salons. Reproaches Brunetière (no. 2743), for his bitter attitude.

Sainte-Beuve, Charles Augustin. Madame de Lambert. *In his :* Causeries du Lundi. *See* 267. 2758

One of first studies on Madame de L. and source of much that has been written

since. Notes in her writings transition to
a new age. Shows her salon as midway
between Madame de Rambouillet's and
Madame Necker's. Somewhat superficial but can be read with pleasure and
profit. Article dated June 1851.

Tilley, Arthur. The decline of the age of
Louis XIV. *See* 1076, p. 239-41, 421-28.
2759

Excellent and well-documented book
on period. Interesting comments on
English translations of Madame de L.'s
works. There seems, however, to be
slight mistake in pointing out the edition
of *Réflexions nouvelles sur les femmes* which
Madame de L. tried to suppress. Tilley
says (note 2, p. 241) that it was 1727
edition, *par une dame de la Cour*, whereas
it was probably edition (n. d.) of 34 pages
which Tilley does not list.

Zimmerman, J. P. La morale laïque au
commencement du XVIIIe siècle; Madame de
Lambert. *See* 268. 2760

Excellent analysis of Madame de L.'s
religion and philosophy. Opposing Sainte-
Beuve (no. 2758), Zimmerman believes
that her salon merely continues 17th
century tradition.

Periodical Literature
(Nos. 2761-2866)

GABRIEL BONNO

Bibliography and General Studies
(Nos. 2761-2769).

The material in this section is, in essence,
of such nature that a logical arrangement of it
on an alphabetical or a chronological basis
seems neither desirable nor possible. Items
can be located by consulting the Volume's
alphabetical Index.

Bonno, Gabriel. Liste chronologique des
périodiques de langue française du dix-
huitième siècle. MLQ 5:3-25, 1944. *See*
10. 2761

Delisle de Sales, Jean-Claude Izouard,
called. Essai sur le journalisme depuis
1735 jusqu'à l'an 1800. Colas. 1811.
302 p. 2761A

Only last 50 pages really bear on
subject for our period; sketchy and
polemical; denounces "le pouvoir des-
tructeur du journalisme"; especially bitter
against Desfontaines and Fréron.

Hatin, Eugène. Histoire politique et littéraire de la presse en France avec une

introduction historique sur les origines du
journal et la bibliographie générale des
journaux depuis leur origine. Poulet-
Malassis, 1859-61, 8 v. 2762

Still remains most comprehensive and
detailed study of subject; stresses exter-
nals more than analytical study of contents; v. 2, 3:1665-1789.

— Les gazettes de Hollande et la presse
clandestine au XVIIe et XVIIIe siècle. Pince-
bourde, 1865. 232 p. 2763

Supplements the *Histoire* (no. 2762)
with results of research conducted in
Belgium and Holland. First part gives
interesting data on circulation of foreign
periodicals in France; second part (p. 135-
225) bibliographical list, with comments
stressing chiefly biographical details
about journalists and external history of
periodicals.

— Bibliographie historique et critique de la
presse périodique française, ou catalogue...
précédé d'un Essai historique et statistique
sur la naissance et les progrès de la presse
périodique dans les deux mondes. Didot,
1866. 660 p. 2764

Largely based on same material as
previous contributions by Hatin (nos.
2762-2763) with additional information on
minor journals.

Mornet, Daniel. Les enseignements des
bibliothèques privées (1750-1780). *See*
2116. 2765

Precise and highly interesting statistical
data on diffusion of 30 literary journals,
based on catalogues of 500 private
libraries. Shows leading periodicals rank-
ing as follows : 1. those of Desfontaines;
2. those of Leclerc; 3. Fréron's *Année
littéraire;* 4. *Journal des savants.*

— Les origines intellectuelles de la Révolution française (1715-1787). Colin, 1933.
552 p. *See* 1062. 2766

Describes growing importance of journals for diffusion of *esprit philosophique*,
especially after 1748; gives many precise
and interesting data on circulation and
prices of more important periodicals; p.
346-56 : *Les journaux provinciaux.*

Reviews : G. Lefèvre in AHRF 11:366-
72, 1934; A. Meynier in Rfr 87:5-16,
1934.

Pienaar, W. J. B. English influences in
Dutch literature and Justus Van Effen as
intermediary. Cambridge univ. press,
1929. 260 p. *See* 2944. 2767

Chapter VI, *The reviews and the further spread of English literature*, gives general account of treatment of English matters by several French journals published in Holland : *Journal littéraire de La Haye; Bibliothèque anglaise; Mémoires littéraires de la Grande-Bretagne; L'Europe savante.* Review : J. Boyd in MLR 25:238-41, 1930.

Reesink, Hendrika Johana. L'Angleterre et la littérature anglaise dans les trois plus anciens périodiques français de Hollande de 1684 à 1709. *See* 1153, 2430.   2768

Deals with : *Nouvelles de la République des lettres* (1684-1687); *Bibliothèque universelle et historique* (1686-1693); *Histoire des ouvrages des savans* (1687-1709). Clearly describes their contribution to diffusion of English literature on continent and gives excellent analytical index of articles and book reviews on English matters. Reviews : G. Ascoli in RLC 13:209-12, 1933. Brief mention in MLN 49:350, 1934, and J. G. Robertson in MLR 28:389-90, 1933.

Weill, Georges. Le journal; origines, évolution et rôle de la presse périodique. La renaissance du livre, 1934. 450 p.   2769

Clear, readable survey; necessarily sketchy on our period (p. 86-103) and mostly based on Hatin (no. 2762); general bibliography of the field: p. 419-32.

Leclerc, Desfontaines, Prévost, Fréron, and Suard
(Nos. 2770-2803)

Leclerc
(Cf. nos. 2425-2431)

Leclerc, Jean (1657-1736). Bibliothèque universelle et historique (1686-1693). Amsterdam, Wolfgang, 26 v. dont 1 v. de tables.   2770

Monthly; collaborators : Cornand de La Croze, Jacques Bernard. Gives detailed and fairly objective reviews of recent books, with special attention to theology, ecclesiastical and civil history, philosophy and the sciences; about one fifth of reviews devoted to English books; officially prohibited but widely circulated in France; analytical index in Reesink, (nos. 1153, 2768), 197-288.

— Bibliothèque choisie (1703-1713). Amsterdam, Schelte, 28 v. dont 1 v. de tables.   2771

Twice or three times a year; similar in scope and character to the *Bibliothèque universelle* (no. 2770); includes important biographical articles by Leclerc (Locke, Burnet).

— Bibliothèque ancienne et moderne (1714-1730). Amsterdam, Mortier; puis La Haye, Husson, 29 v.   2772

Quarterly; chiefly devoted to theology, philosophy, and sciences; shows marked hostility to Descartes, Spinoza, and English deists; strongly supports Newton's views in physics and favorably reviews works of his followers.

Barnes, Annie. Jean Leclerc (1657-1736) et la république des lettres. *See* 1114, 2426.   2773

Precise and thorough study of Leclerc in his many-sided activities and cosmopolitan interests; discussion of his periodicals chiefly stresses their contribution to diffusion of English works on theology, philosophy, and sciences; *Amitiés anglaises* : p. 154-87; good index of names. Reviews : D. F. Bond in MP 37:213-14, 1939-40; D. Mornet in RHL 46:131-32, 1939; briefer mention (in Dutch) in Neo 24:303, 1938-1939.

Desfontaines

Desfontaines, Pierre François Guyot, (1685-1745). Le nouvelliste du Parnasse ou Réflexions sur les ouvrages nouveaux. Chaubert, 1730-1732, 52 numbers in 3 v.   2774

Announced as weekly letter, but not always regularly published. Collaborators : Fréron, Granet. Devotes more space to *belles-lettres* than older periodicals and often takes rather sarcastic tone in discussion of recent books and plays. Praises Voltaire but publishes fictitious letters to editor bitterly criticizing him. Defends French poetry against attacks of La Motte.

— Observations sur les écrits modernes. Chaubert, 1735-1743, 34 v.   2775

Collaborators : Fréron, Granet, Mairault. Similar scope and tendencies to preceding title, but becomes more openly hostile to Voltaire. *Privilège* finally cancelled after complaints from authors and publishers against polemical tone of articles.

— Jugemens sur quelques ouvrages nouveaux. Avignon, Girou, 1744-1745, 11 v.   2776

Published under assumed name of Burlon de la Busbaquerie. Collaborators : Mairault, Destrées. Tone of criticism somewhat milder than in *Observations* (no. 2775).

Boivin, Henri. Les dossiers de l'abbé Des Fontaines aux archives de la Bastille (1724-1744). RHL 14:55-73, 1907.   2777

Based on documents from Bastille archives now kept at *Bibliothèque de l'Arsenal.* Detention at Bicêtre in April-May 1725 of Desfontaines accused of sodomy; prosecution against him in 1736 for "un libelle diffamatoire contre l'Académie"; similar difficulties in 1743, indirectly causing cancellation of *privilège* for *Observations sur les écrits modernes* (no. 2775).

— Deux pamphlets antiacadémiques de l'abbé Des Fontaines (1735). RHL 17:354-63, 1910.   2778

Fictitious speeches ironically attributed by Des Fontaines to abbés Séguy and Terrasson, and ridiculing several members of the Academy.

[Quentin, H.] La mort de l'abbé Des Fontaines. Par Paul d'Estrée, [*pseud.*] RHL 15:126-28, 1908.   2779

Letter from Parisian bookseller Chaubert to Jesuit Cordier, showing pious attitude of Des Fontaines at time of his death.

La Porte, Joseph de, *abbé.* Desfontaines, P. F. G., *abbé.* L'esprit de l'abbé Des Fontaines. London, Clément, 1757, 4 v.   2780

Topical arrangement of short extracts from three journals; biographical sketch and list of works by and about Des Fontaines in v. 1.

Nisard, Charles. L'abbé Desfontaines. *In his :* Les ennemis de Voltaire. Amyot, 1853, p. 1-168.   2781

Discussion of life and works stresses his quarrels with Voltaire; praises the "sagacité exquise" of Des Fontaines, but does not make methodical study of his literary criticism.

Prévost
(Cf. nos. 777-834)

Prévost d'Exiles, A. F., *abbé.* Le pour et contre. Didot, 1733-1740, 20 v. et 2 v. de tables (With Des Fontaines and Lefebvre

de Saint-Marc). *See* 777. (Copies at Harvard and Princeton.)   2782

Weekly. Chiefly literary journal, with much space given to anecdotes and lighter matters. Carefully avoids discussion of religious and political subjects. Still influenced by French classical taste, but with cosmopolitan viewpoint and enlightened appreciation of English literature. Widely read and influential in arousing curiosity and interest in English literature on the continent.

— Le pour et contre. The Hague, 1733-1738, 10 v.   2783

Counterfeited edition printed by Dutch publisher Vanderklotten. Little known in France, but had wider diffusion abroad than genuine edition. Out of its 398 articles, only 296 are reproduced from Paris edition, others being gathered by Dutch publisher from various European periodicals. Shows less sympathy for English culture than genuine edition and reflects Protestant viewpoint in discussion of religious matters. *See* Robertson, no. 2786.

Havens, George R. The Abbé Prévost and Shakespeare. *See* 804.   2784

Important *mise au point*, showing Prévost's real attitude towards Shakespeare much less original and enthusiastic than had been previously maintained. Traces English sources (Rowe, Gildon) of longest article on Shakespeare in *Pour et contre* (v. XIV, Jan. 1738). Shows that Prévost, speaking in his own name is rather lukewarm, although he makes effort to be just and moderate in his criticism.

— The abbé Prévost and English literature. *See* 805.   2785

Systematic and exhaustive discussion of Prévost's references to English literature, with separate chapters on his treatment of : Shakespeare, Addison, Dryden, Milton, Pope, Shaftesbury, Steele, Swift, Lillo. Shows that Prévost, still largely influenced by classical taste, but with open-minded conception of principle of relativity, is most successful in dealing with more classical English writers : Dryden, Steele, Addison, and Pope. Accurate and thorough study superseding all previous discussions of subject.

Robertson, M[ysie] E. I. Quelques notes sur la contrefaçon hollandaise du Pour et contre. RLC 15:111-18, 1935.   2786

Based on careful examination of counterfeited Dutch edition of *Pour et contre* (*see* no. 2783). Points out most significant differences between two editions.

Schrœder, Victor. L'abbé Prévost journaliste. *See* 829. 2787

General description of topics discussed in *Pour et contre*. Superseded by Havens (nos. 2784-85) for references to English literature. Mentions literary judgments of Prévost on several French writers, particularly Montaigne, Molière, Mme de Sévigné, Racine, Voltaire, Marivaux.

Staab, Jakob. Das Journal étranger unter dem Abbé Prévost und seine Bedeutung für die literarischen Beziehungen zwischen England und Frankreich im Zeitalter der Aufklärung. Erlangen, Jacob, 1912. 72 p. (Diss., Strasbourg). 2788

Survey of various references to English literature contained in *Journal étranger* under Prévost's editorship, January-August 1755. Shows curiosity about Chaucer, Spenser, Sidney; mentions references to Dryden, Steele, Swift, and several minor writers. No systematic study of Prévost's critical reaction. *See* no. 2850.

Fréron
(Cf. nos. 2867-2884)

Lettres de Mme la Comtesse de *** sur quelques écrits modernes. Geneva, Philibert (Paris, Prault), September 1745-January 1746, in-12. 2789

Nineteen letters, really printed in Paris, by Prault, but published under imprint of Philibert brothers in Geneva. Suppressed in January 1746, but reprinted with some additions in 1752 (3 v. in 12). Written in light vein and chiefly devoted to literature, with occasional references to erudite and technical works. Shows hostility to Fontenelle and Piron and is mildly critical of Voltaire's poems.

Lettres sur quelques écrits de ce temps. Geneva (Paris, Duchesne), 12 v. 1749-1754. *See* 2791, 2871, 2878. 2790

Published with *tolérance verbale* and widely circulated in provinces. Suspended twice for several months through efforts of Voltaire. Takes strong stand against *philosophes* and defends memory of Des Fontaines against attacks of Voltaire.

Prator, C. H., and F. W. Gravit. The editions of Fréron's Lettres sur quelques

écrits de ce temps. MLQ 1:323-31, 1940. *See* 2871, 2878. 2791

Aims to define variants of different editions of the 13 volumes; first four volumes offer most difficulties, periodical having passed rapidly among several publishers in its early stages.

L'année littéraire. Amsterdam et Paris, Lambert (puis Panckoucke, Lacombe, Delalain, Le Jay), 1754-1790, 202 v. (Chief collaborators : Baculard d'Arnaud, Dorat, Palissot—Continued after Fréron's death (1776) by Fréron fils, Clément, abbé Grosier, abbé Royou). *See* 2867. 2792

Published on weekly basis, but not regularly; usually 40 numbers a year. Mostly reviews in form of letters, and occasionally original articles and letters addressed to editor. About 12,000 books reviewed, of which one third belong to literature proper. Five hundred and fifty-two articles or reviews devoted to foreign literatures (chiefly England, then Germany and Italy, and, to much lesser extent, Spain). Strong defender of religious tradition against *philosophes;* Voltaire attacked it as *L'âne littéraire;* supporter of monarchy, but advocating reforms in fiscal, educational, and social matters; very much interested in development of sciences. According to Van Tieghem (*see* no. 2796) " le plus intéressant, le mieux fait, et somme toute le plus équitable " of literary journals of time.

Cornou, François. Trente années de luttes contre Voltaire et les philosophes du XVIIIe siècle; Elie Fréron (1718-1776). *See* 1707. 2793

Author, a Catholic priest, frankly presents his book as " un essai de réhabilitation " and does not conceal his hostility to Voltaire. Gives precise information on Fréron's career and his relations to his contemporaries but does not overrate his importance. Readable and interesting study, in which absence of an index of names is to be regretted.

Review : E. Magne in MerF 156:729-31, June 15, 1922.

Green, Frederick Charles. Voltaire's greatest enemy. *In his :* Eighteenth-century France. New York, Appleton, 1931. p. 111-54. 2794

Does not add any specific information to Cornou (no. 2793) and reflects same sympathetic attitude towards Fréron.

Nisard, Charles. Fréron. *In his :* Les

ennemis de Voltaire. *See* 2781, p. 171-315.   2795

Chiefly anecdotic; praises Fréron's cleverness and pungency, but severely judges his character. Superseded by Cornou's book (no. 2793).

Van Tieghem, Paul. L'année littéraire comme intermédiaire en France des littératures étrangères. Rieder, 1917. (Thèse complémentaire pour le Doctorat ès lettres). *See* 2884, 3221, 3275.   2796

Gives general survey (p. 3-53) sketching history and literary doctrines of *Année littéraire* (no. 2792), followed by *Index analytique* of more significant articles bearing on foreign literatures.
Reviews : E. P. Dargan in MLN 33:357-58, 1918; J. Kessler in MP 16:223-24, 1918-19; A. Monglond in RHL 27:617-18, 1920; L. Roustan in Rcr ns 84:268-69, 1917.

Suard

Suard, Jean Baptiste Antoine (1734-1817). Gazettes et papiers anglais. David, 1760-1762, (with Palissot).   2797

Monthly. Translations of extracts from English newspapers and periodicals, chiefly devoted to politics. Continuation of similar publication begun in 1757 under title *État politique actuel de l'Angleterre*.

— Journal étranger (q. v.). Edited by Suard and Abbé Arnaud, 1760-1762. 2798

— Gazette littéraire de l'Europe. Imprimerie de la Gazette de France, 1764-1766 (with Abbé Arnaud).   2799

Weekly issues containing announcements, short extracts and brief reviews of foreign books; monthly supplements give longer extracts and more detailed discussions. Chiefly interested in English literature. About 20 articles by Voltaire.

— Variétés littéraires, ou Recueil de pièces, tant originales que traduites, concernant la philosophie, la littérature et les arts. 1768-1770, 1804, 4 v.   2800

Selected articles from the *Journal étranger* (no. 2798) and the *Gazette littéraire de l'Europe* (no. 2799) compiled by Arnaud and Suard.

— Lettres inédites de Suard à Wilkes, publiées par Gabriel Bonno. Berkeley, Univ. of California press, 1932. [161-280 p.] (CPMP, v. 15, no. 2). *See* 2940. 2801

References to some articles written by Wilkes for *Gazette littéraire de l'Europe* (no. 2799); Wilkes also sends English books and periodicals to Suard for the journal.
Review : M. Chazin in RR 24:63, 1933.

Hunter, Alfred C. J. B. A. Suard; un introducteur de la littérature anglaise en France. Champion, 1925. 193 p. (Diss., Paris). *See* 2941.   2802

Statistical data and critical comments on articles, reviews, and references concerning English literature in *Journal étranger* and *Gazette littéraire de l'Europe*; comparison of their tendencies with those of other journals; *Mercure, Journal des savants, Année littéraire, Journal encyclopédique*; shows importance of Suard's journals in French vogue of Ossian and Young.
Reviews : J. G. R[obertson] in MLR 21:235, 1926; A. F. in RLC 5:722, 1925.

Van Tieghem, Paul. Ossian en France. Rieder, 1917, 2 v. (Diss., Paris). *See* 2997.   2803

First revelation of Ossian to French readers through *Journal étranger* (I,104, 121 seq.).
Review : T. P. Cross in MP 16:439-48, 1918; E. P. Dargan in MLN 33:357-66, 1918.

Chronological List of Periodicals with Accompanying Studies
(Nos. 2804-2866)

1631-1792; Gazette de France. 163 v. Weekly : 1688-1761; semi-weekly : 1762-1792. (Special edition in small print, selling at half-price for the provinces between 1762 and 1778).   2804

Founded by Théophraste Renaudot, and called *Gazette* until 1762, when it becomes official organ of the government. Gives miscellaneous news from home and abroad, especially about courts and military events. Purely factual, without any discussion or comments.

Genet, Edme Jacques. Table ou Abrégé des 135 volumes de la Gazette de France. Gazette de France, 1766-1768, 3 v. 2805

Covers period 1631-1765.

Granges de Surgères, Anatole, *marquis* de. Répertoire historique et biographique de la Gazette de France, depuis l'origine jusqu'à la Révolution (1631-1790). Leclerc, 1902-1906, 4 v.   2806

Index of names and subjects (chiefly places and institutions) listing more important news concerning French nationals mentioned in *Gazette*. Vol. 4 has *Index des noms patronymiques et des surnoms* and *Table des matières*.

1665-1792 : Journal des savants. Édition de Paris, 111 v. 2807

Weekly, afterwards monthly (1724). Financed by government from 1702 on and written by anonymous collaborators under supervision of Chancellor of State; signed articles appear in 1779. Subscription : 16 *livres*. Reviews of recent books, with special attention to scientific matters, and also theology, philosophy, and history; limited space to *belleslettres*. Briefer mentions and announcements under title *Nouvelles littéraires*. Cautious and conservative attitude in religious and political matters. Shows growing interest in social and economic questions after 1770, occasionally supporting advocates of moderate reforms.

Table générale des matières contenues dans le Journal des Savans de l'édition de Paris (1665-1750), par abbé A. de Claustre. Briasson, 1753-1764, 10 v. 2808

1665-1792 : Journal des savants. Édition de Hollande, Amsterdam, Janson, and later (1775) Rey, 430 v. 2809

Counterfeited edition, reproducing Paris edition with additional extracts from *Mercure*, *Journal de Trévoux*, *Journal de Verdun*, *Année littéraire* and other periodicals. Forbidden in France, but had wide circulation in provinces.

Table générale alphabétique pour l'édition de Hollande (1665-1753), par T. B. Robinet. Amsterdam, Rey, 1765, 2 v. 2810

La Harpe, Jacqueline de. Le journal des savants et la renommée de Pope en France au XVIIIe siècle. Berkeley, University of California press, 1933. p. 173-215. (CPMP, v. 16, no. 2). *See* 3001. 2811

Based on Amsterdam edition. Clear and interesting discussion of French reception of Pope's works, in light of notices and articles published in *Journal* from 1717 to 1786. Shows how editors were chiefly interested in more philosophical works of Pope.

— Le journal des savants et l'Angleterre

1702-1789. CPMP 20:289-520, 1941. *See* 2950. 2812

Based on Amsterdam edition, but clearly indicates in discussion and tables of references what comes from *Mémoires de Trévoux* or from *Extraits des meilleurs journaux de l'Europe* incorporated by Dutch publishers in their edition. Precise and systematic investigation showing journal largely dependent on French translations for its information about English culture, but devoting more space to England than had been previously maintained. Chief period of interest is 1750-1760, when *Journal* accepts Newton's views on gravitation and extensively reviews works of English writers combatting Locke and Deists. Very cautious attitude in religious and political matters, conservative taste in references to English literature.
Review : D. S. Schier in RR 32:429-30, 1941.

McCutcheon, R. P. The Journal des sçavans and the Philosophical transactions of the Royal society. SP 21:626-28, 1924. 2813

No indebtedness of the *Transactions* to the *Journal*, but rather *Journal* was led by example of *Transactions* to devote more space to scientific contributions.

Morgan, Betty T. Histoire du Journal des sçavans depuis 1665 jusqu'en 1701. Les presses universitaires, 1928. 270 p. 2814

Gives interesting details on external life of *Journal* and activities of its editors. Also describes characteristic tendencies of articles in literature (heterogeneous interests often at variance with principles of classicism), in science (first appearance of experimental approach), and in philosophy (conflicting influences of cartesian spirit and scholastic tradition).
Review : D. Mornet in RHL 37:617, 1930.

1672-1791 : (Mercures) Le Mercure galant (1672-1674); Le nouveau Mercure galant (1677); Mercure galant (1677-1714); Nouveau Mercure galant (1714-1716); Le nouveau Mercure (1717-1721); Le Mercure (1721-1723); Mercure de France (1724-1791). En tout, 977 v. 2815

Monthly, but usually with additional volumes bringing yearly number of issues to 14 or 15. 18th century editors : Thomas Corneille (1690-1710), Dufresny (1710-1714), Lefèvre de Fontenay (1714-

1716), François Buchet (1717-1721), Dufresny with Antoine de La Roque and Fuzelier (1721-1724), De La Roque (1724-1744), Fuzelier and De La Bruère (1744-1748), Rémond de Sainte-Albine (1748-1750), Raynal (1750-1755), De Boissy (1755-1758), Marmontel (1758-1760), De La Place (1760-1768), Lacombe (1768-1778), Panckouke (1778-1791). Published jointly with *Journal politique de Bruxelles* from June 1778 and became a weekly in July 1779. Chiefly literary, with many *pièces fugitives* in verse and prose, announcements and brief reviews of new books, news from the court, Paris, and theaters. Reflects growing influence of *esprit philosophique* after 1750 and often praises works of Voltaire, Rousseau, and Encyclopedists; shows more cautious attitude after 1778, under Panckoucke, and devotes many favorable reviews to defenders of orthodoxy.

Choix des anciens Mercures et autres journaux, par Bastide, Marmontel, de la Place, et de la Porte. Chaubert, 1757-1764, 108 v. Table des matières, 1 v. 1765.   2816

Collection drawing its material from 79 different journals of 17th and first sixty years of 18th centuries. Plan varies somewhat with each successive editor : Bastide (1-15), Marmontel (16-39), assisted by Louis Coste and Suard, De La Place (40 seq.) assisted by De La Porte, but usually includes *pièces fugitives*, scientific articles, observations on political and social matters. Care taken not to admit articles that would incur governmental disapproval. Only a few articles, by famous writers, have their authorship indicated.

Miller, Minnie M. Science and philosophy as precursors of the English influence in France : a study of the Choix des anciens journaux. PMLA 45:856-96, 1930.   2817

Careful study of the collection, in which 37 of 79 periodicals contain some reference to English influence in France. Shows growing interest in English science and philosophy in first decades of century.

Table alphabétique des articles historiques et archéologiques contenus dans le Mercure, in Mémoires de la Société impériale des Antiquaires de France. Dumoulin, 1854. p. 181-238.   2817A

Mercure de France. Indicateur généalogique, biographique et nécrologique (1672-1789), par J. Guigard. Bachelin-Deflorenne, 1869. 142 p.   2818

Index of names of French individuals on whom biographical or genealogical notices are found in *Mercure*, listing scattered references to each name.

Courcel, Georges de. Mémoire historique sur le Mercure de France. BBB 1902:301-13, 402-20, 467-84, 524-29; 1903:29-36, 90-102. Reprinted : Leclerc, 1903, 80 p.   2819

Reproduction of anonymous MS kept at *Bibliothèque de l'Opéra* and written in 1760, then continued later by another author in 1780. Contains biographical data on successive editors of the *Mercure* and lists for each year number of issues with their respective dates.

Lovering, Stella. L'activité intellectuelle de l'Angleterre d'après l'ancien Mercure de France (1672-1778). Boccard, 1930. 324 p. (Diss., Paris). *See* 2954.   2820

Conscientious study of articles, reviews, and references in the *Mercure* concerning English publications in fields of literature, philosophy, religion, science, and medicine. Clearly describes general attitude of *Mercure* during three successive periods : 1672-1724, hostility or indifference; 1724-1756, growing interest and sympathy; 1756-1778, wide-spread interest in all fields of intellectual life. Does not make comparison with other periodicals or prevailing tendencies of contemporary public opinion. Good index of names and titles.

1701-1767 : Journal de Trévoux. Mémoires pour l'histoire des sciences et des beaux-arts. Trévoux, 265 v.   2821

Organ of Jesuits. Chief editors : P.P. Tournemine, Catrou, Rouillé, Charlevoix, Berthier. Published every two months avec *privilège et approbation*. Printed at Trévoux and later (1734) in Paris. Contains original articles, letters to editors, literary news from provinces and various foreign countries, but mostly (about 80 per cent) reviews of about 10,000 books. Covers wide range of subjects, especially theology, ecclesiastical and civil history, philosophy, science, and literature. Maintains conservative attitude in religious and political matters thoughout period.

1701-1705 : Mémoires pour l'histoire des sciences et des beaux-arts. Seconde édition augmentée de diverses remarques et de plusieurs articles nouveaux. Amsterdam, Jean Louis De Lorme, 9 v.   2822

Counterfeited edition; some articles on religious or historical matters followed by critical comments expressing Protestant point of view.

L'esprit des journalistes de Trévoux, ou Morceaux précieux de littérature répandus dans les Mémoires pour l'histoire des Sciences et des Beaux-Arts, depuis leur origine en 1701 jusqu'en 1762, par P. A. Alletz. Hansy, 1771, 4 v.   2823

Selections from articles and reviews published in *Mémoires*.

Mémoires d'une Société célèbre considérée comme corps littéraire et académique, depuis le commencement de ce siècle ou Mémoires des Jésuites sur les sciences, les belles-lettres et les arts, par Abbé J. B. Grosier. Defer-Demaisonneuve, 1790, 3 v.   2824

Selected articles from *Mémoires*. Enthusiastic praise of literary contribution of Jesuits, in Preface.

Table méthodique des Mémoires de Trévoux, par Père P. C. Sommervogel. Durand, 1864-1865, 3 v.   2825

V. 1 : Historical notice (101 p.) and list of 1722 original articles classified according to subject-matter, with Index of names and matters. V. 2, 3 : classified list of 9497 reviews, with Index of reviewed authors in v. 3.

Allard, Emmy. Die Angriffe gegen Descartes und Malebranche im Journal de Trévoux 1701-1715. APG 43:1-58, 1914.   2826

Based on careful examination of articles and reviews of the *Mémoires* up to time of Malebranche's death. Shows how the journal reflects persistent opposition of Jesuits to cartesian ideas (especially in reference to demonstration of existence of God, relations between body and soul, and innate ideas), and also to doctrines of Malebranche, with special references to his *Conversations chrétiennes, Entretien entre un philosophe chrétien et un philosophe chinois sur l'existence de Dieu,* and *Réflexions sur la prémotion physique.*

Dumas, Gustave. Histoire du Journal de Trévoux depuis 1701 jusqu'en 1762. Boivin, 1936. 210 p. (Diss., Paris). 2827

Only an external history of the journal,

with biographical data concerning some of more important editors and account of several controversies, notably with Leclerc and Boileau. Index of names. Review : D. Mornet in RHL 44:280, 1937.

1704-1776 : (Journal de Verdun) La Clef du cabinet des princes de l'Europe. Luxembourg, Le sincère, 5 v. (1704-1706). Journal historique sur les matières du tems, contenant aussi quelques nouvelles de littérature et autres remarques curieuses. Verdun, Muguet, 20 v. (1707-1716). Suite de la Clef ou Journal historique sur les matières du tems. Ganeau, 120 v. (1717-1776).   2828-2829

Successive editors: Jordan, De La Barre, Menehault d'Egly, Briasson. Chiefly political news from France and foreign countries; usually well informed and reliable; widely read. Good index of names and contents in each volume.

Table générale alphabétique et raisonnée du Journal historique de Verdun sur les matières du tems depuis 1697 jusques et y compris 1756, par Dreux du Radier. Ganeau, 1759-1760, 9 v.   2830

1713-1722, puis 1729-1736; Journal littéraire. The Hague, Johnson (1713-1722). Gosse et Néaulme (1729-1732), Swart et Van Duren (1733-1734), 24 v. 2831

Published every two months until 1715, then twice a year. Gap between end of 1722 and beginning of 1729 filled in second part of v. 12. Chief collaborators : Sallengre, Thémiseul de Saint-Hyacinthe, S'Gravesande, Van Effen, Marchand, Alexandre. More of a real literary journal than any other of the time; has a long *Dissertation sur la poésie anglaise* (1717, v. 9, p. 157-217) and numerous references to English literature, showing special admiration for Addison. Supports Newton and his disciples, hostile to Bayle, Spinoza, and English Deists (especially Collins, Tindal, Toland)

1715-1720 : Nouvelles littéraires contenant ce qui se passe de plus considérable dans la République des Lettres. The Hague, Henri du Sauzet, 12 v.   2832

Weekly, and later (May,1719) quarterly. Gives announcements and brief reviews of new books, with *pièces fugitives,* biographical notices and letters to editors. Often contains interesting news from London and reviews many English books; highly praises Newton and his disciples, shows hostility to freethinkers and *libertins*.

1717-1728 : Bibliothèque anglaise ou Histoire littéraire de la Grande-Bretagne. Amsterdam, 17 v. 2833-2834

First edited by Michel de La Roche, afterwards (1719) by Armand de La Chapelle. Well received and praised by contemporary journalists. Has a few scattered references to literature, but chiefly devoted to religion, philosophy, and science. Shows bitter hostility to Toland, Woolston; gives long extracts from *Philosophical transactions of Royal Society.*

1720-1724 : Mémoires littéraires de la Grande-Bretagne. The Hague, 16 v. 2835

Begun by La Roche, when he was obliged to relinquish editorship of the *Bibliothèque*, and wholly edited by him. Gives detailed reviews, with long extracts and little critical comment; about 25 % devoted to theology, only 5 % to literature; about 50 % to sciences.

King, G. V. Michel de La Roche et ses Mémoires littéraires de la Grande-Bretagne. RLC 15:298-300, 1935. 2836

Statistical data on various matters reviewed in the *Mémoires* (no. 2835).

1720-1741 : Bibliothèque germanique ou Histoire littéraire de l'Allemagne, de la Suisse, et des pays du Nord. Berlin and Amsterdam, Pierre Humbert, 50 v. 2837

Quarterly. Founded by Lenfant and inspired by example of *Bibliothèque anglaise.* Long reviews and *nouvelles littéraires* from German and Scandinavian countries; occasionally letters to editors and biographical notices. Chiefly devoted to theology, philosophy, history, and erudite matters. Protestant point of view; moderate tone; often expresses opposition to Bayle's skepticism in religious matters. Tables of names and contents in each volume.

1723-1742 : Bibliothèque française ou Histoire littéraire de la France. Amsterdam, Bernard, 34 v. 2838

Monthly. Somewhat similar in scope to the *Bibliothèque* of Leclerc (no. 2770), but giving more attention to *belles-lettres.* Supports strictly classical point of view in literature against Abbé Du Bos and stresses reservations of French taste in discussion of English authors. Gives

detailed and fairly objective reviews of works of English deists and of their opponents.

1728-1753 : Bibliothèque raisonnée des ouvrages des savans de l'Europe. Amsterdam, Wetsteins et Smith, 52 v. dont 2 v. (1-25 ; 26-50) de tables. 2839

Chief editors : Armand de La Chapelle, Barbeyrac, Desmaizeaux. Quarterly. Long reviews of recent books and *Nouvelles littéraires* (i. e., brief announcements concerning publications or activities of scholars from various European countries). Index of names and subjects in each volume. Gives much space to theology, philosophy, and history; hostile to Bayle, Spinoza, and English deists, especially Tindal and Woolston; praises works of English apologists of Christianity.

1728-1734 : Bibliothèque italique ou Histoire littéraire de l'Italie. Geneva, Marc-Michel Bousquet, 18 v. 2840

Volume of about 300 pages every 4 months; index of names and matters at end of each year. Long reviews of recent books and *nouvelles littéraires* from various Italian cities. Chiefly devoted to history and erudition, with occasional references to literature : e. g., translation of a survey of Italian poetry by Scipione Maffei, in v. 1, 2. Carefully avoids controversial subjects in theology and ecclesiastical history.

1728-1803 : Nouvelles ecclésiastiques, ou Mémoires pour servir à l'histoire de la Constitution Unigenitus. 76 v. 2841

Organ of Jansenists; weekly publication clandestinely printed and circulated; chief editors : Abbés Boucher, Berger de La Roche, Guidy.
Table des noms et matières (1728-1731). Paris.
Table raisonnée et alphabétique (1728-1760). Paris, 2 v.

1733-1747 : Bibliothèque britannique, ou Histoire des ouvrages des savants de la Grande-Bretagne. The Hague, Pieter de Hondt, 25 v. (Table of contents in v. 25). 2842

Chief editor Desmaizeaux, assisted by Jacques Bernard. Two volumes a year, but irregularly published, with a gap between June 1744 and July 1746. Reviews devoted chiefly to books on theology, philosophy, history, and science; keeps a cautious attitude in reviewing books from both sides in Deist controversy, gives long extracts from *Philosophical transactions of the Royal Society.*

Beckwith, F. The Bibliothèque britannique, 1733-47. Libr 4 ser. 12:75-82, 1931-32.
2843

Precise bibliographical description of *Bibliothèque* and interesting details on relations between editors and publisher, from unpublished papers of Desmaizeaux in the Sloane MSS of British Museum.

1748-1752 : Les cinq années littéraires, ou Lettres de M. Clément sur les ouvrages de littérature qui ont paru dans les années 1748, 1749, 1750, 1751 et 1752. Berlin, 1755, 2 v. *Also:* The Hague, De Groot, 1754, 4 v. 2844

Published twice a month by Pierre Clément at The Hague; reviews of recent books and plays; interesting references to English literature. Cautious attitude in religious and political matters, but clearly shows sympathy with Voltaire, Diderot, D'Alembert, and Encyclopedists.

1749-1752 : Observations sur la littérature moderne. The Hague, London and Paris, 9 v. 2845

Published every two months by Abbé Joseph de La Porte. Avoids discussion of religious and political subjects. Shows conservative classical taste in literary judgments; clear exposition and moderate tone in reviews; gives interesting information on relations between writers and publishers.

1750-1757 : Journal britannique. The Hague, Scheurleer, 24 v. 2846

Published by Dr. Matthew Maty. Monthly, 116 p. Index of names and subjects in each volume. Long reviews of recent English books and brief announcements under title *Nouvelles littéraires.* Gives much space to theology, philosophy, and sciences, with long extracts from the *Philosophical transactions of the Royal Society.* Had a considerable circulation on the Continent, especially in Low Countries and at Paris, Geneva, and Rome.

1751-1772 : Journal économique ou Mémoires, notes et avis sur l'agriculture, le commerce, et tout ce qui peut avoir rapport à la santé ainsi qu'à la conservation et augmentation des biens. 43 v. (28 v.; 15 v.). 2847

Monthly; founded under personal patronage of Malesherbes; chiefly devoted to questions of agricultural and national economy and interested in practical reforms; often criticizes Physiocrats for their theoretical and dogmatic tendencies. Chief editors : Baudeau, Boudet, Goulin, Querlon, Dreux du Radier.

1751-1811 : Annonces, affiches et avis divers (Affiches de Paris). 61 v. 2848

Published by office of *Gazette de France;* 8 pages, with occasional supplements, and after 1777, 16 pages, twice a week; after December 1778, 8 pages, daily, under title : *Petites affiches ou Journal général de France.* Commercial announcements and financial news, but much space given to reviews of books and plays. Literary articles written by Abbé Aubert (1751-1781) largely contribute to success of the journal. Carefully avoids controversial issues in all political and religious matters.

1752-1784 : Annonces, affiches et avis divers (Affiches de province), 33 v.
2849

Published by office of the *Gazette de France;* 4 or 6 pages weekly, with occasional supplements. Edited by Meusnier de Querlon, and later (1779) Abbé de Fontenay. Similar to the *Affiches de Paris* (no. 2848), but gives even more importance to literary matters. Sometimes praises talents of Rousseau, Diderot, Helvétius, and other *philosophes,* but maintains cautious and conservative attitude in all religious, political, and social questions.

1754-1759, then 1760-1762 : Journal étranger. 2850

Monthly. Edited successively by Grimm, Toussaint, Prévost (July 1754-August 1755), Fréron (August 1755-November 1756), Deleyre (November 1756-December 1758). Resumed under new *privilège* by Suard and Abbé Arnaud : January 1760-September 1762. Poor choice and presentation of matters during first period, except under editorship of Prévost; much improved and more regularly published under Arnaud and Suard. Publishes article by Turgot on Italian and German versification, discusses Lessing, Klopstock, Kleist, Chiabrera, but interest centers on English literature : Diderot's *Eloge de Richardson,* translations of Ossian, Young, Hume, Smollett, Hurd, Adam Smith; many articles translated from *Monthly review, London chronicle, Critical review.* Shows interest in several pre-romantic tendencies : medievalism, primitivism, *mélancolie*, liberalization of poetic and dramatic rules.

1756-1793 : Journal encyclopédique. Liége, Bouillon, 304 v.   2851

Founded by Pierre Rousseau. Fortnightly; each number (144 p.) divided into five parts : *Littérature; Spectacles; Médecine, Chirurgie, Chimie,* etc.; *Beaux-arts, Manufactures, Establissements nouveaux,* etc.; *Nouvelles, Relations, Avis divers.* Mostly reviews of recent books, giving much attention to natural sciences; conservative taste in literature; cautious attitude in religious and political matters, but sympathetic to the *philosophes* and the *Encyclopédie.* Praised by Voltaire. who sent several letters to editors.

1758-1761 : L'observateur littéraire. Amsterdam et Paris, 17 v.   2852

Monthly. Published by Abbé Joseph de La Porte. Similar in scope and tendencies to his *Observations sur la littérature moderne,* no. 2845.

1760-1773 : L'avant-coureur, feuille hebdomadaire, où sont annoncés les objets particuliers des sciences de la littérature, des arts, des métiers, de l'industrie, des spectacles, et les nouveautés en tous genres. Lacombe, 13 v.   2853

Published every Monday; subscription : 12 *livres* a year. Each number (16 p.) divided into 5 parts : *Arts; Industries; Sciences; Spectacles; Nouvelles littéraires,* the last consisting of brief reviews of recent books. Articles short, factual, give interesting data on growing taste for scientific experiments and on teaching of foreign languages in Paris. Reviews have conservative tone in all religious and political matters; many reviews devoted to books defending Christian tradition against deists and materialists.

1765-1772 : Ephémérides du citoyen, ou chroniques de l'esprit national. Lacombe, 69 v.   2854

Weekly, and later (1767) monthly, with new subtitle : *Bibliothèque raisonnée des sciences morales et politiques.* Founded by Abbé Baudeau, first keeps an intermediate position between the Physiocrats and their opponents, then after 1768, under Dupont de Nemours, becomes official organ of the Physiocrats. Most articles unsigned and followed only by conventional letters; A : Quesnay—B :

Mirabeau—C : Turgot—H : Dupont de Nemours.

1765-1774 : Journal de l'agriculture, du commerce, et des arts des finances. Knapen, 48 v.   2855

Monthly. Founded with governmental approval as open forum publishing articles pro and con about controversial issues in economics. Friendly attitude towards Physiocrats under editorship of Dupont de Nemours (July 1765-October 1766), then attacks Physiocrats and defends mercantilism, then sympathetic again to Physiocrats, under editorship of Abbé Roubaud, after 1770.

1771-1791 : (Journal de physique) Observations et Mémoires sur la physique, sur l'Histoire naturelle et sur les arts et métiers. 38 v.   2856

Published by Abbé Rosier; monthly; divided into four parts : Physics, Natural history, Arts and crafts, *Nouvelles littéraires,* i. e., biographical notices on scientists, announcements of new books and brief reviews. Gives much space to translations of papers from foreign scientists; number of January 1773 gives table of contents of first volume of the *Proceedings of the American philosophical society.*

1772-1818 : L'esprit des journaux françois et étrangers; ouvrage périodique et littéraire. Liége, Brussels and Paris (Valade, avec privilège, 1782-1793), 480 v.   2857

Monthly volume of about 400 pages, but irregularly published; sometimes 9 or only 6 volumes a year. Subscription : 27 *livres* in Paris; 33 in provinces. Compilation of articles taken from various French literary journals or translated from foreign (mostly English and Italian) periodicals, with a few original articles. Contents classified according to subject-matter, with most space given to literature, science, jurisprudence, economics, and music. Chief editors : Abbé Coster, librarian of Bishop of Liége, and later (1775-1793) De Lignac, Abbé Outin, Millon. Importance of this collection was stressed by Sainte-Beuve in his *Portraits contemporains,* III, 465 (edit. Calmann-Lévy, 1876).

Lambinet, Abbé Pierre. Table raisonnée des matières contenues dans L'esprit des journaux. Valade, n. d., 4 v.   2858

Covers period 1772-1784 (inclusive).

1775-1778 : Journal anglais, contenant les découvertes dans les sciences, les arts libéraux et mécaniques, les nouvelles philosophiques, littéraires, économiques et politiques des trois royaumes et des colonies qui en dépendent. Ruault, 7 v. 2859

Published twice a month; yearly subscriptions : 24 *livres*. Each number (64 p.) has biographical article on a famous English writer, scientist, or statesman (first article on Chaucer), an account of activities of the Royal Society, miscellaneous news, chiefly on economic and political matters, and brief announcements of new books.

1776-1783 : Journal de Monsieur. Table générale des journaux anciens et modernes, contenant les jugements des journalistes sur les principaux ouvrages en tous genres. Knapen, 30 v. 2860

Monthly. Edited during first eight months by Gautier d'Agoty and divided into two parts containing extracts from older and from contemporary journals; adds original articles under editorship of Charlotte d'Ormoy (1779-1780); from 1781 on, becomes similar in scope and tendencies to the *Année littéraire* (no. 2792) and is edited by Abbé Royou and Geoffroy ; 18 v. for this third period.

1776-1792 : Courrier de l'Europe, gazette franco-anglaise. London, Boulogne, 32 v. 2861

Published twice a week; mostly based on extracts from various English weeklies; has wide circulation on Continent; first forbidden in France, then authorized and even subsidized by government in expurgated form, printed in Boulogne, under the title : *Courrier de l'Europe, ou Gazette des gazettes, continuée sur un nouveau plan*, and edited by Brissot. Gives little attention to literature; interest centers on English political life, with many references to conflict between Great Britain and American colonies. First complete French translation of American *Declaration of Independence* published in issue of March 11, 1777.

1777-1792 : Annales politiques, civiles et littéraires du dix-huitième siècle. London and Paris, 19 v. 2862

Twice a month, published by Linguet, and from 1780 to May 1782, when Linguet was in the Bastille, by Mallet du Pan and Durey de Morsan, at Geneva. Eight numbers in each volume; index of names and subjects in every third volume. Contains letters addressed to editor and his answers, reviews of recent books, and chiefly long articles on political and social questions. Bitter attacks against *la philosophaille*, especially against D'Alembert, sarcastic tone towards the Physiocrats, Academy, and Parlements; at first paints dark picture of British institutions, but after Linguet's release from Bastille becomes more appreciative of English liberties. Had wide circulation; several counterfeited editions, one in Nantes.

1777-1811 : Le Journal de Paris ou Poste du soir. 2863

First daily paper in France; founded by Corancez, D'Ussieux, and Cadet de Vaulx. Editor-in-chief after 1785 : Suard. New political orientation after a two months' suspension (August-October 1792) under Condorcet, Sieyès, Garat, Cabanis. Price of subscription : 24, and later 30 *livres* in Paris; 30 and later 33 *livres* in the provinces. Avoids controversial subjects in religious and political matters, condemns extremist views, but expresses admiration for Voltaire, Rousseau, Diderot. Conservative taste in literature; shows little interest in foreign literature.

Abrégé des cinq premières années du Journal de Paris. 1782, 4 v. 2864

Collection of extracts from the *Journal*. Chap. III : *Extraits et notices de livres;* IX : *Variétés, morceaux de littérature;* XI : *Spectacles.*

1779-1783 : Journal de littérature, des sciences et des arts. 30 v. 2865

Monthly. Published by Abbé Jean-Baptiste Grosier. Reviews of recent books and occasionally original articles. Tendencies similar to those of Fréron's *Année littéraire* (no. 2792), but gives less attention to foreign literatures. Conservative in all religious, political, and social questions.

1784-1792 : Journal de Lyon, ou Annonces et variétés littéraires concernant la ville de Lyon et les provinces voisines. Lyon, 8 v. 2866

Weekly; 4 pages, sometimes 6 with supplement; 6 *livres* a year. Gives relatively little space to practical announcements, such as mortgages, sales, commodity prices, and devotes its cultural part to anecdotes, *belles-lettres*, morals, sciences. Avoids religious and political discussions, but shows admiration for Rousseau, Voltaire, and favorably reviews books advocating practical reforms.

Elie-Catherine Fréron
(Nos. 2867-2884)

FRANCIS W. GRAVIT *and* CLIFFORD H. PRATOR

Fréron, Elie-Catherine. L'Année litté-raire, ou suite des lettres sur quelques écrits de ce temps. Amsterdam [i. e., Paris], Lambert, 1754-1776, 183 v. *See* 2792.
2867

One of most widely read and most valuable journals of century, since F. was leader of opposition to *philosophe* move-ment. Influential as intermediary for English, German, Italian thought. Re-flects nearly every field of activity of period. Parts of volumes for 1776 probably not by F. Continued 1777-90 by Stanislas Fréron, abbé J.-B.-G.-A. Grosier, and J.-L. Geoffroy.

— Les Confessions de Fréron (1719-1776); sa vie, souvenirs intimes et anecdotiques ... recueillis et annotés par Charles Barthélemy. Charpentier, 1876, XVI-375 p. 2868

Long extracts from F.'s works linked together with commentary by editor. So arranged as to cover F.'s biography and also to give sampling of his opinions on religion, politics, *philosophes*, history, and examples of his literary criticism, which are too generalized and often too removed from context to be conclusive. Reprints some of F.'s verse, including *Journée de Fontenoy* (of 1745). Documented. Very useful as introduction to F.'s work and opinions.

— Journal étranger, ouvrage périodique ... Septembre 1755 [-Septembre 1756]. Lam-bert, 1755-56, 7 v. *See* 2850. 2869

F. was editor of this periodical for time indicated.

— Lettres de Mme la Ctsse de***, sur quel-ques écrits modernes. Geneva, Philibert, 1746. 2870

Nineteen numbers published. Dated Sept. 1, 1745-Jan. 12, 1746. Contained in two volumes in *Bibliothèque nationale*, for which B. N. call numbers are given, as follows : *Lettres* I-XVI [Z. 49195]; *Lettres* I-VIII and XVII-XIX [Z. Beuchot 1283(3)]. Cf. Fréron, *Opuscules*, 2872

— Lettres sur quelques écrits de ce temps. Geneva, 1749 (I-II); Geneva-Amsterdam, Pierre Mortier, 1750 (III); Geneva-Paris, Vᵛᵉ Cailleau, 1751 (IV); London-Paris, Duchesne, 1752-54 (V-XIII). 2871

Reprints exist for vols. I-III, imprinted London-Paris, Duchesne, 1752. *See* nos. 2791, 2878. This is F.'s first great periodical and is directly continued in *L'Année littéraire*.

— Opuscules de M. F***. Amsterdam, Arkstée & Merkus, 1753, 3 v. 2872

Contains reprints of many articles from *Lettres de Mme la Ctsse de***, plus writings by authors other than F., notably the *Parallèle du Lutrin et de la Henriade*, by C. Batteux, an *Extrait, chapitre par chapitre, du livre de l'Esprit des loix*, and some *Observations sur quelques endroits particuliers de ce livre*, by F. Véron de Forbonnais. Available in *Bibliothèque nationale* and British Museum. Volume II in Harvard Law School Library.

Arnaud, Raoul. Journaliste, sans-culotte et thermidorien; le fils de Fréron, 1754-1802, d'après des documents inédits. Perrin, 1909, VI-368 p. 2873

Chapters I and II discuss accurately, although far from completely, chief incidents of F.'s career and his personal life. Chapter III contains much in-formation about the *Année littéraire* after F.'s death.
Review : G. Rudler in RU 19¹:138-39, 1910.

Brunetière, Ferdinand. La direction de la librairie sous M. de Malesherbes. *In his :* Études critiques, Hachette, 1888-91, 2:160-251. *See* 361. 2874

First authoritative voice raised in F.'s defense; marks real beginning of his rehabilitation. Marked *anti-encyclopédi-que* bias. Study dated Feb. 1, 1882.

Chauvin, Paul. Un journaliste au XVIIIᵉ siècle. RPyr 17:46-74, 1905. 2875

Concluding pages represent one of more successful attempts to evaluate F.'s work as critic, from non-Catholic point of view. Author claims F. defended " les droits méconnus de la critique " with " bon sens ", " finesse ", " modé-ration ", " bon goût ". Insufficiently documented.

Cornou, François. ...Trente années de lut-tes contre Voltaire et les philosophes du xviiiᵉ siècle; Elie Fréron (1718-1776). See 1707, 2793. 2876

Most comprehensive, understanding, and therefore valuable study we have at present time. Should make possible in future to pay less attention to F.'s personality and quarrels and more to his role as literary critic and publicist. Frankly an *essai de réhabilitation*, written from conservative and Catholic viewpoint, and hence sometimes overzealous and not entirely trustworthy. Index and systematic bibliography lacking. References sometimes vague and inexact.
Review : E. Magne in MerF, 156:729-31, June 15, 1922.

Gravit, Francis W. Notes on the contents of Fréron's periodicals. RR 34:116-26, 1943. 2877

Attempts to classify F.'s articles in general way. Reveals astounding multiplicity of subject matter dealt with by his three periodicals.

Prator, C. H. and F. W. Gravit. The editions of Fréron's Lettres sur quelques écrits de ce temps. *See* 2791, 2871. 2878

Attempts to determine which portions of *Lettres* were reprinted and extent to which they were rewritten. (V. I was largely revised).

Green, Frederick C. Voltaire's greatest enemy. *In his :* Eighteenth century France. *See* 2794, p. 111-54. 2879

No new material, but fine semi-popular survey of F.'s dealings with Voltaire. Points out broad implications of the controversy. Fair and up-to-date presentation.
Review : G. R. Havens in MLJ 17:225, 1932-33.

Nisard, Charles. Fréron. *In his :* Les ennemis de Voltaire. *See* 2795. 2880

In many respects marks culmination of hostility toward F. This summary of most of accusations against him dangerous because of false air of fair-mindedness with which material is presented.

Prator, Clifford H. E.-C. Fréron in the light of variants in the text of his Lettres sur quelques écrits de ce temps. MLQ 3:105-18, 1942. 2881

Consideration of F. as stylist and critic. Contains new information concerning genesis of his polemics with Voltaire and Marmontel.

Soury, Jules. Un critique au xviiiᵉ siècle, Fréron. RDM 3rd per. 20:80-112, March 1, 1877. 2882

Good biographical sketch which tries to be objective, but relies at times too greatly upon opinions of some of F.'s enemies. On whole is antagonistic. Sees in F. simple Christian incapable of metaphysics, whose gift for irony made him, despite a disordered life, tool of clerical party and defender of religion.

Trévédy, J. Notes sur Fréron et ses cousins Royou. BSF 27:178-96, 220-41, 307-27, 1900; 28:121-44, 154-63, 1901; 29:3-22, 1902. 2883

Aspects of F.'s biography and history of Fréron family, based on Breton documents and correspondence.

Van Tieghem, Paul. L'année littéraire (1754-1790) comme intermédiaire en France des littératures étrangères. *See* 2796, 2945, 3221, 3275. 2884

Important chiefly as first work to evaluate objectively a phase of F.'s literary activity and to avoid all discussion of biographical and personal questions which have nearly monopolized studies of this author. Index of reviews of non-French works in *Année littéraire* is only printed guide to any part of the journal, and quite useful, though arranged in haphazard fashion and lacking completeness.
Review : *See* no. 2796.

CHAPTER XI. FOREIGN INFLUENCES AND RELATIONS
(Nos. 2885-3319)

CHANDLER B. BEALL, DONALD F. BOND, JOHN F. MCDERMOTT, HENRY H. H. REMAK
and CHARLES N. STAUBACH

English
(Nos. 2885-3127)

DONALD F. BOND

This section was originally planned in conjunction with E. Preston Dargan. Before his death, in 1940, Professor Dargan had been able to complete a few critical notes, chiefly on Voltaire; these are signed with his initials. The entries in Chapter XI deal only with the impact of foreign literature upon the French, not the vogue and influence of French authors abroad.

Bibliographies and General Studies

Ascoli, Georges. La Grande-Bretagne devant l'opinion française au XVIIe siècle. Gamber, 1930. 2 v. 894 p.   2885

Indispensable background to study of English-French influence in 18th century. Book I (*Les événements d'Angleterre*) and Book II (*Connaissance du pays et des hommes*) analyze thoroughly French knowledge of English history and customs. Book III (*Connaissance de la langue, de la pensée et des Œuvres*) best available study of English literature and thought in 17th century France. *Bibliographie méthodique* is almost exhaustive listing of French translations of English works.
Reviews : F. Baldensperger in RLC 11:356-59, 1931; Harcourt Brown in RR 22:149-52, 1931; C. Chassé in RAA 8:441-43, 1930-31; H. C. Lancaster in MLN 45:532-34, 1930; R. Pintard in Rcr ns. 98:176-79, 1931; M. E. I. Robertson in MLR 27:103-05, 1932.

Baldensperger, Fernand, and Werner P. Friederich. Bibliography of comparative literature. Chapel Hill, Univ. of North Carolina, 1950. 701 p. *See* 3182A, 3264A, 3308A.   2885A

Indispensable extensive list of titles in field of comparative literature.

Bond, Donald F. American scholarship

in the field of eighteenth-century Anglo-French studies. RR 29:141-50, 1938.   2886

Bibliographical survey of work done by American scholars, with indication of problems awaiting investigation.

— Anglo-French and Franco-American studies : a current bibliography. RR 29:343-72, 1938.   2887

Lists books, articles, and reviews published in 1937 dealing with English-French and French-American relations from 16th century to present. Continued annually in RR, with collaboration of John F. McDermott, Joseph E. Tucker, Joseph M. Carrière, and Edward D. Seeber, through 1948; then in FrAR 2:203-32, 1949; to be continued in FrAR.

Bonno, Gabriel. La constitution britannique devant l'opinion française de Montesquieu à Bonaparte. *See* 1529.   2888

Well-documented survey of influence of English political thought in France in later 18th century.
Reviews : L. Gottschalk in AHR 38:591-92, 1932-33; D. Mornet in RHL 39:468-69, 1932.

— La culture et la civilisation britanniques devant l'opinion française de la paix d'Utrecht aux Lettres philosophiques (1713-1734). Philadelphia, American philosophical society, 1948. 184 p.   2889

Admirable survey of subject, with full, solid documentation.
Reviews : G. R. Havens in AHR 54:582-83, 1949; D. Mornet in RLC 23:589-92, 1949; F. A. Taylor in FS 3:277-79; F. Vial in FR 23:327-29, 1949-50.

Bateson, F. W. The Cambridge bibliography of English literature, edited by F. W. Bateson. Cambridge, University press, 1940; New York, Macmillan, 1941. 4 v.   2890

Lists bibliographical and general studies on Anglo-French relations, intermediaries, and English-French influences (arranged by *genres*).
Reviews : D. F. Bond in MP 39:303-12, 1941-42; A. Friedman in LQ 11:521-24, 1941; C. J. Sisson in MLR 36:247-49, 1941; J. R. Sutherland in RES 17:490-94, 1941.

Cahen, Léon. A propos des origines intellectuelles de la Révolution française : la librairie parisienne et la diffusion du livre français à la fin du XVIIIe siècle. *See* 14. 2891

Important notes on sales and reading of books at end of 18th century.

Gaudin, Mrs. Lois Frances (Strong). Les lettres anglaises dans l'Encyclopédie. *See* 1306. 2892

Chapters I-IV deal with poetry, drama, fiction, and miscellaneous prose; greater part of book studies influence of English philosophy and theology on *Encyclopédie*.
Reviews : D. F. Bond in PQ 22:183-84, 1943; G. R. Havens in MLN 58:303-04, 1943; H. Peyre in RR 34:269-71, 1943.

Green, F. C. Minuet : a critical survey of French and English literary ideas in the eighteenth century. *See* 1042. 2893

Emphasizes throughout essential differences between French and English taste. In spite of some exaggeration in point of view, is a rich and suggestive study.
Reviews : E. H. Carr in Spect 154:308, 1935; A. F. B. Clark in UTQ 4:555-58, 1934-35; P. M. Jones in LM 31:494-95, 1934-35.

Hazard, Paul. La crise de la conscience européenne (1680-1715). *See* 1043. 2894

Important for background of 18th century Anglomania.
Review : B. Munteano in RLC 15:364-78, 1935.

— La pensée européenne au XVIIIe siècle de Montesquieu à Lessing. *See* 1044. 2895

Best general survey of European movements of thought in 18th century, with due attention to influence of Locke, Newton, Pope, and other English writers on Continent.
Reviews : H. C. Lancaster in MLN 62:133-35, 1947; B. Munteano in RLC 21:125-40, 1947; N.L. Torrey in RR 38:271-76, 1947.

— Les origines philosophiques de l'homme de sentiment. RR 28:318-41, 1937. Reprinted in Quatre études, New York, Oxford univ. press, 1940. p. 112-54. 2896

Contributions of 17th century philosophy, including the empirical psychology of Locke, to emotional expansiveness of Diderot and 18th century sensibility.

Killen, Alice M. Le roman " terrifiant " ou roman " noir " de Walpole à Anne Radcliffe et son influence sur la littérature française jusqu'en 1840. *See* 736. 2897

Best work on subject : Horace Walpole, Clara Reeve, Anne Radcliffe, " Monk " Lewis, and others, and their vogue and influence in France, beginning with Maugenet's *Delphina, ou le spectre amoureux* (of 1797). Titles and dates need checking. Includes valuable list of *romans noirs* from 1797 to 1840. Additions by E. C. Van Bellen in Neo 11:251-56, 1926.
Reviews : M. Citoleux in Rcr 91:293-95, 1924; B. Fehr in Litt 2:112-15, 1925; P. H[azard] in RLC 1:174-77, 1921; G. Meyer in RAA 2:253-55, 1924-25; P. Van Tieghem in RSH 38:151-53, 1924.

Lanson, Gustave. Formation et développement de l'esprit philosophique au XVIIIe siècle : l'influence anglaise. RCC 17[1]:721-36, 1909. *See* 1047. 2898

One of earliest studies to note that English philosophy rather than *belles-lettres*, was significant factor in 18th-century Anglomania. Stresses influence of Locke. Important study.

Mackenzie, Fraser. Les relations de l'Angleterre et de la France d'après le vocabulaire. Droz, 1939. 2 v. (Diss.). 2899

Part I *(Les infiltrations de la langue et de l'esprit anglais, anglicismes français)* provides most complete study of effect of English vocabulary on French in 18th century.

Reviews : P. Barbier in FS 1:157-60, 1947; C. Bruneau in Fmod 14:312-14, 1946; F. Mossé in Lmod 40:375-77, 1946.

May, Louis-Philippe. Documents nouveaux sur l'Encyclopédie; histoire et sources de l'Encyclopédie d'après le registre de déliberations et de comptes des éditeurs et un mémoire inédit. Rsyn 15:5-30, 1938. 2900

New material on plan to translate Chambers's *Cyclopedia*.

Miller, Minnie M. The English people as portrayed in certain French journals, 1700-1760. MP 34:365-76, 1936-37.   2901

Useful summary of contemporary opinions.

— Science and philosophy as precursors of the English influence in France : a study of the *Choix des anciens journaux*. PMLA 45:856-96, 1930.   2902

Important study of beginnings of Anglomania as seen in periodical literature.

Offor, R. A collection of books in the University Library, Leeds, printed before the nineteenth century, containing (a) translations from English into French, (b) books written in French on Great Britain and on British affairs. PLPS 1:292-98, 1925-28 ; 2:109-23, 361-76, 1928-32 ; 4:55-76, 1936-38 ; 5:277-93, 403-11, 1938-43 ; 6:111-24, 196-215, 1945-46 (In progress).   2903

Valuable notes on important Brotherton collection of Anglo-French material in Leeds University Library (over 2,500 volumes).

Philips, Edith. The good Quaker in French legend. *See* 1793.   2904

Largely devoted to 18th century, including a chapter on *The Quakers seen by Voltaire.* P. 213-15 : List of Quaker publications which appeared in French translations.
Reviews : L. Cons in RLC 14:591-93, 1934; A. Schinz in RHL 40:447-48, 1933.

Préclin, E. Introduction à l'étude des rapports religieux entre la France et la Grande-Bretagne (1763-1848). RHM 13:126-96, 1938.   2905

Important bibliographical survey, with indication of problems.

Reesink, H. J. L'Angleterre et la littérature anglaise dans les trois plus anciens périodiques français de Hollande de 1684 à 1709. *See* 1153, 2430, 2768.   2906

Analyzes reviews of English books in Bayle's *Nouvelles de la république des lettres*, Le Clerc's *Bibliothèque universelle et historique*, and Basnage de Beauval's *Histoire des ouvrages des savans*. Although only last-named periodical is as late as 18th century, tabulations of all three are important both as check-list for similar investigations of later periodicals and as summary of Continental views of things English at threshold of century.

Reviews : G. Ascoli in RLC 13:209-12, 1933; K. R. Gallas in Beibl 43:380-83, 1932; K. Glaser in LGRP 53:116-18, 1932; J. G. Robertson in MLR 28:389-90, 1933.

Rochedieu, Charles Alfred. Bibliography of French translations of English works 1700-1800. With an introduction by Donald F. Bond. Chicago, University of Chicago press, 1948. *See* 694.   2907-2908

Indispensable work. Titles arranged alphabetically under English authors, with cross-references by French title. Appendixes dealing with anonymous works translated into French, translations of unidentified works, and collections of works translated from English. Classified subject-index.

Rosières, Raoul. La littérature anglaise en France de 1750 à 1800. RPL 3rd ser. 4:234-41, Aug. 19, 1882.   2909

Well-informed account, with emphasis on Richardson. " L'étude des écrivains anglais a été plutôt pour nous une œuvre d'émancipation qu'un travail d'assimilation." Over-emphasizes the " two schools " of English literature (Anglo-Saxon and Anglo-French) but still of some value. Reprinted in *Recherches sur la poésie contemporaine* (in 1896).

Sagnac, Philippe. Les grands courants d'idées et de sentiments en France vers 1789. RHP 2:317-41, 1938.   2910

Emphasizes native rather than English sources of rationalism, empiricism, and mysticism.

Streeter, Harold W. The eighteenth century English novel in French translation : a bibliographical study. *See* 703.   2910A

Bibliography of translations, preceded by a long and able sketch of vogue and influence of English novel in France.
Review : D. F. Bond in MP 35:457-61, 1937-38.

Seeber, Edward D. Anti-slavery opinion in France during the second half of the eighteenth century. Baltimore, Johns Hopkins press, 1937. 238 p.   2911

Study of one aspect of 18th century English thought in France.

Texte, Joseph. Jean-Jacques Rousseau et les origines du cosmopolitisme littéraire; étude sur les relations littéraires de la France et de l'Angleterre au XVIIIe siècle. *See* 740, 831, 2145.   2912

Monumental pioneer work surveying entire field of English influence in 18th century France. Book I *(L'influence anglaise en France avant J.-J. Rousseau)* deals with early intermediaries and three chief *vulgarisateurs*, Muralt, Prévost, and Voltaire. Book II *(Rousseau et la littérature anglaise)* analyzes Rousseau's early interest in things English, including his reading of English books, and traces influence of Richardson upon writing of *Nouvelle Héloïse.* Book III *(Rousseau et l'influence anglaise dans la seconde moitié du XVIIIᵉ siècle* carries on story of English influence as seen in sentimental novel (Sterne), interest in external nature (Thomson), melancholy (Gray and Young), and the *tristesse du passé* (Ossian), concluding with triumph of cosmopolitan spirit in Mme de Staël. Throughout, Rousseau is focal point : " Le cosmopolitisme est né ... de l'union féconde du génie anglais avec le génie de Jean-Jacques " (p. xvi). Texte's writing is brilliant. In certain respects he exaggerates possibilities of English influence; but for breadth of subject-matter, suggestiveness of point of view, and influence exerted on later generation of scholars, his book still deserves careful study. Reviews : *See* 2145.

Van Tieghem, Paul. La poésie de la nuit et des tombeaux en Europe au XVIIIᵉ siècle. Rieder, 1921. 177 p. 2913

Admirable discussion of poetry of Gray, Collins, Young, and " graveyard school " and its vogue on the Continent in latter half of 18th century. Review : F. Baldensperger in RLC 2:667-69, 1922.

Vreeland, Williamson Updike. Étude sur les rapports littéraires entre Genève et l'Angleterre jusqu'à la publication de la Nouvelle Héloïse. *See* 2154. 2914

Still of value for general view of Anglomania in late 18th century, but superseded in details. Reviews : F. B[aldensperger] in Rcr ns 52:177, 1901; Helen J. Huebener in MLN 22:25-27, 1907.

Wade, Ira O. The clandestine organization and diffusion of philosophic ideas in France from 1700 to 1750. *See* 57. 2915

Ch. X lists manuscript translations from English (Mandeville, Bolingbroke, Toland, etc.) and discusses influence of such English writers as Thomas Burnet and Samuel Clarke. Whole book important for study of method of infiltration of English ideas. Reviews : T. E. Jessop in Phil 14:106-07, 1939; J. Lough in MLR 34:105-06, 1939 ; E. Malakis in MLN 54:385-86, 1939 ; A. R. Morehouse in MP 37:214-17, 1939-40 ; N. L. Torrey in RR 30:205-09, 1939.

West, Constance B. La théorie de la traduction au XVIIIᵉ siècle par rapport surtout aux traductions françaises d'ouvrages anglais. RLC 12:330-55, 1932. 2916

Important study of 18th century opposition between theory of " free " translation and that of exact fidelity to original. Throws considerable light on opposition of tastes between English and French.

Intermediaries
a) Travellers, editors, translators, etc.

Berquin

Carrière, J.-M. Berquin's adaptations from English periodical literature. PQ 13:248-60, 1934. 2917

Study of the *Choix de tableaux tirés de diverses galeries angloises* (dated 1775) by Arnaud Berquin. *Choix* contains 27 essays, 16 translated from *Connoisseur* of Colman and Thornton, 5 from Johnson's *Idler*, 2 from the *Adventurer* of Hawkesworth, one from Johnson's *Rambler*, and 3 which are unidentified. *See* no. 2964

Mme Bontemps

La Harpe, Jacqueline de. Intermédiaires et serviteurs littéraires : Mme Bontemps. *In :* Hommage à l'École Vinet 1839-1939, p. 134-40. Lausanne, Imprimerie La Concorde, 1939. 2918

Study of Jeanne-Marie de Châtillon-Bontemps, first translator into French of whole of Thomson's *Seasons.*

Campion

Campion, Charles Michel. Œuvres de Charles-Michel Campion, poète marseillais du dix-huitième siècle, ed. by Edward D. Seeber and Henry H. H. Remak. Bloomington, Ind., Indiana university, 1945. 300 p. 2919

Prints Campion's translations of Goldsmith's *Deserted village* and Thomas Percy's *Hermit of Warkworth.* Introduction and notes provide information on

reputation of Goldsmith and Percy in
18th century France.
Reviews : H. A. Grubbs in RR 37:85-
87, 1946; E. Malakis in MLN 61:142-43,
1946; I. O. Wade in MP 43:211-12,
1945-46.

Chastellux

Varnum, Fanny. Un philosophe cosmopolite du XVIIIe siècle: le chevalier du Chastellux. *See* 356.   2920

Study based in part on unedited
material; emphasizes English background
of Chastellux's thought.
Review : H. Bibas in MLR 33:444-45,
1938 (" More can really be learnt about
Chastellux's main characteristics as a
thinker in the half-dozen pages allotted
to him in Bury's *Idea of progress...* (no.
1031). There is still room for a book on
Chastellux ").

Coste (*See also* Shaftesbury)

Bastide, Charles. The courtship of Pierre
Coste and other letters. *In his :* Anglo-
French entente in the seventeenth century.
London, Lane, 1914, ch. x.   2921

Good account of Coste's literary
activity. Prints letters to Mlle Brun,
from originals in library of Société pour
l'histoire du protestantisme français. For
additional material on Coste see E. Casati,
*Quelques correspondants français de Shaftes-
bury*, no. 1120.

Des Maizeaux (*See also* Shaftesbury)

Daniels, W. M. Des Maizeaux en Angleterre (d'après des manuscrits inédits du
Musée britannique). RG 4:40-49, 1908.
                                     2922

Brief sketch of Des Maizeaux, who
came to England in 1699 : friend of
Shaftesbury, Addison, Halifax, and
others. Calls attention to Des Maizeaux's
correspondence in Birch collection in
British Museum.

Mme du Boccage

Gill-Mark, Grace. Une femme de lettres
au XVIIIe siècle : Anne-Marie du Boccage.
Champion, 1927. 182 p. (Diss.).   2923

Describes Mme du Boccage's visit to
England in 1750, her translation of Pope's
Temple of fame (1749), and her imitation
of Milton (*Le Paradis terrestre*, 1748).
Du Resnel and Yart also treated briefly.

Review : D. Mornet in RHL 36:461-
62, 1929.

Grimm

Ewen, Frederic. Criticism of English
literature in Grimm's Correspondance
littéraire. *See* 2379.   2924

Surveys briefly opinions of Raynal and
Grimm, emphasizing conventional and
rather unoriginal verdicts of the French
critics.

Hunter, Alfred C. Les opinions du Baron
Grimm sur le roman anglais. *See* 2386.
                                     2925

Grimm's admiration for Richardson,
Fielding, Goldsmith, and others, as
exponents of realism—" vérité des caractères, vérité de la parole, vérité du milieu
intellectuel et moral, vérité de l'action ".

La Place (*See also* Shakespeare)

Cobb, Lillian. Pierre-Antoine de La Place :
sa vie et son œuvre (1707-1793). *See* 579.
                                     2926

Excellent study of La Place's translations, especially his efforts to adapt
Shakespeare, *Oroonoko*, and *Tom Jones* to
French standards of " good taste."
P. 138-43 list some of the English books
reviewed in *Mercure* under La Place's
editorship. Chapter on La Place's translations of English fiction ignores certain
problems of authorship which need investigation.
Reviews : A. Brulé in RAA 7:346-47,
1929-30; W. Kalthoff in LGRP 51:369-
72, 1930; P. Van Tieghem in RHL
36:142, 1929; and in RSH 48:88-89, 1929.

La Rochefoucauld

**La Rochefoucauld, François Armand
Frédéric,** *duc* **de.** A Frenchman in
England, 1784. Being the Mélanges sur
l'Angleterre of François de La Rochefoucauld. Edited by Jean Marchand and
translated by S. C. Roberts. Cambridge,
University press, 1933. 256 p.   2927

La Rochefoucauld (1765-1848), son of
duc de Liancourt, visited England in
1784 and left an interesting record of his
visit in form of memoirs, a portion of
which is here translated for first time from
the MS in British Museum. La Rochefoucauld knew Arthur Young, and he
sets down vividly his impressions of
English agricultural life in Suffolk and
Norfolk. Marchand's edition of *Mélan-*

ges has also been published in French
(Le Prat, 1945).
Reviews : in NQ 164:144, 1933; in
TLS, Feb. 23, 1933, p. 121.

Le Blanc (*See also* Shakespeare)

Havens, George R. The abbé Le Blanc
and English literature. MP 18:423-41,
1920-21.   2928

Analysis of Le Blanc's opinions of
English authors, with special attention
to Shakespeare. Fully documented essay
which situates Le Blanc's views in current
of early 18th century Anglomania.

Monod-Cassidy, Hélène. Un voyageur-
philosophe au XVIIIe siècle : l'abbé Jean-
Bernard Le Blanc. Cambridge, Mass.,
Harvard University press, 1941. 565 p.
(HSCL, 17).   2929

Critical edition of Le Blanc's correspondence, preceded by long and illuminating biographical sketch of Le Blanc,
emphasizing his sojourn in England
(1736-38) as background for *Lettres d'un
François sur les Anglois.*
Reviews : D. F. Bond in MP 40:219-
20, 1942-43; J. David in MLQ 3:150-51,
1942; E. Joliat in PQ 21:445-46, 1942;
J. Lough in MLR 38:365-66, 1943; N. L.
Torrey in RR 33:82-84, 1942.

Mühlhöfer, Lisl. Abbé J[ean] B[ernard]
Le Blanc, sein Leben und sein Werk;
ein Beitrag zur Geschichte der Anglomanie
im Frankreich des 18. Jahrhunderts.
Würzburg, Kilian, 1936. 87 p. (Diss.,
Würzburg).   2930

Useful survey of Le Blanc's career and
analysis of his ideas about English and
their literature. Omits discussion of the
Kingston—La Touche affair, for which
see G. Desnoiresterres, *Épicuriens et
lettrés : XVIIe et XVIIIe siècles*, 1879,
p. 359-428.

Le Clerc (*See also* Shaftesbury)

Barnes, Annie. Jean Le Clerc (1657-1736)
et la république des lettres. *See* 1114,
2426, 2773.   2931

Detailed account of Le Clerc's life and
his activities as journalist and controvers-
ialist, with due attention to his importance
in dissemination of English thought on
Continent in early 18th century.
Reviews : D. F. Bond in MP 37:213-14,
1939-40; D. Mornet in RHL 46:131-32,
1939; E. Philips in RR 30:203-04, 1939.

Le Tourneur (*See also* Shakespeare)

Cushing, Mary G. Pierre Le Tourneur.
See 583.   2932

Best account of Le Tourneur's work
as translator, but needs revision in light
of later research.
Reviews : F. Baldensperger in RG
6:75-76, 1910; M. J. Minckwitz in ZFSL
35²:83-85, 1909.

De Lolme

Ruff, S. Edith. Jean-Louis de Lolme und
sein Werk über die Verfassung Englands.
Berlin, Ebering, 1934. 108 p. (HS, 240).
                                           2933

Competent study of De Lolme's
political ideas as expressed in his *Constitution de l'Angleterre* (Amsterdam,
1771) and in relation to his sojourn in
England.
Review : W. M[uller] in AJJR 23:188-
89, 1934.

Mercier

Béclard, Léon. Sébastien Mercier : sa vie,
son œuvre, son temps, d'après des documents inédits. *See* 598.   2934

Treats incidentally Mercier's English
interests, his translation of *Rape of the
lock* in 1764, his versions of Shakespeare,
and his admiration of Milton, Young, and
Richardson.

Zollinger, O. Ein französischer Shake-
speare-Bearbeiter des 18. Jahrhunderts.
ShJ 38:98-117, 1902.   2935

Detailed study of Mercier's adaptations
of Shakespeare. Fails to take into
account, however, his indebtedness to
Ducis.

Muralt

Muralt, B. L. Lettres sur les Anglois et les
François et sur les voiages (1728). Ed. by
Charles Gould. Champion, 1933. 381 p.
                                           2936

Reprints revised text of 1728. Introduction situates *Lettres* in biography
of Muralt, discusses their originality and
importance, and traces their influence in
18th and 19th centuries. Helpful notes.
Excellent bibliography of editions. Supersedes editions of E. Ritter and O. von
Greyerz (both of 1897).
Reviews : F. B[aldensperger] in RLC
14:411-12, 1934; A. Schinz in MLN

49:485-86, 1934; J. Thomas in Rcr ns 100:493-94, 1933; J. M. S. Tompkins in RES 12:228-30, 1936; in TLS, July 6, 1933, p. 459.

Texte, Joseph. Béat Louis de Muralt et les origines du cosmopolitisme littéraire au XVIIIe siècle. RHL 1:8-26, 1894.   2937

Good discussion of Muralt and controversy aroused by publication of *Lettres*. Points out importance of Muralt as a pioneer in 18th century Anglomania.

Rutlidge

Las Vergnas, Raymond. Le chevalier Rutlidge, " gentilhomme anglais " (1742-1794). Champion, 1932. 238 p.   2938

First full-length biography of this cosmopolitan figure. Thanks to his mixed Irish-French ancestry, Rutlidge wrote with equal fluency in French and English. His *Essay on the characters and manners of the French* (of 1770) and his satiric novel, *La quinzaine angloise à Paris* (of 1776) both served to carry out Rutlidge's main purpose, " une fusion du point de vue français et du point de vue anglais " (p. 36). His imitations of Goldsmith and the *Spectator* and his defense of Shakespeare against Voltaire were influential. All these works are analyzed by Las Vergnas and situated chronologically in this carefully documented biography. There is an informative chapter (p. 46-57) on *Le milieu irlandais* in 18th century France.
Reviews : D. Mornet in RHL 39:467-68, 1932; in TLS, Aug. 18, 1932, p. 578.

De Saussure

Saussure, César de. A foreign view of England in the reigns of George I and George II; the letters of Monsieur César de Saussure to his family. Trans. and ed. by Mme B. van Muyden. London, Murray, 1902. 384 p. Lettres et voyages de Monsieur César de Saussure en Allemagne, en Hollande et en Angleterre, 1725-29, ed. B. van Muyden. Fischbacher, 1903.   2939

Interesting record of English life which supplements and parallels Voltaire's. *Lettres* provide good field for further study. *See* René Doumic, *La découverte de l'Angleterre au XVIIIe siècle*, in his *Études sur la littérature française*, 5e sér. (Perrin, 1906), p. 71-85 (originally published in RDM, 15 décembre 1903, p. 909-16); and G. Lanson, *Deux voyages*

en Angleterre : Voltaire et César de Saussure, RHL 13:693-97, 1906 (points out borrowings from Voltaire and raises question of further plagiarism by Saussure).
Review : in Ath June 14, 1902, p. 744.

Suard (*See also* Garrick)

Suard, Jean Baptiste Antoine. Lettres inédites de Suard à Wilkes, publiées par Gabriel Bonno. *See* 2801.   2940

Prints 57 letters, dating from 1764 to 1780, accompanied by a brief introduction, " observations finales," excellent notes and an index. Gives information not only on personal relations of Suard and Wilkes, but also on progress of Anglomania in France between 1764 and 1780.
Review : M. Chazin in RR 24:63, 1933.

Hunter, Alfred C. J. B. A. Suard : un introducteur de la littérature anglaise en France. *See* 2802.   2941

Most important part of this book is series of chapters analyzing English material in *Journal étranger* (1760-62) and *Gazette littéraire* (1764-66), which Suard edited; also a chapter on *Suard traducteur* and a *résumé* of Suard's life. Dates and titles need constant checking.
Reviews : A. Brulé in RAA 3:549-50, 1925-26; L. Cazamian in Rcr ns 93:455-57, 1926; in RLC 5:722, 1925; P. Van Tieghem in RSH 40:134-35, 1925.

Thémiseul de Saint-Hyacinthe

Bastide, Charles. The strange adventures of the translator of Robinson Crusoe, the Chevalier de Thémiseul. *See* 2921, p. 217-27.   2942

Readable account of this cosmopolitan figure, author of popular *Chef-d'œuvre d'un inconnu*.

Horsley, Phyllis M. Thémiseul de Saint-Hyacinthe (1684-1746). CLS 4:6-13, 1942.   2943

Best up-to-date brief sketch.

Van Effen

Pienaar, W. J. B. English influences in Dutch literature and Justus Van Effen as intermediary : an aspect of eighteenth century achievement. *See* 2767.   2944

Important survey of English literature on Continent in early 18th century.

Van Effen, central figure in this study, translated Shaftesbury (in 1710), DeFoe (in 1720-21), Swift (in 1721), and Mandeville (in 1723); he contributed to the *Journal littéraire* (in 1713-22), visited England twice (1715-16, 1727-28), and published three important series of essays in manner of Addison and Steele. Reviews : J. Boyd in MLR 25:238-41, 1930; K. R. Gallas in Beibl 43:184-89, 1932; P. Van Tieghem in RSH 50:125-26, 1930.

Periodicals

Van Tieghem, Paul. L'année littéraire (1754-1790) comme intermédiaire en France des littératures étrangères. *See* 2796, 2884, 3221, 3275.   2945

Important but by no means exhaustive analysis of Fréron's periodical, with useful indications of more important reviews of foreign books.
Reviews : *See* 2796.

Beckwith, F. The Bibliothèque britannique, 1733-47. *See* 2843.   2946

Bibliographical study, with analysis of contents.

Sichel, Julius. Die englische Literatur im Journal étranger. Ein Beitrag zur Geschichte der literarischen Beziehungen zwischen England und Frankreich im 18. Jahrhundert. Darmstadt, Otto, 1907. 75 p. (Diss., Heidelberg).   2947

Describes briefly reviews of English books (*Die Dichtung*, p. 8-41; and *Die Wissenschaft*, p. 41-60). Useful finding list, but with little interpretation or attempt to relate judgments of *Journal étranger* to earlier reporting of English works.
Review : F. Baldensperger in RG 4:605-06, 1908.

Staab, Jakob. Das Journal étranger unter dem Abbé Prévost und seine Bedeutung für die literarischen Beziehungen zwischen England und Frankreich im Zeitalter der Aufklärung. *See* 2788.   2948

Discusses briefly English books reviewed in *Journal étranger* under Prévost's editorship (January-August, 1755).

La Harpe, Jacqueline de. Le Journal des savants et l'Angleterre, 1702-1789. *See* 2812.   2950

Interesting and informative study, emphasizing periods 1702-30 and 1750-

60 as most important for the subject. Findings interpreted with skill and judgment. Serviceable index. Cf. no. 3001.
Review : D. S. Schier in RR 32:429-30, 1941.

Hemprich, Paul. Le Journal littéraire de la Haye, 1713-1737. Berlin, Hermann, 1915. 143 p. (Diss., Berlin).   2951

Brief history of *Journal littéraire*, biographies of its editors, and (p. 34-130) an analysis of contents arranged by subjects. For English literature, chiefly important *Dissertation sur la poésie angloise*, see p. 50-52, 61-64, 66-69, and index.

Helming, Vernon P. Edward Gibbon and Georges Deyverdun, collaborators in the Mémoires littéraires de la Grande Bretagne. PMLA 47:1028-49, 1932.   2952

Analyzes reviews of English books, with extensive quotations and *bibliographical note* (p. 1048-49).

King, G. V. Michel de La Roche et ses Mémoires littéraires de la Grande-Bretagne. *See* 2836.   2953

Statistical table analyzing contents : scientific and theological works most prominent.

Lovering, Stella. L'activité intellectuelle de l'Angleterre d'après l'ancien Mercure de France (1672-1778). *See* 2820, 2901. 2954

Brings together good deal of material relating to English science, philosophy, and literature, as seen in *Mercure galant* and its successors. Documentation uneven and not altogether accurate.
Reviews : Donald F. Bond in PQ 11:213-14, 1932; P. Brunet in Archeion 13:133-34, 1931; A. Digeon in RAA 9:153-54, 1931-32; E. Ellery in AHR 36:859, 1930-31; A. Koszul in Rcr ns 98:264-66, 1931.

The vogue of English authors in France

Addison and Steele (*See also* De Brosses, Marivaux, Prévost, Voltaire)

Price, Lawrence M. Inkle and Yarico album. Berkeley, University of California press, 1937. 171, 38 p.   2955

Excellent comparative study of literary theme stemming from *Spectator* No. 11. Reviews : D. F. Bond in MP 36:81-83, 1938-39; H. Flasdieck in Beibl 49:157-61, 1938; in TLS, Jan. 1, 1938, p. 8.

Bacon (*See also* Diderot)

Adam, Charles E. Philosophie de François Bacon. Alcan, 1890. 437 p.   2956

Book IV (*Influence de Bacon aux XVIIe, XVIIIe et XIXe siècles*) sketches briefly vogue and influence of Bacon in England and France. See particularly ch. ii : *Bacon et les philosophes du XVIIIe siècle*. Though incomplete, is a good starting point for study.

Beckford

Hunter, A. O. Le Vathek de William Beckford: historique des éditions françaises. RLC 15:119-26, 1935.   2957

Useful bibliography. See also G. Jean-Aubry, *Autour du Vathek de William Beckford*. RLC 16:549-52, 1936.

Aphra Behn (*See also* Prévost)

Seeber, Edward D. Oroonoko in France in the eighteenth century. PMLA 51:953-59, 1936.   2958

Study of popularity of Mrs. Behn's novel and dramatic adaptation by Southerne.

Bolingbroke   2959
See Pope, Montesquieu, Voltaire.

Sir Thomas Browne

Leroy, Olivier. A French bibliography of Sir Thomas Browne. London, Harrap, 1931. 97 p.   2960

Reviews : in RLC 11:827-28, 1931; in TLS, Feb. 25, 1932, p. 132.

Chaucer

Hunter, Alfred C. Le Conte de la Femme de Bath en français au XVIIIe siècle. RLC 9:117-40, 1929.   2961

Discusses Voltaire's *Ce qui plaît aux dames* and four other versions of the tale, 1757-1770. Points out these are dependent either on Voltaire's story or on Dryden's modernization of Chaucer. Hence they cannot be taken as evidence for 18th century interest in Chaucer.

Spurgeon, Caroline F. E. Chaucer devant la critique en Angleterre et en France depuis son temps jusqu'à nos jours. Hachette, 1911. 422 p.   2962

Ch. VII (*Chaucer en France*) best survey of subject, though incomplete.

P. 221-43 deal with 18th century and trace growth of knowledge about Chaucer in encyclopedias, journals, and miscellaneous works. It is not until 1803, with Suard's article in *Biographie universelle*, that " nous ... voyons pour la première fois un Français nous laisser entendre qu'il a lu du Chaucer dans l'original." Author's survey of periodicals extends only to *Journal littéraire de la Haye*, *Pour et contre*, *Journal étranger*, and *Journal anglais*.

Reviews : in Ath, Aug. 19, 1911, p. 216-17; in Archiv 127 : 449-50, 1912; F. Baldensperger in RG 7:603, 1911; E. Legouis, *ibid.* 8:75-76, 1912; P. Reyher in RELV 29:431-32, 1912.

Chesterfield

Gulick, Sidney L. Jr. A Chesterfield bibliography to 1800. Chicago, University of Chicago press, 1935. 114 p.   2963

Lists translations (p. 33-39).

Cibber

See Voltaire (no. 3092).   2963A

A. Collins

See Voltaire (no. 3104).   2963B

Thomas Day

Carrière, J.-M. A French adaptation of *Sandford and Merton*. MLN 50:238-42, 1935.   2964

Describes translation of first two parts of Day's novel by Arnaud Berquin (in 1786-87) (*see* no. 2917) and analyzes briefly changes made to suit French taste.

Defoe (*See also* Prévost)

Dottin, Paul. La vie et les aventures étranges et surprenantes de Daniel Defoe... Presses universitaires, 1924. 896 p. 2965

Pt. II, ch. vi (*Robinson Crusoë en France*) provides full and detailed study of vogue and influence of Defoe's novel in France, including material in W. E. Mann's dissertation (of 1916) Reviews : L. Cazamian in RAA 1:438-40, 1924; S. B. Liljegren in Beibl 36:340, 1925; H. V. Routh in MLR 22:104-05, 1927.

Dryden

See Chaucer, Voltaire.   2965A

Fielding

Waldschmidt, Carl. Die Dramatisierungen von Fielding's Tom Jones. Wetzlar, K. Waldschmidt, 1906. 104 p. (Diss., Rostock). 2966

Deals with English, German, and French versions, including those by Poinsinet (in 1765) and Desforges (in 1782).

Garrick (*See also* d'Holbach)

Hedgcock, Frank A. David Garrick et ses amis français. Hachette, 1911. 283 p. (Diss., Paris). A cosmopolitan actor : David Garrick and his French friends. London, Stanley Paul, 1911. 442 p. 2967

Full account, based on original sources, of Garrick's two visits to Paris in 1751 and 1763-65. Contains much information on interrelations between French and English theaters of time, on Anglomania, and on introduction of Shakespeare to French stage. Part IV (*Garrick's French correspondence*) prints letters from such persons as Jean Monnet, Suard, D'Holbach, and Mme Necker. Includes bibliography of French translations of Garrick's works and list of French biographies of Garrick. The " journal kept by Garrick for a short time during his stay in France " (p. 156 n.) is now in Folger Shakespeare Library and has been published (*The Journal of David Garrick, describing his visit to France and Italy in 1763*, ed. George W. Stone, Jr., New York, M. L. A., 1939).
Reviews : F. Baldensperger in RHL 20:450-51, 1913; C. Bastide in Rcr ns 72:90, 1911; H. F. Stewart in MLR 7:387-90, 1912.

Gay

Goulding, Sybil. Eighteenth-century French taste and The Beggar's Opera. MLR 24:276-93, 1929. 2968

Thorough study of Gay's play and its conflicts with French ideas of drama.

Gibbon

Norton, J. E. A bibliography of the works of Edward Gibbon. London, Oxford univ. press, 1940. 256 p. 2969

Includes French translations.
Reviews : D. M. Low in RES 17:361-63, 1941; in TLS, Nov. 16, 1940, p. 584.

Goldsmith

Barwick, G. F. Notes from the first French translation of " The Vicar of Wakefield." Libr ns 5:134-45, 1904. 2970

Carrière, J.-M. Notes on Arnaud Berquin's adaptations from English poetry. RR 26:335-40, 1933. 2971

Goldsmith's *Hermit*, and *The Spanish virgin* from Percy's *Reliques*. In Berquin's *Romances* (of 1776).

Seeber, Edward D. and **Henry H. H. Remak.** The first French translation of " The deserted village." MLR 41:62-67, 1946. 2972

Account of Campion's translation.

Sells, A. Lytton. Oliver Goldsmith's influence on the French stage. DUJ 33:86-101, 1941. 2973

Gray

Northup, C. S. A bibliography of Thomas Gray. New Haven, Yale univ. press, 1917. 296 p. 2974

Includes French translations.
Review : P. Toynbee in MLR 13:343-45, 1918.

Harrington

Lesueur, Théodore. A French draft constitution of 1792 modelled on James Harrington's Oceana : Théodore Lesueur, Idées sur l'espèce de gouvernement populaire qui pourroit convenir à un pays de l'étendue et de la population présumée de la France. Ed. with an introduction on Harrington's influence in France and notes by S. B. Liljegren. (Skrifter utgivna av Kungl. humanistiska vetenskapssamfundet i Lund, 17.) Lund, Gleerup; London, Milford, 1932. 180 p. 2975

Lists translations of Harrington and points out his influence (through Thomas Gordon) on such French writers as Montesquieu, Mably, Condillac, Sieyès, and Lesueur.
Reviews : L. Cazamian in RAA 10:57, 1932-33; W. Fischer in LGRP 55:229-30, 1934; L. Gottschalk in MP 30:232-34, 1932-33; A. Stern in Beibl 43:167-68, 1932.

Eliza Haywood (*See also* Prévost)

Hughes, Helen S. Notes on eighteenth-century fictional translations. MP 17:225-31, 1919-20. 2976

Mainly on English translations of French fiction; but p. 226-27 discuss fortunes of Mrs. Haywood's *Fortunate foundlings* (of 1744), its adaptation by Crébillon *fils* as *Les heureux orphelins* (of 1754), and retranslation into English with changes, as *The happy orphans* (of 1758).

Whicher, George F. The life and romances of Mrs. Eliza Haywood. New York, Columbia univ. press, 1915. 210 p. (Diss., Columbia).   2977

Bibliography (p. 176-204) includes French translations of Mrs. Haywood's novels.
Reviews : C. Bastide in Rcr ns 80:404-06, 1915; C. A. Moore in JEGP 16:163-65, 1917; W. Paterna in Beibl 27:280-85, 1916; D. H. Stevens in MP 14:59-61, 1916-17.

Hobbes
(*See also* D'Holbach, Prévost, Rousseau)

Laird, John. Hobbes. London, Benn, [1934], 324 p.   2978

Includes in Part III (Influence) interesting though too brief sketch of reputation and influence of Hobbes in 18th-century France, particularly with regard to Rousseau.
Reviews : S. P. L[amprecht] in Jph 31:551-52, 1934; A. T. Shillinglaw in Mind ns 44:75-84, 1935; in TLS, May 10, 1934, p. 332.

Hume (*See also* Diderot, D'Holbach, Montesquieu, Rousseau)

[Metz, L.] Les amitiés françaises de Hume et le mouvement des idées. RLC 9:644-714, 1929.   2979

Precise information on Hume's contacts with France and his influence on French thought.
(Author's name mis-spelled as Mertz).

Mossner, Ernest C. The continental reception of Hume's Treatise, 1739-1741. Mind ns 56:31-43, 1947.   2980

Excellent account of reaction to *Treatise of human nature*.

Hutcheson

Aldridge, Alfred O. A French critic of Hutcheson's aesthetics. MP 45:169-84, 1947-48.   2981

Study of *Essay philosophique sur le beau & sur le goût* (1750) of Charles Louis de Villette.

Inchbald

Joughin, G. Louis. An Inchbald bibliography. TSE 14:59-74, 1934.   2982

Lists a few late 18th century French translations.

George Jeffreys

See Voltaire (no. 3116).   2983

Jonson

Grubbs, Henry A. An early French adaptation of an Elizabethan comedy : J. B. Rousseau as an imitator of Ben Jonson. MLN 55:170-76, 1940.   2984

Adaptation of Jonson's *Epicoene*, written c. 1733 but not printed until 1751, under title *L'hypocondre, ou la femme qui ne parle point*.

Charlotte Lennox

Small, Miriam R. Charlotte Ramsay Lennox : an eighteenth century lady of letters. New Haven, Yale univ. press, 1935. 268 p.   2985

Appendix VI (p. 248-60) contains bibliography of Mrs. Lennox's novels, including translations.
Review : C. Rinaker in JEGP 35:291-93, 1936.

Matthew Gregory Lewis

Baldensperger, Fernand. Le Moine de Lewis dans la littérature française. JCL 1:201-18, 1903.   2986

There were two translations of Lewis' novel in 1797, but most material treated here lies in the Romantic movement. Good analysis of elements in *The monk* which made it popular in France during Revolution.

Lillo

Benn, T. Vincent. Notes sur la fortune du George Barnwell de Lillo en France. RLC 6:682-87, 1926.   2987

Lists 18th century translations, with notes on textual changes and performances.

Locke
(*See also* Helvétius, D'Holbach, Montesquieu, Prévost, Rousseau, Sieyès, Voltaire)

Fabre, Joseph. Les pères de la Révolution (de Bayle à Condorcet). *See* 1409.   2988

Book I *(Les précurseurs)* considers Locke's influence on *philosophes*. " Bayle inspira la philosophie française dans son œuvre militante; Locke l'inspira dans son œuvre doctrinale " (p. 38). Good summary, but without references, of Locke's chief ideas; rather sweeping generalizations as to Locke's influence on Montesquieu, Voltaire, and Rousseau.

Mandeville
(See also Montesquieu, Voltaire)

Kaye, F. B. The influence of Bernard Mandeville. SP 19:83-108, 1922.   2989

Study of Mandeville's influence in three fields of literature (particularly on Voltaire), ethics (Helvétius), and economics (Voltaire, Melon, and Montesquieu). *See also* Kaye's edition of *Fable of the bees* (Oxford, Clarendon press, 1924), 2 v.

Milton
(See also André Chénier, Voltaire)

Racine, Louis. Life of Milton, together with Observations on Paradise lost. Translated, with an introduction, by Katherine John. London, L. and Virginia Woolf, 1930. 158 p.   2990

Introduction presents attractively written account of Milton's vogue in 18th century France.
Reviews : D. Saurat in RES 7:474, 1931; in TLS, Oct. 23, 1930, p. 869.

Robertson, J. G. Milton's fame on the continent. PBA 3:319-40, 1908.   2991

Excellent brief sketch.
Reviews : F. Baldensperger in RG 6:73-74, 1910; K. Lincke in Beibl 22:364, 1911.

Stevens, David H. Reference guide to Milton from 1800 to the present day. Chicago, University of Chicago press, 1930. 302 p.   2992

For studies of Milton's reputation in France see section XIX *(Influence)*.
Reviews : H. Fletcher in MLN 46:539-41, 1931; D. Saurat in RES 7:473, 1931; E. N. S. Thompson in PQ 9:317, 1930.

Telleen, John M. Milton dans la littérature française. Hachette, 1904. 151 p. (Diss., Paris).   2993

Rapid sketch of Milton's vogue and influence; chapters II-VI devoted to 18th century (chapter III on Voltaire). Facts need checking and book somewhat weak in interpretation of materials. Remains best single treatment of subject to date.
Reviews : F. Baldensperger in RG 1:718-19, 1905; C. Bastide in Rcr ns 58:397-98, 1904; J. Delcourt in ES 37:244-47, 1907; W. Küchler in ZFSL 29²:52-55, 1906; in TLS, Sept. 2, 1904, p. 268.

Newton *(See also* Voltaire)

Bloch, Léon. La philosophie de Newton. Alcan, 1908. 643 p.   2994

Ch. x *(Voltaire et Newton)* offers substantial analysis of Voltaire's interpretation of Newton and his pioneering effort to substitute scientific point of view for old metaphysical " systems."
Reviews : G. Milhaud in RMM 16:492-506, 1908; J. Sageret in Rph 66:100-04, 1908.

Brunet, Pierre. L'introduction des théories de Newton en France au xviiie siècle avant 1738. Librairie scientifique Albert Blanchard, 1931. 355 p.   2995

Standard account of beginnings of newtonianism in France and cartesian opposition up to publication of Voltaire's *Éléments de la philosophie de Newton*.
Reviews : T. E. Jessop in Mind 41:259-60, 1932; Hélène Metzger in Rph 114:147-48, 1932; P. Wolff in RHP 5:426-27, 1931.

Mouy, Paul. Malebranche et Newton. RMM 45:411-35, 1938.   2995A

Shows Newton's influence on the 6th edition of the *Recherche de la vérité* (of 1712).

Schier, Donald S. Louis-Bertrand Castel, anti-Newtonian scientist. Cedar Rapids, Iowa, Torch press, 1941. 229 p.   2996

Interesting notes on *anti-philosophe* opposition to Newton in France.
Review : G. R. Havens in MLQ 2:639-40, 1941.

" Ossian "

Van Tieghem, Paul. Ossian en France. *See* 2803.   2997

Thorough, definitive treatment. Model for studies of this type.
Reviews : G. Ascoli in RSH 30:191-94, 1920; A. Cahen in RDS 5:93-95, 1918; T. P. Cross in MP 16:439-48, 1918-19; E. P. Dargan in MLN 33:357-66, 1918;

A. Monglond in RHL 27:607-17, 1920;
L. Roustan in Rcr ns 84:263-68, 1917.

Percy, Thomas
(*See* Goldsmith, 2971)   2998

Pope (*See also* Voltaire)

Audra, E. L'influence française dans l'œuvre de Pope. Champion, 1931. 650 p.
2999

Book I, part ii (*Les rapports de Pope
avec la France et les Français*) lists
translations of Pope in French during
first half of century, and quotes extensively from letters and memoirs to show
extent of Pope's reputation in France.
Particularly valuable is the account of
vogue of *Essay on man* and controversy
aroused by Crousaz's attack on Pope
(p. 87-107). Best treatment of subject
to date.
Reviews : J. Butt in MLR 27:481-83,
1932; A. F. B. Clark in RLC 12:903-17,
1932; R. S. C[rane] in PQ 11:200-01,
1932; G. Sherburn in MLN 50:475-77,
1935.

— Les traductions françaises de Pope (1717-
1825) : étude de bibliographie. Champion,
1931. 135 p.   3000
Addenda by F. Beckwith in MLR
29:70-72, 1934.
Review : J. de La Harpe in RR 23:65-
66, 1932.

La Harpe, Jacqueline de. Le Journal des
savants et la renommée de Pope en France
au XVIIIe siècle. *See* 2811, 2950.   3001

Part I (p. 175-96) summarizes briefly
reviews of translations in the *Journal des
savants*, and in *Mémoires de Trévoux*,
which were combined with *Journal des
savants* in Holland edition of 1754-64.
Part II (p. 197-215) interprets and analyzes material, and shows convincingly
that it was Pope as thinker rather than
as poet who interested *Journal des
savants*. Within limits set, excellent
study.

Van Tieghem, Philippe. La Prière universelle de Pope et le déisme français au
XVIIIe siècle. RLC 3:190-212, 1923.   3002

Illuminating analysis of action and
reaction provoked by Pope's poem
(translated by Le Franc de Pompignan in
1741).

Richardson (*See also* Diderot, Prévost,
Rousseau, Voltaire)

Facteau, Bernard A. Les romans de

Richardson sur la scène française. Presses
universitaires, [1927]. 144 p. (Diss.,
Paris).   3003

Useful study of dramatic adaptations
of Richardson's three novels in France.

Purdie, E. Some adventures of Pamela on
the Continental stage. *In :* GSF p. 352-84.
3004

Includes discussion of La Chaussée's
Paméla.

Shadwell (*See* Destouches, no. 3042)
3004A

Shaftesbury (*See also* Diderot)

Casati, Ennemond. Quelques correspondants français de Shaftesbury. *See* 1120.
3005

Includes discussion of Bayle, Leclerc,
Des Maizeaux, and Coste.

— Hérauts et commentateurs de Shaftesbury
en France. *See* 2427.   3006

Best brief discussion of dissemination
of Shaftesbury's ideas in France.

Shakespeare (*See also* M.-J. Chénier,
Prévost, Voltaire)

Baldensperger, Fernand. Esquisse d'une
histoire de Shakespeare en France. *See*
514.   3007

Excellent interpretation, particularly of
influence of Shakespeare on French
writers of later 18th century. Studies of
Havens (nos. 804-05) modify importance
given here to Prévost's Anglomania.
Reviews : Archiv 125:261-62, 1910;
J. Aynard in RG 7:353-56, 1911; D.
Mornet in RHL 18:457-61, 1911; L.
R[oustan] in Rcr ns 70:190-92, 1910;
G. Rudler in RU 20²:145, 1911.

Bösser, Reinhold. Shakespeare's Romeo
and Juliet in französischer Bearbeitung.
Frankfort a. M., Voight and Gleiber, 1907.
(Diss., Rostock). 132 p.   3007A

Assembles data on French translations
and adaptations.

Dargan, E. Preston. Shakespeare and
Ducis. *See* 515.   3008

Critical dicussion of Ducis, with
illuminating analyses of adaptations of
Hamlet, Romeo and Juliet, Lear, Macbeth,
and *Othello*, and an important account
(p. 171-77) of other 18th century attempts
to adapt Shakespeare to the French stage.

Dubeux, Albert. Les traductions françaises de Shakespeare. (Études françaises, 15). Les belles lettres, [1928]. 81 p. 3009

Essay, followed (p. 49-81) by valuable bibliography of *Traductions et adaptations françaises de Shakespeare*, based mainly on Rondel collection at *Bibliothèque de l'Arsenal*, listing translations of complete works and individual plays. Reviews : A. Brulé in RAA 6:64-65, 1928-29; R. Pruvost in Rcr ns 96:40, 1929; P. Van Tieghem in RSH 46:135-36, 1928.

Ebisch, Walther, and Levin L. Schücking. A Shakespeare bibliography. Oxford, Clarendon press, 1931. 294 p. 3010

Standard bibliography of material on Shakespeare (to 1929), with sections on Shakespeare's influence on French writers, and French translations of Shakespeare.

Supplement for the years 1930-1935, Oxford, Clarendon press, 1937, 104 p.

Feuillerat, Albert. Shakespeare's influence : France. CBEL, I, 599-604, 1940. 3011

Best summary bibliography.

Gilman, Margaret. Othello in French. Champion, 1925. 197 p. (Diss., Bryn Mawr). 3012

Part I (p. 1-75) gives an excellent account of first translations of *Othello* by La Place (in 1745) and Le Tourneur (in 1776); first versions intended for the stage by Douin (in 1773), Butini (in 1785), and an unknown author; and Ducis's version, first to be performed in France (in 1792). Specific comments on omissions, changes, and additions. Reviews : L. Cazamian in Rcr ns 93:454-55, 1926; J. Derocquigny in RAA 3:340-43, 1925-26; P. Van Tieghem in RSH 42:136-37, 1926; M. J. Wolff in ES 65:106-07, 1930-31.

Haak, Paul. Die ersten französischen Shakespeare-Uebersetzungen von La Place und Le Tourneur. Steinau, Wolf, 1922. 94 p. (Diss., Berlin). 3013

Gives adequate summaries of prefaces of two editions and detailed study of textual changes made by La Place and Le Tourneur (p. 24-34, 56-84). Review : W. Keller in ShJ 59-60:196, 1924.

Haines, C. M. Shakespeare in France : criticism, Voltaire to Victor Hugo. *See* 516. 3014

Written in uneven, in places brilliant, style, centers around two focal points of Shakespeare's reputation in France, Voltaire and Hugo. " For a hundred years he was unknown; for a hundred years he was despised; for a hundred years he was adored." Facts drawn mainly from Jusserand (no. 3015), not always accurately. Based on insufficient documentation and fails to take into account adaptations and imitations. Bibliography incomplete and inaccurate. Stimulating essay. Needs constant checking. Reviews : in Archiv 150:158, 1926; W. D. Briggs in MLN 42:539-46, 1927; H. T. Price in Beibl 38:113, 1927; A. W. Reed in RES 2:109-11, 1926; J. G. R[obertson] in MLR 21:106-07, 1926; H. Servajean in RAA 4:150-54, 1926-27.

Jusserand, J. J. Shakespeare en France sous l'ancien régime. Colin, 1898, 389 p. English translation, see 518, 812. 3015

Still most readable and generally authoritative survey, summing up a great deal of previous research on subject. Superseded in details, particularly on history of particular plays and on role of Prévost; see 3063-64. Reviews : A. B[randl] in ShJ 36:320-21, 1900; S. Lee in Ncent 45:930-37, 1899; J. Texte in RHL 6:144-45, 1899.

Keys, Allwyn C. Les adaptations musicales de Shakespeare en France jusqu'en 1870. Recueil Sirey, 1933. 237 p. (Diss., Paris). 3016

Chapters II and III deal with 18th century adaptations (1761-1806), published and unpublished. A *Bibliographie des livrets et des partitions* (p. 221-25), arranged in chronological order, provides useful finding-list. Many typographical errors.

Looten, Camille. La première controverse internationale sur Shakespeare entre l'abbé Leblanc et W. Guthrie, 1745-1747-1758. Lille, Université catholique, 1927. 48 p. (MTL, 32). 3017

Precise account of quarrel, summing up arguments and placing controversy in general current of French thought of period. Reviews : F. L. Schoell in RAA 5:361, 1928; P. Van Tieghem in RSH 46:136, 1928.

Saur, Albert. Shakesperes König Lear in Frankreich bis zum Jahre 1827. Ansbach, Brügel, 1910. 48 p. (Diss., Munich). 3018

Careful study of translations and adaptations of *King Lear* in France up to year of Hugo's preface to *Cromwell*. Good remarks on critics' reactions to Shakespeare's tragedy. Still useful.

Review : H. Weyhe in ShJ 48:210, 1912.

Van Tieghem, Paul. Le préromantisme; études d'histoire européenne. III. La découverte de Shakespeare sur le continent. SFELT, 1947. 412 p. 3019

Comprehensive and penetrating account of impact of Shakespeare's drama, particularly the tragedies, on Continent, with emphasis on Shakespeare as a liberating force in 18th century esthetic theory.

Review : L. M. Price in CL 1:88-90, 1949.

Frances Sheridan

See Prévost, 788, 3058A. 3019A

Sidney

Osborn, Albert W. Sir Philip Sidney en France. Champion, 1932. 171 p. 3020

Largely devoted to 17th century. Ch. 8 deals with *Sidney en France pendant le Grand Siècle et depuis* and shows references to Sidney in this period only incidental and indirect.

Reviews : M. S. Goldman in JEGP 23:295-300, 1934; H. C. Lancaster in MLN 48:269-73, 1933.

Smollett

Joliat, Eugène. Smollett et la France. *See* 735. 3021

Excellent study of Smollett's indebtedness to French authors, his contacts with France, and (Part III) Smollett's vogue and influence in France. Deals not only with novels but also Smollett's *History of England*. Good bibliography of translations (p. 255-69).

Reviews : in RLC 15:380, 1935; E. S. Noyes in MLN 52:66-68, 1937; H. W. Streeter in RR 26:357-59, 1935.

Thomas Southerne (*See* Aphra Behn, 2958)

Steele (*See* Prévost, Voltaire) 3021A

Sterne

Baldwin, Charles S. The literary influence of Sterne in France. PMLA 17:221-36, 1902. 3022

Largely concerned with 19th century imitations of Sterne. Considers *Jacques le fataliste* " an imitation not of the tone, but of the method and manner " of *Tristram Shandy*. Cf. J. Robert Loy, *Diderot's Determined Fatalist* (N. Y. King's crown press, 1950, no. 2219A) for a somewhat different view.

Barton, Francis B. Étude sur l'influence de Laurence Sterne en France au dix-huitième siècle. *See* 733. 3023

Limited to somewhat obvious points, but still standard treatment. Good on similarities between Sterne and Diderot. *See* no. 3022.

Reviews : F. Baldensperger in RG 7:605, 1911, and in Rcr ns 72:255-56, 1911.

Swift (*See also* Diderot, Voltaire)

Goulding, Sybil. Swift en France; essai sur la fortune et l'influence de Swift en France au XVIIIᵉ siècle, suivi d'un aperçu sur la fortune de Swift en France au cours du XIXᵉ siècle. Champion, 1924. 210 p. 3024

Excellent survey, comprehensive for 18th century. Shows conclusively that Desfontaines' translation seriously altered conception of Swift for French readers. *Addenda* by C. M. Webster in MLN 47:152-53, 1932.

Reviews : F. Baldensperger in RLC 4:702-04, 1924; C. Bastide in Rcr ns 93:161-62, 1926; E. Pons in RAA 2:348-50, 1925; J. G. Robertson in MLR 20:93, 1925; A. Thibaudet in LM 11:532-34, 1924-25.

Teerink, Herman. A bibliography of the writings in prose and verse of Jonathan Swift, D. D. The Hague, Nijhoff, 1937, 434 p. 3025

Fullest available list of French translations of Swift's works.

Reviews : H. Williams in RES 13:366-73, 1937; in TLS, March 20, 1937, p. 228.

Thomson (*See also* Voltaire)

Cameron, Margaret M. L'influence des Saisons de Thomson sur la poésie descriptive en France (1759-1810). *See* 401. 3026

Important study, though somewhat narrow in its approach; does not always take into account other than English influences (e. g. Virgil's *Georgics*).

Reviews : in RLC 8:599, 1928; P. Van Tieghem in RSH 46:134-35, 1928.

Hirsch, André. James Thomson : ses traducteurs et ses critiques en France. RELV 42:66-75, 105-12, 160-72, 1925. 3027

Good brief analysis of vogue of Thomson in 18th century France. Part 3 (p. 160-72) is entitled *L'influence de Thomson en France.*

Seeber, Edward D. Anti-slavery opinion in the poems of some early French followers of James Thomson. MLN 50:427-34, 1935. 3028

Humanitarian views of Thomson, as seen in poems of Saint-Lambert, Chénier, Delille, and others (1769-1812).

Vanbrugh (*See* Voltaire, no. 3092)

Horace Walpole

Horace Walpole's Correspondence with Madame du Deffand and Wiart. Edited by W. S. Lewis and Warren H. Smith. *See* 128. 3029

Best edition, including much hitherto unpublished material. Volume V contains Walpole's *Paris journals* (1765-75). Contains a wealth of material on personalities of time, both in France and England.

Reviews : F. Baldensperger in VQR 16:308-11, 1940; D. M. Clark in AHR 46:130-32, 1940-41; G. T. Hellman in NY 25:31-41, Aug. 13, 1949; D. M. Low in RES 16:478-81, 1940; R. K. Root in MLN 56:310-12, 1941; H. Williams in MLR 35:543-46, 1940.

Yvon, Paul. La vie d'un dilettante : Horace Walpole (1717-1797) : essai de biographie psychologique et littéraire. Presses universitaires, 1924. 872 p. (Diss., Paris). 3030

Book 5 discusses in some detail Walpole's connections with France, including his travels and his contacts with French contemporaries.

Reviews : H. Buffenoir in Rcr ns 92:49-50, 1925; R. Huchon in RAA 2:248-52, 1924-25; A. M. Killen in RLC 5:698-701, 1925; R. Schneider in RSH 38:174-82, 1924; F. T. Wood in ES 66:285, 1931-32.

Young (*See also* A. Chénier)

Baldensperger, Fernand. Young et ses Nuits en France. *In his :* Études d'histoire littéraire. Hachette, 1907, p. 55-109. 3031

Best study of French translations and criticism of Young from 1762 through Romantic period.

Reviews : Archiv 119:475-76, 1907; J. Aynard in RG 7:353-56, 1911; R. M. Meyer in Euph 17:372-73, 1910; D. Mornet in RHL 15:541-45, 1908.

Thomas, Walter. Le poète Edward Young (1683-1765): étude sur sa vie et ses œuvres. Hachette, 1901. 663 p. 3032

Part II, ch. IX, gives a brief sketch of *Les nuits d'Young en France* (p. 521-51). *See also* p. 650-54 for a list of adaptations and translations.

Reviews : C. Bastide in Rcr ns 55:31-34, 1903; L. Cazamian in RHL 9:157-59, 1902; L. Morel in RU 11¹:277-78, 1902.

English influences on French authors

Bayle (*See also* Shaftesbury)

Courtines, Leo P. Bayle's relations with England and the English. *See* 1123. 3033

Important study, analyzing Bayle's knowledge of England and English thought; his relations with French refugees in England and with Boyle, Gilbert Burnet, Locke, Shaftesbury, and others; and (ch. III) opinions about Bayle in certain English periodicals. Appendices deal with (1) English references in *Œuvres diverses*, (2) articles on Englishmen in *Dictionnaire*, and (3) English references in Articles and Remarks of *Dictionnaire.*

Reviews : D. F. Bond in MP 36:322-25, 1938-39; L. I. Bredvold in JEGP 38:318, 1939; C. E. Engel in BSHP 87:591-92, 1938; E. Philips in RR 30:202-04, 1939.

De Brosses

Michéa, R. Le Président de Brosses en Italie : les sources de son érudition et de son esprit. RLC 14:425-53, 1934. 3033A

Some material on Addison's influence.

Buffon

Brown, Harcourt. Buffon and the Royal Society of London. *In :* StGS p. 141-65. 3034

Important study of Buffon's contacts with English scientists.

A. Chénier

Dimoff, Paul. Une source anglaise de l'Invention d'André Chénier. RLC 1:504-26, 1921. 3035

Calls attention to Young's *Conjectures on original composition* as source.

Kramer, C. Les poèmes épiques d'André Chénier. Neo 5:210-18, 1919-20.   3036

Deals with Milton's influence on *Susanne*.

Legros, René P. André Chénier en Angleterre. MLR 19:424-34, 1924.   3037

Deals with Chénier's sojourn in England in 1787-90 while he was attached to ambassador, Marquis de La Luzerne.

M.-J. Chénier

Liéby, A. Étude sur le théâtre de Marie-Joseph Chénier. *See* 554.   3038

Part II, ch. v, deals briefly with Chénier's *Brutus et Cassius* and its relation to Shakespeare.
Review : J. Bury in RHL 10:698-708, 1903.

Condillac (*See also* Harrington)

Kaye, F. B. Mandeville on the origin of language. *See* 1238.   3039

Discusses possible influence of *Fable of the bees* on Condillac.

Le Roy, Georges. La psychologie de Condillac. *See* 1246.   3040

Studies influence of Locke's ideas in France as background.
Reviews : H. A. L[arrabee] in Jph 34:524, 1937; P. A. Stéphanopoli in Rsyn 14:198, 1937.

Crébillon fils
(*See* Eliza Haywood, no. 2976)

Mme du Deffand (*See also* Horace Walpole)

Toynbee, Paget. Mme du Deffand and Hume. MLR 24:447-51, 1929.   3041

Destouches

Gilman, Margaret. Le Dissipateur and Timon of Athens. MLN 42:162-65, 1927.   3042

Shows that Destouches' play is based on Shadwell's adaptation of Shakespeare.

Wade, Ira O. Destouches in England. MP 29:27-47, 1931-32.   3043

Shows how correspondence of Destouches, who was in England from 1717 to 1723, reflects much the same interest

in English philosophy, science, politics, and literature which Voltaire was later to publicize in *Lettres philosophiques*.

Diderot (*See also* Sterne)

Cru, R. Loyalty. Diderot as a disciple of English thought. *See* 2330.   3044

Incomplete and exaggerated (Diderot " owed more to English than to French thought "), but best general account of Diderot's relations to England in four fields of philosophical and scientific thought, drama, fiction, and criticism. Cru's research done at a time when much information on Diderot was still obscure. " Information is lacking ... on almost every thing concerning his life between 1733 and 1743 " (p. 35).
Reviews : F. Baldensperger in RG 9:598-99, 1913; G. Lanson in RHL 21:443-45, 1914; P. Hazard in RU 23²:63, 1914.

Dieckmann, Herbert. The influence of Francis Bacon on Diderot's Interprétation de la nature. *See* 2334.   3045

Good analysis of method of Bacon's influence and suggestions as to reasons for Diderot's divergence from Bacon.

Legros, René P. Diderot et Shaftesbury. MLR 19:188-94, 1924.   3046

Able discussion of influence of Shaftesbury on *Pensées philosophiques*.

Pommier, J. Diderot avant Vincennes. Boivin, 1939. 119 p.   3047

Discusses influence of Shaftesbury and Swift on development of Diderot's thought. Published originally in RCC beginning 39:193-200, 1937-38.

Taupin, René. Richardson, Diderot et l'art de conter. FR 12:181-94, 1938-39.   3048

Notes particularly influence of *Pamela* on composition of *La religieuse*.

Venturi, Franco. Jeunesse de Diderot (1713-1753). *See* 2284.   3049

Analyzes Diderot's translations of Shaftesbury's *Enquiry concerning virtue* (*Essai sur le mérite et la vertu*, of 1745) and discusses Diderot's debt to Shaftesbury in the *Pensées philosophiques*.
Reviews : D. Mornet in RHL 46:129-31, 1939; A. O. in Crit 37:378-80, 1939.

Vexler, Felix. Studies in Diderot's aesthetic naturalism. *See* 2321.   3050

Relates much of Diderot's dramatic riticism to English philosophical and psychological writers, particularly Hume. Reviews : in RLC 4:160-61, 1924; D. Mornet in RHL 32:609-10, 1925.

Helvétius (*See also* Mandeville)

Keim, Albert. Helvétius : sa vie et son œuvre, d'après ses ouvrages, des écrits divers et des documents inédits. *See* 1332. 3051

Good on Locke's influence throughout, particularly in discussion (chapter XIV) of *Le livre de l'esprit*. Chapter XVIII describes Helvétius' visit to England in 1764.

D'Holbach (*See also* Garrick)

Lough, J. Essai de bibliographie critique des publications du baron d'Holbach. *See* 1346. 3052

P. 227-34 : *Traductions d'ouvrages anglais.*

Wickwar, W. H. Baron d'Holbach : a prelude to the French Revolution. *See* 1355, 3260. 3053

Pays considerable attention to D'Holbach's English friendships (Hume, Wilkes, Adam Smith, and Garrick), his translations of English works, and indebtedness to English philosophers (notably Toland, Hobbes, and Locke). Reviews : J. Lough in RHL 43:307-09, 1936; in TLS, Nov. 23, 1935, p. 759.

Malebranche (*See* Newton, no 2995A)

Marivaux

Gelobter, Hanna. Le Spectateur von Pierre Marivaux und die englischen moralischen Wochenschriften. Limburg, Limburger Vereinsdruckerei, 1936. 94 p. (Diss. Frankfurt.) 3054

Best brief survey of Marivaux's indebtedness to the *Spectator* of Addison and Steele.

Baldwin, Edward C. Marivaux's place in the development of character portrayal. PMLA 27:168-87, 1912. 3054A

Brief consideration of Addison's influence.

Montesquieu (*See also* Harrington, Locke, Mandeville)

Collins, J. Churton. Voltaire, Montesquieu,

and Rousseau in England. *See* no. 3098. 3054B

Dargan, E. P. Recent publications concerning Montesquieu. MLN 30:253-60, 1915. 3055

Discusses Montesquieu's relations with the English after his return from England, and points out his connections with Hume, Warburton, and others.

Dedieu, Joseph. Montesquieu et la tradition politique anglaise en France : les sources anglaises de l'Esprit des lois. *See* 1480, 3101. 3056

Points out number of parallels to Montesquieu's ideas in earlier English writers : Locke, Bolingbroke, Mandeville, Warburton, etc. Too often, however, Dedieu assumes borrowing without real evidence and without inquiring as to common source or coincidence. Reviews : F. Baldensperger in RG 6:75, 1910; H. Barckhausen in RHL 17:405-08, 1910; K. Glaser in ZFSL 26²:272-73, 1910; P. Hazard in RU 23²:62, 1914; G. Rudler, *ibid.* 19¹:137-8, 1910.

Jameson, Russell P. Montesquieu et l'esclavage; étude sur les origines de l'opinion antiesclavagiste en France au xviiie siècle. *See* 1571. 3057

Careful analysis of chapters on slavery in Book XV of the *Esprit des lois* in light of earlier theories, including those by English writers. Reviews : H. Barckhausen in RHL 18:685-89 1911; G. Chinard in MLN 26:227-29, 1911; G. Rudler in RU 21²:324, 1912.

Prévost

Prévost, Abbé. Mémoires et avantures d'un homme de qualité. Tome V., Séjour en Angleterre. *See* 783. 3058

Substantial preface gives summary of Prévost's sojourn in England (1728-30, 1733-34). Miss Robertson demonstrates that the " Chevalier Ey... " whom Harrisse and others had taken to be Sir Robert Eyre was in reality Sir John Eyles, to whose son Prévost was tutor. From the *Middlesex session rolls* she produces evidence to show that Prévost was imprisoned in December 1733 on charge of forging a note in the name of Francis Eyles. Bibliographical introduction and full *Notes explicatives* conclude this excellent edition.

Chew, S. P. Jr. Prévost's *Mémoires pour servir à l'histoire de la vertu.* MLN 54:592-97, 1939.   3058A

Shows that Prévost's novel based on Frances Sheridan's *Memoirs of Miss Sidney Bidulph* (1761) is more faithful to its English original than has generally been assumed.

Cooper, Berenice. An eighteenth century dictatorship. TWA 34:231-36, 1942.
3059

Study of scenes with the Abaquis in Prévost's *Cléveland, ou le Philosophe anglais.*

— The relation of Le philosophe anglais by the Abbé Prévost to the religious controversies in France and England during the early eighteenth century. TWA 32:279-86, 1940.   3060

Useful study of neglected aspect of Prévost's work.

Elissa-Rhaïs, Roland. Une influence anglaise dans Manon Lescaut ou une source du réalisme. RLC 7:619-49, 1927.
3061

Grossly exaggerates claim for Defoe's *Moll Flanders* as source for *Manon Lescaut,* but contains sound remarks on " new realism " of Prévost's novel and kind of English fiction which led the way.

Engel, Claire Eliane. Figures et aventures du XVIIIᵉ siècle : voyages et découvertes de l'abbé Prévost. *See* 810.   3062

Most significant recent work on Prévost's sojourn in England and its effect on his writing. Stresses Penelope Aubin's *Illustrious French lovers* (of 1727) as source for *Manon Lescaut,* but denies that Prévost really understood English character : his work written after English visit shows little change from that written before.
Reviews : C. Bastide in BSHP 88:234-36, 1939; P. Dottin in EA 3:379-80, 1939; G. R. Havens in RR 31:176-78, 1940; H. Roddier in RLC 20:122-25, 1940-46; A. L. Sells in MLR 34:612-14, 1939.

Havens, George R. The Abbé Prévost and Shakespeare. *See* 804, 2784.   3063

Somewhat fuller treatment of subject than in Havens' book (805). Shows that Prévost was not uncritical admirer of Shakespeare that he is usually considered to be. His remarks on Shakespeare

based on Rowe and Gildon : his position " is midway between that of the more enthusiastic among the English and that of the hostile French."

— The Abbé Prévost and English literature. *See* 805.   3064

Detailed analysis of the *Pour et contre* (1733-40) with summaries of Prévost's comments on English authors. Excellent survey of subject. *See* no. 777.
Reviews : F. Baldensperger in Rcr ns 88:431-32, 1921; in RLC 2:157, 1922; V. Klemperer in Archiv 146:272-74, 1923; P. Van Tieghem in RSH 34:143, 1922.

Hazard, Paul, et ses étudiants américains. Etudes critiques sur Manon Lescaut. *See* 807.   3065

L'abbé Prévost et l'Angleterre : état des travaux (p. 85-99) summarizes and evaluates work done and indicates *travaux à faire. See* especially p. 88-99 : *Les influences anglaises sur Prévost romancier,* an admirable discussion of possible influence of Mrs. Haywood, Mrs. Behn, Defoe, Hobbes, and Locke. Shows that no definite conclusions are yet available, but suggests several lines of enquiry.
Reviews : G. Ascoli in Rcr ns 100:328-29, 1933; G. Chinard in MLN 45:184-85, 1930; J. Ducarre in RLC 10:564-68, 1930; K. Glaser in LGRP 51:119-20, 1930; D. Mornet in RHL 37:449-51, 1930; M. E. I. R[obertson] in MLR 26:125, 1931; I. O. Wade in RR 21:252-56, 1930.

— Une source anglaise de l'abbé Prévost. MP 27:339-44, 1929-30.   3066

Shows that narrative of Baron Spalding in Vol. V of the *Mémoires et avantures d'un homme de qualité* resembles main situation in Steele's *Conscious lovers.* For full consideration of Prévost's sources " il faudra parcourir non seulement le roman, mais le théâtre anglais antérieur au séjour anglais de l'abbé Prévost."

Wilcox, Frank H. Prévost's translations of Richardson's novels. *See* 833.   3067

Excellent analysis of kinds of changes made in Richardson's text to suit French taste.
Reviews : G. Ascoli in Rcr ns 94:455-56, 1927; R. S. C[rane] in PQ 7:183, 1928; M. E. I. R[obertson] in MLR 23:114-15, 1928.

J.-B. Rousseau (*See* Jonson, no. 2984)

J.-J. Rousseau (*See also* Hobbes, Locke)

Rousseau, J.-J. La nouvelle Héloïse. Edited by Daniel Mornet. *See* 701, 1898. 3068

Part I of introduction contains excellent analysis of kinds of fiction flourishing in France in 1741-60 with due attention to vogue of English novel (see especially p. 20-24, 35-36, 46-60). Part II *(La composition et la rédaction du roman)* discusses influence of Richardson (p. 93-96) and genesis of Rousseau's conception of English character, mainly through Muralt (p. 100-03). In the admirable bibliography which completes volume I is a brief list of *Traductions de romans anglais.*
Reviews : H. Buffenoir in Rcr ns 92:429-30, 1925; G. Rudler in FQ 8:72-74, 1926; in RLC 6:184-85, 1926.

— Discours sur les sciences et les arts. Édition critique avec une introduction et un commentaire par George R. Havens. *See* 1886. 3069

Notes contain valuable indications of Rousseau's acquaintance with English authors.

Collins, J. C. Voltaire, Montesquieu, and Rousseau in England. *See* 3098. 3069A

Courtois, Louis J. Le séjour de Jean-Jacques Rousseau en Angleterre (1766-1767) : lettres et documents inédits. *See* 1972. 3070

Most detailed account of this aspect of Rousseau's biography, though superseded in part by later studies of Rousseau-Hume quarrel. Useful index.

Erdbrügger, Gustav. Die Bedeutung John Lockes für die Pädagogik Jean Jacques Rousseaus. Würzburg, Stürtz, 1912. 77 p. (Diss., Würzburg.) 3071

Perhaps best of several German dissertations on this topic.

Havens, George R. The sources of Rousseau's Edouard Bomston. *See* 2175. 3072

Important study of Rousseau's interest in English and an attempt to assess various elements derived from reading and conversation which contributed to character of Edouard Bomston in the *Nouvelle Héloïse.* Two books from which parallels are quoted (Prévost's *Cléveland* and Muralt's *Lettres*) are to be taken as suggestions rather than specific sources. On this point cf. A. Schinz in

MLN 35:184-85, 1920; and Havens' reply, *ibid.*, p. 375-76.

Peoples, Margaret H. La querelle Rousseau-Hume. *See* 1998. 3073

Full account, based on recent scholarship, but written before publication of the Greig edition of Hume's *Correspondence* (in 1932); for this see *compte-rendu* by A. L. S[ells] in AJJR 21:265-70, 1932.

Roddier, Henri. La querelle Rousseau-Hume. *See* 2012. 3074

Best survey of subject. Supplemented by Roddier in RHL 46:211-14, 1939 *(A propos de la querelle Rousseau-Hume : précisions chronologiques).*

Schinz, Albert. La pensée de Jean-Jacques Rousseau; essai d'interprétation nouvelle. *See* 1944. 3075

Part II, ch. iv *(Rousseau et les Anglais),* subordinates Rousseau's interest in English to Schinz's thesis of a Rousseau oscillating between two points of view—romantic impulse and need for discipline. In composition of *Nouvelle Héloïse* both of these urges come into play, represented in person of Lord Bomston. " En effet, ce gentleman anglais qui ose planer au-dessus des conventions sociales, nous l'admirons *tantôt* pour son courage à suivre ses impulsions naturelles en opposition aux règles de la morale courante, c'est-à-dire pour son romantisme; et *tantôt* parce qu'il sait opposer la raison à la voix de la passion ou de la nature, c'est-à-dire pour son caractère romain " (p. 330). Schinz holds that Rousseau became interested in English through Diderot, and particularly through reading of *Grandison* and Muralt's *Lettres.* His chapter is less an analysis of English elements in Rousseau's thought than interpretation of Lord Bomston to fit a particular thesis. Appendix to this chapter *(Note sur l'anglomanie de Rousseau)* attacks those, particularly Texte, who perceive an interest in things English on Rousseau's part before 1756-57.
Reviews : G. Ascoli in Rcr ns 98:557-58, 1931; E. P. Dargan in MP 28:117-20, 1930-31; A. O. Lovejoy in MLN 46:41-46, 1931.

Schmidt, Erich. Richardson, Rousseau und Goethe; Ein Beitrag zur Geschichte des Romans im XVIII. Jahrhundert. *See* 2140. 3076

Important 19th century study of influence of Richardson on composition of *Nouvelle Héloïse*. Of the three phases of composition in the novel, *Das Erfühlte*, *Das Erlernte*, and *Das Erlebte*, it is the second, with correspondence between Clarissa and Anna Howe in Richardson's novel as prototype of correspondence between Julie and Claire, which is regarded as significant. Largely superseded by Texte and others.
Review : W. M. in AJJR 16:267-68, 1924-25.

Vaughan, C. E. Studies in the history of political philosophy before and after Rousseau. *See* 107, 1604, 2149.   3077

Analyzes influence of several English authors—notably Hobbes, Locke, and Hume—on thought of Rousseau.
Reviews : A. H. Lloyd in AHR 31:776-78, 1925-26; H. W. Schneider in Jph 23:155-56, 1926.

Van Tieghem, Paul. Le roman sentimental en Europe de Richardson à Rousseau (1740-1761). RLC 20:129-51, 1940-46.   3078

Places indebtedness of Rousseau to Richardson in larger perspective of development of sentimentality in European fiction. Important to understanding of problem.

Sieyès (*See also* Harrington, no. 2975)

Bastid, Paul. Sieyès et les philosophes. Rsyn 17:137-57, 1939.   3079

Important discussion of Locke and his influence on thought of abbé Emmanuel-Joseph Sieyès.

Treyssac de Vergy

Sutherland, Bruce. Pierre Henri Treyssac de Vergy, c. 1738-1774. MLQ 4:293-307, 1943.   3080

On French adventurer and novelist who lived in London in his latter years. Valuable bibliography, adding several titles to novels listed in CBEL.

Voltaire (*See also* Locke, Mandeville, Milton, Newton, Pope, Shakespeare)

Voltaire. Correspondance de Voltaire (1726-1729), ed. by Lucien Foulet. La Bastille, l'Angleterre, le retour en France. *See* 1634.   3081

Provides essential documents for history of English sojourn—the 50 known letters by Voltaire written between April 1726 and April 1729, as well as four letters addressed to him and 18 which concern him. Most had been printed before, but never with such attention to textual accuracy or such useful documentation. Long introduction gives history of the MSS. Nine appendices on such cognate matters as " Voltaire and Bolingbroke," and " Thieriot and Atterbury ". Most controversial of these is *Appendice* VII, *Quand Voltaire est-il rentré en France?* Work of first importance for Voltaire's English contacts.
Reviews : J. Acher, in ZFSL 42²:169-88, 1914; in Ath Jan. 3 1914, p. 36; C. Charrot in RHL 21:777-87, 1914; P. Hazard in RU 23²:61-62, 1914; F. E. Schneegans in LGRP 35:290-91, 1914.

— Letters concerning the English nation. With an introduction by Charles Whibley. London, Davies, 1926. 197 p.   3082

Reprint of Lockman's translation (of 1733), with first-rate introduction.
Review : A. Digeon in RAA 4:356-57, 1926-27.

— Lettres philosophiques. Édition critique avec une introduction et un commentaire par Gustave Lanson. Cornély, 1909. 2 v. *See* 1642; 3112.   3083

Reprint of essential Jore text of 1734, with full introduction (history of publication, filiation of editions), numerous variants, and rich commentary for each letter. Last feature shows *méthode lansonienne* at its best; intellectual environment (not necessarily sources) for each topic treated by Voltaire is reconstituted. A number of English parallels or references given.—E. P. D.
Reviews : G. Ascoli in RSH 20:378-80, 1910; D. Mornet in RHL 17:194-97, 1910.

Alexander, Ian W. Voltaire and metaphysics. Phil 19:19-48, 1944.   3084

Important for influence of Locke.

Arndt, Richard. Zur Entstehung von Voltaire's Zaïre. Marburg, Friedrich, 1906. 55 p. (Diss. Marburg).   3085

Much space devoted to question of influence of *Othello* on *Zaïre*, which A. concludes is extremely doubtful. Rejects Lounsbury's contention (no. 3114) that *King Lear* was influential; accepts Garrick's suggestion that recognition scene in Steele's *Conscious lovers* was imitated by Voltaire. Believes that " *Geschwister-Motiv* " in Steele influenced also *Les originaux* and finds traces of this in other Continental dramatists. Most important elements in composition of *Zaïre* Arndt thinks are the personal experiences of Voltaire; these are ably discussed in ch. v *(Persönliche Erlebnisse des Dichters als Quelle)*.

Ascoli, Georges. Voltaire : Le voyage en Angleterre et les Lettres philosophiques. RCC 25²:275-87, 1924. *See* 1656. 3086

Gives essentials of English sojourn, without stressing debatable points. Accepts three-year hypothesis; holds that visit broadened as well as " ripened " Voltaire's ideas and gave him " une méthode." Ascoli occupies moderate position between the two schools regarding English influence, but holds that Locke finally directed Voltaire's conceptions of the soul and freedom of the will.—E. P. D.

— Voltaire : l'état d'esprit philosophique de Voltaire avant le séjour en Angleterre. RCC 25²:16-27, 128-44, 1924. *See* 1656. 3087

Ascoli derives Voltaire's philosophic status chiefly from the *Épître à Julie* and *La ligue*, but since the first is cited from text of 1738 we cannot be sure that it expresses views formed previously to 1726. *La ligue* offers surer testimony, particularly since Ascoli is careful, as others are not, to quote from edition of 1723, instead of the much altered *Henriade*.—E. P. D. *See* no. 1847.

Baldensperger, Fernand. Voltaire anglophile avant son séjour d'Angleterre. RLC 9:25-61, 1929. 3088

Masses evidence regarding Voltaire's early initiation into pro-English circles, gathering mostly around Bolingbroke. Views latter as personal rather than philosophical influence. Article wanders into dubious bypaths (*re* Voltaire and Prior, etc.) and offers unacceptable conclusion—that Voltaire valued England more highly before he arrived there. Otherwise, develops anticipations of Voltaire's later contacts and interests.— E. P. D.

— Intellectuels français hors de France. RCC 36¹:41-52, 227-38, 289-98, 1934-35. 3089

Last two articles *(Voltaire chez les mylords* and *Voltaire parmi les hommes de*

plume et le théâtre) are most important. As in other studies, B. assumes that Voltaire had connections with British aristocracy before leaving France. Material here on his *entrée* into English society and how that was checked; then his connections with Grub Street and people of the theater, causing him to limit his conception of English drama to externalities. Some side-lights on launching of *Henriade*, from correspondence in Foreign Office.—E. P. D.

Ballantyne, Archibald. Voltaire's visit to England, 1726-1729. London, Smith Elder, 1893. 338 p. Reprinted : London, John Murray, 1919. 3090

Of wider scope than title indicates. Visit to England described in detail, with abundant use of letters and contemporary documents. Ch. vii *(Voltaire on English life and literature)* sums up Voltaire's opinions toward English not only in 1726-29 but throughout his life, including his changing attitude toward Shakespeare; and ch. viii gives a comprehensive account of *Voltaire's later relations with Englishmen*. Texts quoted often inaccurate and need checking with Foulet (no. 1634); dates given indiscriminately in both old and new styles. Remains, however, best general interpretation of subject.

Review : J. Texte in RHL 1:207-10, 1894.

Bédarida, Henri. Voltaire collaborateur de la Gazette littéraire de l'Europe, 1764. MélFB 1:24-38. 3091

Shows that half of Voltaire's contributions to this journal dealt with English affairs or writers and that his Anglomania was thus still active in 1764.—E. P. D.

Böttcher, Erich. Der englische Ursprung des Comte de Boursoufle. Rostock, Adler, 1906. 87 p. (Diss. Rostock). 3092

Thorough treatment of Vanbrugh's *Relapse* as source for Voltaire's play. Shows that only subplot used by Voltaire, who skilfully detaches and adapts his material within limits of French taste. Shows also some connection between *Les originaux* and main plot of the *Relapse*, as well as with Cibber's *Love's last shift*.— E. P. D.

Brunetière, Ferdinand. La jeunesse de Voltaire (1694-1734). *In his :* Études sur le xviiiᵉ siècle. Hachette, 1911. p. 8-145. *See* 1662. 3093

Three chapters of a study begun in

1886 for the GEF series but never completed. Leading argument in support of Voltaire's French, rather than English, derivations, granting that visit sobered Voltaire and gave him object lessons. Minimizes both belletristic and philosophic influence of English authors : former (Queen Anne writers) was too much in French tradition to produce novel impact; latter should be subordinated to the *libertin* undercurrent and particularly to Bayle (useful examples here) and to Fontenelle (scientific curiosity). Special pleading and dogmatic assertions, with little knowledge of English thinkers; also several errors of detail. Remains valuable as counterpoise to excessively pro-English school— E. P. D.

— Voltaire. *In his :* Études critiques sur l'histoire de la littérature française. *See* 1661, 4:267-90.   3094

Originally published in 1889, apropos of Bengesco's bibliography of Voltaire. Argues strongly against view that English visit profoundly affected development of Voltaire's ideas.

Brown, Harcourt. Voltaire and the Royal Society of London. *See* 1696.   3095

Studies Voltaire's shifting attitudes toward English science and scientists.

Chase, C. B. The young Voltaire. New York, Longmans, 1926. 253 p.   3096

As comprehensive view of English question, this essay makes agreeable first impression, not sustained on closer scrutiny. Aims to fill gap regarding " exact influence of [Voltaire's] exile upon the formation of his character," but process and extent of this " crystallization " not closely analyzed. Plays up importance of " advertising campaign " for the *Henriade*.—E. P. D.

Reviews : C. Becker in AHR 32:645-47, 1926-27; in TLS Dec. 16, 1926, p. 931; G. L. Van Roosbroeck in RR 18:160-63, 1927.

Cohn, Adolphe. Voltaire a-t-il écrit en anglais deux essais ou bien trois? MélGL p. 250-53.   3097

Deals with *A discourse on tragedy* printed as by Voltaire in 4th ed. of the *Essay upon the civil wars of France* (London, Prevost, 1731). Cohn shows, on basis of internal evidence, that this English translation cannot be by Voltaire.

Collins, J. Churton. Voltaire, Montesquieu, and Rousseau in England. London, Nash, 1908. 292 p.   3098

Readable account of Voltaire's experiences in England, based in part on new documents. Written for general reader, and largely superseded by later scholarship.

Reviews : In Ath, Apr. 18, 1908, p. 471; F. Baldensperger in RG 6:74-75, 1910; C. Bastide in Rcr ns 73:88-89, 1912; T. de Wyzewa in RDM 5 per. 45:458-68, May 15, 1908.

Dargan, E. Preston. The question of Voltaire's primacy in establishing the English vogue. MélFB. 1:187-98.   3099

Analyzes Voltaire's claims for initiating Anglomania compared with statements by contemporaries and others.

Davis, Rose M. Thomson and Voltaire's *Socrate.* PMLA 49:560-65, 1934.   3100

Demonstrates Voltaire's independence of Thomson.

Dedieu, Joseph. Montesquieu et la tradition politique anglaise en France: les sources anglaises de l'Esprit des lois. *See* 1480, 3056.   3101

P. 113-23 deal with Voltaire's views of English politics, with material drawn from *Lettres philosophiques*, and later works. Finds that while Voltaire is still " le roi des anglomanes " and while he praised at times English toleration, liberty, system of taxation, and abolition of torture, yet he also presented other side of the medal. He doubted whether there was more liberty of person under Stuarts than under Louis XIV; he was often ironical about separation of powers. His contemporaries thought him superficial and ignorant regarding English government, whose prestige in France he did *not* initiate. This is shown by evidence drawn from Voltaire's predecessors. Dedieu does not bring out how Voltaire's ideas may vary according to direction of his propaganda at a given time. It is difficult to accept as ironical the interpretation of the passage in the *Henriade* regarding the " trois pouvoirs." —E. P. D.

Dubedout, E. J. Shakespeare et Voltaire : Othello et Zaïre. MP 3 : 305-16, 1905-06.   3102

In part a review and rebuttal of Lounsbury (no. 3114), maintaining that since Villemain tendency has been to exaggerate impact of *Othello* on *Zaïre*. Holds that *Zaïre* is not primarily a jealousy-play and is absolutely in the French tradition. Dubedout exaggerates here, though his position in the main is well fortified. Would limit Shakespeare's general influence on Voltaire to externalities.—E. P. D.

Duchâteau, Otto. Pope et Voltaire. An essay on man (1734). Discours en vers sur l'homme (1734-1737). Greifswald, Kunike, 1875. 56 p. (Diss. Greifswald). 3103

Largely series of parallel passages between Pope's poem and Voltaire's *Discours en vers sur l'homme* and the *Poème sur la loi naturelle*. After summarizing (p.49-54) points of resemblance and difference between two authors, Duchâteau concludes that in spite of external and superficial differences, Voltaire is in fundamental agreement with Pope at this stage of his career, though his views were later to be modified. Chief value of dissertation is in parallels cited.

Hahn, Joseph. Voltaires Stellung zur Frage der menschlichen Freiheit in ihrem Verhältnis zu Locke und Collins. Borna-Leipzig, Noske, 1905, 53 p. (Diss. Erlangen). 3104

See Voltaire as closest in point of view to these two English philosophers during years 1738-1766. Within its limits ably done, but whole question needs reexamination.

Haxo, H. E. Pierre Bayle et Voltaire avant les Lettres philosophiques. *See* 1139. 3105

Maintains that Voltaire was already Deist—*à la Chaulieu, à la Bayle*—in 1726, but overemphasizes his mental maturity at that time. Chief contribution is textual parallels between Bayle and *La Henriade* (not differentiated from *La ligue*). In controversy regarding English influence on Voltaire, Haxo takes moderate position and gives interesting citations from both sides.—E. P. D.

Havens, George R. and Norman L. Torrey. Voltaire's books : a selected list. MP 27:1-22, 1929-30. 3106

Pending complete publication of the Leningrad catalogue, authors list here some 400 titles owned by Voltaire. Of these, over 100 are English (originally or in translation), representing about 40 authors.—E. P. D.

— Voltaire's library. FortR 132 (ns 126):397-405, 1929. 3107

General article, with some new details.

— The private library of Voltaire at Leningrad. *See* 1768. 3108

Fullest account of pioneering labors of these two joint authors in this rich library (c. 7500 volumes), including numerous English works. Because of Voltaire's habit of using markers and " stickers " there will be many revelations here for future source-hunters. Hints given regarding Bayle, Swift, and several of the Deists.—E. P. D.

Havens, George R. Voltaire's marginal comments upon Pope's Essay on man. MLN 43:429-39, 1928. 3109

Transcribes Voltaire's comments on Vol. II of Pope's *Works* (London, Gilliver, 1735), now in Public Library of Leningrad. Most of remarks rather hostile and appear to have been made in late 1750's or 1760's.

Hoffmann, Arthur. Voltaires Stellung zu Pope. Königsberg i. Pr., Steinbacher, 1913. 95 p. (Diss., Königsberg). 3110

Points out number of similarities in thought and expression, but often sees influence in thoroughly commonplace ideas. Many errors of detail, and too limited in scope and documentation to be satisfactory.
Review : B. Fehr in Beibl 26:369-70, 1915.

Hurn, Arthur S. Voltaire et Bolingbroke : étude comparative sur leurs idées philosophiques et religieuses. Jouve, 1915. 123 p. (Diss., Paris). 3111

Presents a number of undoubted parallels but exaggerates Bolingbroke's influence, without taking into account common sources and possibility of other influences. Insufficient attention to chronology : opinions of Voltaire separated by years are mingled in close juxtaposition, with little attempt to study evolution of Voltaire's ideas.

Lanson, Gustave. Voltaire et les Lettres philosophiques : comment Voltaire faisait un livre. RPar 15:505-33, Aug. 1, 1908. 3112

Material treated more fully in Lanson's introduction to his edition (nos. 1642, 3083). For forty years, Lanson shows text underwent modifications, showing

Voltaire's " sensibility " and his approval of things English—but only until 1756, when (re Dryden) tide began to turn. Voltaire freely handles sources to give a favorable impression of English affairs; hence he exaggerates English liberty, allows certain omissions, glosses over bad and brutal sides of English life.—E. P. D.

Lantoine, Albert. Les Lettres philosophiques de Voltaire. *See* 1832.   3113

As in other studies in this series, an epoch-making book is set into its environment of contemporary opinion and circumstances. Author narrates " biography " of work, deals competently with its genesis, composition, and publication (especially Jore), criticism of the existing order, reception given to the volume, promotion of Anglomania. Contains also chapters on *Voltaire en Angleterre* and conditions there. Essential book, well-documented; emphasizes how Voltaire praised England in order to condemn France.—E. P. D.

Review : H. Sée in Rhist 170:124-25, 1932.

Lounsbury, T. R. Shakespeare and Voltaire. New York, Scribner, 1902. 463 p.   3114

Describes influence of Shakespeare in *Brutus*, *Zaïre*, *La mort de César*, *Mahomet*, *Eriphyle*, and *Sémiramis*, and controversies aroused by Voltaire's criticism of Shakespeare. Believes that " Voltaire really retarded the appreciation of Shakespeare on the Continent, instead of advancing it " (p. 442). Important study, in spite of tendency to exaggerate Voltaire's debt to Shakespeare and annoyingly verbose style.

Reviews : in Acad, Jan 3, 1903, p. 7-8; in Ath, Dec. 27, 1902, 849-50; C. Bastide in JEGP 5:561-64, 1903-05; A. G. Canfield in Atl 90:712-14, 1902; in Dial 34:199-201, 1903.

Merian-Genast, Ernst. Voltaire und die Entwicklung der Weltliteratur. Erlangen, Junge, 1926. 226 p. (RFor, 40).   3115

Thorough treatment, although too metaphysical and repetitious. Upholds *Essay on epick poetry* as notably advancing " organic " conception of *Weltliteratur* (any masterpiece to be judged in terms of its own folk-culture) : Voltaire early supports this type of relativity in appreciating Milton and Tasso. But his theory (in Introduction) better than his practice, and he fell from grace in his

own translation of the *Essai*. Merian-Genast makes full comparisons with this later text, as also with Voltaire's other critical works and *Réflexions* of Dubos. Substantial contribution, though exaggerating " evolution " of world-literature and importance of Voltaire's *Essay*.—E. P. D.

Reviews : F. Baldensperger in RLC 7:361-62, 1927; P. Sakmann in ZFSL 49:364-66, 1927; F. Schalk in NSp 36:152-53, 1928.

Oliver, Thomas E. The Merope of George Jeffreys as a source of Voltaire's Mérope. *See* 1835.   3116

Jeffreys, who made several changes from Maffei's drama in his *Merope* (of 1731), asserted that Voltaire had made use of same changes in *Mérope* (in 1743). Oliver reprints tragedy of Jeffreys from rare 1754 edition and lists alterations made by both Jeffreys and Voltaire so that reader can estimate extent to which Voltaire was influenced by English play. Jeffreys' claims seem exaggerated. Oliver has also edited Voltaire's *Mérope* (New York, Century, 1925), with an introduction summing up versions of *Mérope* theme in Italian, French, and English literature.

Reviews : C. Cestre in RAA 6:268, 1928-29; H. C. Lancaster in MLN 43:561-62, 1928; H. Lüdeke in Beibl 41:89-90, 1930; G. L. Van Roosbroeck in RR 21:257-59, 1930; H. G. Wright in RES 5:484-85, 1929.

Russell, Trusten W. Voltaire, Dryden and heroic tragedy. *See* 1799.   3117

Able presentation of view that Voltaire's ideas of epic or heroic tragedy were inspired not so much by Shakespeare as by Dryden.

Reviews : B. Dobrée in RES 23:366-67, 1947; H. C. Lancaster in MLN 62:492-95, 1947; A. R. R[iddell] in RR 38:105, 1947; F. A. Taylor in FS 2:170-71, 1948.

Sakmann, Paul. Voltaire als Philosoph. AGP 18:166-215, 322-68, 1905.   3118

For Voltaire's attitude toward Locke see especially p. 174-86, 355-65.—E. P. D.

— Voltaire als Ästhetiker und Literarkritiker. Archiv 120:99-120, 1908.   3119

Last ten pages contain judicious *résumés* of Voltaire's opinions regarding Shakespeare, Milton, Addison, Pope, Swift, and others; also on Restoration comedy and contemporary novel. Fairly adequate documentation, except that *Correspondance* is not used. Sakmann synthesizes well, but offers little comment; allows for shift in Voltaire's views.—E. P. D.

Sonet, Edouard. Voltaire et l'influence anglaise. Rennes, Imprimerie de l'Ouest-Éclair, 1926. 210 p. (Diss. Rennes). 3120

Essential though ill-made book; index lacking, faulty table of contents, inadequate bibliography. Comprehensive in scope, but treatment uneven; better on philosophers affecting Voltaire than on belletristic side; not precise as to Voltaire's political views and their sources; chapter on deists superseded by Torrey (no. 1804). But remains only *ouvrage d'ensemble* in its field.—E. P. D.
Review : H. Sée in Rhist 153:280-81, 1926.

Strachey, Lytton. Voltaire and England. *In his :* Books and characters. *See* 230, p. 115-41. 3121

Originally appeared in EdR 220:392-411, 1914. Over-emphasizes Voltaire's visit as marking " a turning-point in the history of civilization " and *Lettres philosophiques* as expressing " the whole philosophy of Voltaire." Takes view that he was formed as thinker before English sojourn; characteristically regrets that social depiction is lacking in *Lettres philosophiques.*—E. P. D.

Toldo, Pietro. Attinenze fra il teatro comico di Voltaire e quello del Goldoni. GSLI 31:343-60, 1898. 3121A

Points out borrowings from Richardson in Voltaire's plays.

Torrey, Norman L. Bolingbroke and Voltaire—a fictitious influence. PMLA 42:788-97, 1927. 3122

Shows how Voltaire used Bolingbroke's work mainly as smoke-screen. Minimizes contacts, personal and intellectual, between the two men. Probable that these have been " greatly exaggerated," and that textual borrowings are not found, even by Hurn (no. 3111). But is it established, as Torrey asserts, that Voltaire " borrowed nothing," that the two thinkers " despised each other," and that " Voltaire's references to Bolingbroke are regularly ' false ' ?" Subject seems to require further probing.—E. P. D.

— Voltaire and the English deists. *See* 1804. 3123

Emphasizes as chief influences Anthony Collins, Woolston, Tindal, Middleton, and Peter Annet, with minor impacts by Toland, Chubb, and Bolingbroke. Work is main authority on this aspect of Voltaire's Anglomania, to be attached henceforth to Ferney period. Based on Voltaire's actual use of deists, convincing on major names. Torrey remains anti-Bolingbroke and tends to minimize Bayle's anti-biblical attacks. It is unsafe to hold Bayle reached later *philosophes via* English channels. Comparative, three-sided, textual work still needs to be done.—E. P. D.
Reviews : F. Baldensperger in RLC 11:568-72, 1931; L. I. Bredvold in MLN 46:419-20, 1931; E. P. Dargan in MP 29:120-25, 1931-32; H. Sée in Rhist 166:151-52, 1931; in TLS July 3, 1930. p. 544.

— Voltaire's English notebook. MP 26:307-25, 1928-29. 3124

Transcription of commonplace book in which Voltaire entered, during his English visit, various quotations from oral and written sources. Supersedes transcriptions published earlier in ER 16:313-20, 1914; and in RU 30²:38-50, 1921.

Wade, Ira O. Voltaire and Madame du Châtelet; an essay on the intellectual activity at Cirey. *See* 1811. 3125

Includes significant study of the *Examen de la Genèse* and its indebtedness to Woolston. Also important discussion of influence of Mandeville, in connection with Mme du Châtelet's translation of the *Fable of the bees.*
Reviews : H. Brown in MLQ 3:340-44, 1942; G. R. Havens in RR 33:80-82, 1942; J. Lough in MLR 37:225-27, 1942; E. Malakis in MLN 57:238-39, 1942; A. Schinz in FR 15:70-71, 1941-42; N.L. Torrey in AHR 47:584-85, 1941-42.

— Studies on Voltaire, with some unpublished papers of Mme du Châtelet. *See* 400, 1812. 3126

New light on question of Voltaire's indebtedness to Mandeville and spread of Newtonian ideas in France.
Reviews : G. R. Havens in RR 39:164-67, 1948; E. Malakis in MLN 62:497-98, 1947; D. Mornet in RHL 48:271-73, 1948.

White, Florence D. Voltaire's Essay on epic poetry: a study and an edition. *See* 1640.   3127

Several useful introductory chapters discussing various versions of *Essay* and its substance followed by annotated reprint of original *Essay* and Appendix listing principal variants made after 1733. Value of text and Appendix obscured by fact that standard of comparison is Moland (Kehl) text of 1784, quite different from that of 1733. Thus in part author works backwards. Yet she indicates gradual change in Voltaire's attitude towards Milton, mentions important shifts in emphasis between the two " firsts," and shows how English text was a step toward Anglomania and general cosmopolitanism.—E. P. D.

American
(Nos. 3128-3177)

JOHN FRANCIS McDERMOTT

Bibliographies and general studies

Barthold, Allen J. French journalists in the United States 1780-1800. FAR 1:215-30, 1936-37.   3128

Includes bibliographical list of 16 papers. More concerned with " journalism " than " journalists."

Bond, Donald F. Anglo-French and Franco-American studies : a current bibliography, 1937. RR 29:343-72, 1938. Continued with various collaborators in RR 30:151-86, 1939; 31:114-46, 1940; 32:176-98, 1941; 33:132-56, 1942; 34:154-72, 1943; 35:186-202, 1944; 36:161-90, 1945; and 37:105-26, 1946 ; 38:97-116, 1947 ; 39: 181-203, 1948, continued by J. M. Carrière and others in FrAR 2:203-32, 1949; 3:79-119, 1950, etc.   3129

First issue of annual survey of books, articles, and reviews dealing with Anglo-French and Franco-American culture and literary history from 16th century to present day. Continued in FrAR (*see* 2887).

Faÿ, Bernard. Bibliographie critique des ouvrages français relatifs aux États-Unis, 1770-1800. *See* 25.   3130

Part I, a bibliography arranged by years with each year divided into three sections : (1) geography, travels, description; (2) history, politics, political documents, pamphlets, and newspapers; (3) literature, philosophy, morals, and religion. Part II (p. 42-94), critical study of these sources. Appendix I presents documents concerning *Courrier de l'Amérique* and Appendix II documents concerning Tanguy de La Boissière.

Review : G. Chinard in RLC 6:371-76, 1926.

Tinker, Edward Larocque. Bibliography of the French newspapers and periodicals of Louisiana. AASP ns 42:247-370, 1932.   3131

Exhaustive lists of newspapers, both of New Orleans and parishes of Louisiana, with brief accounts of each. Excellent account of most important section of Franco-American press.

Intermediaries

Jillson, Willard Rouse. A bibliography of early western travel in Kentucky (with annotations) 1674-1824. RKHS 42:120-38, 1944.   3132

Useful list but omits such expected names as Saugrain, Collot, Perrin du Lac.

Monaghan, Frank. French travellers in the United States, 1765-1932. *See* 43.   3133

Lists 1806 titles, many of them with informative notes. Most valuable bibliography for its subject and period.

Reviews : H. F. Kane in MVHR 20:608-09, 1933-34; J. L. Mesick in AL 5:394-96, 1933-34.

Sherrill, Charles H. French memories of eighteenth century America. New York, Scribner, 1915. 335 p.   3134

American society and manners as seen by French visitors. No documentation. Organized by subjects, not by authors. Chapter I : *Our French visitors;* other chapters on city life, country life, travel, religious observances, learned professions, etc., as seen by visitors. Bibliography of French authorities consulted and records examined, p. 329-35.

Adams, M. Ray. Joel Barlow, political romanticist. AL 9:113-52, 1937-38.   3135

To correct common impression of Barlow, Adams emphasizes changes in Barlow in latter half of his life and shows importance of his revolutionary writings.

Brackenridge, Henry Marie. Views of Louisiana together with a journal of a voyage up the Missouri River, in 1811. Pittsburgh, Cramer, Spear, and Eichbaum, 1814. 304 p.   3136

Sympathetic account of recently acquired territory; p. 132-46 concerned with *Historical character of the ancient inhabitants—Change of government*. Necessary for proper understanding of social and intellectual conditions of colonial days.

Crèvecœur, St. John de. Sketches of eighteenth century America. More Letters from an American farmer. New Haven, Yale Univ. press, 1925. 342 p. 3137

Edited from unpublished Crèvecœur mss. by Henri Bourdin, Ralph H. Gabriel, and Stanley T. Williams; introductions discuss Crèvecœur as a man of letters. A few of these essays published in French editions (1784, 1787) of the *Lettres*. Valuable additions to Crèvecœur's work on America. Indexed.

Reviews : R. W. Kelsey in AHR 31:583-84, 1925-26; F. L. Mott, in HTB, Dec. 27, 1925, p. 8; in SRL 2:253, Oct. 31, 1925.

Crèvecœur, Robert de. Saint John de Crèvecœur; sa vie et ses ouvrages, 1735-1813. Librairie des bibliophiles. 1883. 435 p. 3138

Biography by great-grandson, based on documents in his possession. *Notes et pièces justificatives* include family documents, funeral oration, bibliography (p. 293-309), note on packetboat service (p. 310-17), on steamboat (Fitch and Rumsey—p. 318-24), Comtesse d'Houdetot (p. 325-49); correspondence : extracts or *résumés* of 97 letters to or from Crèvecœur (p. 350-422).

Adams, Percy G. Crèvecœur and Franklin. Phist 14:273-79, 1947. 3139

Shows that chapter in *American farmer* credited to Franklin as speech at opening of Franklin and Marshall College in 1787 made up of extracts from Imlay's *Topographical description*.

— Notes on Crèvecœur. AL 20:327-33, Nov., 1948. 3140

Shows by parallel citations that Crèvecœur in *Voyage dans la haute Pensylvanie* borrowed word for word from Bartram and others and illustrates Crèvecœur's curious acknowledgement of sources; for account of mounds in Georgia and Florida credit should go not to " M. Brown of Kentucky " but to Bartram; likewise credit given to Frederick Hazen should go to Wm. Smith's *Historical account of Bouquet's expedition;* still

another passage taken from Jefferson's *Notes on Virginia*.

Mitchell, Julia Post. St. Jean de Crèvecœur. New York. Columbia univ. Press, 1916. 362 p. 3141

Careful, fully-documented, straightforward biography; not concerned with literary criticism. Numerous documents in appendix.

Rice, Howard C. Le cultivateur américain; étude sur l'œuvre de Saint-John de Crèvecœur. Champion, 1933. 263 p. (BRLC, 87). 3142

Best critical study of Crèvecœur. Biographical summary (p. 7-44). Chapters as follows : I, *La vie d'un homme : Michel-Guillaume Jean de Crèvecœur;* II, *La vie d'un livre : les Lettres d'un cultivateur américain;* III, *Crèvecœur, ami des Noirs;* IV *Scènes de la vie sauvage;* V, *Crèvecœur, historien de la révolution américaine : Triomphe d'une légende;* VI, *L'Amérique : rêve et réalité.* Bibliography of Crèvecœur's publications and manuscripts and of studies concerning him fills p. 231-40; list of sources consulted, p. 241-54. Proper names indexed.

Reviews : G. Chinard in AL 6:210-11, 1934-35; H. F. Kane in AHR 39:580-81, 1933-34; in RLC 13:793, 1933.

Whitehead, James L. (ed). The autobiography of Peter Stephen du Ponceau. PMHB 63:189-227, 311-43, 432-61, 1939; 64:97-120, 243-69, 1940. 3143

Autobiography in form of letters covering life of writer to 1783. Du Ponceau (1760-1844) was, according to editor, " one of the most effective agents for the diffusion both of French culture in the United States and of American culture in France " (p. 169). Very large part of material belongs to 1777-1783 and concerns principal figures of American Revolution. Letters were written or dictated between 1836 and 1844, chiefly to Anne L. Gareschè, his granddaughter.

Potts, William John. Du Simitière, artist, antiquary, and naturalist, projector of the first American museum, with some extracts from his notebooks. PMHB 13:341-75, 1889. 3144

Most extensive biographical sketch of this talented Geneva-born Frenchman, who first came to Philadelphia in 1766.

Franklin, Benjamin. The complete works of Benjamin Franklin, including his private as well as his official correspondence and numerous letters and documents now for the first time printed, with many others not included in any former collection. Also the unmutilated and correct version of his autobiography. Compiled and edited by John Bigelow. New York, Putnam, 1887. 10 v.   3145

Based on Stevens collection of Franklin papers bought by United States Government.

— The writings of Benjamin Franklin. Collected and edited with a life and introduction by Albert Henry Smyth. New York, Macmillan, 1905-07. 10 v.   3146

Based on all Franklin papers "accessible to the editor," including American Philosophical Society, University of Pennsylvania, and other principal collections. Includes 385 letters and 40 articles by Franklin not previously published.

Chinard, Gilbert. Benjamin Franklin and the mysterious Madame G. APSLB 1946, 49-72.   3147

Identifies Mme G. as Comtesse Golowkin and publishes texts of 22 letters from her to Franklin, 1780-84.

Falls, William F. Buffon, Franklin et deux académies américaines. RR 29:37-47, 1938.
                                          3148

Académies are American Philosophical Society of Philadelphia and American Academy of Arts and Sciences of Boston. Most of article concerned with Buffon's relations with American Philosophical Society through Franklin.

Faÿ, Bernard. Franklin, the apostle of modern times. Boston, Little, Brown, 1929. 547 p.   3149

One of most satisfactory lives of Franklin.
Reviews : W. C. Bruce in AHR 35:633-35, 1929-30; C. H. Grattan in NYW Dec. 1, 1929, p. 10; R. M. Lovett in NR 61:147-48, 1929; A. Nevins in SRL 6:507, Dec. 7, 1929.

Van Doren, Carl. Benjamin Franklin. New York, Viking, 1938. 845 p.   3149A

The most fully informed of all Franklin biographies.
Reviews : C. Becker in HTB, Oct. 9, 1938, p. 1 ; J. P. Boyd in AHR 46 :160-61, 1940-41; C. Brinton in SRL 18: 5, Oct. 8, 1938 ; B. Knollenberg in YR 28:430, 1938-39.

Hays, I. Minis (editor). Record of the celebration of the 200th anniversary of the birth of Benjamin Franklin, under the auspices of the American Philosophical Society... April 17 to April 20, A. D. 1906. Philadelphia, American philosophical society, 1906-08. 6 v.   3150

V. 2-6 form Calendar of papers of Benjamin Franklin in library of American Philosophical Society; a most important collection of 18th century Franco-Americana.

Chinard, Gilbert. Les amitiés américaines de Madame d'Houdetot d'après sa correspondance inédite avec Benjamin Franklin et Thomas Jefferson. *See* 261.   3151

Enthusiasm for America on eve of French Revolution.
Review : A[lbert] S[chinz] in MLJ 10:57, 1925.

Jefferson, Thomas. The works of Thomas Jefferson. Collected and edited by Paul Leicester Ford. New York, Putnam, 1904-05. 12 v.   3152

Most complete selection of Jefferson's correspondence and other writings; annotation slight. Will be superseded by new edition now in preparation at Princeton University. *See* no. 3152A.

Jefferson, Thomas. The papers of Thomas Jefferson. Edited by Julian P. Boyd. Princeton, Princeton university press, 1950.
                                          3152A

The definitive edition of Jefferson's papers, to be published in fifty or more volumes. Volumes I and II (679 and 665 p.), issued in 1950, cover years 1760 to 18 June 1779.
Reviews : G. W. Johnson in HTB, May 21, 1950, p. 1 ; D. Malone in TBR, May 21, 1950, p. 1 ; D. C. Mearns in SRL 33:11, May 27, 1950; St. G. Sioussat in AHR 56:118-22, 1950-51.

Bowers, Claude G. The young Jefferson, 1743-1789. Boston, Houghton, Mifflin, 1945. 544 p.   3153

Reviews : Marie Kimball in AHR 50:810-11, 1944-45; D. M. Potter in YR 34:738-40, 1944-45.

Dumbauld, Edward. Thomas Jefferson, American tourist. Norman, Okla., Univ. of Oklahoma press, 1946. 266 p.   3153A

See p. 60-109 for Jefferson's travels in France.
Review : E. Cometti in JSH 12:582-84, 1946.

Moreau de Saint Méry, Médéric Louis Elie. Voyage aux États Unis d'Amérique, 1793-1798. Edited, with an introduction and notes, by Stewart L. Mims. New Haven, Yale Univ. press. 1913. 440 p. (YHP, 2). 3154

Introduction contains biographical sketch of Moreau who, in 1794, established bookstore in Philadelphia, which became important center for *émigrés* and their American friends.

— Moreau de St. Méry's American journey, 1793-98. Translated and edited by Kenneth Roberts and Anna M. Roberts. Introduction by Stewart L. Mims. Garden City, N. Y., Doubleday, 1947. 394 p. 3155

First complete translation of this valuable account of 1790's. Translation good; annotation slight; preface by Roberts personal; introduction by Mims biographical.
Reviews : L. H. Butterfield in WMQ 3rd ser. 5:130-32, 1948; J. C. Goodbody in MVHR 35:119-20, 1948; H. Hatcher in SRL 30:21, July 12, 1947; H. Herring in HTB, May 25, 1947, p. 3.

Elicona, Anthony Louis. Un colonial sous la révolution en France et en Amérique : Moreau de Saint-Méry. Jouve, 1934. 271 p. (Diss., Paris.) 3156

First biography of this Martinique Frenchman who spent early years of Revolution in France and whose bookstore from 1793 to 1798 was center of Franco-American life in Philadelphia (p. 129-215). Lists Moreau's printed works (p. 247-52) and his Mss. (p. 253-56). Bibliography (p. 257-62). Index of proper names.

Kent, Henry W. Encore Moreau de Saint-Méry. *In :* Bookmen's holiday, notes and studies written and gathered in tribute to Harry Miller Lydenberg. New York, New York public library, 1943. p. 239-47. 3157

Brief biographical sketch, most valuable part of which is a summary of private library left by Moreau in 1819.

Rosengarten, J. G. Moreau de Saint-Méry and his French friends in the American Philosophical Society. APSP 50:168-78, 1911. 3158

Emphasis in this sketch on Moreau's intellectual activities in Philadelphia.

Morris, Gouverneur. A diary of the French Revolution, 1789-1793. Edited by Beatrix

Cary Davenport. Boston, Houghton Mifflin, 1939. 2 v. 618, 652 p. 3159

Very detailed record in letters and diary of Morris' residence in France from March 1, 1789 to January 5, 1793. Morris incorrectly described on title page as minister to France "during the Terror." Introduction summarizes ancestry, background, and life of Morris. Volumes moderately annotated; index of 48 pages.
Reviews : H. E. Bourne in AHR 45:138-40, 1939-40; H. L. Fowler in VQR 15:477-78, 1939; H. Gorman in TBR March 26, 1939, p. 1; A. Guérard in HTB April 2, 1939, p. 5; R. M. Lovett in NR 98:357-58, April 26, 1939.

Roberts, John G. The American career of Quesnay de Beaurepaire. FR 20:463-70, 1946-47. 3160

Compact account of this physiocrat in America during 1777-86 and of his French Academy in Philadelphia and New York.

Chinard, Gilbert. Volney et l'Amérique d'après des documents inédits et sa correspondance avec Jefferson. Baltimore and Paris, The Johns Hopkins press—Les presses universitaires, 1923. 207 p. 3161

Based upon hitherto unpublished documents in Library of Congress and Volney's writings viewed in their light. Only study to present in satisfactory detail Volney's sojourn and travels in America. Bibliography and index.
Reviews : G. R. Havens in MLN 39:499-502, 1924; J. A. James in AHR 29:807-08, 1923-24; in RLC 4:162, 1924.

American-French Influences

Billardon de Sauvigny. Vashington ou la liberté du nouveau monde. Tragédie en quatre actes. Éditée avec une introduction et des notes par Gilbert Chinard avec l'assistance de H. M. Barnes, Jr., J.-Jacques Demorest, R. K. Kellenberger, and E. E. E. Sarot. Princeton, N. J., Princeton Univ. press, 1941. 75 p. 3162

Though perhaps not important in dramatic literature *Vashington* (produced and published in 1791) is interesting and valuable piece of Franco-Americana in its presentation of George Washington as model for French republican hero. In a 37 page introduction Chinard gives a full account of author and analyzes in detail historical aspects of this play.

Reviews : O. Fellows in RR 32:431-33, 1941; K. N. McKee in AHR 47:190-91, 1941-42; J. Park in MLQ 2:520, 1941.

Chamfort, S. R. N. La jeune Indienne, comédie en un acte et en vers avec une introduction par Gilbert Chinard. Princeton, Princeton univ. press, 1945. 80 p. 3163

Based on story of Inkle and Yarico, this is first French play with an American setting; a portion of introduction deals with *L'Amérique de Chamfort*. Text reproduced from first edition (Paris, 1764).
Reviews : D. F. Bond in MP 43:147-48, 1945-46; H. C. Lancaster in MLN 60:426-27, 1945.

Chinard, Gilbert. L'Amérique et le rêve exotique dans la littérature française au xviie et au xviiie siècle. *See* 789. 3164

Important study of relation of American backgrounds and French literature. Parts I and II (p. 1-220), 17th century relations, journals, etc., as background for 18th century writings; Part III, American scene in French 18th century theater, pirates and adventurers in the New World, sentimental romance (Prévost and Lebeau), philosophical missionaries (Lafitau, Charlevoix, etc.); Part IV, J.-J. Rousseau, America and the *philosophes*.

— L'exotisme américain dans l'œuvre de Chateaubriand. Hachette, 1918. 305 p. 3165

Discussion of Chateaubriand's travels in America, followed by analysis of characterization and use of local color in his American writings. Bibliography, p. 301-05.

— Quelques origines littéraires de René. PMLA 43:288-302, 1928. 3166

Discusses sources suggested in Chateaubriand's *Défense du Christianisme* and particularly Sébastien Mercier's *L'homme sauvage* (of 1767). *René* does not suffer by comparison.

— La déclaration des droits de l'homme et du citoyen et ses antécédents américains. Washington, Institut français de Washington, 1945. 38 p. 3167

Analysis of influence of American Revolution on political thought in France.

— Eighteenth century theories on America

as a human habitat. APSP 91:27-57, 1947. 3168

Discusses among others, theories of Montesquieu, Buffon, Raynal, Volney.

Church, Henry Ward. Corneille de Pauw and the controversy over his Recherches philosophiques sur les Américains. PMLA 51:178-206, 1936. 3169

Discusses forty-year controversy over degeneracy of things American. Concludes : " De Pauw owes whatever importance he may have largely to the fact that he expressed the views of Buffon in such a violent, exaggerated, and provocative form that controversy became inevitable."

Fairchild, H. N. The noble savage, a study in romantic naturalism. New York, Columbia univ. press, 1928. 535 p. 3170

Principally concerned with noble savage in English literature. Crèvecœur and other French travelers and Rousseau discussed in chap. IV (p. 97-139). Sources consulted : p. 513-23. Index.
Reviews : G. Paine in AL 1:98-100, 1929-30; F. A. Pottle in SRL 5:67, Aug. 25, 1928; Anon. in NNY 127:380, Oct. 10, 1928.

Faÿ, Bernard. L'Amérique et l'esprit scientifique en France à la fin du xviiie siècle. RLC 3:385-406, 1923. 3171

Investigation of American publications and of publications concerning America, 1770-1790. Shows great influence and stimulus of American thought on French.

— L'esprit révolutionnaire en France et aux États-Unis à la fin du xviiie siècle. Champion, 1925. 378 p. (BRLC, 7). 3172

Well-documented study of political, moral, and intellectual relations between France and United States from 1770 to 1800. Works cited : p. 345-62. Index of proper names : p. 363-74.
Reviews : (with his *Bibliographie critique des ouvrages français relatifs aux États-Unis*, 25, 3130) C. Becker in AHR 30:810-12, 1924-25; G. Chinard in RLC 6:371-76, 1926; G. L. van Roosbroeck (*L'esprit* only) in RR 18:158-60, 1927.

Fess, Gilbert M. The American revolution in creative French literature (1775-1937). Columbia, Mo., University of Missouri, 1941. 119 p. (Univ. of Missouri studies, v. 16, No. 2). 3173

This study of impact of American

Revolution on French creative writing divided into two parts : (1) social and political pattern of revolution as seen by French; (2) French literary works concerned with events of that brief period, 1775-1783 and produced between 1775 and 1937. Author does not show any great influence, especially upon important writers; he does show, however, that there was good deal of vague and erroneous " knowledge " of America. This detailed study will be of definite value in writing of an intellectual history of United States in that period.

Reviews : P. Brodin in FR 16:72, 1942-43; H. C. Lancaster in MLN 58:158-59, 1943; L. C. Tihany in JMH 14:570, 1942.

Hawkins, Richmond Laurin. Unpublished French letters of the eighteenth century. RR 21:1-15, 128-31, 209-17, 308-14, 1930.
3174

Letters of Mme de Maintenon, Maupertuis, Buffon, D'Alembert, Diderot, La Harpe, Morellet, La Rochefoucauld, Mirabeau *fils*, Lavoisier, Marat, Grimm, Marmontel, Toussaint Louverture; arranged chronologically, 1700-1798, with very brief introductions and ample footnotes. Five or six letters addressed to Franklin.

Mornet, Daniel. La révolution américaine. *In his :* Les origines intellectuelles de la révolution française, 1715-1787. *See* 45, p. 389-99. 3175

Influence of American Revolution discussed briefly. *See* no. 1062.

Seeber, Edward D. Chief Logan's speech in France. MLN 61:412-16, 1946. 3176

Speech delivered in 1774 " ranks foremost among America's contributions to the literature of the Noble Savage." Traces its various publications in France from Raynal's third edition on.

— Diderot and Chief Logan's speech (Frontières de Virginie). MLN 60:176-78, 1945.
3177

His editors Assézat and Tourneux published as Diderot's a translation of Logan's speech.

German
(Nos. 3178-3264)

HENRY H. H. REMAK

Lack of space has prevented inclusion here of many valuable items dealing with French

influence on German writers originally prepared for this section by Professor Remak. —The Editors.

Bibliography and general studies

Arnold, Robert F. Allgemeine Bücherkunde. 3rd ed. Berlin, W. de Gruyter, 1931. 361 p. 3178

Descriptive and critical reference work, unmatched in compact usefulness for any study of a problem in literary history. While Arnold's critical appreciations of publications in field of Franco-German literary relations are microscopic and inconclusive, his many individualized, well-organized and up-to-date hints on broad literary research still make it an invaluable help in the approach to any problem of comparative literature.

Reviews : A. W. Aron in JEGP 32:620-22, 1933; A. Kleinberg in LGRP 154:209-11, 1933; F. Piquet in RG 22:459, 1931; J. G. Robertson in MLR 27:227, 1932.

A., J. L'étude des langues vivantes en France au 18ème siècle. RG 6:320, 1910. **Fernand Baldensperger.** A propos de l'étude des langues vivantes en France au 18ème siècle. *Ibid.*, 445, 1910. 3179

Interesting facts about rather considerable vogue of German in Paris in 18th century.

Allard, Emmy. Friedrich der Grosse in der Literatur Frankreichs. Halle, Niemeyer, 1913. 144 p. 3180

Diligent study investigating reaction of French public opinion and writers to Frederick the Great, from youth to death, and posthumously. Adds interesting chapter on treatment of Frederick II in French drama.

Reviews : O. Glöde in LGRP 36:221-22, 1915; A. Ludwig in Archiv 133:199-201, 1915.

Baldensperger, Fernand. L'helvétisme littéraire et ses relations avec les grands courants de la pensée occidentale. *In :* La Suisse et les Français, ed. Alexandre Castell, Crès, 1920, p. 429-45. 3181

Finds that European importance of Swiss literature was much more pronounced in 18th than in 19th century. Fruitful, condensed survey.

— Le mouvement des idées dans l'émigration française, 1789-1815. Plon, 1924. 2 v.
3182

Masterly, concentrated, yet highly nuanced. Logical rather than chronological or geographical divisions. Studies influence of German " mysticism " on *émigrés* and rehabilitation of Germany by refugees. No bibliography, but incomplete index in v. 2 which does not list foreign contacts (such as Klopstock, Goethe, Schiller). *See* Eggli, no. 3215.

Reviews : E. Beau de Loménie in RLC 5:708-18, 1925; C. H. Herford in MLR 20:484-87, 1925; H. Lichtenberger in RG 17:482-84, 1926; P. van Tieghem in RHL 32:613-16, 1925.

Baldensperger, Fernand, and **Werner P. Friederich.** Bibliography of comparative literature. *See* 2885A, 3264A, 3308A.

3182A

New standard work superseding Betz (no. 3183). No evaluations or descriptions of items ; lists very few reviews. Franco-German relations amply covered, but not without *lacunae* and errors. Emphasis on originator of influence, not receiver. Austrian and German literature are combined, but Swiss contributions listed separately. Supplement with corrections and additions to be published in 1955.

Betz, Louis P. La littérature comparée; essai bibliographique. 2d edition (edited by F. Baldensperger). Strasbourg, Trübner, 1904. 410 p. *See* 3267. 3183

Although superseded by Baldensperger-Friederich (no. 3182A), still retains historical interest. Despite admittedly tentative character, far superior to first edition of 1900. Clearly arranged and easy to use. Short introduction by J. Texte offers general classifications of comparative literature. No critical or descriptive remarks. Excellent methodical index ; authors treated are included, but, unfortunately, not authors of critical works and articles.

Reviews : (1st edition) : K. Drescher in ZDP 35:138-40, 1903; M. Koch in ZVL 14:224, 1901; R. M. Meyer in Euph 7:796-98, 1900; M. J. Minckwitz in LGRP 23:57-60, 1902. (2nd edition) : Anonymous in MLR 1:77-78, 1905; anonymous in Archiv 113:483, 1904; F. Baldensperger in RG 1:711, 1905, C. S. Northup in MLN 20:235-39, 1905 and 21:12-15, 1906; R. Petsch in LGRP 26:353, 1905; A. Sauer in Euph 13:650-51, 1906; E. Stemplinger in SVL 6:366-68, 1906; W. Wetz in ZVL 16:486-88, 1906.

Boucke, Ewald A. Aufklärung, Klassik und Romantik. Brunswick, Vieweg, 1925. 67 p.

3184

Based on critical appreciation of Hettner's monumental work (nos. 68, 3192). Boucke's study represents one of most remarkable attempts to define, without verbal ballast, great tendencies in German literature and literary criticism on widest possible basis, starting with Enlightenment. Comparative point of view. Indispensable synthesis, not well enough known. *See also* under Hettner, nos. 68, 3192.

Du Bois-Reymond, E. Friedrich II. und Jean-Jacques Rousseau. DR 19:241-68, Apr.-June, 1879. 3185

Stimulating, precisely - documented study of Frederick's and Rousseau's actual relationship and place in their times. Does more justice to Rousseau's literary genius than to his political-social pioneering. Too negative on *Confessions*.

Dupouy, Auguste. Les littératures comparées de France et d'Allemagne. Delaplane, 1913. 300 p. 3186

Sketchy, succinct, subjective, and selective. Stresses French parentage of " anti-French " literary movement in Germany, minimizes penetration of German literature in 18th century France as well as German influences on French *émigrés* (except Villers). Superficial index, no bibliography or footnotes.

Reviews : F. Baldensperger in RG 9:600-01, 1913; L. Morel in Archiv 133:192-94, 1915.

Ernst, Fritz. Die Schweiz als geistige Mittlerin. Zurich, Girsberger, 1932. 191 p. 3187

Compact, brimful with important indications on Swiss mediating role in Franco-German relations, with particular emphasis on 18th century literature. Many curious details, wide ramifications. Critical attitude. No index or bibliography. Very complete, up-to-date footnotes.

Gaiffe, Félix. Le drame en France au 18ème siècle. *See* 542. 3188

Reveals considerable vogue of mediocre German dramas between 1770 and 1790.

Reviews : Anon in Archiv 126:295-96, 1911; F. Baldensperger, in RG 6:589-90, 1910; G. Lanson in RHL 17:644-45, 1910.

Goedeke, Karl. Grundriss zur Geschichte der deutschen Dichtung. Dresden, Ehlermann, 1884-1940. 14 v. (unfinished). 3189

Antiquated, cluttered up with data on second to fifth-rate writers, uneven and devoid of broad coherence, yet remains standard reference work in German literature. Foreign influences and translations given due consideration. Volumes more or less relevant to 18th century Franco-German relations are : (2d edition): v. 3 (384 p., 1887: 18th century up to and including Gottsched; volume index), v. 4, sec. 1 (780 p., 1891 : 18th century from the Swiss up to and including Goethe; volume index); (3rd edition) : v. 4, sec. 2 (748 p., 1910 : Goethe; no index), v. 4, sec. 3 (826 p., 1912 : Goethe, no index), v. 4, (321 p., 1913 : Goethe; comprehensive index); (2nd edition) : v. 5 (565 p., 1893 : Schiller and second half of 18th century; volume index), v. 6 (822 p., 1898 : romanticism, Switzerland, Austria; volume index), v. 7 (883 p., 1900 : Austria, northern, central and southern Germany; foreign influences; volume index), v. 12 (601 p., 1929 : Switzerland, Austria, Bavaria; volume index of names and some titles), v. 13 (629 p., 1938 : Württemberg, Baden, Palatinate, Alsace, Saxony, Thuringia, Anhalt, Silesia, central Rhineland, northwestern Germany, Schleswig-Holstein, Hamburg, Lübeck ; volume index of names and some titles).

Hazard, Paul. La crise de la conscience européenne, 1680-1715. *See* 1043. 3190

Presents vastly and skillfully documented thesis, supported by judicious examples from French, German, English, etc., literature and thought, that main ideas of the 18th century had already been evolved and discussed by 1715. Masterpiece of exposition concentrating on significant rather than obvious. V. 3 contains extremely useful bibliography, readable for good measure.
Reviews : V. Giraud in RDM 8th per. 26:890-912, Apr. 15, 1935; D. Mornet in RHL 42:396-400, 1935; B. Munteano in RLC 15:364-78, 1935; K. Wais in Archiv 167:307-08, 1935.

— La pensée européenne au XVIIIᵉ siècle, de Montesquieu à Lessing. *See* 1044. 3191

Restricts himself to study of rationalism, with special stress on England, France, Germany and Italy. Fascinating guide to 18th century thought, combining scholarship, breadth, clarity,

and charm. Foible for concise, epigrammatic formulation makes for certain limitations. V. 3 contains a critical bibliography (including even World War II publications) of immense value.
Reviews : D. F. Bond in RR 38:98-99, 1947; J. David in MLQ 8:370-73, 1947; H. C. Lancaster in MLN 62:133-35, 1947; B. Munteano in RLC 21:125-40, 1947; N. L. Torrey in RR 38:271-76, 1947.

Hettner, Hermann. Geschichte der deutschen Literatur im 18. Jahrhundert. Leipzig, List, 1929. 1205 p. *See* 68. 3192

Vastness of scope, clearness and warmth of presentation characterize this unequalled survey based on profound knowledge of French and German literature. Excellent for influences of Rousseau and Voltaire, but inadequate for secondary writers like Mercier and Marmontel. Biased in favor of rationalism. Up-to-date bibliography.
Reviews : R. Haym in PrJ 14:468-70, 1864 (first ed.); J. Körner in LGRP 46:354-55, 1925; L. Mis in RG 18:378, 1927. *See also* under Boucke, 3184.

Jellinek, Arthur L. Bibliographie der vergleichenden Literaturgeschichte. Berlin, Duncker, 1903. 77 p. 3193

Short-lived continuation of Jellinek's reviews in SVL on independent basis. Emphasis on history of themes and *motifs (Stoffgeschichte)*. Index of names and titles.

Johnston, Elise. Le marquis d'Argens; sa vie et ses œuvres; essai biographique et critique. *See* 981. 3194

Important in view of D'Argens' long and intimate connection with Frederick II. Biographical part best of the work.
Review : D. Mornet in RHL 36:292-93, 1929.

Klein, Timotheus. Wieland und Rousseau. *See* 2088. 3195

Investigates their relationship from five angles : their ideas about hypothesis of primitive condition, about nature, state, religion and ethics, and, finally, their personal relationship.

Koch, Max. Schriften zur poetischen Theorie des 18. Jahrhunderts. ZVL 2:223-35, 1889. 3196

State of research as of 1889; includes discussion of Franco-German studies.

Körner, Josef. Bibliographisches Handbuch des deutschen Schrifttums. 3rd ed. (rev.). Berne, A. Francke, 1949. 644 p.   3196A

Most up-to-date and compact standard bibliography of German literature, intelligently selective and partly critical. Actually a new work. Considers literature up to March 1st, 1948. Indispensable. Remarkably complete index of proper names and subjects.

Review : F. R. Whitesell in MDU 42: 122-24, 1950.

Kosch, Wilhelm. Deutsches Literatur-Lexikon. 2d ed. (rev.) Berne, A. Francke, 1947 ff.   3196B

Reasonably complete and up-to-date biographical and bibliographical guide to German literature, particularly recommended for secondary writers. Has reached letter H.

Review : H. Schneider in Grev 25:67-69, 1950.

Mornet, Daniel. Le sentiment de la nature en France de J.-J. Rousseau à Bernardin de Saint-Pierre. *See* 868.   3197

Gives due consideration to German-Swiss influences (Ewald v. Kleist, Gellert, Haller, Gessner).

Reviews : F. Baldensperger in RG 4:609-10, 1908; G. Lanson in RHL 15:168-70, 1908.

Navarre, Charles. Les grands écrivains étrangers et leur influence sur la littérature française; morceaux choisis. Didier, 1930. 715 p.   3198

Outline intended as introduction for beginning students.

Review : F. Piquet in RG 22:233, 1931.

Réau, Louis. L'Europe française au siècle des lumières. Michel, 1938. 455 p.   3199

Although superficial, not reliable, and too obviously patterned after Reynaud's prejudiced studies (nos. 3202, 3254, 3255), possesses certain usefulness on account of inclusion of artistic, linguistic, social, and other factors, in addition to literature. Text, appendices (lists of French artists abroad, foreign artists in France), bibliography (handy list of 18th century sources), and index of names excellently organized. Numerous fine illustrations.

Review : F. Baldensperger in RR 30:90-95, 1939.

Revue germanique. 1905-14, 1920-39.   3200

Contains, in first 7 volumes (1905-11), special bibliography of Comparative Literature, edited by F. Baldensperger, covering articles in journals and periodicals as well as books. *See also: Etudes germaniques*, 1946 ff.

Revue de littérature comparée. 1921-40, 1947 ff.   3201

Regularly features extensive but not complete bibliographies, arranged according to countries (French influences, German influences, Swiss influences, etc.)

Reynaud, Louis. Le romantisme : ses origines anglo-germaniques. Colin, 1926. 288 p.   3202

Reynaud stresses " dangerous " implications of Anglo-German romantic influences in France. Study extends well back into 18th century. No index or bibliography. Frequent references, detailed table of contents.

Reviews : G. Chinard in MLN 42:188-94, 1927; L. Mis in Euph 29:289-92, 1928.

Rosenberg, Ralph P. American studies in Franco-German literary relations. CNL 4:18-22, 1945.   3203

Covers theses from 1897 to 1944. Shows steadily increasing interest in this field, excepting war years.

— (ed.). Franco-German studies. A current bibliography. RR 36:191-99, 1945, and 37:346-48, 1946 ; Bbib 19:60-63, 1947, 47-51, 1948 ; 19:228-31, 1949 ; 20:33-38, 1950.   3204

Compiled annually by Bibliography Committee of the Franco-German Literary Relations group of Modern Language Association of America. Covers American and foreign publications. Descriptive, critical; lists reviews of important works; even includes unpublished addresses. Lists, intermittently, research in progress (in 1945, 1948).

Rossel, Virgile. Histoire des relations littéraires entre la France et l'Allemagne. Fischbacher, 1897. 532 p.   3205

Sober, impartial study by Swiss scholar. Valuable *résumé* of previous research rather than original interpretation. More emphasis on names, titles than ideas. Separate treatment of German literature in France and, less fully, French literature in Germany. Good index. No bibliography but numer-

ous footnotes containing titles. *See also*
RHL 2:169-200, 1895.
Reviews : Anon in NNY 64:308-09,
Apr. 22, 1897; L. P. Betz in ZVL 12:264-
80, 1898; B. Schnabel in ZFSL 19²:181-
83, 1897; J. Texte in RHL 4:288-91,
1897.

Schmidt, Erich. Richardson, Rousseau und
Goethe. *See* 2140, 3076. 3206

Thorough comparative discussion of
Nouvelle Héloïse and *Werther*, preceded
by brief survey of vogue of *Nouvelle
Héloïse* in 18th century Germany. Although first published over 70 years ago,
retains but slightly impaired value due to
absence of a definitive study of Rousseau
in Germany.
Review : Anon in Archiv 148:152, 1925.

**Studien zur vergleichenden Literatur-
geschichte.** 1901-1909. 3207

Each issue in volumes 1 and 2 only (in
1901, 1902) contains a bibliography of
research in comparative literature by
Artur L. Jellinek. Registers books,
articles, and important reviews. Not too
reliable, since frequently based on second
and third-hand information.

Süpfle, Theodor. Geschichte des deutschen
Kultureinflusses auf Frankreich, mit besonderer Berücksichtigung der literarischen
Einwirkung. Gotha, Thienemann. V. 1: Von
den ältesten germanischen Einflüssen bis
auf die Zeit Klopstocks. 359 p., 1886. v.
2, part 1 : Von Lessing bis zum Ende der
romantischen Schule der Franzosen, 1888.
210 p. 3208

Should be obligatory reading in
conjunction with Reynaud (no. 3202).
Outdated in details, but still satisfactory
ouvrage d'ensemble, relatively free from
patriotic distortions. Instrumental in
disposing of myth that French acquaintance with German literature began with
Mme de Staël's *De l'Allemagne*. Extensive references, index of names and subjects at end of each volume.
Reviews : O. Knauer in ZFSL 8:218-
26, 1886 (v. I), and 11²:136-43, 1889
(v. II); J. Meyer in ZVL 1:334-39, 1887
(v. I).

Texte, Joseph. Les origines de l'influence
allemande dans la littérature française du
xixᵉ siècle. RHL 5:1-53, 1898. 3209

Luminous, finely nuanced, and impartial. Shows that Mme de Staël's *De
l'Allemagne* fell on fertile soil prepared in
last half of 18th century. Extensive

study of Villers' role. Greater part deals
with 19th century.

Van Tieghem, Paul (ed.). Répertoire
chronologique des littératures modernes.
Droz, 1935. 416 p. 3210

Very helpful tool. Lists principal
works and related facts of all European
(except Turkish) and American literatures
by years (from 1455-1900), which are
subdivided by languages. Alphabetical
index of authors and works.
Review : L. M. Price in Grev 13:300-
02, 1938.

— Le préromantisme. *See* 3019. 3211

Contains three studies : *La notion de
vraie poésie dans le préromantisme européen. La découverte de la mythologie et de
l'ancienne poésie scandinaves* and *Ossian et
l'Ossianisme au XVIIIᵉ siècle.* Scrupu-
lously objective, full of data and names,
somewhat too enumerative. Wide coverage. Index of authors, anonymous and
collective works.
Review : F. Baldensperger in RLC
6:159-62, 1926.

— Ossian en France. *See* 2803, 2997.
3211A

Contains information of value with
regard to the impact of Gessner and
Werther in France, as well as about
intermediary role of Bitaubé, Merian, the
Bridel brothers and French Switzerland.

Zeller, Gaston. La France et l'Allemagne
depuis dix siècles. Colin, 1932. 211 p.
3212

Brief but trenchant and relatively
objective sketch of Franco-German relations with some attention to literature, art,
and thought. Compact critical bibliography. Useful as introduction.
Review : F. Piquet in RG 24:95, 1933.

Intermediaries

Baldensperger, Fernand. Klopstock et
les émigrés français à Hambourg. RHL
20:1-23, 1913. 3213

Many interesting indications, connected
with subtle psychology, about important
episodes in Franco-German post-revolutionary contacts.

Breitinger, H. Heinrich Meister, der Mit-
arbeiter Melchior Grimms. ZNSL, Sup-
plementheft 3:53-77, 1885. 3214

Complements Tourneux edition of the
Correspondance littéraire (no. 2357) with

additional biographical data obtained from Meister's unpublished posthumous papers.

Eggli, Edmond. Un émigré germanisant, l'abbé Hubert (1760-1842). MélFB 1:225-48. 3215

Hubert spent 20 years in Germany. Eggli fills gap in Baldensperger's *Mouvement des idées dans l'émigration française* (no. 3182).

Gärtner, Johannes. Das Journal étranger und seine Bedeutung für die Verbreitung deutscher Literatur in Frankreich. Mainz, Falk, 1905, 96 p. (Diss., Heidelberg). 3216

First systematic treatment of subject since Süpfle. Limitations imposed as a result of author's inability to use materials in French libraries. Concludes that *Journal étranger* made a valuable contribution to spread of German literature in 18th century France despite its insufficient knowledge of German life, language, and literature.
Reviews : F. Baldensperger in RG 2:686, 1906; R. Mahrenholtz in LGRP 28:243-44, 1907.

Heiss, Hanns. Der Übersetzer und Vermittler Michael Huber (1727-1804). RFor 25:720-800, 1908. 3217

Expert account not only of Huber's life and translating activities, but of general popularity of German literature in France between 1760 and 1773.
Reviews : Anon in Archiv 120:483-84, 1908; L. Geiger in SVL 9:257-59, 1909.

Mathorez, Jules. Les étrangers en France sous l'ancien régime. v. 2 : Les Allemands, les Hollandais, les Scandinaves. Champion, 1921, 446 p. 3218

Factual and solid, with considerably more stress on sociological than literary developments. Tendency to consider German literary " infiltration " in France after 1750 as fairly unsuccessful " plot." No bibliography. Numerous explicit footnotes. Alphabetical index of names and places, very complete.

Reynold, Gonzague de. Le doyen Bridel (1757-1845) et les origines de la littérature suisse romande. Lausanne, Bridel, 1909. 550 p. 3219

Interesting study of influence of German Swiss literature (Bodmer, Breitinger, Haller, Gessner etc.) on French Swiss literature *via* Bridel.

Reviews : F. Baldensperger in RG 6:79-80, 1910; D. Mornet in RHL 16:829-30, 1909.

Ulrich, G. Charles de Villers, sein Leben und seine Schriften; ein Beitrag zur Geschichte der geistigen Beziehungen zwischen Deutschland und Frankreich. Leipzig, Weicher, 1899. 98 p. 3220

Gives useful data on Villers' residence in Germany (chiefly Göttingen and Lübeck) from 1792 on. Semi-popular.
Review : R. Mahrenholtz in LGRP 21:293-94, 1900.

Van Tieghem, Paul. L'année littéraire (1754-1790) comme intermédiaire en France des littératures étrangères. *See* 2796, 2884, 2495, 3275. 3221

Consists of *Mémoire*, covering general features and interests of the journal, and Index, listing reviews and announcements of foreign works or their translations, with brief analytical comments. Not very ambitious or penetrating project, but adduces important testimony on vogue of German literature in France, particularly between 1750 and 1770. Index not complete.
Reviews : *See* no. 2796.

Wittmer, L. Charles de Villers (1765-1815); un intermédiaire entre la France et l'Allemagne, et un précurseur de Mme de Staël. Hachette, 1908. 473 p. (Diss., Geneva). 3222

Although Villers' chief activities take place after 1800, this searching study throws much new light on Villers in Germany in the 1790's. Based on unpublished MS material and contemporary sources difficult of access.
Reviews : Anon in Archiv 121:233, 1908; F. Baldensperger in RG 6:80-81, 1910.

The Vogue of German Authors in France

Gessner

Baldensperger, Fernand. Gessner en France. *In his :* Études d'histoire littéraire, 4e série, Droz, 1939. 116-47. 3223

Points out great influence of Swiss poet not only in conquering France for the pastoral *genre*, but in suggesting to France a long-held rustic, idyllic conception of Germany and Switzerland. Splendid article, but occasionally too subtle and far-fetched. Supersedes Baldensperger's *Gessner en France* in RHL

10:437-56, 1903, and *L'épisode de Gessner dans la littérature européenne*, in *Salomon Gessner*, 3225, p. 85-116.

Broglé, Hans. Die französische Hirtendichtung in der 2. Hälfte des 18. Jahrhunderts dargestellt in ihrem besonderen Verhältnis zu Salomon Gessner. I. Idyll und Conte champêtre. Leipzig, Fugmann, 1903. 128 p. (Diss., Leipzig). 3224

Sound analysis of French pastoral poetry, with copious quotations and useful summaries of contents. Bears witness to Gessner's overwhelming influence.

Leemann-van Elck, Paul. Salomon Gessner. Zurich, Schweizer Bibliophile Gesellschaft, 1930. 322 p. 3225

Splendidly illustrated, rare work of an extremely well-informed *bibliophile*; does not claim to be critical evaluation. Very serviceable account of Gessner's French connections (in biographical part) and reception in France (in bibliographical part) including full and detailed list of original French editions (Zurich) and translations. Index.

Rauchfuss, Arthur. Der französische Hirtenroman am Ende des 18. Jahrhunderts und sein Verhältnis zu Salomon Gessner. Leipzig, Glausch, 1912. 168 p. (Diss., Leipzig). 3226

Careful study, with many *résumés* and quotations from sources. Deals chiefly with Florian, Léonard, and Mlle Lévesque. Concludes Gessner's influence mainly formal.

Goethe

Atkins, Stuart Pratt. The testament of Werther in poetry and drama. Cambridge, Harvard Univ. press, 1949. 322 p. 3227

Very important part of this notable, up-to-date work devoted to cult, imitation, adaptation, and interpretation of *Werther* in France. Excellent bibliography, index.

Baldensperger, Fernand. Goethe en France. Hachette, 1904, 383 p. 3228

Masterful, delicately-balanced treatment worthy of subject. Chapter on vogue of *Werther* of special interest. Conclusion contains some of most valid observations on basic trends in Franco-German literary relations ever penned.

Reviews : J. Collin in ZFSL 30²:52-58, 1906; W. Martinsen in SVL 5:382-84, 1905; H. Morf in Archiv 114:222-24,

1905; D. Mornet in RHL 11:337-40, 1904; J. G. Robertson in MLR 3:195-98, 1907-08.

— Bibliographie critique de Goethe en France. Hachette, 1907, 251 p. 3229

Lists and usually evaluates bibliographical items on translations, adaptations, continuations, criticisms, vogue, influence. Good analytical table, useful index. Not absolutely complete.

Reviews : J. Collin in ZFSL 32²:173-74, 1908 ; E. L. in RG 3:429-30, 1907 ; D. Mornet in RHL 14:746-47, 1907 ; J. G. Robertson in MLR 3:195-98, 1907-08.

— Goethe et les émigrés français de Weimar. RG 7:1-28, 1911. 3230

Subtle, judicious treatment covering period 1792-1800, and centering around unpublished letters (Dampmartin, Boufflers, Dumanoir, De Wendel, Chanorier, De Mun, Mounier (Jos.), Duvau, Pernay, Fumel, Fouquet).

Lichtenberger, Henri. Goethe und Frankreich. JGG 18:45-51, 1932. 3231

Eloquent, warm-hearted *aperçu* on Goethe's general attitude toward, and his reception in, France.

Loiseau, Hippolyte. Goethe en France. GRM 20:150-66, 1932. 3232

Contains useful, factual summary of vogue of German literature in France in 18th century prior to Goethe as well as of Goethe's impact on 18th and 19th century France.

Morel, Louis. Hermann et Dorothée en France. RHL 12:627-62, 1905. 3233

Deals mostly with 19th century reaction, but mentions some 18th century French echoes (Mlle de Rathsamhausen, later Mme de Gérando, J. G. Schweighäuser in *Magasin encyclopédique*, Mme de Charrière).

— Les principales traductions de Werther et les jugements de la critique (1776-1872). Archiv 119:139-59, 1907. 3234

Richly documented treatment of early French reception of *Werther*, prepared for by Rousseau (Huber, Wille, Iselin, Frey, Mlle de Waldner-Freudstein, Deyverdun, Xavier de Maistre, Moritz von Putbus, Seckendorff, La Harpe, Grimm, Aubry (Schmettau), Napoleon I, Geoffroy, *Mercure de France*, Baronne de Gérando,

Mme de Charrière, Mme de Staël, Sevelinges).

— Werther au théâtre en France. Archiv 118:352-70, 1907.   3235

Exploitation of *Werther* on French stage from 1775 to 1903 (including Mercier, Sinner, Ramond de Carbonnières, La Rivière, Dejaure).

— Les principales imitations françaises de Werther (1788-1813). Archiv 121:368-90, 1908.   3236

Shows metamorphoses and dilutions of *Werther* in France, in particular generalization of feeling and passion (Arkwright, Chaillet, Mercier, Fleuriot, Pierre Perrin, Gourbillon, Mme de Staël).

— Wilhelm Meister en France. SVL 9:65-94, 1909.   3237

Only p. 65-70 relate to reception of *Wilhelm Meisters Lehrjahre* in 18th century France; rest deals with 19th century.

— La fortune de Werther en France dans la poésie et le roman (1778-1816). Archiv 125:347-72, 1910.   3238

Werther as pacemaker of romanticism.

Strich, Fritz. Goethe und die Weltliteratur. Bern, Francke, 1946. 408 p.   3239

While mainly concerned with 19th century, this warm, wise, and cosmopolitan study encompasses 18th century in its sections dealing with French formative influences on Goethe (Racine, Voltaire, Diderot, but practically ignores Rousseau) as well as Goethe's influence in France. Wealth of material fruitfully and selectively treated; fine balance between facts and interpretation. Condensed apparatus.
Reviews : F. Baldensperger in RLC 21:312-20, 1947; A. Closs in MLQ 7:501-02, 1946; O. Seidlin in Grev 22:150-51, 1947.

Haller

Cunche, Gabriel. La renommée de A. de Haller en France; influence du Poème des Alpes sur la littérature descriptive du XVIIIᵉ siècle. Alençon, Supot, 1918. 153 p. (Diss., Caen).   3240

Reliable study based on sources. Includes account of Haller's personal relationship with Frenchmen. Treats problem within larger framework of reception of German-Swiss 18th century literature in France. Concludes that Haller's influence, while definitely noticeable, must not be overestimated. Badly arranged bibliography; numerous footnotes, no index.

Herder

Tronchon, Henri. La fortune intellectuelle de Herder en France; la préparation. Rieder, 1920, 570 p.   3241

Exhaustive, definitive, and unusually erudite. Discrepancy between elaborate apparatus of learning and the meager, chiefly negative results at which it arrives. Shows however to what extent German literature and philosophy were known in France by 1800. No index.
Review : F. Baldensperger in RLC 1:178-83, 1921; P. Hazard in RHL 28:596-98, 1921; F. Piquet in RG 12:94-96, 1921; M. Schütze in MP 20:331-33, 1923.

— La fortune intellectuelle de Herder en France; bibliographie critique. Rieder, 1920. 70 p. (Thèse complémentaire, Paris).   3242

Selective, critical, profitable, and convenient *répertoire*. Covers everything published on Herder since bibliography by Haym (from 1877-85) to 1914. Alphabetical index.

Klopstock

Chuquet, Arthur. Klopstock et la Révolution Française, *in* : Etudes d'histoire, 2ème série. Fontemoing, n. d. P. 93-187.   3242A

Includes highly revealing and entertaining account of Klopstock's reception in France and among French *émigrés*.

Kotzebue

Thompson, L. F. Kotzebue; a survey of his progress in France and England, preceded by a consideration of the critical attitude toward him in Germany. Champion, 1928. 175 p.   3243

P. 109-35 particularly relevant. Also notes numerous French influences on Kotzebue. General indications on German influences in France toward end of 18th century. Procedure too mechanical; strictly chronological method often confusing. Some literary gazettes have not been consulted. Index of proper names; no bibliography, but numerous footnotes.

Reviews : A. Ludwig in Archiv 157:91-92, 1930; B. Munteano in RLC 10:571-85, 1930 ; H. Tronchon in RG 21:158-60, 1930 ; L. A. Willoughby in MLR 25: 379-81, 1930.

Lessing

Aronson, Alexander. Lessing et les classiques français. Montpellier, Imprimerie de la charité, 1935. 279 p. (Diss., Toulouse).
3244

Unjustly neglected study, which aims at significant syntheses rather than statistical completeness. Vast preliminary and marginal considerations overshadow treatment of subject as such. Bibliography, no index.

Kinkel, Hans. Lessings Dramen in Frankreich. Darmstadt, Otto, 1908. 109 p. (Diss. Heidelberg).
3245

Best and most complete portion of this thesis deals with the 18th century. More French interest in *Miss Sara Sampson* and *Emilia Galotti* (before French Revolution) than in *Minna* and *Nathan*. Takes issue with E. Schmidt's negative verdict on Rochon. Useful bibliography indicates in what libraries and collections rarer 18th century sources can be found. No index.

Reviews : Anon in Archiv 121:488, 1908; F. Baldensperger in RG 6:80, 1910; R. Mahrenholtz in LGRP 30:156-57, 1909.

Schmidt, Erich. Lessing. 4th ed. Berlin, Weidmann, 1923. 2 v.
3246

Standard biography, fully discussing Lessing's many and varied relations with French literature. Rich notes; index in v. 2.

Schiller

Baldensperger, Fernand. La traduction de Don Carlos par Adrien de Lezay-Marnésia. SVL 5 (Ergänzungsheft) : 171-79, 1905.
3247

According to Baldensperger, this is a rare translation, superior to that of La Martelière.

Eggli, Edmond. Schiller et le romantisme français. Gamber, 1927. v. 1. 652 p.
3248

Basic work showing continuity of Schiller's influence in France from 1782

on. Discusses early translations by Bonneville and Friedel, considerable success of *Räuber, Fiesco, Kabale und Liebe* and *Don Carlos. Index des noms de personnes et des périodiques cités,* Gamber, 1928.

Reviews : F. Baldensperger in RLC 8:585-88, 1928; A. Ludwig in Archiv 155:241-43, 1929; L. Mis in Euph 30:579-84, 1929; J. G. Robertson in MLR 23:91-94, 1928.

Gleichen-Russwurm, Alexander von. Schiller und das Ausland. LE 7:1093-1100, 1905.
3249

Summary sketch of Schiller's attitude toward French literature and his reception in France.

German influences on French authors

Baldensperger, Fernand. Les théories de Lavater dans la littérature française. *In his :* Études d'histoire littéraire, Hachette, 1910, 2ᵉ série, 51-91.
3250

Discusses strong echoes, enthusiastically positive and critically negative, of Lavater's theories in France.

Gill-Mark, Grace. Anne-Marie du Boccage, une femme de lettres au xviiiᵉ siècle. Champion, 1927. 182 p.
3250A

Influenced by Haller. Inept imitator of Gessner.

Price, Lawrence M. The relation of Baculard d'Arnaud to German literature. MDU 37:151-160, 1945.
3251

Relates Arnaud's stay in Germany and notes that more than a dozen German plays used him as a source. Contains bibliography called : *Arnaud and the German drama.*

Morel, Louis. L'influence germanique chez Mme de Charrière et chez Benjamin Constant. RHL 18:838-64, 1911; 19:95-125, 1912.
3252

Mass of valuable data (mostly 18th century) on multiple connections with Germany of these precursors of Mme de Staël.

— L'influence germanique chez Benjamin Constant; Benjamin Constant à la cour de Brunswick. RHL 22:86-112, 1915. 3253

Factual account of early German influences on Constant.

Reynaud, Louis. Histoire générale de l'influence française en Allemagne. Hachette, 1924. 3rd ed. (rev.). 570 p.   3254

Most important work available on this subject. Broad approach : political, social, artistic, literary, etc. Powerful, passionate, and excessively Gallophile. Numerous footnotes, extensive bibliography, detailed table of contents. No index.

Reviews : A. Beaunier in RDM 6th per. 25:697-708, Feb. 1, 1915; F. Piquet in RG 10:598-99, 1914.

— L'influence allemande en France au XVIIIᵉ et au XIXᵉ siècle. Hachette, 1922. 316 p.   3255

Outstanding treatment of topic. Incisive and prejudiced. Sees in France legitimate heiress of Greece and Rome (order, beauty, harmony) defending herself against emotional chaos of Teutons. Numerous valuable references, detailed table of contents, no index.

Reviews : F. Baldensperger in RLC 3:485-94, 1923; F. Ernst in LGRP 44:254-57, 1923; F. Piquet in RG 14:85-86, 1923; J. Pommier in RHL 30:113-18, 1923; L. M. Price in JEGP 22:271-90, 1923; A. Thibaudet in NRF 19:329-38, 1922.

Rudler, Gustave. La jeunesse de Benjamin Constant (1767-1794). Colin, 1908. 542 p. (Diss., Paris).   3256

— Bibliographie critique des œuvres de Benjamin Constant, avec documents inédits et fac-similé. 1ᵉʳᵉ partie : 1767-1794. Colin, 1909. 108 p.

Excellent coverage of Constant's stays in Erlangen and Brunswick.

Review : G. Lanson in RHL 16:621-24, 1909.

Scherer, Edmond. Melchior Grimm. See 2409.   3257

Deals not only with German origins of Grimm, but also with his activities in interest of German literature, his relations and correspondence with eminent persons in Germany, and his voyages beyond the Rhine. By no means last word on these subjects.

Schwenke, Walter. Florians Beziehungen zur deutschen Literatur. Weida, Thomas & Hubert, 1908. 153 p. (Diss., Leipzig).   3258

Traces influence of Gessner on Florian, and success of Florian's plays in Germany.

Review : F. Baldensperger in RG 6:78-79, 1910.

Ullman, Helene. Benjamin Constant und seine Beziehungen zum deutschen Geistesleben. Marburg a. d. L., Ebel, 1915. 179 p. (Diss., Marburg).   3259

Contains interesting data on Constant's early sojourns in Germany (Erlangen, 1781-83, and Brunswick, 1788-94), attitude toward German literature and philosophy and influence of Mauvillon and Duke Karl W. F. of Brunswick on him. Bibliography. No index.

Wickwar, W. H. Baron d'Holbach; a prelude to the French Revolution. See 1355, 3053.   3260

Full data on German origin, and youth in Germany, of D'Holbach. Also discusses fortunes of his work in Germany. D'Holbach himself owed very little to German thought. Interestingly written. Bibliography far from complete.

Review : J. Lough in RHL 43:307-09, 1936.

Pange, Pauline Laure Marie (de Broglie) *comtesse de.* Mme de Staël et la découverte de l'Allemagne. Malfère, 1929. 154 p.   3261

Relates Mme de Staël's contacts with Germany before 1800, mainly with and through Goethe. Based to large extent on unpublished material. Pays more attention to Mme de Staël's personality than to evaluation of her literary output. Uncritical.

Reviews : L. Karl in LGRP 53:118-20, 1932; E. Seillière in RG 21:321-31, 1930.

Süpfle, Theodor. Französische Studien über die deutsche Literatur vor Frau von Staël. ZVL ns 1:221-30, 1887-88; ns 2:1-8, 1889.   3262

Complements his *Geschichte des deutschen Kultureinflusses auf Frankreich*. Studies by or on Grimm, Bielfeld, Boulenger de Rivery, Dorat, Hérissant, Mercier, Villers, *Mercure de France*, and *Journal étranger*.

Jordan, Leo. Die Münchener Voltairehandschriften. Archiv 129:388-429, 1912.   3263

Shows important role of Frederick II in composition of the *Pucelle*.

Mangold, W. Friedrich des Grossen Dichtungen aus den ersten schlesischen Kriegen. Archiv 129:188-205, 1912.   3264

Frederick II's creative works of this period attempt to convince Voltaire of justification of Silesian wars.

Italian
(Nos. 3264A-3308)

CHANDLER B. BEALL

Bibliographies and General Studies

Baldensperger, Fernand, and **Werner P. Friederich.** Bibliography of comparative literature. *See* 2885A, 3182A, 3308A.
3264A

Indispensable bibliography for all studies in comparative literature. See particularly chapters III-XVII of Third Part.
Review : R. Wellek in CL 3:90-92, 1951.

Balzo, Carlo del. L'Italia nella letteratura francese, dalla morte di Enrico IV alla Rivoluzione. Turin, Soc. tip. edit. nazionale, 1907. 501 p. 3265

Chapters vii-xv deal with 18th century. Mentions Voltaire, Montesquieu, Terrasson, Chabanon, Rousseau, Mme du Boccage, French travelers in Italy, quarrels on music. Gossipy and disorganized.

Beall, Chandler B. Un recueil italianisant du xviiie siècle français. MLN 55:528-31, 1940. 3266

Discusses *Etrennes du Parnasse* (1770-1790), published by Fétil, which contained sketches of Italian poets, with translations.

Betz, Louis Paul. Essai de bibliographie des questions de littérature comparée. RPF 10:247-74, 1896; 11:22-61, 81-108, 241-74, 1897; 12:45-64, 118-34, 1898. *See* 3183.
3267

Important bibliographical work, with introduction by J. Texte, contains a section dealing with Italian influence. Was republished as a separate volume, with title : *La littérature comparée; essai bibliographique*, introduction by Joseph Texte, Strasbourg, Trübner, 1900. 123 p. This edition elicited several reviews which contained material utilized in a new and enlarged edition, with index, published by Fernand Baldensperger, Strasbourg, Trübner, 1904, 215 p. (*See* no. 3183). Basic bibliography for studies in comparative literature, but is

now superseded by Baldensperger- Friederich. (*See* no. 3264A.)
Reviews (of the 1900 edition) : F. Baldensperger in Rcr ns 50:91-93, 1900; E. Bouvy in Bit 1:56-58, 1901; A. L. Jellinek in LE 3:216-17, Nov., 1900; M. J. Minckwitz in LGRP 23:57-60, Feb., 1902.
Reviews (of the 1904 edition) : Anon in NNY 79:437, 1904; C. S. Northup in MLN 20:235-39, 1905; 21:12-15, 1906.

Blanc, Joseph. Bibliographie italico-française universelle; ou Catalogue méthodique de tous les imprimés en langue française sur l'Italie ancienne et moderne depuis l'origine de l'imprimerie, 1475-1885. Milan, L'auteur, 1886. 2 v. 3268

Early and essential work listing translations from Italian, and French studies on Italian literature.

Hauvette, Henri. L'Italie dans ses rapports avec les autres littératures. Bit 7:266-67, 1907. 3269

Bibliographical article; this installment deals with Franco-Italian literary relations in 18th century.

Neri, Ferdinando. Gli studi franco-italiani nel primo quarto del sec. XX. Rome, Fondazione Leonardo, 1928. 387 p. 3270

Indispensable bibliographical tool for studying literary and cultural exchanges between France and Italy.
Review : P. Hazard in RLC 9:192-93, 1929.

— Gli studi di questi ultimi 35 anni intorno ai rapporti culturali italo-francesi durante il Settecento. Cint 4-5:27-32, 1936. 3271

Supplements his 1928 volume (no. 3270); contains a few titles dealing with Italian influences.

— Italia e paesi di lingua francese. *In :* Un cinquantennio di studi sulla letteratura italiana (1886-1936). SVR, v. 2, p. 65-79. 3272

Further supplement to Neri's 1928 volume (no. 3270).

Robertson, John George. The indebtedness of France to Italy. *In his :* Studies in the genesis of romantic theory in the eighteenth century. Cambridge, University press, 1923. p. 195-218. 3273

Chapter deals in an interesting way with French knowledge of Italian critics in early 18th century.

Review : G. Maugain in RLC 5:522-29, 1925.

Texte, Joseph. L'Italie et la critique française au 18e siècle. RCC 4¹:418-24, 449-53, 1896.   3274

Very brief general study on French critics of Italian writers. Old but still useful. Includes translations.

The vogue of Italian authors in France

Van Tieghem, Paul. L'ouvrage français sur l'Italie. *In his :* L'année littéraire comme intermédiaire des littératures étrangères. *See* 2884, 2945, 3221, p. 129-46.   3275

Very useful study on this important journal. Shows Fréron in a favorable light.

Cioranescu, Alexandre. L'Arioste en France, des origines à la fin du xviiie siècle. Éditions des presses modernes, 1939. 2 v. (Diss., Paris).   3276

Chapters IV and V of v. 2 treat Ariosto's influence on French theater of 18th century and on Voltaire respectively; ch. VI deals with translators and minor imitators. Thorough and useful study.

Reviews : C. B. Beall in MLN 57:234-35, 1942; N. Edelman in RR 31:172-75, 1940; G. Fatini in Rin 2:512-15, 1939; J. Lavaud in HRen 6:396-98, 1939; E. Magne in MerF 291:368-71, Apr. 15, 1939; P. Van Tieghem in RS 60:156, 1940-45.

Keyser, Sijbrand. Contribution à l'étude de la fortune littéraire de l'Arioste en France. Leyden, Dubbeldemann, 1933. 225 p. (Diss., Leyden).   3277

Conscientious but partial study. Superseded by work of Cioranescu listed above (no. 3276).

Review : H. Hauvette in Bit ns 3:352-53, 1933.

Montera, Pierre de. André Chénier et l'Italie. NRI 9th ser. 5:121-39, 402-19, 1921.   3278

Indicates imitations and judgments on Dante, Petrarch, several humanists. Useful sketch.

— Quelques jugements d'André Chénier sur la littérature italienne. NRI 9th ser. 7:140-55, 1922.   3279

Good brief study on Chénier's admiration for Italian poets of Renaissance, particularly Sannazzaro.

Counson, Albert. Le xviiie siècle. *In his :* Dante en France. Erlangen, Junge, 1906. p. 64-101.   3280

Serious piece of work, but clumsily arranged.

Reviews : H. Hauvette in RHL 14:167-70, 1907; W. von Wurzbach in ZFSL 30²:62-63, 1906.

Farinelli, Arturo. Dante e la Francia dall'età media al secolo di Voltaire. Milan, Hoepli, 1908. 2 v.   3281

Good study. Most of volume II devoted to 18th century. Treats French critics and imitators of Dante.

Reviews : J. Vianey in RHL 17:647-50, 1910; J. Wihan in Euph 22:752-75, 1913.

Friederich, Werner P. Dante's fame abroad, 1350-1850 : the influence of Dante Alighieri upon the poets and scholars of Spain, France, England, Germany, Switzerland and the United States. Rome and Chapel Hill (N. C.), 1950. 590 p.   3281A

Contains a section dealing with 18th-century French poets and critics.

Oelsner, Hermann. Dante in Frankreich bis zum Ende des XVIII. Jahrhunderts. Berlin, Ebering, 1898. 106 p. (Diss., Berlin).   3282

P. 34-53 treat allusions to Dante in 18th century French writers. Insufficient.

Reviews : F. X. Kraus in Dlit 19:1880-81, Dec. 10, 1898; E. Sulger-Gebing in ZVL ns 12:485-91, 1898; B. Wiese in Archiv 102:229-30, 1899.

Benoist, Charles. L'influence des idées de Machiavel. ADI 4:131-306, 1925.   3283

Third in this series of lectures delivered at The Hague deals with Montesquieu, Voltaire, and Rousseau. Rather hasty treatment.

Cherel, Albert. La pensée de Machiavel en France. L'artisan du livre, 1935. 350 p.   3284

Useful, but biased and sketchy. Chapter viii deals with 18th century. *See* index of present work for further material on Machiavelli in France.

Reviews : V. Luciani in Ital 15:86-88, 1938; R. Pintard in RLC 17:420-22, 1937.

Sorrentino, Andrea. Storia dell'antimachiavellismo europeo. Naples, Loffredo, 1936. 225 p.   3285

Partly popular, partly scholarly; fairly good summary of general European polemic against Machiavelli.

Bouvy, Eugène. La Merope de Maffei en France et la Mérope de Voltaire en Italie, notes bibliographiques. Bit 2:198-200, 1902. 3286

Mentions French translations from Maffei by Fréret in 1718, Du Bourg in 1743, J. Mangeart in 1845.

Guiet, René. La tragédie française au XVIIIe siècle et le théâtre de Metastasio. PMLA 53:813-26, 1938. See nos. 322, 478. 3287

Important study of Metastasio's influence.

Beall, Chandler B. La fortune du Tasse en France. Eugene, Univ. of Oregon, and MLA, [1942]. 308 p. 3288

Chapters VII-X devoted to critics of Tasso, his imitators and general popularity in France during 18th century; ch. VIII is on Voltaire.
Reviews : V. Luciani in FR 18:231-34, 1944-45; A. T. MacAllister in MLQ 3:467-69, 1942; E. Malakis in MLN 58:157-58, 1943; A. Marni in Ital 20:148-49, 1943; L. Vander Cammen in LR 4:74-76; 1950; J. H. Whitfield in MLR 37:512-15, 1942.

Cottaz, Joseph. L'influence des théories du Tasse sur l'épopée en France. Foulon, 1942. 251 p. (Diss., Paris). 3289

Includes discussion of 18th century epics influenced by Tasso. Sketchy and confused presentation.

Italian influences on French authors

Bezard, Yvonne. Comment le président de Brosses a écrit ses Lettres d'Italie. Eit 4:81-96, 1922. 3290

Indicates mixture of authenticity and mystification in work.

Michéa, R. Autour des Lettres familières du président de Brosses. RHL 42:63-71, 1935. 3291

Discussion of *lettre d'Italie* as literary *genre*. Mentions Lalande's *Voyage* and points out its indebtedness to De Brosses. Contains useful bibliography.

Socio, Giuseppe de. Le président Charles de Brosses et l'Italie. Rome, Marchesi, 1923. 320 p. (Diss., Besançon). 3292

Cites De Brosses' judgments on various Italian literary figures.
Review : E. Champion in RLC 4:365-67, 1924.

Montera, Pierre de. André Chénier et Vittorio Alfieri. Eit 4:32-41, 97-113, 1922. 3293

Sketches personal relations between the poets and Alfieri's influence on *Perfection des lettres*. Good study.

Busnelli, Manlio. Diderot et l'Italie : reflets de vie et de culture italiennes dans la pensée de Diderot. See 2328. 3294

Important study, well-documented. Surveys Diderot's knowledge of things Italian, acquaintance with Italians, judgments on Italian authors, painting, music, philosophy. Ch. iv devoted to his relations with Goldoni.
Reviews : E. Maddalena in Marz, Apr. 18, 1926, p. 1-2; G. Maugain in Rcr 93:404-06, 1926; P. Ronzy in GSLI 91:338-90, 1928.

Faggi, Adolfo. Un traduttore francese del Rolli. GSLI 47:455-57, 1906. 3295

N. Gilbert's *L'amant désespéré* translated from Rolli's *Solitario bosco ombroso*.

Robertson, J. G. Sources italiennes des paradoxes dramatiques de La Motte. RLC 3:369-75, 1923. 3296

P. J. Martelli exerted an indirect influence on La Motte *via* L. Riccoboni's *Dissertation sur la tragédie moderne*.

Toldo, Pietro. Quelques sources italiennes du théâtre comique de Houdar de la Motte. Bit 1:200-05, 1901. 3297

Indicates sources of La Motte's *Le magnifique, Minutolo, Le calendrier des vieillards*, and *Le talisman* in the *Decameron* and use of traditional Italian characters elsewhere in his plays.

Levi-Malvano, Ettore. Montesquieu e Machiavelli. See 1582c. 3298

Old but excellent study, well organized. For other studies on this same general subject *see* nos. 1582, 1596, 1603.

Hazard, Paul. L'Italie de l'abbé Prévost. MélHH, p. 347-52. 3299

Points out Prévost's ignorance of Italy and his purely fanciful descriptions.

Salza, Abdelkader. Alcune relazioni tra poeti francesi e italiani dei secoli XVII e XVIII. Bit 8:56-65, 1908. 3300

Points out sonnet by J.-B. Rousseau imitated from Zappi.

Benedetto, Luigi Foscolo. Jean-Jacques Rousseau tassofilo. ScrRR, p. 371-89. 3301

Essential study on Tasso's influence on Rousseau.

Nicolini, Fausto. La teoria del linguaggio in Giambattista Vico e Giangiacomo Rousseau. RLC 10:292-98, 1930. 3302

Points out similarities between *Scienza nuova* and *Essai sur l'origine des langues.*

Bouvy, Eugène. Voltaire et l'Italie. Hachette, 1898. 368 p. 3303

Basic work on subject. Reviews Voltaire's knowledge of Italian language and literature, appraisals of Italian writers, friendship with Bettinelli, quarrel with Baretti. Old, but very good study.
Review : E. Bertana in GSLI 33:403-21, 1899.

Cioranescu, Alexandre. Tancrède de Voltaire et ses sources épiques. RLC 19:280-92, 1939. 3304

Sources discussed are Ariosto; a novel of Mme des Fontaines called *La comtesse de Savoie,* of 1726; 12th century French poem *Macaire;* certain stories of Bandello.

Dubled, Jean. L'Orlando furioso et La Pucelle de Voltaire. Bit 11:287-315, 1911; 12:50-73, 299-309, 1912; 13:37-47, 1913.

Important study.   3305

Farinelli, Arturo. Voltaire et Dante. SVL 6:88-138, 166-227, 1906. 3306

Surveys Voltaire's acquaintance with Dante's work and indicates its influence upon Voltaire's own writings. Also notes Voltaire's judgments on other Italian authors.

Hazard, Paul. Voltaire et la pensée philosophique de la Renaissance italienne. MélAL p. 473-78. *See* no. 1770. 3307

Hazard finds in Voltaire the last traces of influence of Italian thinkers of the Renaissance.

Maestro, Marcello T. Voltaire and Beccaria as reformers of criminal law. *See* 1783. 3308

Voltaire had prepared ground for reforms; after reading Beccaria he took

direct action. He also gave support and publicity to Beccaria's principles.

Spanish
(Nos. 3308A-3319)

CHARLES N. STAUBACH

Baldensperger, Fernand, and **Werner P. Friederich.** Bibliography of comparative literature. *See* 2885A, 3182A, 3264A
3308A

Contains some items which have appeared since the Gaudin (Strong) bibliography (no. 3310), does not supersede the latter for items published before 1930. Authors not always sure how to classify items ; therefore great care must be taken to check all categories, with repeated reference to table of contents. Franco-Spanish relations, 17 items on p. 369; Spanish influence on France, 27 items on p. 450-51 ; on individual authors, numerous items, p. 469-72 ; French authors of 16th, 17th and 19th centuries appear more often than those of 18th.

Foulché-Delbosc, Raymond. Bibliographie des voyages en Espagne et en Portugal. Welter, 1896. 349 p. 3309

For 18th century, lists 94 travel accounts : 32 originally published in French or written by French authors, and a number of others which appeared in French translation. Important for further studies of the knowledge of Spain in France. Reprinted from Rhisp 3:1-349, 1896.

Gaudin, Mrs. Lois Frances (Strong). Bibliography of Franco-Spanish literary relations. New York, Institute of French Studies, 1930. 71 p. 3310

Basic. Supersedes Betz (no. 3183) in field. Not critical, and occasionally inaccurate, but indispensable. Lists material of importance under *Bibliographies* (nos. 1-16), *General works* (nos. 17-133), *Eighteenth century* (nos. 628-776). Further subdivision by authors, French and Spanish, facilitates its use.
Review : Josephine de Boer in RR 23:350-52, 1932.

Bardon, Maurice. Don Quichotte en France au XVIIᵉ et au XVIIIᵉ siècle, 1605-1815. Champion, 1931. 1:369-527; 2:531-807. 3311

Detailed, documented, basic. Delves

into correspondences, journals, major and minor authors in all genres. Shows there was a wide acquaintance with *Don Quijote*, though understanding was often colored by attitudes of century. Incidental comment on Spanish influence in general. Reviews : G. Le Gentil in Rcr 98:413-15, 1931; P. Mérimée in RLC 11:799-804, 1931.

Claretie, Léo. Lesage. *See* 765.   3312

Goes deeply into Lesage's use of Spanish materials. Not yet outdated in this sense, despite numerous later investigations on specific source questions.

Huszár, Vilmos. L'influence de l'Espagne sur le théâtre français des xviiie et xixe siècles, par Guillaume Huszár. *See* 517. 3313

Interesting introductory chapters on psychology of literary influences; Spanish influence on Lesage, Marivaux, Beaumarchais. In places impressionistic rather than scientific.

Kurz, Harry. The Spanish. *In his :* European characters in French drama in the eighteenth century. *See* 626, p. 45-85.
3314

Chapters concerning Spanish somewhat subjective. Author seems to assume that French treatments represent accurately the Spanish character. Useful in connection with Huszár (no. 3313), if consulted with reservations.

Morel-Fatio, Alfred. L'Espagne en France. *In his :* Études sur l'Espagne. 2nd ed., Bouillon, 1895. 1st ser., p. 1-108.   3315

First published by Vieweg, 1888. Though brief, is mature study. For 18th century author suggests political and historical reasons for Spain's fall from grace in French eyes.

Discussions : F. Brunetière, *L'influence de l'Espagne dans la littérature française ;* In his : *Études critiques sur l'histoire de la littérature française.* 2nd ed., Hachette, 1893-1907. v. 4, p. 51-71; A. Farinelli, *España y Francia.* In his : *Ensayos y discursos de crítica literaria hispano-europea.* Rome, Treves, 1925. v. 2, p. 303-55. First published in RHLE 2:1-21, 1897. Adds data to Morel-Fatio.

Rogers, Paul Patrick. Spanish influences on the literature of France. Hisp 9:205-35, 1926.   3316

General, brief, not documented, but useful for specific listing of French authors and works which show recognized Spanish influences. For 18th century, lists works of 16 French authors. Gives working bibliography.

Salvio, Alfonso de. Voltaire and Spain. *See* 1800.   3317

Documented and detailed analysis of Voltaire's errors concerning Spain. Asserts Voltaire consistently violated his own standards for historical method and search for truth whenever he dealt with things Spanish.

Sorrento, Luigi. Francia e Spagna nel settecento; battaglie e sorgenti di idee. Milan, Società editrice, " Vita e pensiero," [1928]. 300 p.   3318

Study of attitudes of *philosophes* toward Spain, and of defense of Spanish culture in France by certain Frenchmen and others. Firmly built study.

Vézinet, F. Iriarte et Florian (la fable littéraire). *In his :* Molière, Florian et la littérature espagnole. Hachette, 1909. p. 179-252.   3319

Shows that Florian imitated Iriarte both in method and subjects ; credits Florian with more grace and interest; Iriarte with more originality.

INDEX

NOTE. — When entries in this Index are followed by more than three serial numbers, these serial numbers are identified as to content, as briefly as possible.

When the subject of the Index entry is the author of the item represented by the serial number, the number is given in italics.

A

*

THE SAINT-CATHERINE PRESS, LTD. BRUGES, BELGIUM.

Printed in Belgium.